WITHDRAWN

Handbook of Intelligent Sensors
for Industrial Automation

Contributors

George A. Alers, Magnasonics, Inc.
John W. Berthold III, The Babcock and Wilcox Company
Shawn Buckley, Cochlea Corporation
Mark Carlos, Physical Acoustics Corporation
David A. Dornfeld, University of California, Berkeley
Martin R. Hamar, Hamar Laser Instruments
David M. Jankowski, Krautkramer Branson
William A. Kline, Montronix, Inc.
C. S. McCamy, Macbeth
George Mordwinkin, Sensor Corporation
Jack A. Perry, Perry Associates
Steven C. Ross, FLIR Systems, Inc.
Jonathan S. Shapiro, Greenwich Instrument Company
M. W. Siegel, Carnegie Mellon University
Scott Wohlstein, SD Laboratories, Inc.
Nello Zuech, Vision Systems International

Handbook of Intelligent Sensors for Industrial Automation

Nello Zuech
Editor

Addison-Wesley Publishing Company, Inc.
Reading, Massachusetts Menlo Park, California New York
Don Mills, Canada Wokingham, England Amsterdam Bonn Paris
Milan Sydney Singapore Tokyo Seoul Taipei Mexico City San Juan

Many of the designations used by manufacturers and sellers to distinguish their products are claimed as trademarks. Where those designations appear in this book and Addison-Wesley was aware of a trademark claim, the designations have been printed in initial caps.

The publisher offers discounts on this book when ordered in quantity for special sales. For more information please contact:

>   Corporate & Professional Publishing Group
>   Addison-Wesley Publishing Company
>   Route 128
>   Reading, Massachusetts 01867

>   Library of Congress Cataloging-in-Publication Data

Handbook of intelligent sensors for industrial automation / Nello
  Zuech, editor.
    p. cm.
  Includes bibliographical references and index.
  ISBN 0-201-55022-9
    1. Intelligent control systems—Handbooks, manuals, etc.
  I. Zuech, Nello, 1938–
  TJ217.5.H36 1991
  670.42'7—dc20   91-14073
                                                              CIP

Copyright © 1992 by Addison-Wesley Publishing Company, Inc.

All rights reserved. No part of this publication may be reproduced, stored in a retrieval system, or transmitted, in any form, or by any means, electronic, mechanical, photocopying, recording, or otherwise, without the prior written consent of the publisher. Printed in the United States of America. Published simultaneously in Canada.

Cover design by Absolute Design Services
Text design by Webster Design
Set in 11/13 point Times by Compact

ISBN 0-201-55022-9

Printed on recycled and acid-free paper
123456789-MW-9594939291
First Printing, October 1991

Contents

Acknowledgments vii

Overview ix

1. Machine Tool Monitoring Systems 1
   William A. Kline, Ph.D.
2. Fiber Optics 21
   Scott Wohlstein
3. Fiber Optics Applications 33
   John W. Berthold III
4. Nonvision Sensors for Robotics 63
   M. W. Siegel
5. Electro-optical Sensors in Process Control 87
   Nello Zuech
6. Laser Alignment 111
   Martin R. Hamar
7. Infrared Thermal Sensors 161
   Dr. Jonathan S. Shapiro
8. Infrared Imaging 203
   Steven C. Ross
9. Color Sensors 223
   C. S. McCamy
10. Intelligent Eddy Current Sensing Systems 243
    George Mordwinkin
11. Noncontact Ultrasonic Testing with Electromagnetic Transducers 285
    George A. Alers
12. Ultrasonic Hardness Testing 307
    David M. Jankowski
13. Acoustic Emission 321
    Mark Carlos
14. Force-field Sensing 353
    Shawn Buckley
15. Use of Ultrasonic Sensors in Level and Flow Measurements 383
    Jack A. Perry
16. Sensor Fusion 419
    David A. Dornfeld

Credits and Permissions 509

Index 517

Acknowledgments

I wish to acknowledge and express my appreciation to all the contributing authors and their firms. In addition, thanks are due to my editor, Kathy Manley, as well as to those who granted permission to allow their work to be published. I also want to thank my many colleagues and friends who have added to my understanding of sensor technology and helped provide me with the "infrastructure" for this book. And to my wife, Maureen, to whom this book is dedicated. Without her understanding and patience, this book would not have been possible.

Overview

Intelligent sensors are the foundation of industrial automation. The entire concept of Computer Integrated Manufacturing (CIM) in discrete products manufacturing rests on data acquisition. Significantly, intelligent sensors are the data collectors.

A *sensor* has been defined as a device that detects and measures some physical/chemical quantity and outputs its data as an electrical signal to monitor a process or the result of a process. An *intelligent sensor* is one that incorporates electronics (which typically condition the signal from the sensor), does some local interpretation on the signal, and generally includes self-calibration and diagnostics.

Three levels of intelligent sensors have been characterized:

- Level 1:
    - Actions fixed
    - Sensors initiate sequence
    - Operator handles exceptions
    - No data collected

- Level 2:
    - Actions adaptable
    - Data acquired
    - Sensors have intelligence to signal adjustments
    - "Islands" of automation

- Level 3:
    - Integrated "islands"
    - Sensors initiate adjustments to "island" work flow
    - Data acquired and integrated to plantwide systems

Intelligent sensors provide the inputs to data acquisition systems for the purpose of control: process control, machine control, robot control, and quality control. Emerging intelligent sensor techniques include remote/distributed, integratable, programmable, and noninvasive characteristics.

There are many ways to group sensors:

- By the property sensed:
    - Electromagnetic energy (light, x-rays, gamma rays, magnetic fields)
    - Mechanical vibrational energy (ultrasound, acoustic)
    - Thermal energy
    - Particles (electrons, neutrons, protons)

- By the techniques executed:
    - Silicon
    - Fiber optics

- By the application:
    - Presence/absence
    - Positioning
    - Inspection/nondestructive evaluation
    - Condition measurement
    - Identification

Significantly, for any application there are generally many tactics. For example, position can be sensed by any of the following tactics: limit switches, ultrasonics, encoders/resolvers, capacitive, inductive, machine vision, LVDTs, lasers, etc. Another example: identification applications can be addressed by OCR, bar codes, RF, machine vision, fluorescent tags, surface acoustic waves, and magnetic stripes.

Successful application of intelligent sensors requires a thorough understanding of all the variables in a process. These include more than those variables that the equipment must be sensitive to; what generally dictates the optimal sensor to use is what variables the sensor must be tolerant of and, therefore, able to ignore.

Regrettably, the application of intelligent sensors is often accomplished with little or no understanding of the subtle differences between sensor modalities. One of the reasons for this is the fact that few engineering schools offer courses in sensors. Rather, they prepare engineers with a grooming in fundamental principles and expect "on-the-job" experience to give them the background to differentiate among modalities and how those differences are important to a specific application.

This book was conceived to provide a single source that introduces many "hot" intelligent sensor technologies currently being adopted by industry. Each chapter covers the specific sensor technology pragmatically. Discussion of principles and properties is not done from the scientist/mathematician perspective, but in a way that relates the technology to an application. This

helps the reader understand where the specific technology covered can be applied.

Not every sensor modality is included in the book—only those, as suggested above, that are currently "hot" are covered. That is, the book includes those modalities that are currently successful in industrial applications, which are, in general, more demanding than laboratory applications.

Chapter 1 Machine Tool Monitoring Systems*

William A. Kline, Ph.D.

Introduction

Metalcutting machine tools are used to cut, shape, and finish parts and pieces that are used in applications from automotive to aerospace. In the past, machine tools were manually operated; each machine had its own operator responsible for monitoring and controlling the machine movements. The cutting tools used naturally wear out due to the abrasion of the cutting process, and they can also break if subjected to excessive impact or load. With the advent of computer numerically controlled (CNC) machines, the machine movements are controlled by a microprocessor, and the operator's role is more to monitor the process and less to control it.

In recent years, a number of factors have converged to make machine monitoring a critical issue. A CNC machine operates "open-loop"; the servo-drives push the cutting tool from point to point within the work envelope with limited feedback. Advances in cutting materials allow machines to be run at faster rates to shorten cycle times. To achieve higher productivity, more automation devices such as tool and part changers are being used to allow the machine to run longer periods of time with one operator tending multiple machines. Today, the human operator is faced with more complicated machines, operating at a very fast pace. If tooling problems or part program errors occur, the operator has very little time to stop the machine to prevent catastrophic damage.

Machine monitoring systems are essential to improving productivity in automated and minimally tended machining systems. The integrity and condition of the cutting tools on a machine are essential to high-quality production and avoiding workpiece, tool, and machine damage. A typical system to monitor the condition of cutting tools, which consists of a transducer, amplifier, and processing unit, is shown in figure 1.1. The transducer is placed near the cutting action and

---

* Copyright Montronix, Inc. 1990, all rights reserved, William A. Kline, author.

Figure 1.1 Block Diagram for Monitoring System

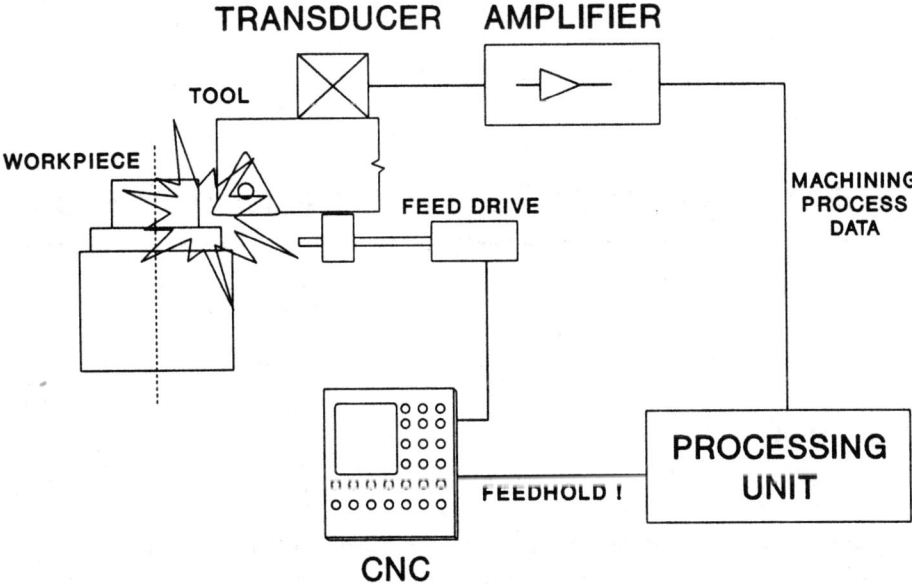

measures a response of the cutting process, such as force, vibration, temperature, etc. The amplifier is the signal conditioning necessary to condition and amplify the transducer output. The processing unit monitors the transducer signal for telltale indications of machining abnormalities. When an event is detected, a signal is transmitted to the machine tool control unit, thus providing feedback about the condition of the cutting tool and the process.

This chapter discusses the basic features of monitoring systems, the factors to consider in the selection of a system, and performance expectations on the shop floor.

Benefits of Tool Monitoring Systems

The benefits realized through the use of tool monitoring systems depend on the features and performance of the system. Commonly available monitoring capabilities include the following:

- Collision or overload detection

- Tool breakage or chipping detection

- Tool wear detection

BENEFITS OF TOOL MONITORING SYSTEMS

The common progression of events during metalcutting is gradual tool wear during the early life of the cutting tool. As the wear level increases, the cutting force on the tool increases and if the force increases to a high enough level, tool breakage can occur. During and after breakage, cutting forces can reach very high levels, which can lead to damage to the machine tool.

Breakage and collision events also occur due to unpredictable circumstances, such as a workpiece of the wrong size, a workpiece that is too hard, the wrong cutting tool, or a part program mistake. Regardless of the cause, an effective monitoring system must detect these abnormal events and prevent damage to the cutting tool, machine tool, and workpiece.

To illustrate the rapid progression of events, a cutting force plot during tool breakage in single-point turning is shown in figure 1.2. In this case, a ceramic cutting tool fractured during cast iron machining, and the operator response time to stop the machine was about 3 seconds. After the initial breakage, the cutting forces oscillate wildly and reach very high levels within a short period of time. Both the tool holder and the workpiece were scrapped. There was no machine damage, but it was necessary to inspect and check the machine carefully. This result demonstrates that events happen unexpectedly and consequential catastrophic damage can occur very quickly.

The true economic benefit of a machine monitoring system is the prevention of catastrophic damage to the tool, machine, and workpiece. Figure 1.3 shows

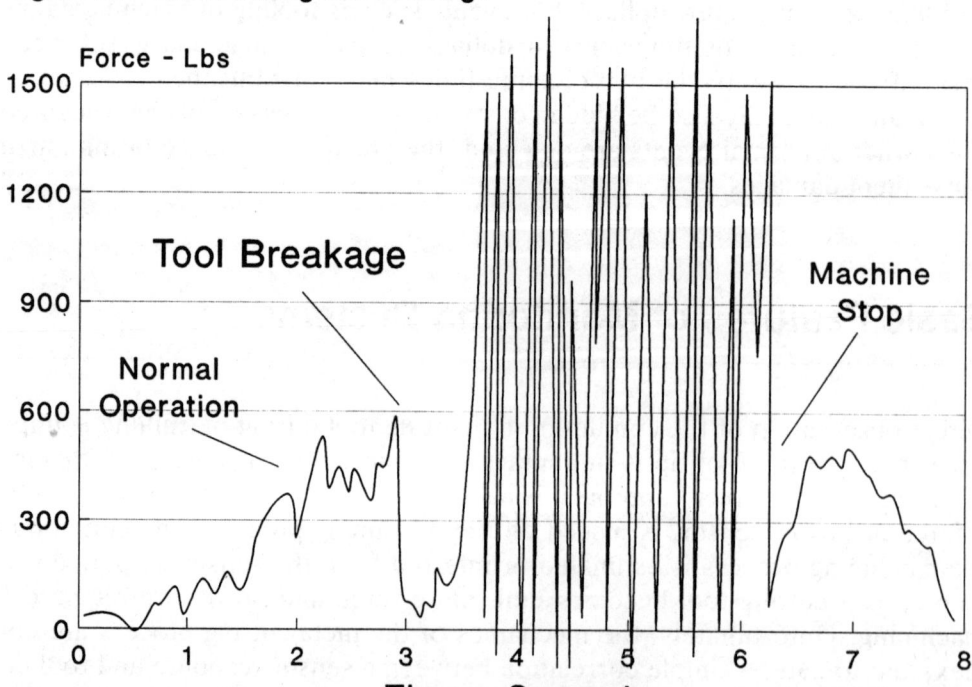

Figure 1.2 Forces During Tool Breakage

Figure 1.3 Cost of Machining Events

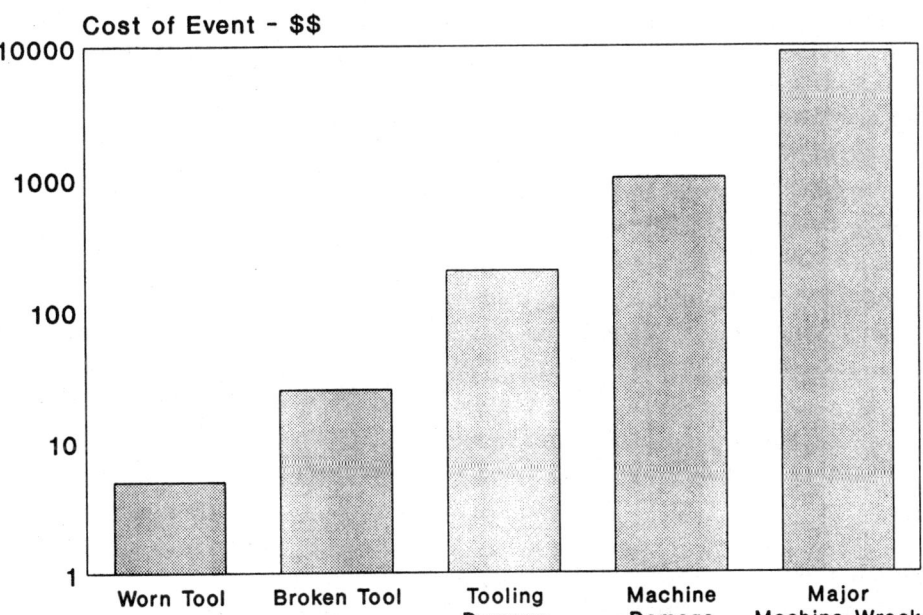

suggested costs of events that may occur on a machine tool. A worn or broken tool may cost only a few dollars, but events such as tooling or machine damage may cost hundreds or thousands of dollars. A serious machine wreck occurs very infrequently—maybe two or three times per year—but the economic cost is high and there may also be hidden costs, such as the loss of machine accuracy. The earlier abnormal events are detected, the greater the chance of minimizing subsequent damages.

Basic Features of Monitoring Systems

Direct observation of the condition of a cutting tool during machining is impossible, because the tool tip is in contact with and hidden by the work material. Therefore, an "indirect" approach is necessary. A sensor or transducer, such as a force or power sensor, is placed on the machining process. The condition of the machining process is estimated or inferred from the sensor output. For example, as a cutting tool becomes dull, more force and power are required for machining. Unfortunately, the mechanics of the metalcutting process are complex, and to date, a simple correlation between a sensor response and tool con-

dition has not been found. Many secondary effects, such as work material condition and changes in machining conditions, are also recorded by the sensor.

Tool monitoring systems consist of a transducer with associated signal conditioning and a processing unit to monitor and analyze the transducer output. The processing unit relays control signals to the machine tool and also displays status information for the operator. A block diagram of a generic system is shown earlier in figure 1.1.

The success of a monitoring system depends on the level of performance of each system component: transducer, signal processing, processing unit, and communication interfaces. If any one of the system components performs poorly, the performance of the entire system will suffer.

Transducers

Many types of transducers have been applied to the monitoring of machine and cutting tool condition. These include force, acceleration (vibration), acoustic emission, temperature, power, and even radioactivity. The factors to consider in evaluating a particular transducer type are sensitivity, response time, ruggedness, and installation. Significant differences of opinion exist as to the suitability of the different transducer types for tool monitoring. Some transducers are better suited to different types of machining operations, such as turning, milling, or drilling, and to detecting particular machining events, such as tool breakage or tool wear.

In selecting a transducer, a basic mechanism must be identified to relate the machining process to a measured signal. For example, "as a cutting tool wears, the cutting force increases," or "when a cutting tool breaks, a burst of acoustic emission energy is produced." Problems arise when secondary effects such as changes in workpiece condition also affect the transducer signal and determination of the tool condition becomes difficult.

The measuring transducer must be installed on the machine tool, and two options are available: either "build into" the machine tool or "add onto" the machine tool. In the first case, the transducer is often installed and hidden inside the machine structure as the machine is being built. The transducer is thus an integral part of the machine tool, but maintenance may be difficult. If a transducer can be "added onto" a machine or retrofitted, installation can be made at any time during the life of the machine, not just when it is being built. The disadvantage is possibly that the transducer is more exposed on the machine surface and prone to damage. Again, different transducer types are more or less suitable for retrofit to a machine tool.

At present, the most widely used and successful technology is cutting force measurement [2–7]. Cutting force has been used successfully to monitor collision, breakage, and wear on a wide range of operations with the only drawback

Table 1.1 Effectiveness of Different Monitoring Techniques

	Collision	Breakage	Wear	Sensitivity	Installation
Force	1	1	1–2	1	2
Power	1	2	3	3	1
Acoustic Emission	1*	1*	3	1	1

*Limited application ranges—mainly drilling
1 = good   2 = fair   3 = poor

being that force sensors may be difficult to install. Other techniques in use include power and acoustic emission. Monitoring cutting power has been found to be less sensitive than measuring force, and acoustic emission has been applied successfully only in limited application ranges (see table 1.1).

Principles of Force Sensing

Because most of the commercially available monitoring systems are based on cutting force, the principles of force sensing are discussed in detail. Two basic technologies are used for force measurement; strain gauge and piezoelectric. Strain gauge techniques have been used for many years for the measurement of mechanical strains. Strain gauges are constructed of a grid of thin metallic film attached to a flexible backing material. The gauge is cemented to the surface of the structure, and as the structure and gauge are strained, the cross section and electrical resistance of the thin metallic film changes. The changes in resistance are measured via a low impedance bridge and amplification circuit, and are calibrated to the applied loads on the structure.

In metalcutting applications, strain gauges may be applied to spindle bearings, leadscrew bearings, or to the machine structure. Figure 1.4 depicts a monitoring system with strain gauges applied to the spindle bearings. The gauges must be applied in a location where significant strains are present. Contrary to this requirement, machine tools are designed to be highly rigid, and thus strain gauge placement is critical. Strain gauges are also sensitive to thermal effects, and they must be placed in a location that is removed from the heat of the metalcutting process or they can be thermally compensated.

Piezoelectric techniques have also been used for many years for force and vibration measurement. Quartz crystals exhibit the piezoelectric effect where the crystal produces an electrical charge output in response to an applied mechanical load. The crystals are fabricated into load cells or washers that are incorporated into the load path of the mechanical structure. The load cells have very high stiffness and usually do not affect the integrity of the structure.

BASIC FEATURES OF MONITORING SYSTEMS 7

Figure 1.4 Block Diagram for Strain Gauge System

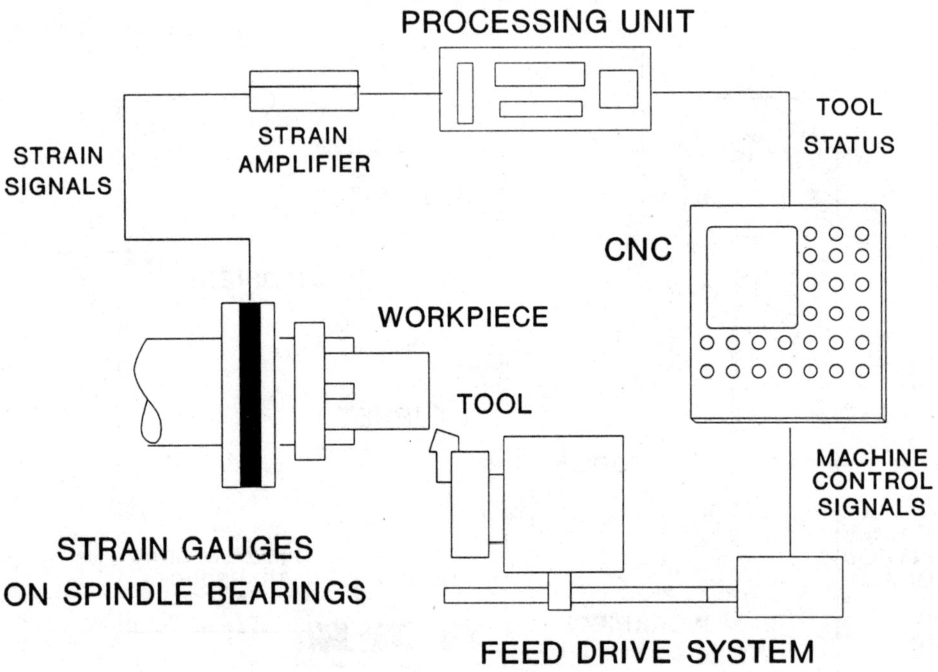

The charge output from the piezoelectric device is processed by a high impedance (10^{12} ohms) charge amplification circuit that produces a low impedance voltage output. The high impedance cables and circuitry must be kept scrupulously clean to prevent charge leakage and inaccurate measurement. Piezoelectric load cells are also sensitive to thermal effects and must be placed in thermally stable locations.

In metalcutting applications, piezoelectric load cells are most commonly designed into transducer plates for turning machines that are mounted in or under the turret, as shown in figure 1.5. This approach permits the development of standard plate designs with measurement ranges and sensitivities that are repeatable from one machine to another.

Both strain gauge and piezoelectric measuring technology have been applied successfully to metalcutting processes. The critical issues for the design and performance of either type of force measurement transducer are as follows:

Measuring range   The highest force that can be measured without damage to the transducer

Figure 1.5 Block Diagram for Piezoelectric System

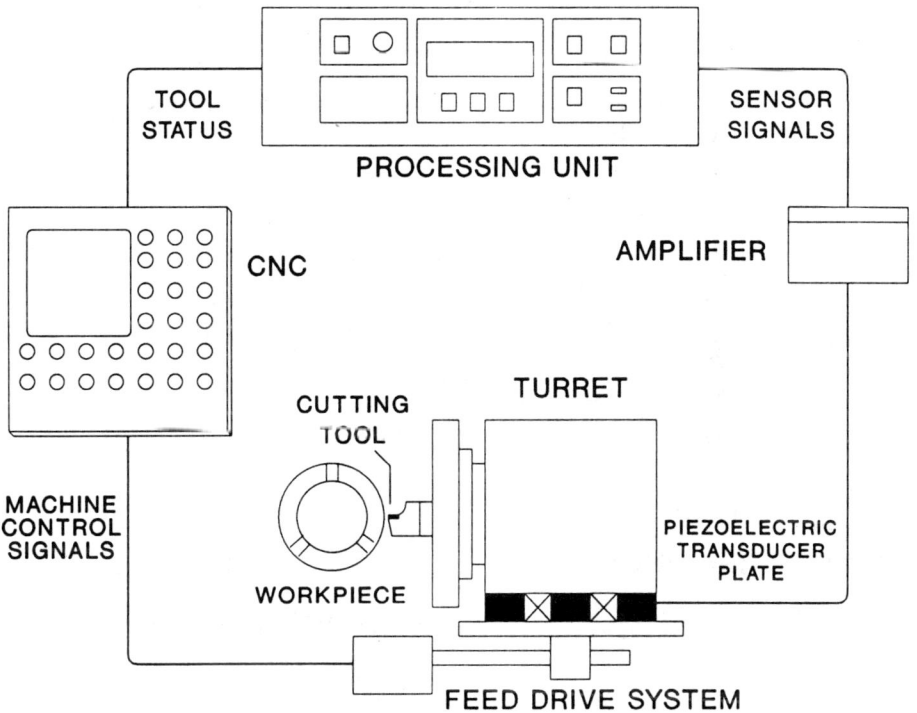

Linearity	The accuracy of the transducer measurements across a range of applied load
Frequency response	The ability of the transducer to measure rapidly changing signals accurately
Crosstalk	When measuring multiple or orthogonal forces, the measured load on one axis must not be affected by applied loads on the other axes

Application of strain gauge or piezoelectric technologies is still an art, so it is necessary to identify an experienced system supplier. When properly designed and installed, either technology can provide an effective force measuring solution.

Processing Unit

The processing unit is the "brain" of the monitoring system. It contains the electronics necessary to monitor the transducer signals, determine the tool condition, display status information to the operator, and communicate with the machine tool. Many commercially available processing units are microprocessor-based and can provide sophisticated monitoring, communication, and display functions. A number of digital signal processing schemes or algorithms (ranging from simple to complex) can be used to determine the tool condition from the transducer data. For example, consider a simple threshold algorithm to determine collision and abnormal events by monitoring cutting force data. The threshold is selected and the "algorithm" consists of two comparisons:

IF Force > Threshold THEN EVENT/STOP !

IF Force < Threshold THEN Continue Monitoring

In this monitoring system, the force data are monitored and evaluated continually with the algorithm above.

Simple processing algorithms such as this can work quite well in some applications. The main problem that arises is secondary effects from normal machining process variations, which include changes in machining parameters or changes in work material hardness, both of which can affect the force level. Such secondary effects are present with all measured signals, not just cutting force. As shown in figure 1.6, changes in the cutting parameters or the condition of the workpiece affect the level of the cutting force. This means that the threshold level must be set higher to avoid false alarms. As the limit is set higher, however, the effectiveness of the system in responding to true events is diminished.

More sophisticated algorithms and processing schemes have been developed to eliminate secondary effects. Signature tracking is an example. With a signature technique as shown in figure 1.7, a "learning" cycle is performed to establish a baseline reference signal, which can be force, vibration, etc. Subsequent operations are compared to this reference, and if significant deviations occur, an event is declared. Signature techniques eliminate some of the effects of change in the cutting parameters but are not totally immune to secondary effects.

Even more sophisticated processing algorithms have been implemented to eliminate secondary effects. These include data normalization, pattern recognition, multiple sensors, and time series analysis. These techniques are often quite effective, but in general, no technique is immune to all secondary effects.

One of the key performance measures of a processing unit is the response time to a catastrophic event. Figure 1.8 shows tool travel distances for typical machining conditions. At normal conditions, a cutting tool may travel 0.42

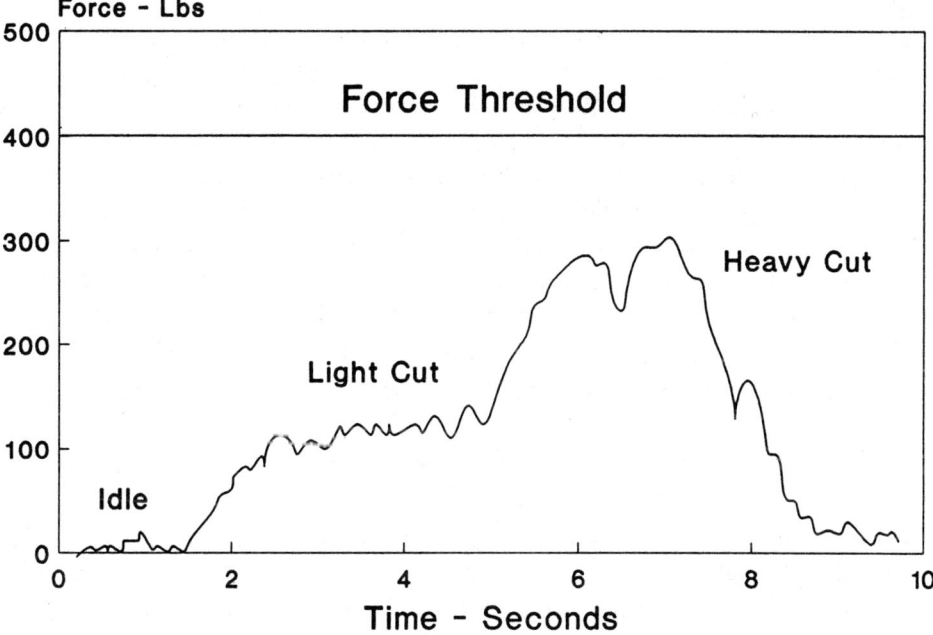

Figure 1.6 Threshold Technique

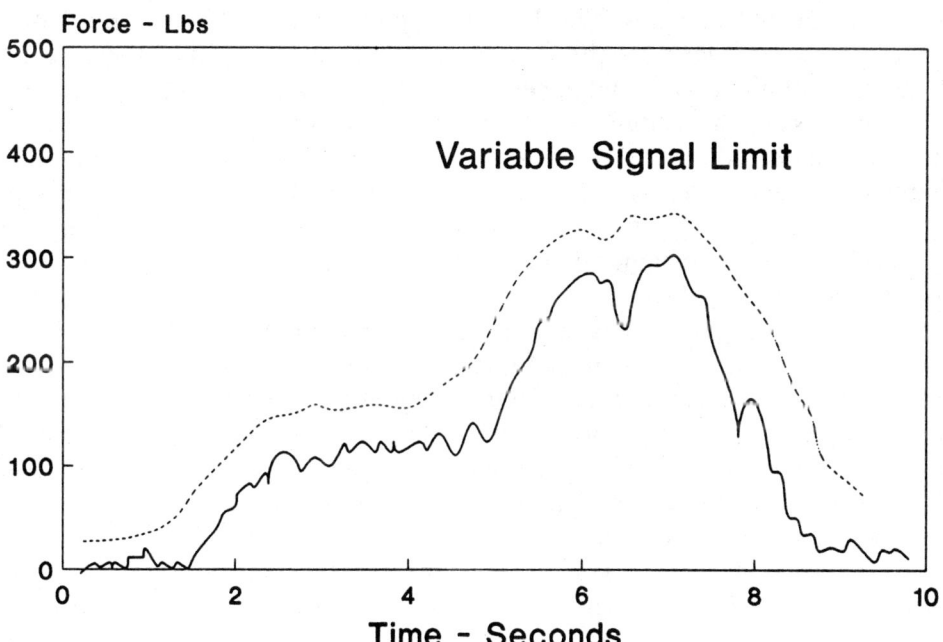

Figure 1.7 Signature Technique

BASIC FEATURES OF MONITORING SYSTEMS 11

Figure 1.8 Tool Travel Distance

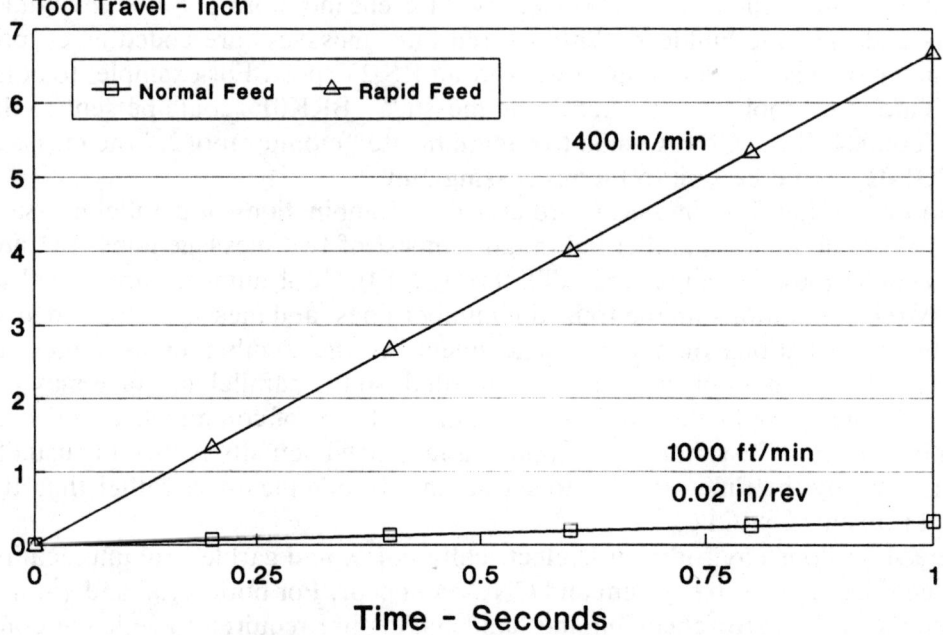

inches in one second, and at rapid feed conditions it may travel 6.67 inches. Rapid response to stop the machine tool after a catastrophic event is clearly necessary. Response times to send "stop machine" signal for monitoring systems are generally specified in milliseconds, and values from 3 to 15 milliseconds are typical.

Machine Tool Interface

Machine tool monitoring systems require a communication interface with the machine tool. This interface is required to transmit status and control signals. For example, the monitoring system may send a "broken tool" signal to the machine tool, indicating that the machine should stop immediately. Similarly, the machine tool may send a "new tool" signal to the monitoring system, indicating that a new cutting tool is being used. Other common commands include tool or sequence numbers, signal conditioning control, and enable/disable commands. Normally, these commands are implemented via "M" codes that are placed in the part program. The monitoring system normally communicates directly with the CNC unit on the machine, and the physical implementation is either a serial link (RS-232) or a parallel link (optoisolated). At the present time, no standards exist for this communication. The Manufacturing Automation Protocol (MAP) is

gaining acceptance for plant and cell communication but is not commonly available on automation devices within the cell.

Different implementations are used by different monitoring system manufacturers and machine builders. With a serial link, messages are coded as cryptic character strings and communicated over an RS-232 port. For example, to communicate that "tool 1 has broken," the message "BRK01" could be sent to the CNC control. If the CNC wished to communicate "monitor tool 2," the message "TOOL02" could be sent to the processing unit.

With a parallel link, messages are coded as combinations of parallel message lines. For example, a parallel link might consist of two message lines (M1 and M2) and four tool number lines (T1 through T4). Tool numbers are coded as binary representations on the four tool number lines, and messages are coded as unique combinations on the message lines. As the number of messages increases, more communication lines are needed, so the parallel interface may not be as flexible or sophisticated as a serial link. In terms of communication speed, both can be quite fast, but the communication speed actually realized is usually determined by the time required to set up and decode messages rather than the actual transmission time.

The shop floor environment is electrically noisy, and garbled communication between the monitoring system and CNC can occur. For both serial and parallel communication, error-checking and handshaking are required for reliable communication. Handshaking ensures that both the monitoring system and the CNC do not attempt to transmit messages at the same time. Error-checking is necessary to check each message for validity, and if an invalid message is received, a request for retransmission can be made. Provisions must also be made to prevent infinite communication loops when errors occur. These are critical considerations for reliable communication on the shop floor.

One of the negative effects of a monitoring system that is often overlooked is the increase in cycle time due to the communication between the monitoring system and CNC. As mentioned above, the communication from the monitoring system to CNC is implemented via M codes in the part program. The addition of these M codes requires additional CNC processing and lengthens the cycle time. Increases may be 0.1 seconds per message and a typical program may require 6 to 10 messages. These increases of 0.5 to 1 second are negligible for larger parts with longer cycles, but they may add 5 to 10 percent for parts with shorter cycles.

User/Operator Interface

Each monitoring system has a user interface that performs two functions: display of system status and entry of data and commands. Again, no standards exist and a variety of designs may be found for the user interface. Useful features are

lights to indicate system status at a glance and an alphanumeric display for more specific text displays. A particular user interface should be evaluated using simple human factors and ergonomic considerations. Is it easy to use and intuitive? Are the displays readable in shop conditions? Do the displays show useful information clearly? Are the buttons easy to use? Will it stand up to shop floor abuse? This is just a matter of "exercising" the user interface to find the good and bad features.

One of the most important things that the user interface can do is display diagnostic information. Murphy's Law applies quite well to machine tools and monitoring systems: things do go wrong. Helpful diagnostic information can allow the user to troubleshoot a problem quickly. Examples of diagnostic information might include an "event log" or a message buffer for the machine tool interface. An event log would record significant events, such as broken tools or collisions, for review at a later time. This record would identify recurring problems, and it would keep an accurate record when events happen very quickly. A message buffer for the machine tool interface would perform much the same function. The communication between the monitoring system and CNC occurs very quickly, and again a record of the messages and responses is useful for troubleshooting.

Performance Expectations on the Shop Floor

Performance of commercially available tool monitoring systems can range from very good to very bad depending on a number of factors. First, the user must consider and define his expectations. What events must be detected: collisions, breakages, wearouts? What levels of missed events and false alarms can be accepted? No system is 100-percent accurate all the time, and if users expect perfect performance, they will be disappointed.

Figure 1.9 suggests relative reliabilities for the detection of different machining events. Gross failures, such as collisions caused by cutting the wrong workpiece or using the wrong cutting tool, produce a significantly different cutting signal and are relatively easy to detect. Events such as small tool chips or slight tool wear are much more difficult to detect repeatedly.

Example of Collision Detection

An example of detection of a collision event using a force-based monitoring system is shown in figures 1.10a and 1.10b. The workpiece machined is a cast iron brake rotor, and in this example, the rotor was miscast, resulting in the height

Figure 1.9 Reliability of Monitoring

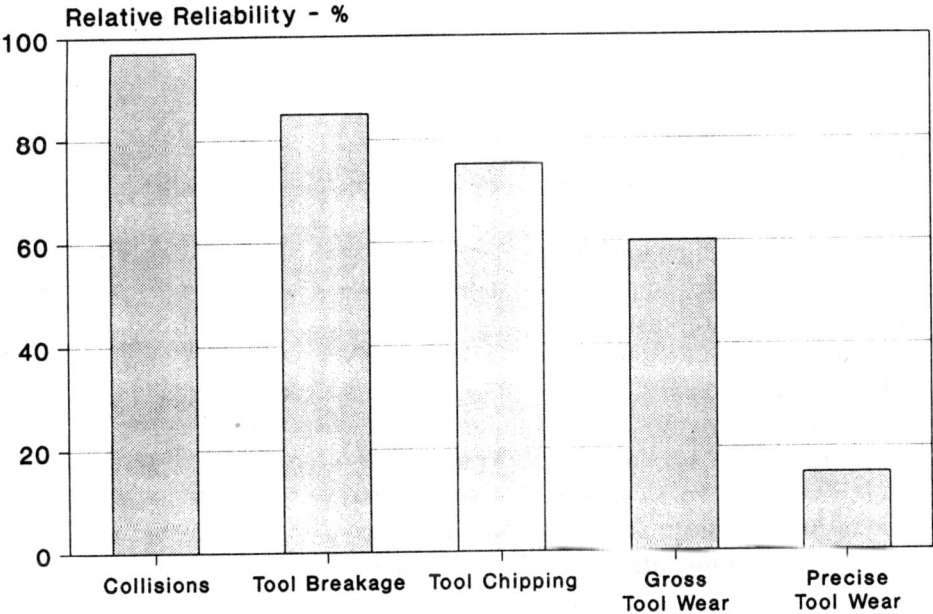

Figure 1.10a Brake Rotor Collision

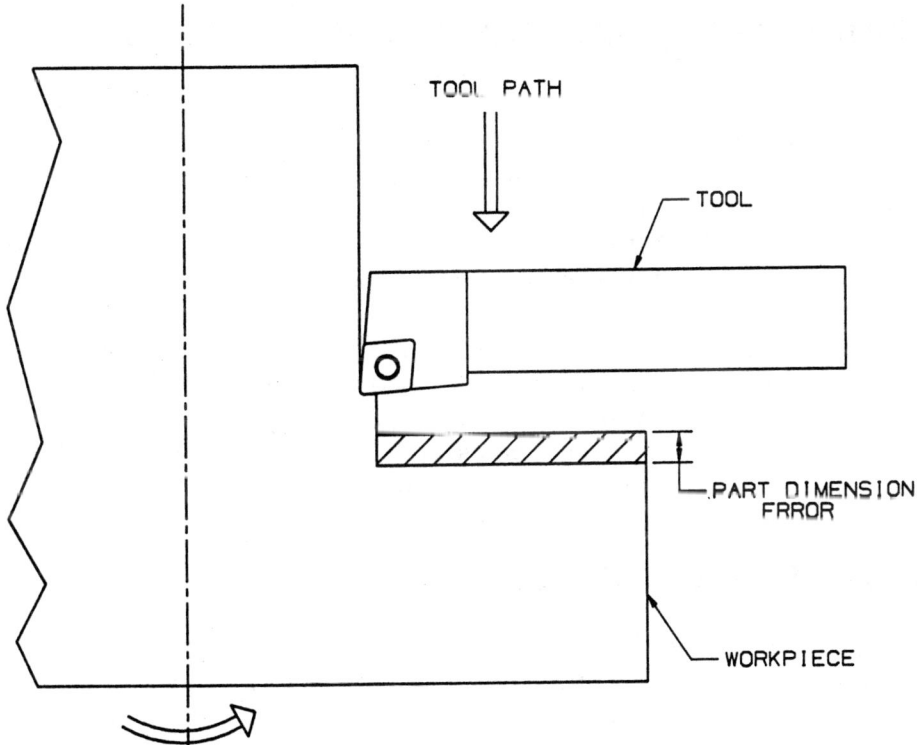

PERFORMANCE EXPECTATIONS ON THE SHOP FLOOR 15

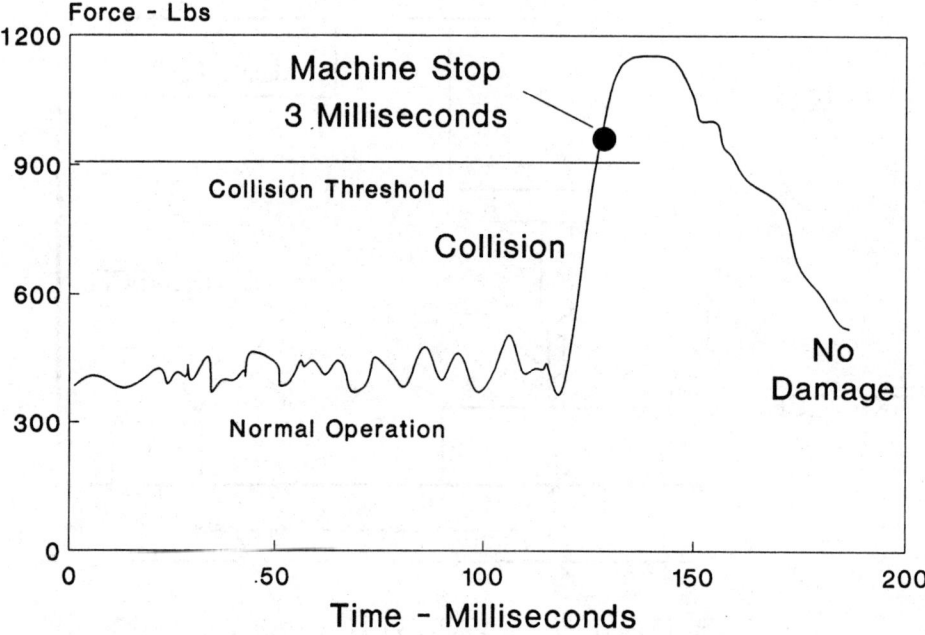

Figure 1.10b Forces for Rotor Collision

dimensions being 0.25 inches too large. During the machining operation shown, because of the oversize dimensions, the cutting tool encountered the top of the "hat" and engaged at a large depth of cut. The tool experienced a sharp increase in forces, overload was declared, and the machine stopped without damage. Without a monitoring system, the tool would have been pushed 0.25 inches farther in the "hat," resulting in a potentially catastrophic event.

Example of Tool Breakage Detection

Tool breakage detection is important in all applications, but especially in small hole drilling. Many drilling machines are multispindle, drilling many holes at the same time, and many are completely automatic with workpiece load and unload. Tool breakage is a greater risk because small diameter drills are used, and if a drill breaks, an operator is not present to detect it. Many pieces may be produced with a missing hole before the fault is detected. Costly manual rework may be necessary.

Acoustic emission monitors are well suited to this application. An acoustic emission transducer is mounted on the machine table, providing an acoustic path

Figure 1.11a AE Drill Monitoring

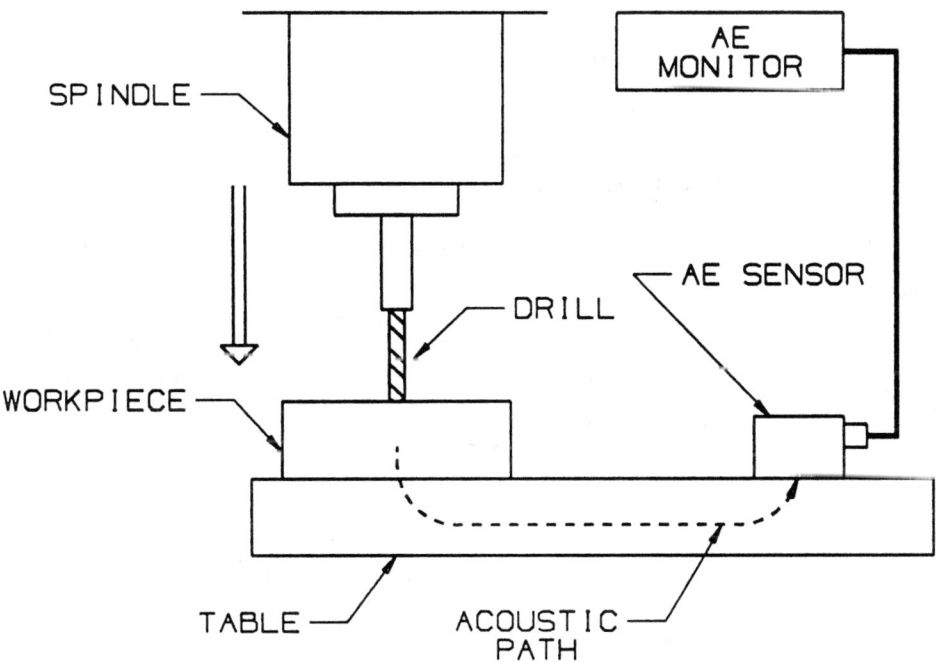

Figure 1.11b AE Data for Drill Breakage

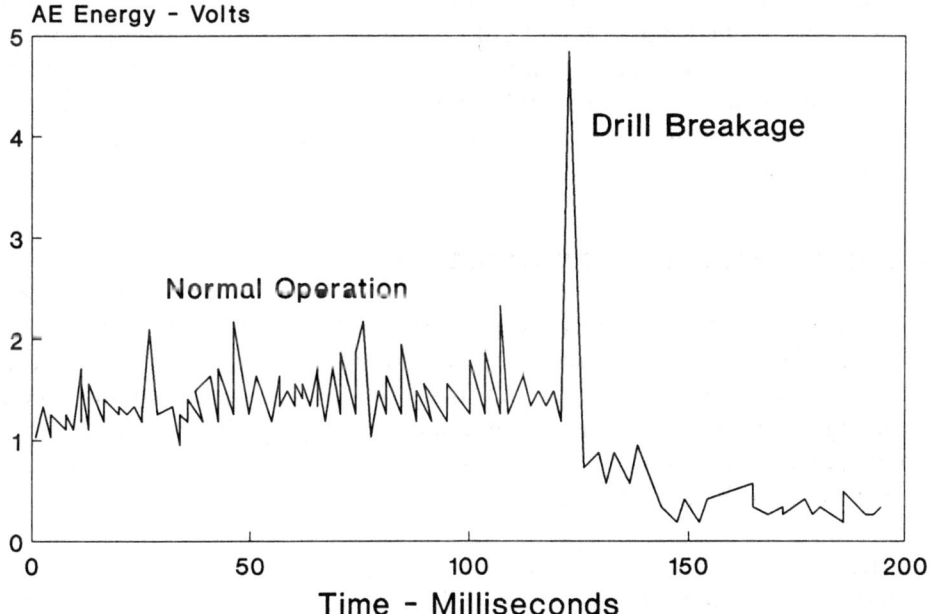

from the workpiece to transducer, as shown in figures 1.11a and 1.11b. When one of the drills breaks, a burst of energy is produced. The system detects the energy spike and stops the machine. The drill can be replaced before many scrap pieces are produced, and for this application, the reliability of the detection system is near 100 percent with almost no missed breakage events.

Example of Tool Wear Detection

Tool wear detection is best demonstrated through repeated tests. A series of wear detection tests was made, cutting 4,340 steel workpieces with variable hardnesses and dimensions with CNMG-543 inserts. A cutting-force-based wear monitoring system was used. Each test was started with a new insert, and machining continued until the wear monitoring system declared a worn tool. The results of the tests in figure 1.12 show that at declared wearout, actual tool wear values range from 0.009 inches to 0.015 inches with no undetected wearouts or failures. Similar wear detection performance has been reported on other materials [1].

Figure 1.12 Tool Wear Test Data

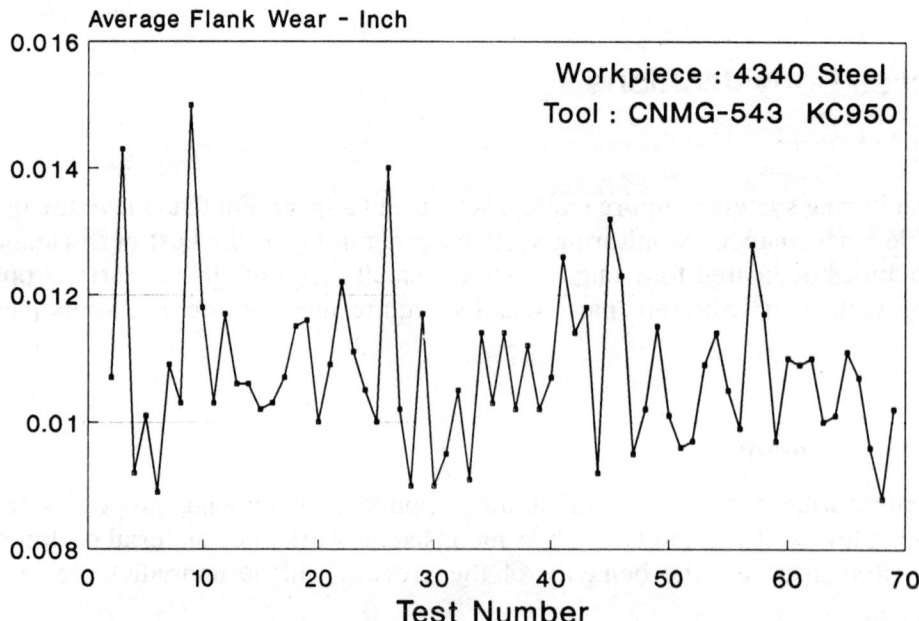

Considerations in the Selection of a System

A number of tool monitoring systems are commercially available. A particular system cannot be labeled "good" or "bad" in all applications, and the selection criteria must go far beyond which sensor or transducer is used. Systems have different strengths and weaknesses, so the performance and user satisfaction of a particular system depends on how well it is matched to the application.

Monitoring Objectives

As mentioned above, the user must define the monitoring objectives and the expected levels of false and missed alarms that are allowable. The user can evaluate different systems with respect to these objectives.

Transducer Considerations

The installation of the transducer for the monitoring system must not adversely affect the capability of the machine. For example, a transducer that weakens the machine structure and that creates vibration or deflection problems is unacceptable. A transducer that is exposed near the cutting action may be damaged during tool or part changing.

Process Considerations

Range of Parts

All monitoring systems require manual set-up and adjustment to achieve the best possible performance. Monitoring systems generally give the best performance on machines dedicated to a single part or a small range of similar parts. Applications with many different parts usually require more set-up and adjustment time.

Process Variation

Tool monitoring systems are sometimes applied to machining processes that have high levels of variability, such as inconsistent workpiece material or dimensions. In such cases, the behavior of the process will be unpredictable, with

unexpected tool wearouts and breakages. A monitoring system may have a higher level of false alarms in these cases, but the system will still detect many of the abnormalities and will be of significant value.

Communication Interface

The communication interface between the monitoring system and the CNC will increase the cycle time, and it is important to estimate these increases and decide how much is acceptable. For example, an increase of 5 percent probably would be acceptable, but 50 percent would not.

The communication interface generally is implemented with commands placed in the part program that is executed by the CNC. The part programming burden must be considered to determine if the required programming changes are acceptable. For example, adding a few "M-codes" to an existing program is probably acceptable, but rewriting an entire part program library to accommodate the communication with the monitoring system probably is not acceptable.

Operator Involvement

The one factor that ultimately determines the success or failure of a monitoring system is acceptance by the machine operator. All monitoring systems require a certain amount of attention from the operator to set up, adjust, and control the system. If the operator finds that the system is confusing, takes too much time, or does not work, he will not work to make it a success. The operator must have confidence that he understands and can control the system and that the system will help him succeed at his job. Adequate documentation and training are necessary.

Construction

The final factor to consider is the construction and design of the monitoring system itself. Any device placed in the shop floor environment must be rugged. The system must be impervious to the dust, mist, and temperature of the shop environment.

In summary, the performance of a monitoring system depends on many factors. No standards exist and no absolute guarantees can be given. When considering a monitoring system, buyers must first carefully define their needs and expectations. They can then evaluate monitoring systems to determine if those systems meet their needs. Buyers should ask for system performance data from similar applications, or they should ask to visit sites where systems are in use.

Summary

Tool monitoring systems are important elements in improving productivity and quality in automated machining systems. Successful application of these systems involves several components: transducer, processing unit, and machine tool interface.

Monitoring systems provide the benefit of detecting collisions, tool breakage, tool wear, or other abnormal events that can lead to catastrophic damage to the workpiece and machine tool.

The majority of commercially available systems are cutting-force-based, but significant differences exist in monitoring objectives and signal processing techniques. The main problem that arises is the presence of secondary effects, such as workpiece or process variations, which make it difficult to accurately assess the true tool condition.

At the present time, monitoring systems are an accessory to a machine tool, but in the future, they will be more integrated into the machining system. Advances in the fundamental monitoring technologies may come from the use of new sensors and/or advanced signal processing techniques.

References

1. Beyer, Peter J. "Tool Condition Sensor for Automated Manufacturing." Eastern Manufacturing Technology Conference, November 10–12, 1987.

2. Dzombak, Ivan, and William Kline. "System Design for In-Process Tool Monitors." Machine Monitoring Sensors—SME Conference, March 7–9, 1989, Detroit, Michigan.

3. Kluft, W. "In-Process Monitoring of Cutting Tools." 2nd Biennial International Machine Tool Technology Conference, NMTBA, Sept. 5–13, 1984.

4. Magadanz, Paul. "Tool Monitoring for Operational Security." Machine Monitoring Sensors—SME Conference, March 7–9, 1989, Detroit, Michigan.

5. McKee, Michael C. "Monitoring Inconsistent Workpieces." *Cutting Tool Engineering* (August 1989):29–32.

6. Powell, John W. "In Process Tool Sensing." *Carbide and Tool Journal* (November–December 1988):17–23.

7. Stockline, Larry E. "Tool and Machine Monitoring Systems," 4th Biennial International Machine Tool Technology Conference, September 7–14, 1988.

Chapter 2 Fiber Optics

Scott Wohlstein

The field of fiber optics has grown exponentially with respect to technological advances in applications and constituent fiber materials. What was once considered a solution aimed primarily at the communications industry has now deeply rooted itself in manufacturing technology that is embedded in sensors for process and quality control.

Fiber-optic "conductors" have advantages over their electrical counterparts:

- Low signal radiation (ideal for high-security placements)

- RFI, EMI, and lightning immunity (ideal for high-voltage or high-magnetic-field placements)

- No ground loops (ideal for spark hazard/flammable placements)

- Low attenuation/high bandwidth (ideal for long-distance, high-volume signal transmission)

- Smaller size/relative volume (ideal for small duct space and limited access areas)

History and Introduction

Although the presence of fiber optics has become pervasive relatively recently, the concept of optical fibers is not new, and in fact, its history spans more than 100 years. The principle of light transmission through a medium (in water), was demonstrated by British physicist John Tyndall. In 1934, Bell Laboratories was

awarded a patent for the "Light Pipe," and in the 1950s, the American Optical Corporation developed glass fibers that had the capability of transmitting light over short distances. In the early 1970s, Corning Glass Works developed the technology to produce optical glass fibers for long-distance applications.

Although other methods have evolved, the majority of techniques used to manufacture fiber-optic fibers are all related to the "drawing" process (refer to figure 2.1). This method uses a furnace to grow a silicon glass boule. During part of the growth process, chemicals can be added to the silica to help attenuate, transmit, or withstand certain environments in the final product fiber.

Once the boule is grown, it is heated to its melting point and drawn through a form (to help mold the fiber into a certain size and configuration). After being formed, the fiber is drawn through a cladding chamber, where the cladding is bonded to the fiber.

Figure 2.1 The Manufacture of Fiber-Optic Cabling

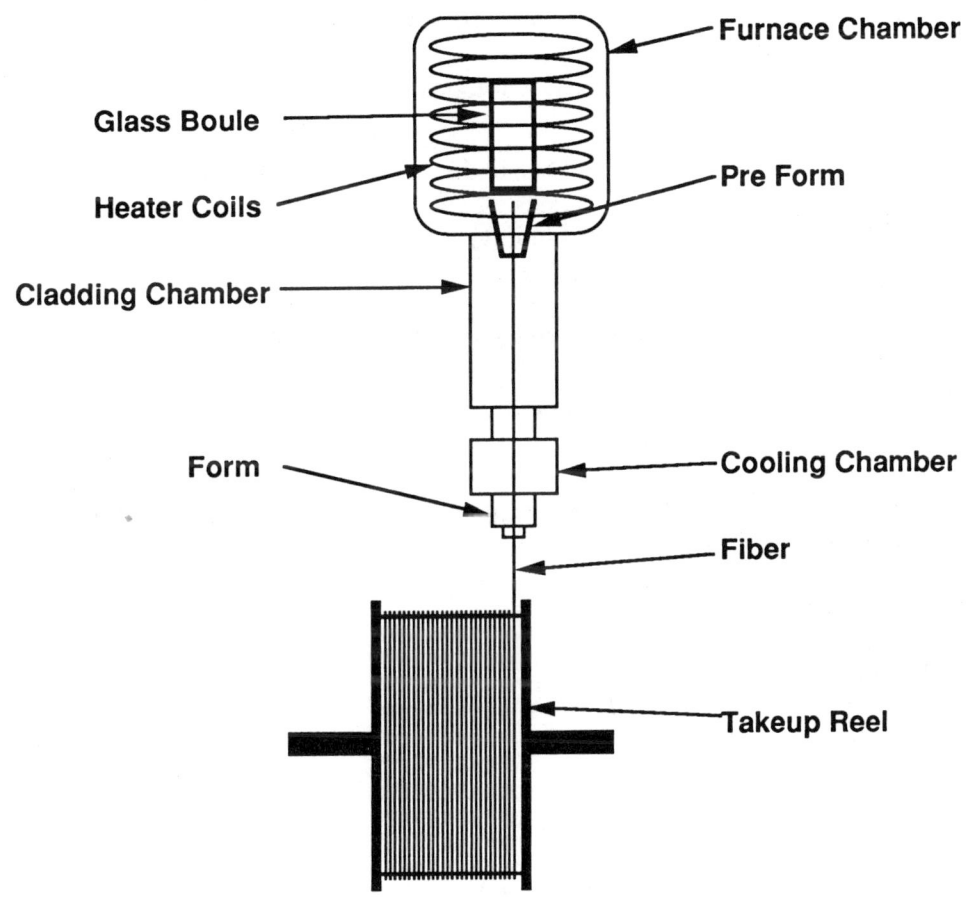

Emerging through the cladding chamber, the fiber is pulled through a cooling chamber, where both the components are cooled to just below melting temperature, before being pulled through a final form (which eliminates excess cladding). Not completely cooled, the fiber is finally wrapped around a large takeup reel for final processing and use.

The whole process is controlled tightly to eliminate any variations in composition and/or form. To produce very consistent fiber-optic fibers, the manufacturing process is conducted in a tall "tower" configuration (hence the term *drawing tower*) that facilitates a much more even drawing process, reducing nonlinear and volumetric forming effects.

Fiber-Optic Theory

The Electronics Industry Association defines fiber optics as "the branch of optical technology concerned with the transmission of radiant power through fibers made of transparent materials such as glass, fused silica, or plastic."

Fiber optics, like all forms of light pipes, rely on total internal reflections (or TIR—the amount of light that "bounces" off the cladding and reflects back through the core material to aid in the transmission of light down the fiber). Losses are kept to a minimum by making the refractive index of the transmitting medium (core) higher than that of the cladding or "containing medium."

Several forms of light pipes exist:

- Liquid light pipes. These consist of a special liquid with a refractive index most suitable to the wavelength of choice. Although the liquid light pipe was the first method of transmitting light, it has seen recent resurgence because it possesses significant transmission and coupling advantages.

- Solid light pipes. These are typically solid pieces of translucent material, such as plastic lenses or bezels that illuminate gauge(s) by transferring light from a bulb through the edge of the lens. This was the first type of mass-manufactured light pipe.

- Fiber-optic light pipes. This category includes the following:
    - Random or noncoherent fiber bundles. Used to illuminate, collect, and transfer light from sources or samples, providing uniform directional lighting.
    - Arranged or coherent fiber bundles. Used for imaging applications, maintaining image property and geometries.

- Single fibers. Used for the transmission or reception of light from LASERs, LEDs (Light Emitting Diodes), or arc sources.

This chapter will focus primarily on single fibers (refer to figure 2.2). Single fibers can be broken down further into either single mode or multimode fibers.

A single mode fiber is characterized as having a small core (light-transmitting center) in the order of $2\mu m$ to $10\mu m$ (this permits only one mode to propagate through the core of the fiber). The core is surrounded by a covering called *cladding* (typically comprised of PVC or TEFLON, although new optically proper materials are being developed), which ranges in outer diameter from $125\mu m$ to $400\mu m$. This cladding is covered by an outer sleeve or protective covering impervious to environmental effects.

The multimode type is characterized as having a large core (light-transmitting center) on the order of $50\mu m$ to $300\mu m$, permitting only one mode to propagate through the core of the fiber.

Three subclasses of fibers help distinguish characteristics further (refer to figure 2.3):

- Step-Index. (Typically single-mode class.) This term describes those fibers in which the core and cladding materials have distinctly different indexes of refraction. This type of fiber configuration has the least loss of light through the cladding material.

Figure 2.2 Light Propagation Through Fiber Optics

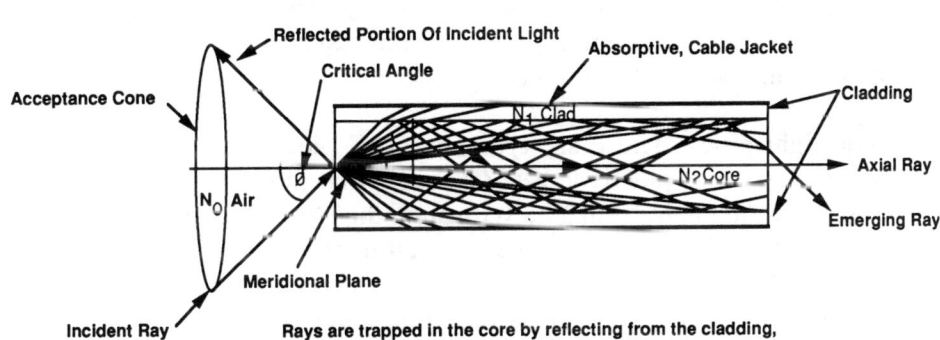

Rays are trapped in the core by reflecting from the cladding, which has a slightly lower refractive index than the core.

$\emptyset$ = Maximum acceptance angle for total internal reflection
N_0 = Index of Refraction of Air = 1.00
N_2 = Index of Refraction of fiber core
N_1 = Index of Refraction of fiber cladding

NA = Numerical Aperture = N_0 Air SIN $\emptyset$ = $\sqrt{N_2 \text{Core}^2 - N_1 \text{Clad}^2}$

FIBER-OPTIC THEORY

Figure 2.3 Fiber Types and Configurations

Multimode

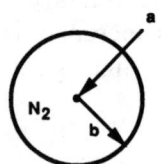

Radius: $= b > a \gg Å$
Index of Refraction: $= N_1 > N_2$, $N_1 - N_2 \approx 0.01$
Numerical Aperature: $= 0.1$
Attentuation: $= 20$ dB/km
Bandwidth: $= 10^9$ Bits/Sec/km (min) {for Graded or low NA Step-Index fiber}
Source: $=$ LASER, SRLED, LED
O.D. (typ.): $= 5$ Mils
Core Dia. (typ.): $= 3$ Mils

Single-Mode

Radius: $= b \gg a \approx Å$
Index of Refraction: $= N_1 > N_2$, $N_1 - N_2 \approx 0.01$
Attentuation: $= 20$ dB/km
Bandwidth: $= 10^{11}$ Bits/Sec/km
Source: $=$ LASER Diode
O.D. (typ.): $= 5$ Mils
Core Dia. (typ.): $= 2$ to 8 μm

Graded-Index

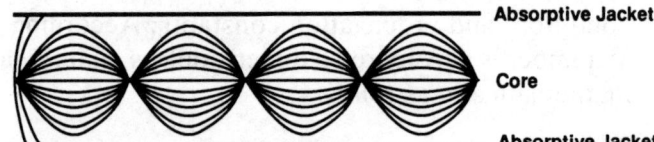

Cross Section

Meridional rays are continually refocused by refraction in the core, which has a refractive index that gets progressively lower away from the center.

Step-Index

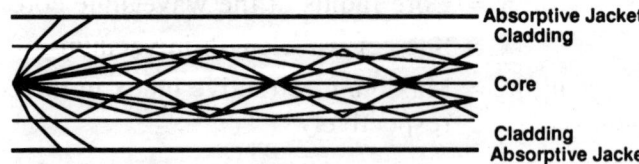

Cross Section

Rays are trapped in the core by reflection from the cladding, which has a slightly lower refractive index than the core.

- Graded-Index. This term describes those fibers in which the core and cladding materials encounter a decreasing index of refraction outward, radially.

- Polarization-Preserving. (Typically of the single-mode class.) This term describes those fibers that are manufactured with birefringent cores to maintain a level of linear polarization.

Related Parameters

Designing any element of a fiber-optic system* properly requires knowledge of the following:

- Numerical Aperture (NA). (Also considered the "light gathering" number for a given fiber optic.) The NA is defined as the sine of the largest angle an incident ray can have for total internal reflection in the core. The NA of a fiber can be determined by measuring the light cone emerging from the fiber when all modes are excited.

    A higher core index with respect to the cladding means a larger NA, although as NA is increased, scattering losses increase as well. As a rule of thumb, the larger the NA, the more "light-gathering" capability.

- Normalized Frequency Parameter (V Number). Several fiber parameters can be expressed in terms of the V number, which can include the number of modes at a given wavelength, mode cutoff condition, and propagation constants. According to the EIA, the V number is considered a dimensionless quantity and is expressed mathematically as follows:

$$V = 2\pi a/\lambda (\sqrt{(n_1^2 - n_2^2)})$$

Where:

a = Core radius of the waveguide core
λ = Subject wavelength in vacuum
n_1, n_2 = Maximum refractive index in the core and cladding, respectively

Engineering Considerations and Related Parameters

Although fiber-optic light guides can be considered immune to most of the problems plaguing their electrical counterparts, they still behave poorly when subjected to certain elements. It is because of these "spoilers" that the following

---

* *System* refers to any/all fiber-optic elements and their related componentry.

considerations involved in the design or engineering of fiber optics and related systems should be understood.

Bandwidth Limitations

The bandwidth of a fiber determines directly the highest transmission rate of information with acceptable resolution (or ability to discern between data). Specifically, a fiber's bandwidth limitation is caused by dispersion. Dispersion can be classified as follows:

- Modal dispersion. Modal dispersion becomes significant when multiple modes are excited in a fiber-optic system. It can be thought of as the function of TIR versus non-TIR. The effect has been shown (in long fibers) to create pulse broadening approximately proportional to the square root of length. Typically, graded index fibers exhibit much less modal dispersion and higher bandwidth than step-index, multimode fibers.

- Material dispersion. Because the refractive index of any material varies with frequency, the different frequency components of a signal can limit efficient bandwidths of transmission as propagated through the fiber-optic material. This affects all types of fibers, although creating a much smaller effect than modal dispersion in multimode fibers. As the source wavelength approaches 1.3μ, and into the NIR (Near Infrared), the material dispersion effects become inconsequential for silica glass (the typical fiber-optic material).

- Waveguide dispersion. Because the group velocity of a waveguide mode is a function of frequency, nonmonochromatic signals will be affected by dispersion even when there exists no material dispersion. This affects all types of fibers, although creating a much smaller effect than modal dispersion (by an order of magnitude).

Attenuation

Attenuation losses through a fiber-optic conductor decay exponentially with length. Losses through attenuation are the single most expensive factor because of the additional required repeaters for those fiber-optic systems with high loss. Specifically, the following are considered the major causes of attenuation:

- Absorption. Small absorption losses appear in silica systems when the source wavelength is in the 800 nm to NIR band.

Impurities (more specifically water in the form of hydroxyl ions) create the majority of absorption losses. Because of recent improvements in production and material purities, systems can deliver attenuation on the order of 0.1 db/km.

- Scattering. Scattering, which can couple energy from guided to radiation modes, is also influenced greatly by Rayleigh scattering (created by minute variations and microbending in the drawing process) and produces attenuation proportional to λ^{-4} (of source).

Microbending Losses

Attenuation in a fiber-optic fiber is increased when force is applied to the surface of the fiber (longitudinally or radially).

Mode Scrambling

Multimode fiber can be subjected to the distribution of optical power among the fiber's modes, leading to power loss.

Polarization Scrambling

Unless they utilize specially designed single-mode polarization-preserving fibers, typical fiber-optic systems will not preserve polarization, leading to transmission/acceptance loss.

Environmental

Environmental factors that affect mode distribution, attenuation (either absorptive and/or scattering), phase, and/or polarization can include the following:

- Temperature. Material breakdown and metallurgical effects can be caused if material is subjected to constant extreme temperatures and/or heating-cooling cycles.

- Pressure. Pressure can cause fatigue in material (as well as in couplings and termination hardware).

- Mechanical stress (bending, twisting, vibrational). Mechanical stress can cause fatigue in material (as well as in couplings and termination hardware).

- Radioactivity. Radioactivity can cause a decay in the material purity as well as creating brittleness.

- Light irradiation. Light irradiation can cause a decay and subsequent attenuation in certain optical materials (UV light can create chaos in certain plastics).

- Chemical. Chemical factors can cause a decay in the material as well as causing mechanical breakdown of coupling cement materials and index matching fluids.

Nonlinear Effects

Nonlinear effects can be caused by irradiating a fiber-optic system with too much optical power. Spectral broadening, distortion, and new frequencies include some of the effects.

Surface Preparation (Termination and Coupling)

Surface preparation includes the polishing, cleaning, and proper handling of fiber-optic components. Proper termination, splicing, and coupling is essential for efficient fiber-optic system operation.

Feedback

Certain systems cannot tolerate feedback (typically through Fresnel reflections). Consequently, solid performance is achieved only through the use of an optical isolator such as a Faraday rotator.

Uses and Applications

Fiber optics have the unique ability to be applied to solve problems in unobtrusive ways. Fiber-optic applications can include the delivery and reception of light and/or images or sensing of changes in intensity, polarization, interference, and phase of propagated light through the system. Relationships among physical effects and changes in optical properties (and typically those effects not desirable for attenuation reduction) are those that produce the most interesting system applications and related solutions. Real-time response from the sensing

system equates to faster correction and control of related conditions. Applications of fiber-optic systems have included sensing the following: magnetic fields, electric fields, rotation, displacement, acceleration, stress/strain, acoustic waves, electric current, fluid current, gas current, temperature, and pressure.

Specific examples in manufacturing process and quality control can include the following:

- Environmental chamber feedback and control. Fiber-optic sensing systems for pressure and temperature can replace standard thermocouples and ionization gauges for use in vacuum chambers, furnaces, and other atmospheres that can contain undesirable elements without degradation to the sensing components.

- Fluid/flow feedback and control. Fiber-optic sensing systems for fluid/flow can replace standard flowmeters and flow sensors for use in fluids that can include undesirable elements without degradation to the sensing components.

- Stress detection, feedback, and control. Fiber-optic sensing systems for stress and/or strain can replace standard stress or load cells for use in applications that can include civil engineering (such as buildings, roads, and bridges), and nondestructive testing apparatus.

- Electrical/magnetic field detection, feedback, and control. Fiber-optic sensing systems for electrical/magnetic field(s) can replace standard magnometers by using the systems' inherent narrow discrimination and real-time analysis capabilities.

- Displacement (acceleration and/or rotation) detection, feedback, and control. Fiber-optic sensing systems for displacement can replace standard methods (such as accelerometers and gyroscopes) for use in navigation/positional applications. Using fiber-optic sensing can eliminate the effects of RFI (Radio Frequency Interference), EMI (Electro Magnetic Interference), as well as EMP (Electro Magnetic Pulse, a tremendous electromagnetic pulse of extremely high energy, created by a nuclear detonation, which creates havoc in electronic and electrical systems). These advantages make fiber-optic sensing systems well suited for military applications.

Conclusions

Although the field of fiber optics has seen mature growth in the communications industries, its adolescent growth in the sensing industry exhibits no sign of foreseeable maturation in the next decade. With the continual advent of new material and optical technologies, fiber-sensing systems will be smaller, more resilient, and more accurate (with better repeatability).

Applications will be seen in more conventional areas, replacing fiber optics' age-old electrical counterparts and related systems. Once optical computing is commonplace, electrical-to-optical (and/or optical-to-electrical) interfaces will be replaced with fiber-optic sensing systems, decreasing conversion times and increasing sensing/detection time (to roughly the speed of light). These advances will truly revolutionize the computer automation, manufacturing process, and quality control fields (just to name a few).

References

1. Bolz, Ray E., and George L. Tuve. *CRC Handbook of Tables for Applied Engineering Science*. 2nd ed. Boca Raton, FL: CRC Press, 1988.

2. Deutsch Fiber Optic Division. *Fiber Optics, Terms and Definitions*. Los Angeles: The Deutsch Company, 1981.

3. McComb, Gordon. *The Laser Cookbook, 88 Practical Projects*. Blue Ridge Summit, PA: Tab Books, 1988.

4. Newport Corporation. *The Newport Catalog*. Fountain Valley, CA: Newport Corporation, 1989.

5. Oriel Corporation. *Light Sources, Monochromators, Detection Systems Catalog*. Volume 2. Stratford, CT: Oriel Corporation, 1989.

6. Weast, Robert C., Ph.D., Melvin J. Astle, Ph.D, and William H. Beyer, Ph.D. *CRC Handbook of Chemistry and Physics*. 69th edition/75th anniversary edition. Boca Raton, FL: CRC Press, 1988.

7. Wohlstein, Scott. "Using Fiberoptics for Practical Sensing." *Lasers and Optronics* (July 1989):73–76.

Chapter 3 Fiber Optics Applications

John W. Berthold III

Introduction

Optical sensing methods have evolved over the past 25 years to the point where practical implementations of many different optical sensors are found in industrial gaging, inspection, and automation systems. The sensing methods used today range from simple light-interruption "photoelectric eye" switches to the more sophisticated methods, such as laser speckle interferometry, digital imaging, and phase shift holography. The inventions of the laser, low loss optical fibers, and charge coupled devices have provided the new technology needed for present-day optical inspection systems. These inventions have enabled optical systems to perform accurate, reliable automatic gaging and inspection with the desirable features of noncontact, on-line, real-time, high-speed operation.

Because the types of optical sensing methods and their applications are so wide-ranging, the scope of any discussion of these methods must be reduced to a manageable size. Many excellent references describe optical measurement techniques and systems [5, 6, 8]. For this chapter, I have chosen to describe optical sensing methods that are application specific. The industrial application areas include furnace control, brazing, welding, and structural strain. The first section provides information on fiber optics that is relevant to the understanding of the subsequent sections. In the next two sections, noncontact radiation pyrometry is discussed, in which optical fibers are used to transmit the radiation from a remote measurement point to the signal processing electronics. The applications are flame temperature measurement for tuning the fuel-to-air ratio of burners in a furnace, and temperature measurement for control of heat input in an induction-heated brazing process. A one-dimensional imaging system for continuous monitoring of the butt-welding of two plates is described in the next section, and the following section focuses on a remote spectroscopic method

for detection of contaminated gases during titanium welding. A practical high-temperature strain gage is discussed in the final section; this gage is used for design verification and for making remaining life predictions for structural components. This fiber optic strain gage is a contact sensor and thus is different from the other noncontact sensing methods described.

Background

Four of the five optical sensing methods discussed in the following sections use optical fibers. Fiber optics is an attractive technology for industrial applications because optical fibers provide the capability to obtain measurements in areas that are remote or difficult to reach, and in hostile environments where high temperatures, pressures, corrosive fluids, or sources of electromagnetic interference (EMI) may be present.

Optical fibers consist of a transparent core with refractive index greater than the surrounding cladding. Light entering the input end is transmitted to the output end via total internal reflection. A buffer layer is placed around the cladding to provide additional mechanical strength and to prevent the intrusion of water vapor, which causes stress corrosion cracking and eventual fiber breakage. For most industrial applications, fiber lengths exceeding a thousand feet are rare. Over these lengths, the light signal losses in optical fibers are, in general, negligible. Losses from connectors, splices, and couplers predominate. Information about the physics of how optical fibers work may be found in many excellent sources on the subject [1, 2]. Detailed descriptions of fiber optic sensors and their applications are also available [15, 4].

Because optical fibers are made from glass-based dielectric materials, these fibers do not emit EMI, nor is the light within them modulated, to first order, by EMI. This means that fibers do not require special shielding or grounding and can be used in the vicinity of high voltage lines. If explosion hazards exist, fibers can be routed anywhere. With electrical cables, the possibility of arcs or sparks requires the use of protective conduits, ground fault protectors, or explosion-proof boxes for safe operation.

Currently, many industrial facilities are installing fiber optics for data transmission to exploit the advantages offered by the technology. These installations help users become familiar with the technology and allow for introduction of fiber optics for measurement and control applications as well.

Three of the fiber optic applications described in the following sections—boiler furnace flame temperature measurement, braze temperature measurement and control, and impurity identification in the cover gas during titanium welding—may be categorized as passive, because the optical fibers are used solely to

gather radiation from the sensing region and deliver it to the optoelectronic signal processing. The fiber optic sensor application also described in this chapter may be categorized as active and intrinsic, because the light intensity signal passing through the fiber is modulated by the external parameter (strain) of interest.

Boiler Furnace Flame Temperature Measurement

The need for reliable, repeatable temperature measurement is pervasive through practically all types of industry. In many industries, such as power generation or basic metals, temperatures are so high that conventional thermometers or thermocouples cannot withstand immersion in flames or molten metal. In these situations, noncontact methods such as radiation pyrometry are used for the temperature measurement.

Several instruments are available that couple a near-infrared radiation pyrometer to an optical fiber. With this approach, the pick-up end of the optical fibers can be routed into hostile or hard-to-reach places for collection and delivery of radiation to the pyrometer. The temperature measurement systems described in this section and the next section are based on this approach.

For power boiler applications, the flame quality analyzer (FQA) diagrammed in figure 3.1 has been used for flame temperature measurement [7]. The FQA is a noninvasive electro-optical device that measures the intensity of flames and determines flame temperature and emittance profiles using two-color pyrometry (see the next section). In operation, an optical probe is installed in an opening in the furnace wall (see figure 3.1). The optical probe, at the furnace end, consists of a two-dimensional array of optical fibers that conveys a two-dimensional flame intensity profile to the processing system: optics, electronics, and signal conditioning. The processing system may be located hundreds of feet away from the optical probe.

The optical probe, which is inserted through the furnace wall, consists of two coaxial tubes separated by an annulus. The inner lens tube contains the flame imaging optics, consisting of a front window, an objective lens, a field lens, and a relay lens. The annulus between the tubes is a flow passage for air, which both cools the objective lens and prevents impingement of coal and slag on the front window. A flange on the back end of the optical probe provides a keyed mounting surface for a mating flange that holds the polished end of the optical fiber bundle. The fiber bundle input is located at the image plane of the relay lens. The optical fibers convey the flame image and radiation to the optoelectronics signal processing.

At the processing end, the fibers are rearranged into a linear array that is encoded with the region of the flame viewed by each fiber. The flame intensity

Figure 3.1 Diagram of Flame Quality Analyzer for Temperature Monitoring in a Boiler Furnace

Inset indicates how flame regions viewed by each fiber are projected onto separate photodiode arrays.

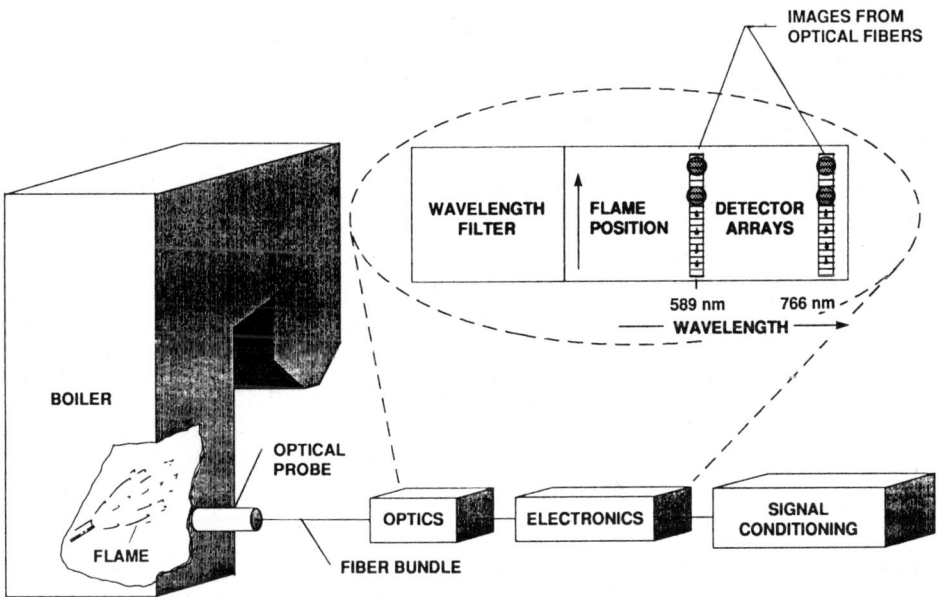

signals from the fibers are scanned by two arrays of photodiodes to determine the intensity at two distinct wavelengths (589 nm and 766 nm). Analysis at two wavelengths helps overcome potential ambiguities caused by emissivity variations. The light image from each fiber spans about five photodiode elements. The output current from each element represents the light energy incident on the photodiode during the integration time. A stable and repeatable measurement of the intensity is obtained by integrating the stepwise approximation of the intensity on the diode elements centermost in the profile (see figure 3.1). The integrated intensity is calculated for each optical fiber at each of the two wavelengths. The intensity signals are processed by a computer, using Planck blackbody radiation laws, to yield the flame temperature and emittance profiles local to each burner of the boiler. This information may be displayed to the operator in several formats or sent by serial interface to a control system.

The FQA has a large, 90-degree, field of view with spatial resolution throughout this field. The spatially resolved temperature information may be used to generate thermal maps and profiles yielding information on a burner-by-burner basis. The temperature measurement range of the FQA is 2000°F to 4400°F. Separate optical fibers view different regions of the flame simultaneously in real time. This configuration permits real-time parallel processing of the temperature

information from up to 40 separate channels at an update interval of 20 ms per channel. These channels may be incorporated into a single probe to provide high spatial resolution or in multiple probes installed in many different remote locations.

Today's utility and industrial boilers have several burners, each feeding into a common combustion chamber (see figure 3.1). Control on a burner-by-burner basis by monitoring the local combustion process at each burner is important for efficient boiler performance. With the FQA, the local combustion process can be monitored and controlled if suitable actuators and other hardware are available on the boiler for controlling fuel and air flow burner by burner. On-line flame characteristics are displayed for operational personnel and are available for input to control systems for control action. Inputs for burner-to-burner load balancing, flame envelope control, and flame condition monitoring are all available from the FQA.

Because flame temperature in furnaces provides an indication of fuel-to-air ratio, the FQA could provide a control signal for manual or automatic control of individual burners and thus balance boiler load. This control scheme is based on the fact that a properly trimmed burner exhibits a predictable flame shape and spatial temperature distribution, both of which are detected and analyzed by the FQA.

To achieve optimum efficiency, present load balancing control schemes based on global measurements of CO and O_2 are unsatisfactory in multiburner furnaces. As shown in figure 3.2, combustion efficiency varies with fuel-to-air ratio. In this plot, exhaust gas carbon monoxide (CO), oxygen (O_2), and combustion efficiency are all plotted versus excess air. At low excess air, incomplete combustion occurs and excess CO is generated. At high excess air, the extra unneeded air must be heated, and thus, heat is wasted. Because present measurements of O_2 and CO in boilers are made in the exhaust, these measurements are averages over all the burners. To allow for the fact that some burners may operate fuel-rich and others lean, operators tend to adjust excess air levels to produce waste heat, rather than allow incomplete fuel combustion. Load balancing in boilers on a burner-by-burner basis, not yet possible with other technologies, could be performed with the FQA. As a result, the boiler could be operated near peak efficiency at excess air levels in the neighborhood of 1 percent. The relationship of flame temperature, measured with the FQA on both burners of a two-burner boiler, and excess oxygen is plotted in figure 3.3.

In conclusion, the FQA has been used to measure local flame characteristics in wall-fired and tangentially-fired boilers [7]. Data taken from these boilers show that local flame temperature and light intensity are sensitive to excess oxygen concentration. These measured parameters also show a significant dependence on measurement location and burner type. This information is vital for burner load balancing, which can significantly improve boiler efficiency and productivity, thereby reducing operating costs (by millions of dollars) for industrial and

Figure 3.2 Plot of Boiler Exhaust Gas Carbon Monoxide, Oxygen, and Combustion Efficiency versus Excess Air

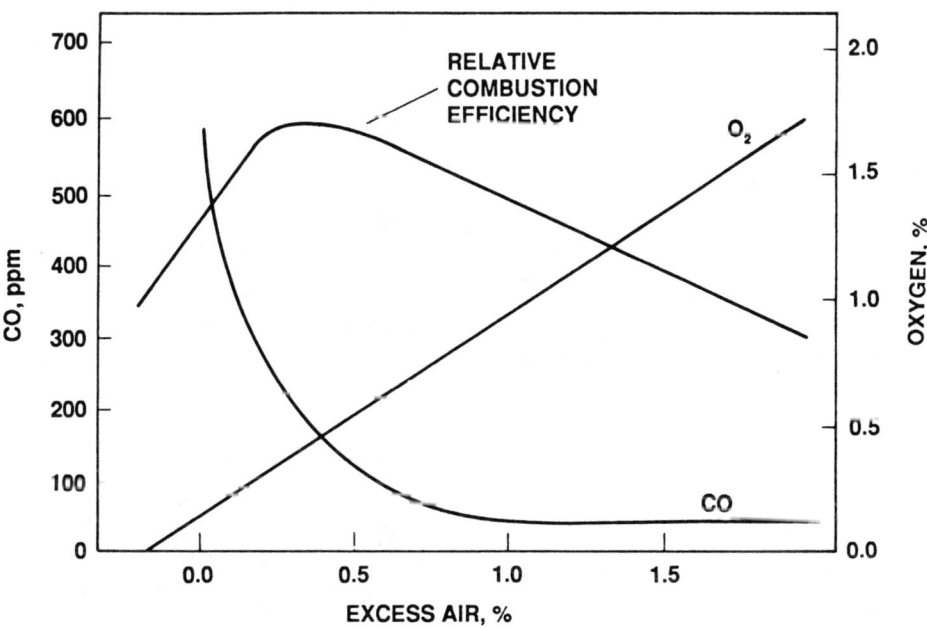

Figure 3.3 Flame Temperature from FQA versus Percent Excess Oxygen from Boiler

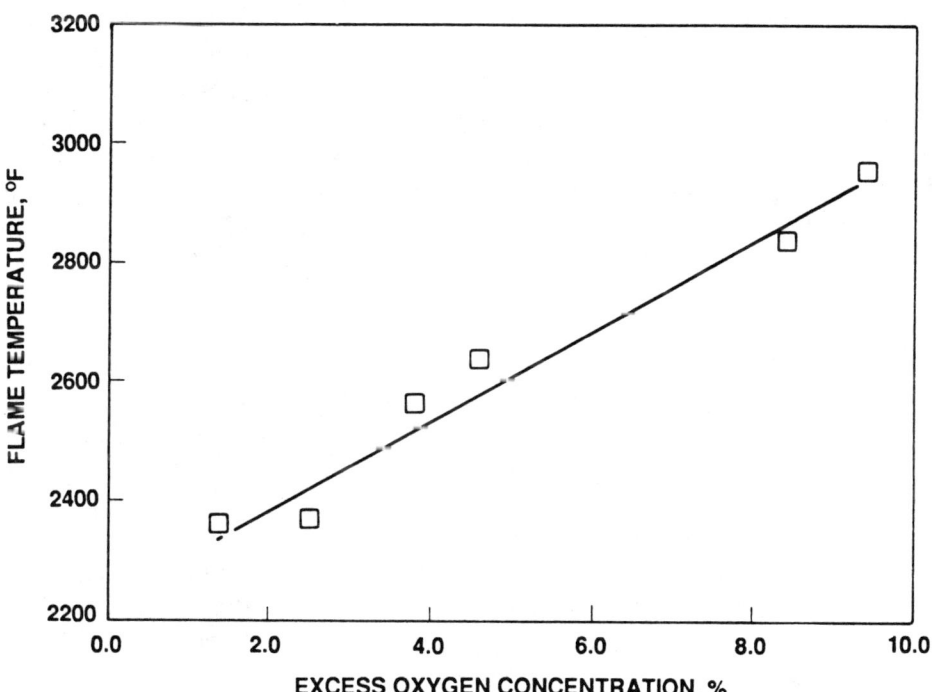

utility plants. Additionally, because flame temperature is an important contributor to nitrogen oxide (NO) formation, the FQA may be used as a tool for the evaluation of special burners used in acid gas emission control strategies.

Braze Temperature Measurement and Control*

This section describes an electro-optic temperature-monitoring and control system that was developed for use in repairing steam generator tubes in nuclear reactors. The repair consisted of spanning the faulty section of tube with an internal sleeve that was then brazed to the tube to seal off the affected section.

One requirement for achieving reliability in this operation is that the tube and sleeve reach the proper temperature. Temperatures higher than that required for brazing promote grain growth, which accelerates subsequent corrosion. Insufficient temperature prevents proper melting of the braze alloy, resulting in improper wetting of mating surfaces. Therefore, successful sleeving requires accurate control of the braze-zone temperature.

The primary objectives were to control the temperature accurately during brazing and during a subsequent annealing period.

The braze control system described here was originally designed, developed, and demonstrated by L. A. Jeffers [9]. The brazing system consists of three main sections: 1) the induction-coil heating element, which is built into a "torch" that is inserted into the sleeve to be brazed, 2) the induction-coil power supply, and 3) the braze system control cabinet.

The power supply is located remotely from the torch. The braze system control cabinet is located in a van outside of the nuclear reactor containment building. These three sections are interconnected (figure 3.4) to provide closed-loop control of the braze-zone temperature. The control signal is based on a temperature measurement derived from an optical pick-up built into the torch and connected to the analyzer in the control cabinet through an optical fiber.

The system housed in the braze control cabinet is intended to do three things:

- Determine the braze-zone temperature

- Use this value to provide closed loop feedback control of the braze torch power supply to achieve the desired time/temperature sequence

---

* Portions of this section have been reprinted with permission. Copyright © Instrument Society of America, 1985. From *Proceedings of the 31st International Instrumentation Symposium*.

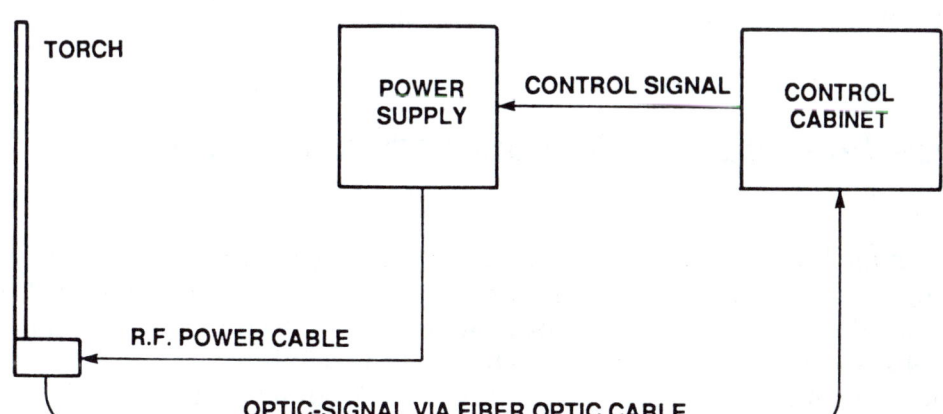

Figure 3.4 Closed-loop Control of the Braze-zone Temperature [9]

- Provide on-line display and permanent recordings of vital information regarding the braze sequence.

The heart of the system is a microcomputer programmed to carry out most of the required functions automatically. Except for various switches that must be activated when power is first brought to the system, all of the operator interaction with the system comes in response to prompts that appear on the video display screen.

Figure 3.5 shows a block diagram of the braze control system. Light from the braze zone is delivered to the detector unit through an optical fiber. Inside the detector unit, this light is separated into two color components that are directed to separate photodetectors. The photodetectors generate voltage signals (X and Z) that are proportional to the intensities of the light. The ratio of these signals is a linear function of the temperature. From the detector unit, these signals go into the microcomputer controller. The computer uses predetermined calibration constants stored in its memory to calculate the braze-zone temperature from the ratio of the X and Z signals.

The temperature is used in a proportional plus integral control equation to derive a control signal that is relayed to the power supply via a remote switching panel located in the control cabinet.

The brazing "torch" consists of a water-cooled, induction coil heater on a 3-foot-long probe that is inserted into the tube/sleeve. Thermal radiation from the heated sleeve wall is gathered by a small gradient-index lens mounted in the gap between the two central turns of this heater coil. This radiation is directed, via a gold-plated turning mirror, onto the end of a single optical fiber with a core diameter of 200 µm. The fiber surface is prepared by diamond scribing and cleaving to produce a "mirror-smooth" surface. The fiber extends down the center of

Figure 3.5   Block Diagram of the Braze Control System [9]

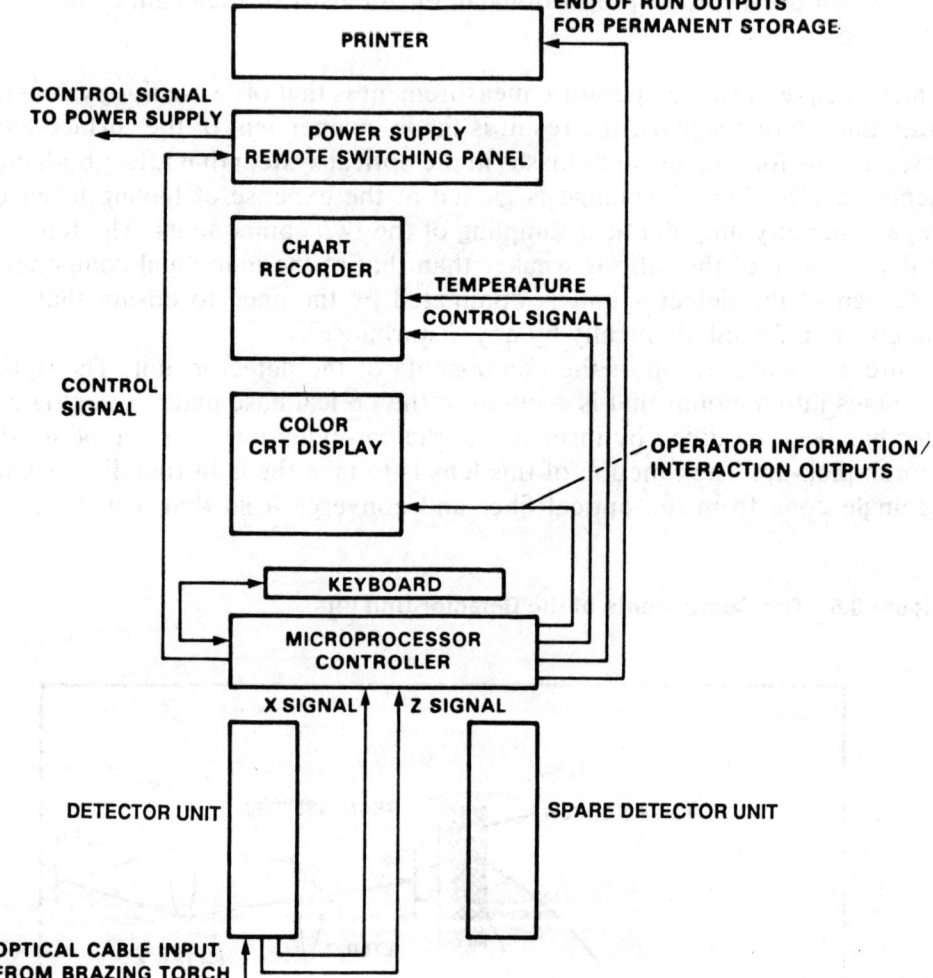

the torch shaft, emerging at the bottom and extending another 7 meters. This pigtail then connects to the 190-meter cable that goes to the instrument van outside of the containment building. The pigtail and fiber in the torch pick-up are made from the same cable as the 190-meter length.

The 190-meter fiber plugs directly into the detector unit located in the control cabinet. The detector unit has three functions:

- To split the light signal delivered by the optical cable into two different color components

- To detect the intensity of each component

- To output a voltage proportional to the intensity of each light component.

The principle of the temperature measurement is that of two-color pyrometry: by ratioing the two signals, the result is made independent of the surface emissivity, window fouling, or other losses in the optical system that affect both components equally. This advantage is gained at the expense of having to ensure high gain stability and identical sampling of the two components. The temperature dependence of the ratio is weaker than that of the individual components. The design of the detector unit is dominated by the need to ensure that both channels are affected identically by any disturbance.

Figure 3.6 is a drawing of the components of the detector unit. The optical cable plugs into a mount that is secured to the optical base plate. The plug connector has been modified by inserting a gradient-index lens of the type used in the torch pick-up. The function of this lens is to take the light that diverges in a wide-angle cone from the optical fiber and converge it so that it will all pass

Figure 3.6 The Components of the Detector Unit [9]

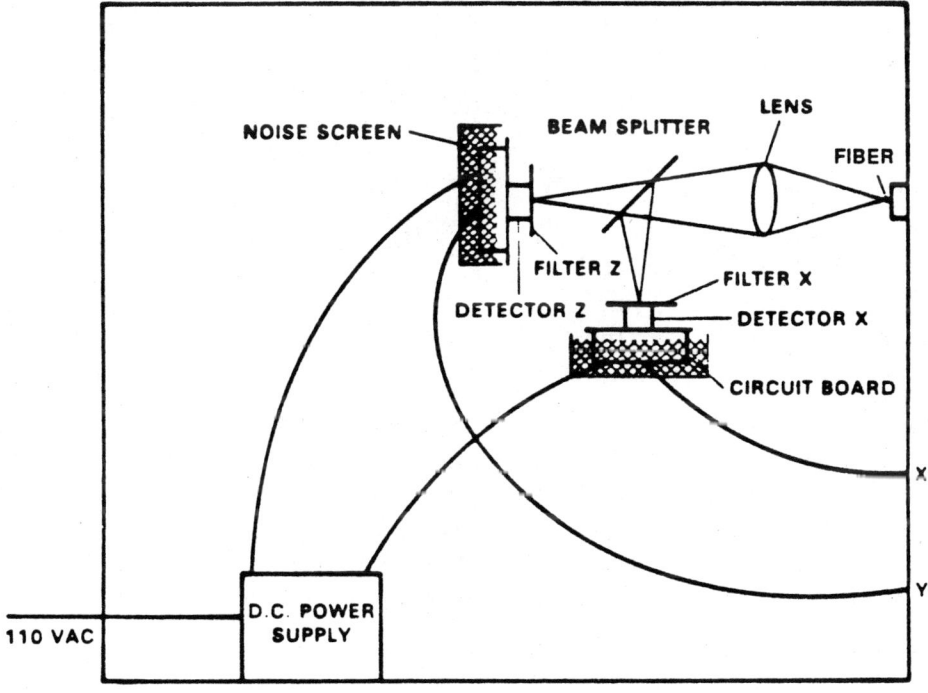

through the focusing lens. The focusing lens takes the light and focuses an image of the fiber onto the detector plane.

Light with wavelength less than 900 nm is transmitted through the beam splitter onto the Z-channel detector, and light of a longer wavelength is reflected toward the X-channel detector. Filters mounted in contact with the detectors restrict the detected light to narrow wavelength bands centered about 812 nm (Z channel) and 974 nm (X channel). Silicon photodiodes with active areas 1 cm in diameter and built-in preamplifiers convert the light to voltage signals. The ratio of these two voltages is given by the following equation:

$$R = \frac{k_1 \lambda_2^5}{k_2 \lambda_1^5} \exp\left(-\frac{C_2}{T}\left[\frac{1}{\lambda_1} - \frac{1}{\lambda_2}\right]\right) \tag{3.1}$$

where:

T = Temperature in K
C_2 = 1.4388 × 10⁴ m · K
λ_1, λ_2 = Effective wavelength of the Z and X channels, respectively
k_1, k_2 = Constants for the Z and X channels, respectively

Equation 3.1 is the standard two-color pyrometry equation [12], which follows from an approximation of the Planck blackbody function.

The temperature may be written as follows:

$$T = T_o + T \tag{3.2}$$

where T_o is some temperature near the mid-range of interest. Equation 3.1 can be manipulated to express the ratio, R, as a cubic equation in temperature. A reversion of series technique [14] can then be used to express the temperature as a cubic equation of the ratio. The linear term of this equation gives the temperature to within 5 K over the operating range of this system 1000–1300 K (1300°F to 1850°F). To this accuracy, then:

$$T = MR + B \tag{3.3}$$

where:

$$M = \frac{T_o^2}{\left(\frac{k_1 \lambda_2^5}{k_2 \lambda_1^5}\right) C_2 \left(\frac{1}{\lambda_1} - \frac{1}{\lambda_2}\right) \exp\left[-\frac{C_2}{T_o}\left(\frac{1}{\lambda_1} - \frac{1}{\lambda_2}\right)\right]} \tag{3.4}$$

and

$$B = T_o \left[1 - \frac{T_o}{C_2 \left[\frac{1}{\lambda_1} - \frac{1}{\lambda_2} \right]} \right] \quad (3.5)$$

Because T_o and C_2 are constants, the slope, M, depends on k_1, k_2, λ_1, and λ_2, whereas the intercept depends only on λ_1 and λ_2. To maximize stability and minimize the variability from one detector unit to another, changes in the effective wavelengths and the k values must be avoided or minimized. The k values depend on emissivity of the source, optical system collection efficiency, the transmission of the filters and other optical components, and detector responsivity and amplification.

Because the two k values appear as a ratio, changes in emissivity and optical system collection efficiency cancel out to the extent that both channels are affected equally. Only differential changes in collection efficiency and emissivity can contribute to errors in temperature prediction with this system.

Figure 3.7 shows a plot of temperature versus ratio as determined in a calibration furnace. The data points from two separate calibration runs are presented. The first run was made from 1850°F to 1770°F and the second from 1580°F to 1500°F. There is more scatter in the lower temperature data simply because the magnitude of the X and Z signals is lower and more affected by the electronic noise.

The two lines are the calculated best-fit lines from two calibrations. At 1530°F, the two lines differ by only 2°F, which is in good agreement with the theoretical prediction that over this range the response should be linear to within 3°F.

Table 3.1 lists data from 13 calibration runs made over a period of one month on one combination of brazing torch, detector unit, and interconnecting fiber optic cable. During the period, this combination was used repeatedly to do various test brazes. The calibrations were run periodically to check for changes brought on by use or handling. The combination was used for at least 50 heating cycles and was transported between a test rig and calibration lab more than five times during the month.

In addition to the calibration constants (slope and intercept), table 3.1 lists $T_{0.9}$ values. These are the values of T computed from the calibration constants at voltage ratio values of R = 0.9. Because of the vagaries of the statistical data fitting, the slope and intercept of two runs can differ in offsetting ways; that is, the slope increase is canceled by a corresponding decrease in the intercept. For this reason, the values of $T_{0.9}$ are used to compare one run to the next.

As can be seen in table 3.1, the values of $T_{0.9}$ ranged from 1839°F to 1821°F over the month. This includes nonrepeatability of the calibration system. This means that if the initial calibration constants had been used throughout the entire

Figure 3.7 Temperature versus Voltage Ratio in a Calibration Furnace [9]

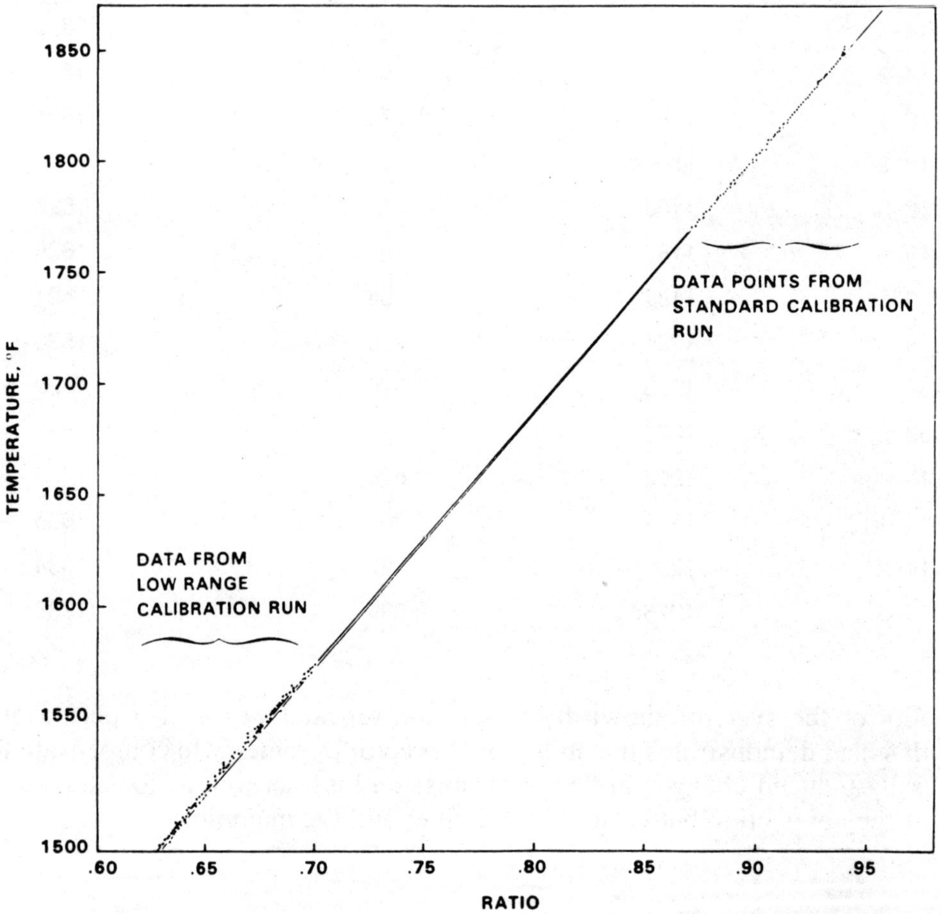

month, the measured temperature in the brazing range would differ from that based on the most recent calibration by a maximum of 18°F. Short-term repeatability over one-day time periods is ten times better.

The desired control cycle was to raise the temperature to the brazing setpoint as quickly as possible, hold at that temperature for 2 minutes and then reduce the temperature to a lower annealing value for a period prior to shutdown. Using the microcomputer control system, the temperature could be brought to setpoint within 30 seconds and maintained at the desired setpoint within 10°F for the entire cycle.

In conclusion, this system has achieved accurate measurement and control of braze-zone temperature over the range from 1300°F to 1850°F. Use of a single strand of optical fiber to convey the thermal radiation made possible a 200-meter separation between the optical detection system and the measurement point.

Table 3.1 Repeatability/Stability of Calibration

Date	Slope (°F)	Intercept (°F)	$T_{0.9}$ (°F)
4/14–1	1173	783	1839
4/14–2	1173	782	1838
4/16–1	1166	775	1824
4/16–2	Aborted		
4/16–3	1165	778	1826
4/19	1185	759	1826
4/23	1186	754	1821
4/28	1225	720	1823
4/30	1225	726	1829
5/03	1223	730	1831
5/13	1262	698	1834
5/14–1	1261	700	1835
5/14–2	1230	727	1834
5/14–3	1276	686	1835

Stability of the system, shown by calibration repeatability over a period of a month's use, demonstrates the ability of two-color pyrometry to compensate for flexurally-induced changes in fiber transmission loss, as well as for changes in loss at the connection between the torch fiber and the main fiber.

Noncontact, Continuous Measurement of Preweld Seam Alignment

In the high frequency electric resistance welding process (HFERW) for mechanical tubing production, plates of flat, strip steel are bent and formed into a smooth cylindrical shape. Before the edges of the strip are butt together, welding shoes contact the strip near each edge. A large electric current from the HFERW power supply passes into the steel to heat the edges close to the melting temperature. The edges are then forged (pressed) together between weld pressure rolls in a special mill. The weld bead is subsequently trimmed from the inside and outside surfaces as the near-finished cylindrical tube exits this mill machine.

The diagram in figure 3.8 shows a tube in the intermediate and final stages of formation. Just prior to forging, the edges of the cylindrical plate converge after the welding shoes to form a V. At the apex of the V (fusion point), forging begins. It is important that the V pattern, as determined by the convergence angle of the plate edges, be maintained constant. Pulsations of the strip caused by slippage during forming can lead to fluctuations in the convergence angle and instability in the position of the fusion point. This instability may result in weld nonuniformities and potential weld defects.

A practical method to monitor the V-convergence uses a line scan camera containing a 1,024-element photodiode array. The set-up is shown in figure 3.8. The hot, glowing edges of the strip following the welding shoes provide ample light intensity so that no external light source is required in this application. The camera is aimed at a known position between the convergence point and welding

Figure 3.8 Installation of Line Scan Camera on Production Tube Mill

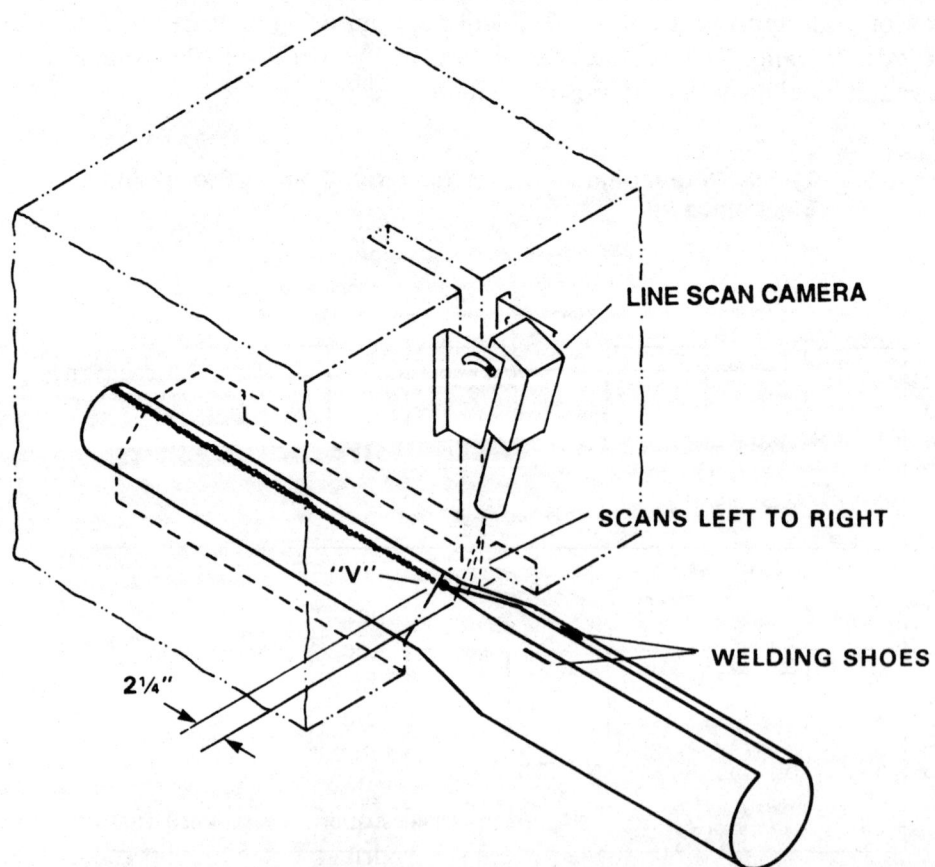

shoes. An image of the gap across the V (from edge to edge) is focused on the photodiode array located at the camera image plane.

Typical output signals from the camera processing electronics are shown in figure 3.9. Regions of high light intensity are received from the hot metal edges of the strip. Regions of low light intensity are received from the gap between the edges. The width of the gap is computed from the dark segment between the hot edges.

In operation, the camera is mounted to the structural frame of the mill machine. The width of the gap is imaged in advance of the fusion point (V apex). As the photodiode array in the camera electronically scans the gap from left to right, the camera electronic processing unit computes the intensity of light at 1,024 photodiode pixels within the field of view (approximately 1.0 inches) at 624 Hz ($1{,}024 \times 624 = 638{,}976$ intensity signals/second). These intensity signals may be archived on magnetic tape in analog form, or processed in real time. Mean values and standard deviation of gap width may be computed and displayed along with the light intensity versus time shown in figure 3.8. The actual width is determined by counting the number of pixels across the gap and multiplying the result by a scale factor. With the line scan camera linked to a microprocessor with appropriate software, on-line monitoring of V gap widths in the $\frac{1}{8}$- to $\frac{1}{4}$-inch range is possible. Resolution in the width of .0015 inch can be achieved at steel strip line speeds of 30 inches/second.

Figure 3.9 Typical Output Signals versus Time from Camera Processing Electronics

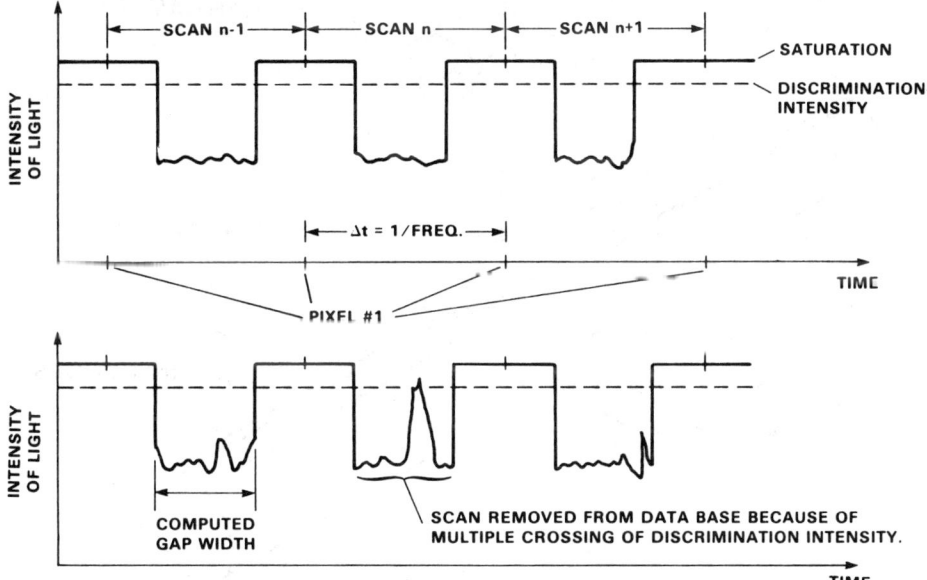

Postprocessing software may be used to "filter" or remove data in situations where noise signals in the dark gap region result in multiple zero-crossings of the discrimination intensity (see the center signal scan on the bottom trace in figure 3.9). These occurrences are rare in practice and amount to roughly 1 in 400 scans. The noise events probably result from the random appearance of droplets of cooling fluid within the gap.

In conclusion, a line scan camera is capable of continuous monitoring of a critical dimensional parameter during an industrial welding process. Imaging is performed in a hostile industrial environment in the presence of smoke and oily sprays. Satisfactory light levels are obtained, which permit operation of a photodiode pixel array at a 624 Hz rate and an overall spatial resolution of .0015 inch perpendicular to the direction of motion.

Impurity Identification in the Cover Gas During Titanium Welding

Shipbuilders are currently interested in titanium welding to reduce the fabrication cost of sea-going vessels. In addition, increased use of titanium will reduce weight, thereby increasing fuel efficiency. However, good welds of titanium metal have been difficult to obtain in the past. Poor strength from porous welds is a common problem. Recently, good titanium welds of reproducible quality have been obtained. This success has been achieved primarily from detailed attention to proper shielding of the weld arc with pure argon cover gas.

In a production environment, means must be provided to ensure that the argon cover gas provides continuous shielding of the arc from the surrounding atmosphere and that impurities in the argon do not exceed acceptable levels. Impurities at sufficient levels cause weld defects. Emission spectroscopy is an easily implemented analytical method for monitoring of impurities in high-temperature arcs. The method described in this section shows that emission spectroscopy may be used to identify low-level impurities in titanium weld arcs.

Spectra are obtained from the titanium weld arc using the apparatus diagrammed in figure 3.10. Light radiation from the arc is reflected by a mirror to a collection lens that focuses the radiation onto a fiber optic bundle. The mirror-lens-bundle end tip assembly is attached to the traversing welding head. The fibers in the bundle conduct the light to the entrance slit of the monochromator. The exit slit of the monochromator is replaced by a silicon intensified target (SIT) camera tube that converts the spectra to electrical inputs to an EG&G PAR Optical Multichannel Analyzer (OMA). The OMA acts as an electronic spectrograph to convert optical spectra to digital electronic signals. The silicon intensified target camera tube converts the spatially dispersed optical spectra

Figure 3.10 Apparatus for Obtaining Spectra from Titanium Weld Arcs

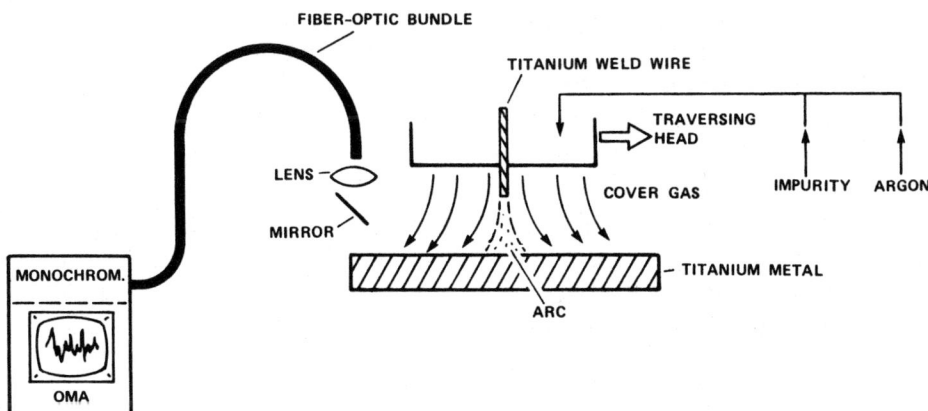

from the monochromator into electrical signals for analysis by the OMA computer. The electrical signal generated at each optical wavelength within the camera tube is proportional to the light intensity at that wavelength. These signals are collected, digitized, and sent to the OMA computer. This method of spectral data collection is convenient and enables data storage, processing, and display on a built-in CRT along with outputs to drive an X-Y plotter for hard copy.

To characterize system performance, measured concentrations of O_2, CO_2, H_2O, and H_2 are purposely injected into the argon cover gas to determine spectroscopic measurement sensitivity and to attempt to induce weld defects. Upon entering the high-temperature welding arc, these molecular impurities are dissociated into their atomic constituents, which in turn are raised to excited electronic states. The spectral emission from radiative decay of the atoms back to the ground state is unique to each constituent and is detected and displayed by the OMA. During welding, a constant cover gas mixture was maintained during the deposition of a weld bead approximately 18 inches long. The oxygen, hydrogen, carbon, and nitrogen concentrations in these beads were subsequently assayed.

Care must be used in operation of this impurity monitoring system. Several variables can change the calibration and introduce errors to the system spectral response. These variables must be controlled and/or compensated. The most important of these variables are listed below:

- Deposit build-up on the light collecting mirror requires that this mirror be cleaned periodically.

- The field of view and hence collection efficiency of the optical system may change. All optical components must be mounted securely and their spacing must be held constant.

- Varying amounts of obscuring smoke may be present between the arc and the mirror. Signal averaging will help reduce uncertainties from this variable.

- The electronic dark-current noise varies due to ambient temperature changes. To correct for this effect, ambient temperature must be measured.

Figure 3.11 shows typical spectra from the OMA in the region of the 777.1 nm oxygen emission line for various levels of added O_2. The oxygen line intensity is measurable down to the 7 ppm level set by the purity of the available argon cover gas. Figure 3.12 shows the normalized emission intensity at 777.1 nm versus oxygen concentration in the cover gas. At concentrations above 950 ppm, surface oxidation of the weld bead is visually evident.

Addition of 2,500 ppm of CO_2 to the cover gas causes a large increase in the observed 777.1 nm oxygen emission, equivalent to roughly 3,000 ppm O_2 alone, but without visual evidence of oxidation.

The data in figure 3.12 is normalized or compensated for in the changes in instrumental variables and deposit build-up on optical surfaces listed above. This

Figure 3.11 Relative Light Intensity versus Wavelength for Three Different Oxygen Concentrations in Cover Gas

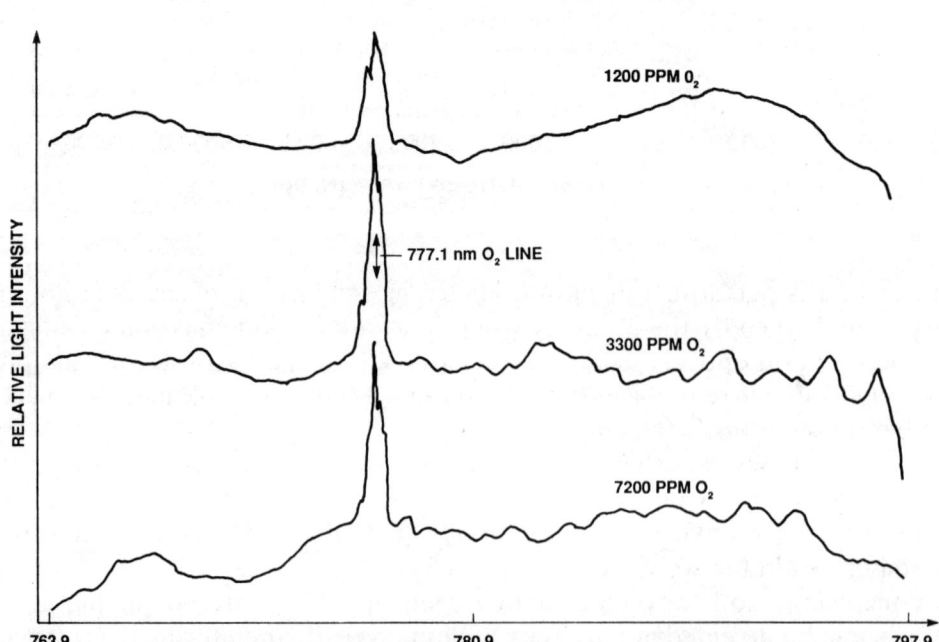

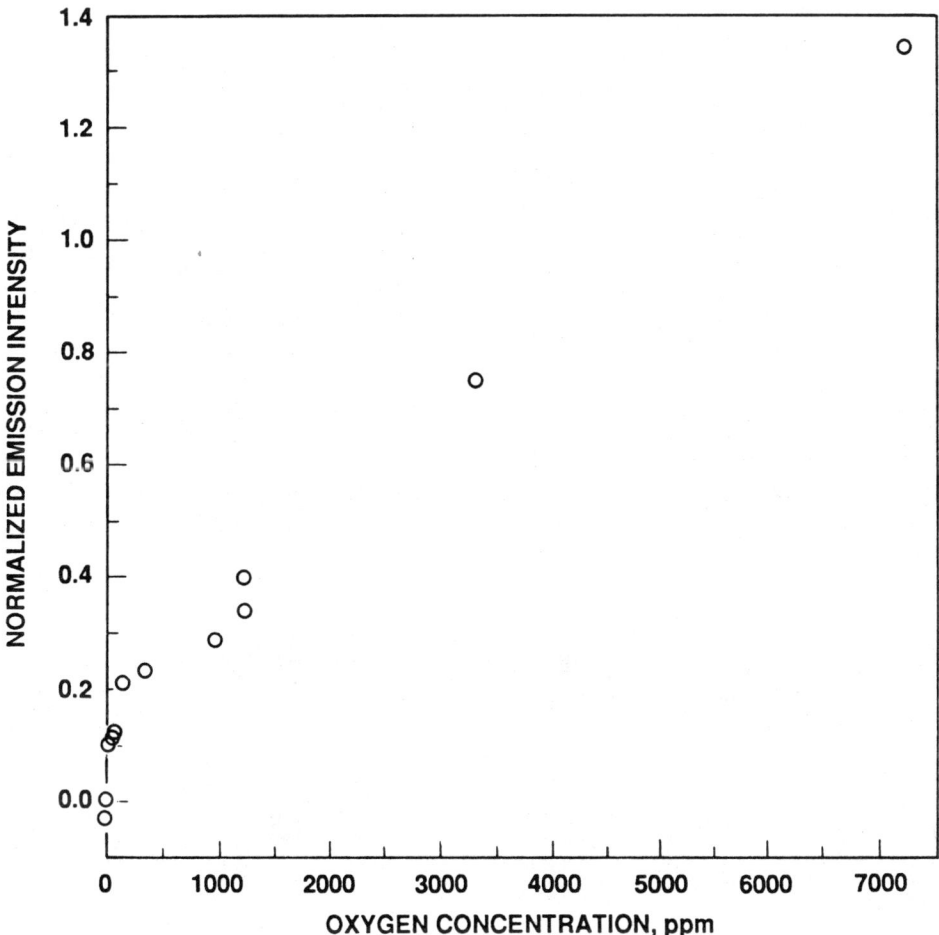

Figure 3.12 Normalized Emission Intensity at 777.1 nm versus Oxygen Concentration in the Cover Gas

compensation is performed using ratiometric normalization of the emission intensity from oxygen by the intensity from the nearby argon emission (see figure 3.13). Deposits on optical surfaces attenuate light at the two wavelengths proportionally. Dark current noise from the SIT camera tube is subtracted from each signal before the ratio is calculated.

Figure 3.14 shows the 656 nm emission intensity from pure H_2 impurity versus concentration in the cover gas. Water vapor and machine oil contamination can be detected at this wavelength via emission from the hydrogen liberated from these impurities in the weld arc.

In conclusion, both oxygen and hydrogen impurities present in the argon cover gas can be detected at parts-per-million levels by monitoring the intensity

Figure 3.13 Spectrum with 950 ppm Oxygen Added to Argon Cover Gas

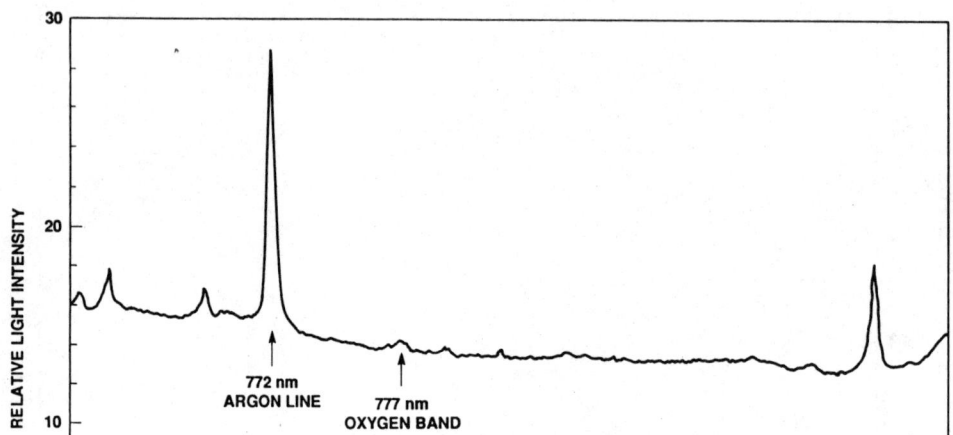

of their respective spectral emission lines. In addition, the concentration of these gaseous impurities can be determined in real-time in the weld arc during titanium welding. Other gaseous impurities, such as CO_2, H_2O, and machine oil vapor can be detected as well, to the extent that products of decomposition in the weld arc include oxygen and hydrogen.

Advanced Fiber Optic Method for Measurement of Strain

Strain measurements are required in the power generation industry for design verification, diagnostic testing, and remaining life assessment purposes. Temperatures of up to 1200°F and hostile conditions of steam/water or hot flue gas are often present at locations where strain data is required and severely limit the measurements that can be obtained. The measurement limitation results because the elevated temperatures affect the materials used in strain sensors unpredictably and often in ways unique to a particular gage/geometry. The effect of the

Figure 3.14 Normalized Intensity at 656 nm versus Hydrogen Concentration in Cover Gas

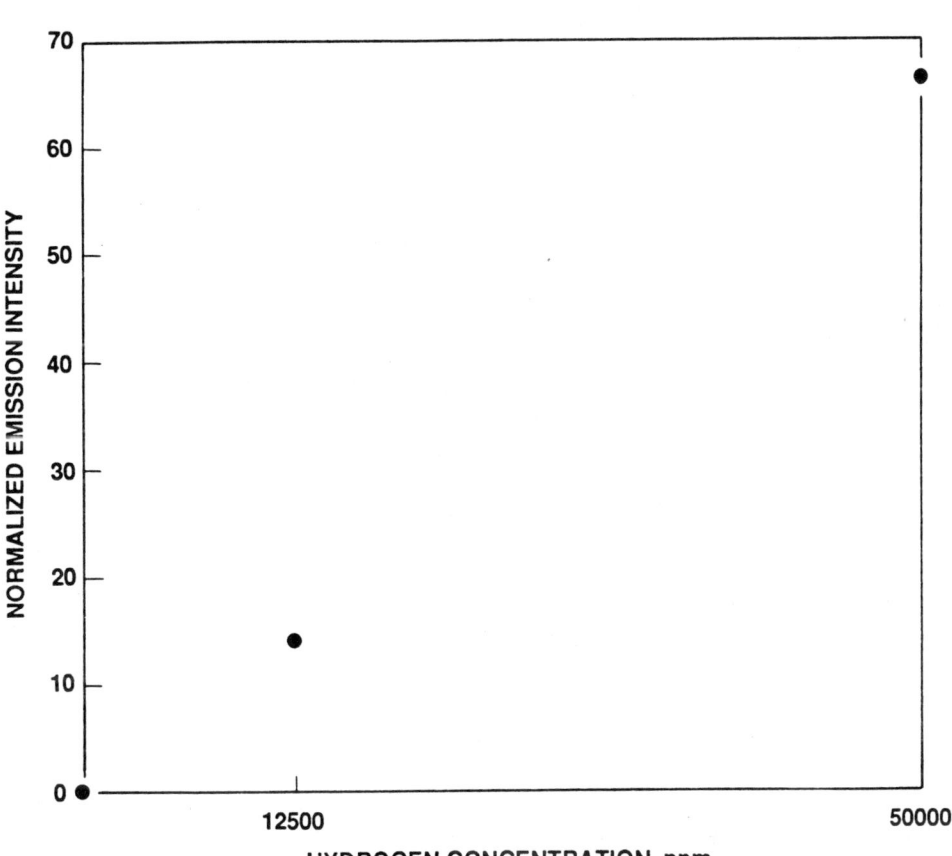

thermal response of strain sensors/material causes a number of problems relative to obtaining reliable static strain data at elevated temperatures. The most important problems are apparent strain (thermal output due to temperature environment) and drift (signal stability)—both of which cause a change in the DC voltage level obtained from a strain sensor.

An "ideal" strain gage could be described as a small, easy to install, high compliance, and low-cost device, with sufficient resolution, range, and accuracy for the anticipated strain measurement and adequate stability, predictability, and durability in the measurement environment for the anticipated test duration. For relatively benign measurement environments, the bonded resistance strain gage approaches the ideal—hence, its widespread use and great commercial success. As test conditions become more hostile, application of the bonded resistance gage becomes more difficult and eventually impractical.

The desired strain gage is intended to make long term (5,000–10,000 hours) static, quasistatic, and dynamic strain measurements at temperatures of 750–

1000°F, with the potential to be extended to higher temperatures. Environments could be gases, pressurized fluids, or particulate-laden gases. Potential applications also include measurements of thermally induced strains, or mechanical strains over a range of temperatures, as well as the potential for both laboratory and field-testing applications. Thus, the gage should have excellent long-term stability at temperature (minimal drift), small or predictable output with temperature (minimal apparent strain), and good repeatability with both thermal and mechanical cycling. In addition, the gage should have inherent immunity to or be readily protected from the expected environments. Our experience with optical-fiber-based sensors [13, 3, 11] indicated that a strain gage based on a fiber optic sensor potentially could meet all of these requirements.

Because free optical access is not always available in the structural areas of interest, a fiber optic contact gage is preferred over noncontact interferometry. An intensity modulated fiber sensor was selected for the strain gage application because it is the simplest and most reliable and has the lowest cost of the various fiber optic modulation techniques. Fiber microbending was chosen as the method of achieving the modulation again for reasons of simplicity and low cost. A microbend sensor is based on the fact that in a graded or step index optical fiber, the light losses between the core and the cladding are changed as the radius of curvature of the fiber is changed [10]. These resulting changes in the light intensity can then be detected with simple optoelectronic components.

To assemble a microbend strain gage, an optical fiber is sandwiched between two corrugated end plates, as shown in figure 3.15, that are made from the same material as the test beam. The fiber is preloaded (bias compression) between the

Figure 3.15 Magnified View of Optical Fiber Clamped Between Corrugated Plates

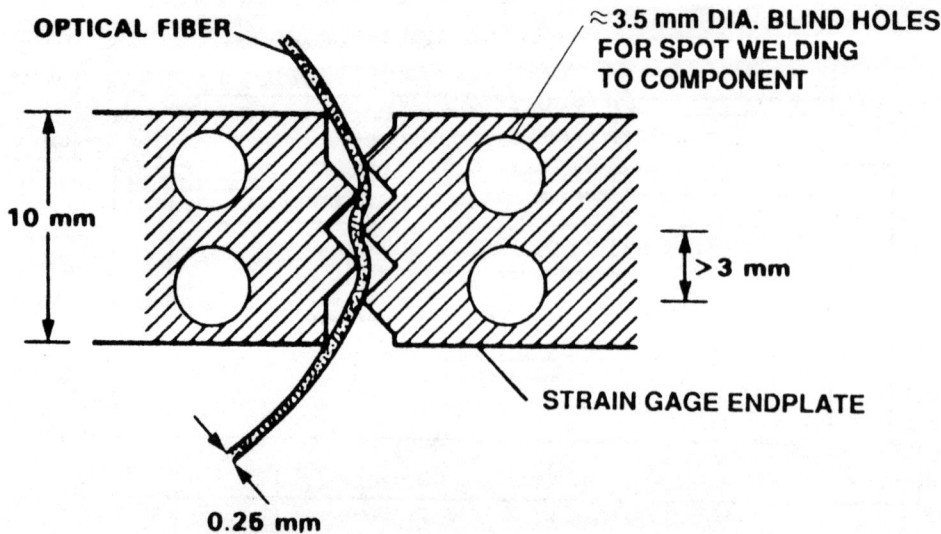

two end plates prior to installation, to provide tensile and compressive measurement capability and to set the fiber-bend amplitude to produce the sensitivity and linearity required.

A prototype gage has been fabricated and characterized based upon the concept shown in figure 3.15. This prototype was designed with two spatial sinusoidal bends in the fiber. Aluminum-coated, step-index fiber was used. The plates were fabricated from stainless steel for testing on a stainless steel beam, to minimize thermal offset from thermal expansion mismatch between the gage and test beam. The gage length was selected to be approximately .2 inch (5 mm), and the width of the gage was about ¼ inch (6.5 mm). In this configuration, the in-plane stiffness of the gage is about 1,000 pounds per inch or about the stiffness of a stainless shim 1 mil thick and 7 mils wide with the same (.2 inch) length. The stiffness of the gage is thus somewhat less than that of a typical weldable resistance type gage, but more than that of a typical capacitance gage.

Figure 3.16 shows the location of the prototype gage installed on the test beam. To install the gage, two holes were counterbored in each end plate to leave a thickness at the bottom of about .010 inch; the plates were then capacitance discharge spot welded to the beam. In addition to the sensing fiber sandwiched

Figure 3.16 Four-Point Bending Test Apparatus and Bending Moment Diagram

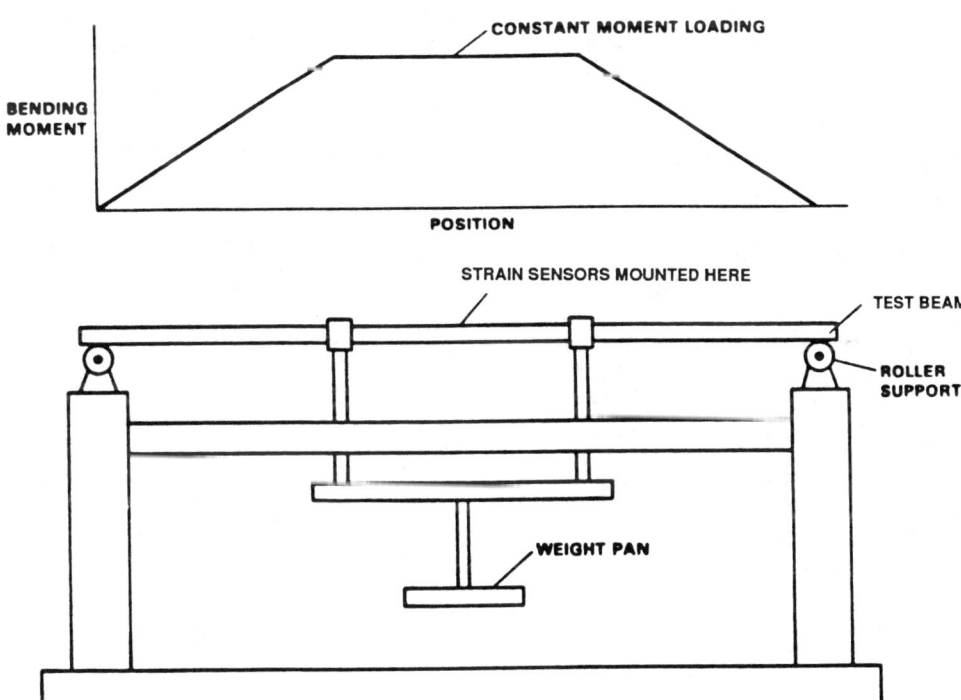

between the plates, an unclamped reference fiber was also installed with approximately the same length in the hot zone. This fiber is used to provide compensation for any thermally induced changes in the sensing fiber or any variations in the intensity of the light source. A reference gage and thermocouples for air and metal temperature measurements were also installed on the beam. The test beam was a stainless beam 1 inch wide by ½ inch thick; it was designed for use in an available four-point bending test rig as diagrammed in figure 3.16. The calibration test rig included a "clam-shell" three-zone furnace for elevated temperature testing.

The optoelectronics used to excite and read the microbend strain gage are shown in figure 3.17. The components used are conventional inexpensive optoelectronics. The light source is a light emitting diode (LED), and the detector is a silicon dual photodetector. A logarithmic radio amplifier is the best choice to amplify the output from the dual photodetector. With this amplifier, the output signal sensitivity is not affected by variations in interconnecting fiber cable length between the gage and the optoelectronics.

The prototype fiber optic strain gage was tested in both tensile and compressive bending at room temperature and in compressive bending at 300°F and 600°F. During each of the tests, deflections were applied to the test beam to produce beam surface strains of about 250, 500, 750, and 1000 microstrain. Measurements were made during both the loading and unloading of the beam, and each loading cycle was repeated three times.

Figure 3.17 The Optoelectronics Used to Excite and Read the Microbend Strain Gage and to Compensate for Thermal Changes and Light Source Fluctuations

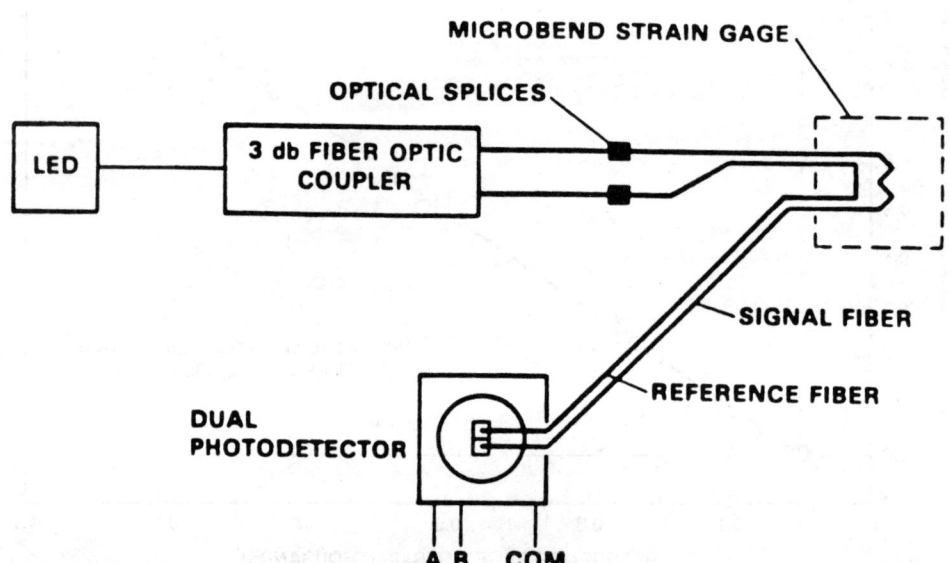

A typical plot of the data for the tensile and compressive room temperature runs is shown in figure 3.18. This plot shows that repeatability of the gage is quite good; the largest contribution to inaccuracy comes from hysteresis. Gage resolution was measured to be better than 3 microstrain.

The beam was thermally cycled three times to 600°F and cooled to room temperature. Strain calibration tests were repeated as described above at room temperature, 600°F, and again at room temperature. Typical calibration results at 600°F are shown in figure 3.19, and they compare favorably with the room temperature results in figure 3.18.

The initial tests at 77°F produced results with .5-percent repeatability and 3-percent hysteresis. There was essentially no drift. Sensitivity of the gage was comparable to that obtained in figure 3.18. The zero shift on heat-up to 600°F was approximately 2000 microstrain. The sensitivity of the gage was about 10 percent greater than the room temperature value (see figure 3.19). During the first thermal cycle, the gage showed a relatively large compressive shift (over −80 microstrain) in zero. Subsequent cycles showed good repeatability and a sensitivity within 2 percent of the room temperature value. Drift of the gage appeared to be minimal; the microbend gage showed a change of −16 microstrain

Figure 3.18 Microbend Strain Gage Output versus Reference Gage Output at 77°F

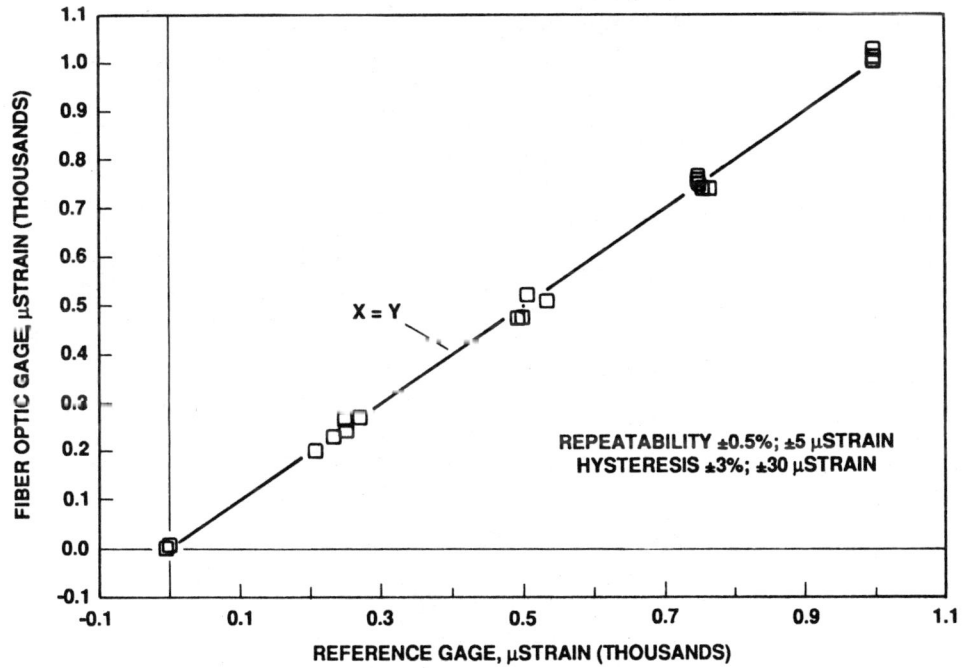

Figure 3.19 Microbend Strain Gage Output versus Reference Gage Output at 600°F

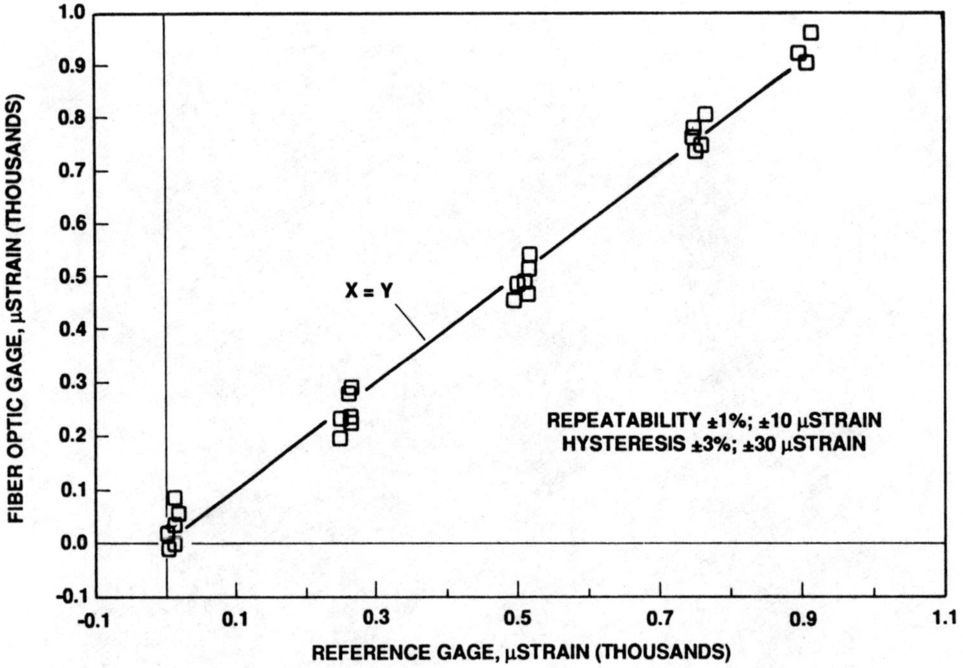

REPEATABILITY ±1%; ±10 μSTRAIN
HYSTERESIS ±3%; ±30 μSTRAIN

during the monitoring period, while the reference gage showed a change of −19 microstrain.

After the last 600°F calibration, when the beam was returned to room temperature, the zero of the microbend gage showed a shift of −250 microstrain compared to its initial room temperature value; the reference gage showed a shift of −150 microstrain. These shifts could have been caused by some small inelastic behavior of the test beam. Drift of the microbend gage was minimal. Hysteresis, repeatability, and sensitivity were comparable to those previously obtained at room temperature.

In conclusion, results to date indicate that fiber optic microbend strain gages have sufficient resolution and repeatability for practical applications. However, care must be taken in hardware implementation. The hysteresis and thermal offsets encountered are both judged to be unacceptably large; past experience with fiber optic sensors indicates that both of these can be reduced by an order of magnitude (or more) with an improved design and mounting method. Based on the test results obtained and presented in this section, an improved design should incorporate features to preclude fiber motion perpendicular to the mounting surface within the corrugations and to isolate the active sensing area from motions

Figure 3.20 Microbend Strain Gage Mounted in the Plane of a Pressure Transducer Diaphragm

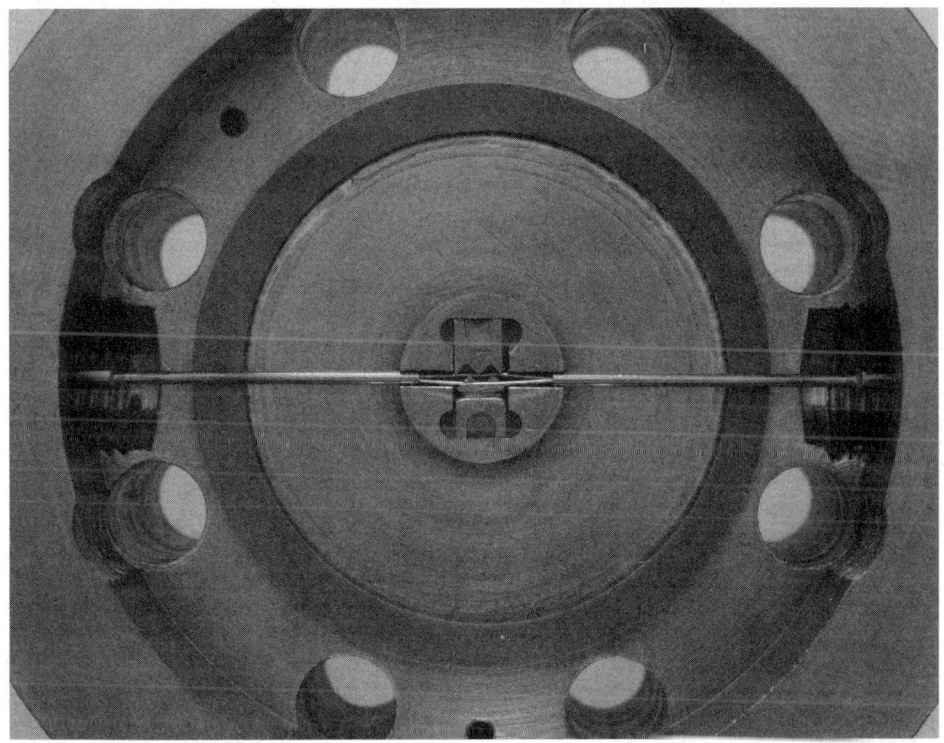

of the fiber optic leads. One such design is illustrated in figure 3.20, where the microbend strain gage is attached to a pressure transducer diaphragm in a configuration for sensing differential pressure. Development of this strain gage package is continuing, with emphasis on extending the maximum operating temperature, improvement of thermal and long-term drift characteristics, and convenient packaging for general applications.

Summary

Several optical sensing methods based on radiation pyrometry, digital imaging, spectroscopy, and microbending in optical fibers have been described. The application of these methods was necessitated by the desire to improve furnace

temperature measurements, braze temperature control, welding methods, and strain measurements. These optical sensors and their application are typical of the varied and widespread opportunities to improve industrial process control, reduce wastage, and increase automation using optical and fiber optic techniques.

The optical methods discussed in this chapter have been applied successfully to solve specific problems. These methods, as well as many other available optical sensing methods and new techniques under development will continue to be applied in situations where optical methods have unique advantages. Chief among these advantages is noncontact measurement capability. Applications of optical sensors and systems will continue to increase in the industrial environment as these systems become more familiar to industrial engineers and as interactive robotics and other adaptive manufacturing methods are implemented.

References

1. Arnaud, J. A. *Beam and Fiber Optics*. New York: Academic Press, 1976.

2. Bailey, R. T., and H. R. Carter. "Flame Quality Analyzer for Temperature Measurement and Combustion Control." *Sensors* 5, no. 7. (July 1988):23.

3. Basch, E. E. *Optical Fiber Transmission*. Indianapolis, IN: Howard W. Sams, 1987.

4. Berthold, J. W., et al. *Journal of Lightwave Technology* LT–5 (1987):870.

5. Dakin, J., and B. Culshaw. *Optical Fiber Sensors*. Boston: Artech House, 1988.

6. Dodd, G. G. *Computer Vision and Sensor Based Robots*. New York: Plenum Press, 1979.

7. Erf, R. K. *Speckle Metrology*. New York: Academic Press, 1978.

8. Jakeman, E. *Optics, Optical Systems, and Applications*. Philadelphia: Adam Hilger, 1988.

9. Jeffers, L. A. "Microcomputer-Based System for Remote Temperature Measurement and Control of an Induction-Heated Process." Proc. of ISA 31st International Instrumentation Symposium, San Diego, CA, 1985.

10. Lagakos, N., et al. *Applied Optics* 20 (1981):167.

11. Miers, D. R., et al. "Design and Characterization of Fiber Optic Accelerometers." SPIE O-E/Fibers '87, Fiber Optic and Laser Sensors V, San Diego, CA, 1987.

12. Quinn, T. J. "Radiation Thermometry." In *Temperature*. New York: Academic Press, 1983, p. 351.

13. Reed, S. E., and J. W. Berthold. "Development of a Microbend Strain Gage." SEM Fall Conference on Experimental Mechanics, Keystone, Colorado, 1986.

14. Selby, S. M. *Handbook of Mathematical Tables*. Cleveland, OH: Chemical Rubber Company, 1962, p. 399.

15. Udd, E. *Fiber Optic Sensors: An Introduction for Engineers and Scientists*. New York: John Wiley & Sons, 1991.

Chapter 4 Nonvision Sensors for Robotics

M. W. Siegel

Introduction

Only a few sensors are both peculiar to robotics, that is to say *not generally found in other automation specialties,* and also mature enough to be commercially available for industrial applications. By far the most mature is the wrist force-torque sensor, in the form of an instrumented coupling inserted between the effector end of the robot elbow-to-wrist link and the robot-end of the hand. Commercial tactile-force-measuring arrays are also available, but their use typically has a research orientation even in industrial applications. Other "robot sensors" are either generic mechanical sensors installed in robots—for example, angle encoders, strain gauges, and optical proximity sensors—or are basically laboratory devices—for example, shear force and slip velocity sensors for grasping. The state of the art is summarized in figure 4.1.

In recent years the term *nonvision sensors* has become standard in the vocabulary of robotics, even occurring routinely in the titles of conference sessions and books. In a NATO Advanced Research Workshop held during the summer of 1989, entitled "Traditional and Non-Traditional Robotic Sensors," the participants for the most part agreed that *nontraditional* and *nonvision* were synonymous in this context [14]. Notwithstanding this predilection of academics and industrial theoreticians to treat all robotic sensory modalities other than machine vision as "alsos," it is in fact nonvision sensors that dominate the industrial practice of robotics. It is these workhorses of present and predicted near future automation that are the subject of this review.

With respect to priorities, more than the usual space has been devoted to navigation sensors, based on faith that the future of robotics is as much in mobile robots as in workcells. This perspective suggests scale and continuity: navigation sensing blends continuously into range sensing, into proximity sensing, and then into touch sensing and the proprioceptive sensory modalities relating to the

Figure 4.1 Sensors Peculiar to Robotics

(**) denotes sensors in use in state-of-the-art industrial applications. (*) denotes sensors in use in research anticipating industrial applications.

Noncontact Sensors
- Navigation
  - (1) Automatic Guided Vehicle (AGV) technology applied to robots on mobile platforms: guide wires, stripes, etc.
  - (2) Beacon systems used for short and long range navigation in military, transportation, and industrial applications

- Range
  - (1) Machine vision techniques
  - (2) Laser radar techniques

- Proximity
  - Conventional proximity sensors (optical beam, fiber optic, inductive, capacitive, acoustic, etc.) adapted to surface mapping via software to conduct data-directed search

Contact Sensors (Touch)
- Wrist Force/Torque
  - (1) Remote Center of Compliance (RCC) is a mechanical approach to assembly
  - ** (2) Several commercially available "six-component" force-measuring forearm-hand couplers with specifications matched to specific robot and hand combinations

- Tactile Arrays
  - Normal Force:
    - (1) Gripper force sensors integral with hand as supplied by manufacturer
    - * (2) Several commercially available tactile arrays—for example, piezoresistive elastomers, photo-occlusive—but typically used in applications research only
  - Slip:
    - Substantial academic interest and prototyping for robotics and prosthetics, but no commercially available sensors

- Self-Sensing (Pose)
  - (1) Joint angle encoders may be incorporated by robot manufacturer
  - (2) Experimentally, strain gauges, accelerometers, etc., are employed to characterize dynamic effects
  - (3) Approached as a calibration issue, approaches are based on methods and instrumentation used in general machine tool location and characterization

configuration of the machine, frequently designated *pose,* and in practical terms being indistinguishable from the universal requirement for calibration. Coverage of sensors that are more related to dimensional measurements during automated machining than to endowing robots with the perceptive essentials for intelligent activity has also been excluded; these instrumentation issues are nearly invariant, whether the instruments are in robot or human hands.

With respect to organization, the prose is descriptive and emphasizes applications near the cutting edge of recent developments in technology and attitude; figures with detailed captions contain the prosaic details of what the more traditional gadgets look like and how they perform. The text's emphasis on the newsy notwithstanding, nothing judged important has been excluded intentionally because of age alone.

Measurement Needs, Sensor Implementations

A robot sensor is a piece of hardware, usually supported by software, that makes a physical measurement and sends it to the robot controller. Sometimes it is a little more complicated—for example, in the case of an "active sense," like touch, which requires data-directed exploration—but these details aside the concept of sensors measuring observables for robot control is necessary and sufficient. Looking too compulsively for one-to-one correspondences between robot sensors and human senses inevitably traps people into creating false and sometimes absurd analogies. For example, sonar-based robot navigation is frequently but falsely equated with the human sense of hearing. Sensory apparatus used primarily for communication rather than for measurement or symbolic understanding of the environment, like hearing, are generally excluded from this discussion.

It is important to separate measurement needs from sensor implementation methods. First ask "what additional information does the control system require?" If you instruct the robot, rephrased in its native language, to "pick up the hammer," you presume that the concept of a hammer, and how to hold it, already resides in the robot's knowledge base. For the request to be an interesting one, it is of course appropriate also to presume that the hammer's location is inexactly known to the robot or to you. The measurement requirement might be expressed as "the robot sensor system needs to find the location of the hammer's center-of-mass, and the hammer's orientation, in the robot's coordinate system." Only after the question of need has been asked and answered is it germane to ask "what physical principles can you use to equip the robot with a suite of sensors that it can use to acquire or infer the missing information?" To find a hammer with a nonvision sensor suite, one might implement a magnetic field sensor to navigate in the direction of increasing magnetic field, which will likely be toward the hammer. The motion might be subject to veto by an optical or ultrasonic proximity sensor to prevent actually colliding with the target. The proximity sensor might then be used to confirm, by mapping the target's shape, that it is indeed a hammer. Trying to do this in the reverse order, identifying the physical principle on which a measurement is to be based before asking very carefully what needs to be measured, usually leads down a dead end road.

Internal, External, and Connecting Sensors

Robots need sensors for three kinds of measurement:

- To measure their own internal states—for example, pose as measured by a set of joint angle encoders incorporated in or installed on the robot. These measurements specify the relationships among the robot's internal configuration coordinates (base-to-shoulder angle, shoulder-to-elbow angle, shoulder-joint-to-wrist-joint distance, etc.) but are not referred to the work space—for example, the set does not include base-to-factory-floor angle.

- To measure the external state of the environment—for example, a range map giving the distance from the robot to the first obstacle in any direction. The robot is in some sense centered in this map, but its pose and orientation in the environment is inexactly known. Ideally, the robot should be a total abstraction at this level—that is, its presence should in no way perturb the environment.

- To measure the transformation connecting the internal and external measurement frames—for example, by means of a robot-base-to-factory-floor angle encoder. These are the sensors used for initialization and calibration. Operationally, they are used to tweak the parameters in the algorithms connecting the robot controller's digital representation of its pose with distance measurements in the workspace, finding at least one coincident point, etc. This level includes sensors to measure the robot's perturbation of its environment.

Some authors find it useful to separate the internal and external spaces in a fuzzier fashion, by the concept of an intermediate "proximity" or "workspace" regime. In fact, a feature of much recent technical literature is a substantial number of articles describing prototype proximity sensors and methods for using them to map the surfaces of three-dimensional objects. This observation will be discussed further in the next section.

A fourth class of nonvision sensors, which are excluded from this review, is nevertheless extremely important in practice: communication sensors. Sometimes the lines cannot be drawn so strictly, and sometimes a communications modality evolves into a measurement modality or vice versa. For example, the human sense of hearing, which for our animal forebears was an environmental

monitoring sense, is for humans almost entirely a communication modality; conversely, television, which began as and is still primarily a communication modality has become the means for implementing machine-vision-based metrology.

Noncontact Sensing: Navigation, Range, and Proximity

The connected concepts of robot autonomy and robot mobility are becoming increasingly prevalent components of robotics research and its technical literature. As robots become more autonomous and more mobile, the range of senses they will need will increase substantially beyond the simple mechanical ones (angles and distances) mentioned. Distance sensing at global, local, and near-contact scales becomes of paramount importance. A hierarchy of sensors for measuring the spatial environment merits systematic discussion: sensors for navigation, rangefinding, and proximity.

Navigation

Navigation sensors tell a mobile device where it is on a map. The sensor systems fall broadly into two classes: inertial systems and beacon systems.

Inertial Navigation Systems

In an inertial system, the initial position and orientation are usually presumed known, and later positions and orientations are inferred from spatial measurements, such as odometers or wheel encoders, or from velocity measurements and the single integration of velocity over time, such as speedometers or Doppler radars, or from acceleration measurements and the double integration of acceleration over time, such as accelerometers and gyroscopes. Alternatively, if the initial position and orientation are inexactly known but it is possible to build a local map of some distinctive feature of the environment, such as an interestingly meandering road that can be followed (using range and proximity sensors, for example) for some distance, then location and orientation can be found by an algorithm able to overlay the locally measured relative map feature and the absolute stored global map. This is a method known as *augmented dead reckoning*.

Substantial progress is being made in laser gyroscopes, which promise small, rugged, and eventually inexpensive alternatives to conventional mechanical gyros. Two types are under development or in early production, one employing a

ring laser and the other a fiber optic interferometer. Both rely on the differential Doppler shift experienced by clockwise and counter-clockwise traveling light waves when the apparatus as a whole is in rotation. The ring laser version is in production, and one model is a key navigational component of Boeing's 757/767 passenger aircraft. However, it is generally felt, or at least hoped, that once some technical details are resolved, the inherent simplicity and ruggedness of the fiber optic system will make it the system of choice in robotic applications.

Beacon Navigation

In a beacon navigation system, the map location of certain easily seen and identified points is known, as in lighthouse-based sea navigation. The mobile system finds its own location on the map by spatial or temporal triangulation. Alternatively, the beacon may be carried by the mobile component, and its location may be tracked by the fixed system. If orientation information is encoded in the beacon's radiation pattern, a distance measurement to a single beacon combined with the observed orientation is sufficient to locate the mobile system.

The Global Positioning System (GPS) uses a method based on precise time and satellite position signals transmitted by the network of NAVSTAR satellites. When four satellites are visible simultaneously, the receiver's microprocessor can solve four simultaneous equations to obtain its own three spatial coordinates and the true time; the Doppler shifts in the received signals can also be translated into the receiver's velocity with respect to ground. Although the original intent was to degrade (by coding and noise) the accuracy available to nonmilitary users to about 100 meters, researchers at CMU using the GPS system to support applications such as the autonomous operation of mining vehicles report being able to obtain 1-meter real-time precision. The military-precision data are sometimes reported to provide absolute three-dimensional positions accurate to about a millimeter. Compact (portable, with shirt pocket size promised) and relatively inexpensive (currently GPS systems are available). In the spring of 1991, a system on a PC card was available for approximately $3,000.

Range

Range sensors may be used as short-range navigation sensors, or they may be used to build local maps at a finer scale than is available from the navigational map. The best known range sensor example in robotic applications is the Polaroid sonar sensor (see figure 4.2), originally developed for autofocusing cameras. It consists of an acoustic transceiver element and an electronic package that measures acoustic transit time. Evaluation kits including a couple of transducers, drive electronics, and an LED range display can be purchased for about $150. Range maps have been produced by scanning a single unit, or by integrating multiple units in an array—for example, a ring. Sonar range mappers for

Figure 4.2 Block Diagram of the Polaroid Sonar Range Transceiver

The transducer is a metallized plastic film that emits an ultrasonic pulse when excited by a voltage pulse and that conversely produces a voltage pulse when acoustically excited. The time between pulse emission and echo reception combined with the known speed of sound gives the range to the target. Originally produced for autofocusing cameras, these transducers have found wide application in navigation and collision avoidance systems on mobile robots and automatic guided vehicles. Recently, they have begun to appear in inexpensive "electronic tape measures" for the home handyman.

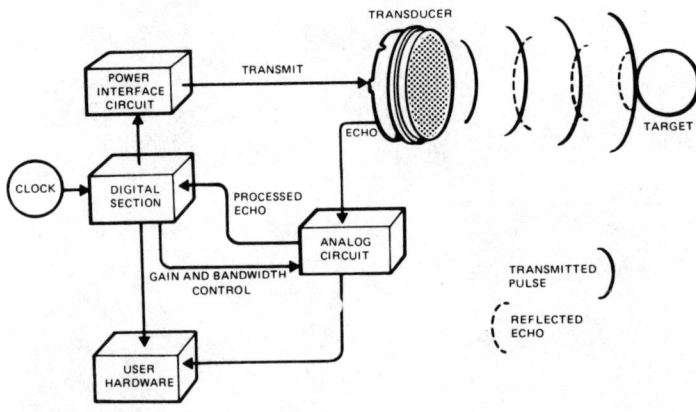

mobile robot applications have several weaknesses, including inherently low spatial resolution, slow scanning speed, and interpretation difficulties that result from the simultaneously high but unknown probabilities of both specular and diffuse echoes from arbitrary targets. Nevertheless, encouraging results have been demonstrated in simple but realistic simulated household and industrial environments [9, 26].

In part because of the difficulties with sonar, there has been a great deal of recent interest in laser rangefinders [19]. One commercial implementation is illustrated in figure 4.3. Unlike sonar, where the acoustic echo time is an easy-to-measure 6 milliseconds per meter of range, the light echo time is a hard-to-measure 6 nanoseconds per meter of range. Thus, somewhat fancier schemes are needed. Two approaches are at or near market.

One method is to amplitude modulate the laser beam, and to measure the modulation phase difference between the outgoing and return beams. In principle, this method, like any phase-measuring method, results in a range measurement that is ambiguous by an unknown integer number of modulation wavelengths. In practice, the integer essentially can be guaranteed to be zero, because the decrease of signal strength with distance means that only relatively close ranges are actually seen. Additional tricks, such as using multiple laser

Figure 4.3 Digital Optronics Corporation's Eagle 3515 FM Laser Radar System for Creating Range Maps, Depicted in a Robotic Package Sorting Application

This system uses the method of modulation of the laser optical frequency, heterodyning the echo with a sample of the outgoing chirp. Competitive systems use amplitude modulation of the laser intensity, measuring the phase difference between the echo and transmitted beam. In either case, distance images are assembled by mechanically rastering the outgoing beam horizontally and vertically.

frequencies simultaneously, can also help resolve ambiguity. ERIM, Odetics, and Perception are marketing devices that use this method. These systems are integrated with horizontal and vertical mechanical scanning devices to raster acquire and display range maps. One of these units is in experimental use on a road following recreational vehicle built at CMU.

The second method borrows from FM radar technology. The laser's optical frequency is sawtooth modulated ("chirped"), and the echoed chirps interfere in the temporal domain with a reference signal that is a sample of the transmitted signal. If the relationship of chirp frequency to time is truly linear, then the frequency difference between the reference and return chirps is constant at constant range, and it is proportional to the target range. Prototype systems using this technology, also including horizontal and vertical mechanical scanning to

display range maps, have been demonstrated, and prototypes are being marketed by Digital Optronics Corporation. Simple estimates suggest that amplitude modulation systems may already be performing close to their theoretical limits, but with further development the more embryonic FM radar systems might be able to give range measurements of machine shop precision over ranges of several meters. However, the practical functionality of systems like these is more often limited by nuisance issues like robustness against specular reflection than it is by esoteric considerations of the limitations imposed by signal theory.

Proximity

Proximity sensors are close-in range sensors. They enforce the distinction between internal and external parts of the system. One-bit (on/off) inductive proximity sensors are applied extensively in automated processing lines for sensing the presence or absence of metal parts and have an obvious if unglamorous place in robotics as limit switches, collision avoidance detectors, etc. Eddy current sensors, essentially the same inductive devices but with a multibit (ranging) capability, are finding increasing applications in metalworking, and perhaps in some robotic inspection applications. There has recently been a proliferation of research designs for proximity sensors specifically designed to be incorporated in robot and effectors. Most of these new devices [28, 6, 17, 23, 15, 16, 26] are optical reflectance sensors, some employing fiber optics. No one of them seems to be a universal solution spanning the range of potential applications, although each is obviously well tuned to the requirements of the developer's specific application. Their intent is to use robot motion under proximity sensor guidance to scan and map a three-dimensional picture of solid objects in the workspace for description, identification, and manipulation. These are "active" technologies, in which the robot scans its workspace along data-driven feeling and groping paths. A typical configuration is shown in figure 4.4.

The substitution of active proximity sensing methods for, on the one hand, shape from tactile sensor arrays, and, on the other hand, shape from TV image interpretation, is a tacit admission that neither of these two classic technologies is in outstandingly good health with respect to this application. Specifically with respect to tactile sensing, it is a wisely motivated attempt to separate the complexities of touch sensors requiring contact from the complexities of architectural and algorithmic methods needed to control robots on the basis of touch data. Because there is no contact involved, the teletouch approach removes artifacts related to the nature of the contact between transducer and surface. It reduces the problem to a strategy for surveying the surface and decoding the survey results from precise measurements of pose (discussed later in this chapter).

Figure 4.4 Robot Hand Equipped with Optical Proximity Sensors on Each Gripper Finger

Proximity sensing is an alternative to tactile (touch, contact) sensing that sidesteps the issue of finding a true tactile sensor with adequate specifications and lifetime for industrial application.

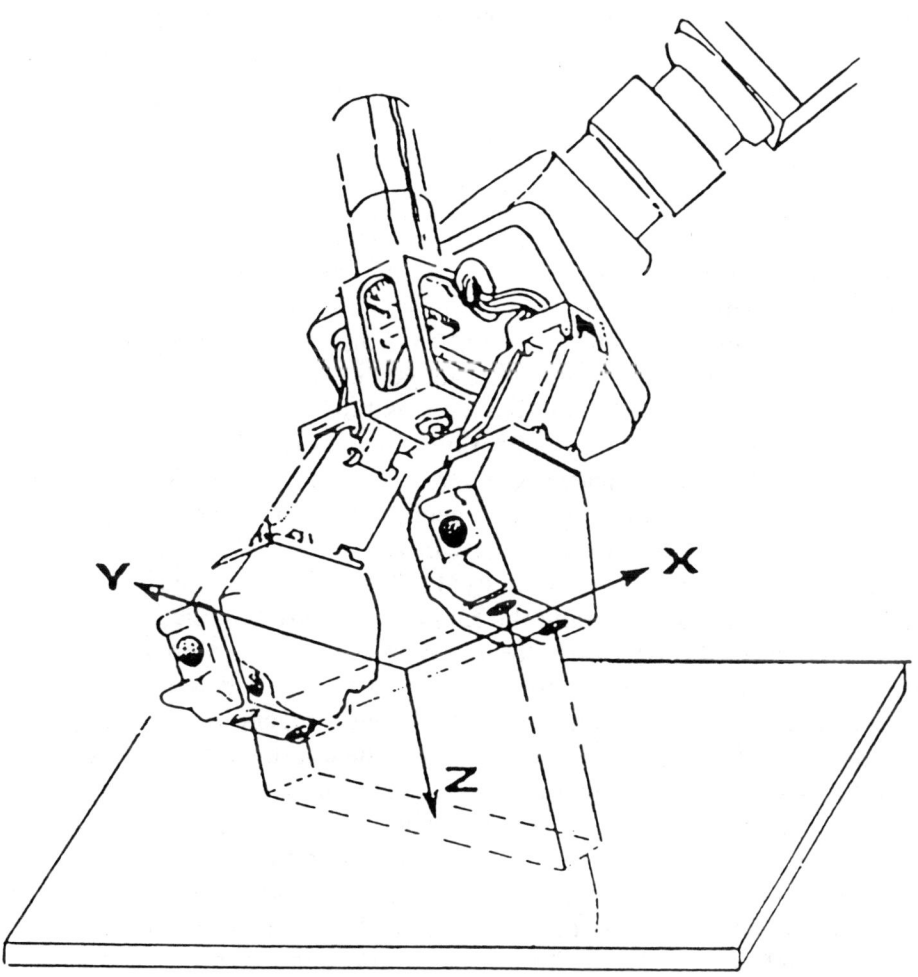

Contact Sensing: Touch

Touch sensors measure physical properties of the contact between parts of the external and internal systems. Force, torque, slip, induced vibration, thermal transfer characteristics, and other quantities analogous to components of biolog-

ical touch dominate the literature of nonvision sensing. Each inventor would like to think that what his particular sensor measures is touch, or at least that it could substitute for the richer suite of senses that constitute human touch. An eloquently presented love for this richness is presented by the late Leon Harmon [13] in the volume edited by Beni and Hackwood [1]. The inadequacy of attempts, on the one hand, to build touch sensors that demonstrate measurement and perception capabilities in any way comparable to biological sensors of the same quantities, and, on the other hand, to demonstrate the utility of tactile sensing in any set of general industrial robotics applications, appears increasingly evident, as shown in part by the recent spectacular growth of the alternative proximity-sensing methods discussed in the previous section. A systematic needs analysis is given by Dario *et al.* [4], and the case for recognizing and using tactile sensors for shear and surface torque in addition to or instead of the conventional normal force sensors is made by Hackwood *et al.* [10] in the volume edited by Alan Pugh [21]. An example of a simple but well implemented research approach to slip sensing integrated with a robot gripper is given in figure 4.5. Most workers concentrate on the transducers *per se*. Some of their approaches, both recent and historical, are summarized in the following sections.

Wrist Force and Torque

Joint force and torque sensing is the most highly developed form of commercially available touch sensing. The sensor is generally a flat cylindrical package designed to be inserted between two robot links, for example, between forearm and hand. One commercial product is described, with specifications, in figure 4.6. Strain gauges bonded to the force and torque transmitting beams measure the vector tilt and twist induced by the load between the endplates of the cylinder. These devices, in principle simple but in practice often diabolically clever [3] have found widespread industrial application, at least in demonstration set-ups of real tasks, and possibly in routine production. A variant on the theme is the instrumented remote compliance center device [5], which combines passive mechanical accommodation to jamming-prone peg-in-hole motions with the potential for active control based on the forces and torques measured by the strain sensors, in this case optical.

A similar but substantially simpler instrumented flexible wrist, in which the force is transmitted through four sheet springs 90 degrees apart, each equipped with a strain gauge, is described by Goto *et al.* [7] as having been in production line use at Hitachi since the early 1970s. In the task of inserting pistons in cylinders with about 20-micron clearance, their data show the robot completing the operation within 0.9 to 1.2 seconds, and human workers completing it in 0.2 to 4.2 seconds, both time distributions being effectively flat and demonstrating a clear statistical advantage in favor of the robot. This report provides convincing evidence of the value of simple instrumentation in a well-chosen narrow domain.

Figure 4.5 The Arbotech Gripper, Modified by SRI International to Incorporate an Experimental Tactile Slip Sensor Based on Thermal Conductivity Detected by Embedded Thermistors

In the steady state, thermal conductivity, usually measured via the power needed to keep the self-heated thermistor at constant temperature, can distinguish between good heat conductors (metals) and poor heat conductors (insulators). Slip is accompanied by a transient increase in power demand as cool portions of the workpiece move into contact with the sensor.

Figure 4.6 Barry Wright Corporation's Astek Model FS6-120A 6-Axis Force/Torque Sensor

Units in this series are available with full-scale ranges of 100 to 600 newtons (25 to 150 pounds) force, 2 to 12 newton-meters (18 to 108 inch-pounds) torque, with 12 bit (1/2000) resolution. Sensors of this type are generally intended to be mounted between the robot *per se* and its end-effector or tooling. It would not be unusual for the robot, the sensor, and the end-effector to be purchased from three separate suppliers and integrated by the user.

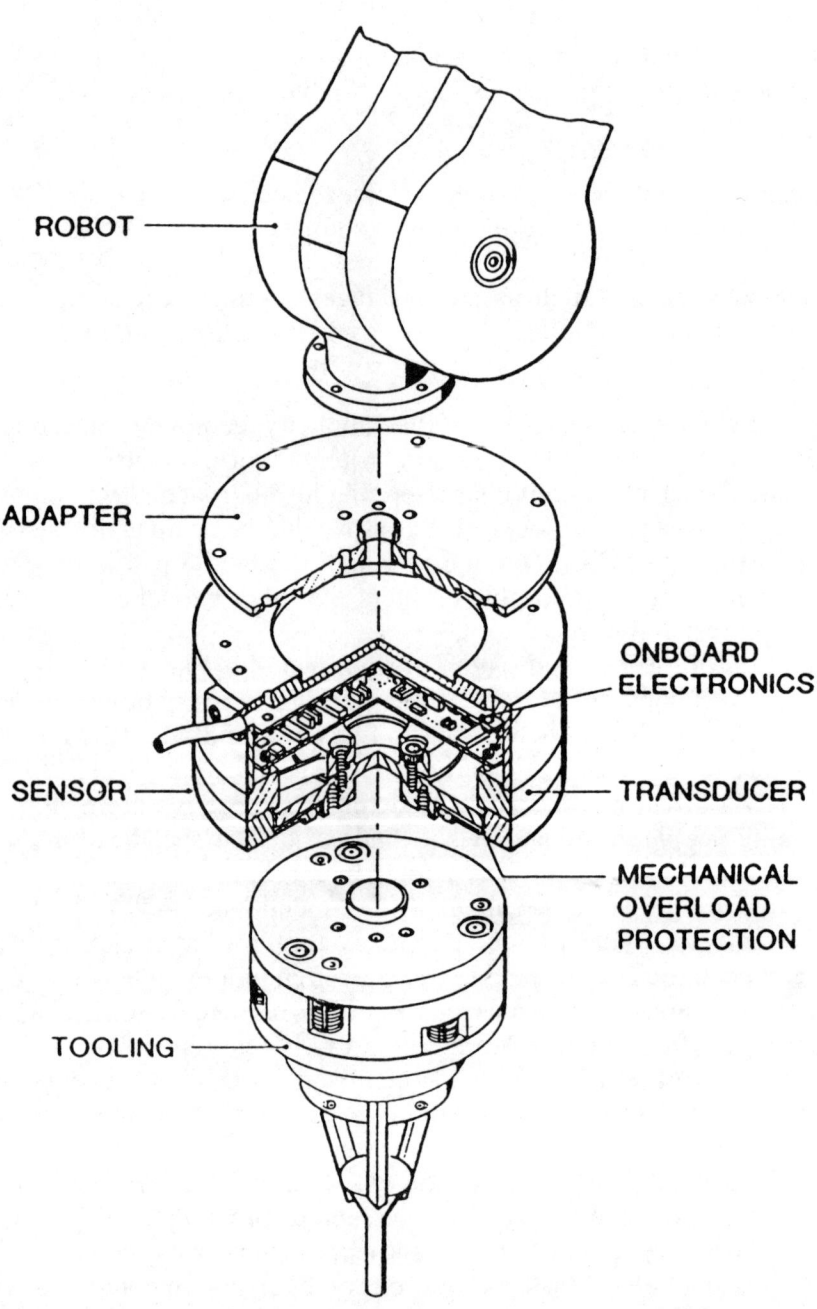

Tactile Arrays

Normal Force

Tactile sensing arrays have traditionally measured the normal force distribution. Sensing schemes are manifold, including the following:

- Parametric mechanisms, such as macroscopic or contact resistance, microscopic or piezoresistance, variable capacitance, and variable inductance

- Transduction mechanisms, such as piezoelectricity (voltage source) and magnetic induction (current source)

- Indirect mechanisms, such as strain gauges, optical occlusion, acoustic path, pneumatic leak rate, and frustrated total internal reflection.

The merits touted by each designer are the simplicity, economy, ruggedness, potential for implementation as a flexible skin, potential for miniaturization, and ease and speed of electrical readout characterizing his approach. Two commercial implementations, one a photo-occlusive approach to finger-tip tactile sensing and the second a piezoresistive approach in which the tactile pad is the work surface rather than an anthropomorphic organ of the robot *per se,* are shown in figures 4.7 and 4.8, respectively.

This proliferation of designs and paucity of real-world applications is symptomatic of a general failure to address tactile sensing in a top-down fashion, asking first what the requirements and possibilities are, and addressing implementation schemes in the context of clearly defined specifications related to utility. Harmon [11, 12] attempted diligently to determine these requirements, but he did it by asking people in industry what kinds of device specifications they thought they needed to replace assembly people with robots, rather than by creating models and testing them experimentally. As mentioned previously, Dario *et al.* and Hackwood *et al.* have attempted to take a top-down approach but have always in the end been limited by specific transducer endpoint implementations.

Some experiments addressing issues of the utility of specific measuring resources and computing architectures to tactile array-based manipulator control were done at CMU several years ago [25]. A tactile array signal processing computer was constructed consisting of a parallel array of sixteen preamplifiers, analog-to-digital converters, and asynchronous microprocessors with local program and data memory, all in communication with a large serial processor via a seventeenth "supervisor" microprocessor. The tactile computer was interfaced to an array of piezoelectric touch sensors, and experiments were conducted to quantify the utility, to a control task, of multibit force resolution compared with

Figure 4.7 The Lord Corporation's LTS 200 Gripper Mounted Force/Torque Sensor

Force sensitivity is about 5 grams. Force transduction is by a photo-occlusive technique in an 8-×-8 array: with increasing normal force a miniature rubber vane below each tactile cell location increasingly occludes the light transmission between a photo-emitter and a photo-receptor associated with that cell. There is a single vector (three-axis) torque sensor whose mechanism is not disclosed.

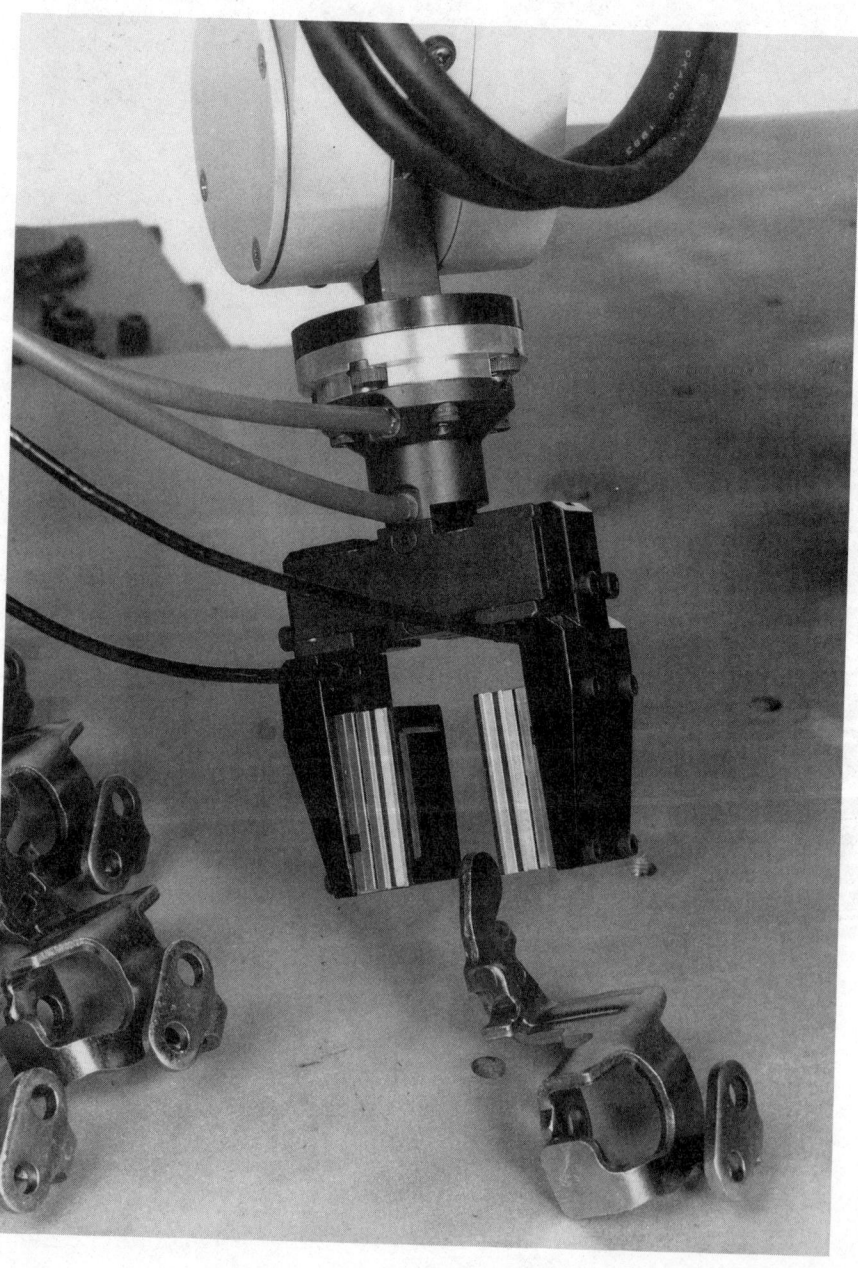

Figure 4.8 The Lord Corporation's LTS 300 Tactile Sensor Pad Is an 80-×-80 Array with 2 mm Spacing

It uses a piezoresistive conductive elastomer for force transduction. In operation, the robot blindly acquires a part, then moves it to and presses it against the tactile pad to produce a force-image that can be used for identification and orientation.

simple one-bit touch/no touch information such as would be delivered by an array of switches. In an experiment with the sensor array mounted on the end effector of a robot and used for closed-loop control, it was found that if the ratio of programmed motion step size to endpoint compliance was about unity, the algorithm's having access to multibit force measurements reduced its convergence time substantially. On the other hand, if the programmed motion step size was grossly mismatched to the endpoint compliance in either direction, one-bit data were as useful as multibit data.

Many more experiments in this spirit, designed to teach what are and what are not really useful characteristics of tactile sensor arrays in manipulator control domains, will have to be done before tactile array sensors become useful for anything more than identification and orientation of parts, tasks that are already done adequately by machine vision anyway.

The technologies that are being pursued for tactile sensing include the following:

- Piezoresistive

- Piezoelectric

- Optically occlusive

- Frustrated total internal reflection

These technologies are discussed in the following sections.

Piezoresistive The electrical resistance of many materials changes in response to mechanical strain. The effect may be either microscopic or macroscopic. Suitably doped silicon, for example, has a resistivity strongly sensitive to strain, making possible the silicon pressure or strain gauge. This is a microscopic effect—that is, it involves the structure of the material at the atomic level. The macroscopic effect is better known. It is, for example, the principle behind the old-fashioned carbon granule microphone in telephone mouthpieces. In a conducting granular or fibrous material (carbon is popular in both granules and fibers), the bulk resistivity is decreased as the grains or fibers are pressed into more intimate contact, effectively increasing the cross-sectional area of the electrical current flow path. Thus the microscopic effect is a true change in resistivity, and the macroscopic effect is just a change in resistance. Piezoresistivity, especially the macroscopic effect, has been used over many years in an impressive variety of laboratory prototype tactile sensor arrays [30]. More recently, the microscopic effect has been exploited, by incorporation of micromachined silicon strain gauges [20] in a tactile surface. However, none of these implementations apppear to have found industrial application except possibly for part identification and orientation.

Piezoelectric Certain crystals, and certain polymers with molecular symmetries similar to those crystals, exhibit mechanical strain in response to an applied electric field, and conversely develop an electric field in response to an applied strain. The first effect can be used to make actuators, such as electronically controlled gas flow valves, and its converse can be used to make sensors, such as tactile sensor arrays. A particularly convenient material for the latter purpose is the polymer polyvinylidine difluoride (PVF2 or PVDF), sometimes known commercially as Kynar, which is available in sheets, optionally metallized on both surfaces. A voltage measuring circuit connected between the metallized surfaces will exhibit a response whenever the material is strained—for example, by a normal force. In principle, the voltage remains as long as the strain is maintained, but in practice, leakage effects in the material and the measuring circuit cause the response to be a transient voltage of one sign when the strain is applied and the opposite sign when it is released. Piezoelectric tactile sensors and arrays thus have good high-frequency response but are unsuitable for directly measuring static or slowly varying loads. This disadvantage can in part be compensated in software. Alternatively, the piezoelectric effect can be used indirectly, as in the ultrasonic array described by Grahn *et al.* [8]. There have been many suggestions for implementing tactile arrays by the direct piezoelectric effect, but apparently there have been only two attempts to actually do so, one by Dario *et al.* [3, 4, 13], and the one at CMU described above. Both of these are research applications with little suggestion of being close to ready for commercialization.

Optically Occlusive A commercially available tactile sensor pad, manufactured by the Lord Corporation, is in essence an array of bumps on a rubber surface. Each bump carries, on its underside, a vane that moves down when the bump is depressed. A photodiode light source is mounted on one side of each vane, and a phototransistor is mounted on the other side of each vane. Each array site produces an analog signal related to how far the corresponding bump is depressed. The system has been shown to be useful in industrial part identification and orientation but apparently has not been demonstrated in a manipulation control task [22].

Frustrated Total Internal Reflection Light moving in a medium of high index of refraction toward a medium of low index of refraction at a sufficiently oblique angle (an angle greater than the critical angle) experiences total internal reflection: 100 percent of the energy remains in the reflected ray, and there is no refracted ray. There is nevertheless some penetration of the light into the low index region, where the energy density falls off exponentially with distance from the interface. If a material with a high index of refraction invades this space—that is, closely approaches or touches the interface—light will leak from the first high index medium into the second high index medium. This is known as frustrated total internal reflection. If two high index of refraction plates, one rigid and flat

and one flexible and knobby, are set up so that the flexible one is a tactile surface and so that scattered light associated with frustrated total internal reflection can be imaged by a TV camera, the image is essentially a tactile force map [31]. Several variations on this recently demonstrated theme have been described.

Shear and Surface Torque

In a discussion of a sensor they built as an array of magnetoresistive elements overlaid by an array of magnetic dipoles in an elastic medium, Hackwood *et al.* [9] argue convincingly that in realistic application scenarios only very simple and spatially gross normal force measurements are needed, whereas the availability of detailed shear and torque information can result in substantial manipulation performance improvements. In the device they describe, each sensor element consists of four magnetoresistive elements associated with one magnetic dipole element. Each sensor element reports three components of shear strain and one component of torque. The authors draw an appealing analogy between this kind of multimodal response and that of the human skin, pointing out that in both cases the pattern discrimination capacity is much greater than that of the two-point resolution because of the multidimensional richness of information available from each sensor site.

Temperature and Thermal Conductivity

Surfaces feel hot or cold by virtue of both their temperature and their thermal conductivity, their ability to absorb heat from or deliver heat to skin. Several groups have recently demonstrated thermally sensitive tactile arrays and noted potential applications, mostly identification and orientation.

The method generally is either to use self-heated thermistors embedded in a skin of appropriate thickness and thermal conductivity or to use a separately heated skin monitored by an array of passive thermistors [24, 23].

Induced Vibration

Rubbing the skin across a surface conveys information about the surface in part because people are skilled at interpreting the vibrations induced by this rubbing action. Neville *et al.* [18, 27] have recently demonstrated a machine counterpart to this sensory component, consisting of a patterned surface, a vibration transducer embedded in the surface, and instrumentation for frequency spectrum analysis of the induced vibration. Impressive discriminating ability has been demonstrated in a few very limited application domains—for example, distinguishing ball bearings of very slightly different diameter.

Self-Sensing: Pose

Measuring pose (or posture), the representation of robot configuration in its own internal coordinate system, involves sensory components variously known as *kinesthetic,*[1] *proprioceptive,*[2] and prosaically, *joint angle* and *link length sensing.* It is accomplished simply and usually reliably by installation of commercial linear and angular encoders on the required links and joints. The accuracy and precision potentially available from off-the-shelf commercial sensors exceeds the requirements of most robotic tasks. However, this method, at least if too inexpensively or too naively implemented, fails when the flexing of the robot under load cannot be neglected.

Except under bizarre circumstances, such as after recovery from a communications failure or computer crash, the pose is known fairly well just from "dead reckoning," the mechanically initialized configuration as modified by the summed effect of all the motion commands. About the only reason for wanting to know the pose any better than this (assuming the mechanics and controls are good enough that gross errors never accumulate) is that precise knowledge of pose may be the only way to know the precise location and orientation of the end effector.

An alternative, given that the purpose of pose measurement is endpoint navigation, is to do endpoint navigation directly. Several systems for this purpose use a beacon, such as a spark source of audible clicks, mounted on the end effector and an array of receiving stations, such as microphones, fixed in the workspace. Colson and Perreira [2] have reported on the general problem in detail and have described several experimental endpoint navigation methods for pose measurement using a variety of sensor technologies, such as corner cube reflectors.

Conclusions

Two key recent developments in nonvision sensors for robotics are (1) the substitution of proximity sensors carried in robot end effectors for both touch- and vision-based mapping of three-dimensional surfaces in the workspace, and (2) the availability or near availability of precise, compact, and inexpensive navi-

---

[1] Kinesthesia: a sense mediated by end organs located in muscles, tendons, and joints, and stimulated by bodily movements and tensions. [29]
[2] Proprioceptive: of, relating to, or being stimuli arising within the organism. [29]

gation and range sensors. The range sensors are especially important because they mitigate the seriousness of stereo vision's fatal flaw, the unsolved corresponding point problem. With immobile robots, constrained to perform more or less the same job in the same place again and again, simple vision and simplistic tactile systems for part identification, orientation, and acquisition, supplemented by simple touch sensors for grasping and tool control, will be enough. The decision between vision and nonvision sensing modalities will remain one of economics and convenience rather than principle: every necessary dimensional and force measurement could be made with a sufficiently high performance vision system. When mobile robots enter the industrial workforce, vision will cease to be enough. A mobile robot has to be wary of the unplanned and the unexpected in the domain of every sensory modality. Threats will be invisible, or by the time they become visible it will be too late. Operating in this inevitably hostile environment will require a suite of sensors paralleling and surpassing our own biological senses. At least an auditory hazard and fault detection method, and a chemical hazard or chemical marker sensor will be needed. Other senses, from the technological world (and sometimes from the nonhuman biological world) will also likey prove useful. These include electrostatic and magnetostatic fields, electromagnetic radiation, nuclear radiation, barometric and hydrostatic pressure, and others. The two most critical current research areas in nonvision sensory robotics are (1) the integration of navigation, range, proximity, and touch sensing, and (2) a clear understanding of the components of touch sensing, aimed at discovering which are important for what kinds of tasks, learning which components are nearly independent and which are tightly coupled, and learning computational architectures for integrating the touch sense components required to perform specific categories of tasks. Specific technologies and inventions for implementing sensory modalities or components will be forthcoming in response to carefully articulated specifications, and are far less problematic than the system integration issues.

References

General References

1. *International Journal of Robotics Research*. MIT Press. A heavily mathematical scholarly journal covering robotics theory, often including articles on the modeling and performance of laboratory prototypes of sensor designs and application techniques.

2. *Sensor Review* (British). A monthly trade journal with modest technical content but excellent sensor business coverage.

3. *Sensors*. North American Technology. A good monthly trade journal.

4. *Sensors and Actuators*. Elsevier. A scholarly journal covering the business end of sensor technology, such as microfabrication of silicon sensor devices.

References Cited in the Chapter

1. Beni, Gerardo, and Susan Hackwood, eds. *Recent Advances in Robotics*. Volume 1: *Recent Advances in Robotics*. New York: John Wiley & Sons, 1985.

2. Colson, James C., and N. Duke Perriera. "Pose Measurement Devices, Pose Error Determination, and Robot Performance." In *Proceedings of the Detroit Meeting,* pages MS85–987–1–18. Sensors '85, SME, Dearborn, Michigan, November, 1985.

3. Cutkosky, Mark. *Robotic Grasping and Fine Manipulation*. Boston, MA: Kluwer Academic Publishers, 1985.

4. Dario, P., A. Bicchi, A. Fiorillo, G. Buttazzo, and R. Francesconi. "A Sensorized Scenario for Basic Investigation on Active Touch." In *International Trends in Manufacturing Technology*. Volume 2: *Robot Sensors: Tactile & Non-Vision*. Alan Pugh, ed. Bedford, UK: IFS (Publications) Ltd, 1986, pages 237–45.

5. DeFazio, T. L., D. S. Seltzer, and D. E. Whitney. "The IRCC Instrumented Remote Centre Compliance." In *International Trends in Manufacturing Technology*. Volume 2: *Robot Sensors: Tactile & Non-Vision*. Alan Pugh, ed. Bedford, UK: IFS (Publications) Ltd, 1986, pages 33–44.

6. Espiau, Bernard. "Use of Optical Reflectance Sensors." Chapter 8 in *Recent Advances in Robotics*. Volume 1: *Recent Advances in Robotics*. Gerardo Beni and Susan Hackwood, eds. New York: John Wiley & Sons, 1985, pages 313–57.

7. Goto, T., T. Inoyama, and K. Takeyasu. "Precise Insert Operation by Tactile-Controlled Robot." Chapter 1 in *International Trends in Manufacturing Technology*. Volume 2: *Robot Sensors: Tactile & Non-Vision*. Alan Pugh, ed. Bedford, UK: IFS (Publications) Ltd, 1986, pages 45–52.

8. Grahn, Allen R. "Robotic Ultrasonic Imaging Force Sensor Arrays." In *International Trends in Manufacturing Technology*. Volume 2: *Robot Sensors: Tactile & Non-Vision*. Alan Pugh, ed. Bedford, UK: IFS (Publications) Ltd, 1986, pages 297–315.

9. Hackwood, S., G. Beni, L. A. Hornak, R. Wolfe, and T. J. Nelson. "A Torque-Sensitive Tactile Array for Robotics." *The International Journal of Robotics* vol. 2, no. 2 (Summer 1983):46–50. Also see reference 10.

10. Hackwood, S., G. Beni, and T. J. Nelson. "Torque-Sensitive Tactile Array for Robotics." In *International Trends in Manufacturing Technology*. Volume 2: *Robot Sensors: Tactile & Non-Vision*. Alan Pugh, ed. Bedford, UK: IFS (Publications) Ltd, 1986, pages 123–29.

REFERENCES

11. Harmon, Leon D. "Automated Tactile Sensing." *The International Journal of Robotics Research* vol. 1, no. 2 (Summer 1982):3–32.

12. ———. "Robotic Taction Industrial Assembly." *The International Journal of Robotics Research* vol. 3, no. 1 (Spring 1984):73–76.

13. ———. "Tactile Sensing for Robots." Chapter 10 in *Recent Advances in Robotics*. Volume 1: *Recent Advances in Robotics*. Gerardo Beni and Susan Hackwood, eds. New York: John Wiley & Sons, 1985, pages 389–424.

14. Henderson, T. C., ed. *Traditional and Non-Traditional Robotic Sensors*. New York: Springer-Verlag, 1990.

15. Idesawa, M., and G. Kinoshita. "New Type of Miniaturized Optical Range Sensing Methods RORS & RORST." *Journal of Robotic Systems* vol. 3, no. 2 (Summer 1986):165–82.

16. Kurahashi, A., M. Adachi, and M. Idesawa. "A Prototype of Optical Proximity Sensor Based on RORS." *Journal of Robotic Systems* vol. 3, no. 2 (Summer 1986):183–90.

17. Masuda, Ryosuke. "Multifunctional Optical Proximity Sensor Using Phase Modulation." *Journal of Robotic Systems* vol. 3, no. 2 (Summer 1986):137–48.

18. Neville, Gale E., Jr., Eric F. Schildwachter, and Keith L. Doty. "Alternative Skin Geometries and Materials for Induced Vibration Touch Sensors." In *Proceedings of the Detroit Meeting,* pages MS85–992–1–7. Sensors '85, SME, Dearborn, Michigan, November, 1985.

19. Parthasarathy, S., J. Birk, and J. Dessimoz. "Laser Rangefinder for Robot Control and Inspection." *SPIE Robot Vision* vol. 336 (1982):2–11.

20. Petersen, Kurt, Carl Kowalski, Joseph Brown, Henry Allen, and Jim Knutti. "A Force Sensing Chip Designed for Robotic and Manufacturing Automation Applications." In *Proceedings of the Philadelphia Meeting,* pages 30–32. Wen H. Ko and Ken D. Wise, eds. Transducers '85, IEEE, June, 1985.

21. Pugh, Alan, ed. *International Trends in Manufacturing Technology*. Volume 2: *Robot Sensors: Tactile & Non-Vision*. Bedford, UK: IFS (Publications) Ltd, 1986.

22. Rebman, J., and K. A. Morris. "A Tactile Sensor with Electrooptical Transduction." In *International Trends in Manufacturing Technology*. Volume 2: *Robot Sensors: Tactile & Non-Vision*. Alan Pugh, ed. Bedford, UK: IFS (Publications) Ltd, 1986, pages 145–55.

23. Russell, R. Andrew. "A Thermal Sensor Array to Provide Tactile Feedback for Robots." *The International Journal of Robotics Research* vol. 4, no. 3 (Fall 1985):35–39.

24. Siegel, David M., and Laurel Simmons. "A Thermal-Based Sensor System." In *Proceedings of the Detroit Meeting,* pages MS85–995–1–14. Sensors '85, SME, Dearborn, Michigan, November, 1985.

25. Toto, Gregory M. *Manipulator Control by Tactile Sensor Feedback*. Master's thesis, Carnegie-Mellon University, February, 1984.

26. Tsujimura, T., T. Yabuta, and T. Morimitsu. "3-D Shape Recognition Method Using Ultrasonics for Manipulator Control Systems." *Journal of Robotic Systems* vol. 3, no. 2 (Summer 1986):205–16.

27. Venugopal, Ravi, Gale E. Neville, Jr., and Keith L. Doty. "Real Time Feature Extraction from an Induced Vibration Touch Sensor." In *Proceedings of the Detroit Meeting,* pages MS85-993-1-7. Sensors '85, SME, Dearborn, Michigan, November, 1985.

28. Wampler, Charles. "Multiprocessor Control of a Telemanipulator with Optical Proximity Sensors." *The International Journal of Robotics Research* vol. 3, no. 1 (Spring 1984):40–50.

29. Webster. *Webster's Seventh New Collegiate Dictionary.* Springfield, MA: G. & C. Merriam Company, 1965.

30. John G. Webster, ed. *Tactile Sensors for Robotics and Medicine.* New York: John Wiley & Sons, 1988.

31. White, Richard M., and Andrew A. King. "Tactile Array for Robotics Employing a Rubbery Skin and a Solid-State Optical Sensor." In *Proceedings of the Philadelphia Meeting,* pages 18–21. Wen H. Ko and Ken D. Wise, eds. Transducers '85, IEEE, June, 1985.

Chapter 5 Electro-optical Sensors in Process Control

Nello Zuech

Laser Gauges

HeNe and semiconductor lasers are used in a variety of ways in industrial settings: to measure dimensions, profiles, position, and velocity. One of the earliest applications, and one in widespread application throughout manufacturing industries, uses the laser to gauge parts. These laser optical measuring systems are effective when the edges of the feature to be measured can be seen in a silhouetted scene of the object.

The general principle involves detecting the amount of time the light is blocked through a sensor during a single line sweep of the laser (figure 5.1). To obtain high accuracies, clever collimated optical arrangements are used both to project the laser from the transmitter onto the object as well as to optically image the silhouette of the object onto the receiving sensor. A rotating mirror arrangement is typically used in the transmitter to create a scanning pattern 120–150 or so times per second. The feature of the object essentially interrupts the scan.

The shadow of the feature is detected by the receiver's sensor. This sensor can be a simple point detector; because the velocity of the laser beam is constant, the distance measured corresponds to the length of time the signal out of the sensor drops to near zero. Alternatively, a linear array or single line arrangement of photosensors can be used as the sensor, and then the number of pixels turned off corresponds to the dimension.

Because the linear array is scanned continuously, the number of pixels turned off corresponds to a time-dependent change in signal level, so again a measurement of time between signal changes results in a measure of dimension. By averaging the results of multiple scans, the accuracy and repeatability of measurement can be improved with any of the methods.

Figure 5.1 Operation of a Scanning Laser

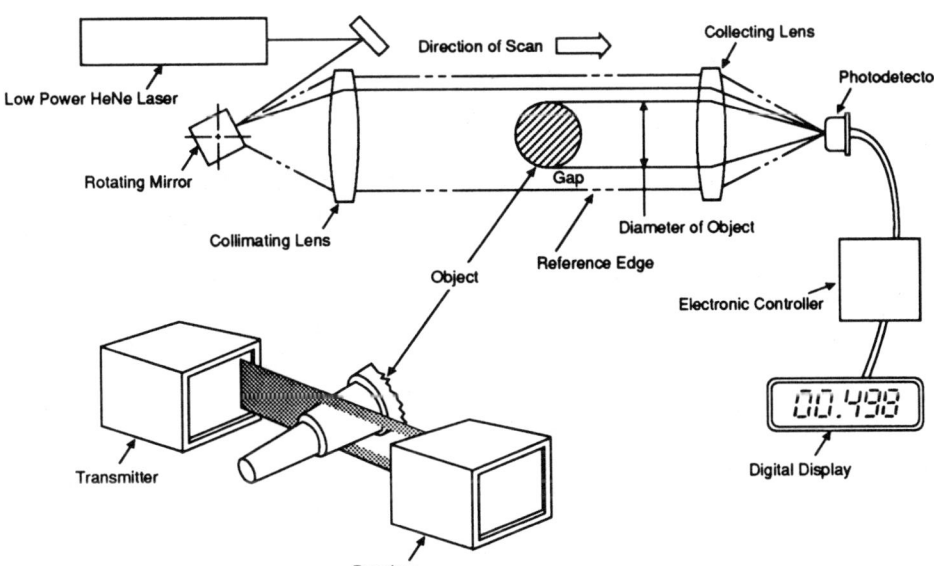

Versions of these techniques can measure parts as small as on the order of 0.005 inch and as large as 20 inches. The accuracy of measurement is a function of the range and is established by calibration against known standards. Consequently, the main concern is repeatability of measurement, and again, this is a function of design execution and measurement range. Typically, repeatability could be optimized to 20 to 30 millionths of an inch with multiple scans.

These techniques are widely used for monitoring diameter during drawing or size reducing processes in wire and fiber operations. The width of web-produced products can also be monitored. Extensions of the techniques can be used to measure all the dimensions of slotted strip steel or perforated strips. They can also be used to measure the diameter and run-out of discrete products that can be rotated about an axis. An extension of this has been their use on grinding machines and lathes, making possible unattended feedback control based on the measured properties of the work piece. IDs and ODs of objects with holes can be measured.

Clever arrangements of multiple scanners make it possible to measure length and width of screw machine parts, for example, or hexagonally shaped bars Although originally designed for laboratory use, these gauges have been successfully adapted to harsh environments, such as steel mills, with proper attention to maintaining clean optics and constant temperatures. Multiple sensor arrangements can be interfaced to a single processor unit. In some cases, these processor units even have the capacity to take measurement data from other sensors. Generally, these processors offer statistical data processing packages.

LASER GAUGES

Figure 5.2a Principle of Measurement of Optal System

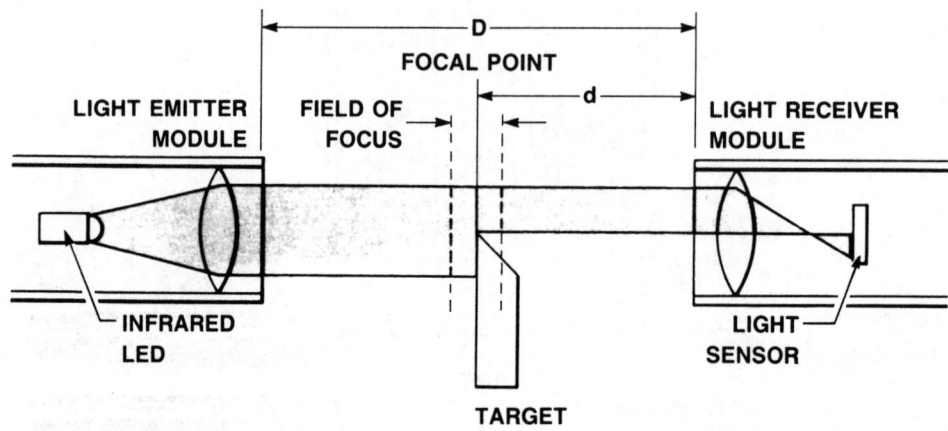

Figure 5.2b Optal System Light Receiver Module Signal

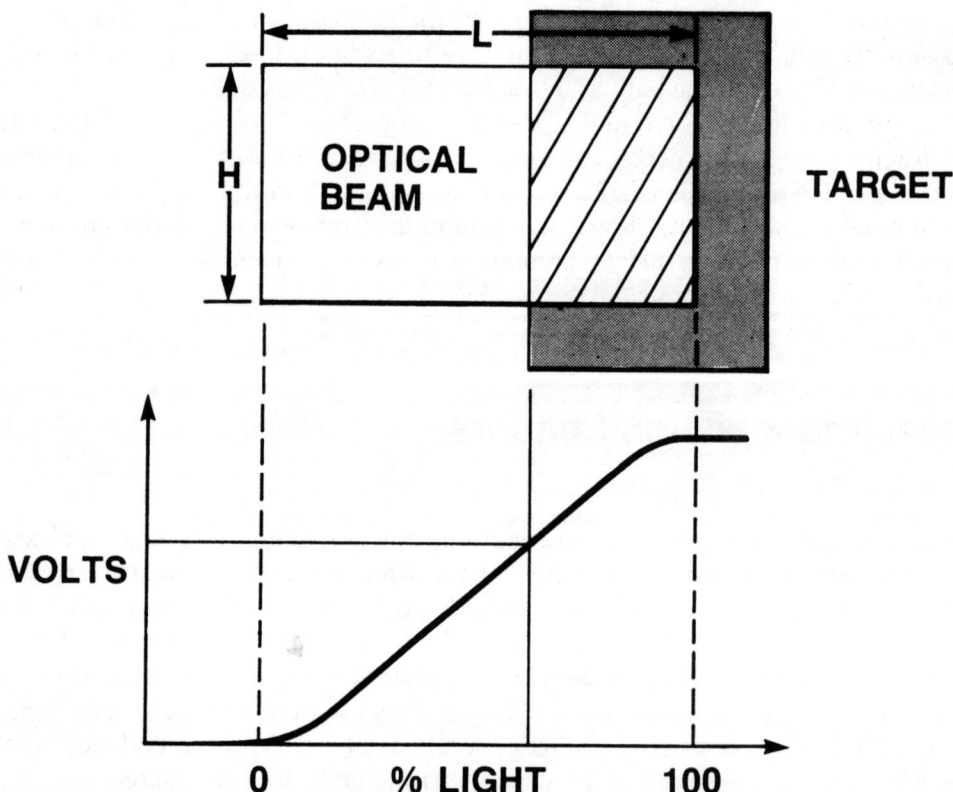

Figure 5.2c Optal System Diameter Measurement Based on Photodetector

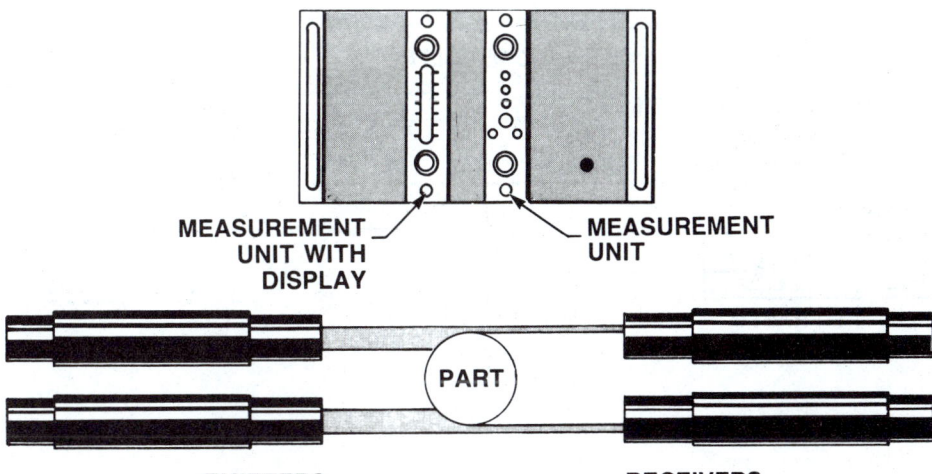

An alternative technique to the laser scanner is one that utilizes collimated light beams and photodetectors with a very linear relationship between light level and output signal (figures 5.2a, 5.2b, and 5.2c). As in the laser scanner, the object is positioned between the light and the detector along the edge or edges of a part. The amount of light interrupted is directly proportional to the size of the part. Accuracies to +/- 1 micron are claimed, and measurements can be made on objects moving at speeds of 120 meters/min. In addition to dimensions such as part diameter and length, clever positioning of arrangements of the collimated light/photosensor allow this technique to measure concentricity, eccentricity, and taper.

Laser Triangulation Sensors

Another popular electro-optical measurement technique is one based on laser, optical triangulation to make measurements to a surface of an object (figure 5.3) If successive or continuous measurements are made, changes in displacement can be measured. This change from a nominal position can be due to a vibration condition to be monitored; a change in a part dimension, such as thickness, surface contour, or height; a change in level in the case of a liquid, etc. The typical triangulation probe consists of: a light source, a camera/detector, and electronics to control the light source and process the raw signals from the detector.

LASER TRIANGULATION SENSORS

Figure 5.3 Laser Triangulation Sensor Techniques

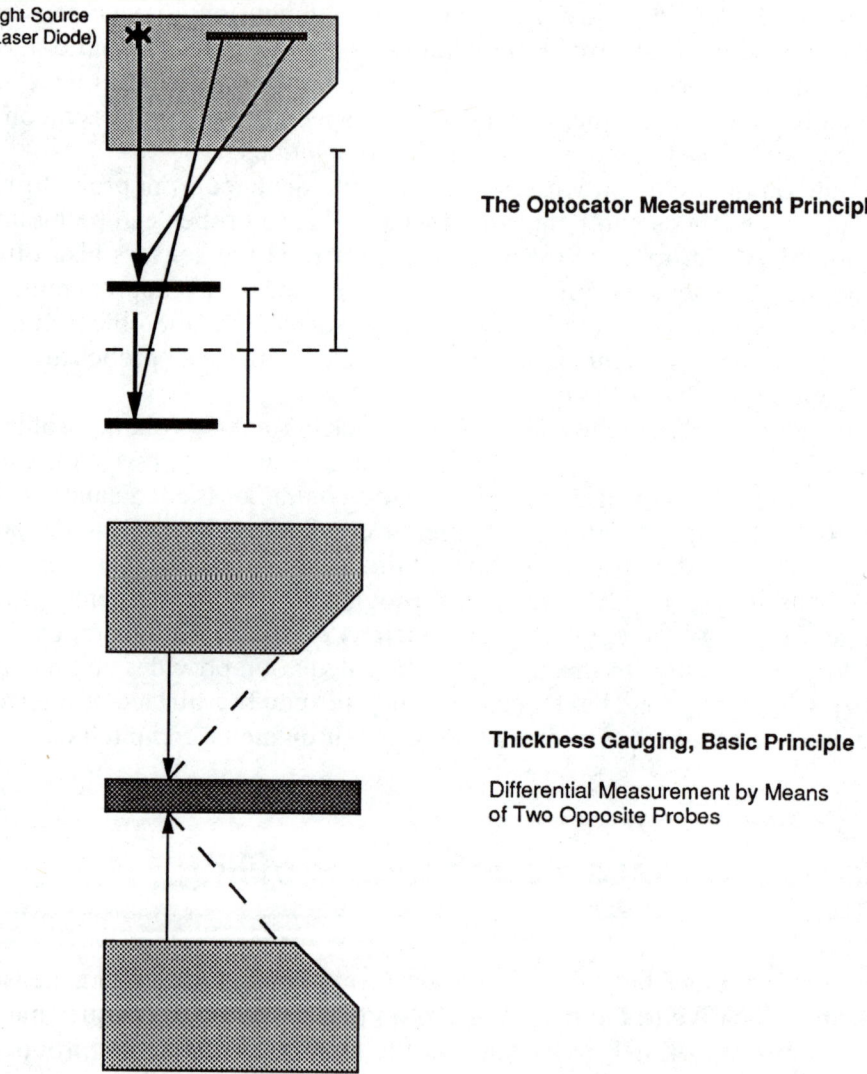

As figure 5.3 shows, a beam of light is projected from the probe onto the surface to be measured. After striking the surface, the beam is scattered (diffused) and optics are used to collect an image of the spot and project it back to a detector. The location of the image on the detector is a function of the distance between the probe and the measured surface. As the surface moves closer to or farther away from the probe, the position of the light spot image on the detector will change. By measuring the location of the light spot image on the detector, it is possible to measure the distance from the probe.

Various lasers, laser diodes, or light emitting diodes are used. Similarly, different executions use different sensor arrangements: lateral effect photodiode, quadrant photodiode, linear array sensor, or two-dimensional image sensor. A major concern with these probes, inevitably, is their ability to handle a wide range of specular, color, and transparency conditions. Again, different executions are more robust than others. Some rely on special image processing on the reflected beam profile. Others use modulation techniques.

Depending on the optics, a variety of stand-offs (distance from probe to part) and measurement ranges can be accommodated. These probes can be mounted a substantial distance (meters) away from the part. These sensors also offer a high-speed measurement capability with response capabilities approaching several thousand hertz. One limitation of these sensors is that the object must be opaque. Typical measurement accuracies associated with these probes are $+/-$ 0.1 to 0.2 percent of the measurement range.

In addition to simple height and thickness measurements, volume profiles of objects can be measured. For example, in the lumber industry, by rotating a log in front of an arrangement of these sensors, the volume of the log can be calculated and that data used to optimize the yield from that log. By moving the probe or the part in front of the probe, one can obtain three-dimensional data regarding objects such as air foils and turbine blades. Moving parts under the sensor allows the volume profile of high-speed objects, such as pouches containing powdered product, to be calculated. In this example, the calculation provides an indication of fill level. Clever versions have been designed to scan the surface of internally threaded holes to obtain data such as: minor/major diameter and pitch diameter.

Noncontact Surface Roughness Profiling

A number of techniques have emerged to perform noncontact profiling measurements as an alternative to tactile/stylus profilometers. These techniques make it possible to perform a timely inspection in the vicinity of the actual production and provide an opportunity for continuous monitoring of the production process. Noncontact electro-optical techniques have the advantages of speed and the ability to measure delicate objects. As with all electro-optical metrology tactics, a major concern is the effect of dirt. Another issue is correlation with existing stylus measurements, and still other issues are those of the color and specularity of the surfaces and the impact these variables will have on repeatability. Again, there are a number of different executions of electro-optical techniques; their results and their ability to handle these concerns vary.

Understanding surface measurements is the first consideration. Surface analysis breaks down into three features: vertical information (amplitude), horizontal

NONCONTACT SURFACE ROUGHNESS PROFILING

information (frequencies), and slope. Most electro-optical probes produce a measurement that embodies all these parameters.

One probe based on scattered light measurements is depicted in figure 5.4. A light emitting diode is used as the radiation source. The one micron laser beam is split in two, with one reference beam focused on a split diode photodetector. The other beam is collimated and focused on the test piece surface by a measuring lens. The back scattered rays from the surface are collected by the

Figure 5.4 A Probe Based on Scattered Light Measurements

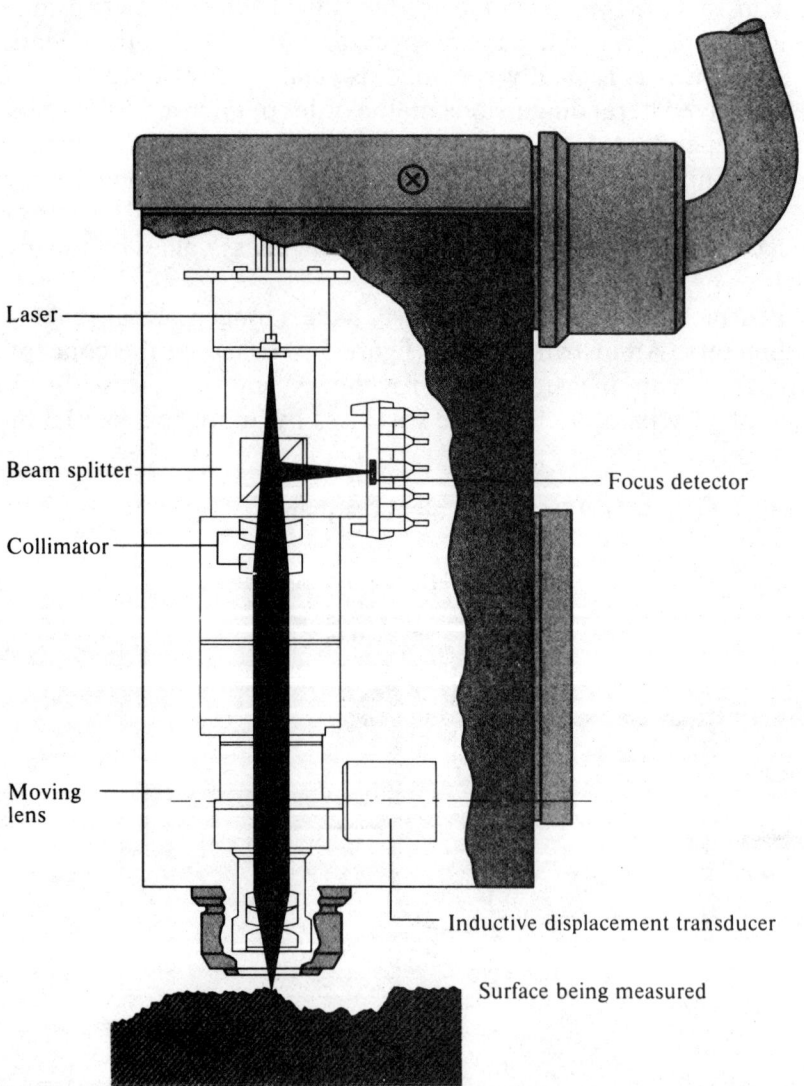

scattered light optical system and passed to a photodiode array via the beam splitter. The optical system is corrected so that individual scattering angles are mapped on corresponding diodes. The electrical signal of the individual diode is amplified, converted from analog to digital, and processed by a microcomputer to generate a signal to refocus the lens. The resultant lens movement accurately follows the surface contour, and lens movement is measured continuously by an inductive displacement transducer to generate the surface profile signal.

The system has a short measuring time of 20 mseconds, and the roughness characteristic obtained is insensitive to changes in distance or inclination of the sample under test. Accuracies range from 0.003 micron for a +/− 3 micron measuring range to 0.3 micron for a +/− 300 micron range.

Another twist in this surface profiling is the optical interferometric microscope. These microscopes can be used to inspect for and control both roughness and waviness. Roughness is typically specified as small microfeatures of a surface—features that have lateral dimensions on the order of microns. Height itself will be application-dependent. For example, optical surfaces will have roughness values from less than an angstrom to several hundred angstroms. Computer hard discs will have typical roughness values on the order of a hundred angstroms. Products produced on grinding machines will have roughness values on the order of 1,000 angstroms.

Waviness of a surface, on the other hand, will have a longer lateral scale—on the order of millimeters. An instrument (see figure 5.5) based on the concept of Nomarski microscopy can measure both roughness and waviness. Surface roughness is quantified separately from the waviness by applying a spatial filter

Figure 5.5 Noncontact Surface Profiler System Diagram

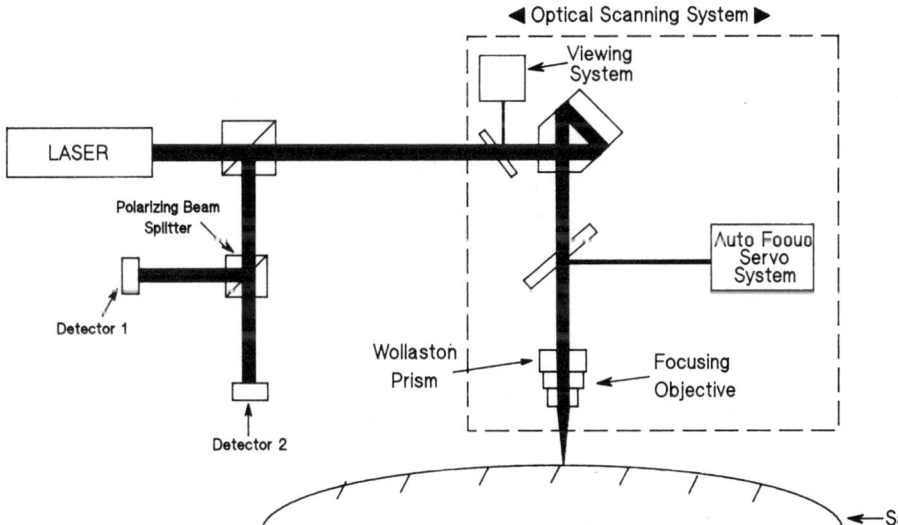

to the surface profile data. The spatial filter typically is defined to have a sampling length long enough to specify features of interest for the sample.

As shown in figure 5.5, the instrument produces an absolute two-dimensional surface profile by projecting two focused 1-micron laser-produced spots onto the test surface, both separated by approximately ¼ of the focal spot diameter. After reflection from the surface, the beams spatially recombine and then ultimately are split into their respective components by the polarizing beam splitter and are directed to either of two detectors. The voltage differences between the two detectors are directly proportional to the surface slope at each measurement point. A translation of the two turning mirrors causes the focal spots to scan across the surface with a maximum scan length of 10 millimeters. Data is collected at 1-micron intervals along the scan line. The results obtained using the instrument have been reasonably comparable to those obtained using tactile stylus instruments.

A somewhat different interferometric approach adapted to flatness measurements is shown in figure 5.6. A laser beam within the interferometer is expanded into an 8-inch column of light. At the hypotenuse of the system's precision prism, the light column is divided into two beams: the reference and test beams. The test beam exits the prism and strikes the specimen at grazing angle. The test beam reflects off the specimen surface and reenters the prism to recombine with the plane reference beam. Where these beams recombine, they "interfere" with one another to create an interference pattern, or a series of light and dark bands.

Figure 5.6 One Interferometric Approach to Flatness Measurement

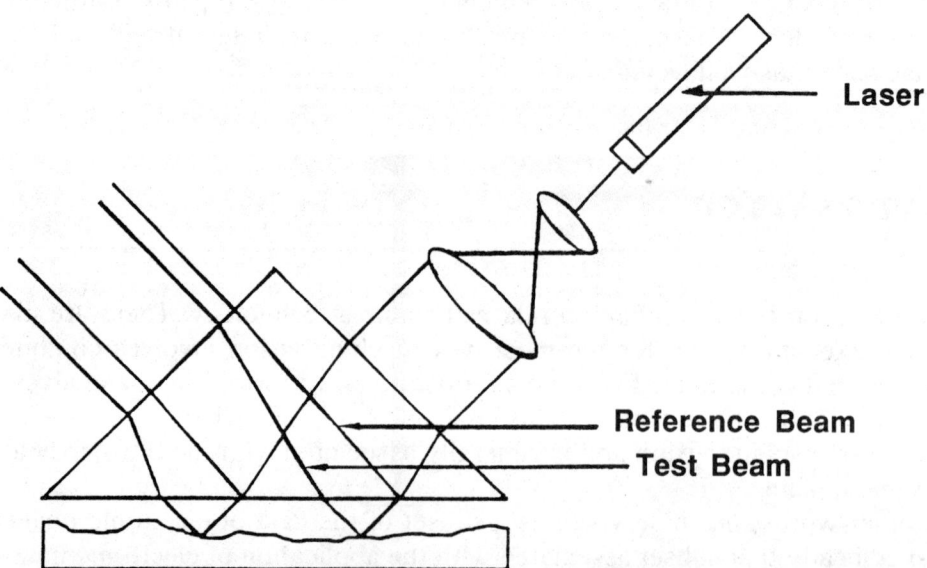

The interference pattern represents the shape of the part surface. The system captures more than two million data points, interprets them, and compiles the data into a three-dimensional image of the test surface. These techniques are well suited to process control of machining processes, such as lapping, polishing, fine grinding, microfinishing, and some surface grinding.

Laser Velocimeter

Another interesting potential use of lasers in production monitoring is based on using Doppler principles to monitor speed (figure 5.7). Velocity measurements accurate to 0.1 percent are possible. Although electro-optical, these instruments have been designed to operate in harsh environments such as those encountered in the production of steel and aluminum.

The laser Doppler velocimeter works on the principle that light scattered from a moving object is frequency-shifted with respect to the incident light. If the source is moving toward the sensor, the received frequency is higher than the frequency of the source. If the source is moving away, the received frequency is lower than the source. By comparing the received frequency to that of the source, it is possible to determine speed. In the laser Doppler gauge, the Doppler shift is between two converging beams. The frequency of the beam pointing toward the source of the product is shifted up, and the beam pointing toward the destination is shifted down. The instrument measures the frequency shift and uses this information to calculate the speed and length of the object. The instrument can make noncontact measurements on almost any type of continuously produced product. The measurements it can make include current speed and average speed, as well as length.

Machine Vision

Machine vision is conceptually a relatively simple technology. There are many different executions, but for the most part machine vision involves combining television and computers. In its most straightforward form, it is the analysis of television pictures by computer. This concept transcends what is commonly referred to as machine vision and is generally associated with the broader field of electronic imaging.

In other words, machine vision is a subset of the field of electronic imaging, and specifically that subset associated with the application of electronic imaging

Figure 5.7 Differential Doppler Implementation

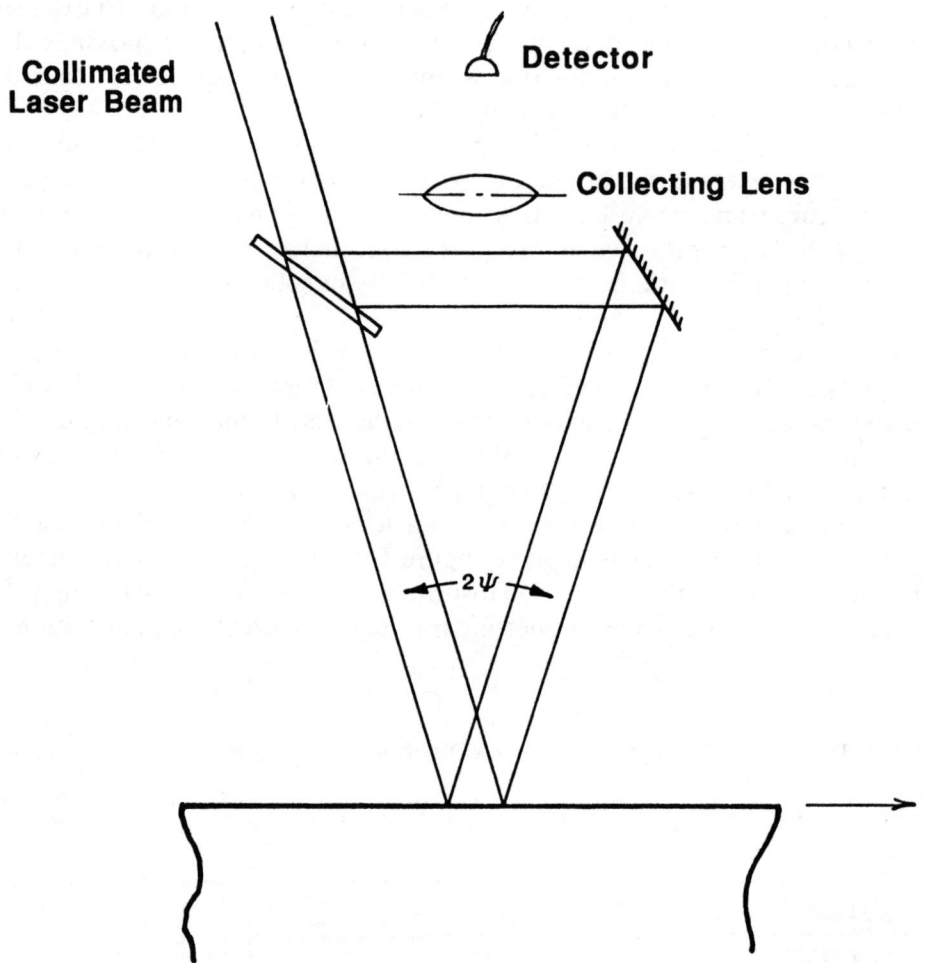

technology or techniques in industrial manufacturing settings. In manufacturing, machine vision is employed for the purpose of control: quality control, process control, machine tool control, or robot control. As much as anything, the application to control distinguishes machine vision from other subsets of electronic imaging, such as applications in medicine, offices, document scanning, etc.

Machine vision begins with an image—a picture. In many ways, the issues associated with a quality image in machine vision are similar to the issues associated with obtaining a quality image in a photograph. In the first place, quality lighting is required in order to obtain a bright enough reflected image of the object. Lighting should be distributed uniformly over the object. Nonuniform

lighting will affect the distribution of brightness values that will be picked up by the television camera.

As is the case in photography, lighting tricks can be used in order to exaggerate certain conditions in the scene being viewed. For example, it is possible that shadows can in effect include high-contrast information that can be used to make a decision about the scene being viewed.

The types of lamps that are used to provide illumination may also influence the quality of the image. For example, fluorescent lamps have a higher blue spectral output than incandescent lamps. Although the blue spectral output is more consistent with the spectral sensitivity of the eye, higher infrared output is typically more compatible with the spectral sensitivity of solid-state sensors that are used in machine vision.

It has been found that the sensitivity of human inspectors can be enhanced as a consequence of using softer lighting or fluorescent lamps with gases that provide more red spectral output; so, too, may be the case in machine vision. That is, the lamps' spectral output may influence the contrast associated with the specific feature one is attempting to analyze.

As in photography, machine vision uses a lens to capture a picture of the object and focus it onto a sensor plane (figure 5.8). The quality of the lens will influence the quality of the image. Distortions and aberrations could affect the size of features in image space. Vignetting in a lens can affect the distribution of

Figure 5.8 General Vision System Block Diagram

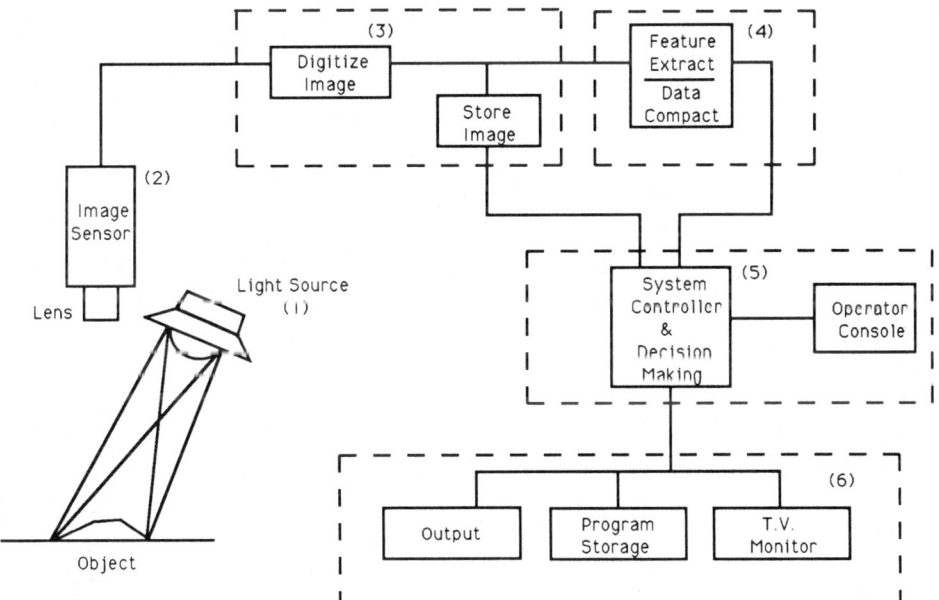

light across the image plane. Magnification of the lens has to be appropriate for the application. As much as possible, the image of the object should fill the image plane of the sensor. Allowances have to be made for any registration errors associated with the position of the object and the repeatability of that positioning. The focal length and aperture have to be optimized in order to handle the depth of field associated with the object.

The imaging sensor that is used in the machine vision system will basically dictate the limit of discrimination of detail that will be experienced with the system. Imaging sensors have a finite number of discrete detectors, and this number limits the number of spatial data elements that can be processed or into which the image will be dissected. In a typical television-based machine vision system today, the number of spatial data points is on the order of 400 to 500 horizontal data points × 400 to 500 vertical data points.

Basically, this means that the smallest piece of information that can be discriminated is a function of the field of view. In photography, if one uses panoramic optics to take a view of a mountain range, although a family might be in the picture in the foothills of the mountains, it is unlikely that one would be able to discriminate the family in the picture. On the other hand, if one uses a different lens and moves closer to the family, one would be able to capture the facial expressions of each member, but the resulting picture would not include the peaks of the mountains.

So, for example, given that an application requires a 1-inch field of view, and given that a sensor with the equivalent of 500 spatial data points is used, one would have a spatial data point that would be approximately .002 inches on the side. Significantly, the ability of machine vision today to discriminate details in a scene is generally better than the size of a spatial data point.

In a manner basically analogous to the way an eye can see stars in a night sky because of the contrast associated with the starlight, so, too, in machine vision techniques exist that allow systems to be able to discriminate details smaller than a spatial data element. Again, contrast is critical. The claims for subpixel sensitivity vary from vendor to vendor and depend very much on their execution and the application.

In all machine vision systems up until this point in our discussion, the information or the image has been in an analog format. For a computer to operate on the picture, the analog image must be digitized. This operation basically consists of sampling at discrete locations along the analog signal that corresponds to a plot of time versus brightness and quantizing the brightness at that sample point (figure 5.9).

The actual brightness value is dependent on the lighting, the reflective property of the object, conditions in the atmosphere between the lighting and the object and between the object and the camera, and the specific detector sensitivity in the imaging sensor. Most vision systems today characterize the brightness into a value of between 0 and 255. The brightness so characterized is generally referred to as a shade of gray.

Figure 5.9 Digitizing an Image

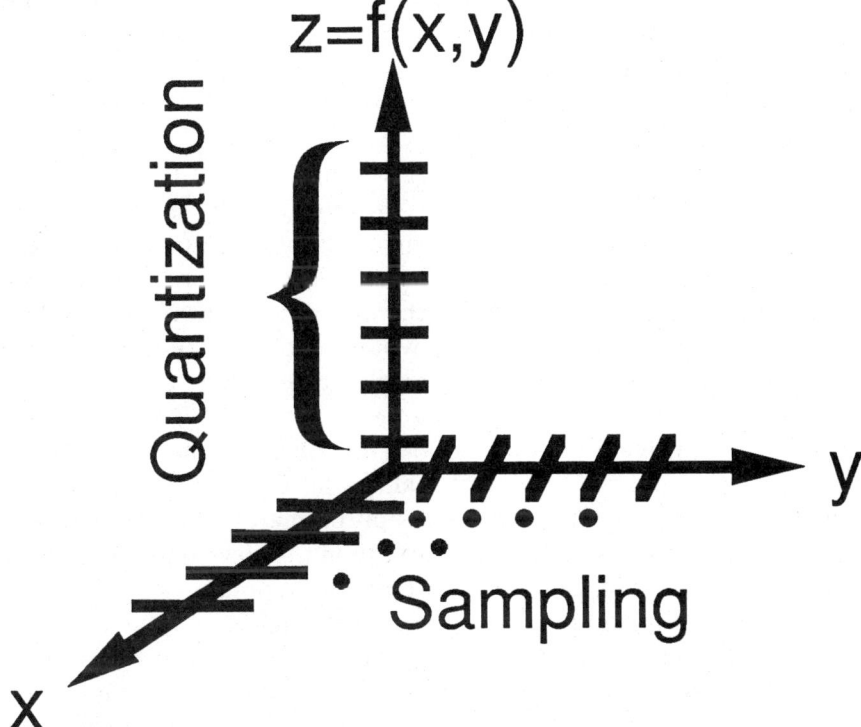

Digital image is obtained by sampling and quantization

Each image element is called a pixel

For the most part today, machine vision systems are monochromatic. Consequently, the color may also be a factor in the brightness value. That is, it is possible to have a shade of red and a shade of green (and so on), all of which have the same brightness value. In many cases where color issues are a concern, filters are used in order to eliminate all colors that are not of interest to the

particular application. In this way the gray shades are an indicator of the saturation level associated with a specific color.

At last we have a picture that has been prepared for a computer. In most machine vision systems today, the digitized image is stored in memory that is separated from the computer memory. This dedicated memory is referred to as a frame store—where *frame* is synonymous with the term used in television to describe a single picture. In some cases, the dedicated hardware that includes the frame store also includes the analog-to-digital converter as well as other electronics to permit one to view images after processing steps have been conducted on the image to view the effects of these processing procedures.

Now the computer can operate on the image. The operation of the computer on the image is generally referred to as *image processing*. In addition to operating on the image, the computer is also used to analyze the image and make a decision on the basis of the analyzed image and perform an operation accordingly. What is typically referred to as the *machine vision system* is the combination of image processing, analysis, and decision-making techniques that are embodied in the computer (figure 5.10).

A good analogy can be made to a tool box. Virtually all machine vision systems today include certain fundamental tools, much like a hammer, screwdriver or pliers. Beyond these, different suppliers have developed additional tools, more often than not driven by a specific class of applications. Consequently, the description frequently given for machine vision as being an "idiot savant" is quite apropos. That is, most of the platforms are brilliant on one set of applications but "idiots" or truly not optimal for other applications.

It is important, therefore, to select the vision platform or tool box with the most appropriate tools for an application. Significantly, no machine vision systems exist today that come anywhere near simulating the comprehensive image understanding capabilities that people have. It is noted that for many applications many different tools will actually do the job, in many cases without sacrificing performance. On the other hand, in some cases, although the tools appear to do the job, performance might be marginal, as if a flat head screwdriver were used in an attempt to turn a screw with a Phillips head.

Image processing is generally performed on most images for basically two reasons:

- To improve or enhance the image and, therefore, make the decision associated with the image more reliable

- To segment the image or to separate the features of importance from those that are unimportant

Enhancement might be performed, for example, to correct for the nonuniformity in sensitivity from photo site to photo site in the imaging sensor, to correct for

Figure 5.10 Steps in Machine Vision

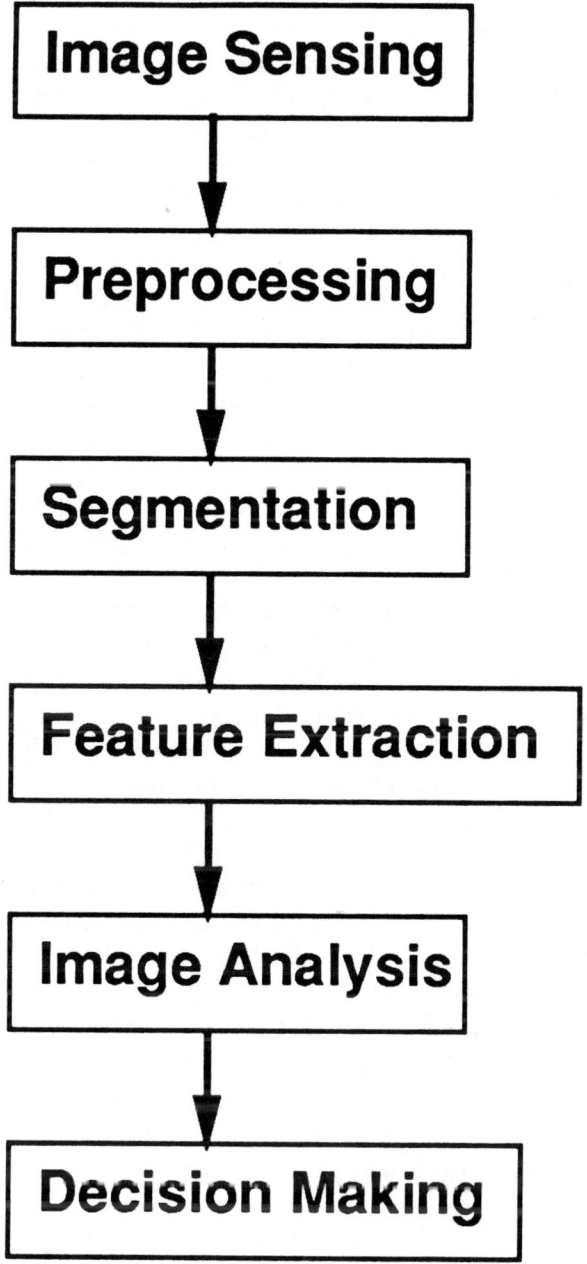

distortion, to correct for nonuniformity of illumination, to enhance the contrast in the scene, to correct for perspective, etc.

These enhancement steps could be as simple as adding or subtracting a specific value to each shade of gray or could involve a variety of logical operations on the picture. There are many such routines. One routine that is commonly found as a tool for image processing in most vision platforms today is a histogram routine. This involves developing a frequency distribution associated with the number of times a given gray shade is determined (figure 5.11).

One use of histograms is to improve contrast. This involves mathematically redistributing the histogram so that pixels are assigned to gray shades covering 0 to 255, for example. In an image with this type of contrast enhancement it could be easier to establish boundaries or easier to establish a specific gray shade level or threshold to use to binarize the image. Binarizing an image, or segmenting an image based on a threshold above which all pixels are turned on and below which all pixels are turned off, is a conventional segmentation tool included in most vision platforms; it can be effective where high contrast exists.

Where contrast in a scene is not substantial, segmentation based on edges may be more appropriate. Edges can be characterized as locations where gradients or gray shade changes take place (figure 5.12). Both the gradient and the direction of change can be used as properties to characterize an edge. Significantly,

Figure 5.11 Histogram May Help Pick Threshold for Making a Binary Image

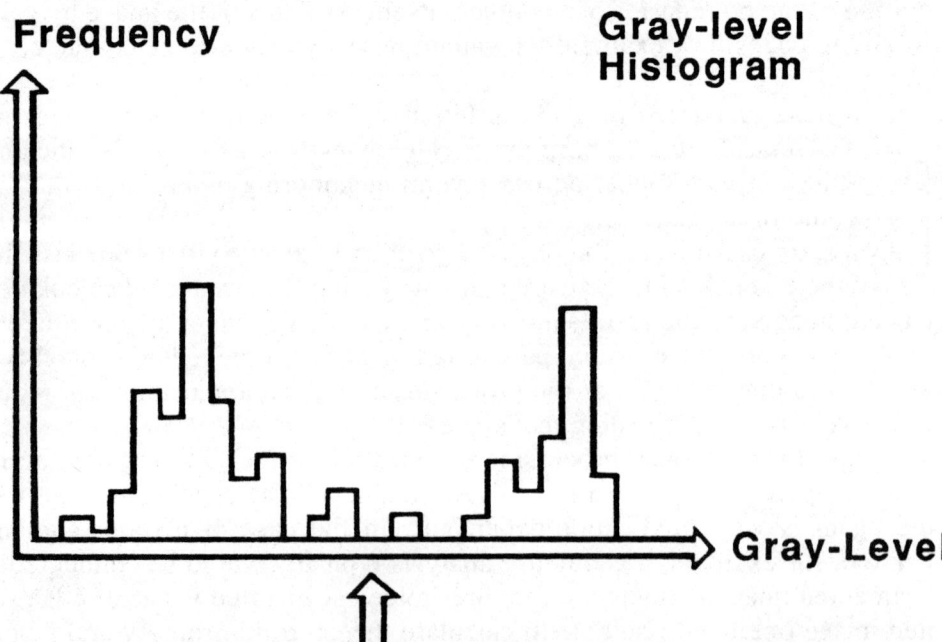

Figure 5.12 Edge Optical Intensity Profile

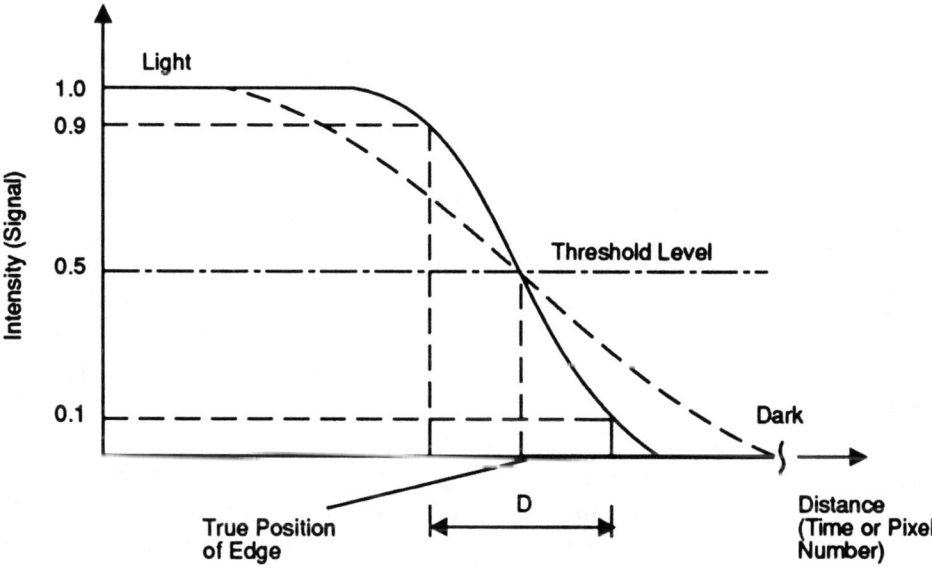

edges can be caused by shadows as well as reflectance changes on the surface in addition to the boundaries of the object itself. Artifacts in the image may also contribute to edges. For example, unwanted porosity may also be characterized by increased edges.

Edges are characterized in many different ways. One of the simplest is just using the fact that there are sharp gray scale changes at an edge. Significantly, however, edges in fact appear across several neighboring pixels, and what one has is a profile of an edge across the pixels. Because of this, there are mathematical ways to discriminate the physical position of an edge to a value less than the size of the pixel. Again, there are many ways that these subpixel calculations have been made, and the results are very application-dependent. Consequently, although claims are made of one part in ten or better subpixelling capability, it is important to understand that the properties of a given application can reduce the effectiveness of subpixelling techniques.

Having performed image processing routines to enhance and segment an image, the computer is now used to analyze the image. The specific analysis conducted again is very application-dependent. In the case of a robot guidance application, for example, a geometric analysis typically would be conducted on the segmented image. Looking at the thresholded segmented image or edge segmented image one would be able to calculate the centroid property and furnish this as a coordinate in space for the robot to pick up an object, for example.

In the case of using vision systems to perform inspections of one type or another, literally hundreds of different types of analysis techniques have emerged. The number of pixels associated with the binarized or thresholded picture, for example, could be counted. This could be a relatively simple measure of the completeness of an object. The number of transitions from black to white can be counted. The distance between transitions can be counted and can serve as a measurement between boundaries of an object. The number of pixels that are associated with an edge can be counted. Vectors associated with the direction of the gradient at an edge can be used as the analysis features. A model based on the edges can be derived where the edges can be characterized as vectors of a certain length and angle. Geometric features can be extracted from the enhanced image and used as the basis of decisions.

These same techniques can be used in conjunction with pattern recognition applications. In each case, a pattern can be defined by one or more of the above-mentioned features extracted from the image. For example, maybe a combination of the transition counts and edge pixels would be sufficient to make a judgment about patterns where that combination is sufficient to distinguish between the patterns. Another approach might be to use geometric properties to distinguish patterns. These might include length and width ratios, perimeter, etc.

The computer, having reduced the image to a set of features used as the basis of analysis, would typically then use a deterministic or probabilistic approach to analyze the features. A probabilistic approach is one that basically suggests that given a certain property associated with a feature, there is a high probability that the object is in fact good. So, for example, using the total number of pixels as an indication of the completeness of an object, one would be able to suggest that if the total number of pixels exceeded, say, 10,000 there is a high probability that the object is complete. If the number is less than 10,000, the object should be rejected because it would be characterized as incomplete. Some refer to this as goodness-of-fit criteria. It is also possible to set a boundary around this criteria. That is, one could say that it should fall between 10,000 and 10,500. An indication of a pixel count greater than 10,500 could be an indication, for example, of excess flashing.

A deterministic approach is one that will use physical feature properties as the criteria. For example, the distance between two boundaries has to be 1 inch +/− .005 inch. The perimeter of the object must fall between 12 inches +/− .020 inch. The pattern must match the following criteria in order to be considered a match: length/width ratio of a certain value, perimeter of a certain value, centroid of a given calculated value, etc.

In a deterministic mode, each of the features can be associated with a vector in decision space. In a pattern-recognition application, the combined feature vector or the shortest distance to the known feature set for each of the patterns is the one that would be selected. This type of evaluation is referred to as *decision theoretic*. Another type of analysis is one based on syntactic techniques. In these cases, primitives associated with pieces of the image are extracted and the re-

lationship between them is compared to a known database associated with the image.

In other words, the primitives and their relationships to one another have to abide to a set of rules. Using syntactic techniques, one may be able to infer certain primitives and their position knowing something about other primitives in the image and their position with respect to one another. This could be a technique for making certain decisions about parts that might be overlapping and that cannot be seen entirely.

As you can see, many vision tools are available, and the specific tools that one requires are application-dependent. Today, machine vision type technology is found in virtually every manufacturing industry. The largest adopter by far is the electronics industry. In microelectronics, machine vision techniques are used to perform inspections automatically throughout the integrated circuit manufacturing process: photomask fabrication, post die slicing inspection, precap inspection, and final package inspection for mark integrity.

Throughout the manufacturing process, machine vision is also used to provide feedback for position correction in conjunction with a variety of manufacturing processes, such as die slicing and bonding and wire bonding. In the macroelectronic industry, machine vision is being used to inspect printed circuit boards for conductor width spacing, populated printed circuit boards for completeness, and post solder inspection for solder integrity.

As in microelectronics, it is also being used to perform positional feedback in conjunction with component placement. It has become an integral part of the manufacturing process associated with the placement of chip carriers with relatively high density pin counts.

In industries that produce products on a continuous web, such as the paper, plastic, and textile industries, machine vision techniques are being used to perform an inspection of the integrity of the product being produced. Where coatings are applied to such products, machine vision is also being used to guarantee the coverage and quality of coverage. In the printing industry, machine vision is used in conjunction with registration.

The food industry finds machine vision being used in the process end to inspect products for sorting purposes—that is, sorting out defective conditions, misshapen product, undersize/oversize product, etc. At the packaging end, it is being used to verify the size and shape of contents, such as candy bars and cookies, to make sure they will fit in their respective packages.

Throughout the consumer manufacturing industries, machine vision is found in various applications. These include label verification—that is, verifying the position, quality, and correctness of the label. In the pharmaceutical industry it is used to perform character verification—that is, verifying the correctness as well as the integrity of the character sets corresponding to date and lot code.

The automotive industry uses machine vision for many applications. These include looking at the flushness and fit of sheet metal assemblies, including the

final car assembly; looking at paint qualities, such as gloss; inspecting for flaws on sheet metal stampings; verifying the completeness of a variety of assemblies from ball bearings to transmissions, etc. It is also used in conjunction with robots to provide visual feedback for sealant applications, windshield insertion applications, robotic hydropiercing operations, robotic seam tracking operations, etc.

Virtually every industry has seen the adoption of machine vision in some way or another. The toothbrush industry, for example, has vision systems that are used to verify the integrity of the toothbrush. The plastics industry looks at empty mold cavities to make sure that they are empty before filling them again. The container industry is using machine vision techniques widely. In metal cans, machine vision looks at the quality of the can ends for cosmetic flaws, presence of compound, score depth on converted ends, etc. The can itself is examined to inspect it for defective conditions internally.

The glass container industry uses machine vision widely to inspect for sidewall defects, mouth defects, and empty bottle states, as well as dimensions and shapes. In these cases, vision techniques have proven to be able to handle 1,800 to 2,000 objects per minute.

Justifying an electro-optical technology project may be an issue. Significantly, justification based solely on labor displacement is unlikely to satisfy the ROI requirements. Quantifying additional savings is more difficult, but in reality may yield an even greater impact than labor savings. Product returns and warranty cost should be evaluated to assess how much such costs will be reduced by the machine vision system. The cost of rework should be a matter of record. In addition, however, a value can be calculated for the space associated with rework inventory as well as the rework inventory itself. The cost of rejects and related material costs, the cost of waste disposal associated with rejects, and the cost of freight on returns are all tangible quantifiable costs.

There are other savings, though less tangible, that should be estimated and quantified. These include items such as the following:

- The cost of overruns to compensate for yield

- The avoidance of inspection bottlenecks and impact on inventory income and inventory turnover

- The elimination of adding value to scrap conditions

- The potential for increased machine uptime and productivity accordingly

- The elimination of schedule upsets resulting from the production of items that require rework

Another observation is that when considering the savings due to labor displacement, it is important to include all the savings. These include savings in the following areas:

- Recruiting

- Training

- Scrap rework created while learning a new job

- Average workers' compensation paid for injuries

- Average educational grant per employee

- Personnel/payroll department costs per employee

Overall, the deployment of sensor technology in production process control will result in improved and predictable quality. This in turn will yield improved customer satisfaction and an opportunity to increase market share—the biggest payback of all.

References

1. Bristow, T. C. "Surface Measurements and Applications for Manufacturing Parts Using Noncontact Profilometer." *Optical Testing & Metrology* 11, C. P. Grover, ed. Proceedings of the SPIE, volume 954, p. 217.

2. ———. "Surface Roughness Measurements Over Long Scan Lengths." *Surface Topography,* vol. 1 (1988):85–89.

3. Bristow, T. C., and Dag Lindquist. "Surface Measurements with a Non-Contact Nomarski-Profiling Instrument." Paper presented at SPIE, San Diego, August, 1987, Proceedings of the SPIE, no. 816.

4. Broadman, R., and W. Smilga. "In Process Optical Metrology for Precision Machining." Proceedings of the SPIE, no. 802.

5. Kaplan, Herbert. "Noncontact Surface Profiling." *Photonics Spectra* (April 1989):78–82.

6. Parks, Linda, Zygo Corporation. Private correspondence, December 22, 1989.

7. Scott, James F. "Measurement Capabilities of the Industrial Flatmaster." Correspondence from GCA Tropel, Fairport, NY, March 13, 1989.

8. Sprow, E. E. "Surface Measurement: New Challenges." *Tooling & Production* (March 1989):115–17.

9. Truax, B. E., *et al.* "Laser Doppler Velocimeter for Velocity and Length Measurements of Moving Surfaces." Paper presented at CLEO '83 Conference, Baltimore, MD, May 17–20, 1983.

10. Wiese, David. "New Non-Contact High Speed Measurement System: Applications for the Food and Packaging Industry." Paper presented at PACK Expo, Chicago, IL, November 17, 1988.

11. Zuech, Nello. "Applying Machine Vision." New York: John Wiley & Sons, 1988.

Chapter 6 Laser Alignment

Martin R. Hamar

Introduction

This chapter is about alignment lasers and how they are used for machine alignment and geometric measurement in general industry. Alignment has been required since the earliest days of construction for proper building of all types of structures and devices. The builders of the pyramids used the human eye extensively with sight lines and sighting stakes. In modern times, the telescope has extended the range and accuracy of such alignment, but the principles have not changed significantly. In recent years, lasers have come on the scene and provided a positive projection of a sight line, removing the human eye from the system. Electronic targets and computers have increased accuracy and utility. A true new generation of technology has been born.

This chapter describes this equipment and how it relates to older methods. Data is given concerning the performance of lasers, and some actual examples of applications have been provided to give "flavor" to the subject. All of these "war" stories are true and have happened in the field. The results will seem amazing. This technology represents a true technological revolution.

Basic Principles

Light, by its very nature, travels in straight lines unless deflected by some outside disturbance. A laser beam is an intense beam of light that has a most important property. It does not diffuse substantially with distance. The center of energy of such a parallel beam is an extraordinarily straight line. It is this principle attribute that is used in alignment laser systems. No periodic or systematic

unstraightness has ever been observed in a laser alignment beam down to the accuracy permitted by atmospheric turbulence.

This extremely accurate laser "straight edge" can be manipulated in a number of ways. If a two-reflection penta prism is used, the laser beam will be bent through an angle of 90 degrees. These prisms can be constructed with sub-arc-second accuracies so that an extremely accurate 90-degree angle can be generated (90° ± 1/3 arc-second). Penta prisms have the chief important property that rotation about an axis perpendicular to a plane containing the input and output beams is effectively cancelled, so the beam always emerges at 90 degrees. Essentially, what happens at the first reflecting surface of the prism "unhappens" on the second surface as the prism is rotated. The two cancel each other out, and the beam still emerges from the prism 90 degrees to the input beam.

If such a prism is rotated about the input beam, an extremely accurate flat plane can be generated. The best spindle-bearing systems will have wobbles on the order of one to two arc seconds (.006 to .012 inch/100 feet). This wobble is compensated for by the use of this penta prism so that these extremely accurate planes may be generated.

The laser beam, whether straight, bent through 90 degrees, or rotated to create an extremely flat plane, is relatively inaccurate in itself. The spot diameter is, in most cases, substantially over 1/4 inch and, in some cases, 3/4 inches. Attempting to locate the center of the beam visually is not an accurate process. However, if a position-sensitive "target" is used (see figure 6.1) the center of the laser spot can be found with a high degree of accuracy (.0001 inch).

Figure 6.1 The Laser Target Concept

The laser target acts like a two-axis dial indicator.

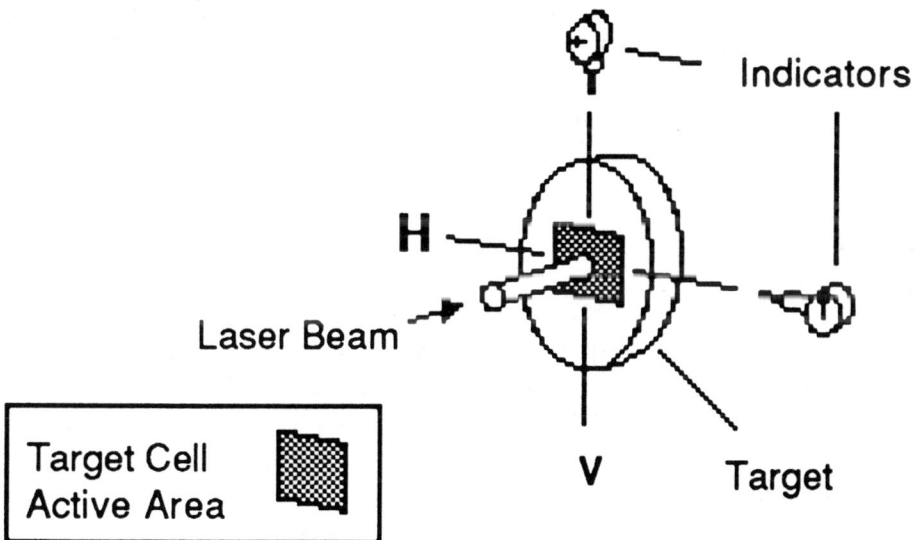

BASIC PRINCIPLES

These position-sensitive targets are generally two-axis devices that generate a voltage both horizontally and vertically proportional to the separation between the center of the laser beam and the center of the target cell. This voltage is amplified and processed by some form of read-out electronics and is presented to the operator in either numerical or analog form so that the operator may observe relative misalignment between the target center and the laser beam center. A computerized read-out can present "processed" alignment information and is useful in many sophisticated alignment situations.

Basic Principle of Laser Alignment

The basic principle of laser alignment, as illustrated in figure 6.2, is as follows: the laser beam center is the "ideal" reference. It is adjusted to be roughly parallel to the machine. The target and its fixture follow the work, line-of-motion, or surface, etc. The difference between them is what is read by the target/read-out combination and shown on the displays. This combination can be thought of in conceptual terms as a two-axis electronic indicator, for that is exactly what it is.

As the target and read-out are central to the accurate use of an alignment laser system, it is important to understand a little more about the target and target cell itself. First, the cell is position-sensitive. That is, it generates voltage in proportion to the displacement between the center of the target and the center of the

Figure 6.2 The Basic Principle of Laser Alignment

The laser beam is the reference. The target and its fixture follow the way surface. The difference is shown by a read-out. Here it would show a + or target high and how high it is, just like an indicator.

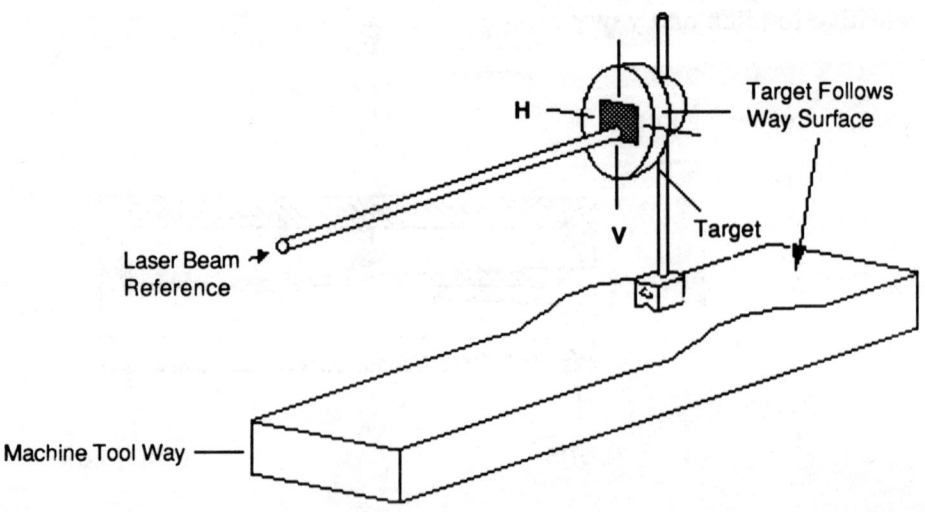

Figure 6.3 Center Measurements and Rotation

Center measurements are not sensitive to the laser beam angle of incidence at the cell plane. Rotation about an axis in the cell plane does not change center [B]. Rotation about any other axis does change center [A].

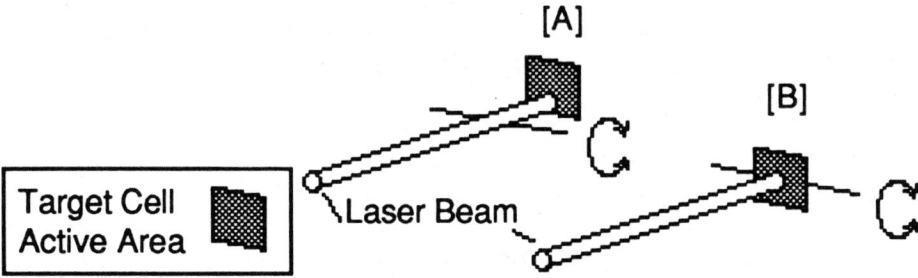

laser beam. In most cases, this target is a two-axis device. That is, it simultaneously finds the center (horizontally and vertically).

The laser spot hits the target cell plane, and that is where the center of measurement is made; therefore, it is important to understand the location of the cell plane. Put another way, if the cell surface is rotated about an axis that lies in the cell surface itself (the active area of the surface), there is no change of the center reading (see figure 6.3).

In other words, the target cells are inherently insensitive to angle of incidence. Tests have been made in which the cell has been rotated as much as 45 degrees to the normal or perpendicular with no change in laser center at all. Such an extreme angle of incidence is usually not possible because of other limitations in the construction of a typical laser target.

In many alignment situations, it is important to be able to measure angle. By putting a lens in front of a target cell with the target cell surface at the focus of the lens, it is possible to create a collimator target (figure 6.4). Such a target is then sensitive to pitch and yaw.

Figure 6.4 Collimator Target

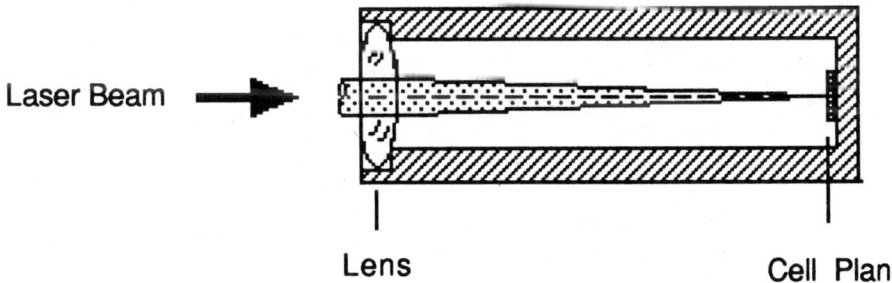

BASIC PRINCIPLES

The accuracy of the system depends entirely on the focal length of the lens. For example, when a target with a 12-inch focal length is used, the read-out presented will be in units of inches per inch with a least resolution of .0001 inches per foot as a typical output from such a target. Lesser sensitivities are possible with shorter focal length lenses.

For convenience, the center and the angle generally are both quantities that must be known, and the functions of center and angular detection can be combined in a single target with a beam splitter. The beam is split into two components, one of which goes directly to a cell for center measurement. The other goes through a lens to a second cell to form a collimator target. (See figure 6.5.)

Such four-axis targets are most convenient and are often used either in spindle alignment and high-production transfer lines or in part alignment on other types of machines.

Perhaps the most important aspect of laser alignment is that, in effect, a coordinate system is constructed that is consistent within itself. The flat plane is perpendicular to a beam from which it is derived. A second beam can be bent through 90 degrees, and another plane may be generated. Vertical and horizontal planes may be generated, and straight lines may be generated perpendicular to those planes. All of these geometries are consistent or are related back to themselves. In effect, what the user has available is a "coordinate system" that can be dropped or put onto a machine, and all aspects of the machine may be measured relative to the same coordinate system. This is an extremely useful function, as prior metrology methods generally require a measurement of one part to an adjacent part to the next part, etc., resulting in accumulated errors. This stair of errors is eliminated in many cases by the use of alignment lasers, as every part is measured individually to the same coordinate system. Thus, it is easy for

Figure 6.5 Four-axis Target

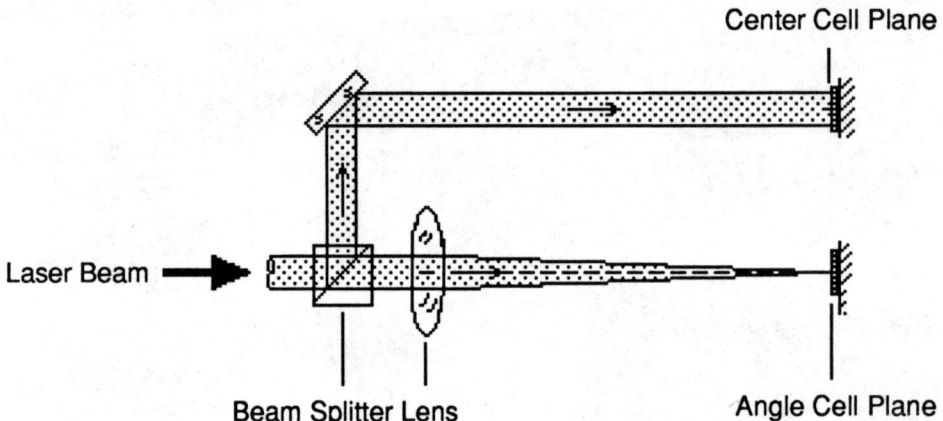

the user to understand what is truly causing the problem in the machine. The operator can more clearly "see" where an alignment problem occurs and can more quickly take corrective action.

Minimum System Requirements

Minimum system requirements are a *laser,* a *target* and a *read-out* (figure 6.6). Those are the fundamental elements required for a laser alignment system. There are many, many types of targets, beam benders, leveling devices and accessories for bore and spindle work, etc. The most fundamental package must consist of these three basic elements before any useful work may be done with the system.

Figure 6.6 Basic Laser Alignment System

Table 6.1 Types of Alignment Lasers

Type	Features	Principal Use
Tooling laser	Cylindrical body with beam on the axis of the cylinder	Used in aerospace for tooling alignment
Sweep tooling laser	Cylindrical body with straight beam and 180° scan plane	Used in aerospace and general industry for assembly and part alignment on machines
Machine tool laser	Levels, horizontal sweep plane, plumb beam	Used for all types of alignments in aerospace and general industry, but mainly for machine tool alignment
Spindle lasers	Small cylindrical body with axial beam	Used for machine spindle and coupling alignment
Coupling lasers	Small laser and target with brackets	Used to align rotary machinery over the couplings

Types of Alignment Lasers

Alignment lasers are available in several different styles depending upon functional requirement. Table 6.1 summarizes the basic types, their uses, and their benefits.

Geometries Possible with Laser Alignment

Figure 6.7 illustrates in conceptual form the various geometries possible with a laser alignment system. They are the following: straight line, right angle, flat plane, and level lines and planes.

Straight Line

The first, and most obvious, geometry possible with a laser alignment system is the straight line. The laser beam inherently is a straight line. More properly said, the center of energy of the laser beam is a straight line. This line is straight with a known accuracy of .0001 inch per ten feet (as a usable rule of thumb). Atmospheric limitations do not permit the use of the laser system to a higher degree of accuracy. If there are any systematic unstraightnesses in the beam, they are of a magnitude of less than ten millionths per foot. The straight line obviously can be used for lining up or checking the straightness of ways of a machine tool,

Figure 6.7 Geometries Possible with a Laser Alignment System

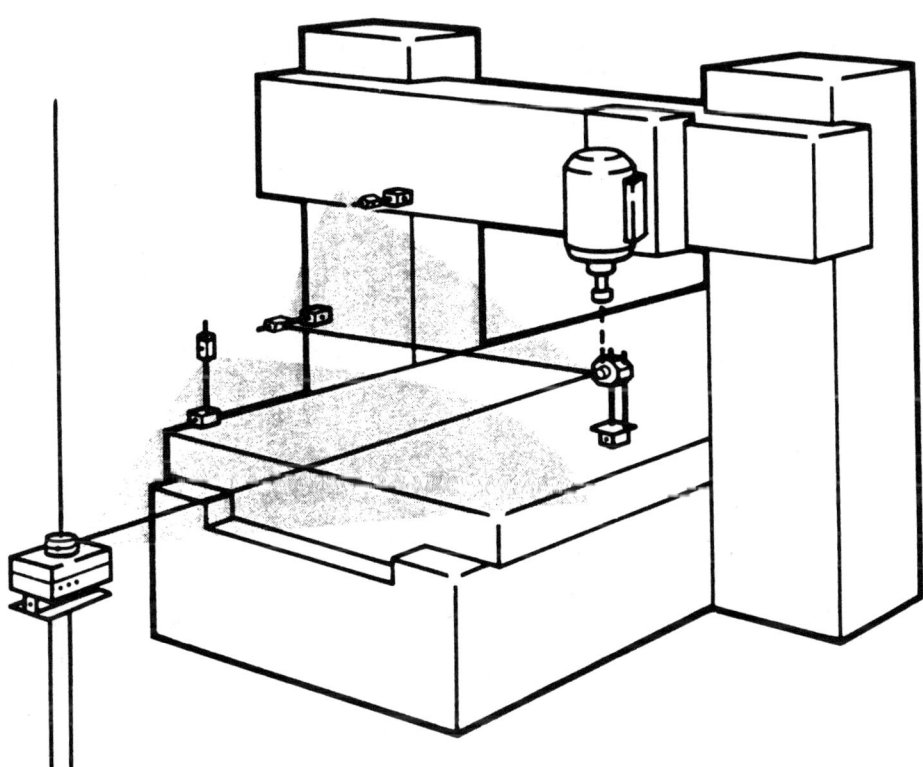

lining up spindles, doing bore measurements, lining up shafts, couplings, and many other applications where an extremely accurate "straight edge" or straight line is advantageous.

Right Angle

As mentioned above, the use of a penta prism to bend the beam to an exact 90-degree angle is one of the cornerstones of laser alignment technology. These prisms create a 90-degree angle because of the two reflecting surfaces positioned at 45 degrees to each other. After two reflections, the beam is deviated 90 degrees. (See figure 6.8.)

The accuracy of that angle depends upon the accuracy of the 45-degree angle. This accuracy may be on the order of 1 arc-second. Special optical corrections may be applied to such a prism to get the 90-degree angle accuracy to approximately ¼ arc-second. (That would be .0015 inch/100 feet or 15 millionths/foot).

Figure 6.8 Penta Prism

Two Reflection Tilt Angle Compensating Prism

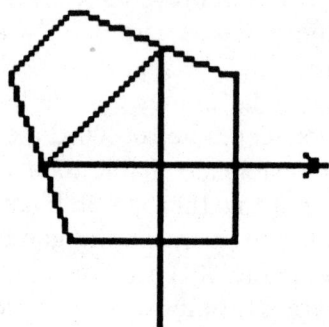

Input Laser Beam

The right angle is a fundamental geometry necessary in a great deal of machine tool and related work. Most axes of machine tools are intended to be perpendicular to each other and must be adjusted periodically. Various slides, spindles, quills, and columns are all intended to be mutually perpendicular; thus, the 90-degree angle is extremely important geometry.

The Flat Plane

A flat plane is another fundamental geometry crucial to alignment problems. If the penta prism mentioned in the paragraph above is mounted on a suitable set of bearings and rotated, it can generate a plane of exquisite flatness (.001 inches/ 50 foot radius). With a shorter radius of 20 feet, if a sweep laser is set in one corner and the sweep angle is limited to 90 degrees, accuracies on the order of .0001 inch are possible over the entire area. Therefore, a sweep laser system can produce a true optical surface plate or laser surface plate. A flat reference plane is crucial for checking the flatness of table tops, verifying the vertical parallelism of two ways, and many other useful applications. Such geometry is critical to a full-function alignment system.

One useful application of such a large area "surface plate" is the ability to level or measure parallelism of two unconnected surfaces. Two table tops may need to be parallel and coplanar, but may be separated by many feet. The sweep laser plane allows the operator to measure or align these two surfaces. This type of alignment cannot be done by an interferometer.

Leveling with Lasers

Many machine tools and other mechanical devices, such as hydroelectric power generation turbine shafts, must be either plumb or level. Levels have historically been used in machine tool alignment, as gravity represents a most convenient transfer reference in that, in the area of the machine, gravity always is in the same direction. Thus, one part of a machine may be made parallel to another part by using levels. Laser straight lines and flat planes can be level and can provide an extremely useful capability. Level accuracies of .0002 inch in ten feet (⅓ arc-second) are possible with alignment systems available today.

The various geometries available can be put together in combinations to perform higher level complex functions for measurement and alignment. For example, in making measurements from a laser plane, it is possible to place a target to intercept a laser beam and "zero" that target (or adjust its elevation above or below the plane so that it is zeroed out) at a given location and then move the target around the plane and measure the *relative elevation* of all of those points relative to the first points. Such a measurement is very useful when it comes to aligning ways, scraping surfaces of ways, etc. It should be appreciated that the target can be lifted up away, the surface scraped, and the target put back down to measure how much material has been removed in the scraping process. This cannot be done with laser interferometers.

In any event, it is also possible to combine lasers, targets, and height-gage elements to actually measure elevation *differences* between various surfaces. This is often important, as certain way surfaces are not coplanar-planer but must be set to a specific dimension between such surfaces. The ability to use the laser plane in conjunction with a distance measurement perpendicular to that plane is a fundamental and important capability of such systems. Targets of various configurations are mounted on, or are used with, height-gage elements to perform such measurements.

Parallel Measurement

One of the more important combination measurements necessary is that of parallel measurement. Examples of this may be found in the measurement of ways of large machine tools or the measurement of bores in gear cases where there are many bores whose axes are parallel, and it is desirable to know the parallelism of those axes relative to one another (see figure 6.9).

Another example is roll alignment in a process mill. A process mill is any mill that conducts almost any material through the use of a collection or series of

Figure 6.9 Gear Case Bore Parallelism—Plan View

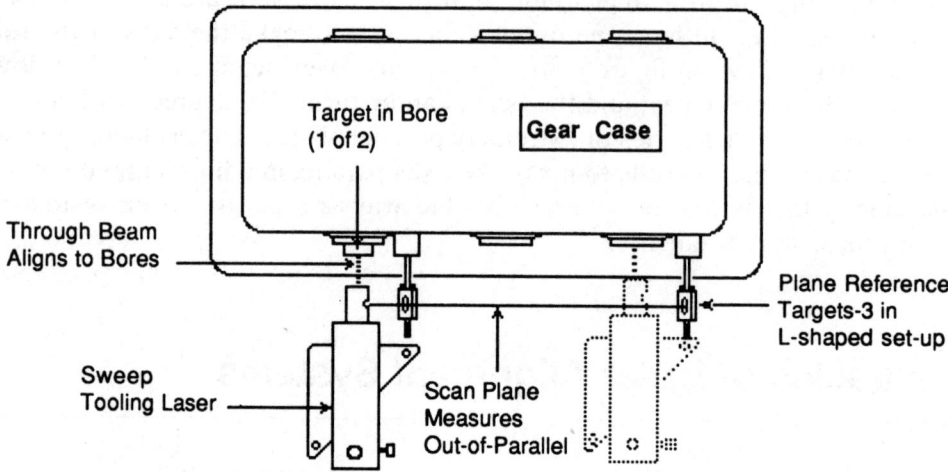

Figure 6.10 Roll Alignment

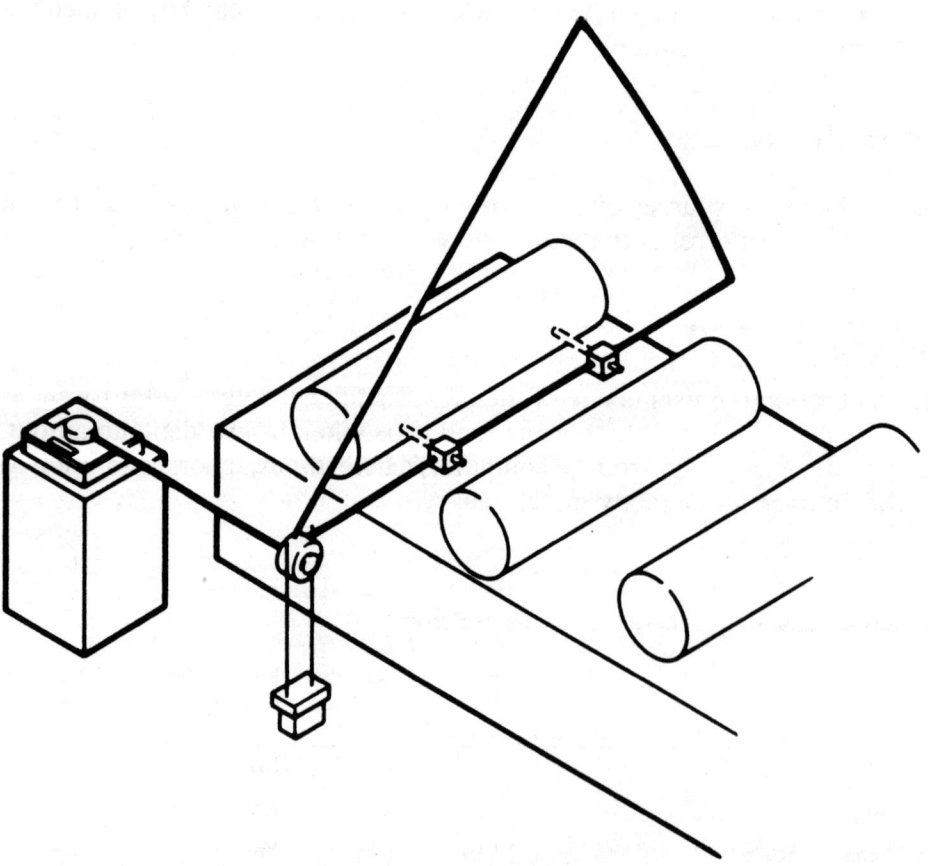

rolls. A printing press, a steel rolling mill or a textile mill are all examples of process mills. They all have in common the need to make the axes of the rolls parallel. As is shown in figure 6.10, the primary laser beam can be shot down the side of these machines, and the beam can be turned 90 degrees with a beam bender, thus creating a series of extremely parallel planes. These planes are used as references to line the rolls to make the axes parallel in a horizontal direction. Illustrated below is one of several possible ways to use the laser system for creating these measurements.

Accuracies of Laser Alignment Systems

An alignment laser system is subject to various errors that affect the accuracy when used in the real world. This section discusses the various sources of error as they are currently known and gives data concerning their magnitude. An error budget is presented at the end of this section as a kind of summary of these errors. Experience has shown that these levels of accuracy can be obtained readily under most field conditions.

System Errors

Table 6.2 shows the sources of error for most laser alignment systems. The largest single source of error is the atmosphere.

Target Calibration

Target calibration represents one of the most significant sources of error in laser alignment measurement. Whether the reading is taken from a digital read-out of target lateral position or from a computerized read-out, poor calibration will make the numbers not exactly match reality.

Table 6.2 Laser Alignment—Sources of Error

	Atmospheric Turbulence	Target Calibration	Target Linearity	Accuracy of Penta Prism	Radial Bearing Runout	Axial Bearing Runout	Bearing Axis Wobble
Straight Line	Yes	Yes	Yes	N/A	N/A	N/A	N/A
Right Angle	Yes	Yes	Yes	Yes	No	No	NO
Flat Plane	Yes	Yes	Yes	Yes	Yes	Yes	Yes

ACCURACIES OF LASER ALIGNMENT SYSTEMS

Although calibration errors can be serious, they are percentage errors. A 5 percent calibration error means a .025-inch displacement will read either .0238 inch or .0263 inch. However, if the displacement is only .001 inch, the reading will be in error by 50 millionths, which is ½ of the minimum system resolution.

Target Linearity Data

The data shown in figure 6.11 is representative of target linearity. The continuous area type of cell usually used today is a single sensitive surface with no divisions. The cell integrates to the center of energy of an incident laser spot and outputs voltages proportional to the position of that center of energy relative to the cell center. These devices are sensitive in two axes.

Figure 6.11 Data Representative of Target Linearity

```
                TARGET NUMBER  1   (Calibrated @ .03)

-.0478 -.0489 -.0499 -.0505 -.0509 -.0510 -.0510 -.0505 -.0499 -.0491 -.0480
0.0476 0.0379 0.0281 0.0185 0.0088 -.0005 -.0101 -.0193 -.0290 -.0382 -.0463

-.0378 -.0388 -.0396 -.0401 -.0404 -.0405 -.0405 -.0402 -.0397 -.0390 -.0383
0.0485 0.0386 0.0287 0.0189 0.0090 -.0005 -.0102 -.0197 -.0294 -.0390 -.0480

-.0281 -.0287 -.0294 -.0297 -.0299 -.0300 -.0300 -.0298 -.0294 -.0289 -.0284
0.0492 0.0392 0.0292 0.0192 0.0092 -.0004 -.0103 -.0199 -.0298 -.0394 -.0490

-.0186 -.0191 -.0195 -.0197 -.0198 -.0199 -.0200 -.0198 -.0195 -.0192 -.0188
0.0498 0.0397 0.0295 0.0196 0.0093 -.0004 -.0103 -.0200 -.0299 -.0397 -.0494

-.0090 -.0093 -.0096 -.0097 -.0097 -.0098 -.0099 -.0098 -.0096 -.0094 -.0092
0.0502 0.0400 0.0298 0.0198 0.0095 -.0002 -.0103 -.0200 -.0300 -.0398 -.0496

0.0001 0.0001 -.0001 -.0000 -.0000 0.0000 -.0001 0.0000 0.0000 0.0001 0.0001
0.0504 0.0403 0.0300 0.0199 0.0097 -.0001 -.0102 -.0200 -.0300 -.0397 -.0495

0.0097 0.0098 0.0099 0.0101 0.0102 0.0103 0.0101 0.0101 0.0100 0.0099 0.0097
0.0504 0.0403 0.0301 0.0200 0.0098 0.0001 -.0101 -.0199 -.0298 -.0395 -.0492

0.0187 0.0191 0.0193 0.0197 0.0199 0.0200 0.0199 0.0198 0.0196 0.0193 0.0189
0.0504 0.0403 0.0301 0.0200 0.0099 0.0002 -.0099 -.0196 -.0295 -.0391 -.0487

0.0280 0.0287 0.0291 0.0295 0.0298 0.0300 0.0299 0.0297 0.0294 0.0290 0.0283
0.0502 0.0401 0.0301 0.0200 0.0100 0.0003 -.0096 -.0192 -.0290 -.0386 -.0477

0.0372 0.0382 0.0387 0.0393 0.0397 0.0398 0.0397 0.0395 0.0391 0.0383 0.0371
0.0497 0.0398 0.0298 0.0199 0.0100 0.0004 -.0094 -.0188 -.0285 -.0378 -.0461

0.0468 0.0478 0.0486 0.0493 0.0498 0.0500 0.0499 0.0496 0.0489 0.0475 0.0460
0.0492 0.0393 0.0295 0.0197 0.0100 0.0006 -.0091 -.0183 -.0277 -.0365 -.0443


Display Format:

#.####  (Y axis value)
#.####  (X axis value)

Note:  Actual Displacements were in .010" increments.
```

These devices are fairly linear (within 5 percent) along any axis. They become progressively nonlinear when the laser spot is off the cell center in both directions. The data given in figure 6.11 shows the linearity of a typical cell when calibrated at .030 inch on each axis and separate + and − calibration factors. Note the roll off in the corners of the active area at .050, .050 inches. This roll off can be compensated for with an error table. A new type of "super linear" cell is now available in the marketplace. These new cells will significantly improve cell linearity, largely eliminating the corner roll off.

If the target is used as a nulling device, such considerations are academic. In 90 percent of laser alignment work, the end goal is to align a surface, slide, or fixture so that all readings are the same. In such cases, the linearity of the target, and indeed calibration, are not very important. The errors are the same for each point measured and thus do not affect the final outcome.

Air Turbulence Errors

Air turbulence is the most significant and serious source of error in both alignment and interferometer laser use. The air is full of pockets of air that are at differing temperatures. Air has a small but noticeable index of refraction (a measure of the power of a transparent medium to bend light). Moreover, this index will change with temperature.

The effect of all this is a bending of the laser line of sight at many points along its path. This usually amounts to one or two arc-seconds (.006–.00012 inch/100 feet). It is random and exerts about an average position. Averaging over a 10-to-20-second period will reduce this value by a factor of 10 or more. Fans, set up along the side of the beam and blowing down the beam, will help "homogenize" the air.

Figures 6.12 and 6.13 below summarize data taken with a straight line laser system. Figure 6.12 summarizes data for a 166-inch (~ 14-foot) shot made under good shop conditions. Standard deviations of .0001 inch can be obtained. Figure 6.13 summarizes data taken in a tunnel at a 100-foot range with the best possible conditions: still air at a constant temperature. Together, these figures show that good alignment lasers work well at both short and long distances.

Note: These figures and many that follow show stability data, which is mainly turbulence data, over various periods of time. They show data taken with various numbers of samples for each average reading (5 to 25) taken. Sample rates over 25 do not seem to improve the standard deviations significantly.

Look particularly at the standard deviations shown at the bottom summary. These represent the standard deviation (1 Sigma) for all the average readings taken. The spreads of the data are also shown.

Figure 6.12 Summary of Atmospheric Effects on Model L-731 Scanner, Straight Through Beam (Average Over 20 Sec.)

# of Samples/ Reading	2	2	5	5	10	10	25	25
Reading #	Vert	Horiz	Vert	Horiz	Vert	Horiz	Vert	Horiz
1	0.0008	-0.0049	0.0009	-0.0046	0.0009	-0.0047	0.0008	-0.0047
2	0.0010	-0.0048	0.0009	-0.0045	0.0008	-0.0047	0.0008	-0.0048
3	0.0010	-0.0050	0.0009	-0.0046	0.0008	-0.0047	0.0009	-0.0048
4	0.0010	-0.0050	0.0010	-0.0045	0.0008	-0.0047	0.0008	-0.0048
5	0.0009	-0.0051	0.0010	-0.0046	0.0008	-0.0047	0.0008	-0.0048
6	0.0011	-0.0050	0.0009	-0.0046	0.0009	-0.0047	0.0009	-0.0048
7	0.0011	-0.0050	0.0010	-0.0045	0.0009	-0.0047	0.0009	-0.0048
8	0.0009	-0.0050	0.0009	-0.0046	0.0009	-0.0047	0.0009	-0.0048
9	0.0009	-0.0050	0.0009	-0.0046	0.0008	-0.0046	0.0008	-0.0048
10	0.0010	-0.0051	0.0009	-0.0046	0.0009	-0.0047	0.0009	-0.0048
Average of Readings	0.0010	-0.0050	0.0009	-0.0046	0.0009	-0.0047	0.0009	-0.0048
STD Dev of Readings	0.0001	0.0001	0.0000	0.0000	0.0001	0.0000	0.0001	0.0000
Spread of Readings	0.0003	0.0003	0.0001	0.0001	0.0001	0.0001	0.0001	0.0001
Min Std Dev/Reading	0.0000	0.0000	0.0000	0.0000	0.0000	0.0001	0.0001	0.0001
Max Std Dev/Reading	0.0002	0.0003	0.0001	0.0001	0.0001	0.0001	0.0001	0.0001
Date	6/3/87	6/3/87	6/3/87	6/3/87	6/3/87	6/3/87	6/3/87	6/3/87
Distance	166"	166"	166"	166"	166"	166"	166"	166"
Place			HLI Fixture Room					
Data Taking			Over 20 Second Period					
Fans on?	Y	Y	Y	Y	Y	Y		
Time Between Readings	1 min	1 min	1 min	1 min	1 min	1 min	1 min	1 min

Figure 6.13   Brookhaven Tests, Model 731 Laser Stability Data, Range = 100 ft.

Reading #	Data of 8/20/87 Avg	Std Dev	Reading #	Data of 8/21/87 Avg
1	-0.0044	0.0015	1	0.0010
2	-0.0057	0.0032	2	0.0005
3	-0.0072	0.0005	3	0.0007
4	-0.0074	0.0005	4	0.0013
5	-0.0074	0.0005	5	0.0007
6	-0.0074	0.0004	6	0.0012
7	-0.0073	0.0006	7	0.0012
8	-0.0073	0.0004	8	0.0012
9	-0.0076	0.0005	9	0.0014
10	-0.0074	0.0005	10	0.0015
11	-0.0076	0.0005	11	0.0016
12	-0.0074	0.0005	12	0.0014
13	-0.0071	0.0021	13	0.0011
14	-0.0076	0.0005	14	0.0011
15	-0.0076	0.0004	15	0.0014
16	-0.0075	0.0005		
17	-0.0076	0.0006		
18	-0.0077	0.0005		
Average	-0.0072	0.0008		0.0012
Std Dev of Avg	0.0008			0.0003
Min	-0.0077	0.0004		0.0005
Max	-0.0044	0.0032		0.0016
Spread	0.0033	0.0028		0.0011
Exclude 1,2				
Average	-0.0074	0.0006		0.0012
Std Dev of Avg	0.0002			0.0003
Min	-0.0077	0.0004		0.0005
Max	-0.0071	0.0021		0.0016
Spread	0.0006	0.0017		0.0011

Figure 6.14 shows data taken at 100 feet in the same tunnel as used to produce the data shown in figure 6.13. Here a different laser was used, representing original alignment laser technology. The data taken on two separate days is approximately twice as noisy as the data shown in figure 6.13. This noise is attributable to internal effects in the laser itself.

Scan Laser Data

Scan lasers have been developed in recent years that produce a very flat plane by rotating the penta prism by a small motor. These scan planes are very useful as they allow the unattended operation of the laser. The planes produced are nearly as accurate as the older manual sweep units. The data summarized in figures 6.15 through 6.18 show turbulence data for these scan planes under various conditions.

Figure 6.15 summarizes short range (166-inch) data taken under good shop conditions. Note how the reading spreads diminish as the number of samples increase.

Figure 6.16 shows some scan data taken at a range of 45 feet under good shop conditions. Note the steady improvement in the standard deviation as the number of samples is increased.

Figure 6.17 shows data taken over a 46-foot range outside. The scan plane swept vertically and the target was mounted about 10 feet in the air on a concrete retaining wall. The shot was over a macadam surface. Note that the data is noisier than that shown in figure 6.16 by a factor of 3. These are much worse conditions than would likely be encountered in any kind of normal alignment.

Figure 6.18 shows further data taken under fair shop conditions. Two sets of data were taken—one at 45 feet and one at 90 feet. Compare these data to those in figure 6.16. Note that the standard deviations are somewhat larger. This kind of variation is quite common in laser alignment, because the entire system accuracy is so dependent on the quality of the atmosphere.

Penta Sweep Errors

The primary reason for using a penta prism is its ability to compensate for slight wobbles in the bearing axis rotation. Basically, a penta prism is rotated about an input laser beam to produce a flat plane. Two kinds of errors, centering and angular, can affect the accuracy of the plane being swept. This section examines the various effects and evaluates their effect on plane accuracy.

Figure 6.14   Brookhaven Tests, Model 711 Laser Stability Data, Range = 100 ft.

Reading #	Avg	Std Dev		Avg	Std Dev
1	-0.0019	0.0015	19	-0.0032	0.0012
2	-0.0010	0.0032	20	-0.0029	0.0014
3	-0.0012	0.0015	21	-0.0024	0.0017
4	-0.0014	0.0021	22	-0.0033	0.0015
5	-0.0018	0.0015	23	-0.0027	0.0015
6	-0.0019	0.0023	24	-0.0030	0.0023
7	-0.0018	0.0014	25	-0.0031	0.0015
8	-0.0016	0.0021	26	-0.0009	0.0031
9	-0.0029	0.0014	27	-0.0029	0.0018
10	-0.0026	0.0024	28	-0.0030	0.0014
11	-0.0021	0.0014	29	-0.0032	0.0018
12	-0.0017	0.0019	30	-0.0025	0.0015
13	-0.0027	0.0018	31	-0.0028	0.0015
14	-0.0022	0.0017	32	-0.0035	0.0020
15	-0.0019	0.0026	33	-0.0032	0.0024
16	-0.0017	0.0023	34	-0.0025	0.0022
17	-0.0019	0.0016	35	-0.0040	0.0015
18	-0.0019	0.0018	36	-0.0032	0.0015
			37	-0.0043	0.0020
			38	-0.0036	0.0015
			39	-0.0034	0.0017
			40	-0.0044	0.0024
			41	-0.0034	0.0020

	Readings 1-18		Readings 19-41	
Average	-0.0019		-0.0031	
Std Dev of Avg	0.0005		0.0007	
Min	-0.0029	0.0014	-0.0044	0.0012
Max	-0.0010	0.0032	-0.0009	0.0031

ACCURACIES OF LASER ALIGNMENT SYSTEMS

Figure 6.15 Summary of Atmospheric Effects on Model L-731 Scanner (Samples Taken Over 20 Sec.)

# of Samples/ Reading	5	10	25
Reading #			
1	-0.0012	-0.0011	-0.0012
2	-0.0013	-0.0012	-0.0012
3	-0.0011	-0.0012	-0.0012
4	-0.0012	-0.0011	-0.0012
5	-0.0013	-0.0012	-0.0012
6	-0.0014	-0.0012	-0.0012
7	-0.0011	-0.0012	-0.0012
8	-0.0010	-0.0012	-0.0011
9	-0.0012	-0.0012	-0.0011
10	-0.0011	-0.0013	-0.0011
11	-0.0013	-0.0012	-0.0011
12	-0.0011	-0.0011	-0.0012
13	-0.0012	-0.0013	-0.0012
14	-0.0011	-0.0012	-0.0011
15	-0.0012	-0.0013	-0.0011
Average of Readings	-0.0012	-0.0012	-0.0012
STD Dev of Readings	0.0001	0.0001	0.0001
Spread of Readings	0.0004	0.0002	0.0001
Min Std Dev/Reading	0.0000	0.0001	0.0001
Max Std Dev/Reading	0.0003	0.0002	0.0002
Date	6/3/87	6/3/87	6/3/87
Distance	166"	166"	166"
Place	HLI Fixture Room		
DataTaking	Samples spread over 20 seconds		
Fans on?	Y	Y	Y
Time Between Readings	30 sec	30 sec	1 min.

Figure 6.16 Summary of Atmospheric Effects on Model L-731 Scanner (Samples 150 msec/Sample Continuous), 45.5-foot Shot Inside

# of Samples/ Reading	5	10	15	20	25
Reading #					
1	0.0002	0.0020	0.0020	0.0020	0.0018
2	0.0021	0.0020	0.0019	0.0021	0.0018
3	0.0022	0.0017	0.0018	0.0018	0.0019
4	0.0018	0.0020	0.0016	0.0018	0.0018
5	0.0019	0.0018	0.0019	0.0018	0.0020
6	0.0018	0.0020	0.0021	0.0018	0.0018
7	0.0021	0.0022	0.0022	0.0018	0.0019
8	0.0021	0.0019	0.0019	0.0019	0.0020
9	0.0017	0.0017	0.0018	0.0017	0.0016
10	0.0019	0.0021	0.0017	0.0019	0.0018
11	0.0018	0.0020	0.0017	0.0017	0.0017
12	0.0021	0.0021	0.0017	0.0019	0.0018
13	0.0019	0.0022	0.0019	0.0019	0.0019
14	0.0022	0.0021	0.0018	0.0017	0.0017
15	0.0015	0.0020	0.0020	0.0017	0.0018
Average of Readings	0.0018	0.0020	0.0019	0.0018	0.0018
STD Dev of Readings	0.0005	0.0002	0.0002	0.0001	0.0001
Spread of Readings	0.0020	0.0005	0.0006	0.0004	0.0004
Min Std Dev/Reading	0.0002	0.0002	0.0002	0.0003	0.0004
Max Std Dev/Reading	0.0006	0.0006	0.0005	0.0006	0.0006
Date	6/6/87	6/6/87	6/6/87	6/6/87	6/6/87
Distance	45.5'	45.5'	45.5'	45.5'	45.5'
Place		HLI Fixture Room to south Wall Inside			
DataTaking		Samples 150 msec/sample continous			
Fans on?	2 Fans	2 Fans	2 Fans	2 Fans	2 Fans
Time Between Readings	1 min	1 min	1 min	1 min	1 min

Centering Errors

The penta prism is mounted on a rotating shaft. It is important that the laser beam be centered exactly on the axis of rotation. If it is not centered, a translational (up or down) shift of the output beam will occur. *Translational* means that

ACCURACIES OF LASER ALIGNMENT SYSTEMS 131

Figure 6.17 Summary of Atmospheric Effects on Model L-731 Scanner (Samples Taken Over 20 Sec.), 46.5-foot Shot

# of Samples/ Reading	5	10	25
Reading #			
1	0.0018	0.0013	0.0018
2	0.0031	0.0014	0.0017
3	0.0010	0.0020	0.0013
4	0.0012	0.0011	0.0013
5	0.0030	0.0019	0.0017
6	0.0017	0.0019	0.0010
7	0.0012	0.0009	0.0018
8	0.0019	0.0015	0.0011
9	0.0013	0.0013	0.0012
10	0.0017	0.0018	0.0016
11	0.0023	0.0011	0.0017
12	0.0014	0.0013	0.0020
13	0.0012	0.0023	0.0017
14	0.0012	0.0012	0.0011
15	0.0011	0.0017	0.0016
Average of Readings	0.0017	0.0015	0.0015
STD Dev of Readings	0.0007	0.0004	0.0003
Spread of Readings	0.0021	0.0014	0.0010
Min Std Dev/Reading	0.0005	0.0008	0.0008
Max Std Dev/Reading	0.0036	0.0025	0.0017
Date	6/5/87	6/5/87	6/5/87
Distance	46.5'	46.5'	46.5'
Place	HLI Fixture Room to north wall		
DataTaking	Samples spread over 20 seconds		
Fans on?	Windy	Windy	Windy
Time Between Readings	1 min	1 min	1 min

Figure 6.18 Summary of Atmospheric Effects on Model L-731 Scanner (Samples 150 msec/Sample Continuous), 45/90-foot Shot Inside w/ Retroreflector

# Samples/Reading	5 45 Ft	5 90 Ft	10 45 Ft	10 90 Ft	15 45 Ft	15 90 Ft	20 45 Ft	20 90 Ft	25 45 Ft	25 90 Ft
Reading #										
1	0.0009	0.0017	0.0008	0.0026	0.0008	0.0006	0.0009	-0.0009	0.0012	0.0018
2	0.0014	-0.0003	0.0018	0.0019	0.0007	0.0001	0.0008	0.0015	0.0014	0.0004
3	0.0009	-0.0009	0.0005	-0.0009	0.0013	0.0007	0.0010	0.0001	0.0008	0.0004
4	0.0016	0.0017	0.0017	0.0019	0.0005	0.0003	0.0025	0.0017	0.0011	0.0005
5	0.0006	0.0025	0.0015	0.0005	0.0015	0.0021	0.0013	0.0002	0.0012	0.0000
6	0.0019	-0.0002	0.0029	0.0052	0.0006	-0.0003	0.0008	-0.0003	0.0012	0.0009
7	0.0021	0.0026	0.0006	0.0016	0.0006	0.0014	0.0016	0.0004	0.0008	0.0006
8	0.0024	0.0004	0.0012	0.0017	0.0012	-0.0002	0.0015	0.0013	0.0008	-0.0004
9	0.0017	0.0054	0.0004	-0.0001	0.0014	0.0004	0.0002	-0.0009	0.0010	0.0003
10	0.0018	0.0017	0.0014	0.0017	0.0014	0.0042	0.0006	-0.0003	0.0005	-0.0015
11	0.0009	0.0008	0.0016	0.0022	0.0015	-0.0004	0.0015	0.0010	0.0011	0.0009
12	0.0012	0.0018	0.0010	0.0008	0.0006	0.0001	0.0009	-0.0008	0.0004	-0.0017
13	0.0019	0.0021	0.0015	0.0000	0.0017	0.0021	0.0004	-0.0002	0.0009	0.0005
14	0.0004	-0.0002	0.0026	-0.0001	0.0006	-0.0006	0.0014	0.0006	0.0007	-0.0008
15	0.0012	0.0004	0.0014	0.0027	0.0007	0.0001	0.0009	0.0016	0.0017	0.0025
16	0.0005	0.0017	0.0014	0.0020	0.0008	-0.0009	0.0010	0.0004	0.0008	-0.0001
17	0.0014	0.0006	0.0018	0.0005	0.0012	0.0008	0.0007	0.0000	0.0014	0.0002
18	0.0017	0.0027	0.0012	0.0041	0.0004	-0.0001	0.0010	0.0004	0.0016	0.0029
19	0.0020	0.0042	0.0020	0.0014	0.0021	0.0023	0.0010	-0.0007	0.0005	-0.0016
20	0.0016	0.0005	0.0010	0.0016	0.0014	0.0010	0.0007	0.0014	0.0008	-0.0005
Average of Readings	0.0014	0.0015	0.0014	0.0016	0.0011	0.0007	0.0010	0.0003	0.0010	0.0003
STD Dev of Readings	0.0006	0.0016	0.0006	0.0014	0.0005	0.0012	0.0005	0.0009	0.0004	0.0012
Spread of Readings	0.0020	0.0063	0.0025	0.0061	0.0017	0.0051	0.0023	0.0026	0.0013	0.0046
Min Std Dev/Reading	0.0001	0.0006	0.0002	0.0004	0.0003	0.0003	0.0004	0.0009	0.0003	0.0008
Max Std Dev/Reading	0.0009	0.0022	0.0007	0.0033	0.0008	0.0054	0.0011	0.0033	0.0009	0.0035

Place HLI Fixture Room to south Wall Inside Readings at 45 and 90 Ft-No Fan
DataTaking Samples 150 msec/sample continous Readings 1 Minute Interval

Figure 6.19 Sweep Errors—Effects of Bearing Runout

Bearing runout produces displacement errors in the flatness of the plane swept by rotating the penta prism. The error produced is in direct proportion to the runout and is the same close to the laser and far away.

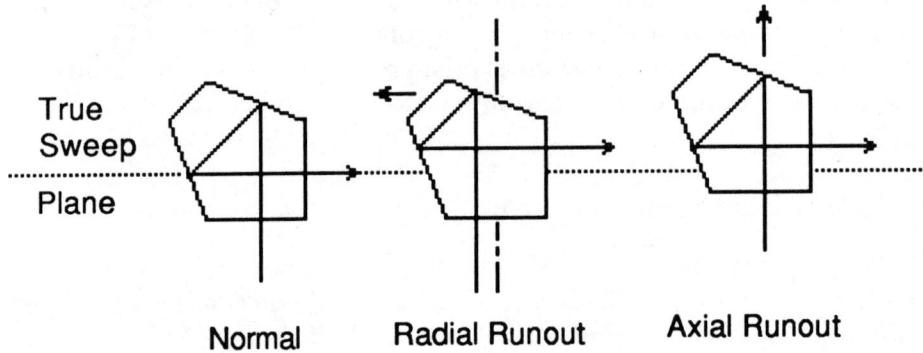

the error is the same at 100 feet as it is at 0 feet. This type of error can readily be adjusted out and should be checked before using such a system.

Assuming that the laser beam is centered accurately on the bearing axis of rotation, there can still be residual errors due to bearing runout. Axial runout is easy to understand and is usually less than .0001 inch for a class 7 matched-pair bearing set. Radial runout will produce the same effect. Examine figure 6.19 to see the reason. This, too, is a translational error and is generally small.

Angular Errors

The effects on plane accuracy of rotations of the prism relative to the input laser beam is a somewhat more complex subject. Although there is only one primary source of error, it is the most significant and subtle error source in the process of sweeping a flat plane. This section deals with these effects, and a formula is given to calculate the primary effect.

Consider three mutually perpendicular axes. These represent the three angular or rotational degrees of freedom for the prism. One axis is the input laser beam, the second is the output laser beam, and the third is an axis perpendicular to the first two. Rotation about the input beam is what is done to sweep a flat plane, so this rotation can have no effect on plane accuracy.

If a mirror were used to bend the beam 90 degrees, the slight wobble of the bearing axis, generally less than 10 arc-seconds, would produce a corresponding tilt of the beam that would be *twice* the tilt angle of the mirror. Rotation about the third axis would then produce unacceptably large errors in the plane. This is

why a two-reflection compensating type of reflector is used. Such a prism is called a *penta prism*. (See figure 6.20.)

The rotation of a penta prism about the third axis when one is perpendicular to the input output laser beams is completely compensated for by the dual nature of the reflection. Basically, as the prism is rotated about this axis, if the first reflection opens the angle, the second will close it by the exact same amount, thus perfectly compensating for this type of rotation. The compensation is exact and can occur over large (many-degree) prism rotations. This compensative ability is the primary reason such prisms are used to sweep flat planes.

The Only Significant Angular Error

Rotation of the prism about the exit beam due to bearing wobble will produce a second-order opening of the 90-degree angle. *Second order* means that the phenomenon varies as the *square* of the rotation angle in radians and is small. For instance, a rotation of .001 inch/inch about the exit beam will produce an opening of the 90-degree angle of 1 micro radian or ⅕ of an arc-second. A wobble of .001 inch/inch is large for a good bearing system, so the effect is not normally noticeable or a problem. Figure 6.21 shows why this effect occurs and gives the formula for calculating its effect.

Figure 6.20 Sweep Errors—Compensation for Rotation of Prism

If a penta prism is rotated about an axis perpendicular to the input and output beams, there is no change in the 90° angle. The angle of reflection closes at A but opens at B in exactly the same amount, so the 90° angle remains unchanged. This capability will compensate for bearing wobble and is the reason these prisms are used to sweep planes.

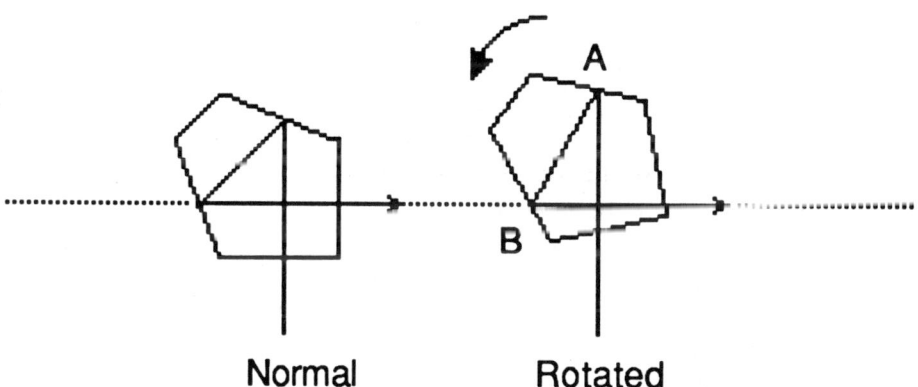

Figure 6.21 Sweep Errors—Effects of Rotating Prism About Output Beam

Rotating a penta prism about the output beam will open the 90° angle. This is a second-order effect. The increase in the 90° angle is equal to the square of the rotation angle in radians. A rotation of 7 arc-minutes will open the 90° angle by 1 arc-second. As bearing wobble is usually less than 10 arc-seconds, the effect is quite small. It occurs because the input and output beams are no longer in the same plane.

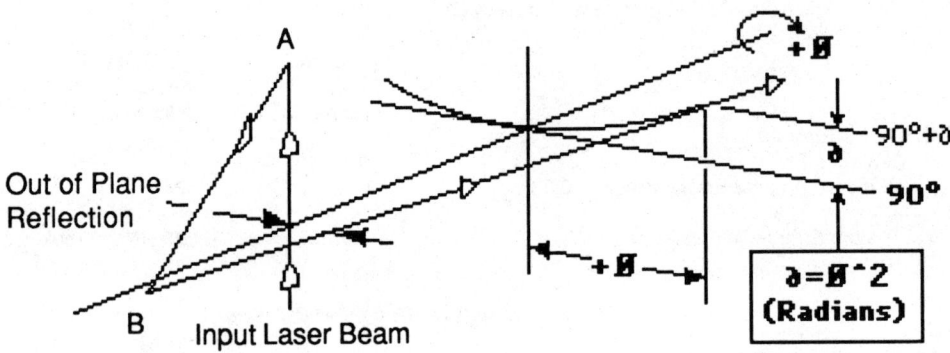

Plane Error Budget

The various sources of error have been discussed above in some detail. What is their cumulative effect on a real plane? Given below are two error budgets for a laser plane.

The first covers only the errors that we described above and provides a ± 3 sigma estimate of plane flatness with all sources of error considered. It is given in two forms, one for 360-degree prism rotation and the second for 90-degree rotation.

The second error budget adds the effects of air turbulence to the overall error of the flat plane. Turbulence influences under average and extreme conditions are given.

Laser Plane Error Budget (No Turbulence)

The error budgets shown in figure 6.22 considers only prism angle and bearing runout errors as they affect plane flatness. Two different budgets are presented, one for 360-degree sweeps and one for 90-degree sweeps. The examination of the geometry of a sweep reveals that limiting the total sweep angle to less than 120 degrees will reduce the residual prism angular error. Figure 6.23 shows that reduction as a function of total sweep angle.

Figure 6.22 Laser Plane Error Budget/Laser Plane Errors Due to Bearing Runout and Prism Angular Errors

Laser Plane Error Budget—360° Sweep

Radius (Ft)	50
Total Sweep Angle (Deg)	360
Sweep Angle Factor	1
Prism Residual Angular Error (Arcsec)	0.33

Laser Plane Errors		±3 Sigma Errors (Inches)	±3 Sigma Errors (Microns)	
Centering Error		0.00010	3	
Effective Angular Error (Arcsec)	0.33	0.0010	24	
Total System Errors—360° Sweep (RSS)		0.0010	25	(No Turbulence)

Laser Plane Error Budget—90° Sweep

Radius (Ft)	50
Total Sweep Angle (Deg)	90
Sweep Angle Factor	0.41
Prism Residual Angular Error (Arcsec)	0.33

Laser Plane Errors		±3 Sigma Errors (Inches)	±3 Sigma Errors (Microns)	
Centering Error		0.0001	3	
Effective Angular Error (Arcsec)	0.14	0.0004	10	
Total System Error—90° Sweep (RSS)		0.0004	10	(No Turbulence)

Laser Plane Error Budget (with Turbulence)

Figure 6.24 shows an error budget similar to the one above except that the influence of air turbulence is incorporated into the error estimates. Estimates for both average and extreme conditions are included. The air turbulence estimates are based upon the data taken in many of the tests shown earlier in this section. The final estimates for average and extreme represent a real-world estimate of the 3-sigma limits of accuracy that are possible with a good alignment system.

Note: These estimates assume appropriate averaging. Operating closer to real time or with a higher response will mean more error in the final plane flatness due to turbulence.

Figure 6.23 Residual Prism Error

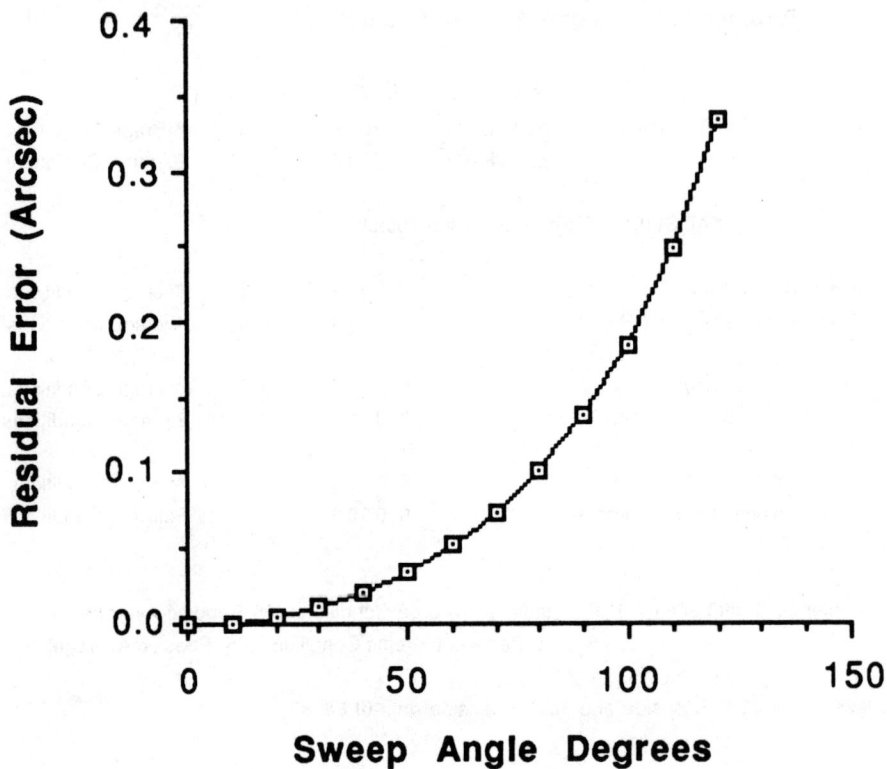

Comparison with Other Systems

Laser alignment systems compare very favorably with most other types of alignment and measuring methods. Lasers readily improve the accuracy, consistency, and overall speed of making alignments. Typically, alignment lasers will allow an actual alignment to be performed in about one-half to one-tenth the time taken with ordinary optical systems. Because of the self-consistent nature of the laser coordinate system "erected" around the part or machine (see figure 6.25), the measurements are far easier to interpret than those produced by ordinary optical systems. A single laser instrument and accessories will perform all of the operations that many separate optical instruments can perform and can do some things optical methods can handle only with great difficulty.

**Figure 6.24 Laser Plane Error Budget
Typical Atmospheric Conditions
Turbulence (±3 Sigma @ 50-ft. Radius)**

	(Radians)	(Inches)	(Microns)	
* Air Turbulence Errors @ Radius	9.00E-07	0.0005	14	Average Conditions
	2.70E-06	0.0016	41	Extreme Conditions

TOTAL SWEEP ERROR (Including Turbulence)

Total Flatness Error			0.0011	28	Average Conditions
(360° Sweep)	(RSS)		0.0019	48	Average Conditions
Total Flatness Error			0.0007	17	Average Conditions
(90° Sweep)	(RSS)		0.0017	42	Extreme Conditions
^Comparison with			0.0003		Average Conditions
single point scan data			0.0009		Extreme Conditions

* Air Turbulence Contribution = ± .9 u-Radians Average Conditions (25 Reading Average)
  = ± 2.7 u-Radians Extreme Conditions (25 Reading Average)

^ Data taken from 45.5 Ft inside and 46.5 Ft outside data of 6/6/87

Interferometers and Alignment Lasers

An alignment laser is frequently confused with an interferometer laser. They both take advantage of a laser beam; however, the principles involved are completely different.

Interferometer Principles

An interferometer (see figure 6.26) is an extremely accurate incremental distance measuring device. Fundamentally, it measures the increment of movement. If a retroreflector is moved from point A to point B with a machine slide, the interferometer will measure the actual movement of that slide to an accuracy of about one part per million. It takes advantage of an optical device known as an interferometer, in which the wavelength of a light is used as the basic unit of measure. An interferometer splits the laser beam into two pieces (or two paths), one of which is a fixed-length path and other of which is a variable-length path.

Both beams are returned from retroreflectors, one in each path. They are recombined in an optical element called a *beam splitter,* and a signal is generated

Figure 6.25 Laser "Coordinate" Box

A laser coordinate box is really a coordinate system that is consistent within itself. Lines are straight, the angles are always 90°, and the planes are flat and square or parallel to the other lines. All measurements are made relative to this coordinate system. Machine misalignments are easy to pinpoint.

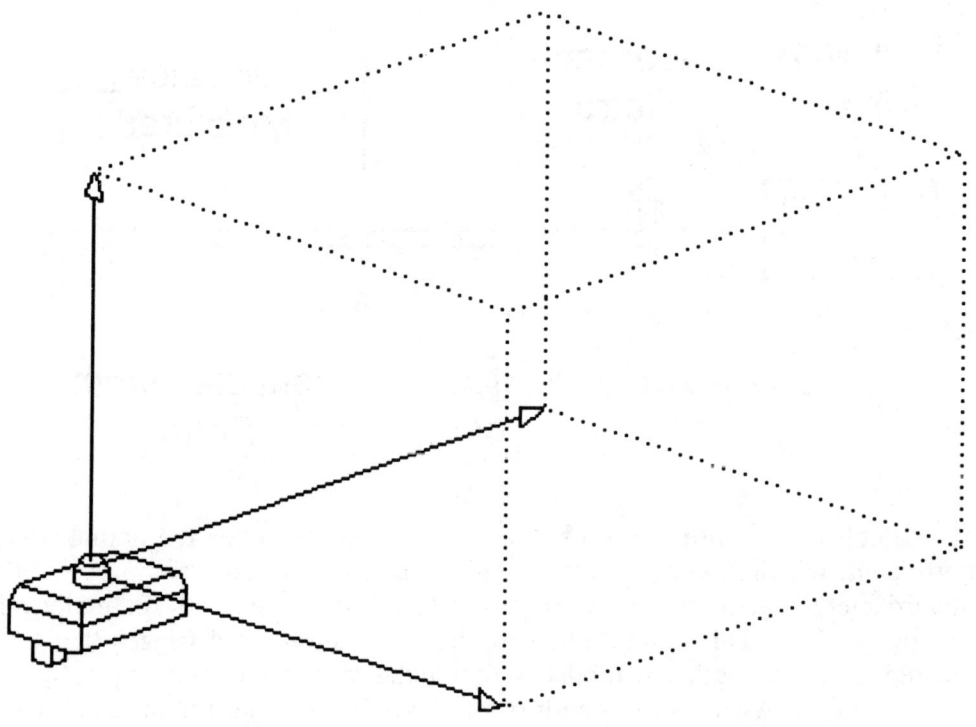

and is detected by two electronic detectors. If you move the variable length retroreflector through one-half of a wavelength, the combined field of the two halves or legs of the interferometer will go from light to dark. Each time the variable path retroreflector is moved by one-half of a wavelength, the field again will change from light to dark.

In reality, there are two fields with 90-degree quadrature, so that the system is capable of detecting if the variable-length retro is moving away from the interferometer or toward it. In any event, a counter in the electronics very accurately counts the number of "fringes" that occur as the variable-length retro is moved from, say, position A to position B.

Note: The beam must not be interrupted while a measurement is being made. An interferometer must continually "count" the fringes to keep track of vibrations of the variable-length retro and the effects of air turbulence.

Figure 6.26 The Basic Principle of an Interferometer

As the measuring retro is moved along the laser beam, the recombined beams vary from light to dark for each ½ wavelength moved. A counter keeps track, and a computer multiplies the count times the wavelength to yield the incremental distance moved.

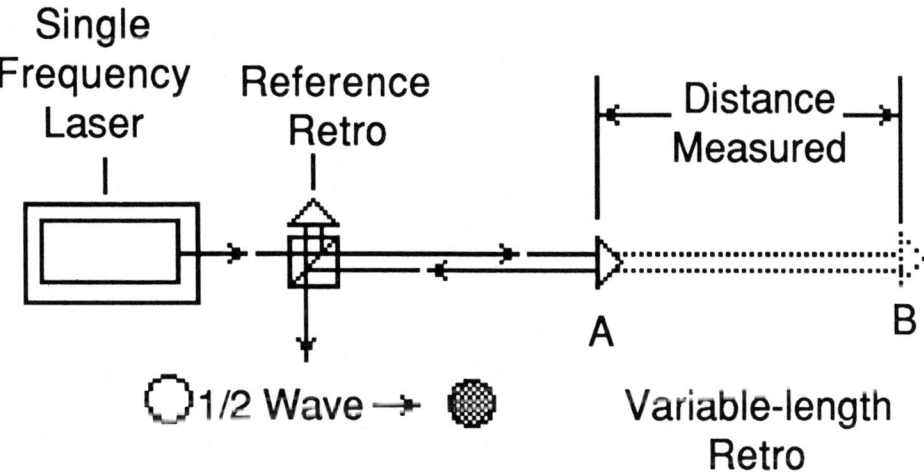

The electronics multiply the number of wavelengths times the actual wavelength itself, which is known to a very high order of precision compared to the standard meter bar at the National Institute of Standards and Technology in Washington, D.C. This is multiplied by the actual number of fringes that have occurred, and the length is established to a high order of accuracy, typically one part per million. As the wavelength of the laser is a standard unto itself and is removed by one step from the standard meter bar at the Bureau of Standards, the interferometer represents an extremely accurate field reference system. Its primary use is for measuring incremental distance.

Geometric Measurement with an Interferometer

Several accessories accompany this system to allow the measurement of straightness, flatness, and perpendicularity. Straightness is measured by using a double interferometer with two beams, separated by some known distance, running parallel to each other. As the return optical system is tilted forward or backward in pitch or yaw, the difference between the two paths represents a measure of the tilt angle. An interferometer can measure straightness and flatness in much the same manner as an autocollimator. The only true difference between the two is that the autocollimator measures the angular tilt of the unit in a different fashion than an interferometer. The results are similar. Mathematical integration of the "steps" yields the straightness or flatness.

In essence, if the return mirror, or retro, is walked in its own footsteps—that is, if the front foot is placed where the rear foot was, and the unit is "walked" as such—an extremely accurate profile may be produced. Typically, with an interferometer, readings at the tens-of-millionths level are possible. Versions are available in which the increment or step is extremely small and, in effect, the signal is integrated so that a continuous output of vertical position as a function of distance is generated. This is a true straightness measurement but suffers a common difficulty with the autocollimator in that any mistake in reading it is carried forward through the remainder of the readings. Such systematic errors do not cancel and are cumulative throughout the course of the measurement.

Flatness is measured by using the "Moody" method, which involves taking four profiles around the edge of a surface plate, two diagonals and two crosspieces all meeting at two cross profiles from the middle of each side to the opposite side. (See Figure 6.27.)

They all form an intersection in the center of the plate. This well-known method has been used for years with autocollimators to measure surface plates for true flatness. Data is reduced by "tilting" all the profiles so that the point measured in the center of the table reads the same for all the profiles. Similarly,

Figure 6.27 Flatness Measurement—Moody Method

Eight linear profiles are taken using the pattern shown below. The profiles are "tilted" so that the intersections for all profiles are coincident. This then describes the surface. No points can be taken in the open areas with this method.

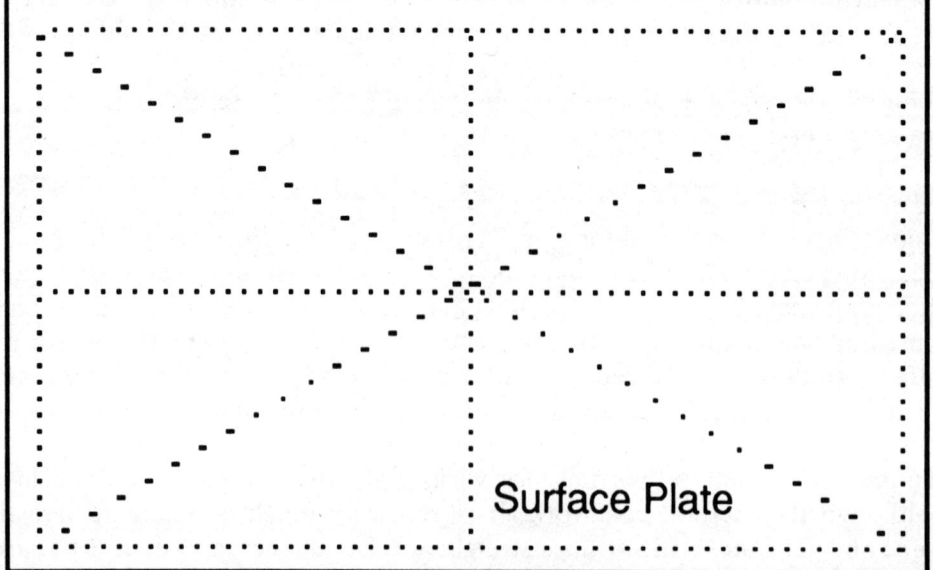

other intersections are adjusted in this manner until a profile of the surface is obtained. The method is very effective, but it is tedious, time-consuming, and benefits greatly from the use of a computer for data reduction.

Alignment and Interferometer Lasers Compared

In general, alignment laser systems and interferometers are far more complementary than they are competitive. The fundamental difference between the two is simple: the interferometers measure incremental distance, such as axial slide positioning. The alignment laser will measure the geometry of the machine, such as straightness, flatness, and squareness. As all of these elements are necessary in order to properly categorize a machine or to realign it and readjust it to an accurate condition, the two systems really complement each other, and most users will end up buying both systems.

A contrast between the two systems is that an alignment laser basically is built to align machines, and an interferometer fundamentally is designed to measure machines. In most cases, when a machine is making bad parts or has too high a reject rate, the operator is more interested in realigning and adjusting the machine so that it will make proper parts. To that extent, the more cumbersome methods of straightness and flatness measurement using the interferometer are prohibitive, because they only measure the amount of misalignment and do not provide a quick and easy method of realigning or rescraping a way or surface that is out of calibration.

Where the interferometer makes its great contribution is in tool or slide positioning. The positioning system of the machine itself commands a move of some distance for the slide of the tool, and the interferometer will verify quite accurately that this move was made exactly as requested. Frequently, such movements do not coincide; that is, the actual movement is not the same as the requested movement. The racks or scales must be adjusted to obtain proper positioning operation from the machine. In this area, the interferometer is king and works very well.

An interferometer can be used to create a machine positioning error "map" that can then be integrated into the controls of a CNC machine in such a way that moves may be corrected for error. This error correction matrix is frequently applied using an interferometer, and the tool is positioned throughout its volume or cubage of machining or measuring space, and an error matrix is generated. This method can be quite effective in correcting errors; however, the problem is that the corrections apply generally on the day when the measurements were made and may vary significantly over weeks and months, depending on average temperature conditions and other environmental factors in the shop. Frequently, such a method is used to "correct" for various geometric errors in the machine, and although the method can work, it is generally much better to realign the machine and get slides and surfaces straight and flat and columns square to bases

COMPARISON WITH OTHER SYSTEMS

rather than attempting to correct them with an error matrix. A final corrective error matrix can be generated after alignment that will be far more accurate than one that is done before alignment.

Atmospheric Effects and Limits on Interferometers and Alignment Lasers

When using any optical instrument, including alignment lasers and interferometers, the atmosphere is the primary limitation on accuracy. Turbulence exists in the atmosphere in all shops, as well as in temperature-controlled rooms. (See figure 6.28.)

The magnitude of this turbulence is generally on the order of about one-half to three or four arc-seconds and is not "seen" by the human eye because the resolution of a fully corrected eye is about 60 arc-seconds. This turbulence consists of pockets of air that pass through the beam and act like a very weak lens and cause the beam to be bent slightly. The effects on an alignment laser and interferometer are different, but the net result is that both systems are affected by the turbulence.

For an alignment laser, the turbulence actually steers the beam slightly or changes its direction. This affects apparent beam straightness. In distances up to ten feet the phenomenon is not readily observable; at distances of 50 to 100 feet, however, such turbulence can be significant. On a typical quiet day in a standard machine shop, turbulence on the order of .010 inch peak to peak at 100

Figure 6.28 Air Turbulence

Air has a small index of refraction that changes with temperature. The atmosphere is full of pockets of air called *turbuls* that deflect any line of sight or laser beam very slightly. The net effect is "noise" or movement of the beam of about 1–3 arc-seconds.

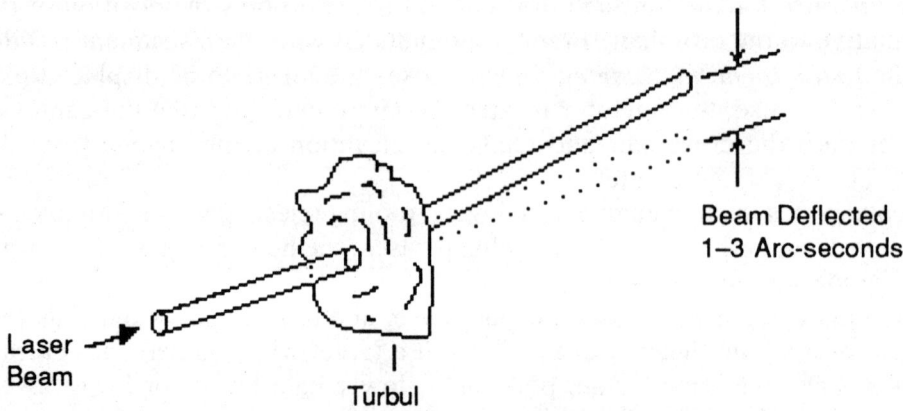

feet can be observed. Such turbulence will average out over a 10-to-20-second period.

This turbulence affects the interferometer in a different manner, although it is the same atmospheric phenomenon. Fundamentally, the wavelength of laser light is affected by the index of refraction of the medium it passes through. Normally, we think of air as having no optical effect, but it does. One needs only to observe the twinkle of the stars to see the turbulence in the air. In any event, one of the consequences of the turbulence is that the air has a slightly higher or lower density and, hence, a slightly different index of refraction. This index of refraction changes the effective wavelength, and an air column from laser interferometer to retro is packed with "turbuls" that change the effective wavelength slightly. The result is simply a movement in the sixth and sometimes the fifth decimal place of a display. Part of this movement is due, of course, to the vibration of the retro itself and part of it is due to the turbulence in the atmosphere. Again, if a sufficient number of readings is taken at any point, such effects can be averaged out to a large degree, but they do represent the limitation on accuracy of both systems.

This so-called turbulence also affects older optical systems. Any line of sight, whether an autocollimator, an engineer level, or theodolite, is affected by exactly the same phenomenon; this represents a significant limitation on the accuracy of such systems.

Comparison of Optical Systems and Alignment Lasers

The so-called standard for alignment has been an optical system. For many years, optical tooling has been employed in the aerospace industry, and to a degree, this same technology and the older technologies of older levels and straight edges have been used to align and make flat various types of machines. Optical systems (see figure 6.29) fundamentally consist of a telescope. Inside the scope at the focus of the eye piece is a crosshair that is projected into space so that the operator looking through the scope at a target notes the position of the target relative to the crosshair. Frequently included with the instrument is a device called an *optical micrometer,* which causes the image to be displaced parallel to itself. In use, the operator rotates the micrometer to bring the center of the target onto the cross hair and reads the elevation of the change from the drum of the optical micrometer.

Optical devices include engineering levels, tooling telescopes, theodolites, autocollimators, and other such devices. In all cases, the human eye is an essential part of the measurement system.

The human eye has a resolution capability of about 60 arc-seconds. This resolution is for a young, healthy eye looking at a target with 100-percent contrast under high light conditions. Age, poor sight, lower light levels, or lower levels of contrast will adversely affect this number and frequently can double or even

Figure 6.29 Optical Tooling Principle

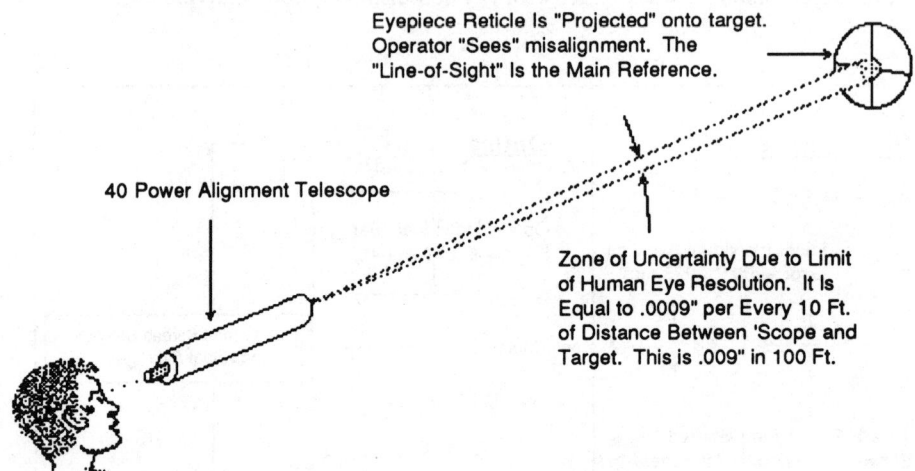

triple it. The significance of the number is this: If you are looking through a 60-power telescope, the human eye will have a resolution of 1 arc-second, or the equivalent of .006 inch in 100 feet. Typically, alignment telescopes, theodolites, and autocollimators use powers up to 40. This means that the typical optical instrument will have a resolution of about 1.5 arc-seconds under ideal conditions. This is equivalent to .009 inch at 100 feet. With lower contrast, poor light conditions, or imperfect eyesight, this number could easily reach .0018 to .0020 inch in 100 feet. In addition, there is a national specification requiring optical tooling telescopes and similar instruments to have a deviation of the crosshair or a lateral shift of the crosshair of no more than .003 inch from close focus to infinity. If all of these errors are added together, it is not possible to use an optical system to an accuracy much better than .010 inch in 100 feet. Contrast this with a laser alignment system that may be used to an accuracy of .001 inch in 100 feet or proportionately smaller in shorter distances, and it is possible to begin to understand the significant improvement in accuracy provided by an alignment system. In fact, atmospheric turbulence frequently makes the use of optical systems nearly impossible at distances of 100 feet in some cases, as the "boiling" of the image is such that the operator cannot achieve an effective focus or a sharp delineation. An alignment laser will still work under such conditions but with reduced accuracy.

Optics/Laser Comparison Test

Some years ago, the following test was performed at a major aircraft manufacturer. A target was placed 100 feet away and a direct comparison was made between an alignment laser and a telescope. In each case, the target was

Figure 6.30 Repeatability Comparison Between Optics and Lasers

Test conditions: distance was 100 ft. with ten centerings by four individuals.

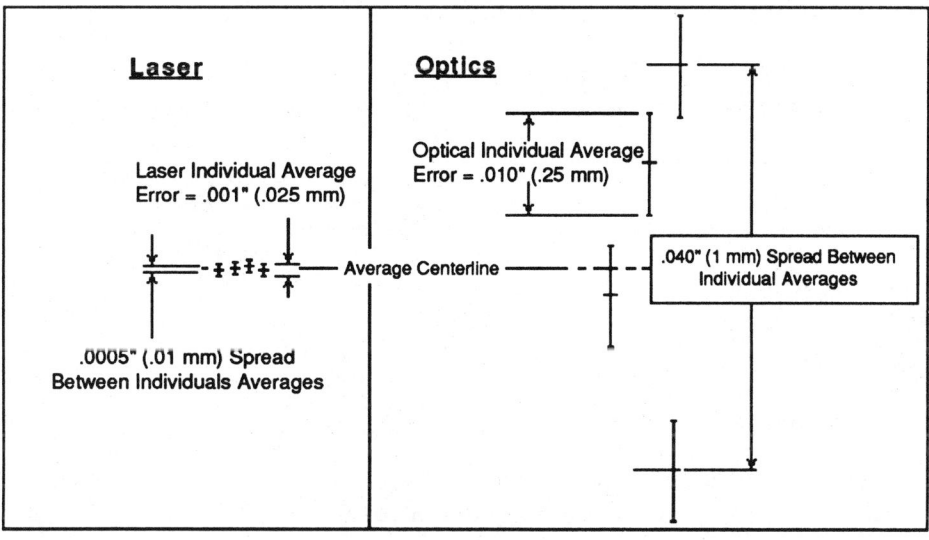

displaced and repositioned at the operator's direction until the target was perfectly centered. The micrometer readings on the X-Y positioning stage were then read and recorded, and the operation was repeated. The same was done both for the alignment telescope with a single operator and for the laser system. The tests were repeated for a number of operators. Figure 6.30 shows the results of the collaboration.

Effectively, the average error for the alignment telescope was .010 inch, which is good agreement with the theory above. More importantly, however, the differences between the average of one operator and another may amount to as much as .040 inch, thereby revealing the significant differences that can occur between different human eyes. Any alignments accomplished by a single operator would be far more accurate than alignments accomplished by a multitude of operators using the same equipment.

By contrast, the alignment laser in the same circumstances had an average error of .001 inch, and the differences between the averages of the four operators was something less than .0005 inch. This dramatically illustrates why laser alignment systems are so much more accurate than visible optical systems.

Comparison of Tight Wires and Alignment Lasers

In comparing alignment lasers to tight wires, it is necessary to understand the older tight wire method. A wire was stretched between two points and weighted to pull it as taut as possible. This was used as a reference for making straightness or flatness measurements. There are many difficulties with tight wires. First, if there is any kink in the wire, no amount of tension will remove it. Second, the wire sags with a catenary sag similar to that observed on a suspension bridge. The loading of a cable resulting from its own weight produces the catenary figure but it represents a very significant departure from a true straight line. Thus, tight wires are rarely used for making elevation measurements.

More often, they are used for making straightness measurements—that is, side-to-side or left and right measurements where there is no sag. Such measurements may have significant errors, as even the slightest wind or breeze can blow a long tight wire off to the side. Problems are further compounded by magnetic effects on steel wires and lack of uniform loading. In addition, tight wires must be moved frequently, as in the case of turbine alignment, to remove internals and then must be reestablished and bucked in again. This process is time-consuming, difficult, and prone to significant error. A laser beam represents a kind of "sagless" tight wire, and parts can be moved through the beam without removing the laser "wire" or affecting the results.

Comparison Conclusions

In many significant respects, the laser is a distinct improvement over older methods of alignment. It is even an improvement in an alignment sense over an interferometer.

Types of Measurements Possible with an Alignment Measurement System

Alignment systems have been used in a variety of applications. Nearly every industry in the United States, from light to heavy and steel to electronics, requires alignment somewhere in the manufacturing process. Machines in all industries are used to build parts, devices, assemblies, components, etc., and in all cases, alignment is central to their accurate manufacture. Discussed below are a number of different categories or applications of alignment in which lasers

have been applied successfully. In each case, the particular needs of the application are discussed, and several examples are given in an attempt to illustrate some of these facets of applying the laser in this particular application.

Machine Tool Geometry Measurement

Perhaps the premier use of the alignment laser is in machine tool alignment. Typically, the larger the machine, the more the process will benefit from using alignment lasers. Self-contained machines, such as Bridgeports, do not generally benefit from lasers. They can be used to check such machines, but cylindrical squares and straight edges are generally adequate for such machines. When the machine is large and is made of several sections bolted together in a line, the alignment laser truly starts to shine. It is not possible to move, much less use, a 100-foot-high cylindrical square, and yet one of the geometries available with the alignment laser is the functional equivalent of a cylindrical square.

The following illustration shows the various geometries possible with a laser system and how they would apply to the alignment of a machine tool. A straight line may be generated and used, a right angle with a functional equivalent of a carpenter's square may be used, a flat plane may be generated and it may be leveled, which is the functional equivalent of a surface plate. The equivalent of a knee square may be generated, as illustrated below. All of these geometries are necessary to ensure that the slides, ways, and table surfaces are straight, flat, and level. Typically, the laser target is mounted on the tool post in the spindle or on the slide and the machine is moved with its own drive mechanisms. A profile of the straightness or squareness of travel is obtained as the machine is moved through its various operations. Beds may be leveled. Way parallelism, surface table flatness, column squareness, spindle droop, and runout may be measured. There are hordes of different types of machine tools built for many purposes. All may benefit from laser alignment. This method represents a type of coordinate system that can be used to measure and align all parts of a machine to a common reference.

Machine Alignment Example

An example of what may be accomplished with an alignment laser is illustrated by the following true story. A customer accepted delivery of a Giddings and Lewis horizontal machine and discovered that the machine was cutting parts out of square. There was a sharp division of opinion among the company employees as to the cause of the out-of-square parts. One group maintained that the horizontal table moving in X and Y was tilting and twisting to cause the out-of-square condition. Another group maintained that the column was out of square. An alignment laser was brought in and set up. A target was placed sequentially in each of the four corners and in the center of the table. The table was moved to

one corner of its movement envelope, and measurements were taken of the flatness of the table. It was then moved to the other four corners and the middle of its movement envelope, and similar measurements were taken. The results were that the surface was flat within .001 and tracked everywhere within its movement envelope within .001 inch. In other words, the machine was in excellent shape. The laser was then picked up and placed under the column with the laser still oriented in the same direction. The unit was releveled, and the plumb beam was used. It should be noted here that the repeatability of some .0002 inch in ten feet makes this type of operation extremely accurate. In any event, the target was mounted on the spindle and carefully centered with the spindle in its lowest position. When the spindle head was driven up the column to its highest position, it was immediately obvious that the column was leaning backward and to one side.

It took approximately 20 minutes to determine that the column was the problem, and it was out of square. At this point, one of the operators left and returned in 5 minutes with a wrench. An additional 20 minutes of adjustment brought the column squareness to within approximately .0002 inch over its length of travel. Giddings and Lewis had built a fine machine, and a quick alignment had produced a truly perfect machine for making parts.

Bore Measurement

One of the primary applications of alignment lasers is measuring the straightness of a collection of bores. Examples of this might be crankshaft bores of an engine block, plastic extruders of a gun barrel or any application where a series of holes must be checked for alignment. In principle, a target is placed in an adaptable fixture and moved down progressively from one bore to the next. If the target is displaced left or right or up and down, this will be determined from the read-out unit, and the misalignment can be readily ascertained.

New Bore Tooling and the "Normin" Method

Tooling is frequently a problem because of size/fit problem that occurs when attempting to build an adaptor to fit into a bore. The size/fit problem is multiplied to a large degree in larger bores. In other words, the problem of making the right size plug to fit in a larger bore becomes a big problem. In any event, a fixturing and data-taking measurement has been developed that involves the use of a device fixturing set-up similar to that shown in figure 6.31.

Basically, two fixed-length measuring arms and an adjustable "jam leg" are used to support the target and bore. With this system, any bore size may readily be accommodated, as the jam leg may be spring loaded. The fixturing consists of three legs of approximately the radius of the bore minus the radius of the fixture and need not be extremely accurate in dimension.

Figure 6.31 The "Normin" Method of Bore Fixturing

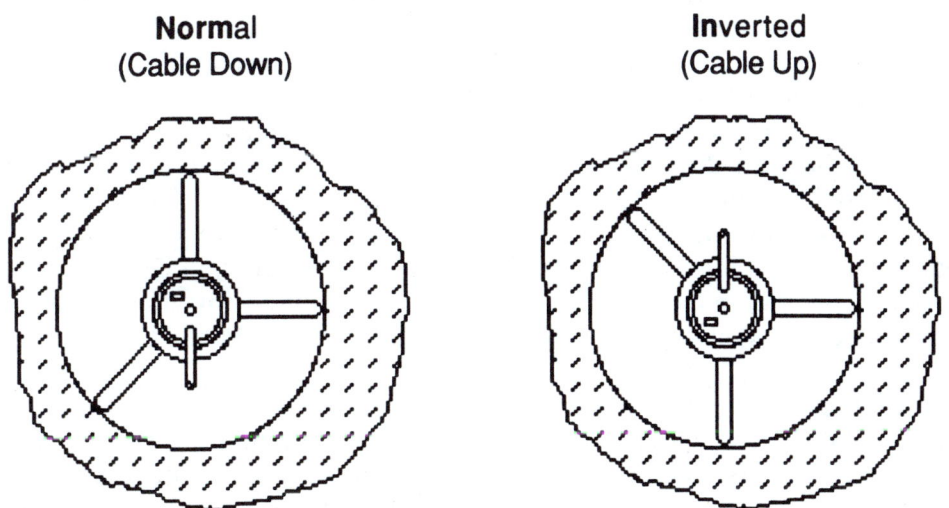

In operation, two measurements are taken. The first is taken in the normal position with the cable down. The second is taken with the entire fixture assembly rotated 180 degrees so the cable is up or in the inverted position. (See figure 6.32.)

This so-called "Normin" method results in a cancellation of all leg length, bore size, and target decentering errors so that a perfect target center is found, regardless of the sources of error. Bore centering errors are calculated by subtracting the inverted reading from the normal reading and dividing the result by two. The result shows the *misalignment of the bore relative to the beam*. The sense of this is for a target in the normal position. That is, a *plus* reading of this result would mean that the bore center is *high* relative to the laser beam center.

This is exactly the same method that is used in tramming bores with an indicator, except that with a two-axis target, it is necessary to take only two measurements at 180 degrees instead of four measurements at 90 degrees. The minus sign arises because the target is upside down and the sign must be changed to get the correct answer. This Normin method is extremely powerful and works down to the tenth levels on very large bores.

Turbine Alignment

One of the specialty applications of the alignment laser system is turbine alignment. Because the beam is a type of sagless tight wire, it allows the user to remove and replace internals without removing the laser. This saves a great deal of time and makes for a far more accurate system. Essentially, in this applica-

TYPES OF MEASUREMENTS POSSIBLE WITH AN ALIGNMENT MEASUREMENT SYSTEM

Figure 6.32 The "Normin" Concept

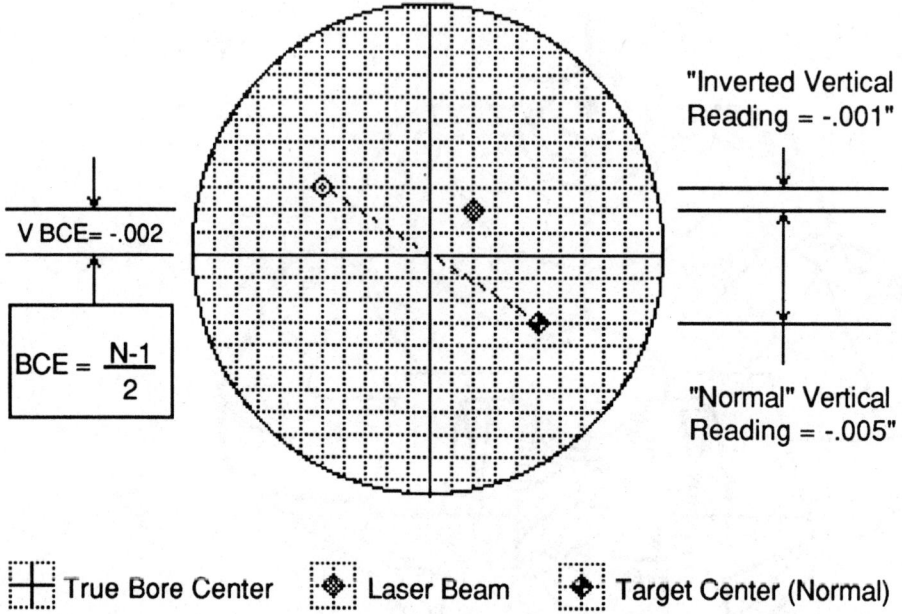

tion, small laser targets are placed in the center of larger holes using various bore sweep devices.

Note: Bore sweep methods are required here because turbines are aligned with the "tops off" and thus the Normin method outlined above will not work.

The laser beam is aligned to the center of the targets, as shown in figure 6.33. Readings may then be taken on bores up to 15 feet in diameter with equipment provided. Generally, with diameters under eight feet, the system will repeat within .001 inch and will repeat within .002 inch with diameters up to 15 feet. Generally speaking, more than a week can be saved on a typical outage using an alignment laser to do the measurement and realignment of the internals.

Vertical Shaft Alignment

This type of alignment is special, because it is a particularly neat and tight application. The plumb beam from the laser is used to measure the verticality and straightness of a vertical shaft, such as a shaft used in a large hydroelectric unit (see figure 6.34). Typically, the water turbine is some distance below the generator and the two are connected by the long shaft upward to 100 feet. For many reasons, it is necessary that these shafts be exactly plumb or vertical.

Figure 6.33 Turbine Alignment

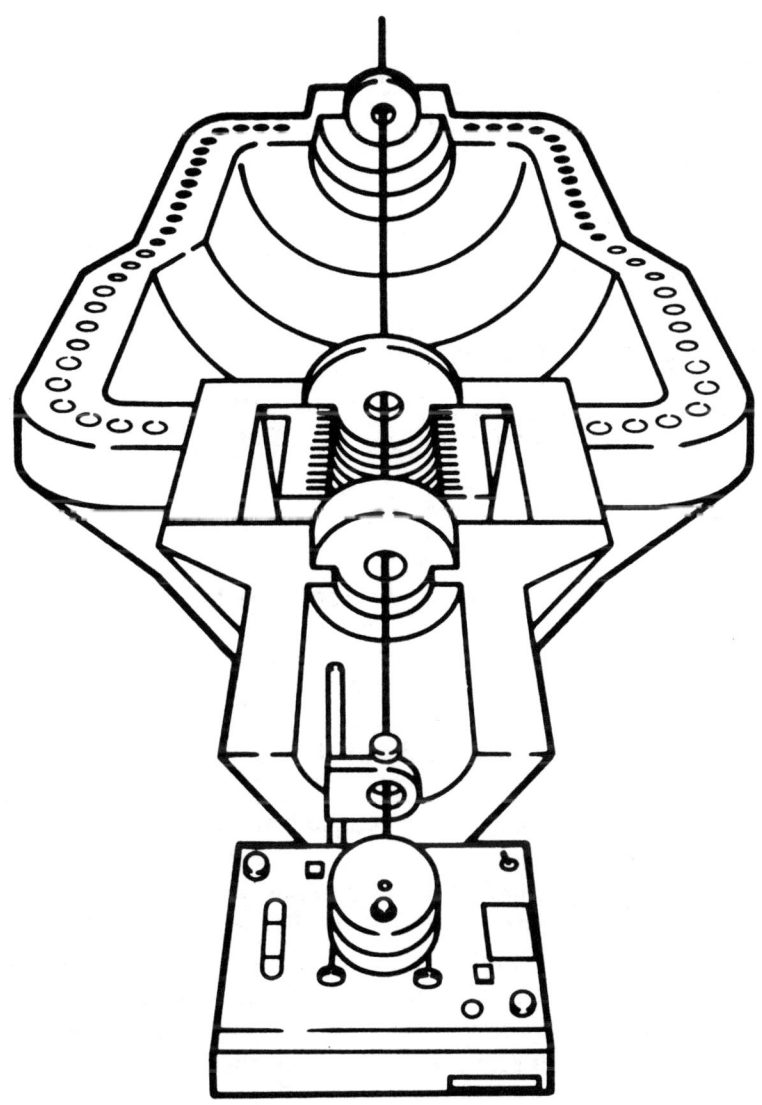

In the past, four tight wires have been hung around the shaft with heavy weights on the ends in buckets of oil for damping. Measurements are made from these plumb bobs to the surface of the shaft using inside mikes and an electrical contact system to determine when the inside mike is just touching the wire. Measurements are generally made around the four sides (north, south, east, west) at a given level, and the operator moves to another level and takes another set of measurements. The data on these measurements is then reduced in the same

Figure 6.34 Vertical Shaft Alignment

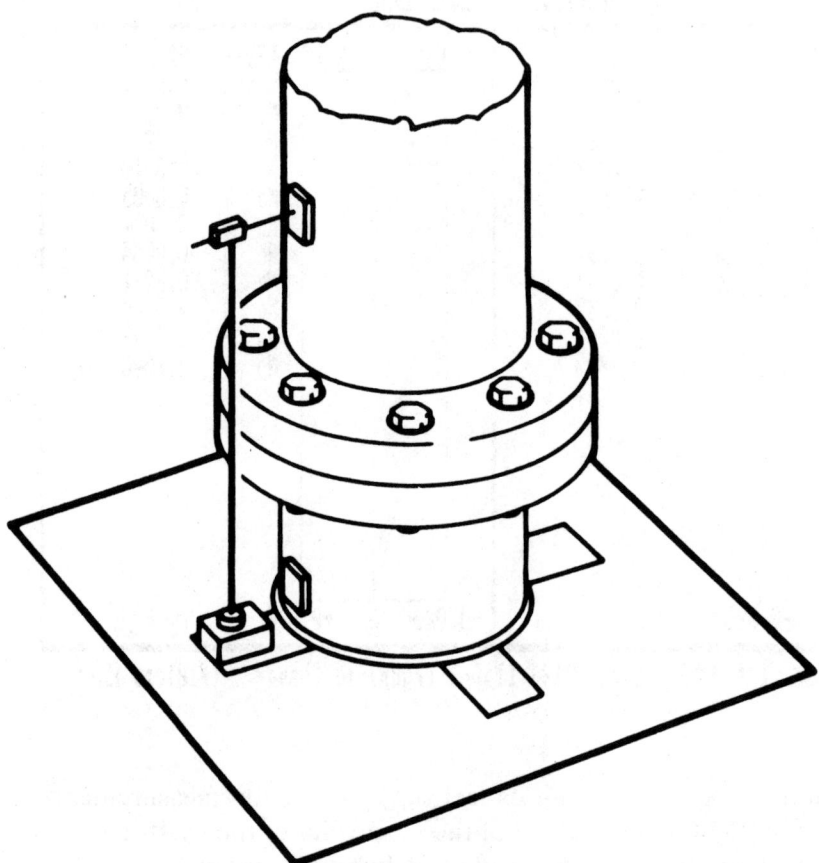

manner as in clocking a bore with a dial indicator. The true verticality of the shaft is then obtained. The process is slow, cumbersome, and can obtain many errors. Not the least of these is that every time the wire is tweaked with the measuring micrometer, it is moved, and the operator must wait until the weight has damped itself out again before taking another measurement.

When an alignment laser is used, the plumb beam is the primary reference. The laser is carefully leveled so that the beam is plumb on, say, the north side of the shaft. In this case, all measurements are taken on the north side before any other side. This is in contrast to the tight wire method where all four measurements at a given level are taken at one time. The laser is then moved progressively to the east, south, and west sides, and measurements at the different levels are repeated.

Note: The same side of the laser is always kept pointing toward the shaft. If this method is followed, and the instrument is carefully leveled each time, errors

Figure 6.35 Typical Printout from Vertical Shaft Alignment Process

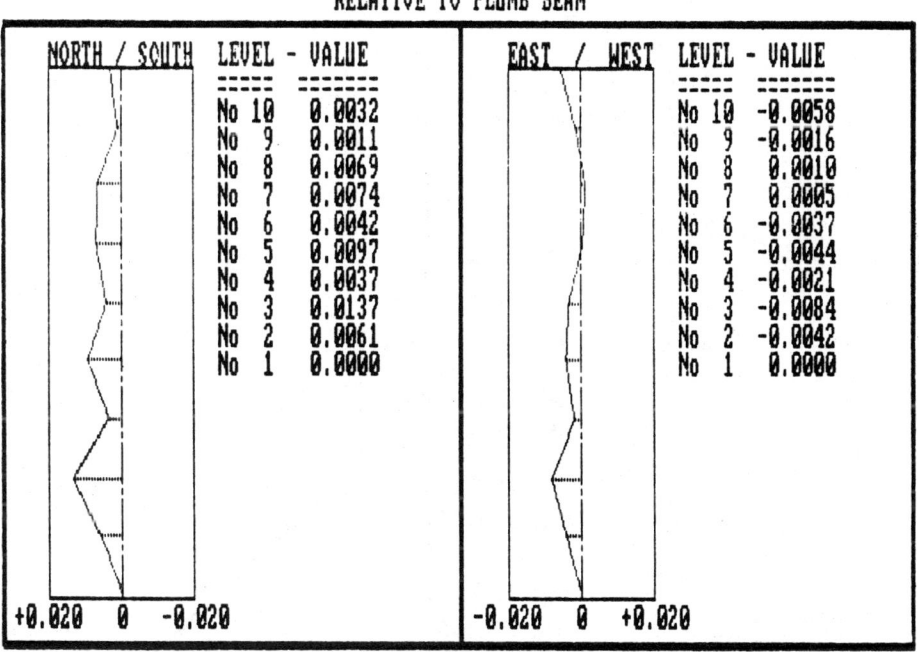

in the true plumbness of the beam cancel out, so that the measurement is, in fact, an extremely tight measurement of the verticality of the shaft. North/south readings are combined in the same way as in bore measurement and east/west readings are combined as a pair. The result is a very accurate measurement of the shaft verticality and the straightness of the shaft at the same time. A typical example of a printout from a computer is shown in figure 6.35.

Process Mill Roll Alignment

There are many types of process mills, such as printing press, steel and aluminum, film production, and textile mills. Many mills produce a high volume of some product. In all cases, it is necessary that the shafts or drums that carry the product through the mill must be made parallel to each other. The leveling of rolls can accomplish this parallelism easily. However, the horizontal parallelism of the rolls is difficult to achieve, especially using conventional optical systems. It is frequently fraught with many compound errors. In fact, over the years of making measurements with alignment lasers, most process mills are found to be

significantly out of parallel in the horizontal direction. In addition, the centerline of the rolls themselves may be significantly out of square with the supposed "centerline" of the entire mill.

A horizontal beam is passed down the side of the machine that is set to be approximately parallel to the centerline of the machine. The laser is then bent through a 90-degree angle, and a vertical plane is established. Experience has shown that rather than trying to pick up the centerline of the machine, it is far better to "buck-in" the laser plane to the surface of the *least movable* roll in the mill, and then proceed with the measurement. Generally speaking, in any of these mills there is one section of the machinery that cannot be moved. It is then sensible to align the movable parts of the machine to the unmovable part. In any event, this primary laser beam is set so that it is perpendicular to the unmovable roll on the machine and is set to level. The remote sweep optical square is then moved progressively down the primary beam and is set up again at intervals down the entire machine, reestablishing a plane perpendicular to the primary laser beam. Because the same prism is used in the same attitude, all of these vertical planes are parallel to one another. Targets placed horizontally from the edges of successive rolls can then measure the roll position relative to the series of parallel planes. The process is quick and quite accurate. Mills aligned with an alignment laser in this manner are found to produce a higher throughput with longer intervals between major maintenance requirements.

Transfer Line and Dial Machine Alignment

Transfer lines and dial machines are both high-volume production machines. Essentially, a transfer line is a collection of machine tools set up on a common line, where sequential operations are performed on a part passing down the line. An example is an engine block that starts as a raw casting on one end of the machine and emerges from the end as a complete engine block.

At each of the so-called stations, a single operation is performed. For example, at one station a hole may be drilled. At the next station a spot face may be done on the hole, and at the following station the hole might be tapped. The alignment of these transfer lines "station" is extremely important. If a tap is put in at an angle relative to a drilled hole, or the hole is out of position relative to where the tap will be, then the tap will break and the entire line must be shut down and the problem corrected. For this reason, spindle alignment lasers are significant.

A spindle laser mounts in the spindle of a machine and is used with conjunction with a target that is sensitive to pitch and yaw to determine the alignment of that spindle relative to a master part.

Note: A master part is machined very carefully to represent what the ideal final part should be.

This master part is positioned at the progressive stations down the line and is used as a reference to align each of the spindles to the same master part at each station. When this is accomplished with a laser system, great accuracy results and significant improvements in machine throughput are obtained.

Dual-Disk Grinder Application

In one recent application, a dual-disk grinder was realigned using a laser system. This grinder is two four-foot diameter disks separated by a fixed interval. They are tilted slightly relative to each other. A piston connecting rod is passed through the grinder, and it progressively grinds the thickness of the connecting rod as it passes through the system. Prior to using the laser, a typical dual-disk grinder might produce 75 to 100 parts before it is necessary to redress the wheels. In this process, the grinding disks themselves are resurfaced to make them flat. When the machine is properly aligned with a laser, it is typically able to produce about 15,000 to 20,000 parts before it is necessary to redress the wheels. This represents a significant improvement in productivity. The same equipment as is used in spindle alignment is used in this process.

Hydraulic Cylinder Machining Application

In another example, a transfer line for making hydraulic steering wheel parts was making a particular part that required three shifts to manufacture enough parts to meet production. A 60-percent reject rate was being suffered in the process. The customer was ready to purchase a new finishing machine, as he was constantly breaking his diamond tools and had to use carbide tools to secure any production from the machine. The problem, in the end, was severe misalignment of the course, or roughing, part of the machine, and when the entire machine was aligned, only one shift was required and the reject rate fell below 1 percent. This is a significant example of the savings that can be expected by the proper use of an alignment system.

Coupling Alignment

In the horizontal sense, the laser may be used to perform coupling alignment using a procedure similar to that described above for vertical shaft alignment. The primary difference is that a laser is mounted on one side of a coupling and the target is mounted on the other (see figure 6.36).

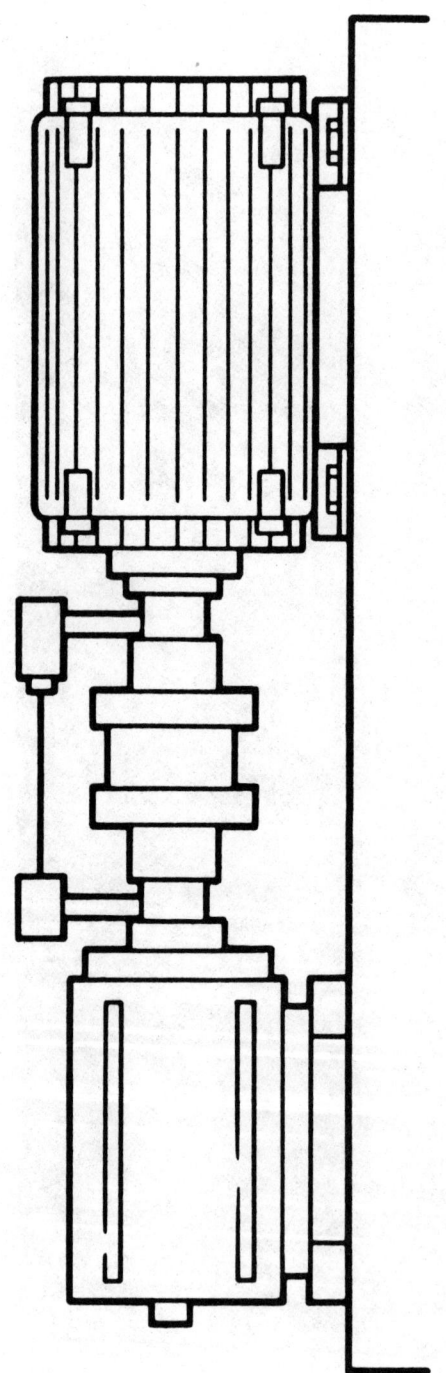

Figure 6.36 Coupling Alignment

Figure 6.37 Digital Height Gage Target

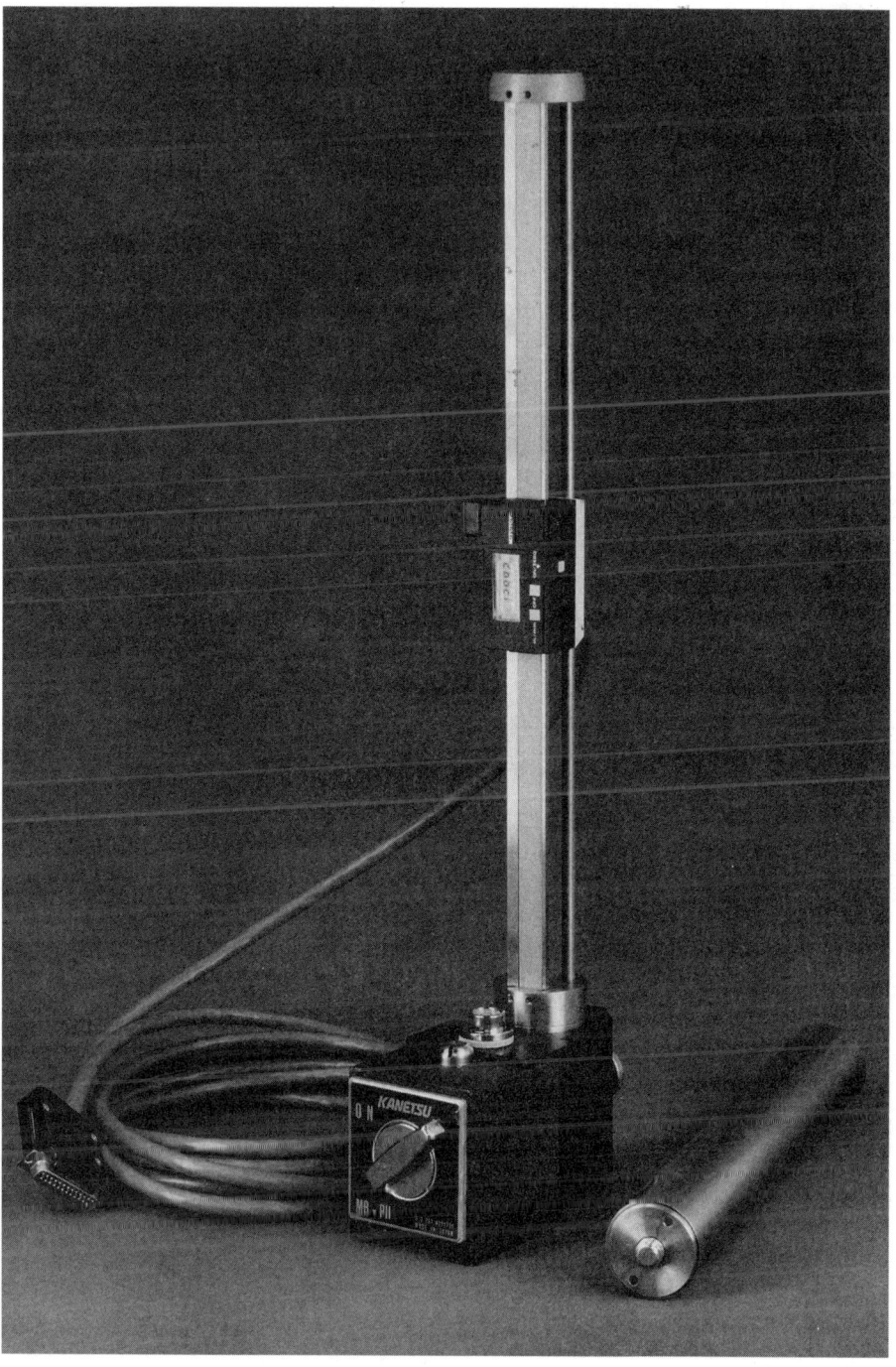

Two, three, or four sets of readings at 12, 6, 3, and 9 o'clock are taken to determine the misalignment of the two shafts. Using a computer allows automatic calculation of the shims necessary to align one part of the system to the other.

Measuring Offset Perpendicular to the Laser Plane

A final application involves the actual measurement of distance from a surface to the laser measuring plane. This is applied in a steel mill in a process of rebuilding the roll sections from a continuous caster. Figure 6.37 shows an example of the system used for this application. The result is a significant improvement in the accuracy with which the rolls are aligned. This accuracy is critical to the proper functioning of such a mill.

Summary

In this chapter, alignment using lasers has been discussed in detail. The basic principles have been given, including the many geometries possible with this exciting new technology. Comparisons for speed and accuracy have been made with optics and tight-wire methods of alignment. Comparisons and contrasts between interferometers and alignment lasers have been made.

The theory of penta prisms, used to sweep flat planes and right angles, the Normin bore measurement method, and several other alignment methods have been discussed. Data on accuracy-limiting air turbulence has been given, together with several error budgets.

Laser alignment is real, valuable to the end user, and proven in more than 25 years of application.

Chapter 7 Infrared Thermal Sensors*

Dr. Jonathan S. Shapiro

Introduction

Infrared sensors are used for noncontact measurement of surface temperatures. These sensors can probe inaccessible objects such as molten glass, iron in a rolling mill, textiles or paper in a dryer, or a tool bit in a plasma coater.

There are numerous other applications for infrared sensing, ranging from remote measurement of power transformer temperature or heat loss from a building, to the measurement of the heat balance of the Earth from outer space or the temperature profile of an integrated circuit.

In this chapter, the underlying principles of infrared temperature will be discussed, along with technical data that will help readers determine what infrared sensing technique is best for their needs.

Infrared radiation is generally considered to have a wavelength between 0.7 and 100 microns (see figure 7.1). The majority of infrared instruments built today operate somewhere between 0.7 and 14 microns.

Infrared Theory

In order to make the proper use of infrared temperature sensors, it is necessary to understand a few basic principles of physics.

---

* The author would like to thank Linda Armino and Celeste Sheppard of EDO/Barnes Engineering for their assistance with the illustrations in this chapter. I would also like to thank Mr. Robert Astheimer for his technical assistance and his permission to use material from his book, *Handbook of Infrared Measurements*.

Figure 7.1 The Location of the Infrared Region in the Electromagnetic Spectrum

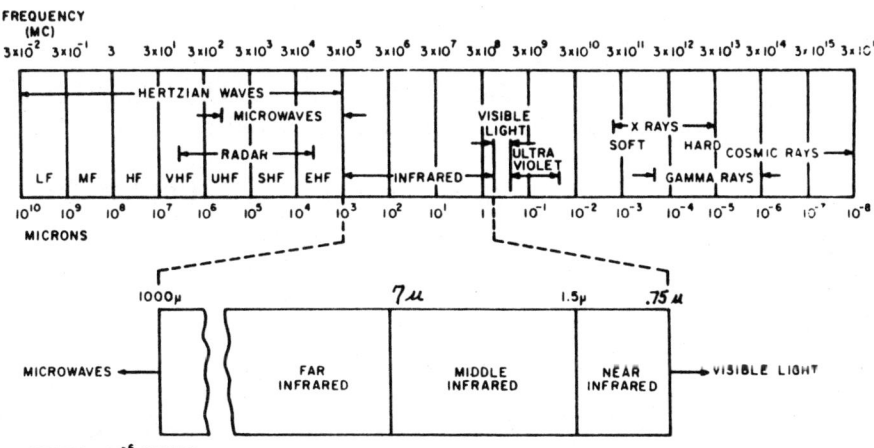

Energy Balance

All objects have thermal energy. There is a balance of energy between an object and its surroundings. Assuming that there is no internal source of energy, when radiant energy (light, for example) is incident on a surface, the energy may be reflected, transmitted, or absorbed. The sum of these coefficients must be 1:

$$t + r + a = 1 \qquad (7.1)$$

where t, r, and a are the transmittance, reflectance, and absorptance coefficients of the surface. (See figure 7.2.)

If a surface is opaque, such that there is no transmission of energy through the surface, the incident energy is equal to the absorbed energy plus the reflected energy. If there is no incident energy on the surface, the radiated energy must come from the internal energy of the object.

If the object neither reflects nor transmits energy, then $t = 0$ and $r = 0$, and $a = 1$. This defines a perfect *black body*. All energy incident on the object would be converted to a temperature rise, until equilibrium exists between incident energy and radiated energy.

A satellite in outer space, having no conduction losses to the atmosphere, is subject to this energy balance. The radiated and absorbed energy is equal to the incident energy:

$$Wr + Wa = Wi \qquad (7.2)$$

INFRARED THEORY

Figure 7.2 Energy Balance at a Surface

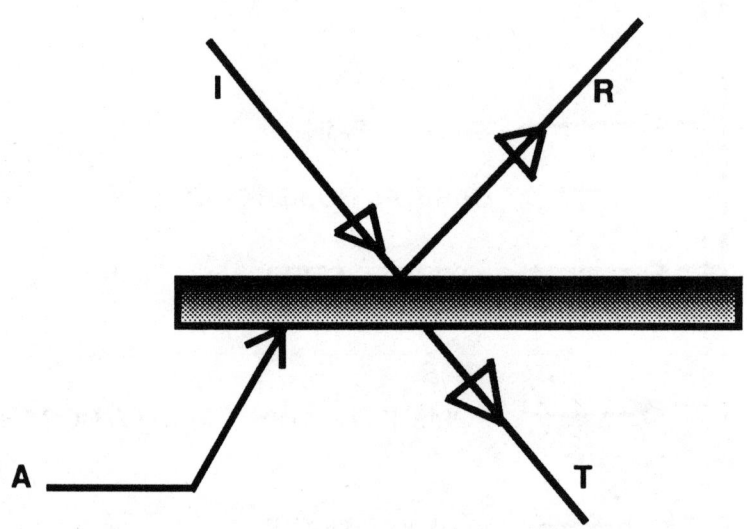

(I) INCIDENT ENERGY **(R) REFLECTED ENERGY**

(A) ABSORBED ENERGY **(T) TRANSMITTED ENERGY**

I = T + R + A

where Wr is the radiated energy, Wa is the absorbed energy and Wi is the incident energy. It is for this reason that extensive use of highly polished surfaces is made on the side facing the sun. If another side of the satellite is always facing away from the sun, it may be black, to radiate the energy to the cold space.

Emissivity is the ratio of the radiant emittance, W', of an object to the radiant emittance of a black body at the same temperature, W:

$$e = W'/W \qquad (7.3)$$

Figure 7.3 Emissivity Values for Various Common Materials

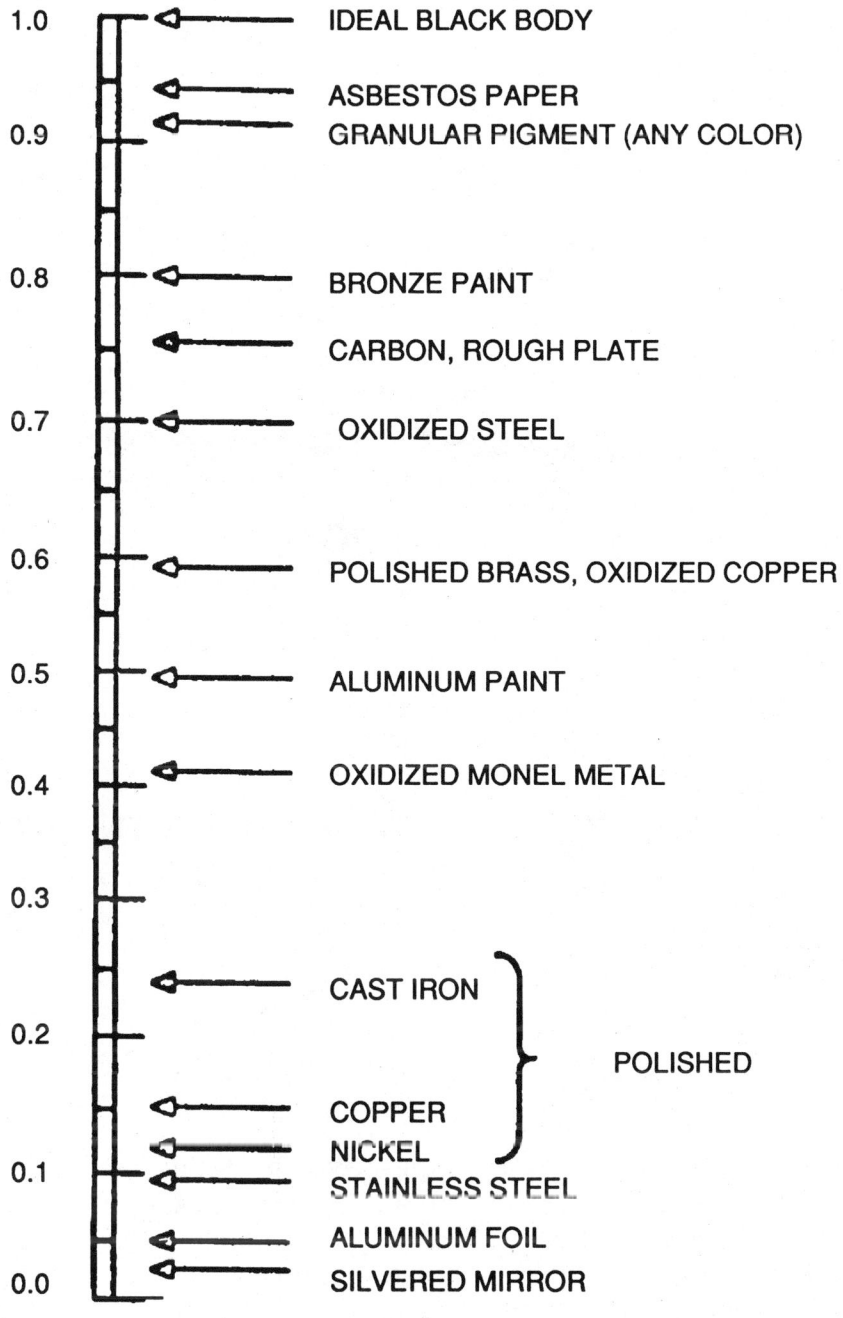

INFRARED THEORY

Emissivity may range from zero to unity. It may be shown that emissivity is equal to the absorbance at every wavelength. This is known as Kirchoff's Law:

$$a = e \tag{7.4}$$

Although a perfect black body has an emissivity of 1.00, and a gray body has emissivity that is less than 1 but that is constant as a function of wavelength, most real materials have an emissivity that is a function of wavelength and temperature. Figure 7.3 is a chart of the emissivity of various common materials in the infrared region. The big surprise is that paint, both white or black, has high infrared emissivity values. Certain black paints may have emissivities as high as 0.97 or 0.98, and white paints may range from 0.7 to 0.92. A material such as tungsten has a total emissivity ranging from 0.032 at 30°C to 0.334 at 3000°C. The emissivity of tungsten changes with wavelength.

The Stefan-Boltzmann Law

The total energy radiated by an object over all wavelengths is defined by the Stefan-Boltzmann Law:

$$W = e s T^4 \tag{7.5}$$

where e is the emissivity, s is the Stefan-Boltzmann constant (5.67×10^{-12} watts cm^{-2} K^{-4}), T is the absolute temperature in Kelvin (K = C + 273), and W is the radiant flux emitted per unit area, watt/cm².

Planck's Equation

Infrared temperature measurements are made in fairly narrow energy bands. Planck [5] calculated the energy that is radiated at any wavelength as follows:

$$W_\lambda = \frac{2\pi h c^2}{\lambda^5} \frac{1}{e^{ch/\lambda kT} - 1} \tag{7.6}$$

which is usually written as

$$W_\lambda = \frac{c_1}{\lambda^5} \frac{1}{e^{c_2/\lambda T} - 1} \tag{7.7}$$

where

W_λ = spectral radiant emittance, W cm^{-2} μ^{-1}
λ = wavelength, μ
h = Planck's constant = 6.626×10^{-34} W sec^2
T = absolute temperature, °K
c = velocity of light = 2.998×10^{10} cm sec^{-1}
c_1 = $2\pi h c^2$ = first radiation constant
    = 3.7415×10^4 W cm^{-2} μ^4
c_2 = ch/k = second radiation constant
    = 1.439×10^4 μ °K
k = Boltzmann's constant = 1.3805×10^{-23} W sec °K^{-1}

Figure 7.4 shows the spectral characteristics of black body radiation from objects at different temperatures. The rapid fall-off of energy from the peak, and the spectral shift of the peak to longer wavelengths, are additional reasons to be careful when selecting a sensor package for an application.

Wein's Displacement Law

The peak energy radiated shifts to shorter wavelengths as the temperature increases.

$$Lm = b/T \tag{7.8}$$

Where Lm is the wavelength of maximum radiation in microns, b is the Wein displacement constant 2897 microns K, and T is the temperature in Kelvin.

Infrared Sources

Infrared radiation is emitted from all objects. The quantity of this radiation is a function of the surface emissivity, the temperature, and the geometry of the object.

A flat object, such as a hot plate that is painted with flat black carbon-based paint, may have an emissivity of 0.97. Using a calibrated infrared pyrometer and a thermocouple thermometer, one could measure the actual surface temperature and the infrared temperature. By adjusting the emissivity control on the pyrometer until the two readings agree, one could measure the surface emissivity. The same argument would apply if the hot plate were half painted, and half bare

INFRARED THEORY

Figure 7.4 Spectral Characteristics of Blackbody Radiation from Objects at Different Temperatures

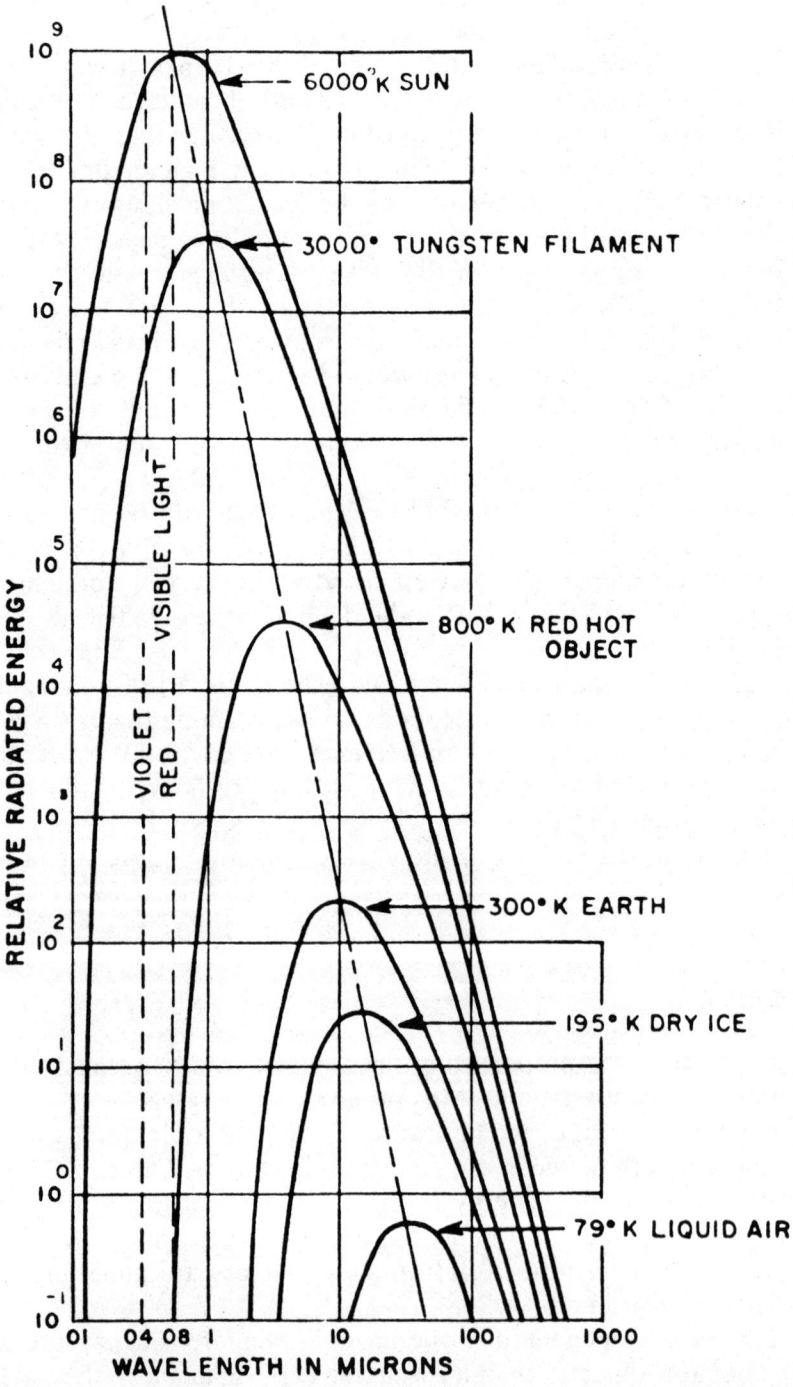

metal. The emissivity of the bare metal could be ascertained by first measuring the temperature of the painted surface with the pyrometer, and then measuring the bare surface. By using a table that converts temperature to radiance, the emissivity can be derived from the ratio of the radiance from the unknown surface to the radiance of a black body at the same temperature.

If the surface being measured has an emissivity of less than 1, it will reflect radiation from its surroundings. If the object is radiantly heated, or is located within an oven that has wall temperatures substantially greater than the object being measured, the pyrometer will indicate an erroneously high reading.

When the surface is more complex, such as a spherical, conical, or cylindrical cavity in which the walls are all at a constant temperature, the emissivity of the cavity is highly dependent on the ratio of the exit port surface area to the total surface area of the cavity. For example, a conical cavity that has a length of 6 units and a diameter of 2 units and that is made from a material with an emissivity of 0.1, which would appear to be reflective, would have an effective emissivity of 0.53. This is because of the multiple reflections of the energy within the cavity. For further details, refer to reference 3 in the "References" section at the end of this chapter.

If the surface is very rough, the emissivity of the object will be further increased. Gouffé's analysis concludes that for a given L/r, the cavity with the largest surface area has the highest effective emissivity, where L is the dimension of the major axis and r is the radius and D is the diameter of the radiating aperature. (See figure 7.5.)

The emissivity question is more than academic. The entire art of making accurate measurements with a pyrometer depends on ascertaining the emissivity of the surface, or in some instances the emissivity of the cavity [3]. Measurements made by viewing inside a furnace or cement kiln are heavily influenced by reflections from the walls or flames. Knowledge of the emissivity of the sample being measured is required, as well as the wall temperature of the surrounding cavity.

Material Properties

As was discussed earlier, three properties are associated with materials: emissivity (or absorptance), reflectivity, and transmission.

Infrared measurements are influenced not only by the material under test but also by the transmission path between the source and detector. Figure 7.6 illustrates the transmission of infrared energy through a 1,000-foot horizontal path through the atmosphere. The absorption bands shown are real, and unless there are mitigating reasons to the contrary, infrared pyrometers are generally designed to operate in the clear bands.

Long-wavelength pyrometers generally operate at 8–14 microns to capture the energy peaks of common objects: people, houses, cars, machinery. Short IR

INFRARED THEORY

Figure 7.5 The Effect of Geometry on Emissivity

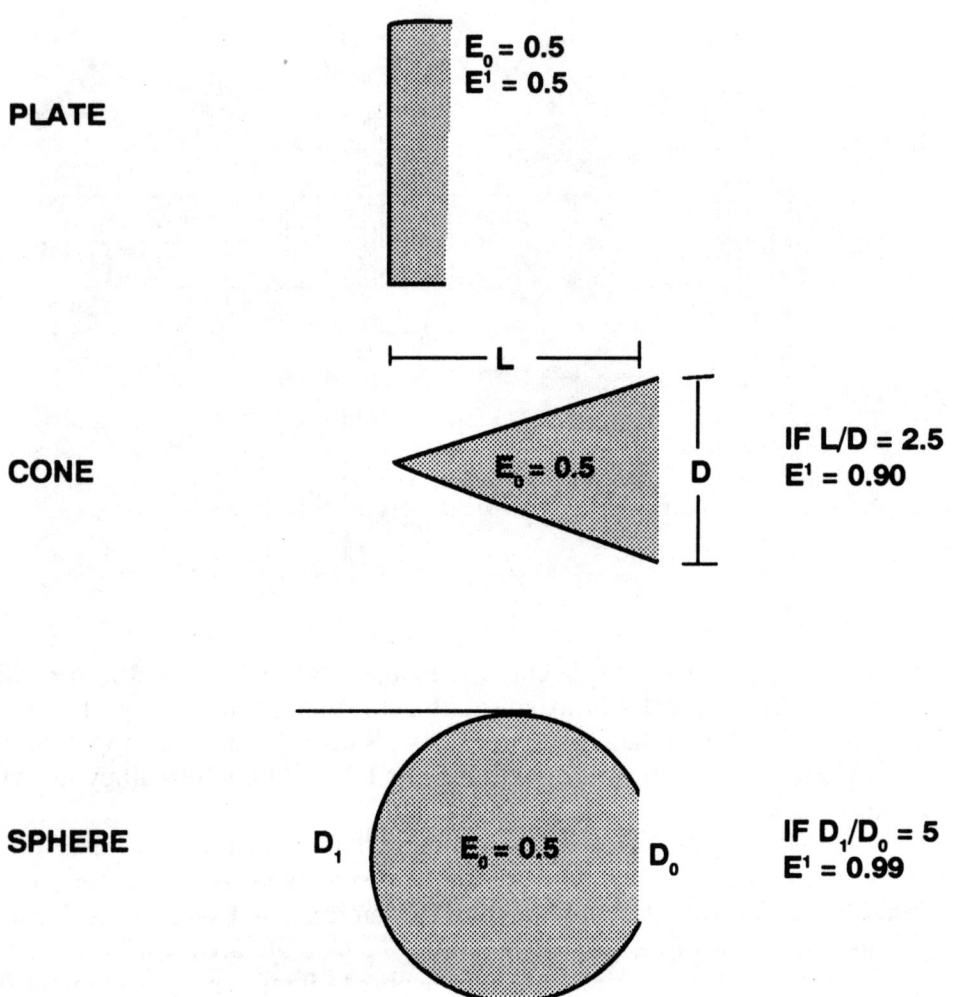

wavelengths, 0.7–1 microns, are used when measuring very hot objects such as blast furnaces, metal refining, silicon wafer diffusion, or other processes occurring above 600°C. Intermediate wavelengths are used for special applications.

Many plastic materials are transparent, both in the visible and infrared regions, yet it is possible to measure their temperatures accurately by using narrow hydrocarbon absorption bands. Figure 7.7 illustrates the transmission spectra of various plastic films. Polyethylene absorbs at 3.43 +/− .05 microns. Instruments are available that use narrow-band transmission filters to detect the emission from this band; such instruments are used in the printing and plastic processing industries.

Figure 7.6 Transmission of 1,000-foot Horizontal Path Through the Atmosphere

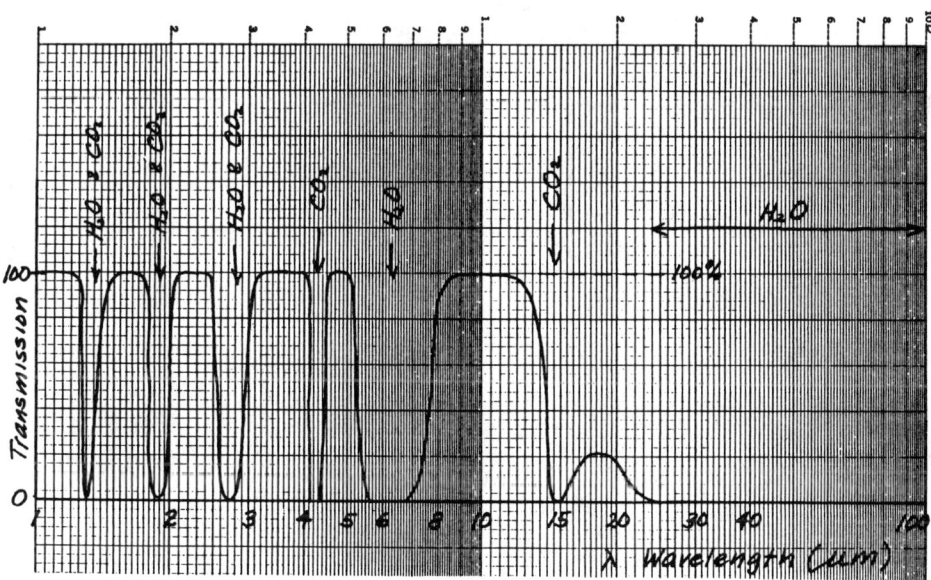

Measurement problems may occur if the object being measured is partially transparent. When a partially transparent object is viewed, the background may generate more signal than the object under test. Silicon wafers may appear to be visually opaque, but to infrared radiation from 1.2 to 10 microns, they are virtually transparent.

If the sample being measured is in a vacuum chamber or pressure vessel, it is necessary to specify the window properly. Borosilicate glass will cut off at 2.5 microns, fused silica will attenuate beyond 3.7 microns, and sapphire will transmit to 5 microns (figure 7.8). For longer wavelengths there are a variety of more exotic materials, such as calcium fluoride (usable to 9 microns), germanium (to 15 microns) and KRS-5 (to beyond 35 microns). Each material poses problems such as strength, cost, or toxicity. A number of infrared transmitting materials are toxic, such as arsenic trisulphide, zinc selenide, or thallium bromide-iodide (KRS-5).

These problems significantly influence the design of the infrared pyrometer. For this reason, it is necessary to define completely the environment in which a system will be placed.

Materials with a low emissivity generally have either a high reflectivity or a high transmittance. Errors may occur when radiance data is taken from these objects because of energy reflectances from other objects. Case in point: When using a device with a short wavelength (0.6–2 microns) outdoors in sunlight, many surfaces, such as cars, glass, people, etc., will read over 600°C. This is because of the influence of the background, the sun.

INFRARED DETECTION

Figure 7.7 Spectral Transmission Characteristics of Some Common Plastics

These materials have low emissivity in the regions where they transmit well and approximate black body emission in the regions of their bands of absorption.

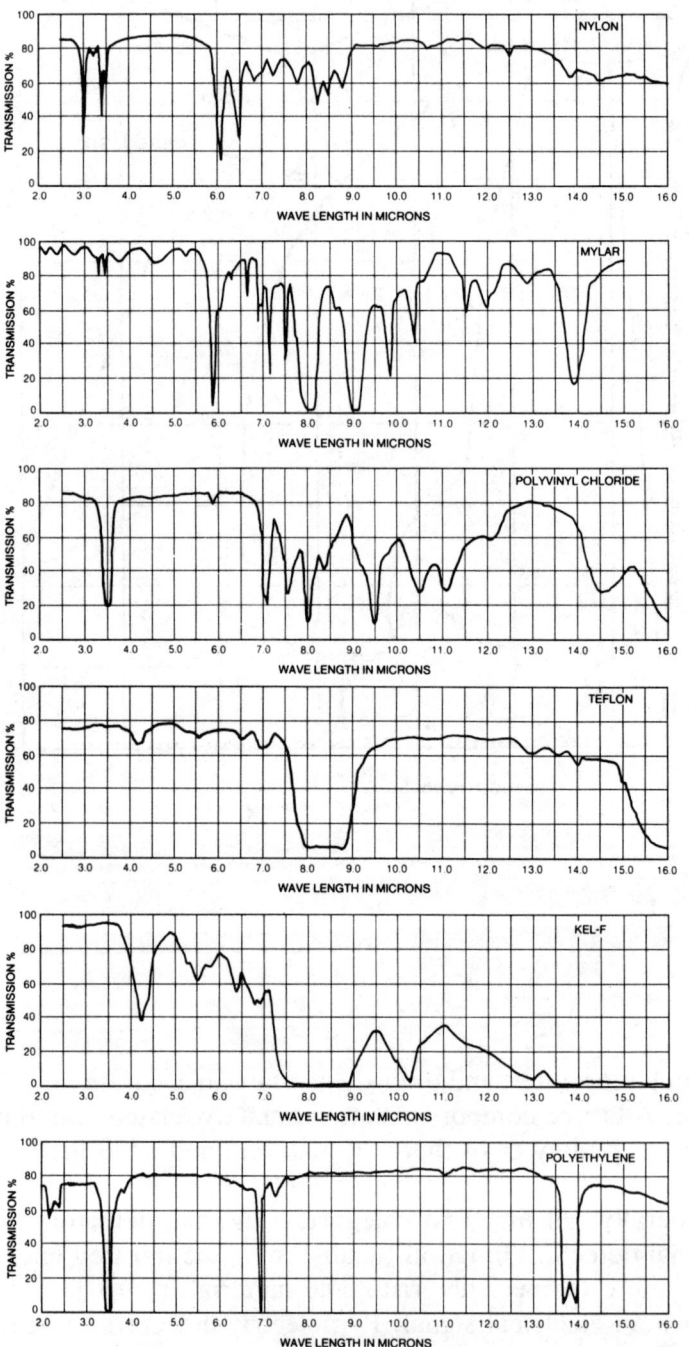

Figure 7.8 Transmission of Glass, Quartz, and Sapphire

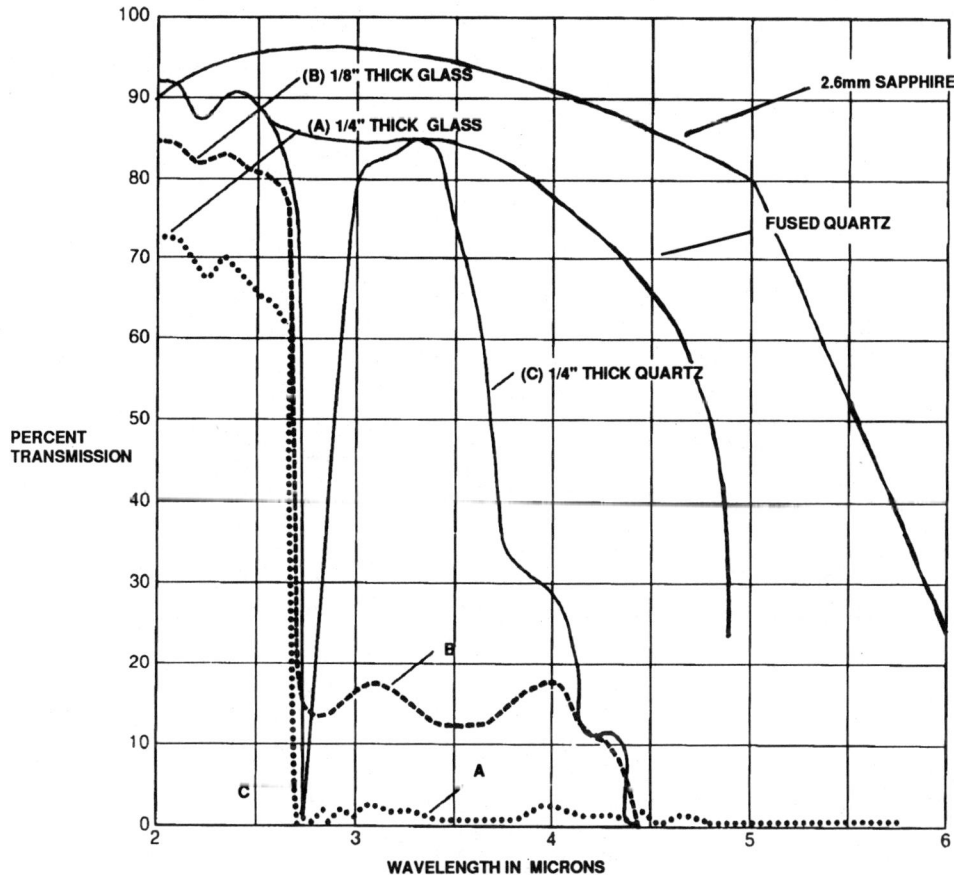

Infrared Detection

Introduction

The proper selection of detector, filter, and optics will allow an accurate infrared system to be constructed. All three components are intimately related, and their proper selection depends on a number of thermal, material, and environmental conditions.

Infrared detectors generally fall into two categories: thermal detectors and photon detectors. Thermal detectors function by absorbing the infrared energy and converting it to a minute temperature rise. The material from which the detector is made provides an electrical signal. Pyroelectric detectors, bolometers, and thermopiles are members of this class. Thermal detectors have a wide

spectral response. They usually have a limited bandwidth, with peak sensitivities up to 20 Hz. Pyroelectric detectors may operate substantially more quickly.

Photon detectors fall into two classes, photoconductive and photovoltaic. In either class, there is an interaction between the incoming photons and the electronic structure of the material, liberating electrons, and holes. Photon detectors usually have a narrow spectral response. Their operation is often greatly enhanced by cooling with liquid nitrogen.

Thermal and Photon Detectors

Thermistors (see figure 7.9) are heat-sensitive resistors that exhibit large changes of resistance with temperature. When radiation heats the thermistor flakes, a large change in resistance occurs. Thermistor bolometers usually have two elements in a bridge circuit. One thermistor receives radiation, and the other is blocked. The difference signal is due to incoming radiation. Thermistor bolometers are often used in satellite infrared systems.

Another popular thermal detector is a *pyroelectric detector* (figure 7.10). Made of a material such as lithium tantalate or TGS (triglycine sulphate), a rapid change in temperature causes the material to generate a surface charge spontaneously. A very high impedance (>10E13 ohms) FET amplifier is required to measure this charge. Once equilibrium is established, the output signal disappears. For this reason, pyroelectric detectors must be used with either a mechanical chopper or with a pulsed source, such as in laser detection applications. Pyroelectric detectors are also used as motion detectors in intrusion alarms.

Thermopile detectors are based on the Seebeck effect, which causes a voltage, dependent on temperature, to appear across a junction of dissimilar metals. Thermopile detectors are formed by the vacuum deposition of two metals onto an insulating film such as mylar. The greater the number of junctions, the greater

Figure 7.9 Basic Features of Thermistors

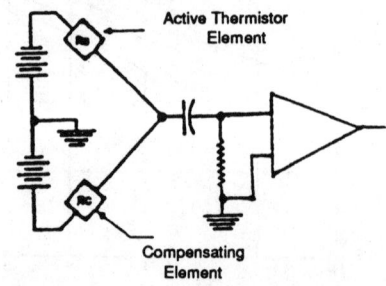

Figure 7.10   Basic Features of Pyroelectric Detectors

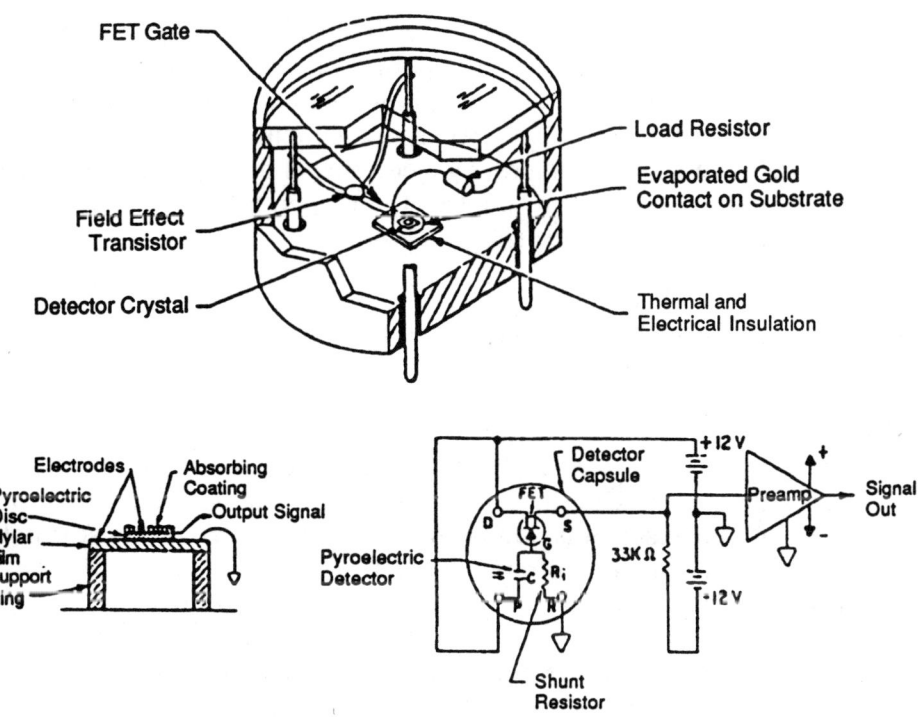

Figure 7.11   Spectral Sensitivities of Other Infrared Detectors in General Present-day Use

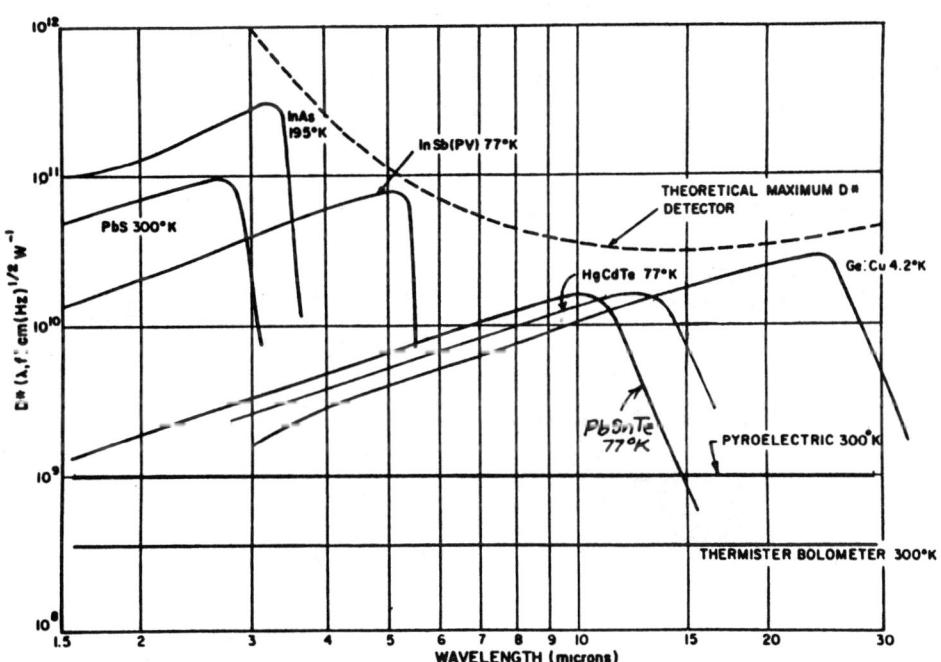

the output voltage. Within reason, thermopile detectors can track changes in ambient temperature without producing spurious signals. For this reason, they are commonly used in unchopped, DC radiometric systems. Figure 7.10 shows the spectral response of the most commonly used infrared detectors. Although the highest performance photon detectors offer two decades of performance improvement over thermal detectors, it comes at the price of cooling requirements, as well as product cost.

Another class of detectors includes *photon* or *quantum detectors*. These detectors directly convert the energy contained in the photons arriving from the target to raise electrons from nonconducting to conducting states. An electrical signal becomes directly available for further amplification. The outstanding characteristic of photon detectors is their high, but wavelength-dependent sensitivity compared to thermal detectors, as well as their much faster response times.

Silicon photodiodes, among the most efficient detectors, have a relatively low cost because of the advanced state of silicon technology, and they operate over a wide ambient temperature range. They may have a detectivity of 5×10^{12}, which approaches the theoretical limits of detectivity. They operate in the 0.7- to-1-micron band, making them useful only for measurements where the target temperature exceeds 600°C. They operate uncooled, which is an advantage for industrial applications.

Indium gallium arsenide phosphide offers the prospect of high detectivity as well as low leakage currents, a useful property for room temperature detectors in the 1-to-1.6-micron range.

Indium antimonide, indium arsenide, lead selenide, and lead sulphide are among the band-limited photon detectors available for either room-temperature or cooled applications. Mercury cadmium telluride is a very high performance detector material that is usually cryogenically cooled. HgCdTe is a class of material that can have its spectral characteristic altered by changing the proportion of mercury to cadmium.

Detector cooling may be obtained either by using liquid nitrogen at 77 K or by using a multistage thermoelectric cooler, which may attain 145 K.

Detector Parameters

Detectors are characterized by their detectivity or by their noise equivalent power, NEP. Detectivity, or D* (Dee star), is the predominant performance specification for a detector. It is defined as:

$$\text{D}^* = \frac{\sqrt{Ad\ \Delta f}}{NEP} \text{ cm Hz}^{0.5}/\text{watt} \qquad (7.9)$$

where Ad is the detector area in cm^2, and Δf is the bandwidth [1, 3].

D*, the detector preamplifier, and the optics ultimately determine the sensitivity of a given instrument. There are theoretical limits to D*.

Responsivity is another important characteristic. This determines the amount of amplification required, and hence the usefulness of the detector. A detector requiring exceptionally high amplification is not very useful, as the noise from the amplifier may be excessive and irreducible. Responsivity is usually expressed as volts/watt, or amperes/watt.

The Influence of Optics on Infrared Temperature Sensing

Optical systems for infrared systems fall into two classes: reflecting and refracting.

Reflective optics use front surface mirrors to collect and focus the IR radiation onto the detector. The IR characteristics are determined solely by the mirror coating. The optics will pass both visible and IR energy. It is generally difficult to seal a mirror system against the environment without placing a window in front of the mirror. A thin plastic film is used by some manufacturers of hand-held pyrometers as a window in order to protect the instrument. Reflective optics, also used in infrared microscopes, allow a wide variety of detectors and spectral filters to be used.

Figure 7.12 Composite Visible/Infrared Lens—Barnes CompuTherm 1X Objective

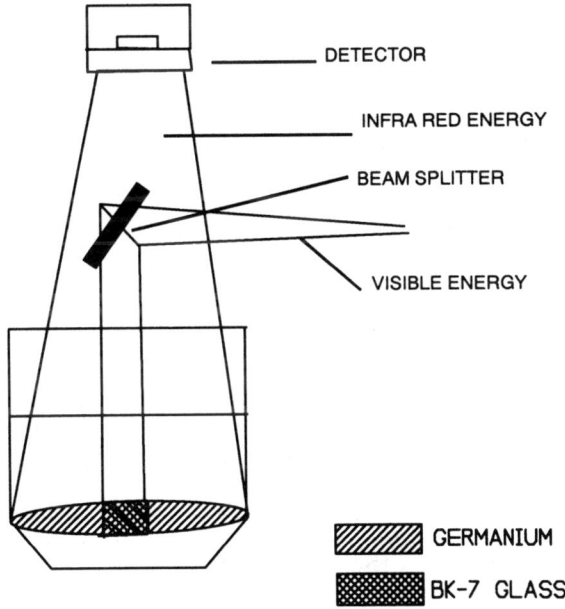

Refractive optics generally imply that one or more solid lenses are used to focus the target energy onto the detector. These lenses must be made from a material that transmits IR radiation in the spectral band of interest. Most lenses require an antireflection coating.

The various materials available for lenses include glass, quartz, sapphire, calcium fluoride, germanium and KRS-5, to name but a few. There are literally hundreds of glass types, with most exhibiting energy cutoff at 2.2 microns. Many IR transmitting compounds contain arsenic or selenium, which are toxic materials and must be carefully handled. Other long wavelength transmitting materials are salts, such as sodium chloride, which must be protected from moisture.

A high-quality radiometer must have optics that 1) collect the energy efficiently, and 2) focus that energy onto the detector. The field of view (F.O.V.) of the radiometer is defined by these elements. In many cases, as will be described later, the F.O.V. is critical for accurate measurements.

Optics pose a special problem when it is necessary to view the infrared target. Many infrared transmitting materials such as silicon and germanium do not transmit visible light. Materials that do transmit visible light have unique problems of their own. The index of diffraction of "light" is a function of wavelength. There can be a 10-percent shift in the index of refraction from 0.5 to 10 microns. This will cause a corresponding shift in the focal length of the lens, making it difficult to track the visible and IR focal planes over any extended change in distance.

One way to work around this problem is to build a composite lens. A composite lens may have a germanium annulus and a clear glass center section (figure 7.12).

The germanium element can be designed optimally for IR transmission. It may be antireflection-coated (AR-coated) for optimal transmission in the desired band. Uncoated germanium lenses reflect 50 percent of the incoming infrared radiation. The visible lens, being made from different material, may be ground to match the IR focal length at the design wavelength. The visible lens can be an achromat and can be AR-coated if necessary. A beam-splitting mirror (dichroic mirror) made from coated germanium can be used to separate the infrared and visible beams.

Energy Collection

The accuracy and stability of the measurement is dependent on the detector, lens, and amplifier. The greater the energy reaching the detector, the more stable the reading will be, unless the linear dynamic range of the detector is exceeded or significant heating of the detector element occurs. Greater energy means lower amplification, less noise contribution from the detector, and less overall drift. Depending on the temperature and wavelength, the energy reaching the detector can increase as T^n where $1 < n < 10$.

The total energy radiated by a black body is as follows:

$$N = K T^4 \tag{7.10}$$

In a narrow spectral band this may take the following form:

$$N' = aK T^n \tag{7.11}$$

where a and n are the best fit to the integral of Planck's Law:

$$N' = \int_{\lambda_1}^{\lambda_2} W_\lambda \, d_\lambda \tag{7.12}$$

where N' is the radiated energy between the two wavelengths (λ_1 and λ_2) and W_λ is Planck's spectral distribution.

Generally, at 8–14 microns, the exponent, n, is low (1–2). At 0.7 to 1 micron, the exponent is high ($n \sim 5$–10).

When viewing an extended target, the detector will receive energy equal to the following:

$$P = N A \Omega \tag{7.13}$$

where Ω is the solid angle subtended by the detector. For a circular detector:

$$\Omega = \pi \sin^2 (\Theta/2) \tag{7.14}$$

where Θ is the conical angle and N is the spectrally filtered radiance reaching the detector in the desired wavelength. (See figure 7.13.)

For the above equation to be satisfied, the source must fill the optical field of view. In a nonimaging system, the detector will receive a signal that is independent of distance (neglecting atmospheric absorption), as long as the subject fills the field of view of the optics. When targets smaller than the diameter of the lens are viewed, precise focusing is required.

Manufacturers often specify their instruments in terms of field of view (F.O.V.) ratio (figure 7.14). This is the ratio of the target diameter to the distance from the target to the lens, and it varies typically from 20:1 to 200:1, or more. The actual field of view will often be larger than the theoretical value because of internal reflectances and scattering. Manufacturers may specify the F.O.V. by measuring the field size that yields 95–99 percent of the energy of an infinitely large target.

The higher the field of view, the smaller the solid angle subtended. This reduces the collected energy. The energy collected is reduced by $1/(F.O.V.)^2$. Thus a 200:1 F.O.V. instrument will collect 1/64th the energy of a 25:1 instrument. Most instruments are energy limited at the lower limits of the useful temperature range. If a narrow field of view at a given temperature is needed, a longer wave-

INFRARED DETECTION

Figure 7.13 Calculation of Radiation Focused onto Detector

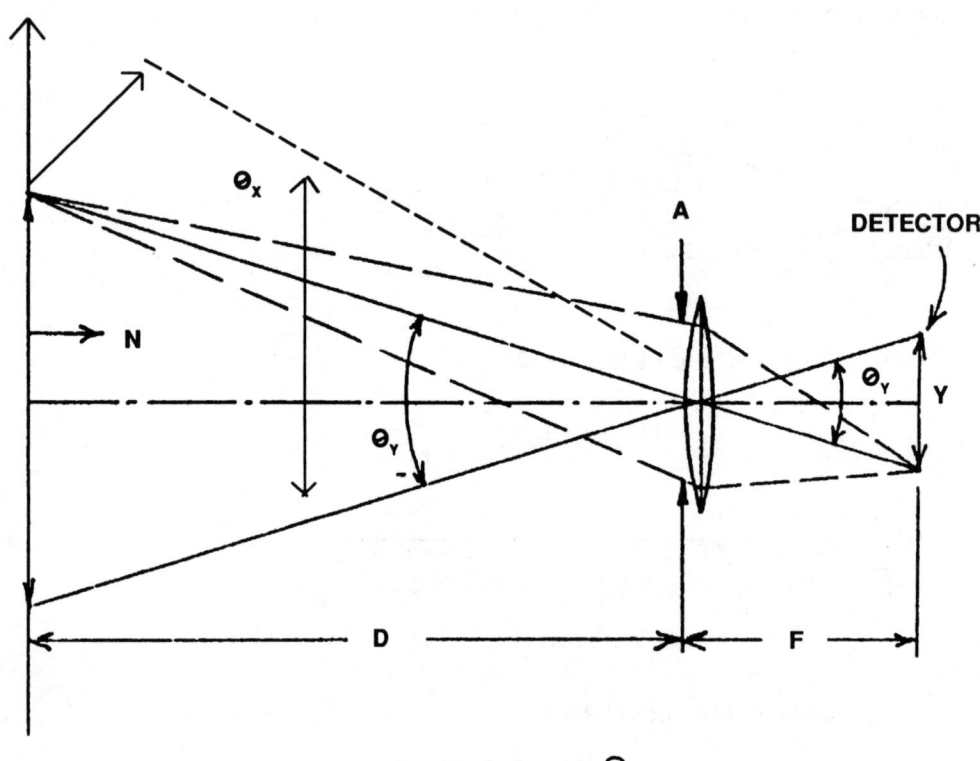

$$P = NA \, \Theta_x \Theta_y = NA \, \Omega$$

$$\text{IF } \Theta_x = \Theta_y \text{ THEN } \Omega = \pi \sin^2 \frac{\Theta}{2}$$

length may be required. There are, however, mitigating reasons to use a particular band. These are discussed in the later section called "Applications."

Band Pass Filters

Band pass filters are needed to limit the spectral response of an infrared instrument. Often, the long wavelength response of an instrument is limited by a sharp but temperature-dependent characteristic of the detector. The short wavelength response may extend to the visible. It may be desirable from a system viewpoint to stabilize the long wavelength cut-off and limit the short wavelength response. In most systems, little performance gain is achieved by having a short wavelength less than 50 percent of the long wavelength.

Infrared filters are usually multilayer thin films deposited on a germanium, silicon, sapphire, or glass substrate. Thin film filters can be designed for virtually any band pass and blocking characteristic.

Figure 7.14 Field of View of a Pyrometer

The target must be at least the diameter of the hatched area for accurate temperature measurement.

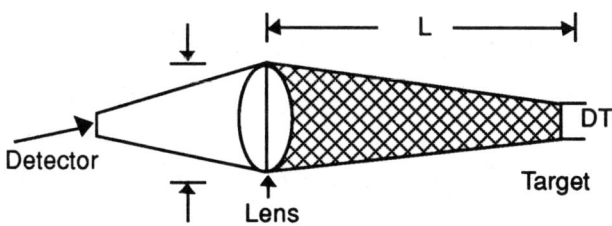

Case 1: Close Focus DT< DL

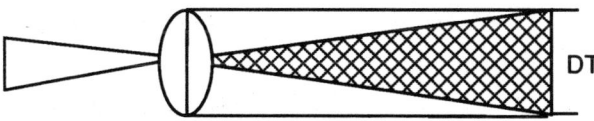

Case 2: Mid Focus DT=DL

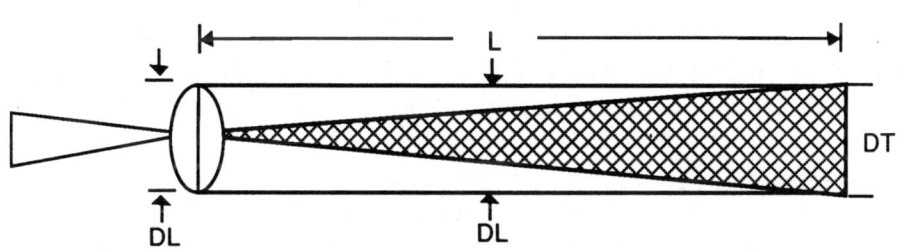

Case 3: Far Focus DT>DL

$$F.O.V. = \frac{L}{DT}$$

Figure 7.15 Typical Spectral Shift of a Photon Detector

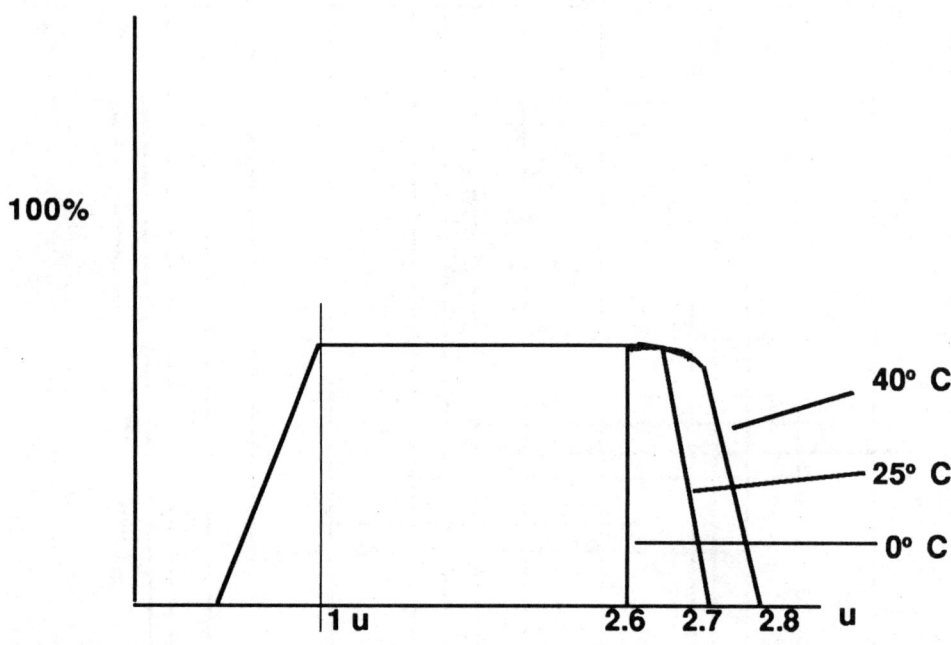

The absorption edge of photon detectors is a function of temperature. Long wavelength detection efficiency increases at higher ambient temperatures (as do noise and leakage effects). A band pass filter will limit the infrared response of a detector to a fixed band that is relatively insensitive to temperature changes. Responsivity is a function of temperature as well. (See figure 7.15.)

IR Component Selection

Figure 7.16 illustrates the spectral band pass of a number of commonly used room temperature detectors and the more common materials from which lenses, filters, and windows are made. Although there are many more materials, it would be safe to say that 95 percent of industrial applications are best served from this list.

Infrared Circuitry

An infrared temperature-sensing instrument must perform a number of basic electronic functions in order to indicate temperature. This section will discuss these operations and explain how an instrument is constructed from them. Figure 7.17 shows a diagram of a pyrometer.

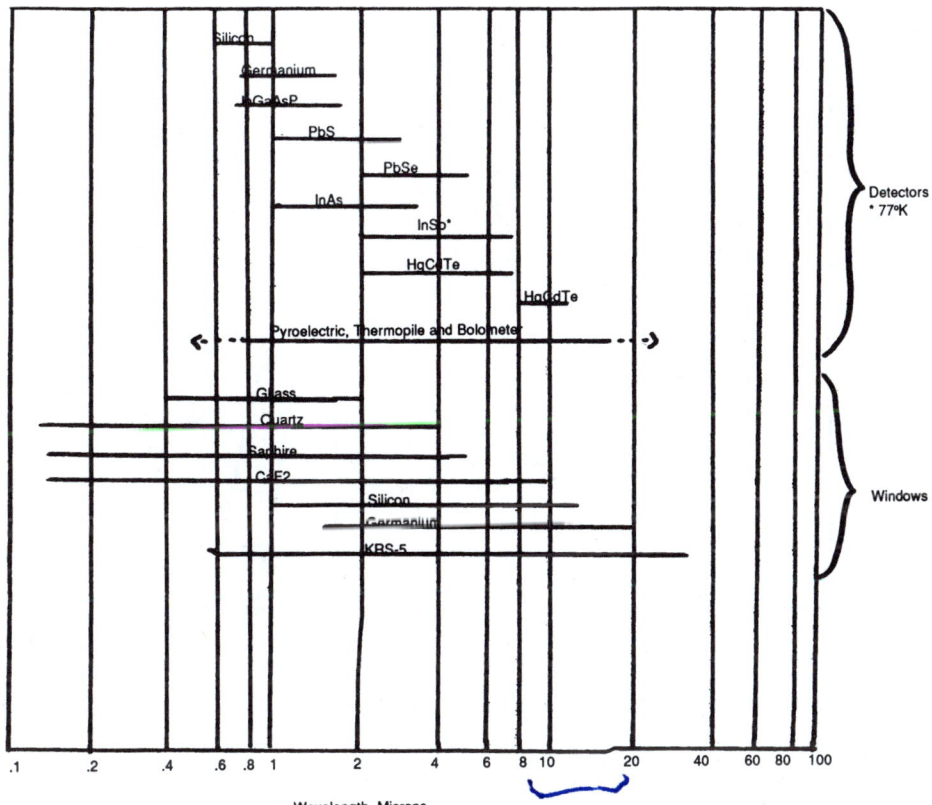

Figure 7.16 Useful Range of Infrared Detectors and Windows

The Preamplifier

The preamplifier is the single most important stage in an IR system. The electronic stability of the unit is determined here. In addition to detector noise, there is preamplifier noise. Mercury cadmium telluride, photoconductive lead sulphide, lead selenide, and thermistor bolometers require bias. The bias curcuit must be stable and noise-free.

Preamplifiers may be configured as voltage amplifiers for photoconductive, pyroelectric, or thermopile detectors, or as current amplifiers for pyroelectric detectors and junction photodiode detectors such as silicon, germanium, or InGaAsP.

The amplified signal is then processed by additional gain stages that compensate for the ambient temperature and the target emissivity.

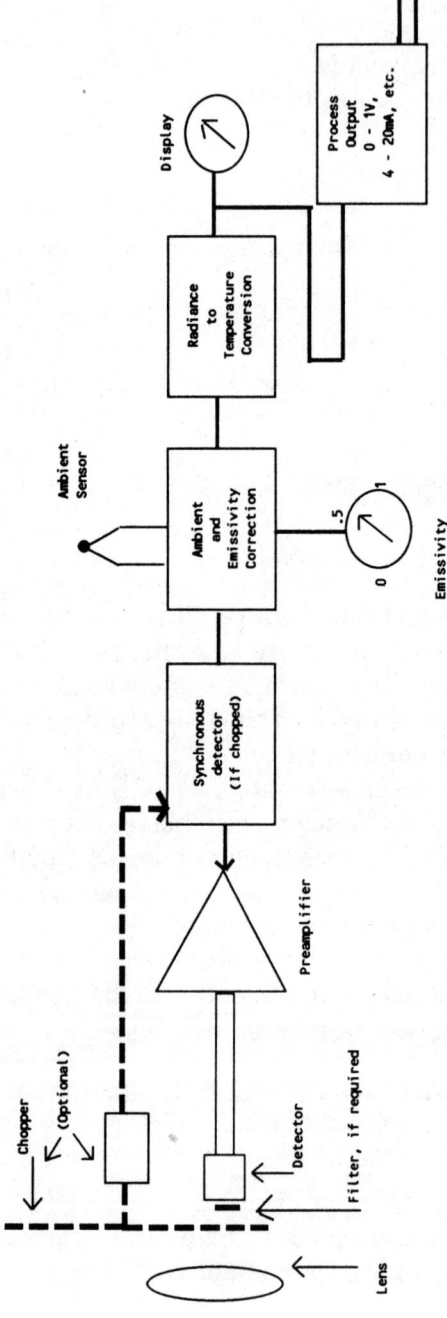

Figure 7.17 Block Diagram of Infrared Temperature Sensor

Synchronous Detection Circuits

The DC output of an infrared detector is usually a very small voltage or current that is the result of a number of stimuli, such as the following:

- The desired target radiation

- Undesired stimuli, such as radiation from inside the instrument or detector housing

- Bias current changes and noise

- Preamplifier offset current drift and noise

- Heating of a narrow band absorption filter

- Heating of the lens

An optomechanical chopper introduced in the light path between the detector and source will eliminate many of these problems by separating slowly varying signals, such as DC drift, from the target signal, which is modulated at a much higher frequency. If the chopper is placed between the lens and detector, as is usually the case, heating of the lens will not be canceled.

A chopper either may be a rotating wheel with a number of slots to pass and block the IR beam or it may be a tuning-fork type in which blades open and close in a narrow slit at a resonant frequency. The maximum chopping frequency is limited either by the frequency response of the detector, which may be 10Hz for a thermopile, or by the practical limit of motor speed and blade design, which is several kHz. The peak-to-peak amplitude of the AC detector signal is the difference in radiation between the clear and the opaque sections of the chopper.

A synchronous detector may be phased to operate in conjunction with the chopper position. A synchronous detection system not only eliminates many causes of DC drift but also improves the signal to noise (s/n) ratio of the system by as much as 3 db [3, p. 410].

The synchronous detector compares the data when the detector is open to the signal to the data when the detector is blocked. This difference signal is then low-pass-filtered to remove the chopping frequency component. The resultant signal is then processed to indicate radiance or temperature.

Emissivity and Ambient Compensation

When a target has an emissivity less than 1 and the emissivity of the target is known, the radiance signal may be compensated by increasing the gain of its amplifier by 1/emissivity. If the emissivity of the object was 0.5, the gain is dou-

bled; if the emissivity was 0.1, the gain is increased by 10. When the emissivity is low, not only is the signal strength increased, but the detector noise is amplified as well. In a DC coupled system such as an unchopped thermopile, detector and amplifier drift increases as well. For this reason, it is necessary to understand one's application fully when selecting equipment and reading data sheets.

To the emissivity-corrected signal, an ambient compensation signal adds the DC component that is removed by chopping, the background temperature. When high temperatures are measured at short wavelengths, the ambient energy content is small in comparison and is often neglected.

Radiance-to-Temperature Signal Processing

The radiant energy generated by an object, given its temperature, is governed by Planck's Law, which was discussed earlier. As the energy is a function of the spectral characteristics of the source, optics, and detectors, it is generally a nonlinear characteristic.

Early pyrometers or temperature sensors used an analog meter, and the meter scale was made to track the theoretical or measured temperature reading.

With the requirement for remote readout of temperature, several electronic means were derived for conversion of radiance to a linear voltage proportional to temperature. Various types of nonlinear circuits, including zener diode breakpoint circuits, logarithmic converters, and log ratio circuits, have been used. It is possible to create a best fit to the nonlinear radiance-versus-temperature relationship by assuming the following form:

$$P = k\, T^n \qquad (7.15)$$

This may work over a fairly large temperature range, depending on the wavelengths involved. A fit can generally be made for a power ratio of 1000:1, with 1-percent accuracy.

A third means for converting radiance to temperature would be through the use of a microprocessor. The data would be stored in memory, and conversion could be made via the use of look-up tables or by formula.

The output of the conversion circuit may be 0 to 1 volt, 1 millivolt per degree (C or F), or a current loop output. A microprocessor will operate a display and will control a digital-to-analog converter.

Current Loops

In order for a radiometer to be interfaced to commercial control systems, a current loop output of 4 to 20 milliamperes is often used. The current loop reduces the effect of induced noise. It interfaces to a number of commercial process controllers.

Some sensors are loop powered, meaning that 4 milliamperes or less is required to operate the basic instrument. The remainder of the current (4 to 20 milliamperes) is consumed as signal current, without affecting the device performance. These devices usually require a minimum supply voltage of 20 volts DC. Other sensors use a separate power supply for the instrument and provide a separate two-wire output. Current loop indicators may provide loop power, may be driven by loop power, or simply may provide conversion of the 4-to-20-mA signal to degrees C or F. It is important to match all components of a current loop in order to ensure compatibility.

Other Remote Output Formats

It is important to select the correct output format for your application. The 4-to-20-mA format is most popular for industrial applications because of its high noise immunity. It can be used in situations where the sensor is located several thousand feet from the data processor.

The 0-to-1-volt format, or one of a similar scale factor, may be supplied as an output linearized to the temperature scale, or it may be supplied as the nonlinear detector output.

Other common output options include 1 millivolt/degree (C or F), RS-422, or RS-232. Serial data formats are often used for data logging either directly to a printer, or to a computer.

IEEE-488 format is used for the remote control of instrumentation systems, as well as for data transfer. It is used in infrared microscopes and cameras for a digital transfer of data or image to a remote computer, but it is not used industrially because of the relatively short cable lengths allowed.

Temperature-sensing Products

A wide variety of equipment is available for noncontact temperature sensing. Although the mechanical configuration and packaging may vary widely, the optoelectronic configurations of the instruments have much in common.

Industrial Fixed-Location Sensors

Industrial infrared temperature sensors are designed as remote noncontact sensors. Their primary physical characteristic is their ruggedness. Most are environmentally sealed. Industrial environments pose numerous problems to infrared

sensors. Ambient temperature changes, dust, reflections, electrical noise, gas fumes, and obstructions in the optical path must all be taken into account.

The ambient temperature limits of a sensor must be observed strictly, not only because of gross electronic failure but also because of the limitations of infrared detectors. They are, in general, responsive to energy from any source, internal or external to the sensor assembly. Their sensitivity is also a function of ambient temperature. The transmission of germanium, which is widely used as an infrared lens, will also decrease with temperature.

Certain high-temperature sensors using silicon diode detectors may operate to 65°C with degradation. However, 40°C is a practical limit without cooling.

Reflections from adjacent hot surfaces and glare into the lens as well as reactive gases in the optical path may also cause erroneous readings. To minimize these problems, an open-ended sight tube with purge gas may be used. It is important that the optical configuration of the sensor be such that it is not sensing the walls of the sight tube, especially if the walls are hotter than the object being measured. Sight tubes allow the purge gas to keep the optical path between the source and lens free of the contaminating atmosphere. The sight tube also provides basic alignment of the sensor and subject. Additional IR transmitting windows may be placed within the sight tube assembly to further isolate the sensor from the subject.

Portable Instruments

The selection process for portable instruments is different. Such instruments generally provide a direct readout of temperature on a digital or analog indicator (figure 7.18). Sighting may be provided either by a separate sighting arrangement or by through-the-lens optics.

Coincident sighting through the sensing lens can provide improved registration and freedom from parallax. The majority of applications for portable units are general-purpose in nature, such as the measurement of machinery temperature, the sensing of roller temperatures, and the location of hot spots in insulation. These are best served by a long wavelength unit operating in the 8-to-14-micron band, where there is a minimum of atmospheric absorption and there is sufficient infrared energy being emitted from common objects. Such portable instruments may span a temperature range of -50 to $+1000$°C, or a subset thereof.

For higher temperatures, such as those normally encountered in metallurgical applications, short wavelength sensors are preferable. A 10-percent error in the emissivity setting will produce a 1-percent temperature error, whereas with a long wavelength unit (8–14-microns), a similar emissivity error will result in a 10-percent temperature error.

Portable instruments may also have recorder or printer outputs. Some versions may be equipped with registers for calculating min and max (peak and valley) and for averaging.

Figure 7.18 Typical Portable Infrared Temperature Sensor

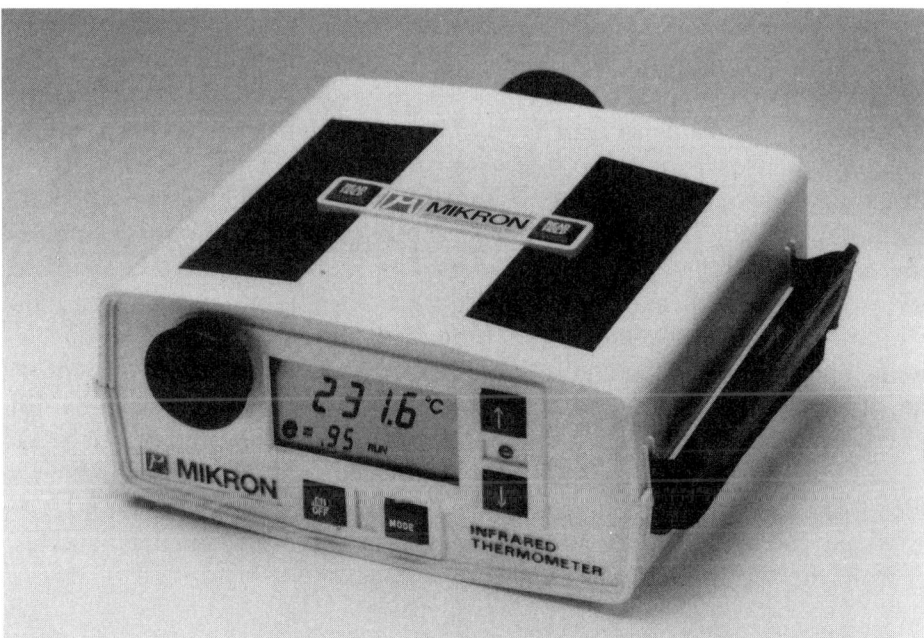

Two-color Temperature-sensing Systems

Two-color temperature sensing provides an excellent means of determining the temperature of an object without knowing its emissivity. It also can make a measurement system relatively immune to the effects of dust on the lens or contamination on a window.

The two-color principle works because the ratio of the radiance at two temperatures is a unique function of the temperature for a given spectral band. When two spectral bands are used, the ratio of the detected energy is a unique function of temperature. In order to convert this ratio to temperature, however, the detectors must receive a minimum signal level. At the lower temperature limit of an instrument, the accuracy may suffer when targets with low emissivity or systems with badly blocked optical paths are involved.

High-temperature two-color instruments may operate from 500° to 3000°C. These instruments typically use silicon detectors and sense at 0.8–0.9 and 0.9–1 micron.

Two-color instruments have been built, customized for specific applications, at various bands throughout the infrared spectrum. When wide variations in IR bands are utilized, spectral variations in emissivity will introduce material-

sensitive measurement errors. Low-noise detectors or high signal levels are required to prevent detector noise from being magnified by the two-color conversion process.

Non-gray-body materials—those materials with emissivity that varies as a function of wavelength—require special care. For example, the spectral emissivity of tungsten is a function of temperature and wavelength.

Fiber Optic Infrared Sensors

Fiber optics provide another class of noncontact sensors (see figure 7.19). They allow the sensing head to probe into confined areas. Measurement of the temperature of a jet engine turbine blade in operation would be possible only with a fiber optic sensor, as would measurement of the dynamic processes in an internal combustion engine. Measurement of plastic temperature in an injection molding machine can be done with fiber optics.

Fibers offer advantages over thermocouples. Glass and sapphire fibers are generally chemically inert; they are not subject to electromagnetic interference, and they are electrical insulators. They have been embedded into the windings of high-power electrical transformers to monitor core and winding temperatures.

Although thermocouples provide remote measurement of temperature in a process, they do not have the fast response time of an infrared fiber system. Thermocouples may take seconds to reach equilibrium with a dynamic process. Infrared fiber systems can respond in milliseconds, or microseconds when necessary.

When the ambient temperature is too hot to locate a sensor in the region, a fiber probe may solve the problem. The temperature of a PC board traveling through a wave solder machine could be monitored in this fashion.

Several types of fiber are available. When high temperatures are to be monitored, clad glass fiber can be used; these fibers transmit short wavelengths. Glass fibers in conjunction with a silicon photodiode will measure temperatures greater than 600°C. The fiber itself should not be overheated. Sapphire fibers may be used in environments as hot as 1800°C.

Fluoride glass, chalcoginide glass, or sapphire fibers will allow measurements to be made to temperatures as low as 35°C, when a suitably sensitive and low-noise detector is used. These fibers will transmit infrared radiation to 5 microns.

On the other hand, optical fibers may have a limited bending radius that is dependent on the fiber diameter and materials, as is the case with fluoride and chalcoginide fibers. Various fiber types also have temperature limits beyond which transmission losses increase or damage to the fiber occurs.

Passive infrared fiber optic temperature sensors are available in two basic types: 1) single wavelength radiometers and 2) two-color radiometers. As described earlier, two-color systems will eliminate the effects of emissivity and

Figure 7.19 EDO/Barnes RM2A Infrared Microscope with Fiber Optic Attachment

The RM2A infrared microscope can make spot temperature measures with 6-micron spatial resolution or can be coupled to a long-wavelength infrared fiber with the attachment shown.

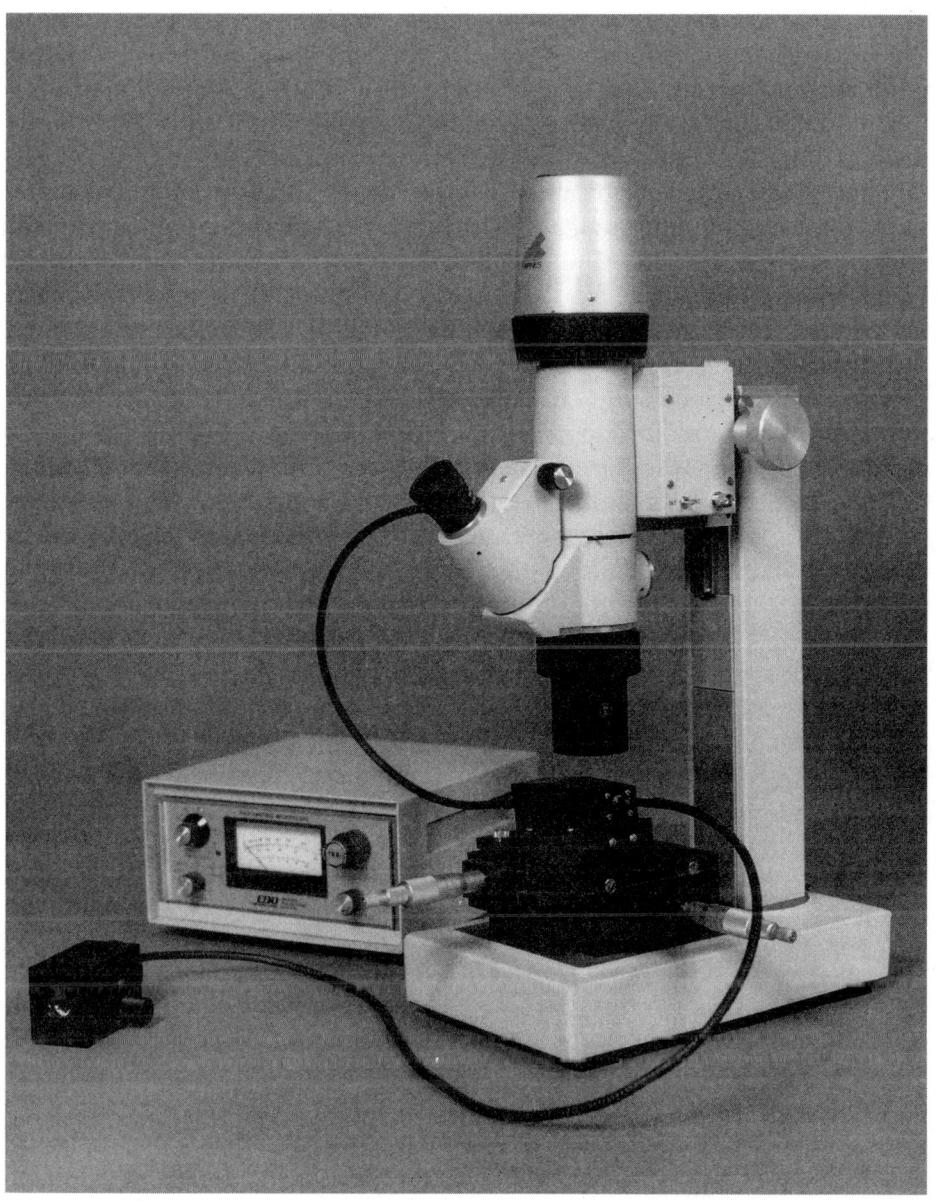

transmission variations. When used with fiber optics, a two-color system and a spectrally neutral fiber bundle become relatively immune to changes in transmission characteristics.

Infrared Microscopes and Imaging Systems

Infrared imaging instruments are divided broadly into two categories: cameras and microscopes. The distinction has as much to do with mechanical design and optics as it does with application software in a computer-controlled instrument.

Infrared cameras are generally designed to look in a horizontal plane. The more sensitive instruments are cryogenically cooled. Liquid nitrogen dewars, when required, are generally operated in one orientation. Stirling cycle cryogenic refrigeration units are available for applications in which the use of liquid nitrogen would be impractical. Infrared cameras generally provide emissivity compensation for the entire image. The optics are optimized for distances ranging from 0.5 meters to infinity. (At very long distances, errors will be introduced.) Close focusing attachments and right-angle mirrors are available to overlap some microscope functions. The cameras do not require through-the-lens sighting for alignment, as their field of view is quite large.

Infrared cameras may also be designed for mobility. Many of their applications are in the industrial troubleshooting or security areas. In these applications, visualization is more important than analysis.

Infrared microscopes (see figure 7.20) are generally designed to look down. They are provided with lenses optimized for magnification. The lenses are usually designed to be diffraction-limited for the infrared band in question. Through-the-lens sighting provides the means of centering the image on a desired feature.

Microscopes are commonly used in the design and test phase of integrated circuits, hybrid devices, and microwave components, where significant power levels may be reached and thermal design is a major consideration. The devices under examination may have a wide range of emissivity, and measurement of this parameter is essential to accurate temperature mapping.

Microscopes require special optics. Infrared microscopes can easily reach their diffraction limits at moderate magnification. The limiting resolution of a microscope when two point objects, separated by a distance Y, are viewed with incoherent illumination and a circular aperture is as follows:

$$Y = 0.61 \lambda/n \sin\theta \qquad (7.16)$$

where λ is the wavelength and $n \sin\theta$ is the numerical aperture of the objective. It is for this reason that microscopes generally operate in the 3-to-5-micron band.

Cameras and microscopes are available with either cooled indium antimonide detectors (2–5 microns) or cooled mercury cadmium telluride detectors (8–14

Figure 7.20 EDO/Barnes CompuTherm III Infrared Microscope

microns) with mirror scanning systems. One- and two-dimensional arrays of cooled indium antimonide or platinum silicide are also available. Arrays will allow real-time imaging at 30 frames per second. The detector may be cooled by liquid nitrogen, closed stirling cycle, or thermoelectric means. Thermoelectric coolers rarely reach 77 K, the temperature of liquid nitrogen.

Installation and Applications

Installation and Care of IR Systems

There are several fundamental problems associated with the use of infrared temperature sensors:

- Surface emissivity

- Optical path length and obstructions

- Background temperature and reflections

- Ambient and environmental limitations

Earlier in this chapter, the subject of emissivity was discussed from a theoretical viewpoint. From a practical standpoint, the emissivity of the target may change as it is being processed. For this reason, the choice of sensor may be dictated by the need to suppress emissivity variations. Using a sensor with as short a wavelength as possible will minimize the effect of emissivity on the temperature reading. If an object is 1000°C, for example, and measurements were made with a long-wavelength, 8-to-14-micron unit, an emissivity error of 10 percent would result in approximately a 10-percent temperature error. If the measurements were made at 0.8 to 1 micron, the same 10-percent emissivity error would produce a 1-percent temperature error. One must be careful in extrapolating from this example. There *is* a lower useful temperature limit for each detector type and spectral range.

The *optical path* can influence a reading significantly. If there are significant concentrations of water vapor, carbon dioxide, or hydrocarbons, certain spectral bands will be adversely affected. For this reason, many long-range IR systems operate at 8 to 14 microns.

Smoke and dust will absorb and reradiate energy. Dust will also obscure a lens. In some systems, it is necessary to focus on a position other than the target in order to avoid an interfering structure, such as a heating element or baffle (figure 7.21).

If the object being measured is inside an enclosed chamber, such as a vacuum system, a window must be provided that transmits in the band of interest. Unless an exotic window, such as KRS-5 or lead selenide, is used, shorter wavelengths should be considered. It is important to know the minimum useful temperature in a process control system, or needless expense may be incurred. Short wavelength windows cost less, are generally stronger, and can withstand temperature and other environmental abuse. Conversely, an IR system may be purchased to operate within the window's spectral transmission characteristics. The spectral

Figure 7.21 Typical Field-of-View Problem

Adjust focal point so as to miss obstructions.

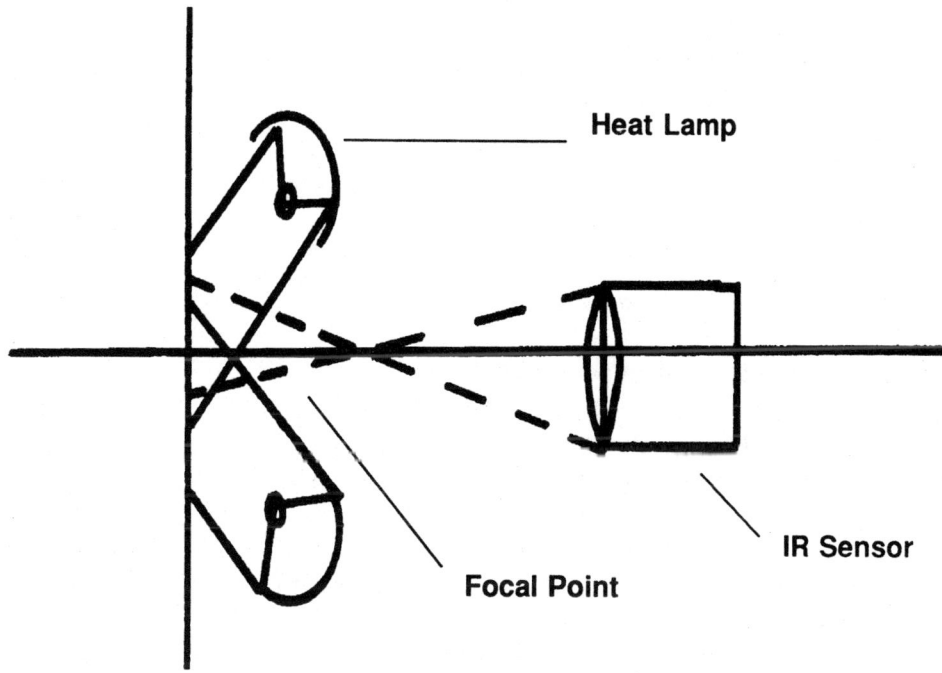

characteristics of the window will help set the minimum detectable temperature, along with tne design of the radiometer.

From the information in table 7.1, it is easy to see the progression of lowest usable temperature as the detection wavelength increases. Most applications at or near room temperature are best served by a long wavelength sensor, as long as the material has a high emissivity or one that is known.

Reflections

When the material has a low emissivity, the signal reaching the detector is a composite of radiation from the surface of the material and the reflection of the ambient radiation (see figure 7.2). In room light or sunlight, an instrument running on short wavelengths, in the 0.8-to-2-micron bands, will respond to this light. A cold metallic surface may indicate 300°C in tungsten light indoors. A cold car may indicate 650°C outdoors on a sunny day. When the material has a high emissivity, it absorbs incoming radiation, and the emitted energy is truly that of its surface temperature.

Table 7.1 Selection of Room Temperature Infrared Windows

Wavelength (Microns)	Application	Window Type	Minimum Source Temp (Est.)
.8–1	High temp metals	Glass	500
1–1.8	Medium/high temp metals	Glass	250
2–2.6	Metals, plasma	Quartz	80
3.43 N*	Plastic films	Quartz	100
4.5 N*	Flame temperature	CaF2, sapphire	250
4.8–5.2	Glass blowing	CaF2, sapphire	50
7.9 N*	Plastic films	CaF2, Ge	0
7–10	Various	CaF2, Ge	0
8–14	Low temp, food, textiles, distance	Germanium KRS-5	−50

*(N = Narrow band filter, typically 5-percent bandwidth)

Flames and radiant heaters in a process can also introduce errors. Some systems can compensate for this background energy.

In extreme conditions, it may be necessary to monitor the temperature of the workpiece and the background environment in order to eliminate the effects of these reflections.

Ambient Considerations

Uncooled infrared photon detectors suffer from degradation of performance when operated above 30°–40°C. This degradation may take the form of increased dark current, reduction in sensitivity, or change in spectral response. Long wavelength responsivity of photon detectors actually increases with temperature. Compensating circuitry is usually employed to reduce these effects, but it is necessary to adhere strictly to the manufacturer's operating and storage temperature specifications. Permanently mounted industrial sensors can function in hot environments if a water-cooled housing for the sensor is used.

Rapid changes in ambient temperature will result in a temporary increase in measurement error. This error may persist until the internal temperature of the sensor has reached equilibrium.

Pyroelectric detectors have a Curie temperature (Tc), beyond which they will cease to function and will lose the polling voltage. Lithium tantalate has a Tc of 618°C, DTGS (deuterated triglycine sulphate) has a Tc of 61°C, and TGS has a Tc of 49°C. Circuits using TGS and DTGS employ a polling circuit that will allow

the detector to recover, should its ambient temperature exceed its Curie point. A form of DTGS, DLaTGS, which is lanthanum doped, is permanently polled and will recover once it has cooled below its Curie temperature.

Other Environmental Considerations

Temperature, humidity, and dust all can cause problems with most measurement systems, including infrared. When a system is operating with a cooling jacket, excess cooling may cause condensation on the outer surface of the lenses or windows.

Dust may settle on the lens. Air purge assemblies are available to prevent dust from settling on the lens.

Figure 7.22 shows an infrared temperature sensor mounted in a cooling jacket and supplied with an air purge assembly and cooling coil for lens mount.

If significant concentrations of reactive gases exist in the path between the sensor and target, there may be attenuation of the IR signal. In this case, a sight tube and air purge can be used to reduce the amount of contaminated air in the sight path.

Sight tubes are also used to provide a thermal break between a hot target, such as a furnace, and the sensor. The sight tube keeps the sensor path clear, prevents anything from breaking the path, provides an alignment means, and sets the distance of the sensor from the furnace. Figure 7.23 illustrates how a sight tube can isolate the optical path from external disturbances.

Closed-end ceramic sight tubes may be inserted and sealed into a hot gas or liquid stream. The IR sensor measures the end of the hot tube, yet is not subject to thermal breakdown problems as might occur with thermocouples. The pyrometer measures the average temperature of the end of the sight tube, which is in equilibrium with the gas or fluid stream. The energy is averaged over the end cross-section of the sight tube.

Applications and Instrument Selection

Table 7.2 lists commonly used infrared detection bands. The trade-offs of short-wave and long-wave radiometers were already discussed. The reasons for choosing a specific instrument for several applications will now be discussed.

IR cameras are used to locate defects in circuit boards. By comparing the IR signatures of good and bad boards 30 seconds after power-up, defects can be found [6]. Shorts in power supply runs, electrolytic capacitors with reversed polarity, and shorted ICs will all produce a characteristic signature. CMOS ICs generally have a very low temperature rise, unless they have an internal short.

IR microscopes are used extensively both in the design and in the failure analysis of microelectronic circuits. They may be used to locate defects in wafers, if used with a probe station, or in open IC packages. With emissivity correction

Figure 7.22 Infrared Temperature Sensor Mounted in Cooling Jacket

Air purge assembly and cooling coil for lens mount is also illustrated.

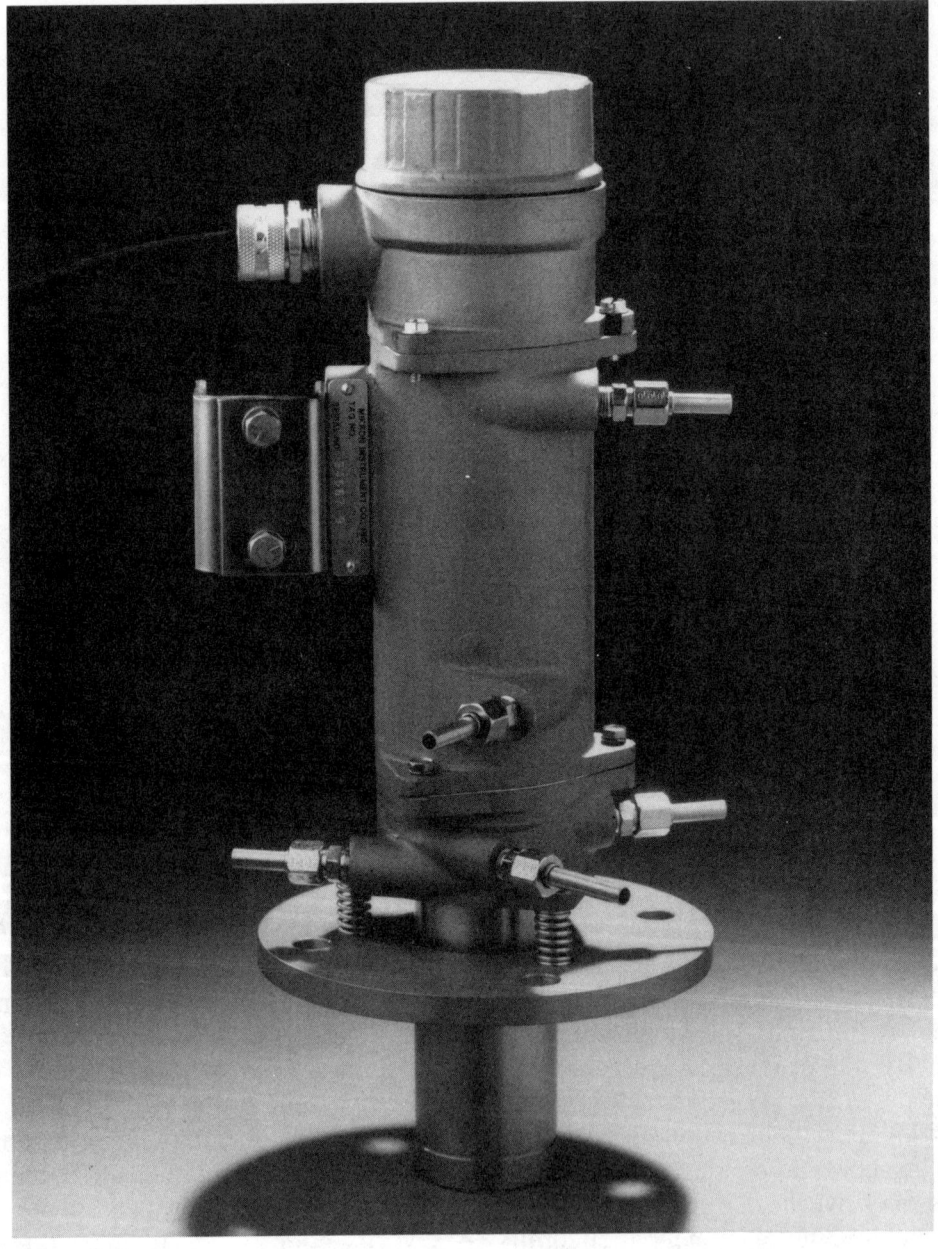

Figure 7.23 Application of Sight Tube

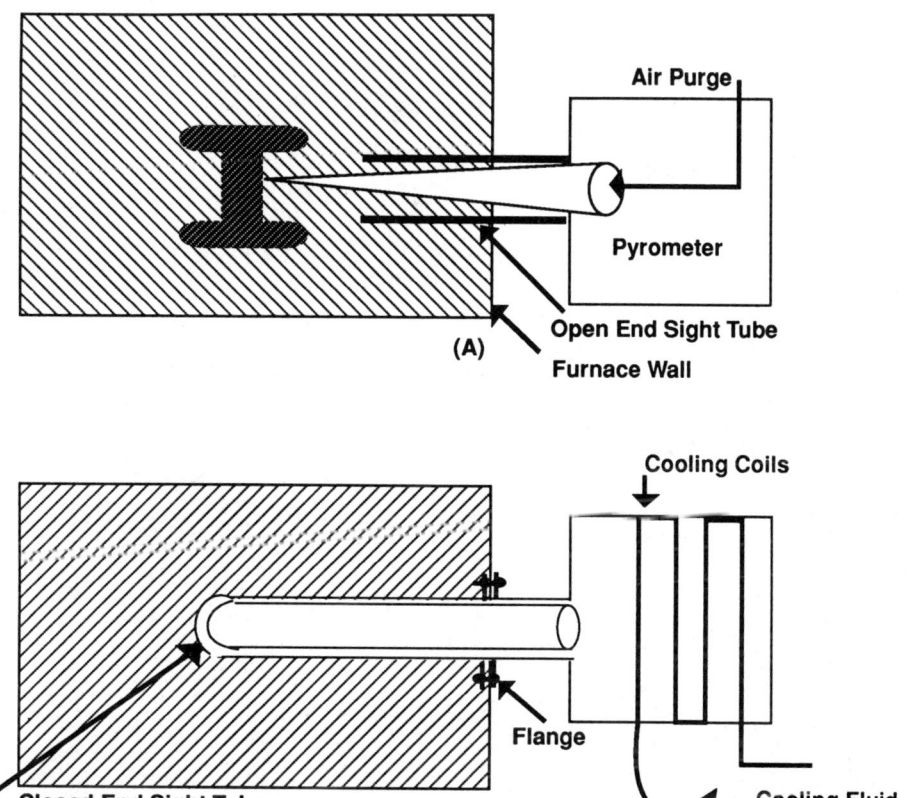

software, the microscope shown in figure 7.20, shown earlier, is capable of resolving temperature differences as small as 0.1°C in various portions of an IC. Isothermal measurements are made at two temperatures with the power off. Data collected at two temperatures can be analyzed, and the emissivity can be computed. A third measurement will eliminate any background reflections from the data. By this process, measurements with temperature differences of 0.1°C can be made without regard for the original emissivity profile of the IC [6].

MIL STD-2194(SH) requires that electrical and mechanical components on a ship be surveyed regularly to find abnormalities. Electrical contacts and connections may overheat if loosened by vibration or corrosion. Motors and bearings may be running at or near their limits. A severity code of one to four stars is assigned to each measurement (see table 7.3).

In a similar fashion, electric utility companies use a long-wavelength (8–14-micron) IR sensor to measure the temperature of pole-mounted power transformers and switches. Special IR thermometers with large-diameter, long-

Table 7.2 Typical Infrared Bands for Temperature Measurement[1]

Application	Temperature Range[2] Low	High	Wavelength[3]
Long-distance, low temperatures. Textiles, food.	−50	[4]1000	8–14
Low temperature. See through calcium fluoride window.	0	2000	7–10
Thin plastic film: polyester.	0	2000	7.9 (5% BW)
Thin plastic film: polyethylene, polystyrene, also quartz window.	65	2000	3.43 (5% BW)
Glass surface.	50	2500	4.8–5.2
See through flames.	250	2200	4.5 (5% BW)
High temperatures: metal foundaries.	500	3000	0.78–1.06
Medium to high temperatures: ferrous/nonferrous metals. See through glass.	2200	3000	0.9–1.8

[1] Data extracted from Mikron M210S data sheet
[2] In degrees centigrade.
[3] In microns.
[4] The high low temperature limits are not necessarily available on a single instrument.

focal-length reflective optics are available to maintain a small region of interest at long distances and yet provide adequate energy collection.

Another application might be the measurement of the temperature of a thin plastic film such as polyethylene. This might be in a printing or coating application. Many plastics have a strong absorption band at 3.43 microns because of the hydrocarbon bonds. At a thickness of 1–2 mils, this material has a very high absorption coefficient, and hence, a very high emissivity at this wavelength with a 1-percent bandwidth. An instrument with a 3.43-micron narrow band filter and a suitably sensitive detector would suffice. An instrument with a 7.9-micron narrow band response should be considered as well.

A jet engine or other flame source would have a very high emittance from hot carbon monoxide at 4.5 to 4.8 microns. Atmospheric CO_2 has its major absorption band at 4.3 microns, but hot CO_2 emission is spectrally shifted [7, pp. 2–76]. An instrument with a narrow band pass at 4.5 microns could be used to measure flame or exhaust temperature.

When annealing or blowing glass, accurate temperature measurements are required. The glass is often in a flame. The problem: measure the glass temperature, not the flame. Glass and quartz are both opaque at 4.8 microns. This is also beyond the shifted CO_2 absorption band (4.5 microns) of combustion sources.

Table 7.3 MIL-STD-2194 (SH)
12 February 1988
Severity code[1,3]

Severity Code	Temperature Above or Below Reference Temperature (°C)	Remarks
****	70 and above	Component (electrical) failure imminent.[2] Stop survey. Inform cognizant officers.
***	40 and above to less than 70	Component (electrical) failure almost certain unless corrected.
**	25 and above to less than 40	Component (electrical) failure probable unless corrected.
	Above 0	Component (electronic) failure probable unless corrected.
*	10 and above 0 to less than 25	Component (electrical) failure unlikely but corrective measure required at next scheduled routine maintenance period or as scheduling permits.
*	Below 0 to ambient	Component has probably failed or degraded or been affected by an upstream component or equipment.

[1] Applies to electrical, electronic, or I.C. equipment.
[2] Some components, such as coils, resistors, and thermal overload heaters, may have high temperature readings which are normal.
[3] The above general criteria have been determined by past field experience for maintenance scheduling. Final decision as to priorities and order of temperature, the type of component, and the critical nature of the equipment or system involved.

When measurements are being performed at exceptionally high temperatures, such as in the metalworking and refining industries, a short wavelength pyrometer would be the best choice. An instrument with a sensor based on a silicon detector (0.8–1 micron) will operate from 600°C to 3000°C, or beyond. Narrow fields of view are easily achieved at these temperatures. Two-color instruments may also be used to mitigate the effects of emissivity variations on the readings. These detectors are fairly insensitive to ambient temperature variations and will work well in the hot environment of a foundry or steel mill. These instruments are available as either portable or permanently mounted instruments. At short wavelengths, accurate readings can be obtained through glass or quartz windows.

Beyond these basic examples, the choice of instrument must be made by weighing the numerous influences of the material and surrounding on the measurement. Notwithstanding the many potential problems, infrared temperature sensors are an essential part of the industrial measurement tool box.

References

1. Astheimer, Robert W. *Handbook of Infrared Radiation Measurement*. Stamford, CT: Barnes Engineering Co., 1983. A monograph providing a condensed version of IR theory and application.

2. Born, M., and Wolf, E. *Principles of Optics*. 3rd ed. Elmsford, NY: Pergamon Press, 1965, p. 419.

3. Hudson, Richard D., Jr. *Infrared System Engineering*. New York: John Wiley & Sons, 1969. Covers all aspects of IR sensing in great depth.

4. Kaplan, Herbert. "IRAMS Progress Report." 1988 Proceedings of the SPIE, no. 934.

5. Planck, M. *Theory of Heat Radiation*. New York: Dover, 1959.

6. Shepherd, Jay W. "A Discussion of Emissivity Correction and Its Application in Infrared Microimaging." 1987 Proceedings of the SPIE, no. 780.

7. Wolfe, William L., and George J. Zissis. *The IR Handbook*. Ann Arbor, MI: Office of Naval Research, Environmental Research Institute of Michigan, 1985. A text with comprehensive coverage of all aspects of IR sensing.

Chapter 8 Infrared Imaging

Steven C. Ross

Introduction

This chapter covers the technology of infrared (IR) imaging. The following topics are included:

- What is infrared energy?

- How is IR imaging performed?

- Effects and influences of IR imaging

- Examples of IR imaging applications

With all of the different imaging modalities, it is becoming increasingly difficult for a user to know which one of the vast array of technologies to utilize in solving a particular problem. This chapter introduces the concepts of IR imaging, presents several potential applications, and provides a general explanation of how IR imaging may be able to address a specific application.

The IR imaging device creates a "picture" based on the amount of IR energy detected from objects in the scene. Depending on the specific IR imaging device utilized, the "picture" is generated in times ranging from several seconds to real time—that is, 30 frames or more per second. Like data generated from a visual light "picture," data from the IR "picture" can be utilized for both process and quality control. This can include on-line inspection for 100-percent examination or off-line sample inspection, consistent with a statistically sound sample.

Electromagnetic Energy

Our environment contains many different forms of energy that are propagated through space at the speed of light. These forms of energy are differentiated as a function of their wavelength.

The world people naturally perceive is in the visible light spectrum (360–830 nanometers). Infrared radiation begins just above the visible light spectrum and continues up to wavelengths of one-thousandth of a meter. Above infrared are radio waves. The electromagnetic spectrum is illustrated in figure 8.1.

All objects above absolute zero in temperature, −273 degrees Celsius, emit infrared radiation. This natural occurrence is caused by thermal agitation of the object's molecules. Because molecules are composed of electrical charges, the oscillations of the molecules create the radiation of electromagnetic energy.

The amount of infrared radiation emitted by an object is related directly to its temperature. In addition, the hotter the object becomes, the infrared energy emitted becomes shorter and shorter in wavelength. The burner of an electric range can be used to provide a graphic example of these properties. At a low temperature setting, the stove's burner radiates electromagnetic energy we can sense as heat but cannot see with our eyes. At a very high temperature setting, the burner emits greater amounts of electromagnetic energy and the radiation occurs at shorter wavelengths. This is portrayed by the red glow of a very hot burner. The wavelengths of a portion of the radiation have become short enough to enter the visible light spectrum.

How can a visual light image be created from infrared energy? An infrared imaging device contains one or more detectors that convert energy in the infrared spectrum into an electrical signal. The more energy detected, the greater the

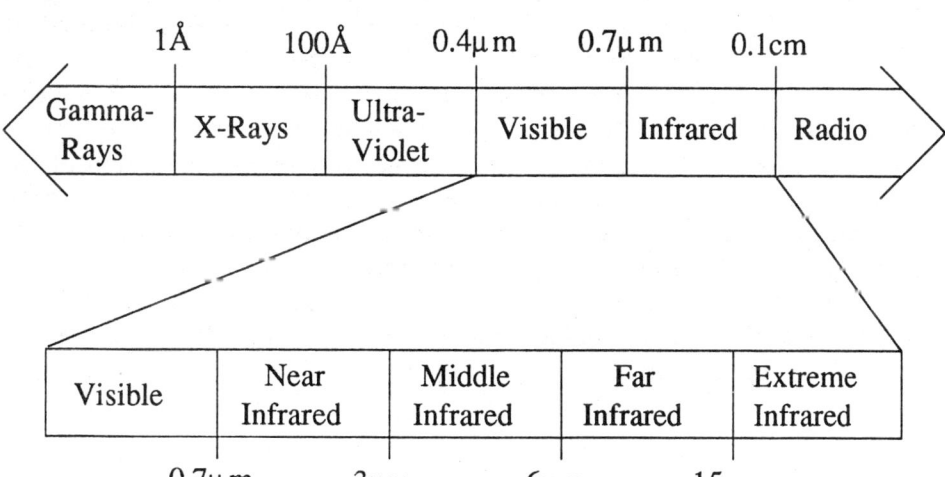

Figure 8.1 Electromagnetic Spectrum

INTRODUCTION

electrical signal output. The electric signals typically are formatted into a video signal and displayed on a CRT. The amplitudes of the electrical signals are then displayed as varying intensities on the CRT, thus creating a gray scale image of the scene. The gray scale value represents the amount of infrared energy detected from a given point in the scene of view.

Examine the image in figure 8.2. Is it an infrared image of a Corvette automobile or is it a normal black and white visual light photograph? It depicts an incredible amount of detail, including reflections of the sun and shadows of a nearby tree. In summary, it does look much like a normal visual light photograph.

The image is an infrared image (thermogram) of the automobile. The particular instrument utilized to create the thermogram senses the infrared wavelengths of 8 to 12 microns.

Take a close look at the front windshield. Unlike that of a visual light photograph, this thermogram portrays the windshield glass like a mirror. Visual light passes readily through normal glass; however, normal glass is a very good reflector of 8-to-12-micron infrared energy. The shadowing on the front of the car is caused by reflections and shading of the sun's tremendous source of IR energy.

What follows is a discussion of the basic properties of IR energy and IR imaging.

Figure 8.2 Infrared Image of an Automobile

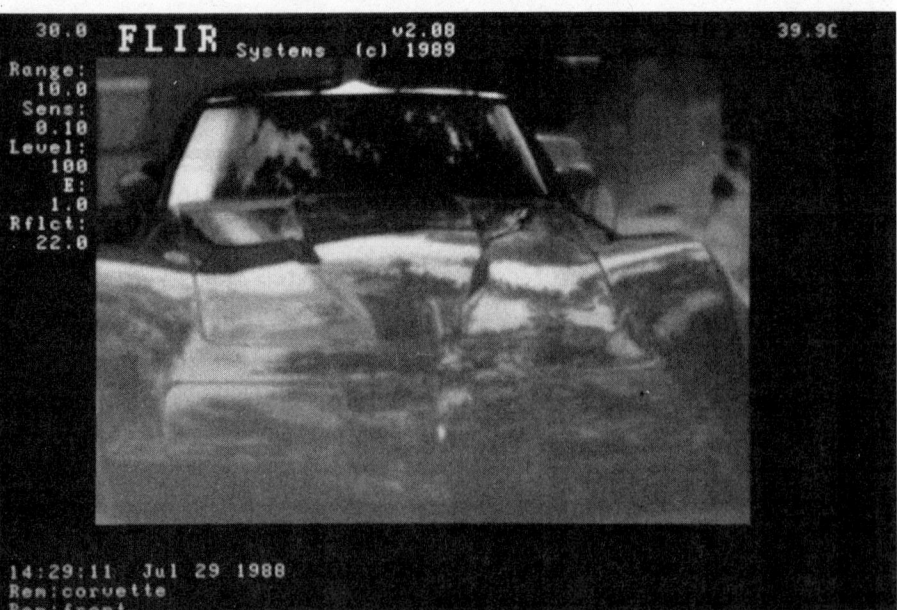

Energy Transfer

As was mentioned previously, one factor that determines the amount of IR energy emitted by an object is its temperature. The hotter an object becomes, the more IR energy it emits.

Objects are heated through the forms of conduction, convection, and/or radiation:

- Conduction   Transfer of energy by molecular agitation within a solid object—an electric stove's burner, for example. Physical contact is required.

- Convection   Transfer of energy within a fluid or gas by density variations—air within an oven, for example.

- Radiation   Transfer of energy in the form of electromagnetic waves of photons—the sun warming the earth, for example.

With IR imaging, the sensor or scanner is only detecting radiated energy. However, it is important to remember the properties of conduction and convection because these forms of energy transfer can be utilized to alter/enhance, to your advantage, the radiated energy emitted by an object. Likewise, if not properly controlled or considered, convection and/or conduction can result in a misleading IR image.

Infrared Imaging Energy

Only radiated energy is detected by the IR imaging device. The radiated energy from an object can be the result of the object's temperature, IR energy being reflected from the object, and/or IR energy being transmitted through the object.

- Transmissivity   The percentage of IR radiated energy that is transmitted through the object.

- Reflectivity   The percentage of incident energy that is reflected from an object.

- Emissivity   The percentage of energy, of an IR black body at the same temperature, that is emitted by the object.

When IR radiated energy strikes an object, the total amount of energy is transmitted, reflected, or absorbed by the object. According to Kirchoff's Law, the

INTRODUCTION

energy radiated by an object equals the energy absorbed when the object is at equilibrium. Because of this, we can assume that the total energy is the sum of the radiated, reflected, and emitted energy (figure 8.3).

A common term used when referring to IR imaging is *black body*. An IR black body is a perfect IR or thermal emitter. Its emissivity is 100 percent, its reflection is zero, and its transmissivity is zero. In addition, these properties hold true regardless of the spectral characteristics of the radiated energy. The black body is a specially designed instrument for the purpose of calibrating and verifying the performance of an IR imaging or measurement instrument.

As you have probably guessed, natural objects are not perfect black bodies. A percentage of total energy will be the result of reflections and/or transmissivity. To complicate the issue, the reflection and/or transmissivity characteristics for a given object may change based on the object's temperature and/or the wavelength of IR energy.

For most common materials, the spectral emissivity is nearly independent of the object's temperature. However, significant changes in spectral emissivity typically occur whenever the object undergoes a state change, such as vaporization, melting, or oxidation.

An object that is not a perfect emitter, but that has emissivity that is independent of wavelength is referred to as a *gray body*.

The emissivity of a gray body is the relationship between the quantity of photons emitted from a black body and the gray body when both are at the same temperature (figure 8.4).

Figure 8.5 shows approximate emissivity values for several common materials. If a material you are interested in observing does not appear in the chart, please refer to a comprehensive emissivity chart found in an IR-related text or data book [1, 2].

Figure 8.3   Total IR Radiated Energy = Reflected + Transmitted + Emitted

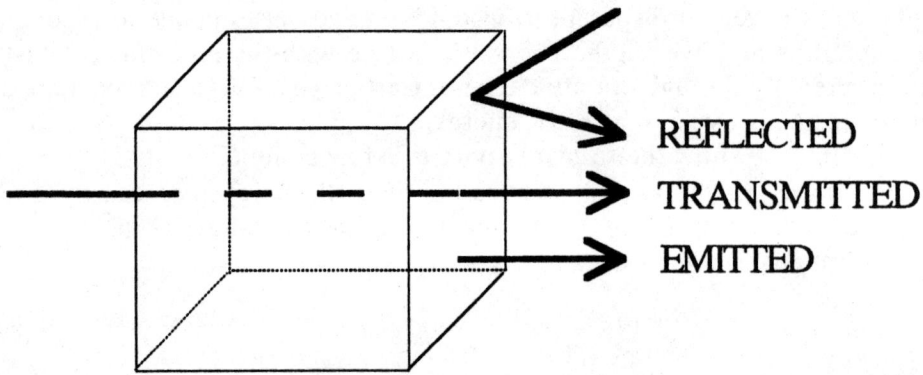

Figure 8.4   Emissivity of a Gray Body

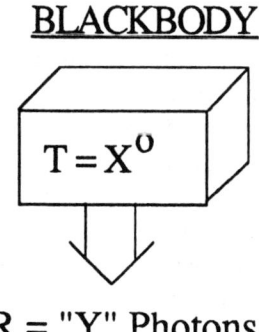
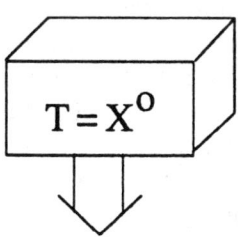

If very accurate emissivity values are required, refer to detailed sources on this subject, which consider aspects such as the precise temperature of the material and spectral characteristics. An alternative method would be to determine the material's emissivity through controlled laboratory measurements.

Transmissivity

When considering whether a material is transparent or opaque to IR, a common mistake is to base that judgment on the visual light spectrum, because that is what can be seen with human eyes. Because of the different wavelengths of visual light energy and IR energy, they may react differently to materials.

Items such as wood, steel, and aluminum are opaque to both visual light and IR energy. The same is not true for items such as plastics, glass, and quartz. For example, glass is very transparent to visual light and very opaque to IR energy above 3 microns in wavelength. The same is true with the atmosphere. Visual light passes readily through our atmosphere. Certain gases in the atmosphere are opaque to certain wavelengths of IR energy.

Figures 8.6–8.10 show the transmissivity of a few common items.

Considering all of the aspects covered above, IR energy received by an IR imaging/measuring device can be summarized as shown in figure 8.11.

These formulas:

$$W_o = eW_t + rW_{rb} + tW_{tb} \tag{8.1}$$

INTRODUCTION

Figure 8.5 Emissivity Factors

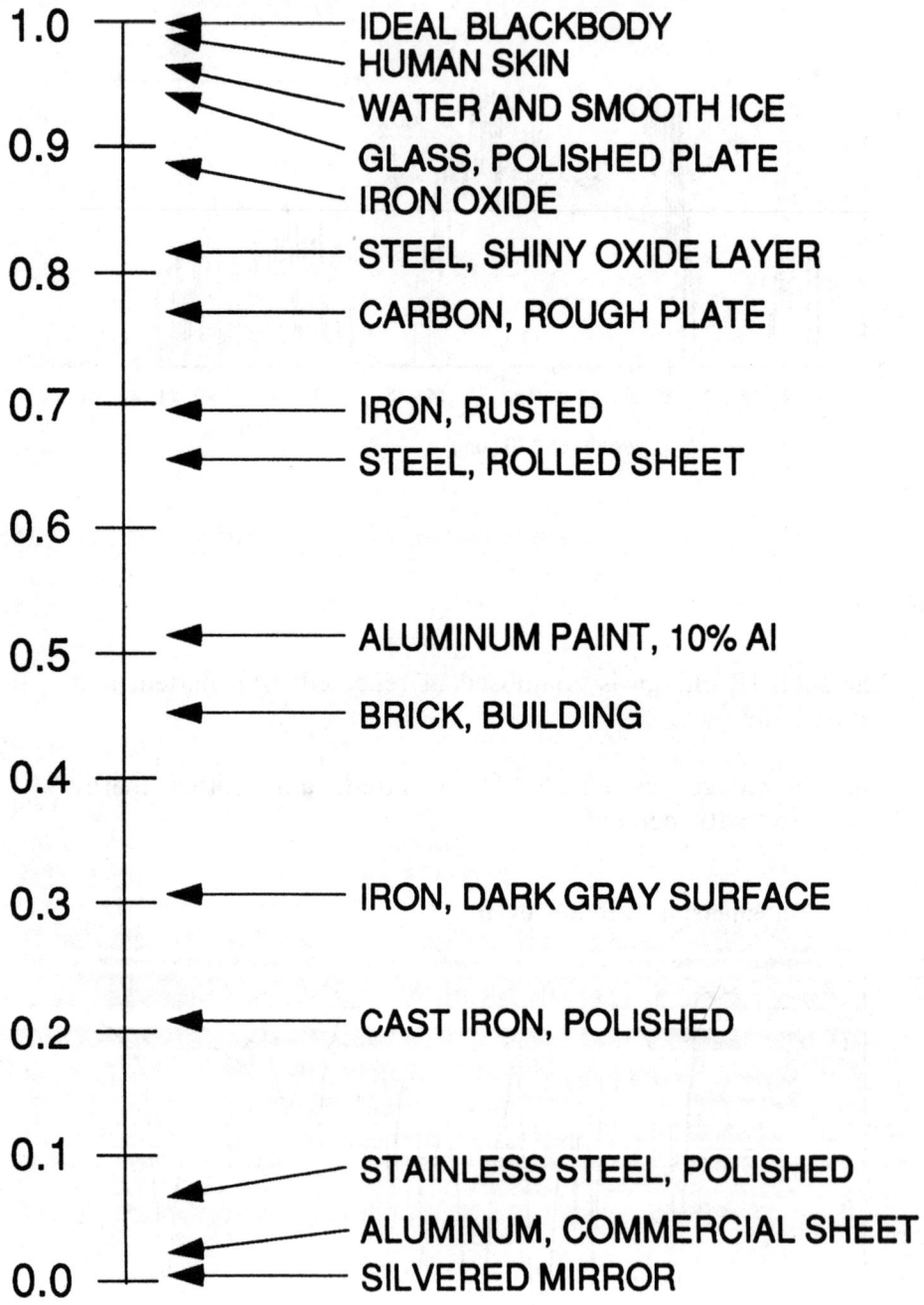

Figure 8.6 Transmission Through 1,000 Feet of Atmosphere

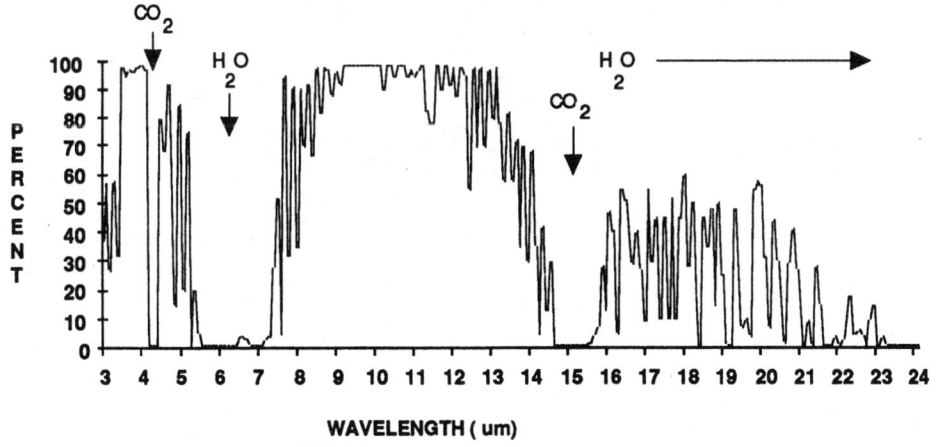

$$1 = e + r + t \tag{8.2}$$

tell us:

- The total IR energy is composed of reflected, transmitted, and emitted energy.

- The percentages of reflected, transmitted, and emitted energy must add to 100 percent.

Figure 8.7 Transmission Through Mylar

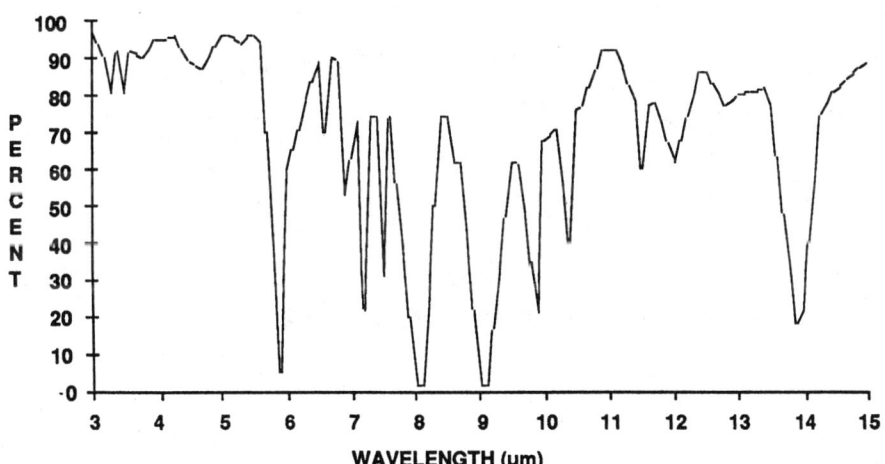

Figure 8.8 Transmission Through Nylon

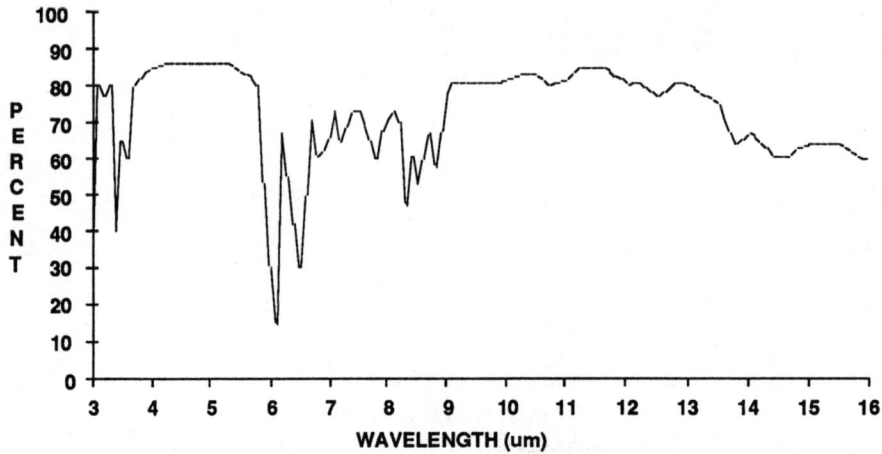

- The amount of reflected energy detected is a function of both the radiation source being reflected and the reflection properties of the object of view.

- Transmitted energy is a function of the transmissivity of the object of view and the radiation source being transmitted through the object.

- Emitted energy is a characteristic of the object's temperature and emissivity value.

Figure 8.9 Transmission Through Polyethylene

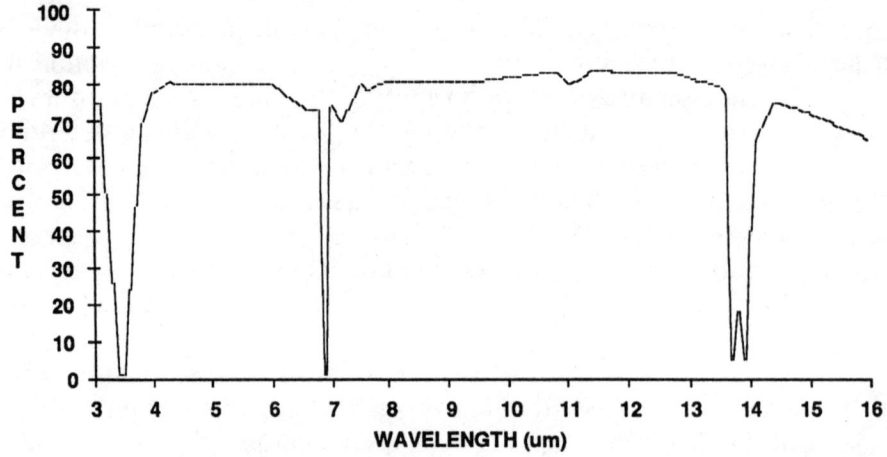

Figure 8.10 Transmission Through Glass and Quartz, ¼ Inch Thick

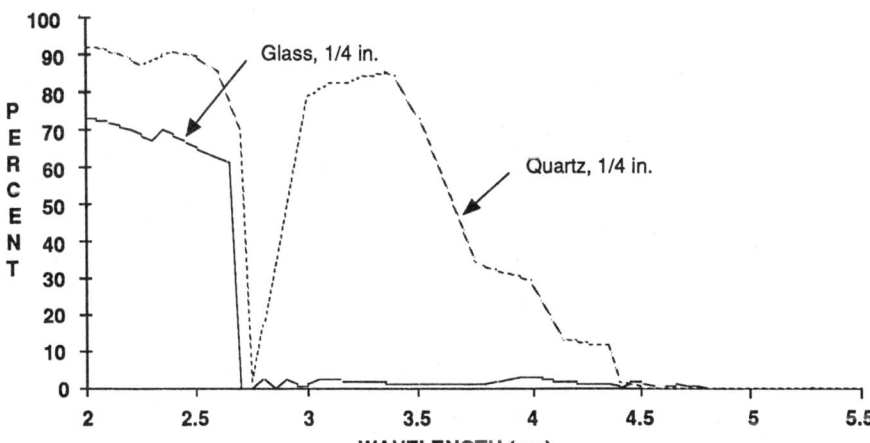

Industrial Applications

Throughout all phases of industrial activity we use heat, control heat, apply heat, remove heat, etc. Heat is everywhere. Because of this, IR imaging has many applications. Some applications are easy, and others are somewhat more difficult. When considering possible applications, one should understand the convection and conduction energy transfer properties. These properties alter the energy being radiated and can be used to observe something with more detail.

What follows are some potential applications for IR imaging.

Heating and Cooling Devices

IR imaging instruments are excellent for observing heating and cooling devices. They can be utilized to measure critical temperatures without contacting the object, to form a visual picture of the uniformity of the object's temperature, or simply to provide you with a "temperature picture" so that you can determine whether the device is functioning properly. This is possible because the amount of IR energy emitted from an object is directly related to its temperature.

The thermograms in figure 8.12 show the front and rear window defrosters of an automobile. In both cases, heat from the source is being conducted through the glass. The IR image is actually IR energy being radiated from the glass as a result of heat being conducted through the glass.

This concept works on applications from those shown above, to determining fluid levels in containers, to observing conveyer bearings to see if any are creating excessive heat. The specific applications are numerous.

Figure 8.11   Summary of IR Energy Received by an IR Imaging/Measuring Device

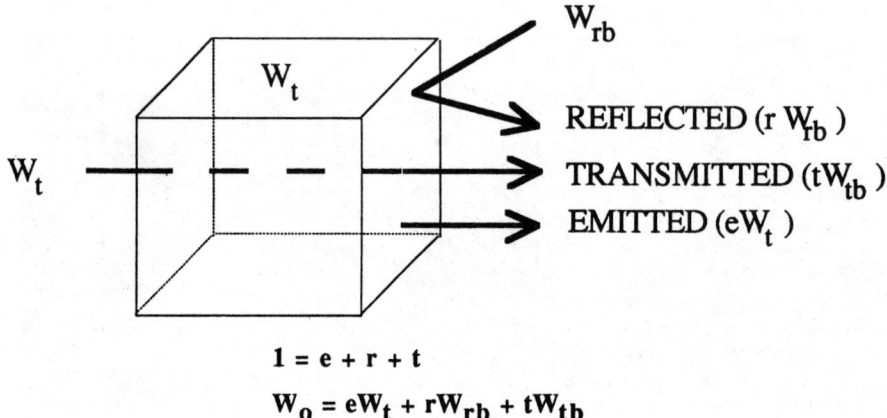

$$1 = e + r + t$$
$$W_o = eW_t + rW_{rb} + tW_{tb}$$

W_o = Total IR received

W_t = Radiation of a blackbody at same temperature as object.

W_{rb} = Radiation source being reflected from the object.

W_{tb} = Radiation source being transmitted through the object.

e = Emissivity of the object.

r = Reflectivity of object.

t = Transmissivity of object.

Electronic Components

As electrical current passes through an object, heat is generated as a result of the electrical resistance of the object. Because of this, all electrical components will have a "thermal signature." With a malfunction, there is either too little or too much heating because of a change in current, voltage, and/or resistance. The defective component will be either cooler or warmer than its normal "thermal signature." An IR image of the component(s) provides a visual thermal signature.

This concept applies to devices ranging from power lines to hybrid circuits. With IR imaging, you can perform the following tasks:

- Perform absolute temperature measurement

- Calculate the reliability of the component(s) based on operating temperature

Figure 8.12 Thermograms of the Front and Rear Window Defrosters of an Automobile

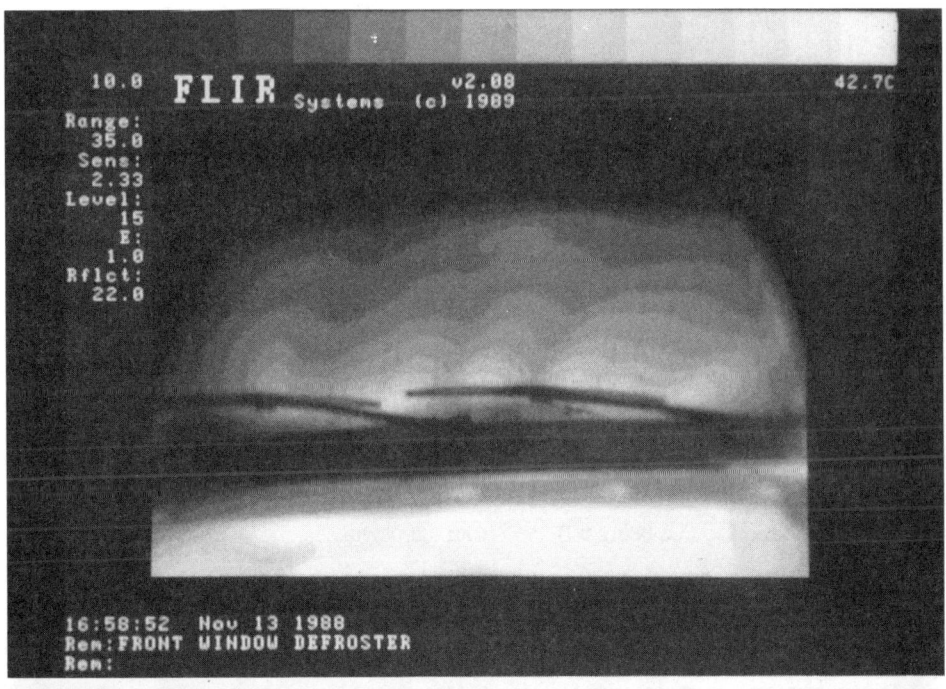

INDUSTRIAL APPLICATIONS

- Calculate the reliability of an entire electronic circuit board

- Screen systems for proper operation based on the operating temperature of each component

- Utilize thermal signatures as a troubleshooting aid by locating components operating at an abnormal temperature

Moisture

Water is a very good conductor of heat. Water conducts heat at a much faster rate than materials such as building insulation, wood, and paper. Because of these great differences in the rate of thermal conduction, IR imaging can be utilized to detect water or moisture presence.

Figure 8.13 further explains this process. In this example, if a heat source is applied to the top of this surface, with an IR imager you will observe a hot spot at the location of the moisture. If a cold source is applied to the top surface, the IR image will show a cold spot at the location of the moisture. This is because of moisture's rapid rate of conduction as compared to insulation.

The same concept applies to detecting moisture in any object/material that has a different thermal energy conduction rate than water. To maximize the IR energy differential, make sure there is a temperature differential between the two sides of the object of view.

Figure 8.13 Energy Conduction Through Moisture

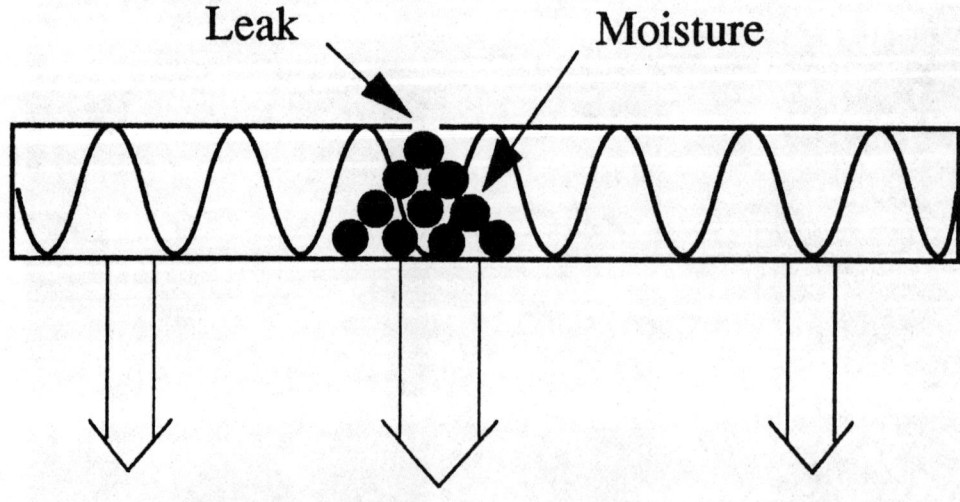

Leaks

One way to tell whether there is a leak in a container is to apply a vacuum or pressure and see if there is a pressure change over time. Another method is to utilize IR imaging.

Movement of a gas, liquid or solid will create a temperature differential. This temperature differential can be observed with IR imaging.

The thermogram shown in figure 8.14 identifies air leaks around the window of an automobile's door. To maximize the thermal differential, the car's defroster was activated to create a slight pressure inside the auto and to make the air warmer than ambient. As the air escapes through the leaks, the IR image shows the leaks as areas of higher temperature than the surrounding areas.

Bonding/Delamination

IR imaging is very effective at locating bonding voids and delaminations. This is possible because of variations in the rate of heat conduction through a good bond/lamination and a void area. The conduction rate varies, because a void is

Figure 8.14 Air Leaks Around an Automobile's Window

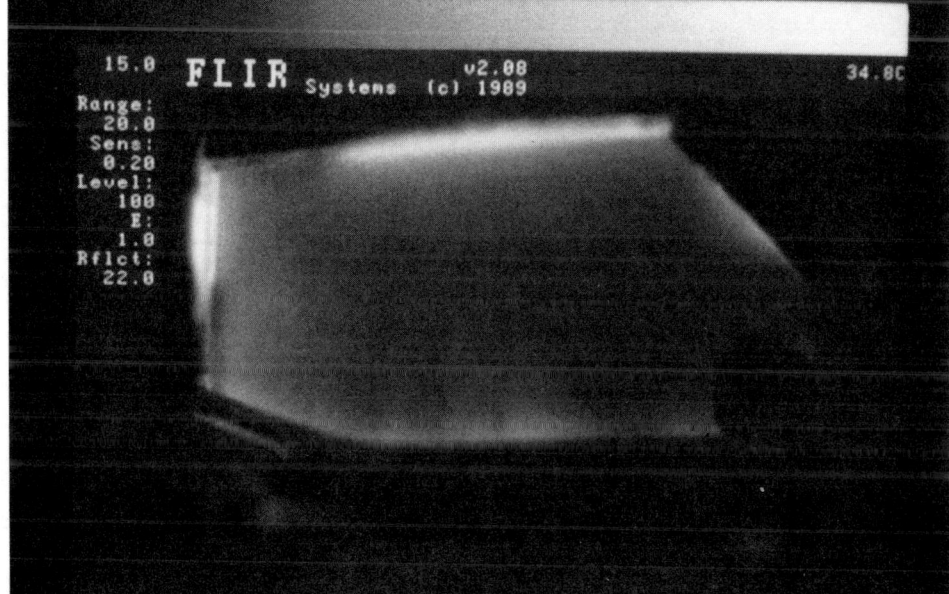

Figure 8.15 Bonding Voids and Delaminations

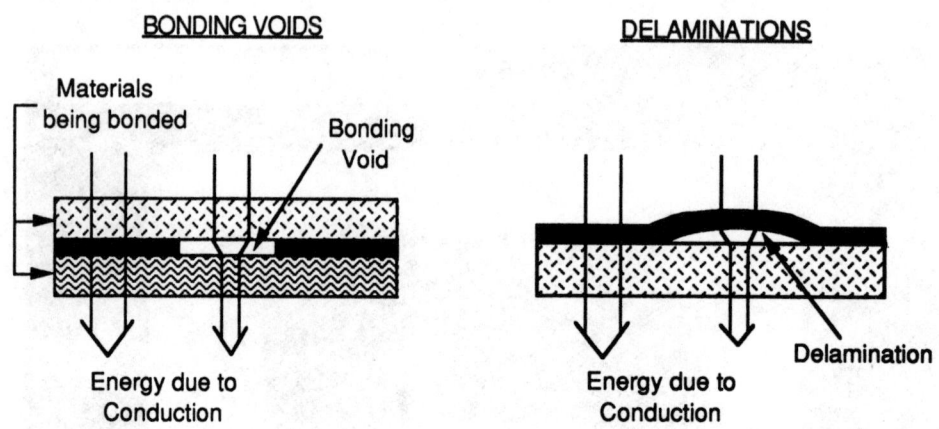

typically a pocket of air and a pocket of trapped air is a relatively poor conductor of heat energy. Voids and delaminations are depicted in figure 8.15.

The thermogram in figure 8.16 shows an example of a bonding defect. The image is of two sheets of aluminum bonded together, with a bonding void in the middle. A heat source has been applied to the bottom of the sample so that differences in the rate of conduction can be observed. The defect is shown as cool temperatures relative to the surrounding area. The void slows down the rate of energy conduction, thus showing up as a cold spot.

Cracks and Voids

It is possible to utilize IR imaging to detect cracks and voids in objects. A crack or void may have a different surface area than the surrounding areas and thus a different rate of cooling or heating. The crack or void may have a different emissivity value than the surrounding area. The angle of reflection relative to the imaging device may be different for the crack/void and the surrounding area. These factors couple together such that the defect emits/reflects a different amount of IR energy than the surrounding area. However, note that the size of the crack or void that is detectable varies depending on the resolution of the IR imaging device utilized, its field of view, and the IR characteristics of the material being observed. One cannot assume that IR imaging can be utilized to detect any crack in any material. Experimentation is required, as with any imaging device.

Figure 8.17 shows two thermograms of complex aluminum castings. The thermograms were captured while the parts were still hot after being removed from the casting mold. The thermogram on the top is that of a good part, which is

Figure 8.16 Thermogram of a Bonding Defect

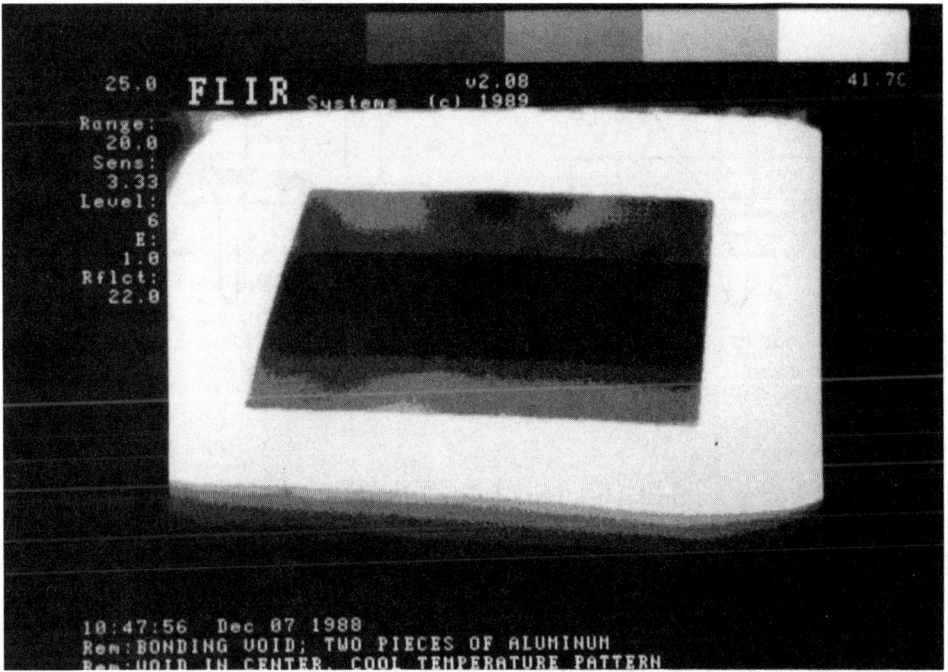

used for comparison. The thermogram on the bottom shows a defect in the lower middle of the part. The defect is surrounded by a box for easy identification.

In these images the video is inverted: white is cold and black is hot, as depicted by the temperature/gray scale bar at the top of the thermogram. The defect shows up as a warmer temperature than the surrounding area. A combination of actual temperature, emissivity variations, and reflections is creating the results:

- The void area is cooling at a slower rate than the other top surface areas, because it is being heated by the walls of the surrounding cavities.

- The void area has a surface that is rougher than a good surface. The rough surface has a higher emissivity.

- The relatively smooth surface of the good areas is reflecting the cooler ambient IR energy.

Figure 8.17 Thermograms of Complex Aluminum Castings, Showing a Good Part (Top) and a Defective Part (Bottom)

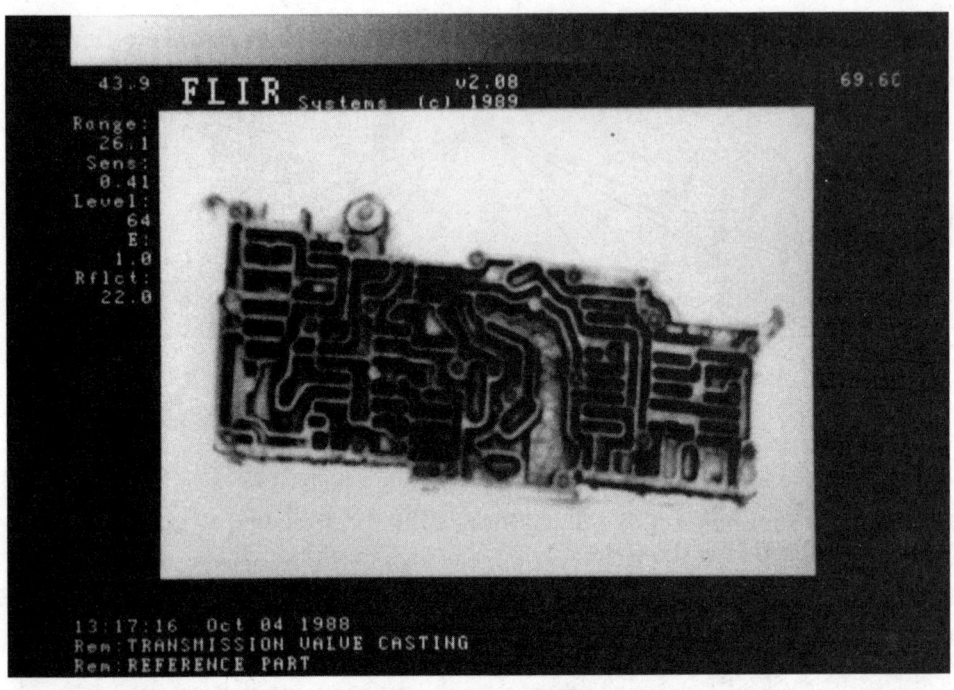

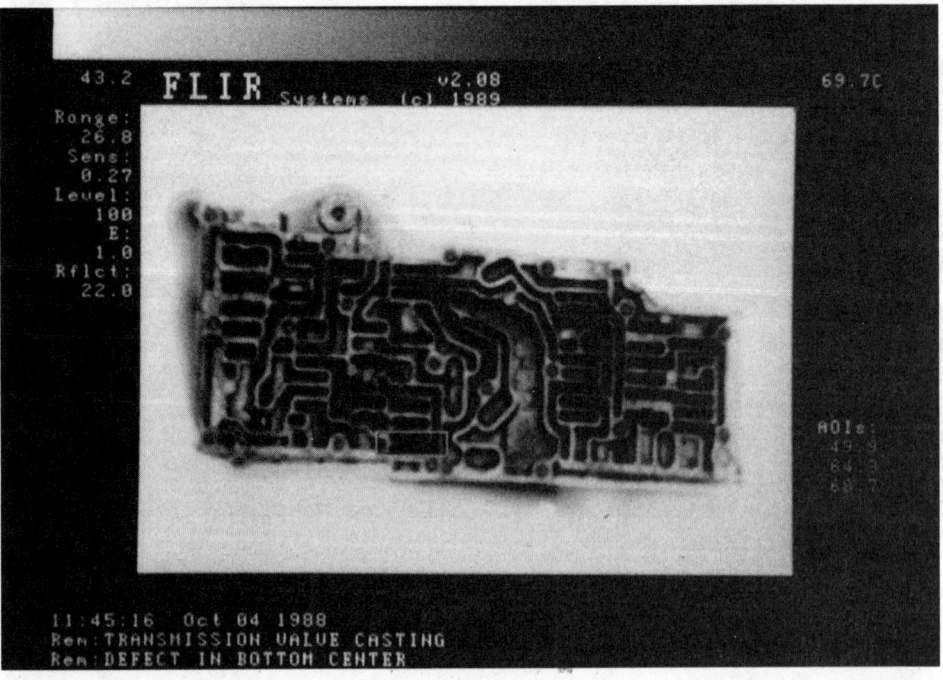

Figure 8.18 Reflection of IR from Smooth and Flawed Surfaces

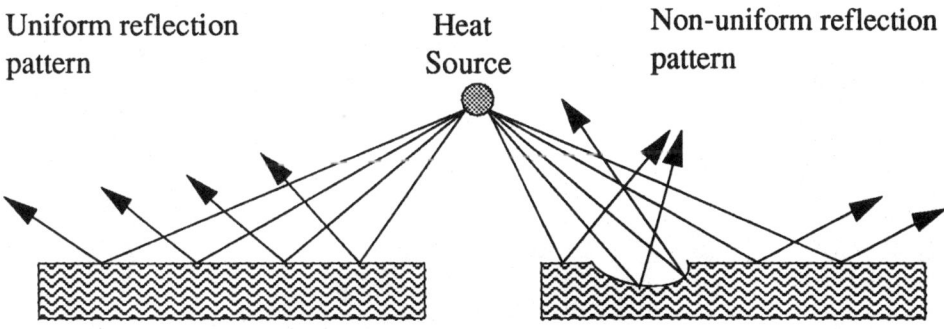

Figure 8.19 Thermogram of a Small Piece of Highly Polished Metal with a Small Defect in the Center

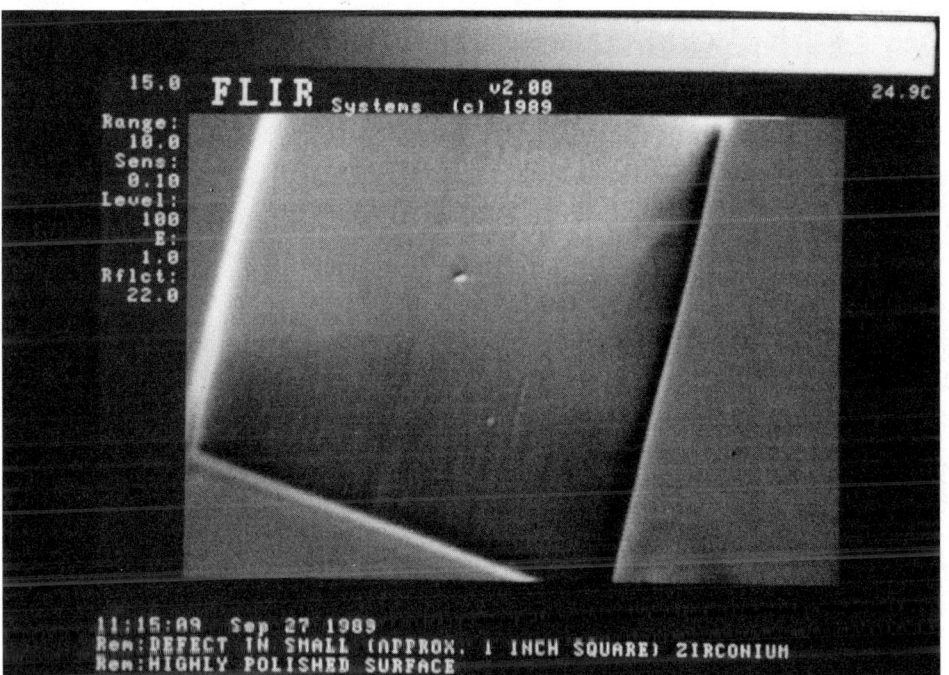

Surface Uniformity

IR imaging can be utilized to detect defects such as dings and dents in a surface. The method for doing this makes use of the material's IR reflective properties. Observe the diagram in figure 8.18.

With a uniform surface, the IR energy will be reflected in a uniform pattern. The IR imaging device is positioned to observe this reflected energy. When a nonuniformity is present, the IR energy will be reflected in many different directions. The nonuniformity can be seen with an IR imaging device as a difference in temperature.

Another advantage to this technique is that the same principles apply even if the material has a coating over it. For example, a piece of bare sheet metal, sheet metal with primer paint applied, and the same material with a final coat of paint will all yield the same pattern to the IR imaging device. The only compensation that may be necessary is that the instrument's sensitivity might need to be adjusted to compensate for the varying reflectivity of the surfaces.

Figure 8.19 is a thermogram of a small piece of highly polished metal, approximately one (1) inch square, with a very small defect in the center. Because of differences in emissivity and reflected energy, one side of the cavity appears colder (black color) than the surrounding surface, and the adjacent side of the cavity appears warmer (white color) than the surrounding area.

Conclusion

Infrared (IR) imaging is an imaging modality that generates an image from the infrared energy emitted by an object. Because all objects above absolute zero temperature naturally emit IR energy, IR imaging is a useful imaging modality. In addition to the object's natural emitted IR energy, you can use the energy transfer properties of conduction and convection to alter the object's temperature and thus the amount of IR energy being emitted. As with other imaging modalities, you can also utilize the properties of reflection and transmittance to enhance the image.

In the body of this chapter, several potential applications for IR imaging were introduced. These examples were used to show a variety of imaging ideas using the various aspects of naturally emitted IR energy, conduction, convection, and reflection to enhance an object to obtain a useful IR image. The list is by no means conclusive. The potential applications are virtually endless.

Like visual light cameras and other imaging modalities, IR imaging devices are being combined with machine vision technology. The result is automated inspection without human intervention for IR image or data interpretation.

References

1. Hudson, Richard D., Jr. *Infrared Systems Engineering*. New York: John Wiley & Sons, 1969.

2. The Infrared Information and Analysis (IRIA) Center, Environmental Research Institute of Michigan. *The Infrared Handbook*. Prepared for Office of Naval Research, Department of the Navy, Washington, D.C., 1978.

Chapter 9 Color Sensors

C. S. McCamy

Introduction

Color is one of the most obvious aspects of appearance, so it is of great aesthetic and commercial importance. The science of measuring color is called *colorimetry*. It is used to specify colors precisely, to provide a means of communicating color information internationally, to preserve color identity long after specimens have faded, to establish numerical tolerances and determine whether they are met, to compute amounts of colorants needed to make a color, and to monitor processes that produce color. Some color processes can be controlled by an optical method of sensing the contributions of the colorants used. Most industrial sensors measure quantities such as length, mass, or time—quantities defined without direct reference to human perception. Color science is part of the interdisciplinary science, part psychology and part physics, known as *psychophysics*. It involves the most complex of all human perceptions. Though most scientists and engineers know there is some relationship between the spectrum and color, few know that two radically different spectra can evoke the same color sensation. An understanding of color instrumentation begins with an understanding of color order, light, and human color vision.

Color Order

In 1900, there was no generally accepted way of identifying colors. People compared colors to the colors of animals, vegetables, minerals, etc. A color wasn't accurately described by calling it "rose," because a rose may be any of a variety of colors. In 1905, an artist, A. H. Munsell, published a booklet describing a

system of specifying the color of any surface in terms of three attributes: hue, value, and chroma [1a].

Hue is the attribute of color that distinguishes red from green, or yellow from blue. Munsell named five principal hues—red, yellow, green, blue, and purple—and five intermediate hues—yellow-red, green-yellow, blue-green, purple-blue, and red-purple. He arranges the hues in natural progression around a circle. He further divided each of these ten into ten parts, making 100 parts. These divisions were made equal, in the sense that they were *visually perceived to be equal*. Any hue could be specified by a number from 1 to 100, starting at the beginning of the red region and numbering in the yellow-red direction. This scale is convenient for use in computers. However, Munsell knew it would be difficult to associate a hue with a number, so he used the number of the subdivision within a region, and the initial letter as a symbol for the hue region. For example, 5R is the fifth step in the red region, the middle of the region, and 9R is a red near yellow-red. The hue scale is continuous, so decimals, such as 5.67R, may be used to make fine distinctions. The symbols for the regions, in order, are R, YR, Y, GY, G, BG, B, PB, P, and RP. Yellow-red is commonly called orange, but Munsell chose to name the intermediate hues in a consistent way. By continuously changing hue in one direction, one returns to the starting hue. The closed hue circuit is a fundamental property of human color vision.

In the Munsell system, the hue arbitrarily designated 0 is chosen so that the center of the red region 5R is a hue, known as *unique red*, which is neither bluish nor yellowish. Because hue divisions are visually equal and the zero point is set, a given hue can be at only one place on the circle. Unique yellow and unique green fall near 5Y and 5G, but unique blue is not at 5B. It is at about 2.5PB, a fact that is well known and therefore presents no problem. The Munsell hue circle is illustrated in figure 9.1.

Munsell value denotes the lightness of a color: the lighter the color, the higher the value. Munsell let the darkest conceivable black have a value of 0 and the lightest conceivable white have a value of 10. The range of lightnesses was divided equally, *as perceived visually*. The use of decimals permits lightness to be expressed on the Munsell value scale to any degree of precision. Munsell value is often illustrated by a series of colors from black through grays to white, but value is used to describe the lightness of any color.

The third attribute of color is *chroma*, which is the difference from a gray of the same value. Imagine having a can of gray paint, removing a small amount, replacing it with yellow paint of the same value, and mixing it well. If this process were repeated many times, the paint would gradually shift from gray to yellow. It would gradually increase in Munsell chroma. Munsell arbitrarily assigned a chroma of 10 to the color of a paint made with vermilion pigment and divided the scale into *visually equal parts*. He later found colors with higher chromas but retained the initial scaling. Materials are available today with a chroma of 20 or more. The use of decimals permits chroma to be specified pre-

COLOR ORDER

Figure 9.1 The Munsell Hue Circle

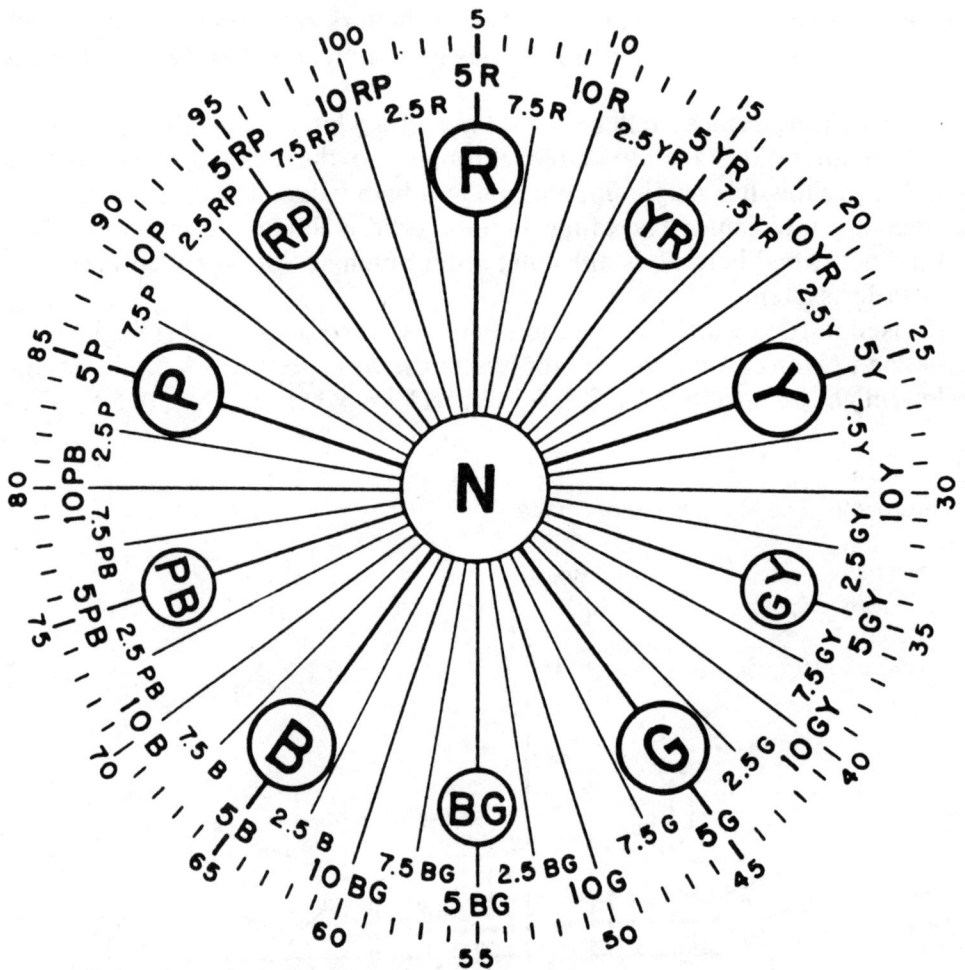

cisely. (Recently, some authors have defined *chroma* as colorfulness relative to white and *saturation* as the colorfulness of an area relative to the brightness of the same area, but in the qualitative sense, the terms are often used interchangeably.)

Black, white, and all shades of gray are called neutral colors, because they have no hue. Their chroma is zero, so they differ only in value. Colors are often considered neutral if the chroma is very low, not necessarily zero, so many colors called gray have some perceptible hue.

Munsell plotted the three attributes in a three-dimensional space known as the Munsell color space. The neutral colors are arranged along a vertical line, known as the *neutral axis,* from black at the bottom to white at the top—like the axis

of the earth. Hues are arranged angularly around the axis, like longitude lines on the earth. Chroma is measured outward from and normal to the neutral axis. This is a cylindrical coordinate system. Like colors are brought together and all colors are represented, with a continuous gradation. The Munsell color space is illustrated in figure 9.2.

The blackest surfaces reflect some light, the whitest ones absorb some, and there are limitations on attainable chromas, so the color space is naturally bounded. Yellow has maximum chroma at a high value, and blue has maximum chroma at a low value. The Munsell color solid is illustrated in figure 9.3. The method described here of establishing order among colors is called the Munsell color order system.

Munsell introduced a neat notation to describe colors. Using H for hue, V for value, and C for chroma, his notation is in the form: H V/C. A bright greenish-yellow might be specified by 5.52GY 7.65/11.35, where the hue is 5.52GY, the

Figure 9.2 The Munsell Color Space

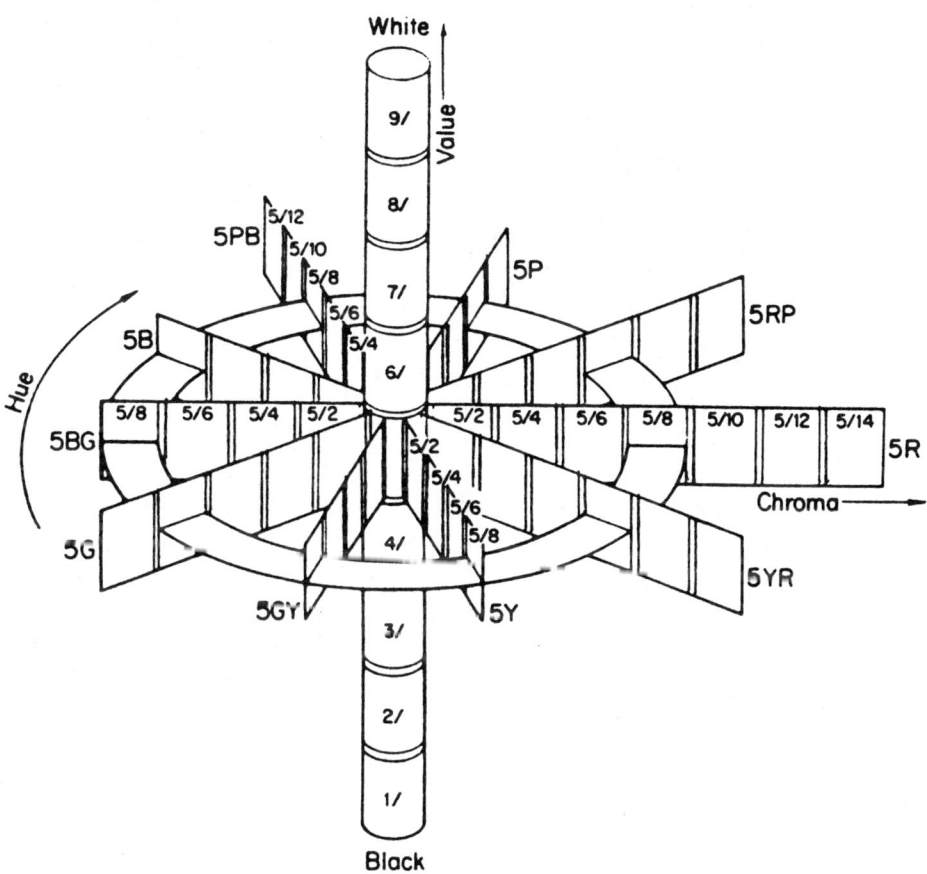

Figure 9.3 The Munsell Color Solid

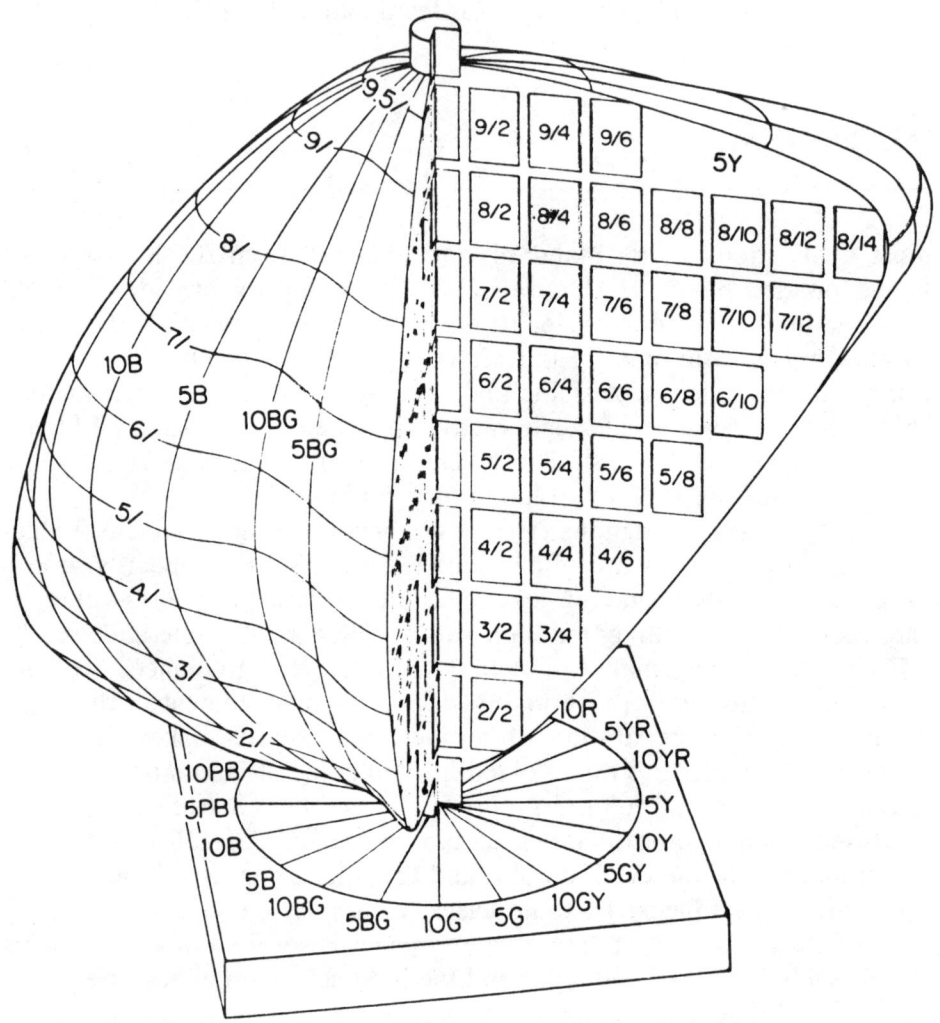

value is 7.65, and the chroma is 11.35. For neutral colors, there is no hue and the chroma is zero, so the notation is simply N, for "neutral," plus the value and the slash—for example, N 7/. For centuries, it was "known" that colors could not be described accurately with words, so the ability to specify any color very precisely, in the space of one long word, is a remarkable achievement.

There are other color order systems, but the Munsell system is the best known and is widely used in scientific studies of color. The system was refined by a committee of the Optical Society of America [12]. A description of the system, with colored illustrations, is given under the entry *color* in the third unabridged

edition of the Merriam-Webster dictionary [14]. Details of the system and its use are given in a standard issued by the American Society for Testing and Materials (ASTM) [3]. This system has been standardized nationally in Japan.

Color Standards

For most applications, color standards are obtained from the Munsell Color Company, founded by A. H. Munsell [10]. The company provides standards made by coating a very durable paint on paper. The Munsell *Book of Color,* displaying samples from most of the Munsell space, is available in both matte and glossy finishes. The most stable and accurately calibrated color standards available today are ceramic tiles calibrated and issued by the National Physical Laboratory of Great Britain [8]. These standards are used to establish the accuracy and monitor the stability of laboratory equipment.

Color is often assessed in industry by visually comparing specimens with colored standards. Tolerances are often exhibited by a set of standards, one the desired color, and others having just tolerable deviations in hue, value, and chroma. Such a set of seven color standards is called a color tolerance set. The Munsell Color Company makes such sets to order. The tolerances are established by consultation with those involved in color management in the organization requesting the preparation of the set. Such a set makes the chosen tolerances clearly evident to all involved in the choice of colors or the production, buying, or selling of colored products. Even when instrumental methods are to be used, such a color tolerance set is very useful in establishing this common understanding of the desired color and the tolerances. It can be measured to set numerical tolerances. In some cases, a product has a natural variation along some straight or curved line in color space. If so, the color tolerance set may simply include the desired color and the limit colors on either side.

Color Inspection

Visual comparisons must be made by normal observers. The Farnsworth-Munsell 100-Hue Test, available from the Munsell Color Company, is used to test the color vision of potential inspectors.

Proper lighting is essential, because the light reflected from a surface depends not only on the surface but also on the nature of the light illuminating the sur-

face. The color may change when the illumination is changed. *More importantly, two surfaces may match in color under one illuminant but not match under another.* This phenomenon is called *metamerism,* and such a conditional match is called a *metameric match.* The principal problem in color matching is to find a mixture of dyes or pigments to produce a color that matches a given standard under all illuminants likely to be important. Viewing booths that provide standard illumination and viewing conditions are specified by an ASTM standard [4].

The Spectrum

The specification of illumination and much of the rest of color science depend on the concept of wavelength. A disturbance in an electric field produces an oscillation of the field that radiates out through space as waves, transmitting radiant power. The distance from the crest of one wave to the crest of the next is called *wavelength.* The usual unit of length used is the nanometer (nm), which is 1/1,000,000,000 meter. Gamma rays and x rays have extremely short wavelengths. With increasing wavelength, the radiation is known as ultraviolet rays, light, infrared rays, microwaves, or radio waves. The nature of light is specified by the relative amount of radiant power in each narrow wavelength band.

Light is radiant power to which the human eye responds. The sensitivity of the eye is greatest at a wavelength of 555 nm and falls off gradually to zero at 360 nm and at 830 nm, the two ends of what is called the visible spectrum. The sensitivity of the eye as a function of wavelength is known as the *spectral luminous efficiency function* or the *visibility function.*

Lights of different wavelengths produce different color sensations, 360–420 nm appearing violet, 420–480 blue, 480–560 green, 560–590 yellow, 590–630 orange, and 630–830 red, with continuous and smooth variation. The colors of lights depend on their spectral power distributions, and the colors of transmitting and reflecting materials depend on the way they are illuminated and the amounts of light transmitted or reflected at various wavelengths in the spectrum.

Standard Illuminants

Illuminants for visual color matching and color measurement have been standardized by the International Commission on Illumination, which is known by the initials of its name in French: CIE. In 1931, they adopted CIE Illuminants

A, B, and C. CIE Illuminant A is a specified incandescent lamp, about like a standard 100-watt household lamp. Illuminants B and C, representing sunlight and daylight, were later replaced by a series of illuminants representing daylight of various colors. The colors of daylight, observed throughout the day in different places, are similar to the colors of a glowing body at various temperatures, so these phases of daylight can be identified by simply referring to a temperature. It is known as the correlated color temperature, expressed on the international temperature scale, in kelvins, with the symbol K. Average daylight has a correlated color temperature of 6,500 K, the light from a lightly overcast sky 7,500 K, and direct sunlight about 5,500 K. To denote the various phases of daylight, the CIE adopted the symbol D with a subscript 1/100 of the correlated color temperature. (For most practical purposes, the temperature can be rounded to the nearest multiple of 100K) [7]. For most color measurements, CIE Illuminant D_{65} is used. In most countries, colors are usually judged using artificially produced D_{65}, but in the United States, artificial D_{75} is usually used.

Color Vision

The retina of the eye has three different kinds of light sensors to differentiate colors. The three have maximum sensitivities to light in different parts of the spectrum. A well-known demonstration illustrates the three-dimensional nature of color vision and provides a basis for color measurement. Let three spotlights with colored filters project blue, green, and red spots of light. If the spots overlap, one can see what happens when light of two or three different colors are added. When blue and green lights are mixed, they produce a bluish-green light. Red and blue lights produce purple. The mixture of red and green light is orange or yellow light. (This fact often surprises people with experience in mixing paints. Here, light is being mixed, not paint.) The mixture of blue, green, and red light in the right proportions produces white light. Various proportions of the components produce all hues. In a gradual progression from all red to all green, for example, the mixture passes through all gradations of red, orange red, orange, yellowish orange, yellow, greenish yellow, to green.

Color television employs this process. The face of the picture tube has an array of tiny dots of three kinds of phosphors that emit blue, green, or red light, the brightness of each depending on an electron beam striking it. The dots are too small to be resolved by the eye, so the color mixture is observed.

Visual Colorimetry

In the first colorimeters, adjustable lamps with filters were used to illuminate half of a screen with a mixture of blue, green, and red lights, called primaries. Some light to be measured was projected on the other half of the screen. The brightness of the primaries were adjusted until the two halves of the screen matched. Sometimes, a light could not be matched. However, if one of the primaries was shone on the other half of the screen so that it mixed with the test light, a match was obtained. The amount of that primary was considered negative. When such negative amounts were permitted, any light could be matched. Three numbers, representing the brightnesses of the primaries, identified the color of the test light. These three numbers are called *tristimulus values*. Instruments with different primaries gave different results, but if enough measurements were made on two instruments, it was possible to derive a transformation equation to compute the values obtained with one instrument from those obtained on the other. This is called a *transformation of primaries*.

The Standard Observer

In the 1920s, visual colorimeters were built, using easily reproduced, very narrow spectral bands or "lines," as primaries. Observers found the mixture needed to match light of each narrow wavelength band in the visible spectrum. For each primary, they found a curve representing the relative amount required as a function of wavelength, known as a *color-mixture function*. Some negative values were found. The primaries were transformed mathematically to eliminate the negative values. This provided convenience in calculation but resulted in a set of theoretical primaries that were not real light sources. A further transformation made the color-mixture function for the "green" primary correspond to the visibility function. These transformed color-mixture functions were standardized internationally by the CIE in 1931 and are known as the CIE 1931 Standard Colorimetric Observer. The three color-mixture functions are given the symbols $\bar{x}$, $\bar{y}$, and $\bar{z}$. The transformations caused the $\bar{x}$ function to have two lobes, the major one in the red region of the spectrum and a small one in the blue region. The $\bar{y}$ function represents the green primary (and the visibility function) and the $\bar{z}$ function represents the blue primary. The visual colorimeters displayed the lights to be judged in a small area, subtending only 2 degrees at the eye of the observer, about like a thumbnail viewed at arm's length.

Data more representative of the observation of larger surfaces was later obtained with fields subtending 10 degrees at the eye, about like one's hand viewed at arm's length. These slightly different data, denoted by $\bar{x}_{10}$, $\bar{y}_{10}$, $\bar{z}_{10}$, were standardized as the CIE 1964 Standard Colorimetric Observer [6].

Filter Colorimeters

All of these elements now come together in a simple method of measuring color. A specimen to be measured is illuminated by a standard light source. The light reflected by the specimen passes through a colored filter to a photosensor that provides an electrical signal proportional to the amount of light incident on it. The filter is one of a set that may be used in succession with the same sensor or simultaneously with separate sensors. The filters and sensors are designed together so that each combination provides a spectral sensitivity matching one of the color-mixture functions of the CIE Standard Colorimetric Observer. The $\bar{x}$ function is often simulated with two different filters to match the two lobes of the distribution.

A white standard, such as a white ceramic tile, is placed in the specimen position and readings are made with the various filter-sensor combinations. The responses for the two lobes of the $\bar{x}$ function are added. Then the specimen is put in place and readings are taken again. The readings for the specimen are divided by the corresponding ones for the white standard to obtain three numbers that represent the amounts of the three primaries needed to match the specimen under the standard illuminant. The three numbers, X, Y, and Z, are tristimulus values, corresponding to the values obtained with the $\bar{x}$, $\bar{y}$, and $\bar{z}$ simulators, respectively. The tristimulus values specify the color, but other quantities, derived from them, are more useful. They will be discussed later.

Filter colorimeters are simple, but they have inherent defects that prevent their achieving the stability and precision usually required. It is difficult to find filter materials to convert lamplight to a standard illuminant as precisely as is required for industrial color work. There is large variation among filters and lamps. Lamps and filters may change with time. Lamps burn out and must be replaced. Similar problems are encountered with the filter-sensor combinations. Nonetheless, the method is useful in applications not demanding high precision, such as the recognition of one of a few colors.

Spectrophotometry

The basic limitations of a filter colorimeter are overcome by the use of a spectrophotometer. In this instrument, the specimen is illuminated and the reflected light is directed to an optical system known as a *monochromator* or *spectral analyzer*. This usually involves a prism or grating that disperses the light to form a spectrum. By measuring the amount of light as a function of distance along the spectrum, the amount of light reflected at each wavelength is determined. As with the filter system, the readings are reported relative to those for the white standard. (The CIE has adopted the convention that the white standard be calibrated by a basic standards laboratory and that measured values be reported relative to a perfect white diffuser.)

Each measurement is made using a narrow band of wavelengths. For that measurement, the power of the illuminant and sensitivity of the sensor at other wavelengths is of no consequence (with an important exception to be discussed later). Therefore, the basic problems of matching ideal illuminants and sensors, so critical in filter colorimetry, are avoided.

Computation of Colorimetric Quantities

The spectrophotometer measures the relative spectral reflectance factor of a surface but does not provide tristimulus values directly, as a filter colorimeter does. The tristimulus values must be computed by numerical integration. For the most precise color work, spectral reflectance factors are measured and integrated at intervals of 1 nm wavelength, but virtually all industrial colorimetry is done at 10 or 20 nm intervals.

The tristimulus value X is computed by summing, for all wavelengths in the visible spectrum, the product of these factors: the spectral power distribution of an ideal CIE illuminant, the spectral reflectance factor of the specimen, the color-mixture function $\bar{x}$ of the CIE standard observer, and the wavelength interval. The tristimulus values Y and Z are computed in the same way, using the $\bar{y}$ and $\bar{z}$ functions. Tables of values for use in these integrations are given in an ASTM standard [2].

Recall that the experimental data for the standard observer were transformed to make $\bar{y}$ match the luminous efficiency function. The computed tristimulus value Y represents the integrated effect of the reflected light at all wavelengths, weighted by the spectral sensitivity of the eye, so it is related to the lightness of the color.

The hue and chroma, which describe what is called *chromaticity*, depend on the relative proportions of X, Y, and Z. Two chromaticity coordinates are defined as follows: $x = X/(X+Y+Z)$ and $y = Y/(X+Y+Z)$. A plot of x versus y, called the CIE chromaticity diagram, is illustrated in figure 9.4. The chromaticities of glowing bodies at various temperatures, in kelvins (the Planckian locus), and the chromaticities of CIE Illuminants A, B, C, and D_{65} are shown. The point E on the diagram is the chromaticity of a source emitting the same amount of energy at all wavelengths. A plot of Y at right angles to x and y defines a three-dimensional space similar to Munsell space. Munsell value is related to Y by an equation. There are no known equations relating Munsell hue and chroma to x and y, but hue and chroma have been plotted on the CIE diagram. Lines of constant hue are slightly curved, and contours of constant chroma are smooth but irregular. Such plots, or a computer having the plots in memory, can be used to convert chromaticity to Munsell hue and chroma [3].

Many problems involving color vision and the mixture of colored lights can be solved conveniently using the diagram. However, a given distance on one part of the diagram may not represent the same perceived color difference as the same distance on another part of the diagram. Industrial color management is mainly concerned with the color differences involved in process control. For this reason, there have been many attempts to find a way to transform CIE x,y,Y space to a uniform color space—a space in which distances correspond to perceived color differences. It has been shown that an ideal transformation is not possible. The color space most widely used is the CIELAB space, described by a rectangular coordinate system in which L^*, a^*, and b^* are plotted at right angles to each other. L^* represents lightness. Positive a^* is in the red direction, negative a^* in the green direction, positive b^* in the yellow direction, and negative b^* in the blue direction. In this system, color differences are fairly well represented by geometric distances [1].

The CIELAB space can be represented in cylindrical coordinates, using L^*, a hue angle $h = \arctan b^*/a^*$, and chroma $C = (a^{*2} + b^{*2})^{1/2}$. These coordinates are quite similar to Munsell value, Munsell hue, and Munsell chroma, respectively. This coordinate system is particularly well suited to the task of setting industrial color tolerances. People accept slight mismatches in lightness or chroma more readily than an equivalent mismatch in hue. With the slightest shift in hue, people see a "different color." The tolerance in h can be set tighter than the tolerance in L^* or C, and the tolerances on L^* and C might also differ. Careful management of tolerances is of great commercial importance, because it helps assure that all acceptable items are delivered (and paid for) and that no unacceptable ones are (with costly consequences) [13].

It may be noted that the term *lightness* is used to describe reflecting surfaces, whereas *brightness* is used to describe luminous surfaces. (*Luminous intensity* is the amount of light emitted per unit solid angle, so it is properly applied to a source small enough to appear as a "point.")

Figure 9.4 The CIE Chromaticity Diagram, Showing the Planckian Locus and the Chromaticities of CIE Illuminants A, B, C, D$_{65}$, and the Equi-energy Point E

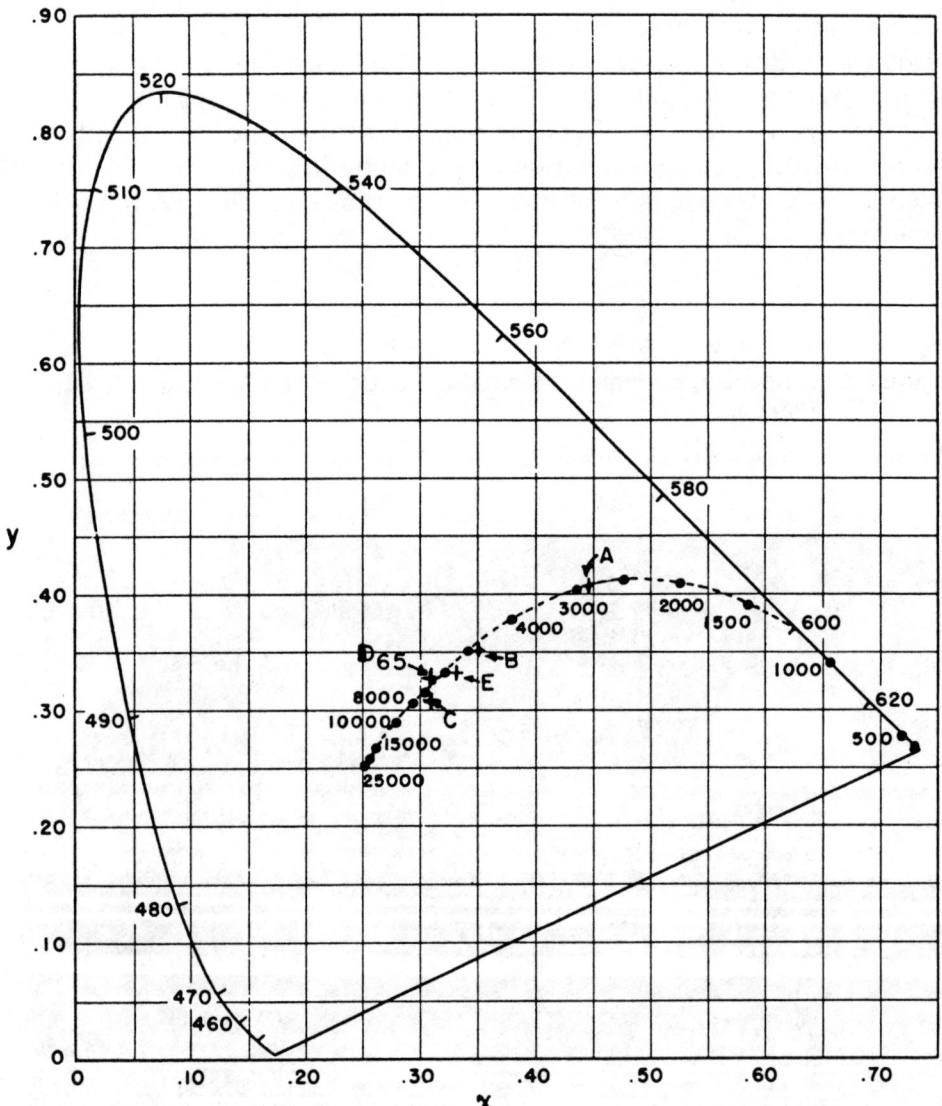

Spectrophotometric Methods

There are several approaches to spectrophotometry. When a prism is used to form a spectrum, the variation of wavelength with distance is not linear. A grating produces a linearly dispersed spectrum. The spectrum can be scanned by varying angular relationships with respect to prisms or gratings. Narrow-band filters, such as interference filters, may be used to isolate wavelength bands. Scanning provides readings for various wavelengths in series. Measurements can be made at many wavelengths at one time, by projecting the spectrum onto an array of sensors [9].

Figure 9.5 A Spectrophotometer Measuring the Color of a Textile in a Dyeing Plant

The device traverses the web, to measure near the edges and in the middle.

Illumination

The source of illumination may be an incandescent lamp, a continuous gas-discharge lamp, or a flash lamp. In on-line applications, as shown in figure 9.5, it is desirable to be able to measure at a specific place on the web, rather than measure an average color over some distance. This is done by the same method that is used to stop action in photography—the use of a flash source that provides very bright illumination for a very short time, about 30 microseconds. Pulsed-xenon flash is usually used. If the photometric system is synchronized with the flash, the system is insensitive to ambient light, even full sunlight on the web. Such a system can have a high signal-to-noise ratio, because of the high instantaneous illumination level. It does not heat the specimen, because the total energy is much smaller than that applied when an incandescent lamp illuminates the specimen continuously. Such heating can change the color of some specimens, a phenomenon known as *thermochromism*.

Fluorescence

Some materials absorb radiant power in one band of wavelengths and emit the power at longer wavelengths. This process is called *fluorescence*. It can greatly exaggerate the chroma, causing materials to seem to glow. White textiles, paper, and plastics tend to yellow with age, so fluorescent dyes are added to these materials to make them whiter. The dyes absorb power in the ultraviolet spectrum and re-emit the power in the blue region of the spectrum, where yellowish materials absorb light. Here is the important exception to the general rule, mentioned earlier, that the spectral power distribution of the illumination is of little consequence in spectrophotometry. When fluorescent materials are measured, it is essential that the spectral power distribution of the illumination closely simulate that of CIE Illuminant D_{65}, including the ultraviolet component. Only in that way can the fluorescent material contribute the same amount to the blue region as it would if illuminated by standard daylight. If the specimens to be measured are not fluorescent, the spectrum may be scanned by illuminating with light of one wavelength at a time and measuring the reflected light at all wavelengths. However, this option is not permissible for fluorescent specimens. In the case of paper with a fluorescent whitening agent, measurements in the blue region would not have the fluorescent component, because the specimen would not have been irradiated by the ultraviolet power needed to excite fluorescence.

Densitometry

In photography, color is produced by developing varying amounts of colored dyes in three layers. In color printing, images are printed with inks of three different colors. In both cases, the primary colors are yellow, magenta, and cyan. Yellow dyes and inks absorb blue light, magenta absorbs green, and cyan absorbs red. Systems, like color television, that add various amounts of red, green, and blue primary lights, are called additive systems. Systems that produce color by using varying amounts of yellow, magenta, and cyan colorants to subtract blue, green, and red light are called subtractive systems.

Photographic and color printing operations are monitored and controlled by simply measuring the transmission or reflection of light in three narrow spectral bands in the blue, green, and red regions, where the yellow, magenta, and cyan colorants absorb most strongly. The results of measurement are not reported in terms of the transmittance factor T or the reflectance factor R, but rather in terms of optical density. Transmission density D_T is defined as $D_T = \log_{10} 1/T$. Transmission density is related directly to the mass of colorant per unit of area, so it was a natural choice of photographic scientists who wanted to quantify images. By analogy, reflection density D_R is defined as $D_R = \log_{10} 1/R$. The higher the density, the darker the image. Such measurements are favored in photography and the graphic arts, because the blue, green, and red densities correspond to the amounts of the colorants being used to produce color. Knowing the deviation from normal, an operator knows which part of the process to adjust.

An instrument to measure optical density is called a *densitometer*. It consists of a light source focused on a small area, appropriate filters, a photosensor, a circuit to convert the output signal to a logarithmic scale, and a display. Densitometers are designed for bench use and for measurements on-line. On-line measurements are facilitated by the use of electronic flash illumination that may last only 10 microseconds per flash. With the proper triggering device to sense when a measurement should be made, a control patch a few millimeters in diameter on a web moving 60 miles per hour can be measured.

Densitometers do not measure color, because the three filters are not designed to simulate the human color-mixture functions. Printers printing advertising or packaging often find it necessary to measure color, to be sure that specifications are met.

Though densitometry is theoretically applicable to the monitoring or control of any coloring process based on a few specific colorants, it is rarely used outside the technologies mentioned.

Geometric Conditions

The color of a surface depends on the direction or directions of illumination and the direction from which the surface is observed. Where color is concerned, it all depends on how you look at it! Correspondingly, measured values depend on the geometry of the illuminator and receiver. The CIE has standardized two general kinds of geometric arrangements of the measuring system.

The sphere method employs an integrating sphere, which is a hollow sphere painted flat white inside. Light is admitted through a small hole, and the interior of the sphere becomes uniformly bright. A sample placed at a small aperture in the sphere is illuminated uniformly from just about every direction. It is diffusely illuminated, like a specimen exposed to the unobstructed hazy sky. The color of the light reflected from the specimen, through another small hole, is measured.

In the other method, known as 45/0, the specimen is illuminated at 45 degrees to the normal and the light reflected along the normal is measured. When this geometric arrangement is used, light specularly reflected from the top surface of the specimen is not measured. Such specularly reflected light is the color of the light source, because it has not penetrated to the interior of the specimen, where pigments or dyes impart color. The color of that light is not considered typical of the color of the specimen. This method does not require instrumentation in contact with the specimen, as is necessary with the sphere method. For this reason, 45/0 geometry is favored for on-line applications. Sometimes, nonstandard geometry is used and, when it is, there is no assurance that on-line measurements will accord with measurements made with standard laboratory equipment. Nonetheless, for process control, such geometry may be useful.

Process Monitoring and Control

A color-production process may be monitored with an on-line colorimeter or spectrophotometer. Usually the colorimetric data are displayed on a video display terminal, to assist an operator in controlling the process. In some cases, processes have been controlled directly by signals from color sensors.

To monitor color variation from the center to the side of the web, as well as end to end, several sensors may be used or a single sensor may be scanned from side to side. Some processes require color measurement on both sides of the web, using two or more sensors.

Any of the colorimetric quantities can be used for color control. The CIELAB quantities L^*, a^*, and b^* or L^*, C, and h are often used. Data are often displayed

in the form of control charts—displays of the variation of colorimetric quantities with respect to time, data being shown relative to upper and lower control limits. The percentage of approach to the limits may be indicated on the display by a change in color of the points or bars representing variables, and the existence of a point out of tolerance may trigger an alarm. Careful attention to the displayed data may permit correction of a trend before a variable exceeds the tolerance, with costly consequences.

Inevitably, operators attentive to variables displayed in real time come to recognize influences that would not be noticed if charts were not seen until some time later. The effect of a sudden draft or other such influence may be observed as it happens and the connection may be established. Thus the contribution of on-line color measurement to the ability to control a process often exceeds expectations.

Measurement as a Process

The color-measurement process can be controlled like any production process. Stable standard colors are measured periodically and the results are plotted on control charts. In this way, data can be accumulated to ascertain the precision of the method. Realistic tolerances can be set, and there can be a statistical basis for knowing when measured values deviate significantly from normal. Drift or other failure of the measurement process becomes apparent as significant deviations when the standards are measured.

References

References Cited in Text

1. American Society for Testing and Materials. *Recommendations on Uniform Color Spaces, Color Difference Equations, and Psychometric Color Terms.* Supplement No. 2 to CIE Publication No. 15(E–1.3.1)1971/(TC–1.3.)1978. Philadelphia, PA: American Society for Testing and Materials.

2. ———. *Standard Method for Computing the Colors of Objects by Using the CIE System.* ASTM E 308–85. Philadelphia, PA: American Society for Testing and Materials, 1985.

3. ———. *Standard Method of Specifying Color by the Munsell System.* ASTM D 1535–89. Philadelphia, PA: American Society for Testing and Materials, 1989.

4. ———. *Standard Practice for Visual Evaluation of Color Differences of Opaque Materials*. ASTM D 1729–89. Philadelphia, PA: American Society for Testing and Materials, 1989.

5. Central Bureau of the CIE. *CIE Standard Colorimetric Illuminants*. CIE Publication No. CIE S001. Vienna, Austria: Central Bureau of the CIE, 1986.

6. ———. *CIE Standard Colorimetric Observers*. CIE Publication No. CIE S002. Vienna, Austria: Central Bureau of the CIE, 1986.

7. ———. *Colorimetry*. 2nd ed. CIE Publication No. 15.2. Vienna, Austria: Central Bureau of the CIE, 1986.

8. Division of Quantum Metrology, National Physical Laboratory, Teddington, Middlesex, U.K.

9. Kishner, S. J. "A Pulsed-Xenon Spectrophotometer with Parallel Wavelength Sensing." *Proc. Color 77*. Proceedings of International Color Association. Bristol, England: Adam Hilger, 1977.

10. Munsell, A. H. *A Color Notation*. 14th ed. Baltimore, MD: Munsell Color Company, 1981.

11. Newhall, S. M., D. Nickerson, and D. B. Judd. "Extension of the Munsell Renotation System to Very Dark Colors." *J. Opt. Soc. Am.* vol. 46 (1956):281.

12. ———. "Final Report of the OSA Subcommittee on the Spacing of the Munsell Colors." *J. Opt. Soc. Am.* vol. 33 (1943):385.

13. Society of Automotive Engineers. *Recommended Practice: Instrumental Color Difference Measurement for Exterior Finishes, Textiles, and Colored Trim*. SAE J 1545. Warrendale, PA: Society of Automotive Engineers, 1986.

14. *Webster's Third New International Dictionary of the English Language Unabridged*. Springfield, MA: G. & C. Merriam Co., 1966, p. 448 *et seq*.

Additional Reading

1. Billmeyer, F. W., Jr., and M. Saltzman. *Principles of Color Technology*. 2nd ed. New York: Wiley-Interscience, 1981.

2. Judd, D. B., and G. W. Wyszecki. *Color in Business Science and Industry*. 3rd ed. New York: Wiley, 1975.

Chapter 10 Intelligent Eddy Current Sensing Systems

George Mordwinkin

Eddy Current Sensors: Basics

Eddy current sensing devices are the "intelligent" sensor types used in metal-sensing applications. They are used for a variety of sensing tasks, such as noncontact distance measurement, proximity limit switch applications, crack and defect detectors, metal sorting, material and plating thickness, noncontact temperature measurement, and monitoring of metallic microstructures (table 10.1).

The unique feature of the eddy current sensor is its ability to receive instantaneously from the metallic sensing target information about its microstructural condition. It does this by measuring its electromagnetic characteristics (table 10.2) without making physical contact. In real-life situations, the knowledge of microstructural characteristics of metal parts is often more important than the knowledge of their chemical composition, because the physical behavior (hardness, for example) depends on the microstructural condition and not necessarily on the chemical composition.

Principle of Operation

A basic eddy current sensing system consists of a sensing coil (single- or multiple-winding type), an oscillator, an amplifier, and a phase and/or amplitude discriminator (figure 10.1). The detailed front end of an absolute (single-winding) circuit used in a digital eddy current system for monitoring the microstructure and for metal grade sorting is shown in figure 10.2. Systems used for crack and

Table 10.1 Eddy Current Sensors: Typical Applications

Detection Principle	Applications
Metal Presence	Metal detectors
	Limit switches
	Speed monitoring
	Broken tool detection
Sensing Gap	Noncontact positioning control
	Eccentricity measurement
	Vibration measurement
	Plating thickness measurement
	Gauging
	Plastic film thickness measurement
	Noncontact sequence control generator
Conductivity	Conductivity measurement
	Sorting nonmagnetic metals
Resistivity	Resistivity measurement
	Temperature measurement
	Metal sorting
	Hardened case thickness measurement
	Weld detection
	Weld integrity monitoring
	Stress detection
	Defects detection (cracks)
	Metallic grain size monitoring
Permeability	Magnetic/nonmagnetic metals sorting
	Curie point detection
	Hardness testing
	Weld integrity monitoring
	Stress detection
	Defect detection (cracks)

defect detection, such as that shown in figure 10.3 use a differential input sensing circuit.

The eddy current sensor operates similarly to an electrical transformer. The sensing coil is the primary winding of the transformer. The secondary windings are the small eddy current loops induced by the variable magnetic field of the sensing coil in the metallic sensing target. The size of the eddy current loops, which determine the "penetration depth," are determined by the sensing frequency and the type of metal. A typical eddy current penetration chart is shown in figure 10.4.

PRINCIPLE OF OPERATION

Table 10.2 Electric Characteristics of Metals (at 70°F)

Metal	Conductivity (% IACS)	Resistivity (microhm/cm)	Permeability (u)
Copper	100	1.7	1
6061-T6 aluminum	42	4.1	1
7075-T6 aluminum	32	5.3	1
Magnesium	37	4.6	1
Lead	7.8	22	1
Uranium	6.0	29	1
Zirconium	3.4	50	1
304 stainless steel	2.5	70	1.02
High alloy steel	2.9	60	750
Cast iron	10.7	16	175

As in an electrical transformer, the electromagnetic load characteristics of the metal under test are reflected back to the primary winding (sensing coil). These metal characteristics change the phase and amplitude of the sensing coil. These changes are detected and used as control variables. The phase change in the eddy current sensing circuit is similar to the "power factor" change in a power transformer. By reading the resistance and permeability characteristics of the metal under test, eddy current instrumentation can monitor the metallurgical characteristics of metals.

When a metal is introduced in the magnetic field of the sensing coil of an eddy current instrument, the permeability of the magnetic material will change the inductive reactance, and the resistivity of the material will change the resistance of the sensing coil. Figure 10.5 shows the mathematical formula of the sensing coil impedance for nonmagnetic material and figure 10.6 shows the formula for magnetic materials.

Figure 10.1 Typical Eddy Current Sensing Device

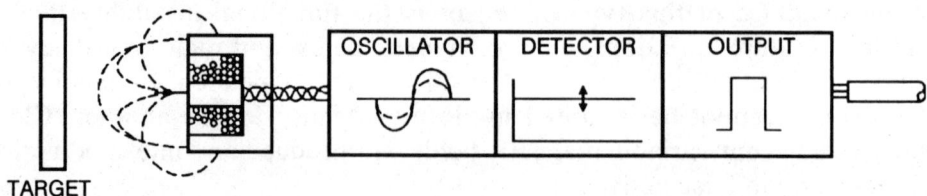

TARGET

Figure 10.2 Basic Eddy Current Sensor: Absolute Type

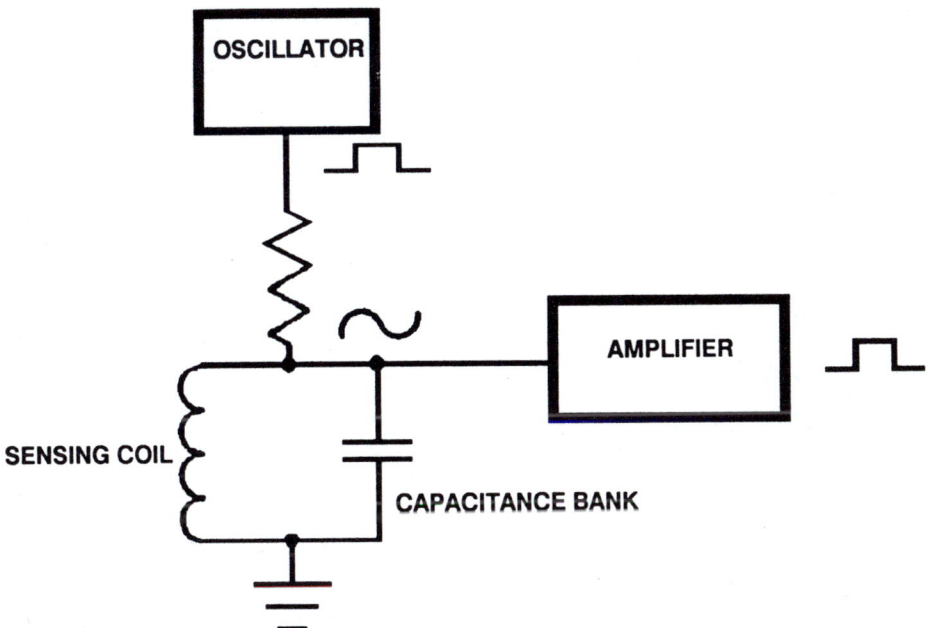

Frequency Sources

There are a number of different methods to generate the excitation power for eddy current sensing devices.

Simple devices, such as proximity limit switches, usually use an oscillator, with the sensing winding being an active component of the oscillator. The change in the inductance of the sensing coil caused by the presence of a metal will cause a variation in the oscillator frequency and/or amplitude. These variations are detected and the output circuit is activated.

The advantage of this approach is its simplicity. A complete limit switch assembly can be packaged in a small enclosure. This method typically is used in two-wire proximity limit switches and is used as a direct replacement for the conventional mechanical limit switches.

The disadvantage of this type of sensor is the functional instability due to ambient temperature variations, electromagnetic fields, and radio-frequency interference. In addition, eddy current sensors using independent frequency excitation sources cannot be mounted in close proximity to one another. Close proximity of adjacent variable magnetic fields will produce an "intermodulation effect," resulting in false activations.

FREQUENCY SOURCES 247

Figure 10.3 Basic Eddy Current Sensor: Differential Type

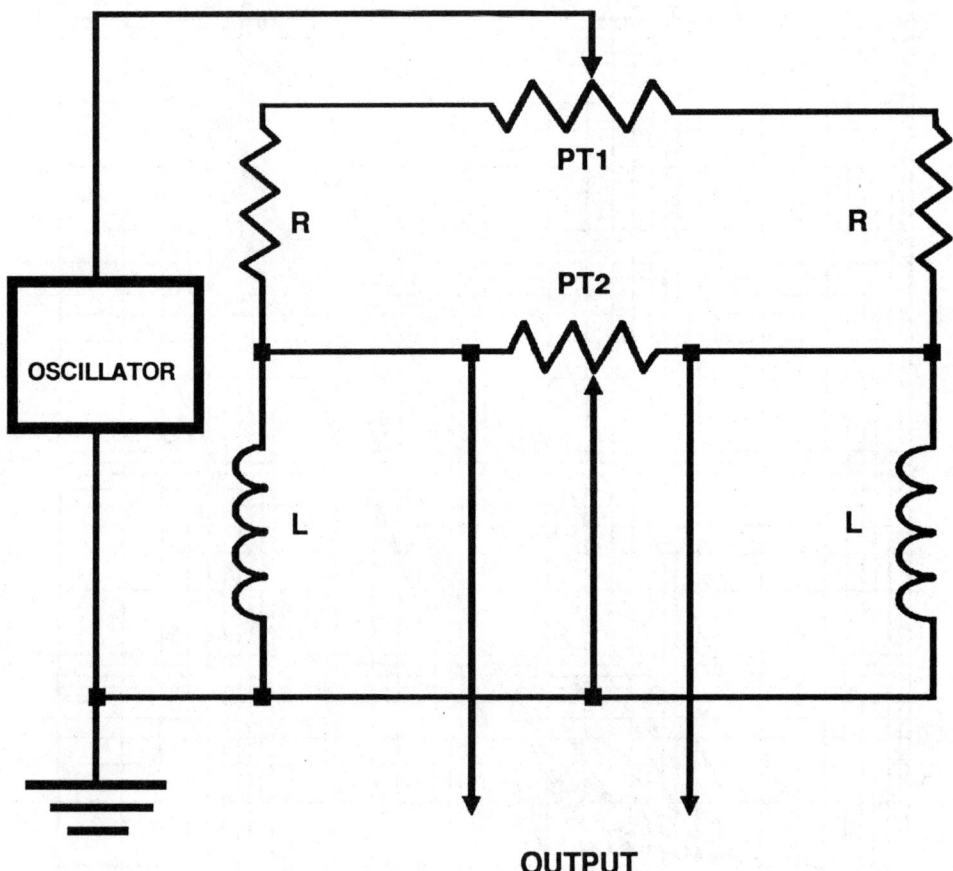

In certain applications, such as metal detectors used for treasure hunting, the stability of the frequency generator may not be too important. The operator of the metal detector is constantly tuning and optimizing the sensitivity and selectivity of the instrument. In an industrial environment, however, the operator has neither the time nor the desire to optimize the detector's performance constantly. An ideal industrial eddy current instrument should operate reliably for years without recalibration.

The most advanced eddy current sensing systems use an independent crystal-controlled oscillator. The same frequency source can be used for a multiple sensing system. This approach eliminates problems with temperature instability and substantially improves noise immunity. The most attractive feature of this method is the ability to use multiple sensing elements in close proximity to one another. Using the same frequency source eliminates the "intermodulation effect."

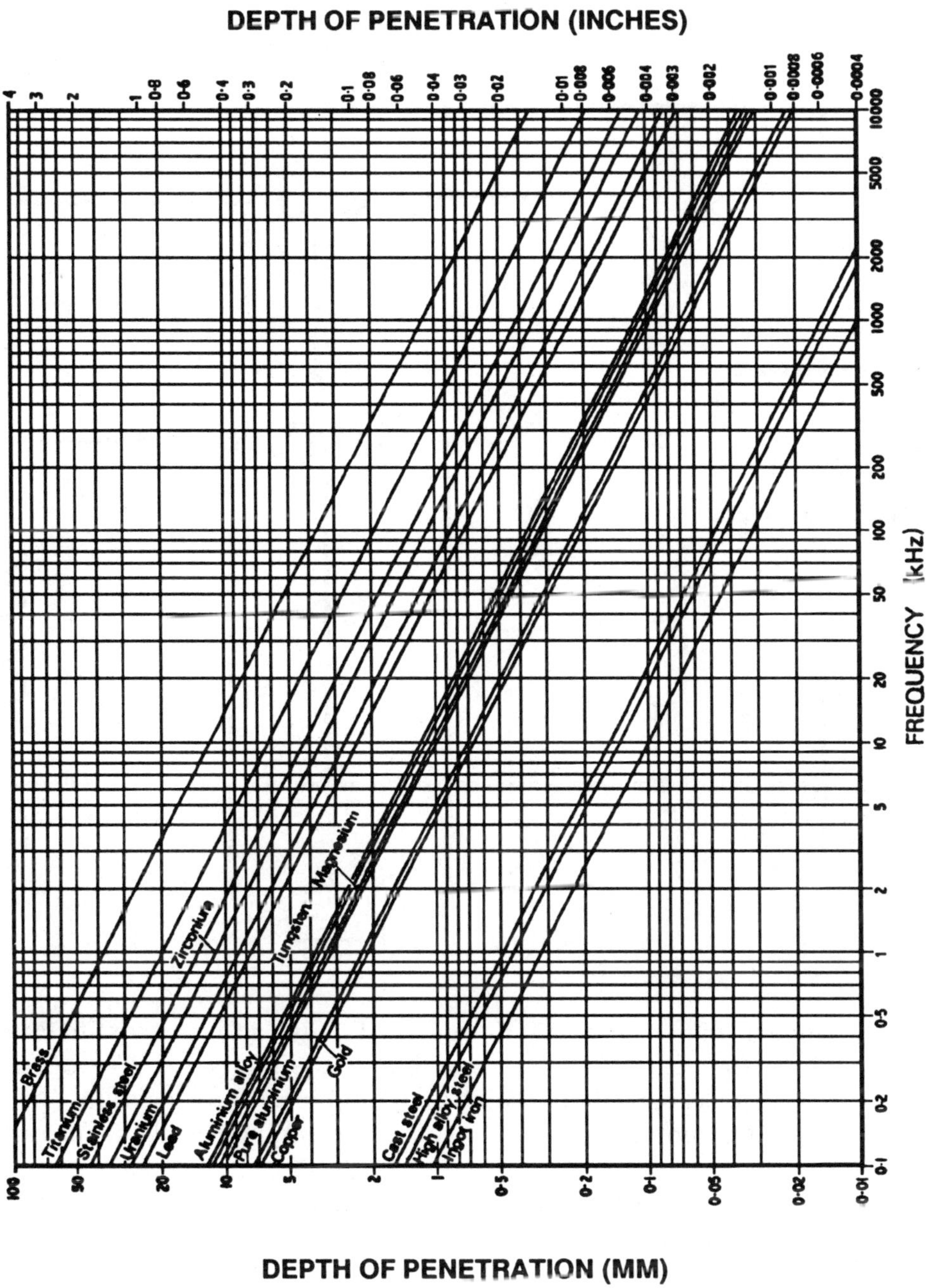

Figure 10.4 Effective Depth of Penetration of Eddy Currents

FREQUENCY SOURCES

Figure 10.5 Sensing Coil Impedance for Nonmagnetic Metals

$$Z = \sqrt{X_L^2 + (R_{COIL} + R_{METAL})^2}$$

WHERE:

- Z = SENSING COIL IMPEDANCE
- X_L = INDUCTIVE REACTANCE OF THE COIL
- R_{COIL} = SENSING COIL RESISTANCE
- R_{METAL} = REFLECTED RESISTANCE OF METAL UNDER TEST

More advanced eddy current instrumentation typically will require a range of available frequencies to optimize performance for the specific application. The frequency source should be one that includes a provision for easy frequency changes.

Figure 10.6 Sensing Coil Impedance for Magnetic Metals

$$Z = \sqrt{(X_{COIL} + X_{METAL})^2 + (R_{COIL} + R_{METAL})^2}$$

WHERE:

- Z = SENSING COIL IMPEDANCE
- X_{COIL} = INDUCTIVE REACTANCE OF THE COIL
- X_{METAL} = INDUCTIVE REACTANCE OF THE METAL UNDER TEST
- R_{COIL} = SENSING COIL RESISTANCE
- R_{METAL} = REFLECTED RESISTANCE OF METAL UNDER TEST

Sensing Coils

Basic sensing coil designs are the probe and encircling types. The probe design uses a *pancake-type* sensing winding, in which the sensing target is located in front of the coil. The V-*groove* and *Fork* designs are basically modified probe types. When the encircling sensing coil is used, the sensing material is passed through the coil winding. From an application point of view, sensing heads are classified as either *absolute* or *differential* types. Absolute sensing heads are used to monitor metallic microstructure by reading the resistivity and permeability of the metal. Absolute sensing heads can be of single- or dual-winding construction. The single-winding type combines the function of the driver and sensing winding. The dual type uses a separate winding as a driver. The dual-winding type is usually more sensitive.

The differential type of sensing head is used for defect-detection applications. This type of sensor ignores the same kind of material and detects only dissimilarities by comparing the signals between two sensing windings. Differential sensors use a construction of two, three, or four windings. In a two-winding design, the same windings are used as drivers and sensing coils. In a three-winding design, one winding is a driver and the other two are sensing windings. In a four-winding design, two windings are drivers and the other two are sensing windings.

Sensing Coil Design

The performance of any sensing system, and especially the eddy current type, is only as good as the quality of the sensing head. The most significant part of the design is related to the quality of the winding. Unfortunately, some designers treat this part of the design trivially and typically use magnet wire wound loosely on bobbins. Any physical impact or temperature change will cause movement of some of the loose turns of the sensing winding, disproportionally changing the inductance of the sensing windings. When this occurs (particularly in a differential sensing head) the signal becomes unbalanced, which results in false activation and/or a dramatic decrease in sensitivity.

With an absolute sensing system, any change in the inductance value of the sensing winding will prevent repetitive test results, thereby rendering previously stored reference data useless. The reference data would then have to be replaced each time the inductance of the coil changes.

A well-designed sensing winding uses special magnet wire that permits the fusing of outside insulation layers to the adjacent turns, resulting in a solid con-

struction with no loose turns. This type of winding will not permit any change of inductance values in the sensing coil resulting from temperature or mechanical shock.

Signal Detectors

Signals from the eddy current sensing heads are discriminated by both their amplitude and their phase changes. To detect these signal variations, separate detection circuits are used. Implementation of these circuits could use either an analog or a digital design.

Typical analog phase and amplitude detector circuits are shown in figures 10.7 and 10.8. In both cases, the sensing frequency carrier is converted into a DC signal level. To implement this function, a resistor/capacitor network is used. The capacitor stores the signal level, and the resistor is used to discharge the capacitor and allow a new signal value to be acquired.

The drawback of analog circuits is the effect of the RC time constant introduced by the resistor and capacitor for capturing the signal amplitude or phase level. These time constants are optimized to the sensing frequency and speed of response. An analog differential system is not reliably able to detect a standing or slowly moving target.

Figure 10.9 shows a typical digital phase detector and figure 10.10 shows a digital amplitude detector. Digital detectors do not use any resistor/capacitor networks. The speed response of the digital system is directly related to the sensing frequency and the number of sensing cycles required to identify a legitimate signal. A digital detector circuit is equally sensitive to standing or to fast-moving targets.

Filters

Filters are electronic circuit components that eliminate unwanted noise and signal frequencies. They permit passage or suppression of a certain range of frequencies. Filters are classified as low-pass, high-pass, and band pass. Depending on the type of electronic components used, a filter could be either a passive or an active type. The passive filters, as shown in figure 10.11, use resistors, capacitors, and inductors as circuit components. The active filters, as shown in figure 10.12, use operational amplifiers in addition to passive components.

Figure 10.7 Analog Phase Detector

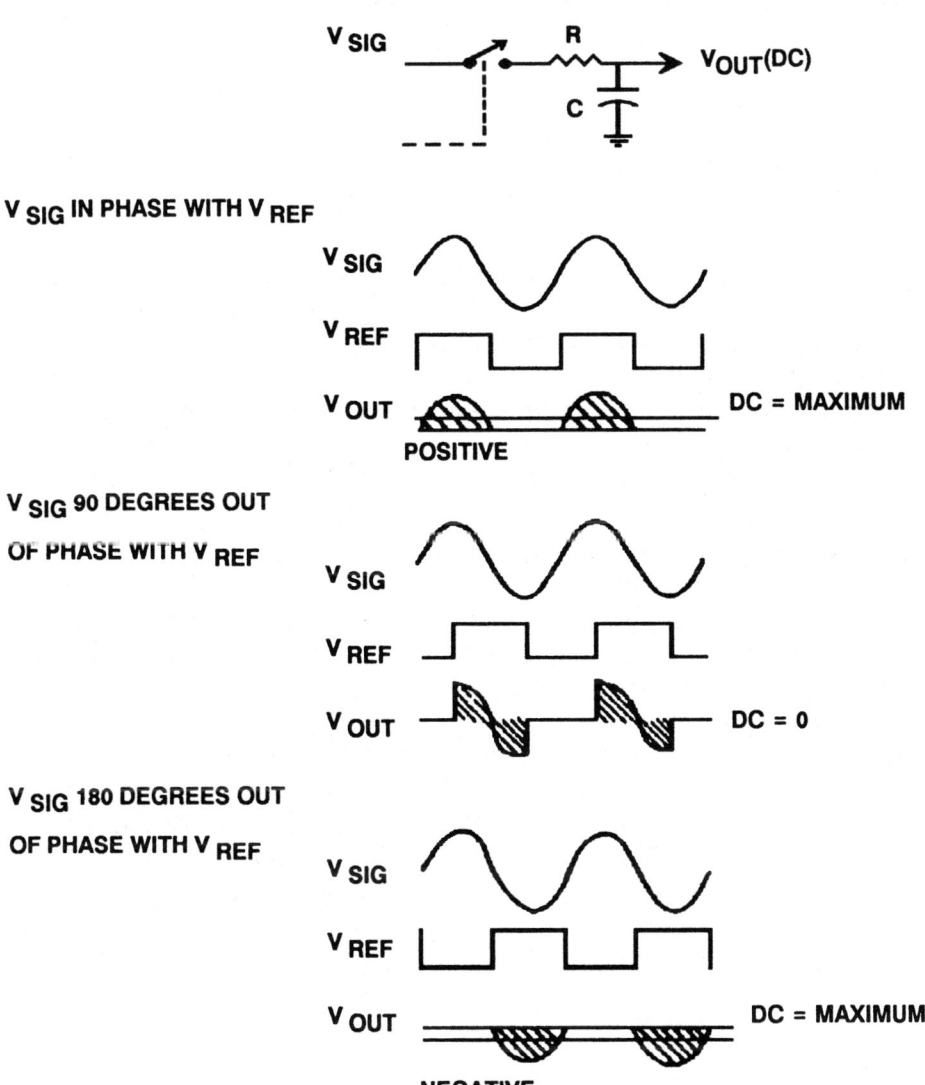

A passive filter causes a decrease in the amplitude of the signal at the output. An active filter usually restores and sometimes increases the amplitude of the output signal. Active filters display sharper response than passive filters. Filters are usually needed with analog circuitry. In digital eddy current instrumentation, hardware filters are seldom used.

Figure 10.8 Analog Amplitude Detector

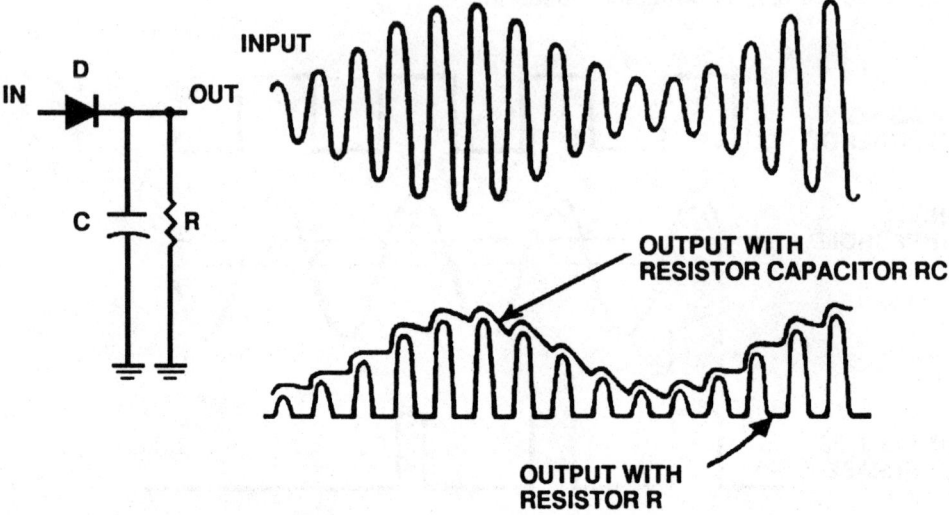

Figure 10.9 Digital Phase Detector

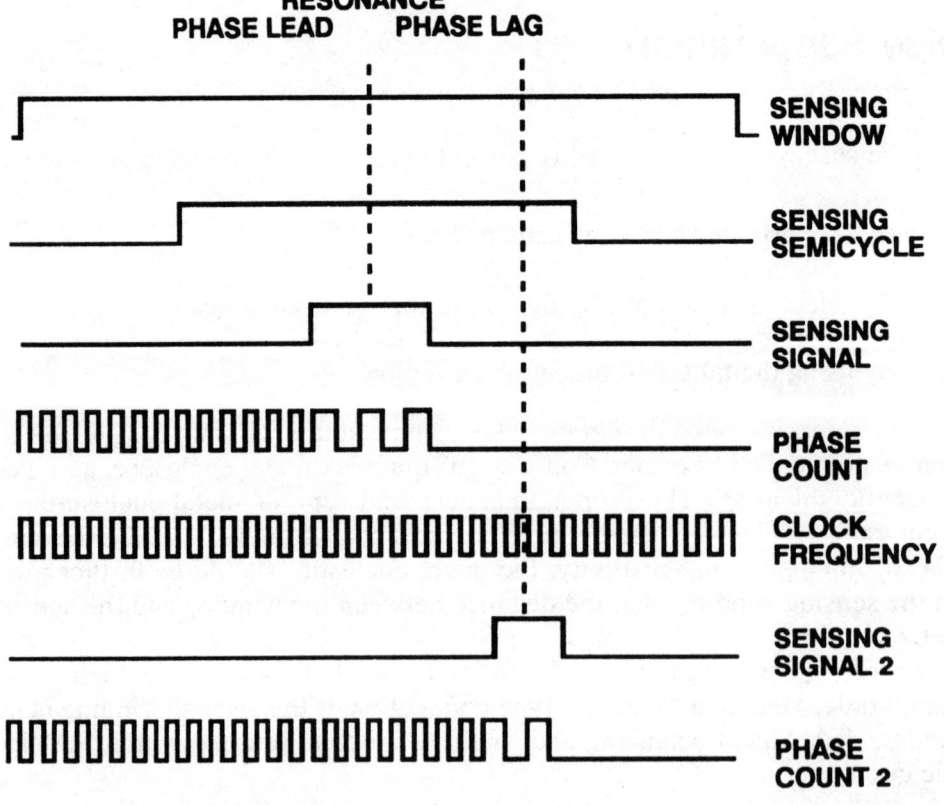

Figure 10.10 Digital Amplitude Detector

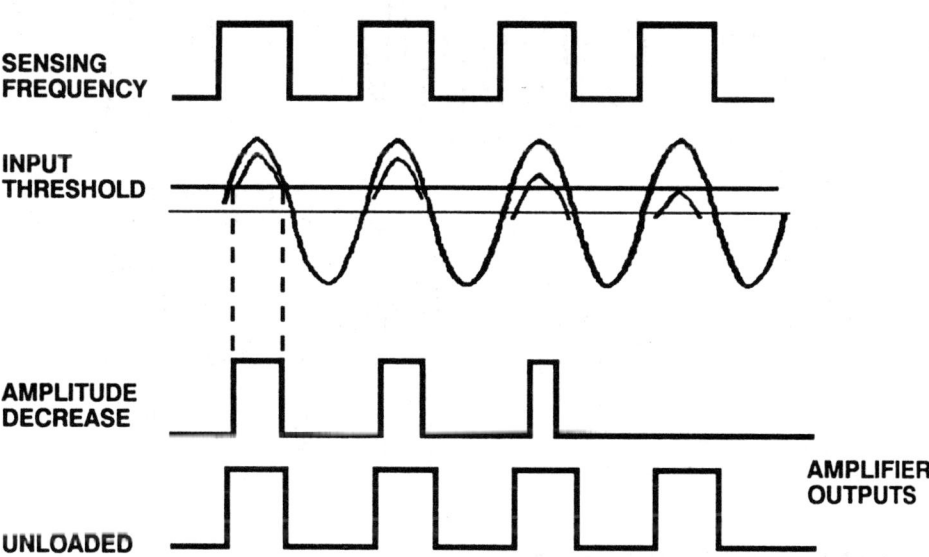

Noise Suppression

The noise susceptibility of the eddy current system can be reduced as follows:

- By properly designing the sensing head

- By selecting a suitable configuration for the sensing head

- By using digital signal processing circuitry

A proper sensing head design includes using a stable winding design (see the earlier section called "Sensing Coil Design"), a thick metal enclosure, and electromagnetic shielding. The proper thickness and type of metal enclosure will prevent external electromagnetic interference signals from penetrating the sensing head. For optimum sensitivity, the metal enclosure should be farther away from the sensing winding than the distance between the winding and the sensing target.

The preferred sensing head configuration is one that results in the highest signal amplitude. Hence, a "nulling" type connection of the sensing winding is not recommended. Signal balancing and "nulling" should be done within the electronic circuitry.

NOISE SUPPRESSION

Figure 10.11 Passive Filters

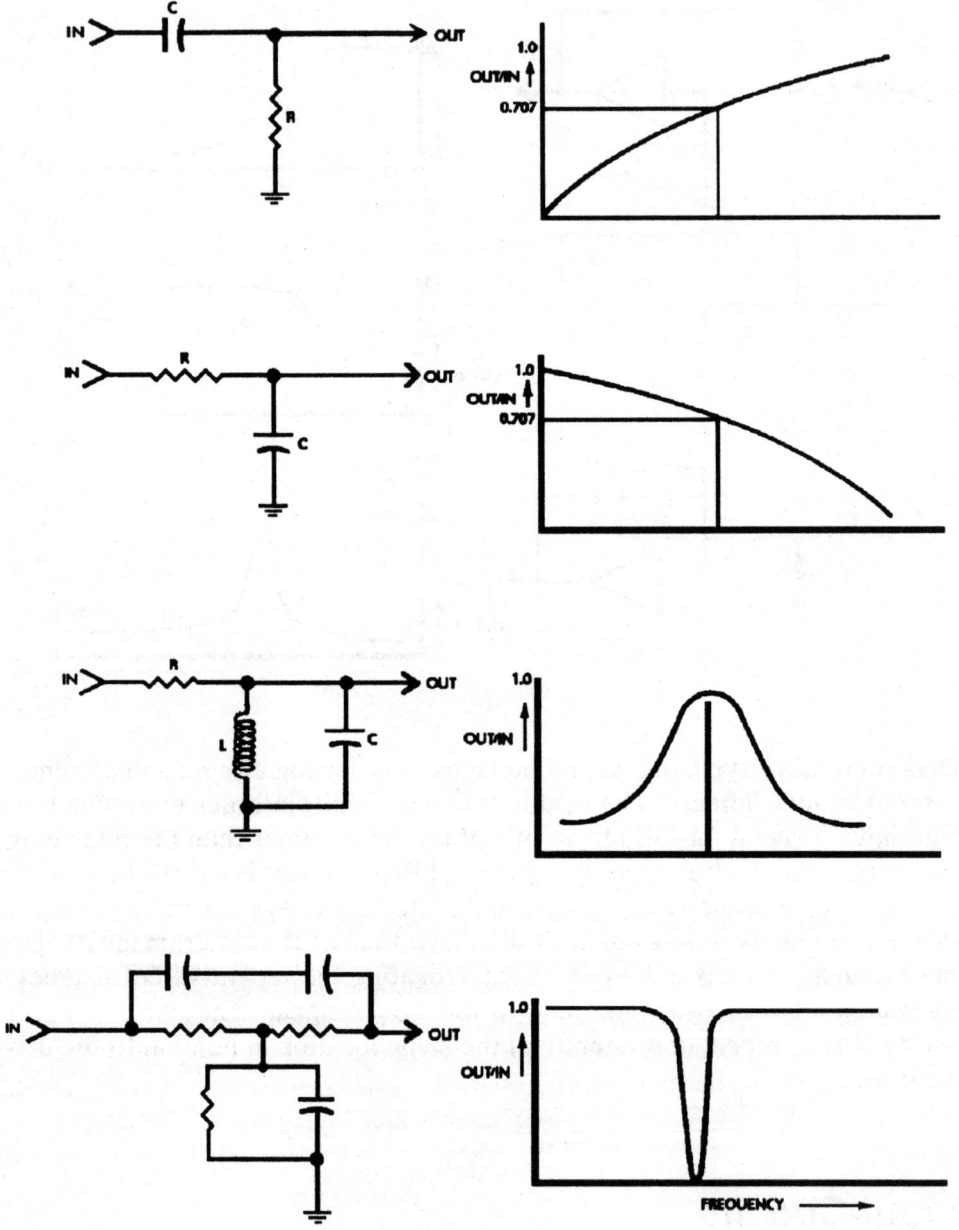

Figure 10.12 Active Filters

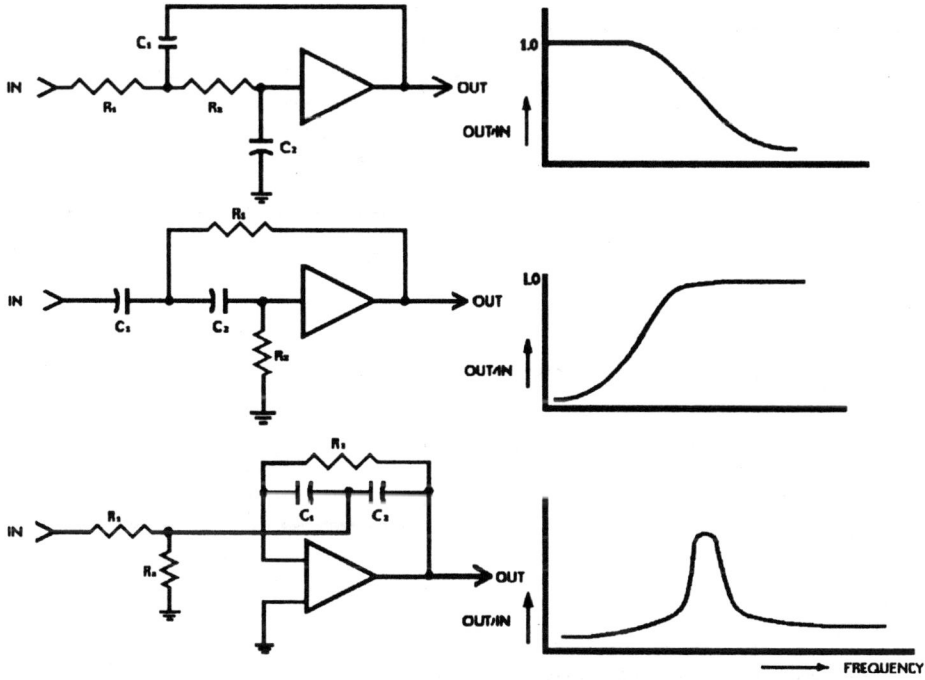

Digital circuitry typically has advantages over analog circuitry in eliminating interference noise effects. The analog sensing circuit, in order to be functional, should have a signal magnitude at least three times larger than the interference signal; otherwise, malfunction will occur. This coefficient is called the *signal-to-noise ratio*. In a properly designed digital circuit, the system performance can be made completely independent of the magnitude of the electromagnetic interference signals. This is achieved by interrogating the repetitive consistency of the signal waveform with reference to the driver signal. The noise signal will never be able to repeat consistently at the same location in relation to the driver waveform.

Output Circuits

The purpose of the output circuit is to indicate the detection of the preselected occurrence, such as the presence of a metallic object or the detection of the defect. The output device could be a mechanical or electronic relay used to dis-

play or activate other devices, such as solenoids, counters, clutches, brakes, motors, and lights.

In analog eddy current instrumentation, the output sorting criteria is usually based on the differentiation of DC signal levels (phase and/or amplitude related). In digital eddy current instrumentation, the output discrimination criteria is based on the digital values of the phase and/or duty cycle (the digital equivalent of amplitude) in absolute systems. In differential systems (defect detectors), the output discrimination is correlated to the location of the defect signal in reference to the driver waveform, also called *output gate control*. The signal position with reference to the driver waveform is described in the "noise" section of this chapter.

Applications

Overview

The following applications are described in this chapter to illustrate how different features of eddy current sensors are utilized to achieve maximum operating efficiency for specific applications.

As described, eddy current sensors feature unusual capabilities for detecting a variety of metallurgical characteristics in metallic objects. When these unique characteristics of eddy current sensors are combined with advanced electronic technology, including computer science, these systems can reach an unprecedented level of sophistication and usefulness.

Eddy Current Systems

Cable Splice Detector

The cable splice detector (figure 10.13) is an example of a differential eddy current instrument design. Safety regulations require manufacturers of wire and cables to eliminate splices, and the eddy current method is an ideal approach to resolve this problem.

Cable splices can be of various types. Some can be natural; others can be specially marked to secure reliable detection. Natural splices are twisted ends and butt or braze welds. Specially marked splices usually use ferrous wires, splice ferrules, or magnetic tapes. Some cable defects, such as a braid "bunching effect," are not rejectable defects and are ignored by using lower sensing frequencies and splice markers of dissimilar metals.

Figure 10.13 Eddy Current Cable Splice Detector

Selection of the sensing frequency is determined by the type of the splice used. When natural butt welds are to be detected, the selected sensing frequency should not be sensitive to individual cable strands and should detect only welds. Welds represent a larger metallic mass than individual cable strands; therefore, eddy current flow can be used to detect them. Detection of the welds is usually practical when wires of AWG 18 and larger gauges are involved. The sensing frequency used for detection of the natural butt welds is in the range of 40 to 100

KHz. For smaller wire sizes the insertion of a ferrous marker is recommended. The ferrous marker is also very helpful in the detection of splices in multiconductor and shielded cables.

The eddy current cable splice detector system uses a differential three-winding encircling sensing coil. Differential sensing windings ignore all identical electromagnetic characteristics of the conductor present in each sensing coil and detect only the splices and other conductor defects, which produce a dissimilar effect at both sensing windings.

The instrument works by sensing phase and amplitude changes in the sensing head. These changes may be caused by the presence of ferrous markers, welded and brazed splices, increased metallic mass due to twisting of conductor's ends, broken conductors, and missing shields or conductors.

The overall electronic circuitry of the cable splice detector is shown in figure 10.14. Some features include the following:

- Sensing frequency generated by the crystal controlled oscillator (labeled "U1" in figure 10.14) and the frequency divider (labeled "U2"). Twelve different sensing frequencies can be selected, ranging from 150 Hz to 150 KHz.

- To achieve a signal balance ("null") when no splice or other electromagnetic dissimilarities are present in the sensing field, the amplitude and phase compensation potentiometers PT1 and PT2 are used. The amplitude is controlled by varying the resistance to ground, which changes the loading effect to each sensing winding. The phase balance potentiometer PT2 controls the capacitance effect at each sensing input, which corrects any phase shift imbalance. When the resistance between the capacitor and ground is decreased, the capacitance effect is increased, thus controlling the phase relation between two input signals. This feature precludes changing sensing heads during operation. In a more advanced unit, manual potentiometers are replaced by electronic digital potentiometers. When the automatic circuit is used, the recalibration procedure takes only a fraction of a second and is activated by pushing a button.

- Another feature of this instrument is the selective output gate control, consisting of an AND gate (labeled "U6"), a set/reset generator (labeled "U3"), and a latch (labeled "U7"). The purpose of this output gate control is to allow only the desired signal to activate the output relay. The output control gate will allow passage of the signal, which is located in the preselected area of the sensing frequency cycle. This feature will eliminate the

Figure 10.-4 Cable Splice Detector: Block Diagram

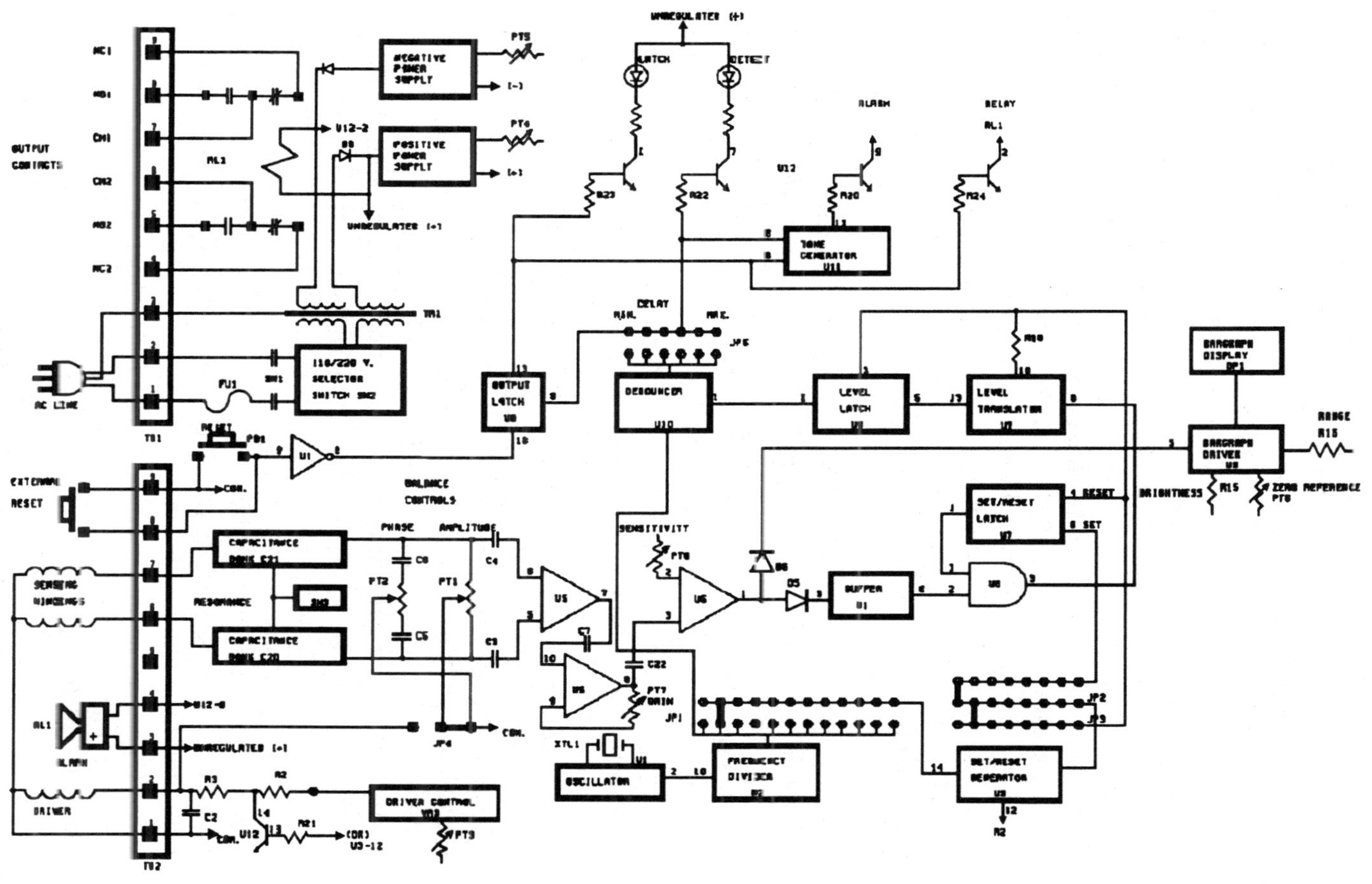

influence of noise spikes, regardless of their magnitude in comparison to the acceptable signal. The noise spikes do not appear in the same place within the sensing cycle as the legitimate signal pulses do. This phenomena allows reliable discrimination between noise spikes and acceptable signals.

- Calibration of the output control gate requires the use of the oscilloscope. The calibration is performed by generating a reference accept pulse, which matches timewise the acceptable signal window when the splice marker is present in one of the sensing windings. This allows reliable detection despite noise in the environment. In the newest eddy current cable splice detector model, the calibration of the output gate is done automatically. When the calibration button is pushed and the calibration cable splice is passed through the sensing head, a special electronic circuit records the "fingerprint" of the splice and stores it as a permanent reference in the nonvolatile memory. Automatic calibration eliminates the need for calibration at the factory and allows field recalibration at any time if required.

- Noise immunity of the device is further improved by the debouncer circuit (labeled "U10"). The signal from the output gate (labeled "U6') is converted to the 0 or 1 level, latched during the whole sensing frequency cycle, and presented to the input terminal labeled "U10". Clock pulses synchronized with the sensing frequency propagate the input signal level through the shift register circuitry of the debouncer by the number of cycles selected by jumper JP6. When the same input level is maintained during the preselected timing, the output of the debouncer will indicate the signal level (presence or absence). If the input signal level changes before the preselected number of the timing pulses is completed, the output level will not assume the new value.

Alloy Monitor

The alloy monitor is an eddy current instrument used for metal grade sorting (figure 10.15). This instrument uses an absolute sensing head and digital electronics (figure 10.16). The advantages of digital electronics have been described previously.

Figure 10.15 Eddy Current Alloy Monitor Instrument

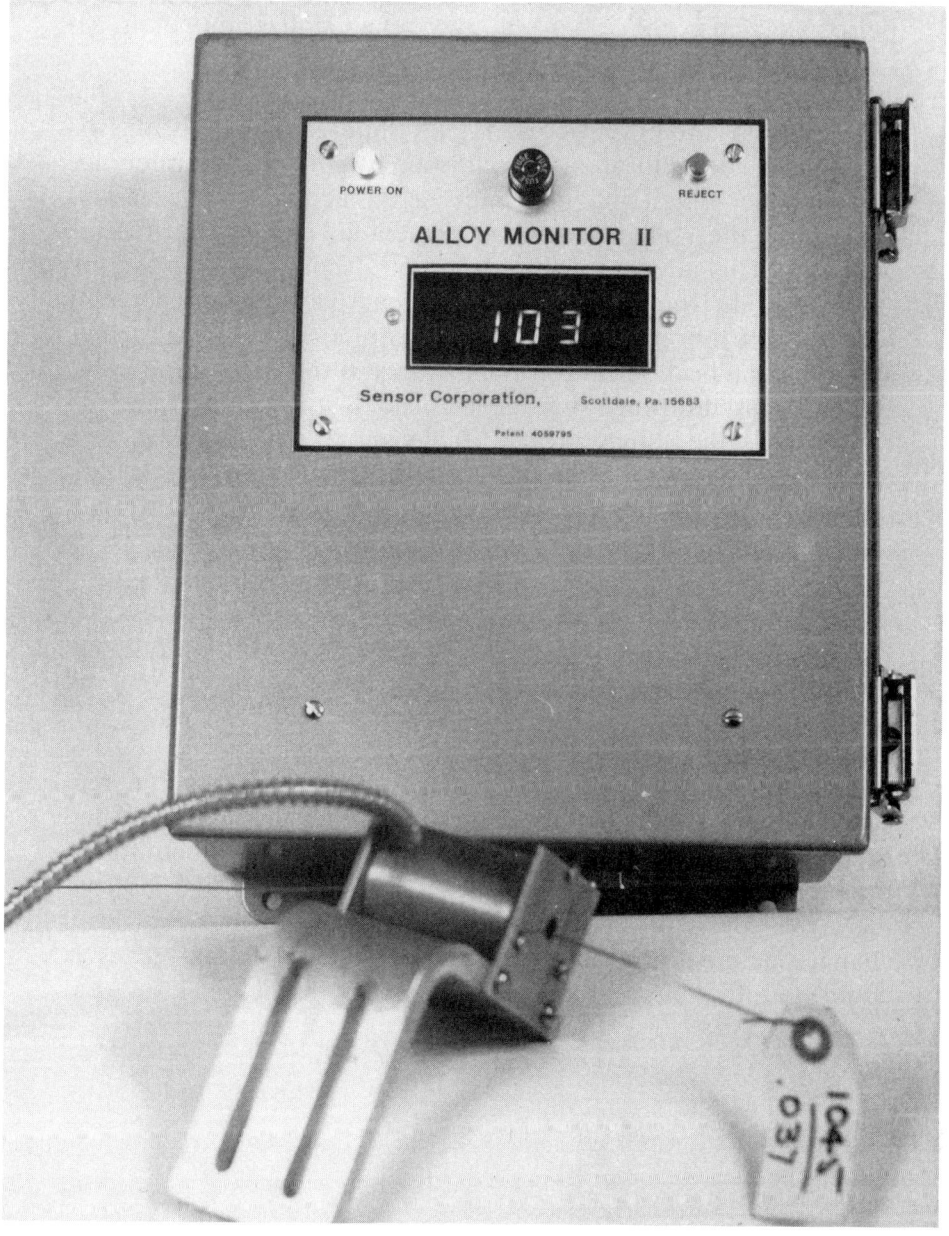

Figure 10.16 Alloy Monitor: Block Diagram

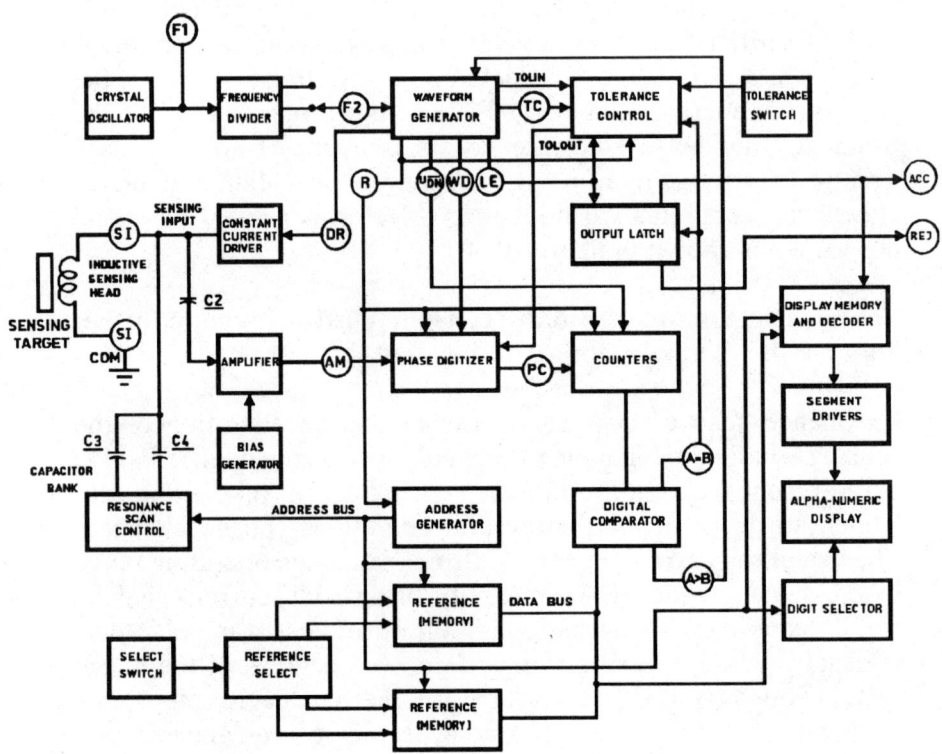

Each metal grade generates a unique three-digit code that is indicated on an LED display. This code represents the phase shift caused when the sample is inserted in the sensing field of an eddy current coil. The *acceptance code* is set by three thumbwheel-switches for each grade. Up to eight different codes can be set at one time, and a particular grade is selected by pushing a button marked with the corresponding grade number.

When the unknown metal sample is placed inside the sensing field, if a match occurs, the "accept" indicating light is energized. When the alloy monitor is used in the automatic mode, the noncoincidence with the preset code will activate the output relay, warning the operator or automatically stopping the production line.

The alloy monitor is a relatively easy instrument to use in the industrial manufacturing environment; it requires only minutes to learn how to use it. Its main application is in nondestructive inspection of incoming batches of new material to prevent accidental mix-ups. It is also an ideal instrument for "in-line" inspection of the production quality.

Some features of the instrument include the following:

- The sensing frequency is generated by a crystal oscillator (see figure 10.16), a frequency divider, and a waveform generator. A single sensing frequency is selected by connecting the input of the waveform generator (labeled "F2") to the proper output of the frequency divider. Usually up to six frequencies are available. The waveform generator, in addition to providing the driver waveform, generates various other waveforms needed for signal digitizing, as shown in figure 10.16.

- The sensing coil driver is of a "constant current" type to further improve the thermal stability of the input.

- Resonance scan control varies the resonance condition of the sensing winding by changing the value of two capacitance banks. If the resonance condition of the sensing coil is varied, the sensitivity to different microstructural conditions can be changed. The use of the capacitance bank also expands the operating range of the sensing head. The sensitivity of an eddy current sensing head to the microstructural condition of the tested metallic part is usually within the range of $+45$ to -45 degrees of the phase shift between the driver waveform and the signal across the sensing head. The capacitance bank controls this relation and expands the operating range of the sensing head.

- The phase digitizer block is a circuit that converts the sensing signal waveform directly into a digital format without using analog-to-digital converters. The basic digitizing principle is shown in the waveform diagram of figure 10.17. The waveform labeled "AM" is the signal, the position of which changes within the sensing window "WD" depending on the metal being tested. The width of the signal "AM" is related to the signal amplitude and should not influence the phase angle value. To eliminate the amplitude effect, this phase digitizing technique uses only the center of the signal waveform as a reference. The digitizing frequency (labeled "F1") begins its count with the rising edge of the sensing window waveform (labeled "WD") and is switched to the half frequency (labeled "F2") when the leading edge of the signal waveform appears. It continues counting until the end of the signal. In this way, the digital value of the phase angle is measured to the center of the signal pulse and will repeatedly show the same value regardless of variations in the signal amplitude. This digitiz-

Figure 10.17 Alloy Monitor: Digitizing Waveforms

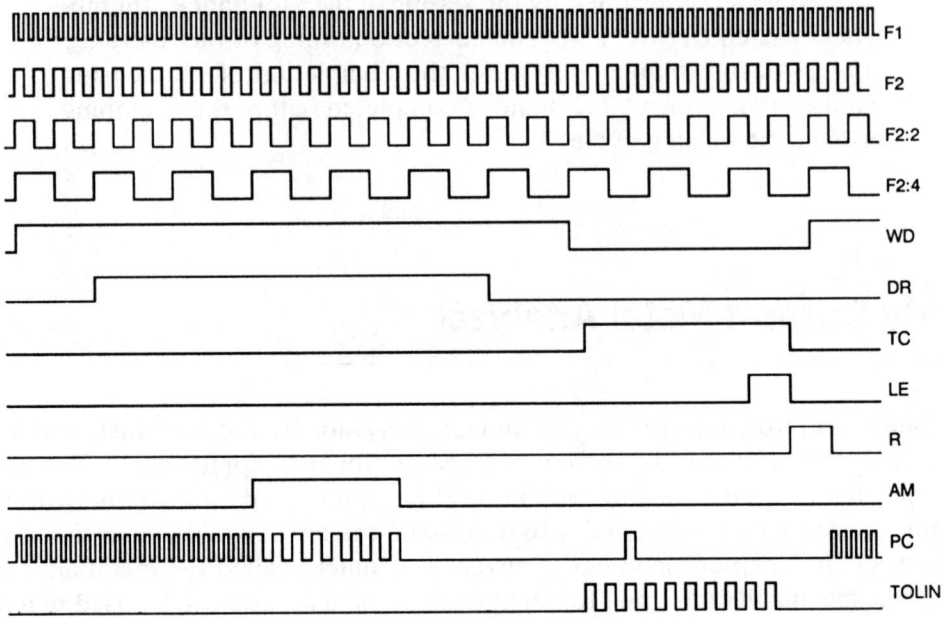

ing technique is suitable for relatively low sensing frequencies with an upper frequency range of 50 to 100 KHz (depending on the digitizing frequency "F1"). The digitizing resolution of this method decreases as the sensing frequency increases. Most metal-sorting applications require a sensing frequency up to 20 KHz; therefore, the alloy monitor operates within an acceptable digitizing resolution range.

- The digital comparator compares the digital value of the unknown metal against the memory stored or preset values of the code switches. When the values match, the output relay is energized, as described above.

- The tolerance control determines the allowed deviation between the preset and the read values. The operation of the tolerance control is determined by output signals $A=B$ and $A>B$ of the digital comparator. The $A=B$ signal inhibits the tolerance control. The output $A>B$ signal level controls the "up" or "down" counting mode of the phase digitizer and will allow the tolerance control to generate additional count pulses (see the "tolout" pulse

"tolout" pulse shown in the phase count waveform "PC" of figure 10.17). The maximum number of pulses generated by the tolerance control is controlled by the setting of the "tolerance" thumbwheel switch (+9 to −9). The correction timing of the tolerance control occurs immediately after the completion of the sensing window (waveform "TC") and is completed before the beginning of the next sensing cycle.

Eddy Current Metal Analyzer

The alloy monitor, despite its advantages, may not be the best instrument to determine the proper eddy current parameters for new applications. The eddy current nondestructive testing technique still requires experimentation with the samples of known characteristics to determine the best suitable operational parameters. The computerized eddy current instrument called the metal analyzer has been specifically designed for such evaluation tasks and can be used in manual ("laboratory") or automatic modes.

The metal analyzer (figure 10.18) utilizes an IBM-compatible personal computer. By installing proprietary eddy current instrumentation hardware and software, the IBM PC can be converted into an eddy current multifrequency scanning instrument (figure 10.19).

The computerized eddy current instrument includes features such as automatic digital scanning of frequency and capacitance, (figure 10.20)—each controls 65,000 points—automatic calibration, and the storage and retrieval of generated metallurgical signatures (figures 10.21, 10.22, 10.23, 10.24).

By incorporating computer control of the critical operational variables of eddy current nondestructive testing procedures, this tool speeds up scientific research and fully utilizes the power of the eddy current nondestructive testing technique. With the computer's help, scientific knowledge of the relationship between the microstructure of metals and eddy current behavior can be accelerated and expanded to fully utilize this method.

Conventional eddy current instruments are usually used as "crack detectors." Crack development in most cases is the last stage before the complete failure of a part occurs. It is usually the result of the formation of improper microstructure. The use of an eddy current instrument capable of monitoring the microstructure of metals can prevent the formation of the cracks by correcting the manufacturing process or detecting the formation of an undesirable microstructure before the cracks occur.

The metal analyzer is an instrument capable of reading the susceptibility to cracks, and it can play a leading role in making nondestructive testing techniques

Figure 10.18 Eddy Current Metal Analyzer

Figure 10.19 Metal Analyzer: Hardware and Software Kit

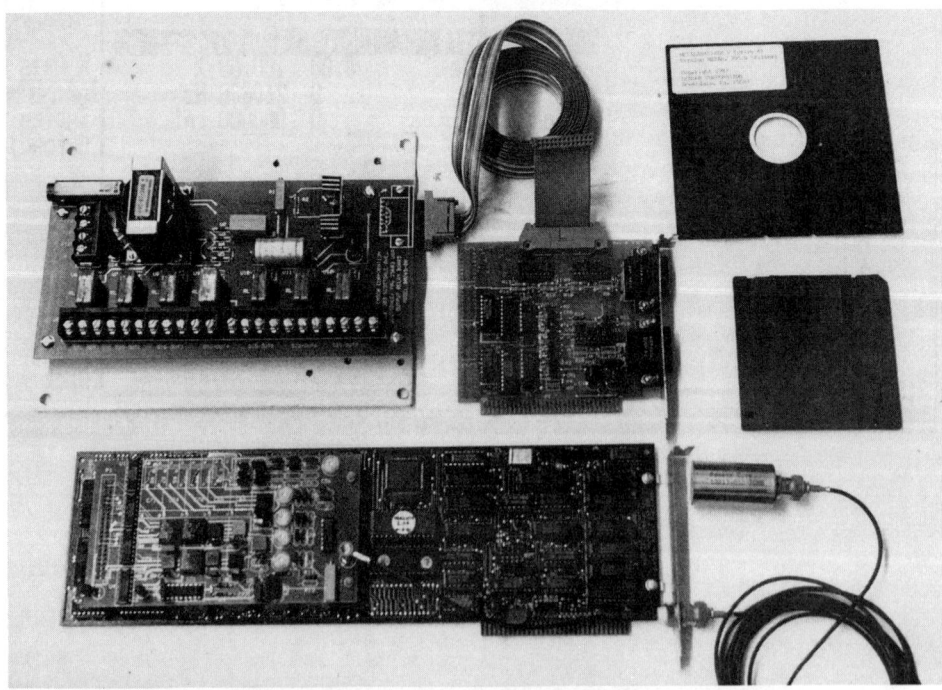

Figure 10.20   Metal Analyzer: X-Axis Parameters Menu Display

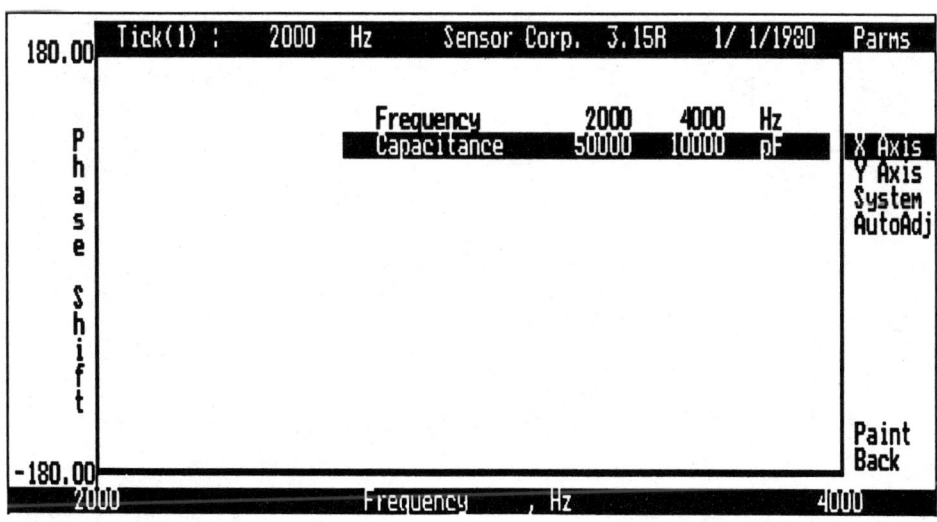

Figure 10.21   Metal Analyzer: Y-Axis Parameters Menu Display

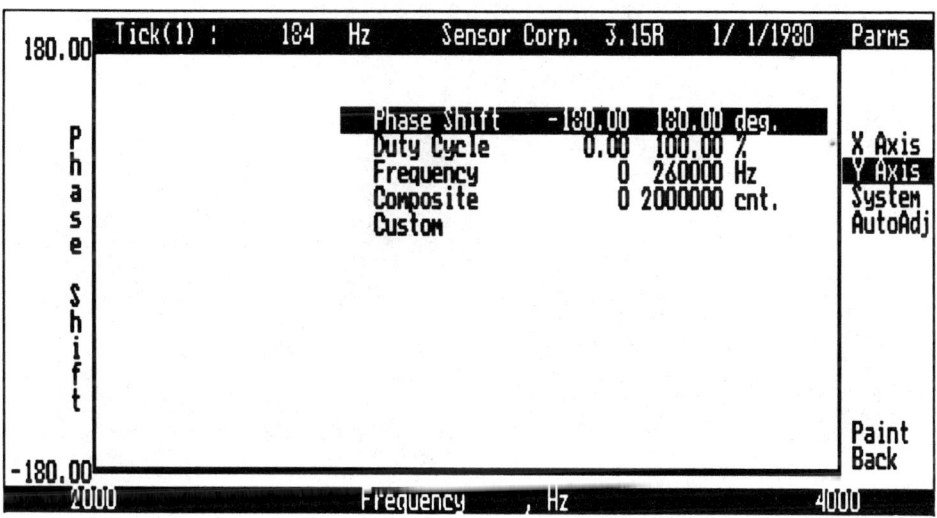

Figure 10.22   Metal Analyzer: Typical Phase Shift Signature

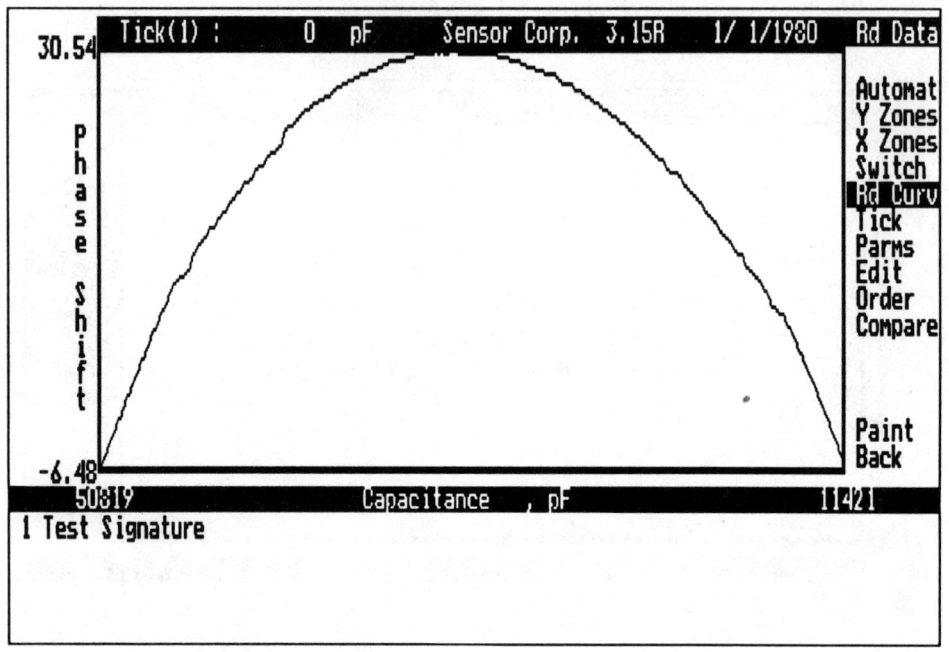

Figure 10.23   Metal Analyzer: Typical Frequency Signature

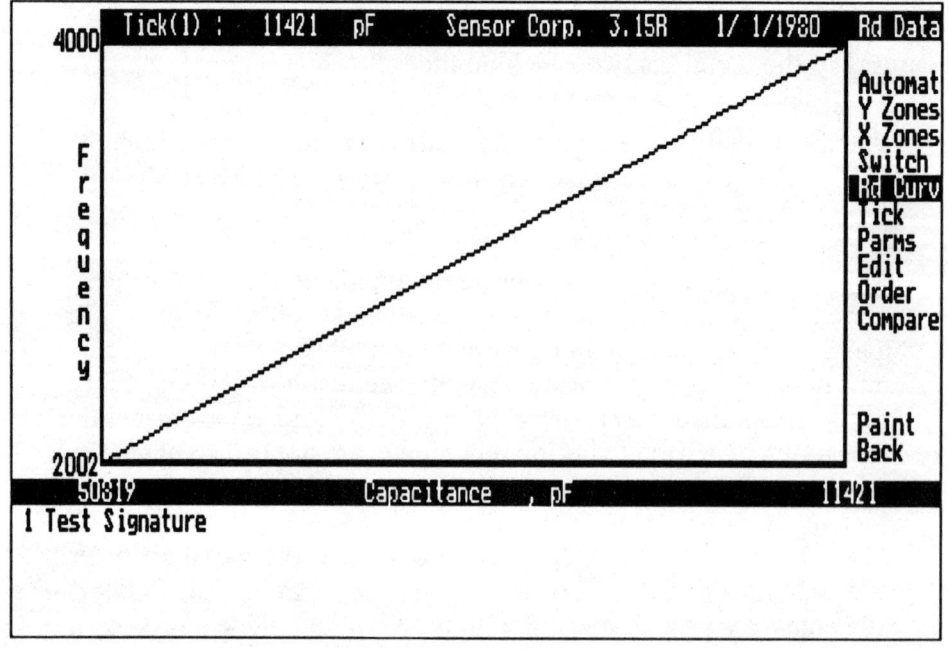

Figure 10.24 Metal Analyzer: Typical Composite Signature

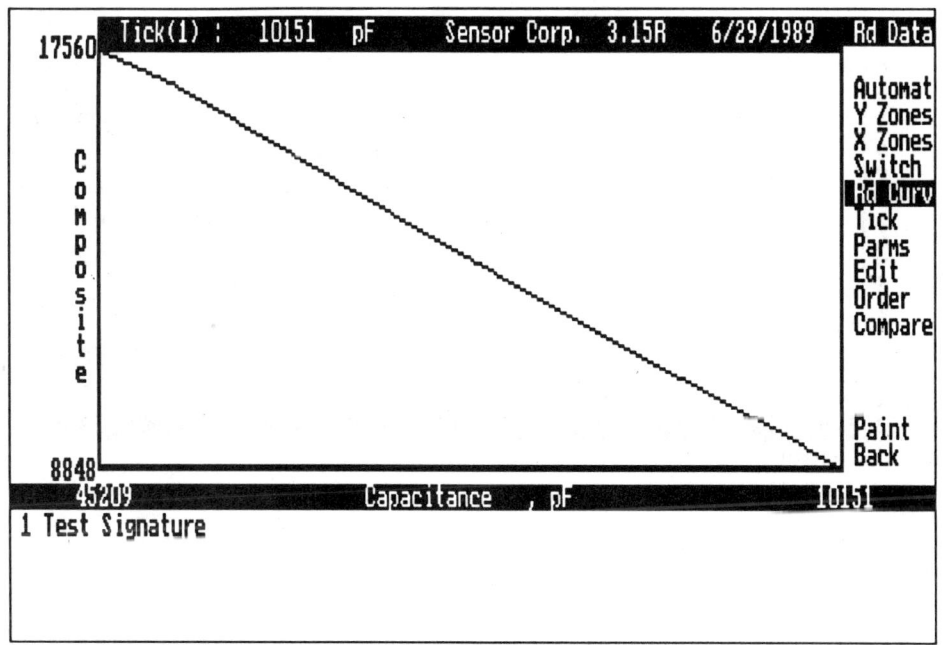

more effective in failure-preventive analysis. This instrument is an ideal link between the metallographic laboratory and process control, allowing 100-percent quality control testing in the manufacturing environment.

Features of the metal analyzer include the following:

- The metal analyzer instrument is controlled through the computer keyboard utilizing various pull-down menus. The Main Menu is shown in figure 10.25.

- Signal filtering techniques: During the digitizing process, the generated signature curves may show a noise effect, which will dampen the resolution and accuracy capabilities of the eddy current instrument. This noise is usually the result of the instability of the sensing signal carrier ("jitter effect") and electromagnetic interference. Various filtering techniques are applied to eliminate this detrimental phenomena.

- The following filtering techniques are used in the metal analyzer instrument: high pass software filtering, low pass software filtering, signal averaging, and smoothing. Each technique has its own

Figure 10.25 Metal Analyzer: Main and Switch Menus

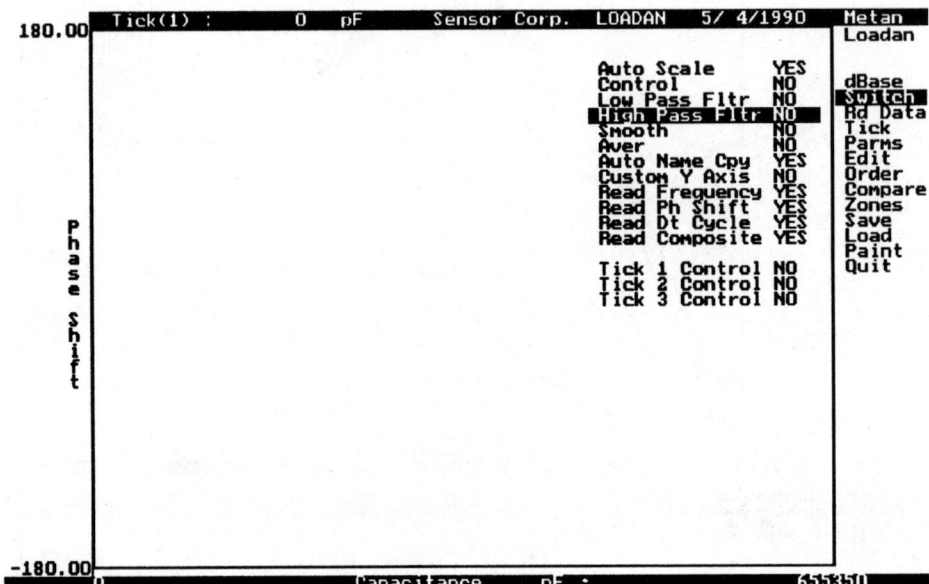

advantages and disadvantages, and the optimum results are usually achieved by combining all three techniques at the low settings.

- Figure 10.26 shows the effect of the high pass filter. This filter is software implemented and not of the hardware type. A hardware filter is not suitable for this application, because to optimize its performance for each frequency range, the filter components must be changed physically, which is very cumbersome. When this technique is used, any setting below 20 will distort the signature substantially.

- Figures 10.27 and 10.28 show the effect of signal averaging. In order to be efficient, this technique requires between 30 and 100 sensing cycles. This may take too much time to digitize, especially at low sensing frequencies. At a higher frequency, where the introduced digitizing delay is not noticeable, this technique is very effective.

- Figures 10.29 and 10.30 show the effect of the smoothing technique. The smoothing procedure is controlled by specifying a

Figure 10.26 Metal Analyzer: The Effect of High Pass Filtering

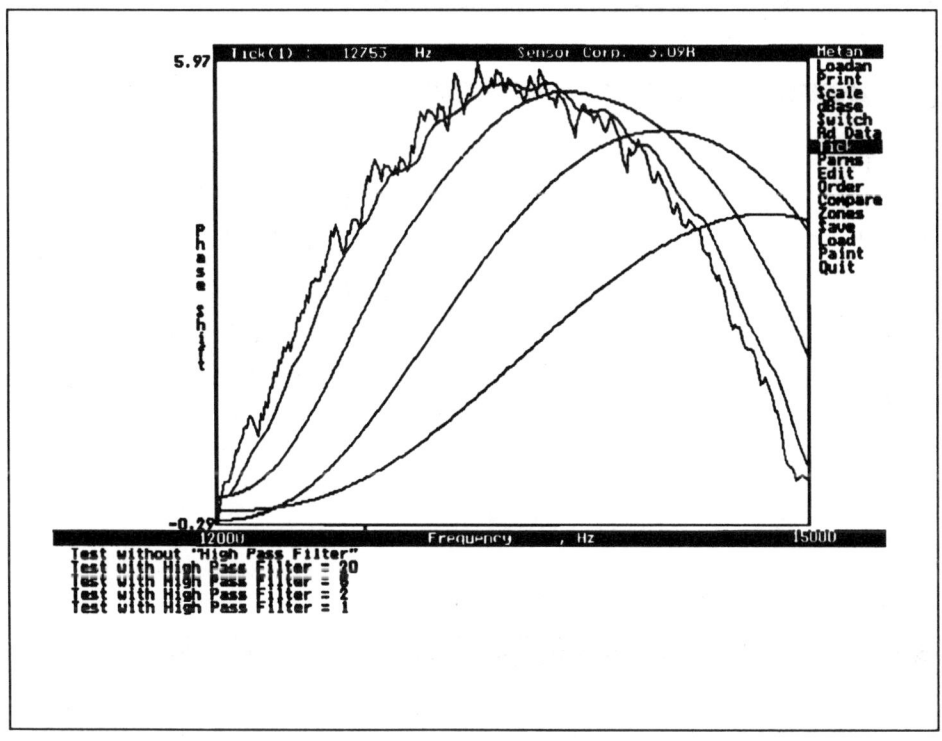

Figure 10.27 Metal Analyzer: Signature with 1 Cycle Averaged

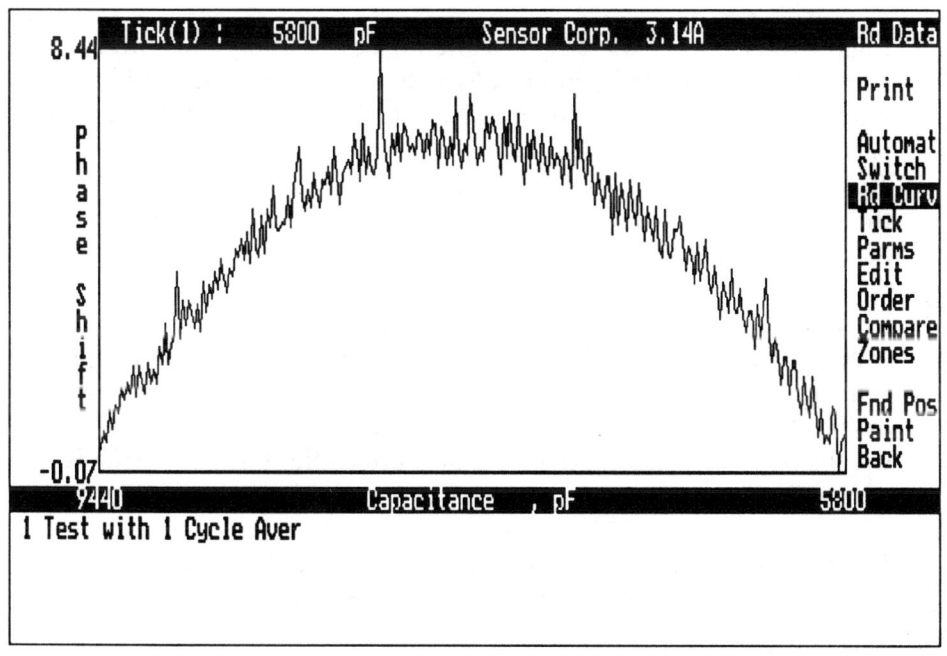

Figure 10.28 Metal Analyzer: Signature with 20 Cycles Averaged

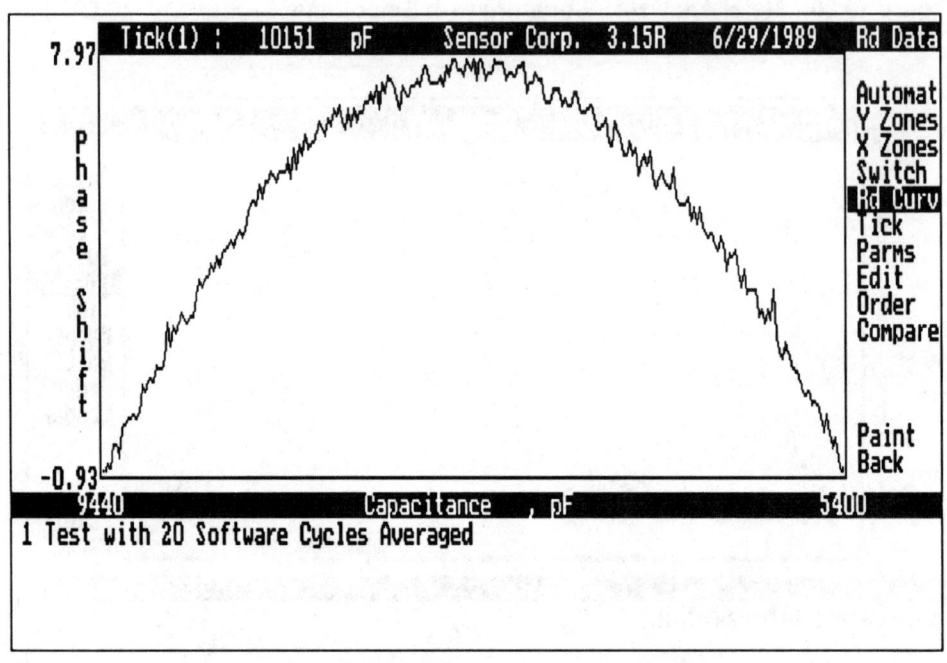

Figure 10.29 Metal Analyzer: Signature without Smoothing

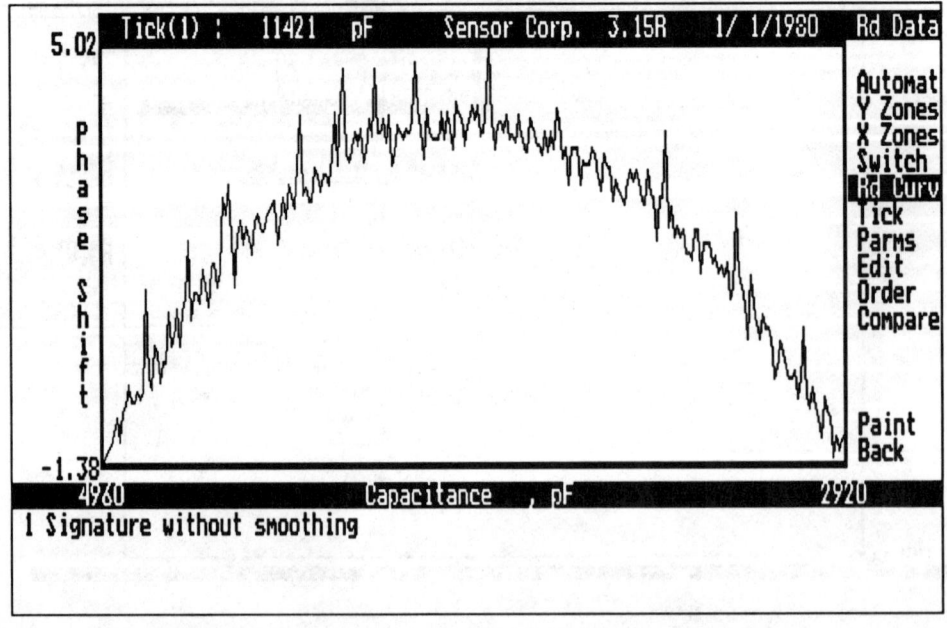

Figure 10.30 Metal Analyzer: Signature with Smoothing

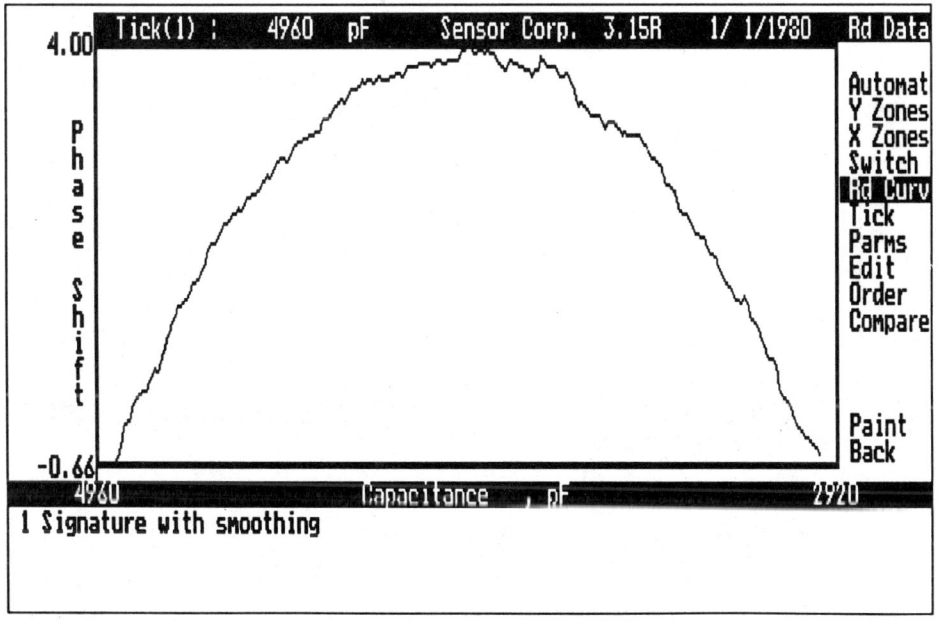

Figure 10.31 Metal Analyzer: System Parameters

number of data points applied to the smoothing cycle. As indicated in figure 10.31, the signature uses 3-point smoothing.

- When using these three filtering techniques, the most effective method is to use the longest averaging cycle possible first. This avoids any signal distortion, but causes a delay in digitizing time. The resulting digitized data should then be subjected to the smoothing procedure, and lastly, the high pass filter should be applied.

Automatic Control of the Induction Heating Process

Certain industrial processes utilize eddy current as a method to achieve goals other than sensing. One of these processes is the induction heating process, used for heat treating and melting of metals. Induction machines use high power levels and, therefore, the eddy currents in these processes were not considered as a sensing media. In the mid-1980s, a new method in the field of induction heating, called *load signature analysis* [1] was developed. In this method, signals are taken directly from the induction coil of the machine. Eddy currents generated in the heat-treated metal are then used as the sensing media to monitor the microstructural transformation of the heated metal during the induction process.

The load signature analysis method also concluded that the sensitivity is not determined by the applied power, but by the ratio of the total number of magnetic lines generated by the induction coil to the number of magnetic lines affected by the treated metal. In the induction heat-treating process, practically all of the generated magnetic lines are affected by the changes in the treated metal part, and therefore, the sensitivity is at its maximum. On the other hand, when a stand-alone eddy current sensing system is used, the applied energy should be at such a level that it does not cause any temperature rise in the part.

By being an integral part of the process, the induction load analyzer system based on the load signature analysis method offers a more efficient approach than other quality control methods. The real-time feature allows it to be used as an instant feedback for process control. When the load analyzer detects the occurrence of the secondary phase transformation point in the heat-treated part, the load analyzer stops the process, forcing all parts, regardless of the starting "prior structure," to be treated to the same uniform condition.

By monitoring the permeability and resistivity changes, this system can be used to monitor temperature, metallurgical phase transformation points,

Figure 10.32 Induction Load Analyzer System

position, and "prior structure" of the heat-treated part. The load signature also reflects the performance of the whole induction system: the power supply, the induction coil, and the heat-treated part. Because it can detect the malfunction of any system component, including intermittent failures not detectable by conventional diagnostic programs, the load analyzer can be used as a more efficient diagnostic tool.

The load analyzer system (figure 10.32) is similar to the metal analyzer system described previously in this chapter. It uses an IBM personal computer. The digitizing and interface boards are connected to the motherboard of the computer. Other interfaces and the output relay boards are mounted in the enclosure of the induction machine or in an auxiliary industrial enclosure. The operating frequency is generated within the induction machine; therefore, the load analyzer is not required to generate this frequency.

The induction load analyzer software differs from the software of the metal analyzer mainly by substituting the frequency/capacitance scan with "heat time" as the X-axis parameter (figures 10.33 and 10.34). The "heat time" parameter is the time required for a complete induction heat cycle. During this time, the power is applied to the heat-treated metallic part. A typical composite signature is shown in figure 10.35, a typical frequency signature is shown in figure 10.36, and a phase shift signature is shown in figure 10.37.

Figure 10.33 Load Analyzer: Main Menu Display

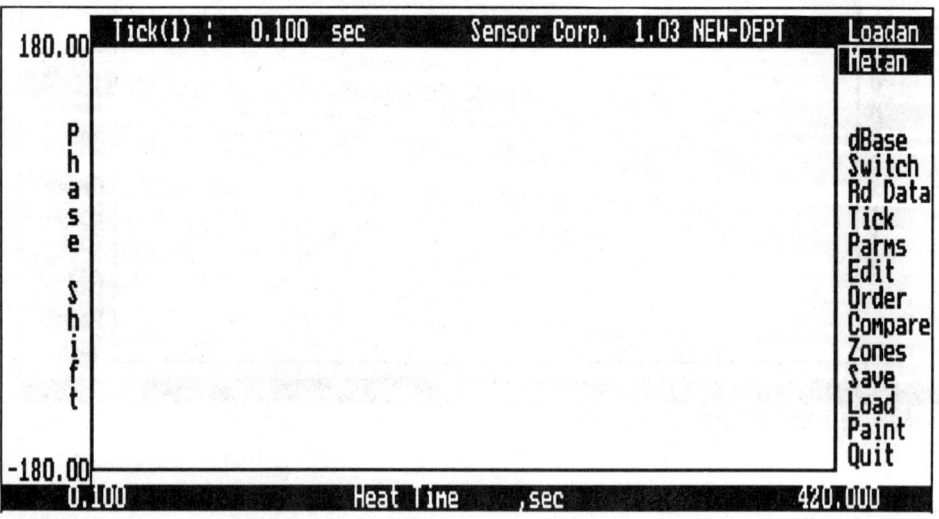

Figure 10.34 Load Analyzer: X-Axis Parameters Menu Display

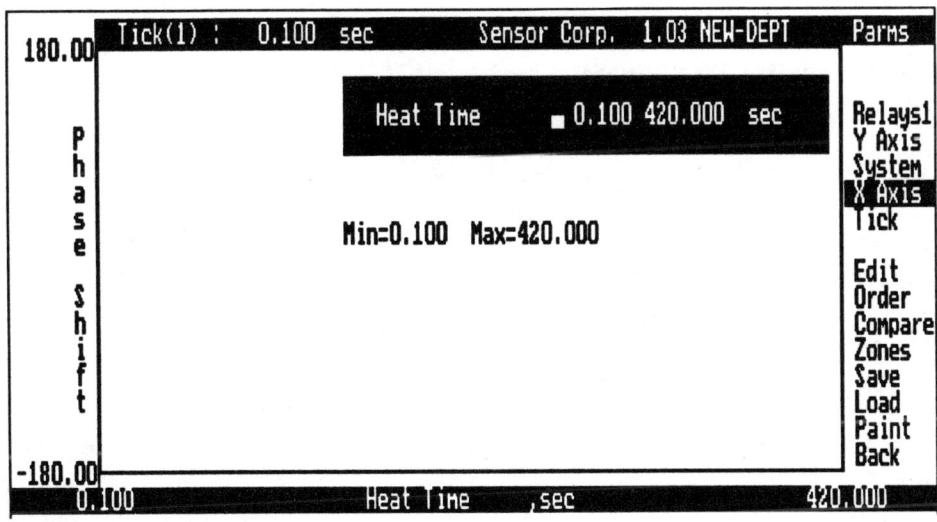

Figure 10.35 Load Analyzer: Typical Composite Signature

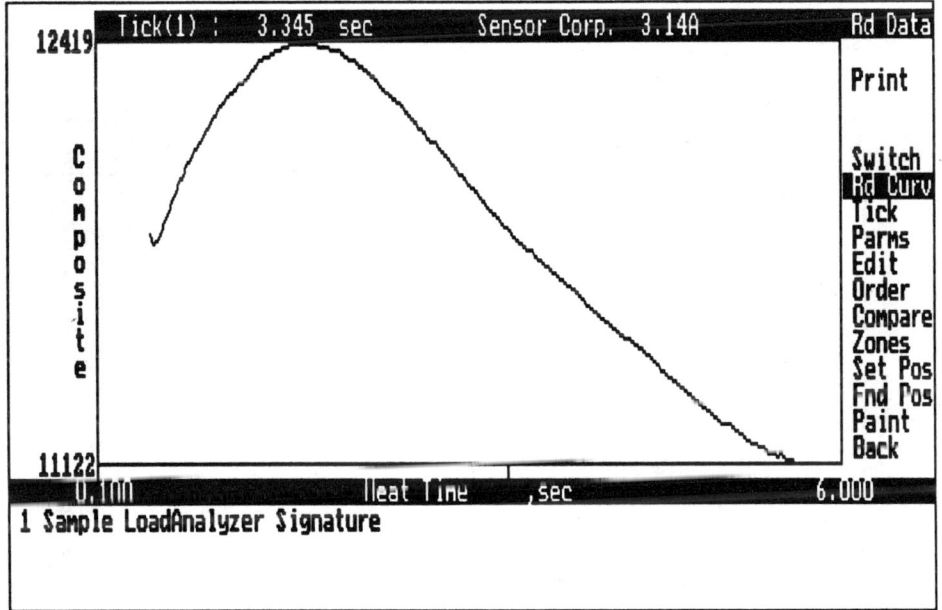

Figure 10.36 Load Analyzer: Typical Frequency Signature

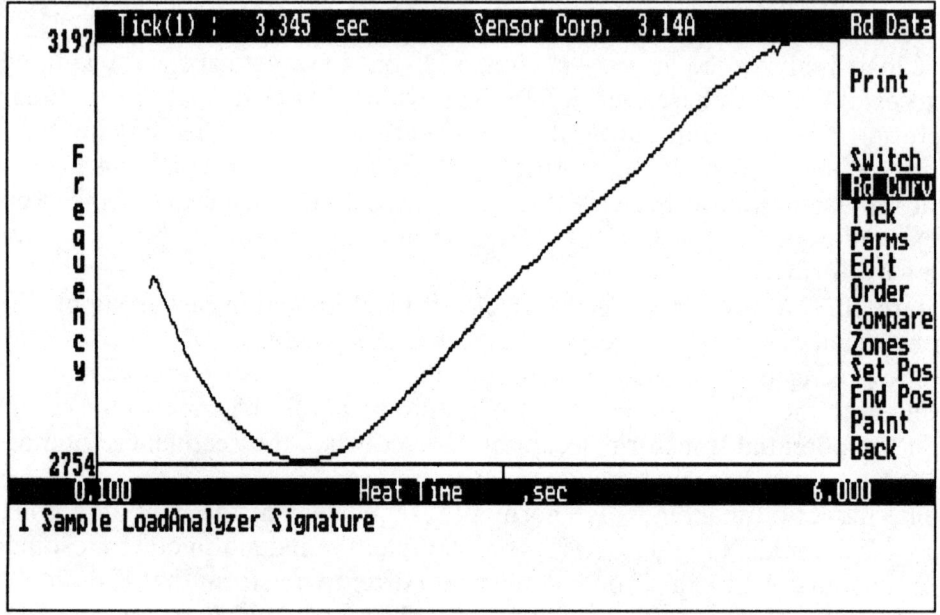

Figure 10.37 Load Analyzer: Typical Phase Shift Signature

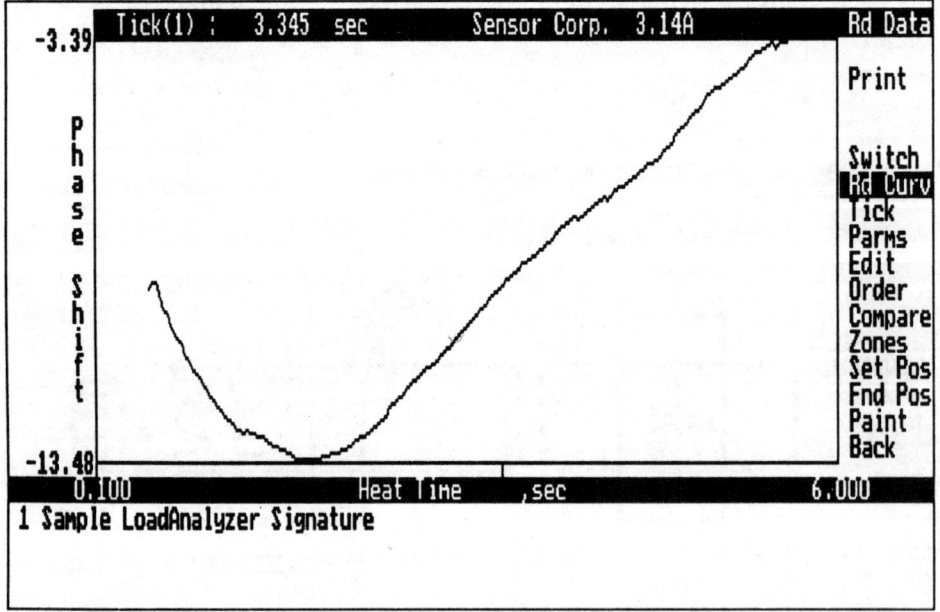

Interfacing with Induction Machine

A typical interface schematic between the load analyzer and the induction machine is shown in figure 10.38.

The load analyzer requires the current and voltage waveforms of the induction coil to establish the phase shift value. This value relates directly to the microstructural transformation during the heat-treating process. The absolute values of current and voltage are not critical for the load analyzer, but an accurate digital representation of the waveform is essential. The selection of the proper current and potential transformers is also important to prevent any distortion of these waveforms.

Figure 10.39 shows an inside view of a typical induction power supply. The current signal can be picked up at the secondary winding of the current transformer by using an oscilloscope current probe. The potential transformer can be connected to the secondary leads of the output power transformer. This connection of the potential transformer cannot be used when the secondary winding is only one turn or when dual induction coils are used.

Some induction machines use harmonic frequencies at the induction coil. If the power supply is fired at 3 KHz, for example, the induction coil is resonated at 9 KHz. This results in a nonsymmetrical current waveform that is difficult to digitize and synchronize. In such situations, the current waveform was replaced by the firing pulse driver waveform of the power supply. This waveform provides exact synchronization between the voltage and current signals. It is also recommended that fiber optics be used to interface between the induction machine and the load analyzer. This will eliminate the pick-up noise and keep the signature clean.

Figure 10.38 Load Analyzer: Interface Schematic

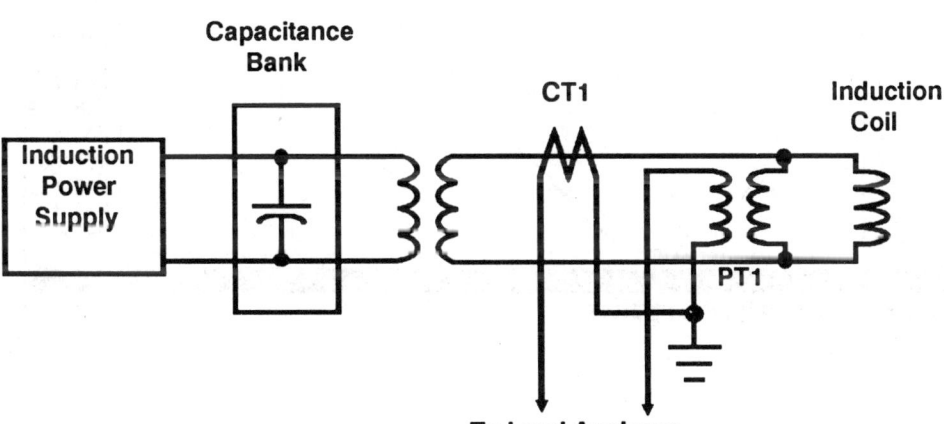

AUTOMATIC CONTROL OF THE INDUCTION HEATING PROCESS

Figure 10.39 Induction Machine: Inside View

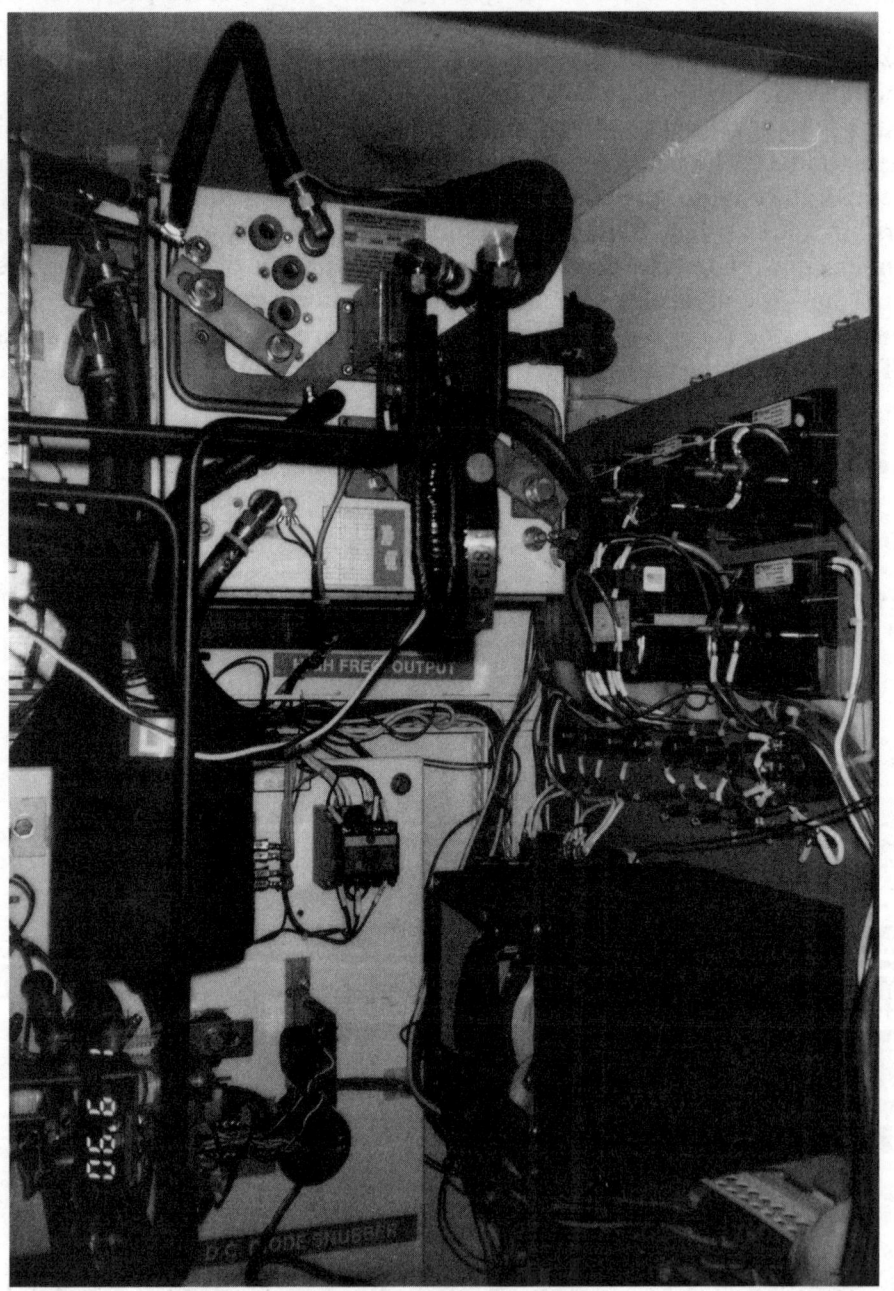

Heat-treating Algorithm

When the load analyzer is used, the quality of the heat-treated part is usually determined by comparing the absolute values of the preselected signature points of a new part against the same points of a reference signature stored in the computer memory. Through analysis of the data collected from heat-treated parts of magnetic steels, it was discovered that the occurrence time of the Curie Point and the secondary phase transformation point (caused by an excessive austenitizing temperature, resulting in austenite grain coarsening [6]) could be used in an algorithm that can serve as a real-time quality control feature. The Curie Point is a temperature-related point at which the permeability of the magnetic steel drops to 1 and the steel loses its magnetic characteristics. The Curie Point is represented on the phase shift signature curve (figure 10.40) as the lowest data point. The Curie Point can be used to indicate the point at which the "prior

Figure 10.40 Load Analyzer: Phase Shift Signature with Curie and Phase Transformation Points Used by Heat-treating Algorithm

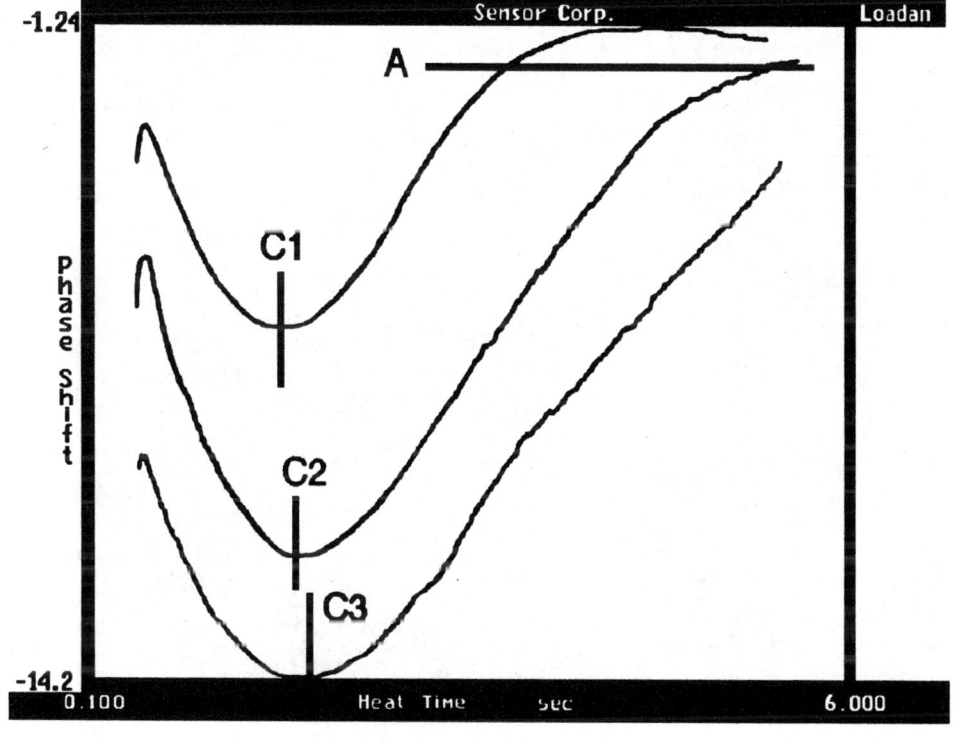

C - Curie Point
A - Phase Transformation

structure" effect is completely eliminated and the remaining heat-treating cycle can be controlled by time. The secondary phase transformation point (figure 10.40) indicates that the highest desired austenitizing temperature has been reached. As soon as the slope change of the signature curve is detected, the load analyzer stops the process at this temperature level, preventing unwanted austenite grain coarsening and assuring heat-treating uniformity of the part. The heat-treating algorithm can eliminate the waiting period for metallographic analysis and the initial set-up time. With the heat-treating algorithm, the induction load analyzer can be used to determine the proper heat-treating parameters (power and time) for new parts, without the need for computer-stored "reference signatures." The instrument eliminates the need to wait for sectioning and metallographic analysis of the heat-treated part. This ability is especially advantageous for fast selection of working parameters for small batches (commercial induction heat treaters) or expensive parts (locomotive crankshafts and large gears, for example).

By monitoring the microstructural changes of the heat-treated part during the process, the induction load analyzer relaxes or completely eliminates the need for preprocessing of materials for microstructural uniformity. It also relaxes the accuracy requirement for the design of induction power supplies, because it automatically compensates for variations by monitoring the overall effect of the whole system on the heat-treated part. In addition, the induction load analyzer can replace the functions of the diagnostic program of the induction machine: it detects the malfunction of any component, including intermittent failures, where conventional diagnostic programs cannot.

Conclusions

The overview of eddy current sensing equipment design and applications included in this chapter is dedicated mainly to helping potential users make technically sound decisions when selecting equipment for their specific needs.

This chapter also should provide some new ideas to designers of eddy current devices and encourage them to search for and apply the new technology.

References

1. American Society for Nondestructive Testing. *Nondestructive Testing Handbook.* Vol. 4: *Electromagnetic Testing.* 2nd ed. Columbus, OH: American Society for Nondestructive Testing, 1986.

2. Hassell, Peter, and George Mordwinkin. "Loadmonitoring—Another Dimension for Induction Heating." *Industrial Heating Magazine* (December 1986):17–20.

3. Krauss, George. "Steels—Heat Treatment and Processing Principles." Metals Park, OH: ASM International, 1989, pp. 169, 180, 285.

4. Mordwinkin, George. Digital Eddy Current Apparatus for Generating Metallurgical Signatures and Monitoring Metallurgical Contents of an Electrically Conductive Material. U.S. Patent No. 4,230,987, 1980.

5. ———. "LoadAnalyzer—New Induction Heating Real Time Quality Control Tool." Proceedings of the 6th International Congress on Heat Treatment of Materials, ASM International, Chicago, IL, September 28–30, 1988.

6. ———. "New Equipment Brings Eddy Current NDT into the Computer Age." *Metal Progress Magazine* (September 1986):53–56.

7. Mordwinkin, George, Arthur Vaughn, and Peter Hassell. "New Induction QC Method Uses Eddy Current Principle." *Heat Treating Magazine* (November 1986):34–38.

8. Zinn, S., and S. L. Semiatin. "Elements of Induction Heating: Design, Control, and Applications." 1988. Metals Park, OH: ASM International, 1988, pp. 160–162.

Chapter 11 Noncontact Ultrasonic Testing with Electromagnetic Transducers

George A. Alers

Introduction

Because ultrasonic waves can penetrate deep into the interior of a body, they can be very useful as measuring tools to monitor the state of the material and to detect hidden flaws within it. Their speed of travel enables them to identify both the composition and the microstructure of the material. Their amplitude is capable of indicating the presence or absence of flaws and inhomogeneities that may be detrimental to the performance of parts fabricated from the material. Because of these properties, ultrasonic waves are now being used to monitor processes in a fabrication mill, so that automatic machine adjustments can be made through feedback loops and so that the mass production of parts can be maintained with minimum rejection rates.

To exploit these capabilities, the sound waves must be introduced into the material and extracted from it by a transducer that interconverts electrical and ultrasonic energy in a rapid, convenient manner. Conventional transducers are based on piezoelectric crystals or ceramics that vibrate mechanically when an alternating voltage is applied to them or they convert mechanical vibrations into electrical signals when sound waves fall on them. No matter what the application, the mechanical vibrations must be conducted to or from the piezoelectric element by a liquid or solid medium that connects the transducer with the part being tested. It is this conducting medium—usually water—that injects limitations into ultrasonic testing and that restricts its applicability to a narrow range of temperatures, surface conditions, and product speeds. It also puts some restrictions on the types of sound waves that can be used and the directions in which they can travel within the part being inspected. These restrictions are now being removed, and the range of applications of ultrasonics to industrial

automation is expanding because of a noncontacting transducer that operates across an air gap without a coupling medium.

In the late 1930s [13], scientists used electromagnetic coupling between a coil of wire and a metal bar to excite vibrations in the bar across an air gap, and thus demonstrated an electromagnetic type of transducer that made no physical contact with the bar. This principle's more modern and familiar manifestation is in the electromagnetic loud speaker, where a coil attached to the diaphragm of the speaker is driven with an electric current and experiences a force because it is suspended in the field of a nearby permanent magnet. It was not until the late 1960s [5] that another group of scientists working with very high magnetic fields, high-purity metals, and very low temperatures showed that high-frequency ultrasonic pulses could be launched and detected in large blocks of ordinary metals in a manner exactly analogous to the piezoelectric transducer used in ultrasonic nondestructive testing. Subsequent developments during the last fifteen years [9] have led to electronic circuits specifically designed for this class of transducer, to the introduction of more powerful permanent magnets, and to the engineering of geometric shapes for the coils that combine to overcome the problems of low efficiency with electromagnetic coupling across small air gaps. Today these transducers are referred to as EMATs (Electromagnetic Acoustic Transducers), and they are finding their way into industrial applications for which liquid coupled, piezoelectric transducers are inapplicable because of the environmental conditions [1].

This chapter first gives a short review of EMAT theory and then summarizes the industrial applications of EMATs, with special attention devoted to those examples that solve manufacturing and control problems in factories and power plants. The first part of the applications section focuses on process control, in which ultrasonic waves are used to monitor the condition of metals during the forming of useful shapes and products. The last section, entitled "Materials Characterization," discusses how the ability of EMATs to excite and detect special kinds of sound waves is used to measure the stress in steel structures and to measure the hardness of armor plate.

EMAT Theory

An EMAT in its most elementary form is shown in figure 11.1. It consists of a loop of wire held close to the surface of a metal part and a magnet that subjects the area under the loop to a magnetic field. As a transmitter or generator of ultrasonic waves, an alternating current I is sent through the wire loop and an eddy current that follows the shape of the loop is induced in the surface. By the Lorentz force law of physics, this eddy current exerts a force F on the surface

EMAT THEORY

Figure 11.1 Schematic Drawing of the Basic Elements of an EMAT

The loop-shaped coils carry an RF current, I, that induces eddy currents in the surface. The interaction of these currents with the magnetic field B produces a force, F, on the surface of the part, which launches an ultrasonic wave.

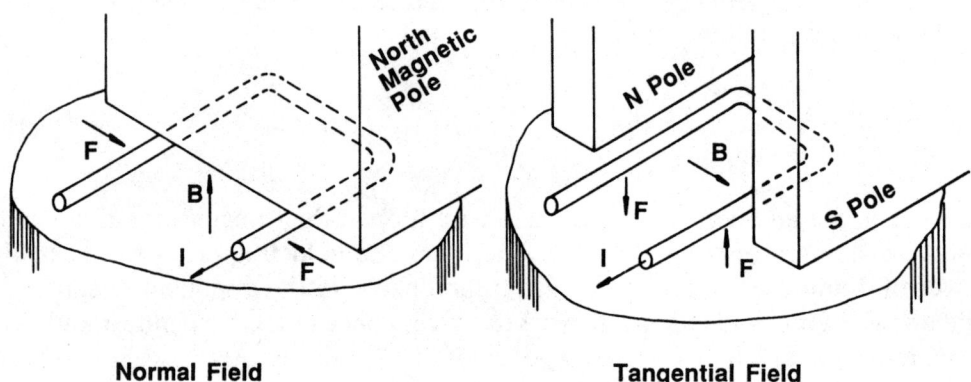

Normal Field   Tangential Field

proportional to the product of the eddy currents magnitude I^* and the magnetic field B. If the field is normal to the surface, this force is parallel to the surface and the surface feels a shearing force that launches a shear wave, as shown on the left side of figure 11.1. If the field is tangential to the surface, the force is perpendicular to the surface, as shown on the right side of figure 11.1, and the resulting normal force launches a longitudinal wave from under the wire. Mathematically, the force on the surface, and hence the intensity of the ultrasonic wave, is proportional to the product of the eddy current magnitude I^* and the magnetic field B. Because there is an air gap under the wire, the eddy current in the surface is smaller than the drive current I by an exponential factor [16] related to the dimension D of the wire loop and the size G of the air gap. That is:

$$I^* \sim I \exp(-2\pi G/D) \qquad (11.1)$$

Clearly, it is advantageous to keep the air gap as small as possible to induce the maximum eddy current I^* for a given amount of drive current and thus to increase the force that generates the ultrasonic wave.

To receive ultrasonic waves, the same geometrical configurations can be used, except that now the acoustic wave under the coil causes the surface of the part to move in the magnetic field. This motion generates an eddy current on the surface by the same mechanism that an electric generator uses to produce power. The eddy current, in turn, induces a voltage in the coil by electromagnetic induction across the air gap. Unfortunately, the voltage is reduced by the same exponential factor shown in equation 11.1.

The overall efficiency of an EMAT transmitter/receiver pair is measured by the voltage V on the terminals of a receiver wire loop that results from a driving current I in the transmitter loop. This ratio of output voltage per unit of input current has the units of ohms and is called the transfer impedance of the transducer pair. Under optimum conditions, when no acoustic power is lost in traversing the space between the transmitter and receiver, this transfer impedance can be written as follows [18]:

$$V/I = 2\frac{N^2 B^2 A}{\rho v} e - 4\pi G/D \qquad (11.2)$$

where N is the number of turns in each wire loop at the transmitter and receiver and A is the area of the wire loop. The magnetic field B appears raised to the power of 2 and the air-gap factor has a factor of 4 in the exponent because the field and gap enter the induction process twice—once at the transmitter and once at the receiver. The mechanical response of the metal supporting the sound wave enters the efficiency equation through the term ρv in the denominator of equation 11.2. This quantity is the acoustic impedance of the metal and is equal to the product of the metal density ρ and the velocity of sound v. For normal values of all the parameters in equation 11.2, the transfer impedance is about 10 $\mu\Omega$. Thus, a current of 100 A in the transmitter will produce a 1 mV signal at the receiver.

The discussion above applies to any metal with an electrical conductivity no worse than a factor of a hundred below the conductivity of copper. Metals with such poor conductivities (titanium alloys and some stainless steels) may require special coil designs and electronic circuits in order to exhibit acceptable performances. Ferromagnetic metals, on the other hand, have magnetostrictive properties that can be utilized to get much higher transduction efficiencies than can be obtained through the eddy current mechanism described above [17]. Steel, in particular, shows a maximum EMAT efficiency at moderate applied fields if these fields are tangential to the surface, as shown on the right-hand side of figure 11.1.

The fact that equation 11.2 contains many different terms reflects the number of variables available for the design engineer to apply to a given problem. Thus, it is this versatility in design that makes EMATs so powerful in difficult-to-solve inspection problems. By adjusting the direction of the magnetic field, the shape of the EMAT coil, and the type of sound waves to be used, an engineer can optimize the transduction efficiency for a particular application. Figure 11.2 shows two coil shapes that are particularly well suited for generating waves that enter or leave the metal perpendicular to the surface in a direct analog to the conventional piezoelectric transducer. If these coils are placed under a single pole piece of a magnet, a shear wave is generated whose polarization is in the radius direction of the spiral. Figure 11.3 shows examples of the so-called mean-

Figure 11.2 Coils for Launching and Detecting Waves that Propagate Perpendicular to the Surface

Spiral Coils

Figure 11.3 Coils for Launching and Detecting Waves that Propagate Along the Surface or at an Angle to the Surface

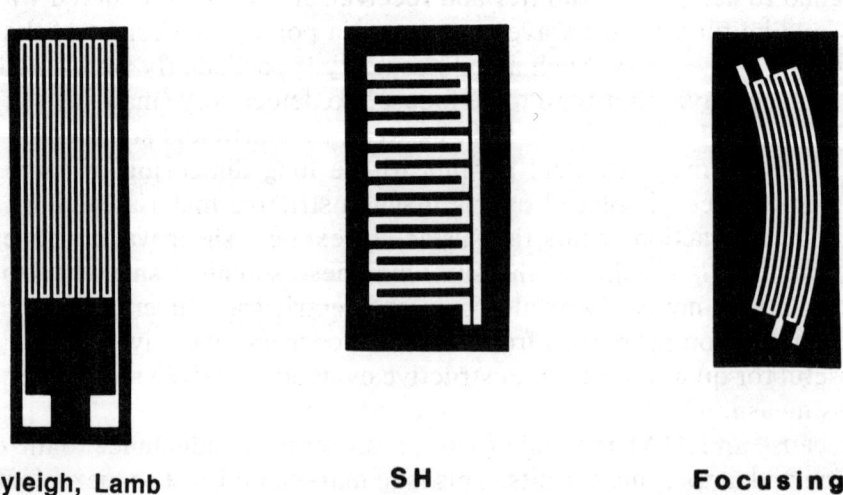

Meander Coils

SV, Rayleigh, Lamb   SH   Focusing

der, or serpentine, coils that are wound in such a way that the direction of current flow (and hence the surface force) switches direction under adjacent wires [20]. This imposes a periodic force on the metal surface and establishes a wavelength for the wave launched by this coil. If the frequency of the drive current is chosen to satisfy this equation:

$$F = v/2D \qquad (11.3)$$

where D is the spacing between adjacent wires, a wave with a phase velocity v will be launched. In most cases, the phase velocity is a uniquely defined number for a given material and part geometry, so equation 11.3 defines the frequency at which a meander-type EMAT coil must be operated to achieve efficient transduction of the wave with the phase velocity v and the wavelength $2D$. A simple shear or longitudinal wave propagating at an angle θ relative to the surface normal can be made to satisfy equation 11.3 if the angle θ satisfies this equation:

$$\sin \theta_c = \frac{V_c}{2DF} \qquad (11.4a)$$

or

$$\sin \theta_s = \frac{V_s}{2DF} \qquad (11.4b)$$

where V_c and V_s are the propagation velocities of longitudinal and shear waves, respectively, in the part.

The right-hand side of figure 11.3 shows a pair of curved meander coils that is designed to act as a transmitter and receiver of waves with curved wave fronts, as would be the case for waves focused to a point at the center of the radius of curvature of the wires. Such a coil geometry is particularly well suited for plate and surface waves that need to be focused to detect very small flaws. The center coil in figure 11.3 is designed to fit between the north and south poles of a magnet, with the magnetic field parallel to the long dimension of each meander. When such a coil is placed over a magnetostrictive material such as steel, the magnetic interaction shears the surface to excite a shear wave whose polarization direction is parallel to the surface. These so-called shear horizontal (SH) waves [23] are not easily excited by piezoelectric transducers and can have very simple reflection properties from surfaces, corners, and flaws. Hence, they can be useful for quantitative nondestructive evaluation (NDE) requirements and for stress measurements, as will be discussed later.

Because an EMAT is a coil of wire, it presents an inductance to the electronic driving and amplifying circuits. This is in marked contrast to piezoelectric transducers that appear electrically as capacitors. EMATs present a low resistance to

the electronics and therefore demand high currents; piezoelectric transducers require high voltages. As a result, the electronic engineering and circuit designs for the two types of transducers are fundamentally different if the designs are to be optimized for particular applications [19]. Most EMAT transmitter circuits generate a tone burst of 4 to 16 cycles duration in the frequency range from 100 kHz to 10 MHz and are able to drive up to 100 A (peak-to-peak) through coils similar to those shown in figures 11.2 and 11.3. The receiver "front ends" must be capable of matching to a wide range of input impedances and must also be capable of rapid recovery from the overload produced by the triggering of the transmitter.

Applications in Industry

Process Monitoring

Noncontacting transducers enable ultrasonic measurements to be carried out in high-production environments because no liquid couplant need be maintained between the transducer and the object being interrogated. Thus, the object can be at an elevated temperature, moving past the transducer at a high speed, or covered with dirt, scale, and rust. Once the sound energy passes through the material, its transit time and its amplitude can be measured and used to give information on the status of the product and hence provide a real-time process control signal. Three examples of the use of the transit time to monitor the internal state of steel and aluminum products are discussed below as they have been used by production line management to control the process and thus meet tight specifications.

Internal Temperature Sensing

During recent years, the steel industry has been turning increasingly toward continuous casting techniques for the preparation of the raw steel that feeds the hot forming of bars, plates, and special shapes. A key requirement for controlling the process is the determination of the temperature on the inside of the hot steel strand a few feet away from the point at which the steel emerges from the casting mold. Clearly, the surface is below the melting point, but the location of the liquid-solid interface inside the strand is vitally important to keeping the molten steel from breaking out or the strand from becoming too stiff to manipulate. Because the ultrasonic wave velocity depends on the temperature, a measurement of the time it takes for a sound wave to propagate across the thickness dimension of the strand can be used to infer the internal temperature distribution

[24]. In a cooperative program between the Department of Energy and the American Iron and Steel Institute, a high-temperature EMAT probe was developed that could withstand continuous exposure to temperatures in excess of 2000°F (1100°C) and that could act as either a generator or a receiver of ultrasonic waves [3]. For this EMAT, the magnetic field was produced by a flat, pancake-shaped coil driven with a pulse of very high current, and the eddy current coil was housed in a ceramic cup. The magnetic field generating coils were flat pancakes with their planes parallel to the surface of the steel and located in heat exchangers that were less than 0.1 inches from the steel. A pulse of very high current (approximately 800 amperes) through these coils applied a magnetic field of 5,000 gauss to the steel. A separate, spiral coil sandwiched between the heat exchanger and a ceramic cover plate formed the EMAT coil that induced or detected eddy currents in the steel surface. The coils and heat exchanger were surrounded by ceramic tubes about one foot in length to protect the wires and coax cables from the radiant heat generated by the nearby hot ingots.

Figure 11.4 shows these ceramic tube EMAT probes mounted on either side of a 4-inch square sample of continuous cast stainless steel placed on top of the instrument package that was taken into a steel mill for testing under actual operating conditions during 1988. The results of these tests are described in reports [4], and laboratory tests are now being carried out using the EMAT probes to develop data on the temperature dependence of the velocity of sound in a wide variety of steels.

Texture Monitoring

During the rolling of thin sheet metal, a texture or preferred orientation of the microscopic crystalline grains inside the metal is developed that makes the physical properties of the sheet vary as a function of angle relative to the rolling direction. When this sheet is used to stamp out parts with practical shapes (such as automobile bodies and beverage cans), this texture must be controlled to yield a minimum of wasted material and to ensure that the metal flows in such a way as to produce a shape with uniform thickness. Several years ago, it was demonstrated that the drawability of steel could be correlated with the angular dependence of Young's modulus in the plane of the sheet, and slow, destructive techniques were developed to make the necessary measurements off-line in sheet rolling mills [11]. Very recently, it has been shown [6] that the same result could be obtained rapidly, nondestructively, and on-line by using EMATs to excite and detect in the sheet a special wave mode called the So Lamb Wave Mode. Non contacting probes with transmitter and receiver EMATs separated by a known distance are held over the sheet, and the transit time required for the So mode to propagate over the separation distance is measured at three angles relative to the rolling direction. A computer then combines the information and outputs a measurement of the drawability parameter commonly used in the industry.

APPLICATIONS IN INDUSTRY

Figure 11.4 An EMAT System for Measuring the Internal Temperature of Continuous Cast Steel Bars at Temperatures Exceeding 2000°F

The tube-shaped EMATs are shown here on each side of a cast bar sitting on top of the instrumentation package.

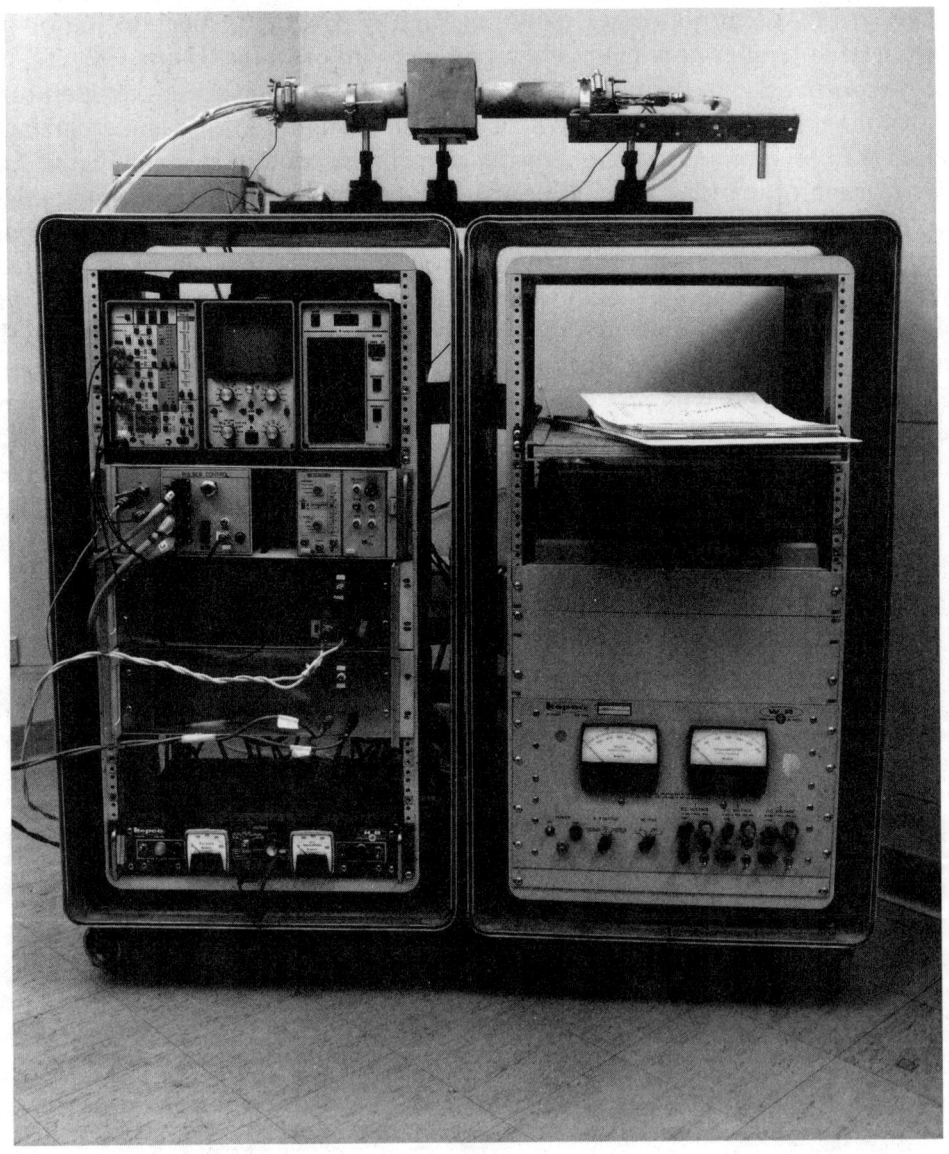

Thickness Measurements

Seamless steel tubing is manufactured at speeds approaching 200 feet per minute, and abnormal variations in the wall thickness represent the major cause for rejection. Thus, on-line monitoring of the wall thickness is very desirable. Unfortunately, the monitoring technique must be able to operate on rough, scale-covered surfaces that not only are moving rapidly past the inspection station but that may be at temperatures above the boiling point of water. Using EMATs, the inspection process can be made independent of the surface speed, temperature, and cleanliness. Furthermore, the sensors can be mounted on simple carriages that can track the pipe as it bounces through the inspection station. Figure 11.5 shows a graph of the thickness contour measured by an EMAT ultrasonic thickness gage positioned to record a thickness value every ⅛ inch along a longitudinal path on a 30-foot-long tube that was moving past the sensor at 180 feet/minute in an operating steel mill. An accuracy of better than ±1 percent was obtained in the installed unit, which had eight EMAT sensors located around the circumference to yield eight thickness profile graphs like that shown in figure 11.5. All of this data was processed in real time by a dedicated personal computer so that the operator could be given a display of the results of the inspection immediately after the pipe had passed through the station. This rapidly displayed report provided the average wall thickness, the length of the tube, its true weight per foot, the minimum wall thickness detected, and the maximum eccentricity of the center bore hole.

Figure 11.5 Output Graph of Wall Thickness versus Position Along a 30-foot-long Seamless Steel Tube that Moved Past the EMAT Sensor at 180 Feet/Minute

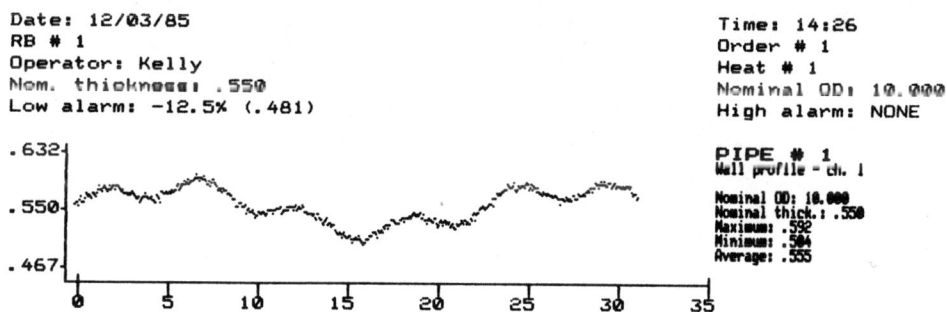

Flaw Detection

Certainly the most common application of ultrasonics in a manufacturing plant is for the detection of flaws in the material that is being processed. Cracks, laps, and seams in sheet or bar stock can cause the parts made from these materials to fail in service, or they can cause failures in the subsequent processing steps that can do damage to the processing machinery, resulting in loss of productivity for the entire facility. Once the final product is made and shipped to the customer, it is often inspected again to make sure that corrosion or accidental damage have not introduced defects that can cause failure of the final user's product. For example, large engineering structures are inspected periodically to assure their continued safe operation, and ultrasonics is quite often used. Therefore, ultrasonic transducers that can operate without couplant liquids can and do provide faster and more reliable inspections of large engineering structures. In the paragraphs that follow, many applications of EMATs to automated inspections of large structures and to production lines will be presented.

Corrosion in Pipelines

Buried gas pipelines are carefully protected from external corrosion attack, but to be sure no small patch develops into a catastrophic failure, instrumented inspection robots called *pigs* are sent through the pipeline at regular intervals to detect and locate the loss of metal that characterizes corrosion damage. Although magnetic sensors are commonly used on these inspection pigs, ultrasonic techniques can give more information on the nature and depth of the damage. The noncontact nature of the EMAT makes it the only way to insure reliable coupling to the inside surface of the pipeline over the long distances involved and the variety of surface conditions encountered. Figure 11.6 shows a photograph of an inspection pig suitable for performing just this sort of inspection. This particular device was designed to inspect 30-inch-diameter pipelines with eight individual EMAT sensors distributed around its circumference. By taking advantage of the fact that an EMAT can be designed to excite and detect Lamb-type ultrasonic waves in plates very efficiently [15], the pig shown in figure 11.6 located corrosion in the walls of the pipeline by detecting echoes when the Lamb wave propagating around the circumference reflected from areas of irregular pitting. Eight sensors were needed to ensure adequate sensitivity in those areas where coal tar coatings on the outside of the pipe caused high attenuation of the waves. Because the device had to be self-contained and had to withstand the pressure of the gas in the line, its central structure consisted of a heavy walled tube that contained batteries, signal-processing electronics, and data recording devices. The magnetic field required by the EMATs was generated by special permanent magnets mounted on wheels to magnetize just the region around each

Figure 11.6 A Robot Vehicle, Called a *Pig*, for Inspecting Buried Gas Pipelines for Corrosion Damage

Eight EMAT sensors are distributed around the circumference of the device.

of the eight EMAT coils. After an inspection run, off-line computers analyzed the information recorded by the on-board computer to produce a map showing the location of suspect areas so that remedial action could be taken by the pipeline owner.

Surface Inspection of Bars

Laps and seams rolled into the surface of bars during their fabrication are a common type of flaw that should be detected and marked by an on-line inspection system capable of operating at product speeds of 200 feet per minute or more. If such flaws are found, it is customary to hand grind the surface until the defect is no longer visible. By using surface acoustic waves (Rayleigh waves), it has been shown that very small cracks can be detected and their depths can be

measured automatically [12]. Thus, an accept/reject decision can be made immediately, and the bars with deep flaws can be diverted to a rework facility without slowing down the production of flaw-free bars. Although conventional, piezoelectric transducers can be made to excite and detect surface acoustic waves, the couplant fluid introduces a random damping factor and limits the speed of inspection. EMATs, on the other hand, are very reliable surface wave transducers and can easily meet the 200-feet-per-minute inspection speed requirement. Figure 11.7 shows a photograph of a simple bar inspection system that can be easily inserted into the production line of a bar mill. Two EMATs and an electromagnet fit under the bar at the 4:30 and 7:30 positions so that they can send the surface waves around the circumference and provide 100-percent coverage from two localized sensor positions instead of requiring sensors that encircle the bar. The wheel on top of the bar in the figure is an odometer wheel that provides the control computer with location information along the length of the bar.

Through-wall Inspection of Pipes and Tubes

If more EMAT coils are added to the magnet installation used to inspect the surface of bars, the interior volume of the walls of tubes and pipes can be inspected by ultrasonic pulse-echo techniques. This capability is of particular interest to the manufacturer of welded pipes and tubes, in which the weld line must be inspected very carefully. For such cases, the weld line is passed between the EMATs, where it is inspected from both sides with both surface waves and by angle beam shear waves that detect flaws on the ID. Such an approach is pictured in figure 11.8, which shows two EMATs and their individual electromagnets located on top of the tube to straddle the weld line. If the location of the weld line is unknown, such as would be the case for oil country tubular goods being inspected in the "oil patch" away from the manufacturing plant, an array of eight EMATs like those shown in the figure, positioned at 45-degree intervals around the circumference, is sufficient to inspect the entire pipe for longitudinal flaws anywhere in the walls.

Ultrasonic Inspection Inside a Vacuum Chamber

Exotic alloy parts used in the manufacture of rocket and gas turbine engines must often be welded together by electron beam welding machines under vacuum conditions. When the weld is critical, it must be inspected by removing it from the chamber, inspecting it at a special facility, and returning it to the chamber if a reweld is found necessary. Such a slow process has been eliminated by using EMATs to perform the inspection inside the vacuum chamber immediately after the weld is formed. This is possible not only because the electromagnetic

Figure 11.7 A Unit for Inspecting Bar Stock in a Production Line

Two fixed EMAT sensors are located under the bar, and the wheel tells the computer where the flaw is located along the length of the bar.

Figure 11.8 EMATs Located on Each Side of the Weld Line on Top of an ERW Tube Are Able to Detect OD Flaws with Surface Wave EMATs and ID Flaws with Angle Beam Shear Waves

Two sensors are used in order to inspect the weld from both sides.

coupling mechanism can operate across a vacuum-filled gap but also because the EMAT can be constructed from materials that can withstand the temperature of the part immediately after the weld. This temperature can be as high as 350°C. Because the wall thickness of the part is only about 0.2 inches and the sensitivity specification requires detecting a $1/32$-inch-diameter flat bottom hole, the EMAT coil wires were curved and positioned to focus 7 MHz ultrasonic waves at the center of the wall thickness dimension. This focal spot was scanned over the total weld volume by translating the transducers perpendicular to the weld line while the part was rotated. A personal computer controlled the entire operation, and it took about five minutes to collect all of the echo amplitude and position data as well as to make the accept/reject decision. Hard copy C-scan images of the joint can be prepared off-line at any time using the data stored in the computer's memory.

Butt Weld Inspection at a Pickle Line

In the mass production of parts from sheet steel, individual ingots are hot rolled into flat plate and then wound up into small coils for cooling and storage. Later, several of these coils are welded together end-to-end to form one large coil, which is trimmed to an exact width and chemically cleaned (pickled) before being rolled into a very long strip of thinner sheet in a high-speed, cold-reduction mill. If the weld is flawed and breaks during the cold rolling process, much of the large coil can be destroyed and the roll surfaces can be scarred to the extent that they must be replaced. Thus, it is very cost-effective to inspect each weld immediately after it is formed and to reweld those whose strengths may be suspect. Unfortunately, space around the newly welded joint is limited and the metal is very hot, so scanning the weld line with conventional NDT sensors immediately after the weld is completed is difficult. Although small EMATs that operate at elevated temperatures can be constructed, a special property of the noncontact devices was utilized that allowed the transducers to be placed well away from the hot zone, outside the clamps that hold the plate during the welding process. This property is the ability to excite and detect a shear horizontal (SH) type of wave that stays trapped between the top and bottom surfaces of the plate and does not leak into the clamping mechanism. Thus, the sound energy can be inserted several inches away from the weld and can be made to pass under the clamps without attenuation so that it can reflect from any discontinuities in the weld line that might decrease the strength of the welded joint. A schematic drawing of the transducer and weld line configuration used for inspecting the weld with SH wave EMATs is shown in figure 11.9. Note that the transmitter and receiver are separated so that the acoustic energy inserted by the transmitter passes under the receiver to produce a signal that measures the amplitude of the wave impinging on the weld. Any reflections from the weld can be referred to this incident intensity to produce a normalized output signal that is independent of the transducer coupling and dependent only on the severity of the flaw. Because the EMATs are scanned across the width of the plate by a mechanical system coordinated with a knife blade that removes the weld bead or flash, the weld is actually inspected a few seconds after the trimming step, and very little time is added to the total weld production time. Using this system being to point out which welds should be cut out and rewelded, the total amount of weld breakage was decreased by an order of magnitude—from 0.4 percent to 0.04 percent.

Small Parts Inspection by Self-aligning EMATs

In order to inspect small parts that are produced at rates approaching one per second, the ultrasonic transducer and the part must be positioned accurately relative to one another and then a 100-percent scan must be performed in a frac-

Figure 11.9 Schematic Drawing of an EMAT System for Inspecting the Butt Weld Between Two Sheets When They Are Clamped in a Jig for Trimming the Weld Flash or Bead Off of the Welded Joint

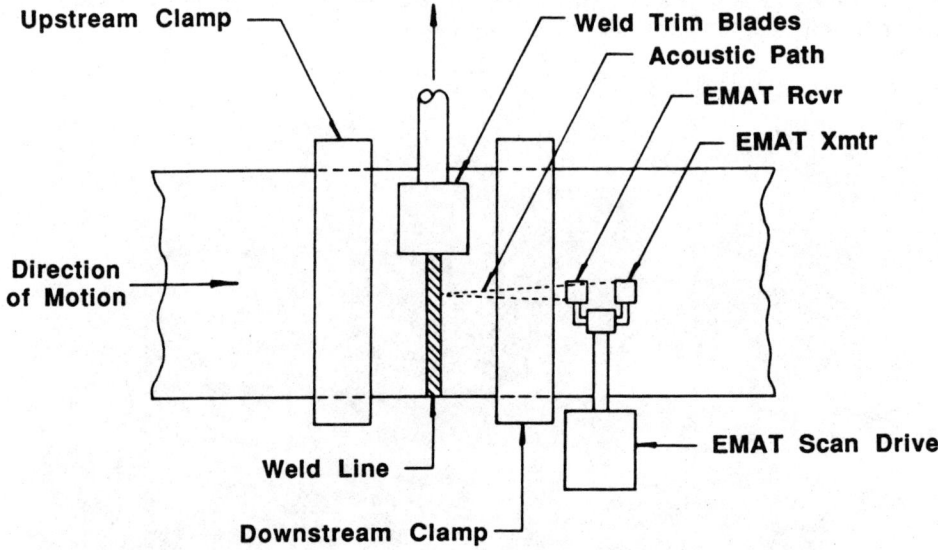

tion of a second. If EMATs in air are used instead of piezoelectric transducers in water, the parts can be kept dry and the positioning mechanism does not have to be kept in precise alignment because there is no refraction of the ultrasonic beam at the surface of the part. An example of the use of these simplifications is a system for inspecting machine gun projectiles as they are produced [10]. The inspection machine shown in figure 11.10 consists of a rotating drum that picks up each projectile from a feed line and delivers it, rotating, to the gap between the pole pieces of a DC electromagnet. Three separate EMAT coils mounted on compliant substrates slide into light rubbing contact with the projectile surface as it enters the gap. Because the compliance of the substrate allows the coils to conform to the curved surface, the ultrasonic waves enter the part over a well-defined curved area and generate a sound beam with a well-defined direction inside the part. Each sound beam interrogates a different, critical part of the projectile body with a pulse-echo technique, and the rotation ensures that every part of the circumference is brought into this inspection volume several times during an inspection cycle. If any one of the EMATs detects an echo that is larger than a preset limit for that channel, the part is rejected and the control computer records the event so that at the end of a production run, a printout of the number of rejections in each channel can be made available to management.

Figure 11.10 Inspection Machine Designed to Detect Flaws in Machine Gun Projectiles as They Are Produced at Rates Approaching One Projectile per Second

Three EMAT coils are located in the gap of the electromagnet. The projectiles are delivered to the gap by a carousel that rotates around a horizontal axis.

Materials Characterization

The rapid expansion of materials science during the past ten years has produced a great demand for sensors that can quickly measure various physical and metallurgical properties of both ferrous and nonferrous materials. This information can be used to recognize the deterioration of structures caused by their operating environment and to monitor the state of alloys at an incoming materials inspection station. Two examples of materials characterization that are unique to the ultrasonic waves produced by EMAT sensors are given in the following sections.

Stress Measurement

The fact that the velocity of sound is linearly dependent on the level of stress in the sound beam has often been used as the basis for instruments that measure stress in bolts [7] and near welds [8]. However, achieving reliable coupling to the part is usually difficult and often sets limitations on the accuracy of stress measurements that can be made in practical situations. If EMATs are used, these restrictions can be removed or minimized, especially if the popular technique of measuring the acoustic birefringence [14] induced by the stress is used. In this method, the velocity difference between shear waves polarized to be parallel and perpendicular to the stress axis is measured and compared to calibration data obtained on the same material under laboratory conditions. It is necessary to use the same material for the laboratory calibration because texture or preferred orientation in the grain structure of the material can and does introduce a birefringence in the shear wave velocities that is not representative of the stress and that therefore must be accounted for in the calibration experiments. During the last several years, the theory of ultrasonic wave propagation in materials with both a texture and a stress has become highly developed and methods of separating the two effects have been discovered [21]. Most noteworthy of these new methods is the use of surface-skimming SH waves generated and detected by EMATs to exploit a symmetry property of the stress tensor that allows the stress to be measured independent of the texture and without any laboratory calibrations [2]. In this technique, the velocity of shear waves along the surface of the part is measured as a function of the angular orientation of the sound path relative to the stress axis. That part of the angular dependence that exhibits twofold symmetry determines the stress level, and that part that exhibits fourfold symmetry determines the texture.

Hardness Measurement

At the completion of manufacture, armor plate must be heat treated to a rigid hardness specification before it is acceptable to the purchasing agency of the military. Because the plate is delivered in the form of massive blocks, it is slow and inconvenient to measure the hardness using the conventional indentation method, especially if several locations on the same block must be monitored. Part of this inconvenience is caused by the necessity for preparing the surface for the test. When surface waves generated and detected by EMATs are used, the sound velocity in a subsurface layer of the metal can be measured accurately with little surface preparation, and the velocity value can be correlated with the hardness level to provide a hardness measurement technique that is independent of the thin dirt and rust layers on the surface [22]. As is quite often the case with correlations between physical properties and hardness, the correlation function

with the surface wave velocity turned out to be double-valued, so the possibility for an ambiguity exists if a wide range of hardness values is encountered in practice. In order to remove this possibility, the EMAT probe used to make the surface wave velocity measurement was equipped with magnetic field sensors and SH wave velocity EMATs so that other physical properties could be measured simultaneously and a multifunctional correlation technique could be used to remove the ambiguity.

Summary and Conclusions

This chapter has described a new type of transducer that can both excite and detect ultrasonic waves in metals across a small air gap without any couplant fluids or greases. As a result, ultrasonic nondestructive testing can now be carried out on parts moving through a manufacturing facility at very high speeds, at excessively high temperatures, or even inside a vacuum chamber. In addition, the design of the internal structure of the transducer allows a wider variety of sound waves to be utilized than are available to the conventional piezoelectric transducer. Therefore, more applications for process monitoring and materials characterization are being developed as the transducer gains wider acceptance as a viable industrial sensor.

References

1. Alers, G. A., and L. R. Burns. "EMAT Designs for Special Applications." *Materials Evaluation*. vol. 45 (1987):1184.

2. Alers, G. A., et al. "Application of Surface Skimming SH Waves to Stress and Texture Measurement in Steel." *Rev. of Prog. in QNDE* vol. 8B. D. O. Thompson and D. E. Chimenti, eds. New York: Plenum Press, 1989, p. 1895.

3. ———. "Electromagnetic Acoustic Transducer." U.S. Patent 4,777,824, issued October 18, 1988.

4. Cook, J. R., et al. "Sensing As-Cast Billet Temperatures with EMATs." *Proc. of AISE Conference*, Cincinnati, Ohio, April 24–26, 1989. AISI CTU–5–4 Program.

5. Gaerttner, M. R., et al. "Experiments Relating to the Theory of Magnetic Direct Generation of Ultrasound in Metals." *Phys. Rev.* vol. 184 (1969):702. See also U.S. Patents 3,583,213 and 3,460,063.

6. Hirao, M., and H. Fukuoka. "Ultrasonic Propagation in Textured Polycrystalline Metals." In *Elastic Wave Propagation*. M. F. McCarthy and M. A. Hayes, eds. Amsterdam: Elsevier Science Publishers, 1989.

7. Holt, A. C., et al. "Sensitivity of an Ultrasonic Technique for Axial Stress Determination." *Rev. of Prog. in QNDE* vol. 7B. D. O. Thompson and D. E. Chimenti, eds. New York: Plenum Press, 1988, p. 1405.

8. Husson, D., et al. "Measurement of Stress with Surface Waves." *Materials Evaluation* vol. 43 (1985):92.

9. Maxfield, B. W., and C. M. Fortunko. "Design and Use of Electromagnetic Acoustic Wave Transducers (EMATs)." *Materials Evaluation*. vol. 41 (1983):1399.

10. Miller, Dave, "An EMAT Inspection System for Small Projectiles." Aerojet Ordnance Company, Downey, CA. Also Thompson, R. B., and C. M. Fortunko. "Ultrasonic Inspection of a Cylindrical Object." U.S. Patent 4,184,374.

11. MODUL-r Instrument, Manufactured by Tinius Olsen, Willow Grove, PA.

12. Palanisamy, R., et al. "On the Accuracy of AC Flux Leakage, Eddy Current, EMAT and Ultrasonic Methods of Measuring Surface Connecting Flaws in Seamless Steel Tubing." *Review of Progress in QNDE* vol. 5A. D. O. Thompson and D. E. Chimenti, eds. New York: Plenum Press, 1966, pp. 215–23.

13. Randall, R. H., et al. "Intercrystalline Thermal Currents as a Source of Internal Friction." *Phys. Rev.* vol. 56 (1939):343

14. Smith, R. T. "Stress Induced Anisotropy in Solids—The Acousto-Elastic Effect." *Ultrasonics* (July 1963):135.

15. Thompson, R. B. "Electromagnetic Generation of Rayleigh and Lamb Waves in Ferromagnetic Materials." *Proc. IEEE Ultrasonics Symposium,* 1975, IEEE Cat. No. 75-CHO-994-4SU.

16. ———. "A Model for the Electromagnetic Generation and Detection of Rayleigh and Lamb Waves." *IEEE Trans. Sonics and Ultrasonics* vol. SU–20 (October 1973):340.

17. ———. "A Model for the Electromagnetic Generation of Ultrasonic Guided Waves in Ferromagnetic Metal Polycrystals." *IEEE Trans. Sonics and Ultrasonics* vol. SU–25 (1978):7.

18. ———. "Noncontact Transducers." *Proc. 1977 Ultrasonics Symposium*. IEEE Cat. No. 77, CH 1264–ISU, 1977, p. 74.

19. Thompson, R. B., and C. M. Fortunko. "Optimization of EMAT Systems." Interdisciplinary Program for Quantitative Flaw Definition, Second Year Report, DARPA and AFML Report on Contract F33615–74–C5180.

20. Thompson, R. B., et al. "Method for Ultrasonic Inspection." U.S. Patent 3,850,028, issued November 26, 1974.

21. ———. "Microstructure Independent Acoustoelastic Measurement of Stress." *Appl. Phys. Let.* vol 44 (1984):296.

22. Tittman B. R., *et al.* "Determination of Physical Property Gradients from Measured Surface Wave Dispersion." *IEEE Trans. Sonics, Ferroelectrics, and Frequency Control* vol. UFFC–34 (September 1978):500.

23. Vasile, C. F., and R. B. Thompson. "Excitation of Horizontally Polarized Shear Waves by EMATs with Periodic Permanent Magnets." *J. Appl. Phys.* vol. 50 (1979):2583.

24. Wadley, H. N. G., *et al. Phil. Trans. Roy. Soc. London* vol. A320 (1986):341.

Chapter 12 Ultrasonic Hardness Testing

David M. Jankowski

Introduction

Hardness testing is the most popular, and the simplest, mechanical test performed in industry. The measurement indicates not only a material's hardness but also physical properties such as tensile strength, abrasion resistance, flexibility, and machinability. Although many of these other properties can be tested directly, determining them through hardness testing is often less time-consuming, less expensive, and less destructive.

Additionally, in today's quality-conscious industrial environment, hardness testing is a fast, economical method for many daily quality-related functions. A typical hardness test can be completed in less than 2 seconds, allowing economical testing of large volumes of parts—for example, qualifying parts for further processing and releasing components for shipment to the end user. Hardness testing is also used frequently as a reliable statistical process control tool.

Hardness Test Methods

The most commonly used hardness testing methods are based on indentation measurement. Other techniques, such as eddy current-based systems, indirectly measure hardness by evaluating a component's microstructure and then relating the system's microstructural response to an empirically determined hardness value.

With indentation hardness testing, a diamond-tipped or hardened-steel indenter is pressed with a predetermined force into the test material. The indentation size, as quantified by the depth or the area of the permanent plastic

deformation, is combined with the applied load to determine the hardness value. For example, the Brinell hardness number (BHN) is defined as follows:

$$\mathrm{BHN} = \frac{P}{A} \tag{12.1}$$

BHN = Brinell hardness number
P = applied load (kg)
A = area of spherical impression in the metal (mm²)

The area (A) can be calculated from the diameters of the ball indenter (D)—usually 10 mm—and the impression (D_1).

$$A = \frac{\pi D^2}{2} - \frac{\pi D}{2} \sqrt{D^2 - D_1^2} \tag{12.2}$$

D = ball indenter diameter (mm)
D_1 = impression diameter (mm)

A convenient equation to calculate the Brinell hardness number is easily obtained by combining equations 1 and 2.

Indentation hardness test methods can be divided into two categories: macroindentation tests, such as the Rockwell and Brinell hardness tests, and microindentation tests. In both the Rockwell and Brinell tests, the test load is fairly large—ranging from 15 kg for a superficial Rockwell hardness test to 3000 kg for a Brinell hardness test. The resulting indentation diagonals and depths are in the range of 1 mm (0.04 in.) or greater.

Microindentation Hardness Test Methods

Microindentation hardness tests employ substantially lower test loads (300 to 1000 grams) than macroindentation tests. Special diamond indenters—defined as *Vickers* (also called *diamond pyramid*) or *Knoop geometries*—are used to optimize the shape and minimize the size of the indentation (figure 12.1). Vickers and Knoop microindentations typically have depths of less than 0.05 mm (0.002 inch). The Vickers or Knoop hardness numbers are calculated using equations 3 and 4. The indentation diagonal(s) are measured. From the diagonal(s), the projected area (Knoop) or surface area (Vickers) of the indentations can be calculated. The Vickers (HVN) or Knoop (HK) hardness numbers are then determined by dividing the area into the test load.

HARDNESS TEST METHODS

Figure 12.1 Hardness Indenter Geometries and Indentation Shapes

(Note: The indenters are not drawn to scale.)

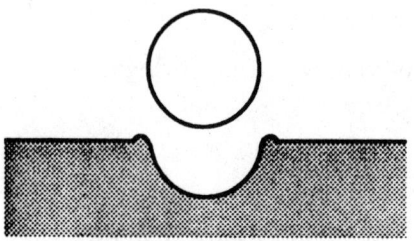
Brinell

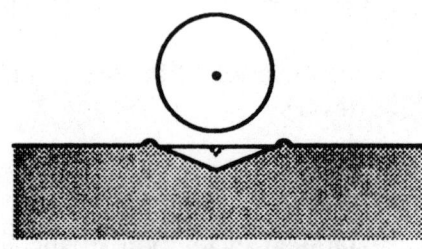
**Rockwell
(Conical Diamond)**

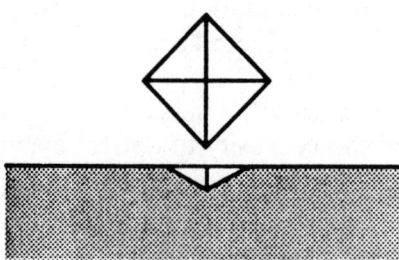
**Vickers
Microhardness**

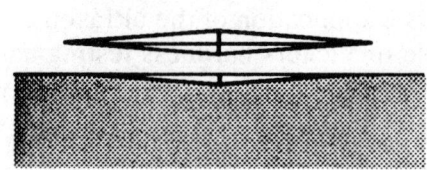
**Knoop
Microhardness**

$$\text{HVN} = \frac{C_1 P}{d_1^2} \tag{12.3}$$

HVN = Vickers hardness number
P = Applied load (kg)
d_1 = Mean diagonal of indentation (mm)
C_1 = 1.8544 = indenter geometry dependent constant

$$\text{HK} = \frac{C_2 P}{d_2^2} \tag{12.4}$$

HK = Knoop hardness number
P = Applied load (kg)
d_2 = Long diagonal of indentation (mm)
C_2 = 14.229 = indenter geometry dependent constant

Look-up tables such as those provided in standards developed by the American Society for Testing and Materials (ASTM standards E 92–82 and E 384–84) are provided to facilitate the calculation of the hardness numbers.

A microindentation hardness test generally consists of three steps:

1. Application of the test load by means of dead weights, springs, or levers

2. Removal of the test load

3. Optical evaluation of the indentation diagonal(s) with a microscope or calibrated eyepiece

Because of the necessity of optical evaluation of the indentation and the low test loads, a microindentation hardness test is generally considered a laboratory procedure.

The application of the ultrasonic contact impedance (UCI) measurement principle to Vickers hardness testing has eliminated the necessity of optical evaluation of the indentation, substantially improving the measurement accuracy and repeatability and decreasing testing time.

Ultrasonic Contact Impedance Measurement Technology and Hardness Testing

The ultrasonic contact impedance (UCI) operating principle was described initially by Kleesattel. It is based upon the relationship of the mechanical impedance between two elastic bodies and their contact area. In principle, a rod-shaped resonator is excited to its natural frequency by a pair of piezoelectric crystals. The rod is oscillated sinusoidally at approximately 80,000 Hertz. The fixed rod length limits the oscillations to the first harmonic, effectively eliminating destructive interference. The resonant frequency of the rod increases when it contacts another object. The frequency shift is measured by a second pair of crystals mounted on the rod. The contact area can be determined from the measured frequency shift and the elastic constants of the rod and the test object. Equation 12.5 defines the relationship:

$$A = g(E_d \mu_d E_p \mu_p) \bullet h(\Delta f / f_0) \qquad (12.5)$$

A = contact area
E_d = Young's modulus of rod
μ_d = Poisson's ratio of rod
E_p = Young's modulus of test piece

HARDNESS TEST METHODS

μ_p = Poisson's ratio of test piece
Δf = frequency shift
f_0 = initial frequency

The quantity $g(n)$ can be determined by calibration with an appropriate standard or by optically measuring the indentation contact area.

The mounting of a Vickers diamond indenter on the tip of the rod-shaped resonator and the application of a load to press the indenter into the test piece allows Vickers hardness measurement as defined by equation 12.6:

$$\text{HVN} = \frac{F}{A} \qquad (12.6)$$

HVN = Vickers hardness number
F = applied load (kg)
A = indentation surface contact area (mm^2)

After calibration for the elastic constants—defined by the function $g(n)$ in equation 12.5—the frequency shift defines the contact area and subsequently the hardness.

An Operational UCI-Based Hardness Tester

A schematic of a UCI-based hardness tester is shown in figure 12.2. The rod-shaped resonator is excited by a feedback amplifier through a pair of crystals. A Vickers diamond indenter is mounted on the end of the rod-shaped resonator. A static load of approximately 800 grams is produced by a constant load tension spring. The rod assembly is lowered and raised by an electric motor. A frequency discriminator measures the frequency shift. The load application time is adjustable from a minimum of two seconds to a maximum exceeding thirty seconds.

An operational UCI-based hardness tester (figure 12.3) consists of the probe and the instrument. The probe has been previously described. The instrument contains the power supply, operating controls, electronic processing components, and display. The hardness can be displayed directly in Vickers hardness numbers or converted to Rockwell values.

The UCI principle allows a significant transformation in the application of microhardness tests—from the laboratory to field, on-site testing applications.

Calibration of a UCI Hardness Tester

Because of the elastic (Young's) modulus dependency of UCI-generated hardness values, a simple calibration procedure must be performed prior to testing. The same material, or a similar material with a known hardness, must be

Figure 12.2 Schematic of a UCI-based Hardness Tester

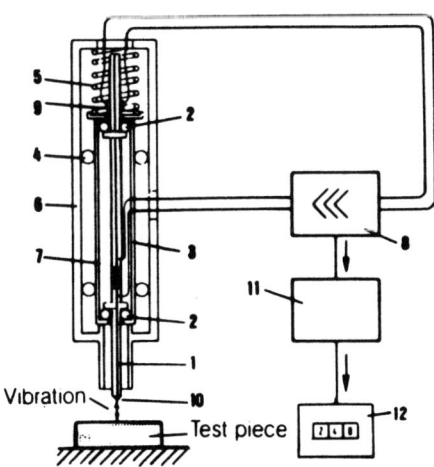

1. = oscillating rod
2. = rubber seal
3. = metal sleeve
4. = ball bearing bushings
5. = special spring
6. = housing
7. = oscillation converter
8. = amplifier
9. = oscillation detector
10. = diamond tip
11. = frequency discriminator
12. = ammeter

Figure 12.3 Operational UCI-based Hardness Tester

available for the UCI calibration. For example, you cannot calibrate with a stainless steel calibration coupon and then test aluminum. In general, material families (such as stainless steels, dies steels, precipitation hardened aluminum, mild or plain carbon steels) can be calibrated with one material within the family. The calibration procedure consists of three steps:

1. Take a hardness reading on the calibration coupon with the UCI tester.

2. Electronically adjust the function $g(\dot{n})$—most easily with a potentiometer—so that the displayed UCI tester value is equivalent to the calibration coupon value.

3. Repeat steps 1 and 2 to "fine-tune" the probe and the display unit.

The frequency response of a UCI-based hardness tester is fairly linear following a third-order relationship; however, it is best to calibrate within the expected hardness range of the test piece.

Experimental Results

A comparison of Vickers hardness values measured by a UCI-based hardness tester and a conventional microhardness tester was conducted on a series of 17 steels, ranging in composition from a plain carbon 1010 to alloyed Cr-Ni-Mo 4340. The steels were in the quench and tempered or annealed heat treatment conditions. The UCI-based hardness tester was calibrated with a 560-HVN block prior to the tests. The experimental results (figure 12.4) show an excellent 1:1 correlation between values measured with the two techniques. Kising, *et al.*, have shown similar results in the 550-to-800-HVN range [2].

Hardness Measurement Under Load

Another primary advantage of the UCI method is indentation evaluation under load. A perfect indentation made with a perfect Vickers indenter would be a square (figure 12.5). However, anomalies are frequently observed with a pyramid diamond indenter. The pincushion indentation shown in figure 12.5 is the result of sinking-in of the metal around the flat faces of the pyramid. This condition is observed with annealed metals and results in an overestimate of the diagonal length. The barrel-shaped indentation shown in the figure is found in cold-worked metals. It results from ridging or piling up of the metal around the faces of the indenter. The diagonal measurement in this case produces a low value of the contact area—the hardness numbers are erroneously high.

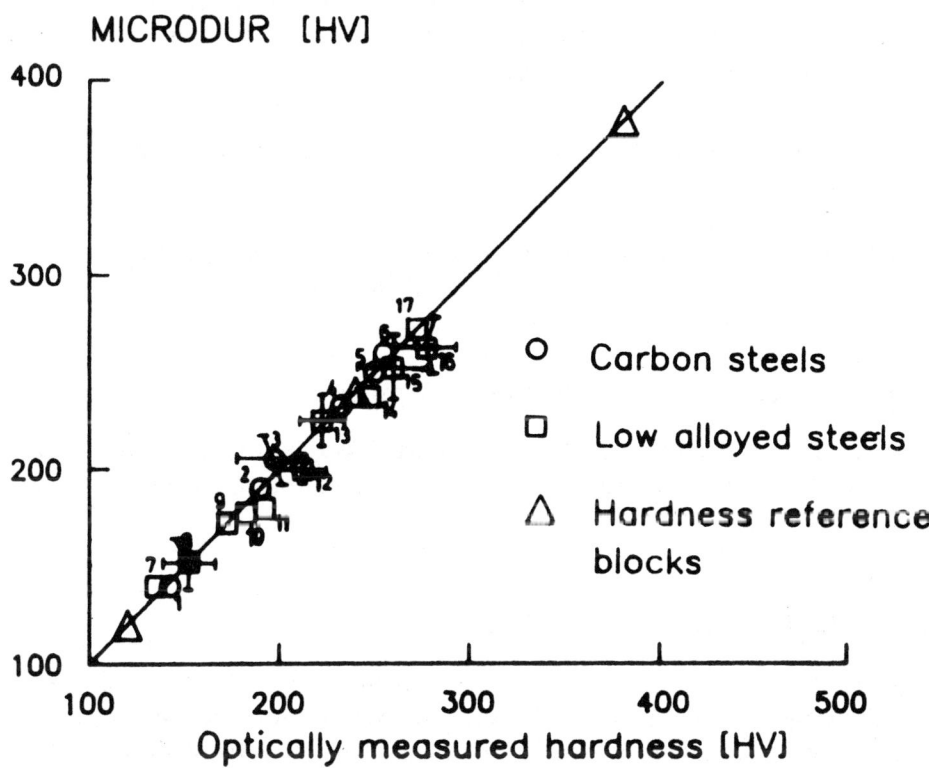

Figure 12.4 Comparison of UCI-generated Vickers Hardness Values to Conventional Optically Measured Vickers Hardness Values

Consequently, indentation evaluation under load eliminates errors due to elastic recovery upon unloading, dramatically improving the accuracy and repeatability of the Vickers microhardness values.

A typical application in which indentation evaluation under load is critical is hardness measurement of thin, brittle coatings such as pyrolitic carbon on a carbon substrate. The brittle nature of the coating prohibits accurate indentation measurement after load removal because of "ghost lines" or corner fracturing.

UCI Hardness Testing Benefits

UCI-based hardness testing provides several benefits, beyond increased accuracy, when compared with conventional indentation hardness testing. With a motor-driven indenter, the probe can be held in any direction and still take accurate readings. This feature, coupled with the portability made possible by compact electronics, allows the probe to be used on large parts, on the production line, and in many other previously inaccessible locations. The probe can also be placed in a test stand or a fixture to test parts of complex geometries.

Figure 12.5 Vickers Indentations Under Load and After Unloading

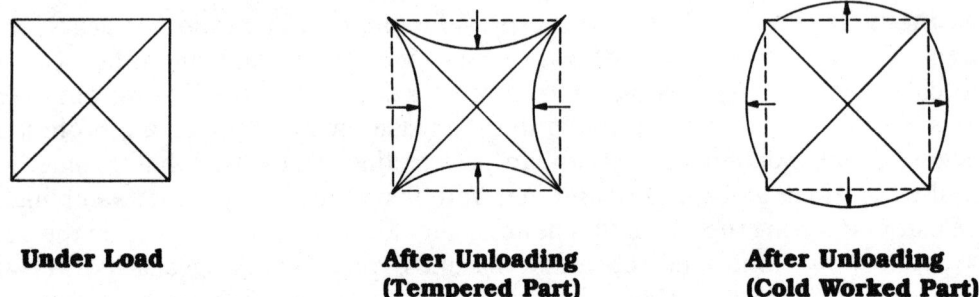

Under Load   After Unloading (Tempered Part)   After Unloading (Cold Worked Part)

UCI Hardness Testing Applications

Typical applications of UCI hardness testing are in the automotive, nuclear, petrochemical, aerospace, and machinery manufacturing industries. These include finished parts with hardened surfaces, thin case-hardened parts, and platings. Often 100-percent inspection is possible on critical components.

Surface Hardness Measurement of Ion-Nitrided Components Several factors must be considered during surface hardness measurement of ion-nitrided components. The indentation depth must be substantially less than the thickness of the hardened layer. A material thickness-to-indentation ratio of 7:1 to 10:1 is often recommended to minimize the effect of the core material on the measured hardness value. For a typical ion-nitrided component with a surface layer depth of 0.025 to 0.100 mm (0.001 to 0.004 inch), the maximum indentation depth should be 0.0035 to 0.010 mm (0.0002 to 0.0004 inch).

Many ion-nitrided components have finish machined or ground surfaces. Consequently, the depth of the hardness indentation should be minimized to eliminate the need for and the cost of corrective machining.

Large ion-nitrided components, such as automotive panel stamping dies, may be difficult or impossible to move to a stationary hardness tester. Sectioning of the die is obviously not desirable. In addition, sample coupons or shims included in the furnace batch may have significantly different properties than the die.

These three factors indicate the need for a low-load, portable hardness tester. A UCI hardness tester allows surface hardness measurement of shallow-cased ion-nitrided components. A surface layer hardened to 780 HVN (approximately 63.5 Rockwell "C") will have an indentation diagonal length of 0.041 mm (0.0016 inch) and an indentation depth of 0.0055 mm (0.0002 inch) when tested with a Vickers indenter and a 0.8 Kg test load. The indentation depth is substantially less than the thickness of the hardened layer. UCI measurement eliminates the

need for optical evaluation of the indentation. The small Vickers tip allows testing in radiused or difficult-to-access areas.

Hardness Testing of Gears In the manufacture and inspection of gears, it is often necessary to test the hardness of gear teeth on the flank and root areas. In the past, such testing was difficult on most gears and impossible on fine pitch gears. Conventional indentation hardness measurement methods are prohibited because of the indenter size. Microhardness testing can be used, but this method requires sectioning of the gear and therefore is practical only for lot sampling.

Custom fixturing (figure 12.6) that holds and locates the UCI probe on the gear tooth allows accurate and repeatable hardness readings. A special fixture was fabricated by molding a fast-curing urethane plastic around the teeth. After curing, the plastic was machined, and locating holes for a probe adaptor were drilled.

To perform ultrasonic hardness testing on fine-pitch gear teeth (10 to 14 pitch), a special diamond indenter was used. The small diameter and 120° included-angle Rockwell-style indenter gave the indenter access to the root and flank without touching the sides of the adjacent teeth. The UCI-generated hardness

Figure 12.6 Custom Fixturing to Locate UCI Probe Perpendicular to Gear Tooth Root or Flank

readings can be displayed digitally in either the Rockwell C or the Vickers scales on the instrument. Average test cycle time for gear teeth testing is 8 to 10 readings per minute. The test is virtually nondestructive with an indenter penetration depth of 0.005 mm (0.0002 inch) at 64.0 HRC.

Ultrasonic Hardness Testing of Bearings During the manufacturing and in-process inspection of ball and roller bearings, it is often necessary to measure the hardness of raceways. Conventional hardness test methods are not suited for this application, because the test surface is inaccessible and the penetration depth renders the test destructive. With special fixturing, the ultrasonic hardness test probe can be adapted for access to ball or roller bearing inner and outer ring raceways. Hardness testing on the raceway is conducted after finish grinding, prior to final honing or polishing. Generally, the stock removal in this operation is sufficient to remove the indentation. The depth of indenter penetration at 64.0 HRC is 0.003 mm (0.0002 inch).

The ultrasonic testing system could be adapted to test roller bearing raceways on a production line. A robot arm could be used to hold and manipulate the probe. Hardness test readings would be fed via an RS-232C or SPC interface to a computer. Such a system could monitor the hardness of roller bearing raceways on a continuous basis.

Ultrasonic Hardness Testing of Engine Components Hardness testing is required on wear surfaces of internal combustion engine components. This includes camshaft lobes, crankshaft pins and fillet radii, and valve tips. Testing for hardness is often a critical requirement for components used for reconditioned or rebuilt engines. Soft spots due to grinding burns or removal of excessive material during the regrind operation are potential problem areas. The ultrasonic hardness tester with special contoured fixtures (figure 12.7) can be taken to the grinding machine for in-process testing of the camshaft lobes or crankshaft pins and fillets.

Engine valve manufacturers are interested in checking the hardness of valve tips. With the length-to-diameter ratio of a typical valve (approximately 15:1), hardness testing on a conventional instrument is often difficult. The indentation left by a conventional hardness tester is also undesirable on the tip. Typically, the valve material is a steel forging with a hardness of 58 to 62 HRC. In some cases, the valve tip is a different material and hardness from the rest of the valve. The tip may be brazed or welded to the valve stem, or it may be hard coated.

A special bench-mounted fixture can be fabricated to locate the UCI probe in the vertical position with probe penetration from the bottom. This allows the inspector to insert the valve with the tip down. A foot switch can be used to trigger the probe and initiate the test. This enables the inspector to have both hands free, allowing a hardness-testing rate of 10 valves per minute.

Figure 12.7 Contoured Probe Shoes Designed to Locate a UCI Probe Perpendicular to the Camshaft Lobe Surface

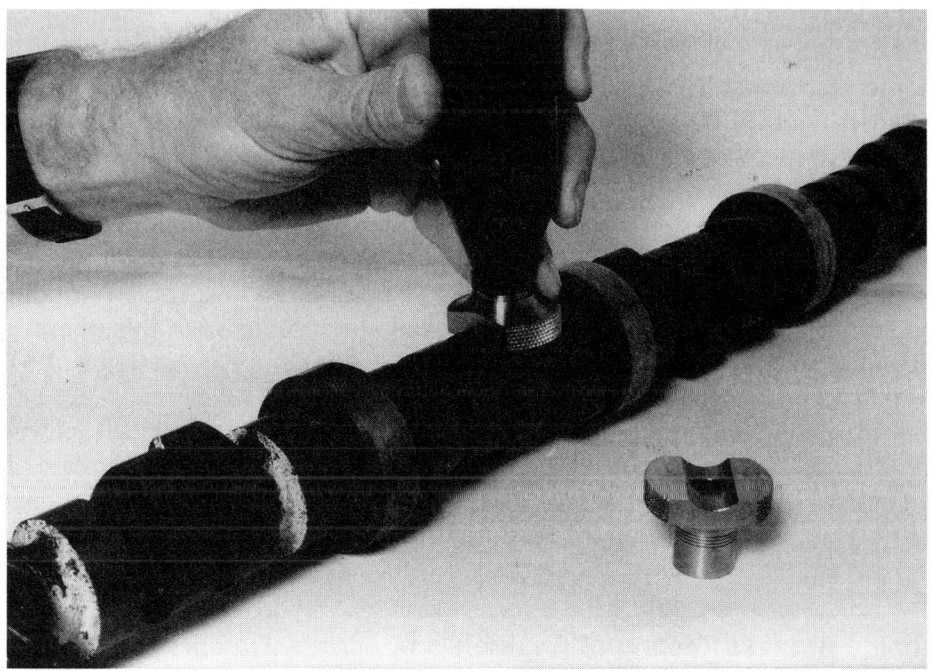

Hardness Testing of Rotogravure Printing Cylinders Rotogravure printing cylinders, used to print magazines and newspaper supplements, are assembled from copper-coated metal printing blocks. The copper coating is engraved with the ink-carrying indentation "cups"; the volume of the cup determines the intensity of the print. The hardness of the copper coating is a critical factor, both for the clarity and "readability" of the imprinted image and for the operable life of the cylinder. If the copper layer is too hard, the engraving needle has difficulty penetrating. If the layer is too soft, the copper will be smeared into the cups, dramatically decreasing print quality.

The thin coating, low hardness (180 to 210 Vickers), and creep properties of the copper dictate a microhardness test. The large diameter and length of the assembled cylinders prohibit testing on a conventional microhardness or standard hardness tester. A UCI hardness tester applies a light load of approximately 300 grams for 30 seconds. The Vickers hardness is then displayed. The test probe can be mounted in a test stand with V-block shoes to allow easy alignment and perpendicularity to the cylindrical test surface. With a copper hardness of 200 Vickers, the indenter will penetrate approximately 0.011 mm (0.00045 inch).

Hardness Testing of Chromium Plating Chromium plating continues to be used as both a principal manufacturing step to increase surface hardness and as a refurbishing technique for worn, out-of-size components. After the plating operation, hardness is often measured to ensure that the proper amount, composition, and thickness of plating was applied on the component. Chromium plating hardnesses can range from approximately 58 RC to more than 68 RC; most typical applications are greater than 65 RC. A Vickers-based hardness tester is particularly valuable for this application. The continuous Vickers scale extends above the conventional HRC scale. The portability of a UCI hardness tester allows on-site testing of the chromium-plated rolls.

Hardness Measurement of Case Depth Hardness Profiles When measurement of the complete surface-hardened profile is required, a UCI hardness tester can be coupled with a motorized traversing stage for fully automated hardness traversing of cross-sectioned samples. The UCI principle eliminates optical evaluation of the indentation, decreasing testing time and improving the accuracy and reproducibility of the hardness measurements. A complete profile can be generated, analyzed, stored, and printed in less than two minutes.

Conclusions

A UCI hardness tester combines the benefits of ultrasonic contact impedance measurement technology and microhardness testing, allowing both on-site and laboratory hardness testing of many types of components. Specifically:

- Work by Kleesattel has established the relationship among contact impedance, indentation contact area, and Vickers hardness.

- The contact impedance has been measured effectively with a rod-shaped resonator oscillating at a frequency of approximately 80000 Hertz.

- A UCI hardness tester has been manufactured that incorporates a Vickers diamond-tipped resonator with a constant load spring applying the load.

- The shallow indentation of the UCI-based hardness tester, coupled with the portability of the unit, has opened many new hardness application areas.

References

1. Jankowski, D. M. "An Automated Method for Measuring Hardness of Large Components." *Heat Treating* (May 1989):35–37.

2. Kising, J., W. Weiler, and I. Winckler. "The UCI Principle." *VDI Berichte* no. 583 (1986):371–91.

3. Kleesattel, C., and G. M. L. Gladwell. "The UCI-Testing Method." *Ultrasonics* vol. 6 (1986):175–80.

4. Larson, P. D., and P. A. Meyer. "The Ultrasonic Method—A Hardness Testing Alternative." *Heat Treating* (May 1987):42–45.

5. Szilard, J. "Quicker, Simple Hardness Testing Using Ultrasonics." *Ultrasonics* vol. 10 (1984):174–78.

6. "Ultrasonic Microhardness Testing." In *Metals Handbook*. 9th ed. Vol. 8: Mechanical Testing. John L. Herron, ed. Metals Park, OH: 1985, pp. 98–103.

Chapter 13 Acoustic Emission

Mark Carlos

Introduction

In today's industrial environment, there is a twofold push: first, to assure product quality at the front end, and second, to automate. Manufacturing lines are producing products at unprecedented rates. Maintaining quality in this environment is a challenge. Where visual inspection cannot keep up, factories are relying more on statistical process control. However, what good is a sampled inspection and process control after the fact? Automation also exacerbates the problem. Unless carefully scrutinized, an automatic machine can start producing scrap at these high line rates. Because the purpose of automation is to reduce the reliance on human factors, an automated and cost-effective way of monitoring and controlling the process is needed.

Acoustic emission (AE) sensors are one solution. This technology has been applied successfully since the early 1970s in many industrial manufacturing (and automated) applications. Successful implementations include: crack detection, weld quality and feedback control, leak detection, machine and tool monitoring, process monitoring, bond analysis, and cure monitoring, to name a few. Acoustic emission lends itself readily to automated applications: it is low in cost, it is easy to apply, it adapts readily to existing manufacturing equipment, and it operates in real time (during the process) to detect anomalies in the production process. AE systems can monitor every part going through the production process, giving instant information on product quality.

What Is Acoustic Emission?

Acoustic emission is defined as energy released in the form of mechanical vibrations from a material as it undergoes stress (figure 13.1). A material that is under stress (via applied heat, force, etc.) emits acoustic emission from a flaw or source as it acts to relieve the stress that caused it. The acoustic emission is an omnidirectional wave that travels from the source to the AE sensor, which is in contact with the material being monitored. The AE sensor converts the mechanical vibration or acoustic emission into an electronic signal for further processing from the AE instrumentation.

In industrial manufacturing applications, AE relies on the process itself to provide the stresses that excite the part being monitored. Figure 13.2 depicts process stresses being induced by a resistance spot weld. The stresses stem from the pressure maintained by the upper and lower electrodes and the heat generated by current flowing through the parts being welded. The AE sensor need not be in direct contact with the parts being welded, provided there is a suitable path for the acoustic emission to travel. Most production processes apply stress in one form or another to shape, attach, or finish the product.

As a result of the applied stress, mechanical vibrations and acoustic emission are generated from the part being processed. Some of these vibrations are infor-

Figure 13.1 Acoustic Emission Generation Model

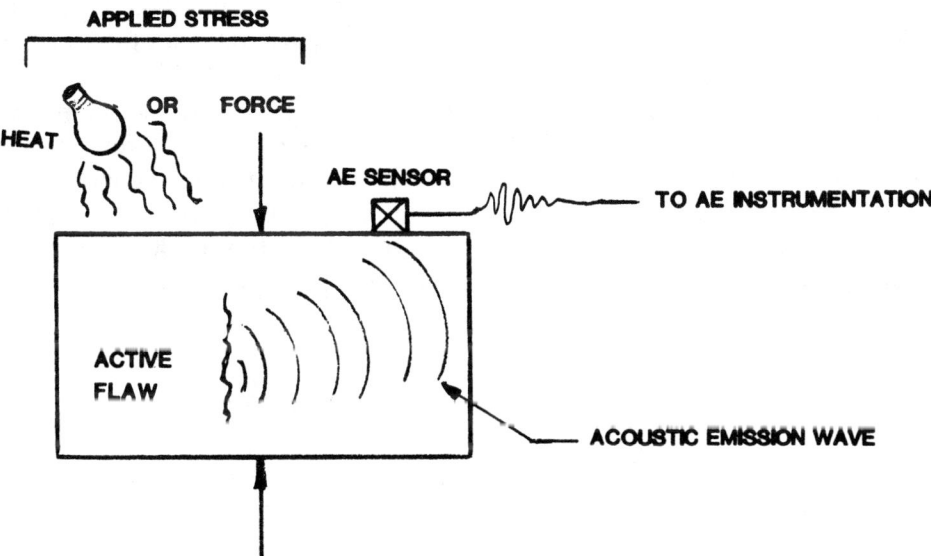

WHAT IS ACOUSTIC EMISSION?

Figure 13.2 Spot Welding Stress Application

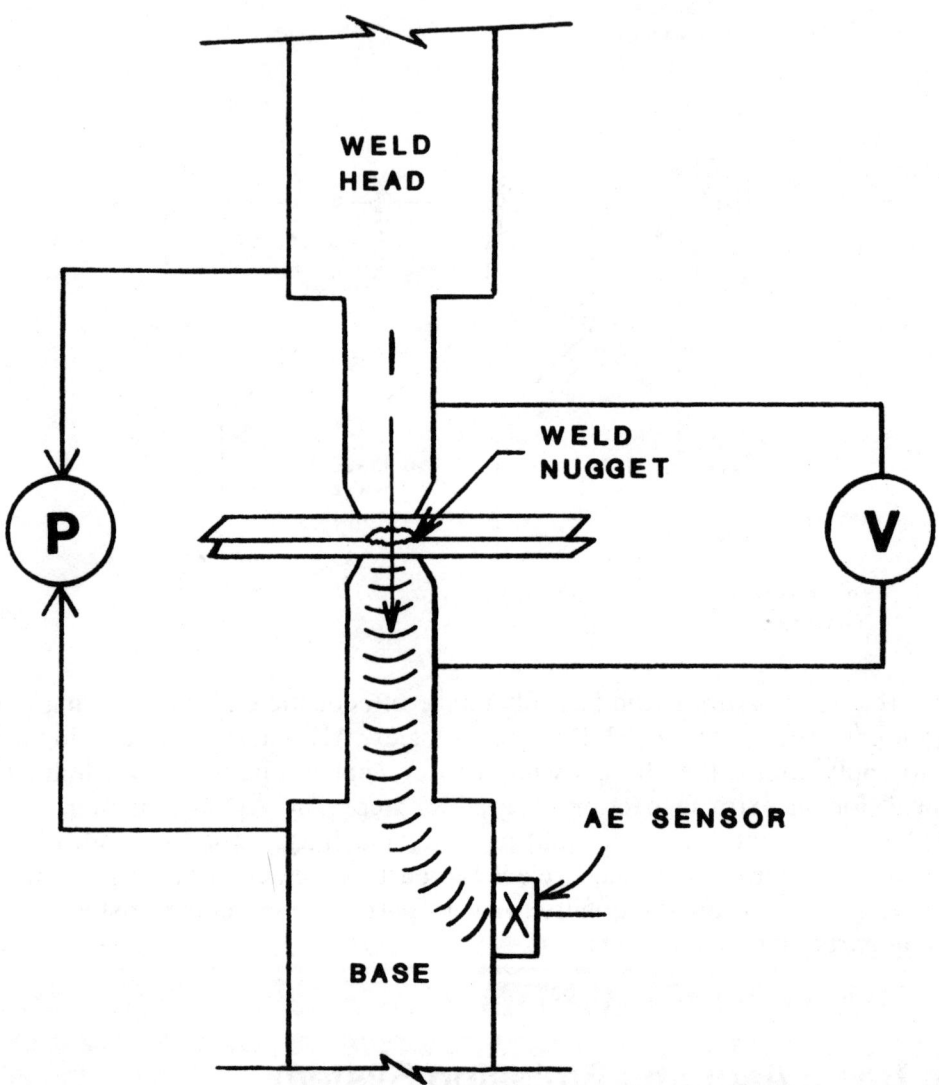

mative and indicate that the process is behaving normally. (Figure 13.3 shows an example of AE waveforms and their time relationship during a resistance spot-weld.) Other vibrations are indicators of harmful and unacceptable conditions that are occurring (such as cracking, expulsion in welding, leaking, etc.). The important factor is that mechanical vibrations occur in real time. This gives the means for instant feedback about the quality of the part being manufactured as well as the process.

Figure 13.3 Typical AE Response Signals During Resistance Spot Welding

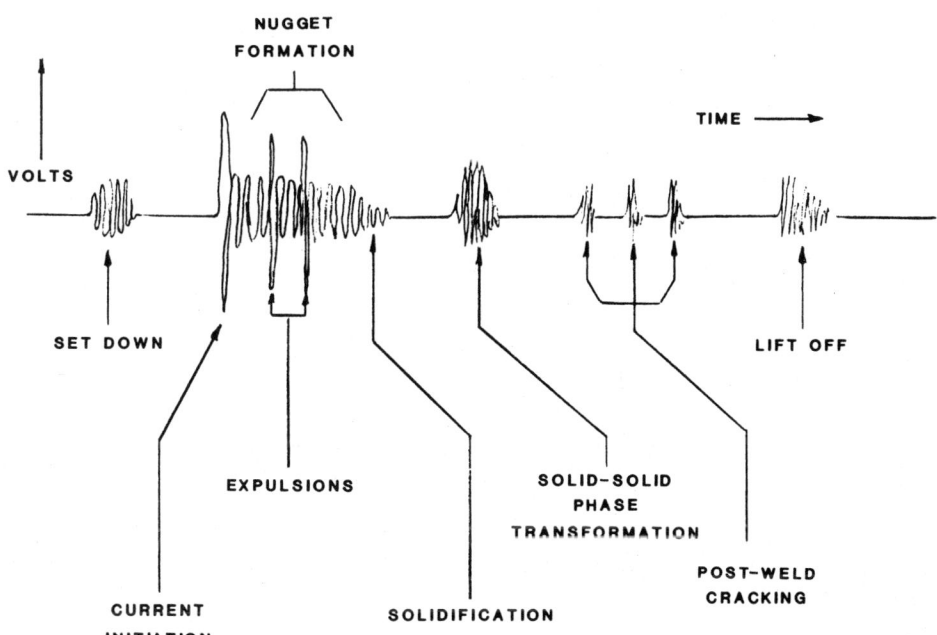

This real-time nature is the key advantage of acoustic emission sensing over other nondestructive testing (NDT) technologies. AE relies on the existing process to apply stress, thereby allowing it to be applied directly. This eliminates the need for an extra inspection or process step. The AE information, being immediate, gives the process instant feedback (such as, "stop the weld, it's acceptable") or control (such as, "reject the part, it's cracked"). This results in cost savings by assuring the quality of every part and eliminating wasteful extra steps on parts that have defects.

The Basic Acoustic Emission System

Acoustic emission sensor systems come in many varieties, shapes, and sizes. They range from simple single-channel boxes with an analog meter to complex multichannel, multiprocessing units that link directly to process computers. A simplified block diagram of the acoustic emission system is presented in figure 13.4.

The basic AE system consists of an AE sensor and a preamplifier (per channel), which is connected to an AE processor. The AE processor receives signals

THE BASIC ACOUSTIC EMISSION SYSTEM

Figure 13.4 Block Diagram of an AE System

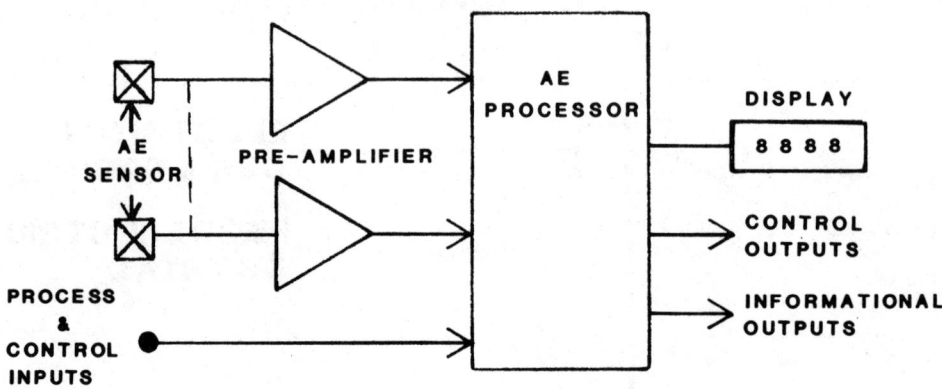

from the AE sensors, indicators of one or several process parameters and control inputs. The AE processor makes a quality decision from these inputs and feeds the results to a display for viewing purposes and to the control and informational outputs. Each of these parts of the AE system are discussed in further detail below.

The AE Sensor

The sensor makes contact with the part being monitored and converts the detected mechanical waves into electrical signals that can be processed by the AE instrument. The most typical AE sensor is constructed using undamped piezoelectric ceramic crystals. The piezoelectric effect was first demonstrated by the Curie brothers in 1880. Piezoelectricity is the phenomenon whereby applying pressure on certain crystals causes an electric charge or potential to appear across the faces. These devices have proven the most sensitive and cost-effective and are generally used in the detection of AE signals. Other methods, such as laser interferometry or capacitive transducers, have been used as well, but they suffer from lower sensitivity and higher cost. Figure 13.5 shows the simplified construction of an AE sensor for reference purposes.

Factors that must be considered when choosing and installing a sensor for a given application include the following: frequency response, sensitivity, coupling to the part being monitored, temperature, size, shape (see figure 13.6), protection, internal or external preamplifier, etc. Through the years, AE companies have seen many applications and have available many different standard sensors already designed with these factors in mind for a given application. Table 13.1 shows typical specification ranges for the sensor factors identified. These ranges

Figure 13.5 Construction of an AE Sensor

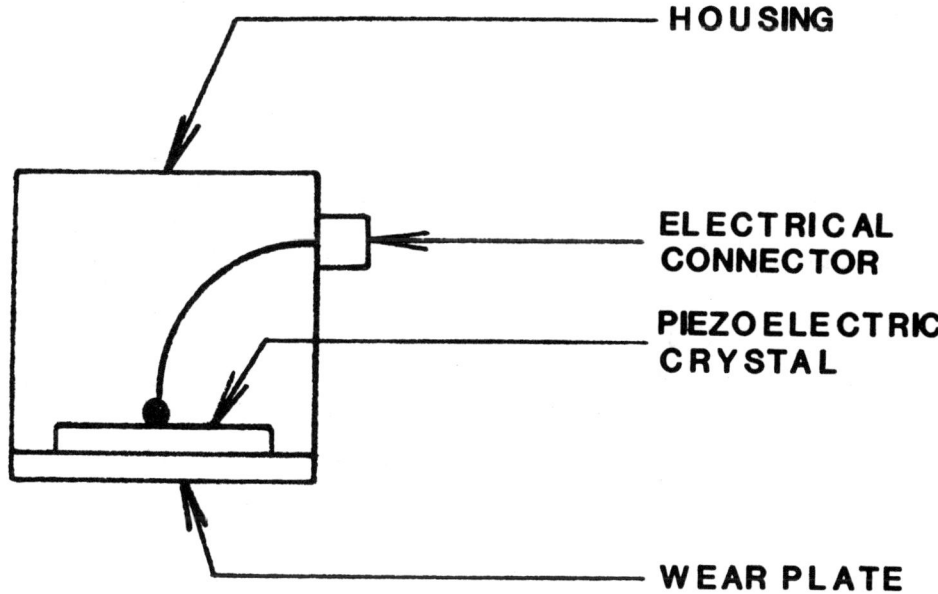

Figure 13.6 Acoustic Emission Sensors

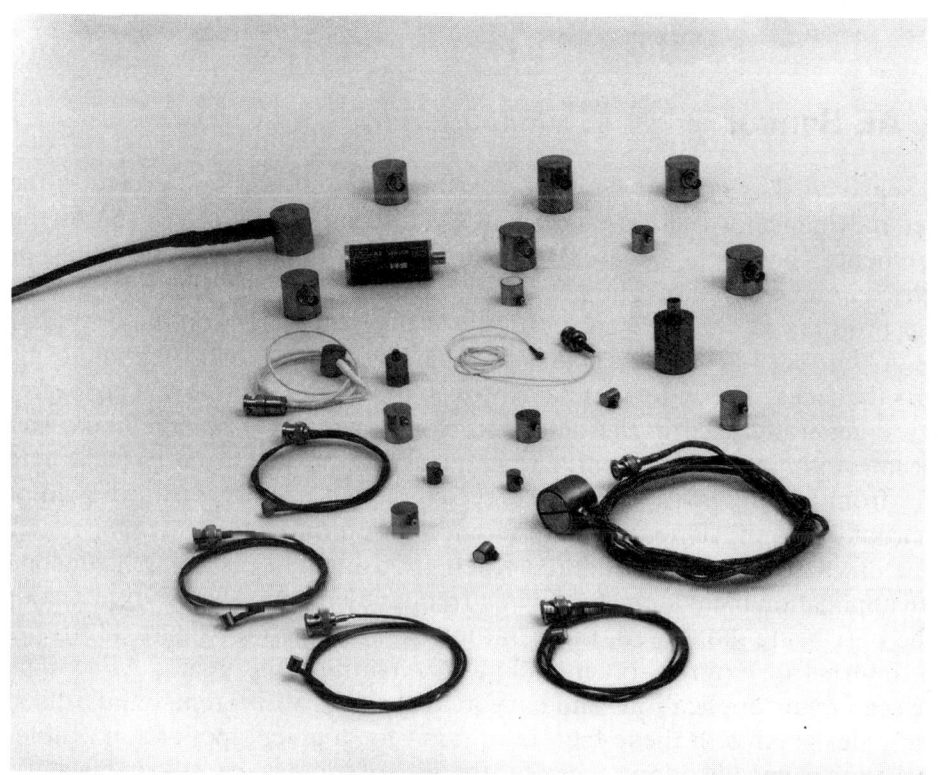

THE BASIC ACOUSTIC EMISSION SYSTEM

Table 13.1 Typical Sensor Specification Ranges

Characteristic	Specification Range
Frequency Range	20 kHz–1 MHz (or even greater)
Wear Plate Types	Ceramic, epoxy, stainless steel, aluminum, brass
Temperature Range	−154°C to +540°C
Shape	Typically cylindrical
Size (small)	0.14 inch in diameter × .095 inch in height
Size (large)	1.125 inch in diameter × 1.16 inch in height

are not achieved in a single sensor; rather, they reflect the properties of a range of products that are commercially available.

Over the last few years, AE sensors have improved in all the areas indicated above. Noteworthy achievements are sensitivity improvements, extended temperature range operation, and miniaturization. These improvements have led to more use of AE systems in demanding process control situations.

Other sensor developments have even simplified AE systems, therefore making AE easier to apply in some applications. One notable achievement is the "rolling sensor" designs, which are found in automated applications (see figure 13.7). These sensors consist of a compliant tire and a barrel rotating around a stationary axle, which has a sensor element attached to it. A fluid between the barrel and the axle assures good acoustic contact. In this arrangement, the sensor element always maintains the same relationship and distance to the part and the process being monitored, even though the part (or process) may be moving.

Some ideal applications for a rolling sensor are described below. In a web process, the sensor will stay in the same relative position to the process, even though the material is moving continuously. In a welding process (such as MIG, TIG, Electron Beam, or Laser Weld), a rolling sensor can be attached to the welding head. In this way it can follow the process, always remaining a constant distance from the weld.

The rolling sensor design offers several key advantages in these and other automated and process control applications. First, the compliant tire makes contact with the part being monitored. This provides the all-important coupling factor and eliminates the need for a grease or other couplant. Second, the rolling sensor assures a consistent distance and relationship (and therefore sensitivity) to the process. Older techniques required that multiple sensors be placed from one end of the part to the other end. Detection sensitivities changed constantly with distance to the sensor. Third, the rolling sensor can be applied automatically for each new process. It need not be removed and replaced by an operator as a fixed sensor would be.

Figure 13.7 Rolling Acoustic Emission Sensor

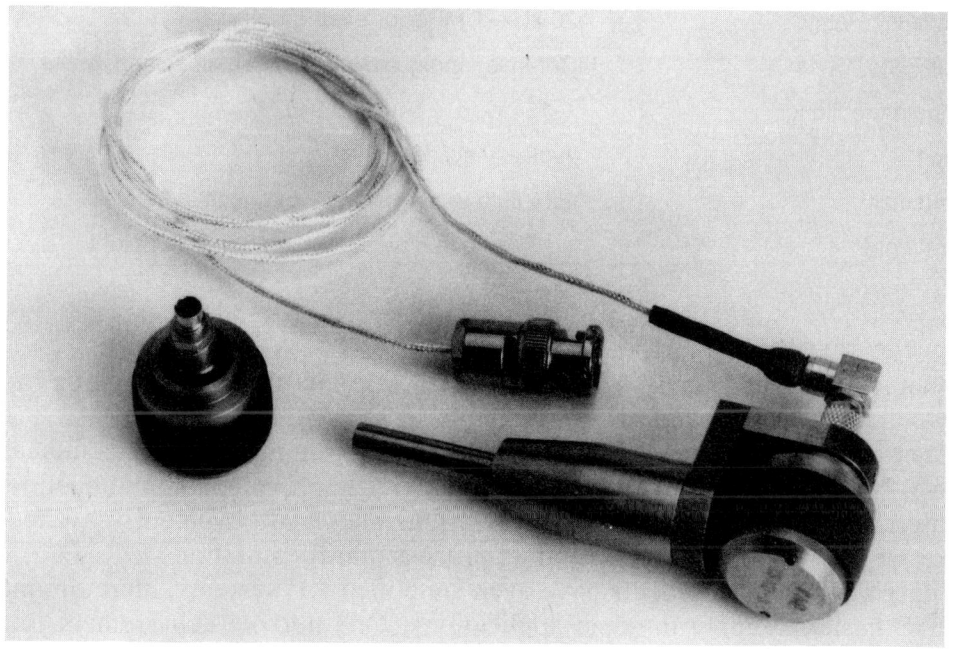

The AE Preamplifier

The AE preamplifier's job is to receive the low-level voltage from the AE sensor (typically microvolts), amplify and filter it, and provide a low impedance output drive to the AE instrument. The preamp supplies a gain of 40–60 dB to increase voltage to a range that can be effectively processed. Application-specific filtering is typically included in the preamp design to emphasize certain frequencies for processing. Finally, the amplified signal is conditioned to drive a 50-ohm terminated coaxial cable to the AE instrument. It is important that the preamplifier be as close to the sensor as possible to minimize the attenuation and noise pickup of the AE signal as it travels down a cable to the preamplifier. Because the sensor impedance is high, it is easy for this line to act as an antenna, picking up electrical noises. Keeping this connection path as short as possible (less than 36 inches) assures the highest signal-to-noise ratio.

Some sensors employ an integral preamplifier. This is ideal, because it eliminates extra parts (separate sensor and preamp) and keeps the amplifier within the shielded cavity. This eliminates any chance for noise pickup.

THE BASIC ACOUSTIC EMISSION SYSTEM

In AE systems being employed today, a single coaxial cable provides both DC voltage to power up the remote preamplifier and an AE signal path to the instrument. This single cable simplifies the installation and makes the system more industrially hardened.

Many times an AE instrument cannot be placed close to the sensor. The preamplifier is usually able to drive well over 500 feet of cable. This makes it possible to create remote AE system installations.

The AE Processor

The AE processor (instrument) is the main part of the AE system. It is here that the AE signals are gathered up with the other process inputs; a decision is formulated and communicated. This decision can range from a "reject" relay closure and a light to a computer communications path, indicating a decision and how the process should be altered. The processor or instrument can be as simple as a small single-channel hand-held instrument or as complex as a large rack-mounted multiple-channel, multiple-computer system.

A simplified block diagram of what goes on inside an AE system is shown in figure 13.8. AE input is accepted from one or more channels. Extra amplification and filtering of the AE signal is performed. Real-time AE signal feature extraction is then performed on the AE signals. These features describe one or more parameters about the AE signals detected. (See the next section, "Description

Figure 13.8 AE Processor Block Diagram

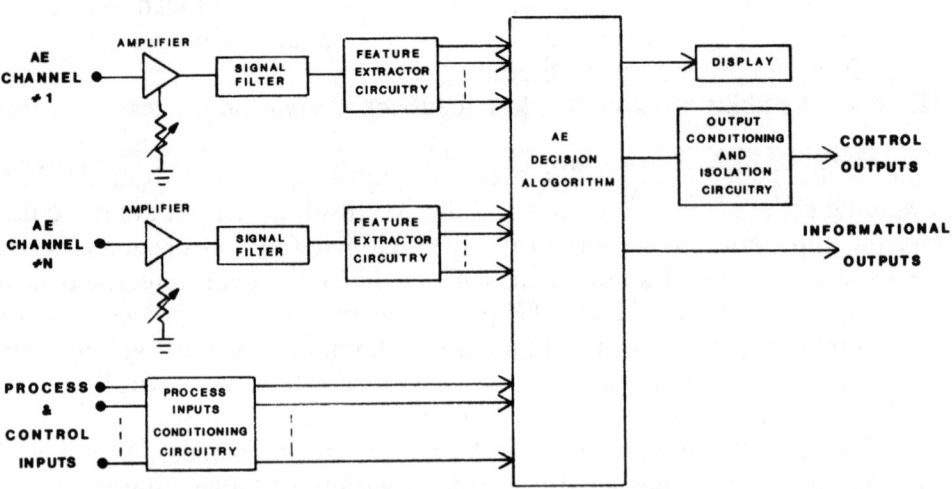

of AE Features," for a more complete description of features.) The AE decision algorithm processing section collects these detected features, operates on them along with the other process and control inputs, and decides on the process. It outputs this information in the form of a display, control output, or informational output for the user or the machine interface to handle accordingly. If, for example, the decision algorithm determines that the process has exceeded a reject condition, it activates an alarm by turning on its control output. This usually actuates a relay that causes a reject mechanism to fire or an alarm to sound.

Over the last several years, there have been many exciting advances to AE systems that make them ideally suited in today's automation and process control applications. Some of the notable achievements include the following: computerization, miniaturization, reduction in price, high data-storage capability, higher reliability in industrial environments, Statistical Process Control (SPC) capability, and ability to incorporate adaptive and artificial intelligence (AI) capabilities.

Monitoring and Integration of Other Process Inputs

Acoustic emission should be looked upon as another key process parameter that must be monitored with the other process parameters. If the process parameters being controlled in today's automated systems were enough, there would be no rejects. However, that is not the case. Even though process controllers are monitoring key inputs very carefully, variables still cause the process to go out of control. In spot welding, for example, it is not enough that the appropriate voltage, current, and force be applied to the materials to assure a good weld every time. Electrode degradation, material changes, and other uncontrollable variables in the on-going welding process will quickly turn what was once a good weld into a cold weld. Controlling the input variables is not enough to guarantee an acceptable result. Again, it is desirable to have a technique that can provide feedback from the process more directly.

AE offers the ability to give this key feedback *during* the process—feedback that verifies the appropriateness of the input variables. The AE parameter signals that a change is needed in the process control inputs. For example, in the spot welding process described above, if the AE result determines that it did not receive the appropriate AE energy from the weld itself, it will signal an increase in the welding current. Examples of sensors that have been integrated in the process control situation with the AE parameter include: time/process synchronization, pressure, force, strain, temperature, humidity, current, voltage, position, weld feedback energy, speed of process, feed rate of weld wire, time, etc. In a given application, some of these sensors must be used with the AE parameter to make a better judgment as to the quality of the process. Significantly, today's AE systems are designed to handle a variety of these different process inputs, condition them, and incorporate them into the AE decision algorithm.

Interface to the Process Controller

In order for the AE system to be an effective part of the process, it must be able to communicate to other peripherals that are part of the processing equipment. It must be able to accept inputs from the process controller and it must be able to output information to direct or change parameters in the process.

To accomplish this, the AE system must have a variety of inputs and outputs. As far as inputs are concerned, the AE system needs analog and digital inputs for monitoring the various status and parametric information about the process. Status signals, such as a process "on" synchronization signal, error conditions from other sensors, etc., are sometimes important information that must be monitored by the AE system. Parametric data, such as sensor data, that has already been implemented into the process controller can be tapped from it also. This data can be in analog or digital form or as pulse trains of data. These parametric inputs are the ones that were discussed previously (such as temperature, pressure, position, etc.). The AE system must be versatile enough to handle different signal levels and, of course, the different types of signals.

Other forms of inputs to the AE system from the process include a computer communications path to the process controller. In this situation, the AE system must be able to accept computer communications or commands from the controller to carry out and coordinate with the process. These types of communications can be via a simple three-wire RS-232 interface, an IEEE-488 interface, or a local area network (LAN).

Outputs to the process can be as simple as relay or DC voltage outputs to indicate status, faults, or reject conditions. They can be as complex as a computer communications output to indicate the status of the process or the type of correction needed to bring the process back into control. Other outputs usually required by the AE system include the ability to provide statistical reports in the form of shift reports, defect reports, etc.

In addition, depending on the process controller capability, the AE system may be expected to act as a master or slave processor to the controller. A master is usually desired when the process controller has no computer capability and does not have the ability to alter the process itself. In those cases, the AE system will tap into the controller and effectively take over the control of the process. In a slave situation, the controller has the ability to coordinate the AE system, accept the outputs from it, and control the process itself.

It is not a matter of supremacy whether the AE system is master or slave in a given process control system. It always comes down to a matter of economics. The most efficient and cost-effective way of implementing a process control system using AE is the important matter.

The successful process control system using AE is one that can easily handle the input and output considerations presented above without much added cost. Today's industrial AE systems have the above-mentioned capabilities and are consequently becoming more widely used in industrial automation.

Process Control Algorithm

The AE sensor, the AE system, and the need for the AE system to monitor other sensor inputs have all been discussed. These factors must be brought together to form a reliable decision that can be used to provide correction information to the process. An algorithm is simply a procedure that is followed to arrive at a solution or decision. An algorithm can be implemented in the system hardware, system software, or a combination of both.

In current AE process control systems, the data collection process (including AE and other sensor inputs) is usually done by computer. The computer reads the values of all inputs, collects all AE information, and then combines and operates on the data to reach a decision. It is here that the full computing power incorporated into modern-day AE systems is required. The AE system must be programmed to think and to compensate appropriately for any change in input parameters, as well as the AE parameter. Many times, under normal operating circumstances, the AE parameter will correlate with one or more of the input variables. If these correlation factors change, the AE system must detect this and correct for it. This is where the AE system must incorporate artificial intelligence techniques. It must survey its input sensors and its AE parameter and must make an informed judgment.

This kind of power was not available several years ago. Systems at that time were carefully adjusted to operate over a very narrow range of input conditions. If an input changed (for example, weld speed in a MIG or electron beam weld), the AE parameter would vary in direct proportion to that input. The result is that the AE system might make a misinformed judgment about the quality of the process. Systems that must operate in a factory environment cannot be "fooled" in this manner. They must be able to operate over many changing conditions without operator interaction.

The appropriate AE algorithm must, therefore, have the following attributes:

- It must operate over a wide range of conditions.

- It must be able to accept inputs from other sensors and incorporate these inputs into the decision process.

- It must be foolproof.

- It must operate in real time.

- It must decide on its own, without human intervention.

- It must have the ability to feed back to the process.

AE Signals and Features

Acoustic emission was defined as energy released due to stress, in the form of mechanical vibrations. The energy release can occur in two ways, causing different acoustic emission signal types. The first type is AE bursts and the second type is continuous AE.

AE Bursts

AE burst are discrete in nature and last a very short time (usually on the order of microseconds). This is the most common form of AE. The nature of material structure is such that energy is not released until a certain amount of stress has been applied. When that stress has been reached, the material gives way suddenly and movement in the form of slip, cracking, etc. occurs. This is a momentary release that causes a shock wave (AE) that propagates throughout the material and gets detected by a sensor. The material then realigns and will not emit until another stress limit is reached. One of the key properties that AE depends upon is that cracking or emission will occur from the weakest areas of the materials. These are areas where small defects or voids exist and applications of stress at a much lower level than material yield or deformation will cause the defects to grow and AE to be detected.

Because the energy release that causes AE bursts to occur lasts a very short time, this gives a very broadband response in the frequency domain (analogous to impulse response in electrical engineering). A second property of AE signal propagation is that the higher the frequency of the AE burst, the faster it attenuates. Most AE signals coming from material deformation or cracking are of a very high frequency. Therefore, the AE sensor should be placed close to the material being processed for maximum sensitivity. These facts are used to the AE system's advantage in an industrial application. First, the manufacturing process is producing machine vibrations at very low frequencies, typically less than 50 kHz. Secondly, AE signals from defects are broadband. If AE sensors and a signal-filtering scheme that is above 50 kHz (the higher, the better) are selected, the machine noise is virtually eliminated and the AE detection sensitivity is enhanced. Typically, industrial applications operate with frequencies in the range of 150–500 kHz. Actual frequency selection is based on the distance/attenuation relationship.

Another property of AE signal propagation is the capability of locating the source by triangulation methods, in which the difference of burst arrival time between several sensors is analyzed. This permits analysis of the severity of the defect and at the same time allows the system to determine the source of the

defect. This information is available in "real time," not as a separate step after the process.

How does the AE system process these signals? The AE system receives the AE burst and breaks it down into signal features. A typical AE burst is depicted in figure 13.9. With it are described measurements that are taken by the AE system in real time and stored as a description of that burst. These features are similar to electrical engineering signal description terms but are based upon the signal's exceeding a preset signal threshold. The following features are described:

AE hit   Each AE burst detected is referred to as a *hit*.

AE amplitude The maximum amplitude in dB, referenced at 0 dB = 1 microvolt at the sensor.

AE counts   The number of times the AE signal exceeds a set threshold.

Figure 13.9 Single AE Burst Showing Measurable AE Features

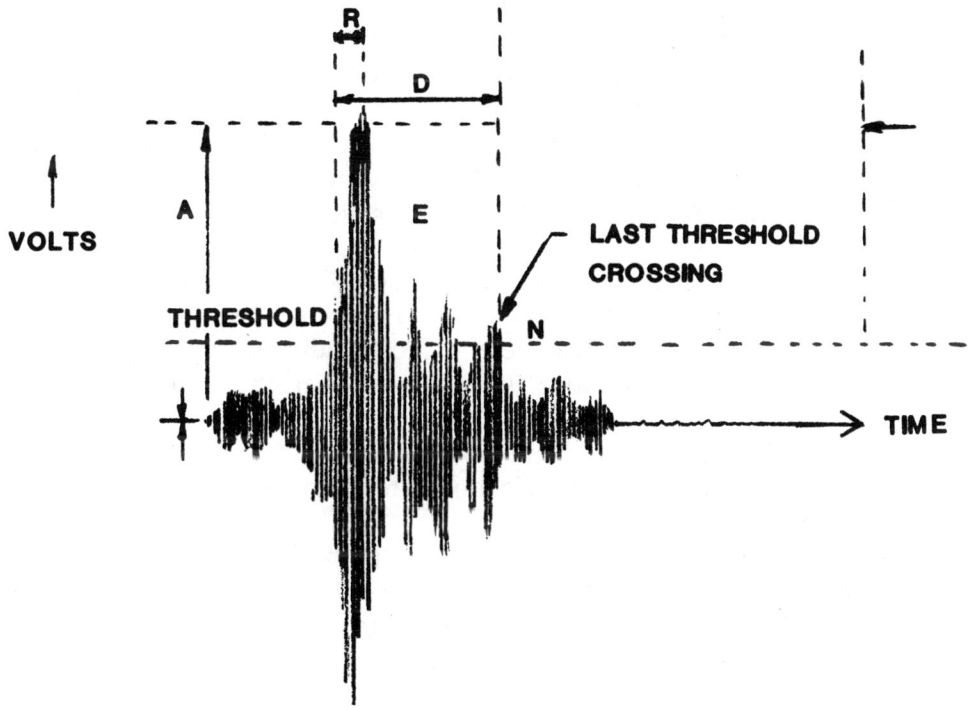

AE rise time	The time from the first threshold crossing to the peak.
AE duration	The time from the first threshold crossing to the last in a burst.
AE energy	The relative energy of an AE burst.
Average freq	The weighted average frequency derived from AE counts to peak divided by rise time.
Arrival time	The time of test at which the first threshold crossing occurred.

Some AE systems are able to operate on all of these features, but industrial systems typically require only a small subset to analyze the process. Using only one or several of these features results in a faster and lower-cost system. Energy has been found to be the most useful of all AE parameters, because it is a measure of the amplitude and time relationship. This is the most common parameter utilized in industrial AE processing systems.

The way in which an acoustic emission system would utilize these features is described in the previous section. Features are formed on each burst as it is received and collected by the AE decision algorithm processing section. The AE decision algorithm processing section then coordinates this data with the other received process control inputs and does the necessary normalization and discrimination functions to decide. Dealing with AE features that are collected in real time is easier and faster than trying to deal with the entire waveform. Accuracy is maintained because a combination of features uniquely describes the waveform received.

Continuous AE

Continuous AE is just that—energy released continuously in the form of mechanical vibrations. Common types of continuous emission are found in leaking, machining (as with drills and lathes), AE due to flow noise, and continuous welding.

There are several ways of measuring continuous AE signals in industrial processes. The first continuous AE feature is RMS, or Root Mean Square. This comes directly from the electrical engineering definition and is a measure of the average of the squared peak amplitude over time. RMS is a measure of the energy of the continuous waveform and is usually reported as a voltage.

The second continuous AE feature is that of ASL, or Average Signal Level. ASL is a measure of the averaged peak amplitude in dB. This is useful for

applications in which a high dynamic range is required. AE amplitude has a dynamic range of over 80 dB, which can be managed easily by ASL.

The final continuous AE feature is called the rate feature. This one is formed by reading burst AE features, such as AE count or AE energy, but reporting the values detected in a given period. For example, the accumulated AE energy counts (in one second) would be reported as an energy rate of 1000 (energy counts per second).

Of the three continuous AE features, the energy rate feature has been found to be the most sensitive and useful in industrial applications, because the energy rate feature reports real values as received from the process. In contrast, because the RMS and ASL features provide an averaged value, they do not respond to important AE bursts that have occurred.

Industrial AE Applications

The sections that follow provide a summary of some of the more popular industrial and automated applications of AE systems.

AE in Crack Detection and Electronics Applications

Crack Detection

One of the oldest and most successful applications of acoustic emission has been in the electronic industry in the detection of cracking in ceramic and semiconductor bonding process. AE systems have been in use in these applications since the early 1970s, monitoring each bonding process and automatically rejecting parts that have cracked. Areas in which this technology has been used include thermocompression bonding on leads and lead frames. These early systems were very simple. A sensor was placed close to the bonding process and would monitor for cracking only during the bonding process itself. The process input was driven from a cam operated microswitch. This would enable AE monitoring after the bonding head had came to rest on the part being bonded (see figure 13.10). Monitoring would cease just before the bonding head came off the part. This allowed for a quiet and sensitive crack-detection period. The heat and pressure of the thermocompression bond would provide the stress necessary to join the materials but in some cases would also cause the part to crack. When cracking occurred, a reject mechanism would mark the defective part. These systems are used widely in today's electronic manufacturing facilities.

Figure 13.10 Bonding Crack Detector Timing Diagram

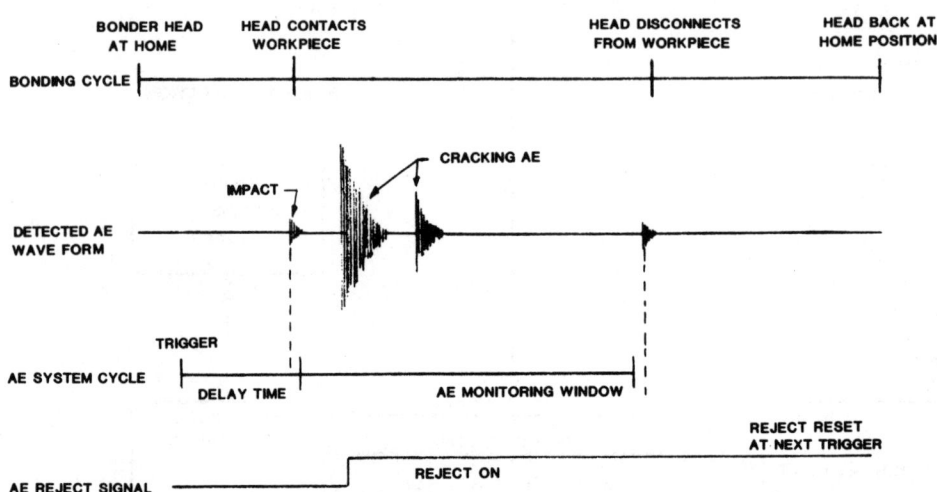

Nondestructive Bond Pull Monitoring

Another successful application of AE in this industry is in the nondestructive bond pull test on wire bonds. A semiconductor industry test must determine if the tiny wire bonds (less than .001 inch) used in integrated circuits are acceptable. The test requires that the bonds be pulled to a force close to their destructive limit. If they don't pull out, the test is successful. However, pulling these bonds in this way can weaken even those bonds that do pass. AE has been instrumented on this application to determine if the bond itself is emitting AE as a signal of impending failure. A good bond has been found *not* to emit AE during this pull test, whereas a poor or failing bond does emit AE. A system has been instrumented that monitors the bond pull load, pull distance, and the AE signal. The AE system determines whether there was a detectable reject and feeds back a response as to whether that bond passed the pull test (see figure 13.11). An advantage of this method is that there is no need to second-guess whether the pull test damaged the bond. In addition, the bond need not be pulled to as high a stress to determine its integrity. Semiconductor manufacturers can be sure of the integrity of their parts.

Particle Impact Noise Detection (PIND)

Particle Impact Noise Detection (PIND) is a standardized MIL SPEC test for the semiconductor industry. It is presently a required testing procedure on 100 percent of all aerospace integrated circuits. The principle is straightforward. The cleaning of semiconductor circuits mounted in ceramic packages can leave small

Figure 13.11 AE Bond Pull Test System Block Diagram

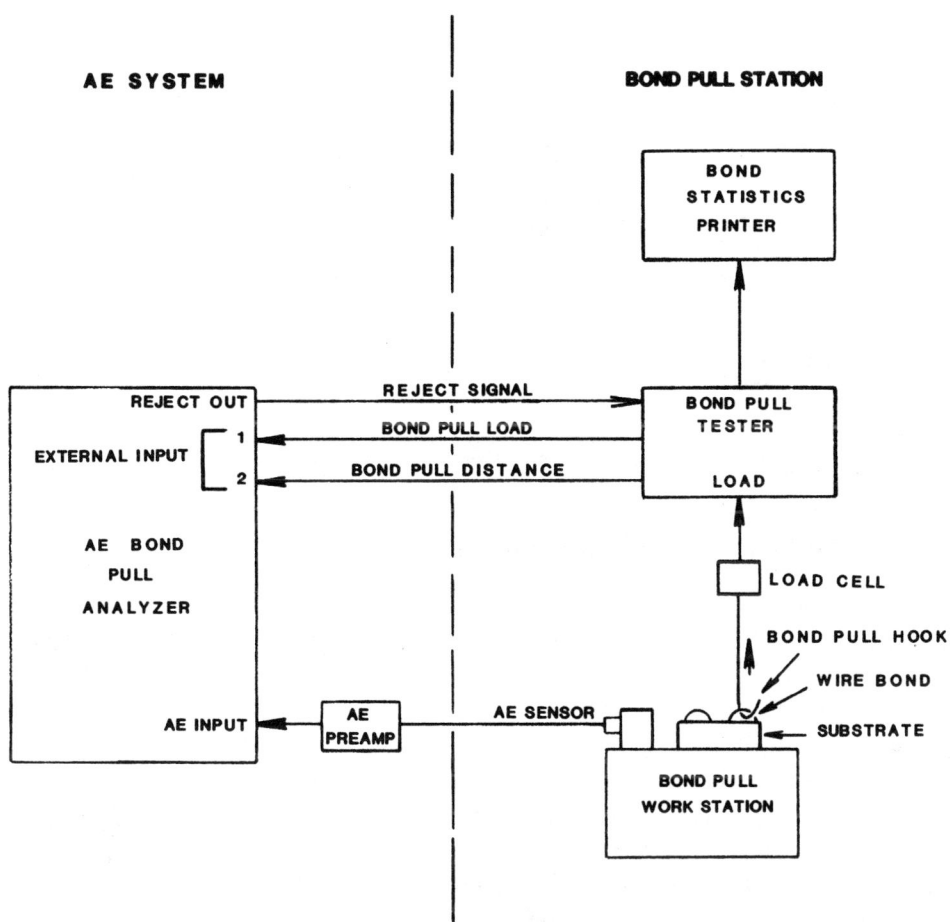

particles lodged into the integrated circuit cavity, where the circuit and all its wire bonds exist. If any of these particles are conductive and big enough, it is possible that during extreme environmental abuse, these particles can dislodge. This can cause a short circuit between two very close traces or bonds on the integrated circuit. Loosened particles have been found to cause failures on actual aerospace equipment. To avoid this possible problem, a special test was developed that stressed each of these ICs in a final inspection called a PIND test. The stress consists of applying large mechanical shocks and then shaking the integrated circuit. During shaking, an acoustic emission system listens for the high-frequency noise caused by loose particles impacting against the cavity walls of the IC. Every MIL SPEC supplier of aerospace ICs uses this method and acoustic emission systems in their final inspection of the parts.

INDUSTRIAL AE APPLICATIONS

This is one application of acoustic emission systems that has its own process step and has not been integrated into an existing application. This is because there were no existing process steps that put the IC through the stress required to cause dislodgement of any particles.

Head Disk Interference Detection on Hard Disk Media

Acoustic emission systems are presently being used for head/disk interference detection during the burnish and glide tests on hard disk drives in the assembly process. In this case, the AE technique can detect asperities on the surface of rigid media during standard burnish/glide testing. The AE technique employs a tiny transducer that is bonded to the existing burnishing head arm (figure 13.12). The resonance of the transducer is above 100 kHz, which makes it sensitive to the high-frequency acoustic emission component of the head disk interference signal.

Figure 13.12 Subminiature AE Sensor Attached to Burnishing Head Arm

Note needle for size reference.

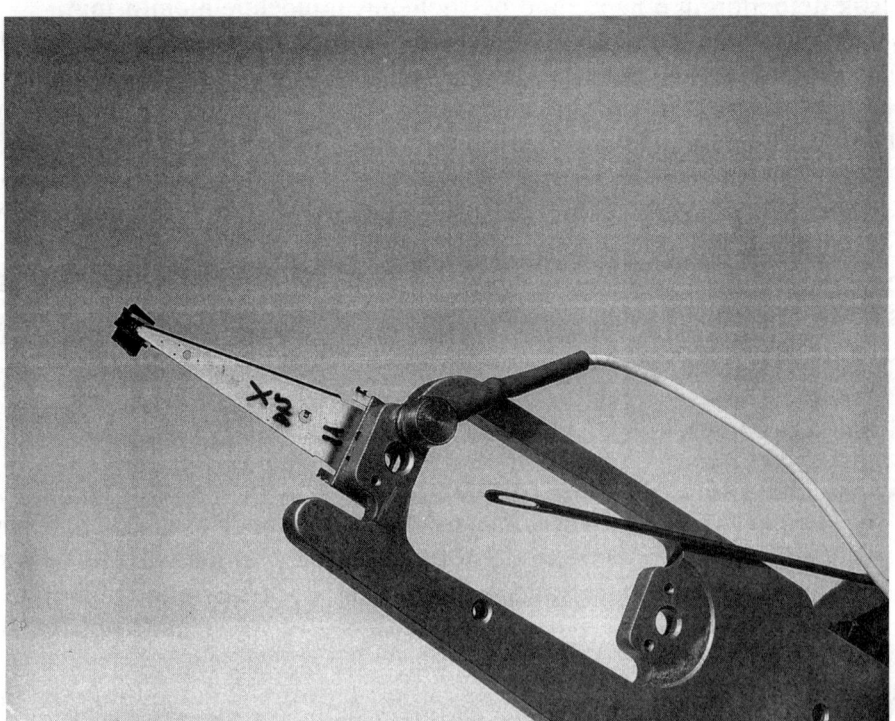

This eliminates low-frequency spindle-bearing noise, air turbulence, and stepper motors process noises. The AE technique listens for these surface defects in real time, during the burnishing process, and can indicate an anomaly.

AE in Leak Detection for the Utility and Chemical Industry

The utility and chemical process industry is extremely concerned about the integrity of all aspects of their plant vessels, piping, pumps, and valves. Plant life extension and industrial safety requirements have led to increased use of acoustic methods for detection of leakage, valve and bearing condition, and crack growth. Although the assessment of pressure vessels is not discussed in this article, it is noteworthy to mention that several ASME codes exist today in the AE testing of metal and composite pressure vessels and storage bottles.

Leak Detection Systems

In leak detection, the instrumentation detects the AE signal that is generated from the turbulent or cavitational flow through a crack, seal, or orifice. Acoustic energy is transmitted through the air or the structure to a piezoelectric sensor. The signal is then processed, filtered, and compared to a leak profile. Existing units are being used in such applications as process monitoring of acid manufacturing, leak detection in boilers, and petrochemical pipeline monitoring.

These systems can connect and monitor multiple sensors throughout the plant. The systems can be operated on a stand-alone basis, they can interface to programmable controllers, or they can tie into plantwide distributed control systems. They also can plot plant piping and vessel drawings on CRT monitors (figure 13.13). These graphic devices show the location of sensors on the structure and indicate those sensors in red at the time of an alarm. This helps operators pinpoint the source of a problem without hesitation so that the problem can be immediately addressed. The systems monitor continuous-level AE signals, such as RMS and energy rate, and they turn on an alarm whenever the preselected leak criteria conditions are exceeded (figure 13.14).

Valve Leak Detectors

Valve leak detectors are portable instruments that detect leakage through closed valves. In the utility industry, where there are many valves close to one another, plant personnel may not be able to determine uniquely which valve is leaking. The AE valve leak detector operates by attaching a sensor on the valve at the suspected leak source and by putting a second sensor upstream from the suspected leak (figure 13.15). The sensor at the valve will detect both noise from the leak and background pipe noise. The second sensor will detect only the pipe

Figure 13.13   Computerized Leak Monitor with RMS Display

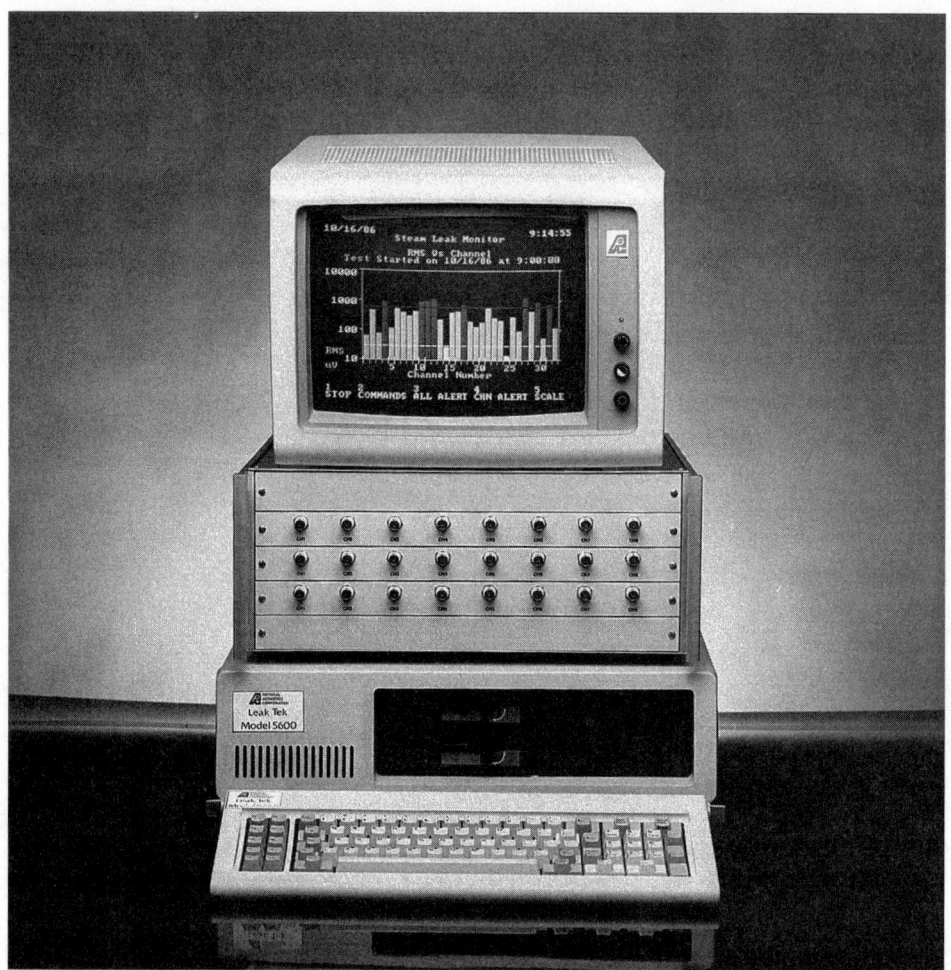

background noise, because any leak noise is attenuated due to its high frequency and distance from the sensor. The difference between the two signals received is calculated, and the result will be just the noise of valve leakage. This system has avoided many costly teardowns undertaken to find a leak source.

Bearing Monitoring and Incipient Failure Detection

Another key AE tool used mostly in the utility industry (but not limited to this industry) is that of bearing monitoring and incipient failure detection. The utility and heavy industry uses very high horsepower pumps in moving fluids around

Figure 13.14 Modular Low-cost Energy-rate-based Leak Monitor

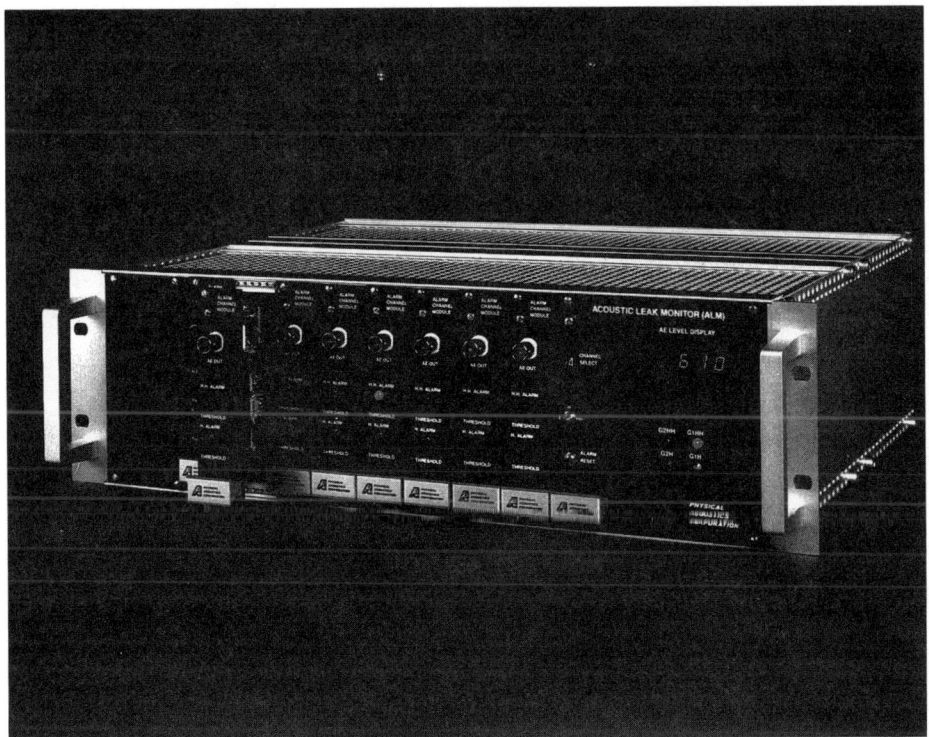

the plant. These pumps put much stress on the bearings that keep the pumps rotating smoothly. In time, because of friction and lack of lubrication, the bearings (whether roller or ball) start to wear and pit, and the races may even crack. If these bearings fail before they can be replaced, the damage to the motor can be costly, and the plant may have to be shut down until the pump can be repaired or replaced. To avoid this situation, acoustic emission systems have been employed—both hand-held portable units for routine sample inspection (figure 13.16) and large multiple-channel data-acquisition and on-line monitoring systems. Each can keep track of bearing and motor integrity.

Acoustic emission is generated in ball and roller bearings at a low level when they are new and undamaged. This low level is due to the friction of the ball or roller on the races. When failure occurs, and the balls roll across cracks in the races or pits in the balls strike the races, the elements are stressed and the emission increases drastically. Because this process takes time, if AE is monitored carefully, plant personnel can have more than enough warning. This gives them plenty of time to order the necessary parts for repair and to schedule mainte-

Figure 13.15 Valve Leak Detection System

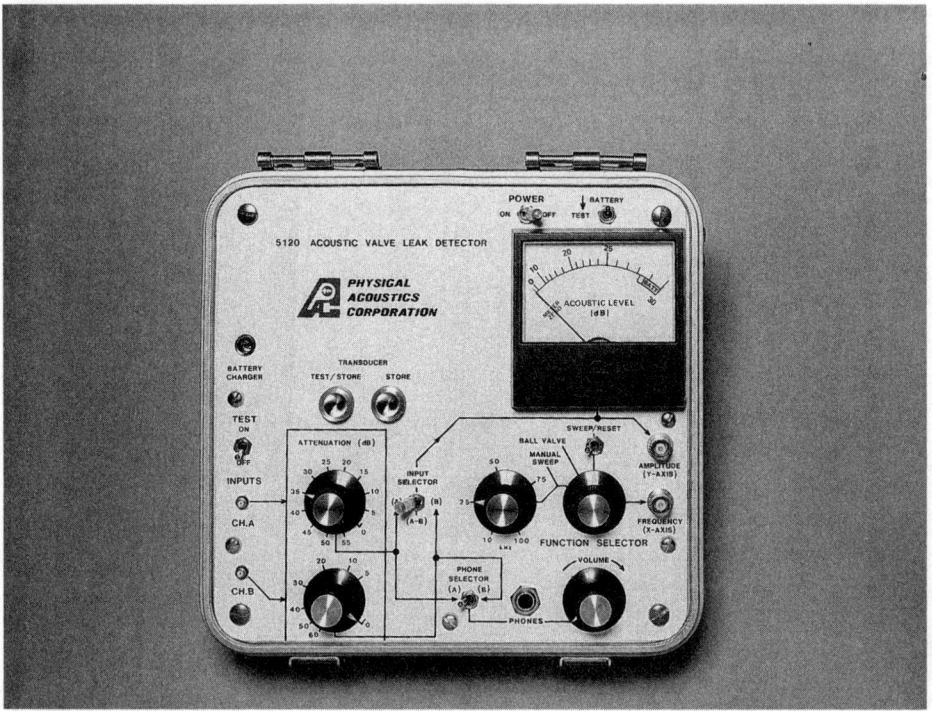

nance outside of the production schedule. Therefore, it is important for the maintenance staff to schedule regular measurements using the portable instrument.

Bearing condition can be monitored using a manual plotting and trending approach. When a data-acquisition and monitoring system is in place, this trending can take place automatically.

AE in Machining and Machine Tool Monitoring

There have been many successful applications of AE in machining and machine tool monitoring. Some of these are described in the sections that follow.

Tool-touch Monitor

A tool-touch detection system exists for metalcutting systems. Severe damage can occur to expensive machinery and workpieces when tool contact is made at too high a speed. AE has been put to work in detecting the frictional noise generated at tool contact. An AE sensor is placed directly on the tool, "hears" the

Figure 13.16   An Operator Performs a Bearing Test with a Portable Bearing Analyzer

noise, and alerts a signal processor card within the machine controller. The controller then automatically decelerates the tool's approach. This system has been implemented as a card solution that can be placed directly in the machine controller (figure 13.17).

Tool Wear and Rupture Monitoring

Much research has been done in evaluating the AE signals received from a machining process to determine tool wear caused by dulling and chipping of the tool. AE is an alternative to other approaches, such as force monitoring. In this case, the cutting process produces elastic waves that are propagated in the material. The AE sensor (in contact with the tool holder) receives these waves, and the system analyzes them (figure 13.18). A signature is determined based on a sharp tool and the material it is machining. This signature is based on some of the AE features that have been discussed previously. During machining, these

Figure 13.17 An AE Card-based System and Sensor Is All that Is Required to Install Tool-touch Monitor to Existing Machine Controllers

features are monitored continuously and compared with this reference signature. Any signs of abrupt change are caused by tool chipping or breakage and require instant stopping of the machining process to minimize damage to the part. Longer-term changes are due to the tool wear and can be monitored and controlled as well. These systems result in automatic monitoring and control.

Punch Press Monitoring

AE monitoring of the punch press operation has also proved fruitful. The approach here is similar to that used to monitor tool wear and rupture in that the system is first trained on the signature of a good punch press cycle. The AE system then monitors for changes to that signature. This approach has been able to detect various process changes and anomalies that are useful to the punch press industry. This includes detection of misfeeds (less material is punched, so the AE signal decreases), material fold over, material hardness changes, delamination, and tool and die wear. This technique has worked on simple punching

Figure 13.18 An AE Sensor Attached to a Lathe Tool Holder Monitors the Machining Process

applications and even on progressive dies and punch-and-stretch operations, in which AE can detect the tearing and cracking during stretching. Again, the AE system is integrated into the workcell to stop the punching operation and sound an alert as soon as it detects a defect.

AE in Welding

Acoustic emission has been applied successfully to welding applications for many years. Many standard AE systems address solutions to real-time control and weld quality analysis, such as the following:

- Resistance spot welding (AC and DC)

- MIG/TIG welding

- Electron beam welding

- Laser Welding

- Friction Welding

Every burst of AE received from the welding process has a logical source and meaning. By targeting in on the expected occurrence of a given weld phenomenon through time, frequency, and feature discrimination, this information can be isolated and used as a control or feedback on the process. This can assure ultimate control of the welding process.

In resistance spot welding, the key user of AE systems has been the automotive and sheet metal industry. Hundreds of systems have been implemented in factories all over the world (figure 13.19). Often, these AE systems are implemented on robotic welders, which further accentuates their capabilities (by eliminating the human factor). These systems were tied into the weld feedback loop and stopped the weld upon receiving the necessary AE indication of a good weld.

Usually this indication was the onset of expulsion. Expulsion occurs in welding when the weld is fully formed and is beginning to overheat. The molten metal pool that lies between the two metals being welded begins to vaporize. This gas starts building up in pressure, being held back from escaping by the electrodes that are pressing against the metals (see figure 13.2, shown earlier). Finally, when the gas pressure exceeds the force applied by the electrodes, it pushes the molten metal violently from the sides of the parts being welded. This expulsion sounds like an explosion to acoustic emission. The AE system is normally set to detect the onset of expulsion and sends a signal that stops the weld immediately. Because the expulsion process is avoided and the weld is stopped before full expulsion, the solid weld nugget remains intact. This results in the strongest weld. In addition, stopping the weld earlier results in a quicker welding process, longer electrode life, and lower overall energy requirements for running the plant. These added benefits are positive incentives for using AE as well.

AE systems in the spot weld application consist of an AE sensor, a current trigger, and an output control relay. The sensor is placed permanently on one of the electrode holders. The current trigger indicates to the AE system that weld current is being applied and that the weld has started. The output relay is connected to the weld/no-weld input of the spot welder (all weld controllers have this or an equivalent) to turn off the weld automatically. When weld current is applied, the AE system detects this and blanks out the early part of the weld AE signals. This eliminates AE caused by current initiation and surface burn-off AE signals (see figure 13.3, shown earlier). After this blanking period, the AE system begins monitoring the AE signal for the onset of expulsion. Upon detecting this (the energy feature is normally processed), the AE system opens up the weld/no-weld relay, which terminates the weld immediately.

MIG/TIG welding has also benefited from the use of AE. Some of the benefits of using AE in this application include the detection of lack of penetration,

Figure 13.19 AE Resistance Spot Weld Feedback Controller

Note industrial packaging.

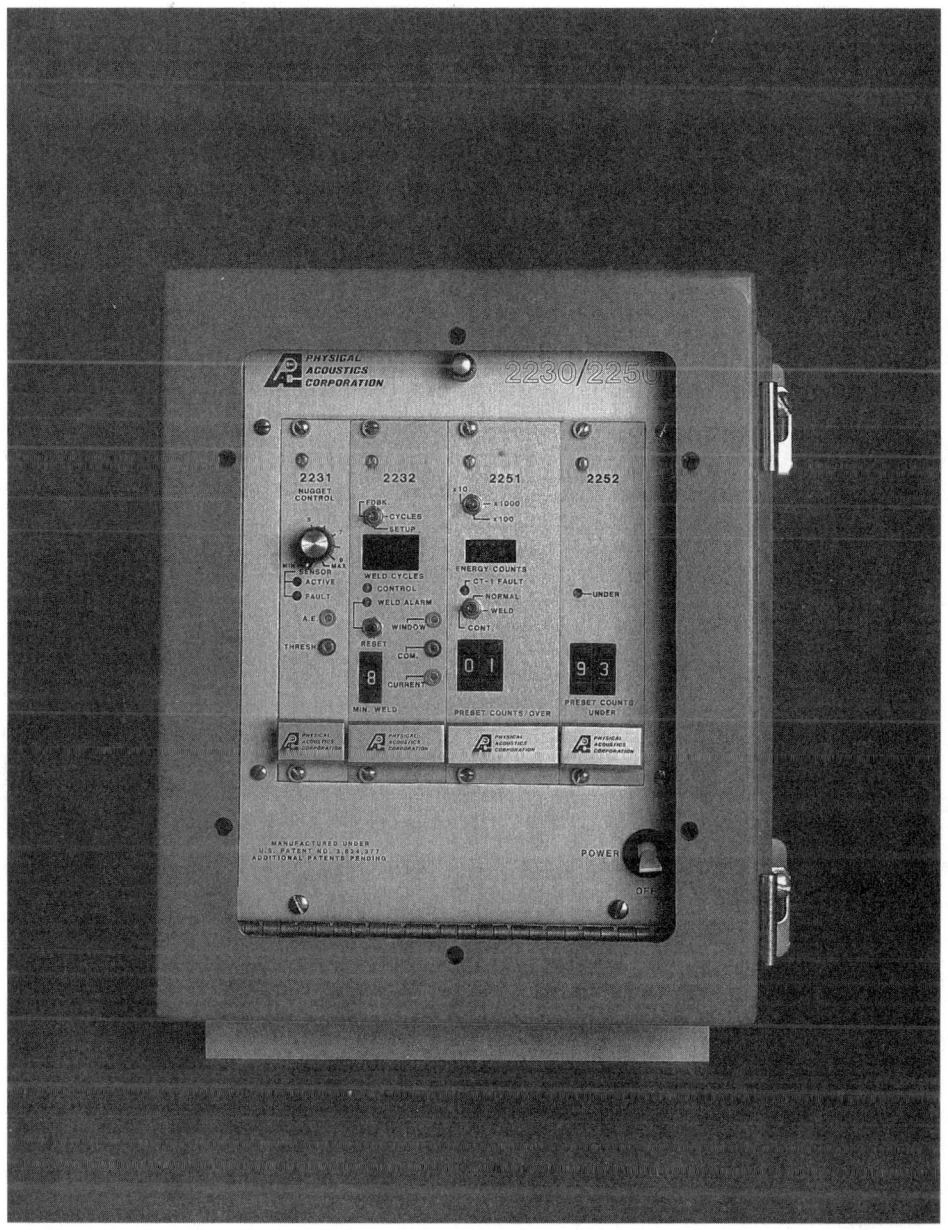

misjoint or misfeed of weld wire, cracking, and porosity. In addition, using multiple sensors, AE systems have been able to locate the exact areas where these discontinuities take place. These systems require high-power AE systems that are able to analyze AE features from multiple sensors in real time and output results to a process computer.

The use of AE in laser welding applications has proved interesting, offering the capability of detecting the amount of material interaction in the weld. This is a function of the weld size and quality. The AE system can also determine whether the laser struck the right spot and if cracking took place.

Case Study: An Electron Beam Weld Inspection System

An electron beam inspection and turnkey process control system is examined here as a detailed example of how to set up and use an effective AE system.

An AE system was developed for a very high quality, low-volume electron beam weld production facility that must 100-percent ultrasonically test each part after the weld process. This ultrasonic inspection is time-consuming and can take place weeks after the actual welding has taken place. The concern was mainly one of determining the quality of the weld while the part was still in the vacuum chamber, thereby eliminating the costly time it takes to load and unload parts into the system, pump down the vacuum again, and reweld the part. If quality could be detected during the weld while the part was still in the chamber, much time and money could be saved. In addition, if the process and AE data could be stored on archival floppy disks for each part monitored, the conditions of the test could be available. This would provide complete documentation on each weld.

A block diagram of the solution system is shown in figure 13.20. The main components of the process control system are the electron beam welder, the cell controller computer, and the AE system. The electron beam welder controls the rotating of the cylindrical part and the welding process. Because the welder is computer-controlled, it can take commands from the cell controller. Other test equipment and peripherals are also being controlled in the process, so a cell controller was necessary to coordinate the workcell. In this case, the AE system acts as a slave, carrying out and responding to the commands the cell controller sends out over the RS-232 serial port. Some of the commands on data sent back and forth include Calibrate, Send Calibration Results, Weld, Send Weld Results, Status, Reset, and file-name data for the naming of calibration and welding storage files.

Figure 13.20 Electron Beam Process Control System Block Diagram

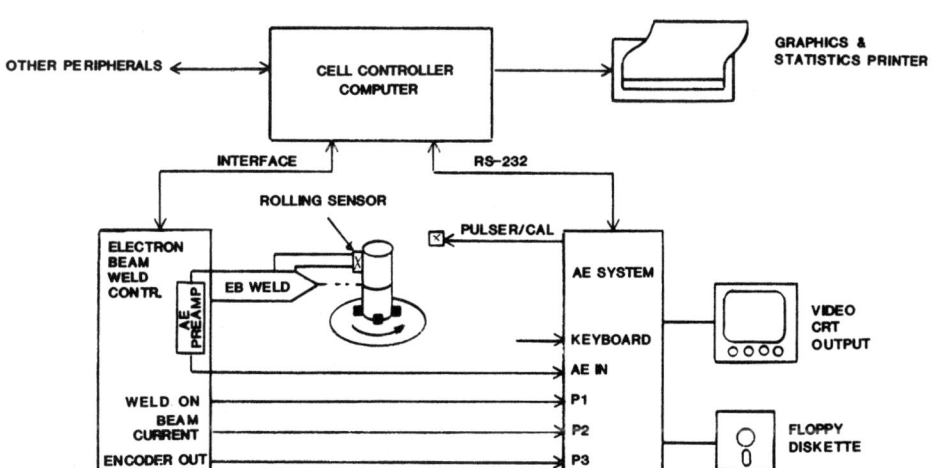

The AE system operates automatically and needs little, if any, user interaction. Upon power-up, it initializes, performs its own diagnostic routines, loads its own set-up information from disk and proceeds to a state where it can accept either keyboard commands or serial port commands from the cell controller.

During the weld process, when the AE system has received a command that a weld is about to start, it sets up a data file with a file name that has been sent by the cell controller and then begins monitoring its inputs for the start of the weld. The system monitors the AE signal coming from a rolling sensor that is physically mounted upon the weld head. This assures that, upon the positioning of the weld head before the weld, the sensor is automatically positioned on the part. The rolling sensor stays in physical contact during the complete rotation of the part, staying a fixed position from the weld taking place. Inside the evacuated weld chamber is a preamplifier that has been modified to operate within the vacuum chamber. The signal from the preamp is routed to the AE system. In addition, several inputs are tapped off the weld controller. These signals help in synchronizing the AE system with the weld process and give more information about the weld process itself.

The additional inputs include a relay-actuated "weld on" signal that changes state upon the start of the weld and returns to its "off" state at the end of the weld. The encoder output is used to let the AE system keep track of the position of the part as it is being welded. Finally, the beam current is an analog signal that is proportional to the energy being delivered to the part. This signal is useful in qualifying the welding process and correlating the AE data.

By using these inputs along with the received and processed AE signal, the AE system can monitor the active part of the weld for conditions such as incom-

plete penetration, overwelding, missing the seam, and hot cracking. After the weld, the system monitors for postweld cracking. The result of the test is that the AE system reports, on its screen and to the cell controller, the quality of the weld. If the weld is faulty, the system reports the position of the detected defects and the type of defect condition. The AE system also stores the complete AE data file to disk for storage and archival purposes. The cell controller then decides whether to reweld the part based on the AE system feedback.

For calibration verification, the AE system is directed by the cell controller when to calibrate the system. Because a special calibration fixture is used along with a special calibration sensor, this piece must be installed each time the system is calibrated. The cell controller leads the user through the calibration process, and after the part has been installed, the AE system is commanded to calibrate. During calibration verification, the part is rotated 360 degrees to evaluate the coupling to the rolling AE sensor. Upon completion, the AE system automatically determines if the calibration is acceptable and compensates for any change, if necessary. The calibration verification (pass/fail) result is then sent back to the cell controller. Calibration data is stored to disk using a special file-naming sequence determined by the cell controller.

All the key ingredients for an effective AE process control system have been incorporated in this example. The AE system itself was a standard unit with no hardware changes. Changes that were made to adapt it to this application included the serial port slave mode, the special weld quality algorithm, and the calibration procedure.

Conclusion

This chapter has described the technology and application of acoustic emission. This technology has proven to be an effective real-time process control sensor that is ideally suited for automation and process control environments. Acoustic emission has been found to provide insights into the process that have been unmatched by other means of evaluation. Every burst of AE coming from the process reveals important information about the immediate status of the process. An acoustic emission system is an interpreter of the process; it hears the "cries" of the process and acts accordingly to control it.

Acoustic emission systems have been operating successfully for many years in the electronics industry, automotive industry, utilities, petrochemical industry, machine tool industry, aerospace industry, and welding industry, to name a few. The use of this sensor technology has led to proven cost reductions and cost avoidance. It has also saved human lives and reduced environmental catastrophes.

Acoustic emission technology lends itself directly to industrial and automated applications. The key benefits are that it operates in real time and that it depends upon the stress applied by the existing process. This stress causes the signals that can be used to evaluate the integrity of the part and the process.

Because of these characteristics, AE technology can be applied into existing processes, rather than being added as an extra step after the process, as other NDT methods require. Keeping these principles in mind, AE systems are designed to be connected directly into the process with programmable controllers and process computers. This makes acoustic emission sensor systems proven excellent technology to be used in today's industrial and automated environments and those of the future.

References

1. Bolotin, Y. I., and Belov, V. M. "Welding Quality Control by Acoustic Emission during Electron Beam Welding." *Welding Production* vol. 23, no. 4 (April 1976).

2. Carlos, M. F., E. P. Lowenhar, C. Fotopoulos, B. E. Gilbert. "Process Control Modeling with the AE Parameter." Presentation at the 1988 Fall ASNT Conference, September 1988.

3. Cole, P. T. "Acoustic Emission." Part 7: "The Capabilities and Limitations of NDT." Northampton, England: British Institute of Non-Destructive Testing, July 1988.

4. Miller, Ronk, McIntire, and Paul, eds. *Nondestructive Testing Handbook*. Vol. 5: *Acoustic Emission Testing*. American Society for Nondestructive Testing, 1987.

5. Sales brochures and literature from Physical Acoustics Corporation.

6. Vahaviolos, S. J. "Method and Apparatus for the Real Time Monitoring of a Continuous Weld Using Stress Wave Emission Techniques." U.S. Patent 3,986,391, October 1976.

7. Vahaviolos, S. J., M. F. Carlos, S. J. Slykhous, S. J. Ternowchek. "Adaptive Spot-Weld Feedback Control Loop via Acoustic Emission." *Materials Evaluation* (October 1981): 1057–60.

Chapter 14 Force-Field Sensing

Shawn Buckley

Overview

Force-field sensing is a technology that has its roots in the work of the great physicists of the last several centuries: Oersted, Faraday, Maxwell, and Hertz in electromagnetic fields and Prandtl, Von Karman, and Rayleigh in pressure fields. Although force-fields were known to exist in nature and could be analyzed mathematically, their use in the inspection of production parts has emerged in only the last two decades.

In the late 1960s, aerodynamicists at the University of California-Berkeley first noticed a relationship between an object and the field around it [7, 9]. An object such as an automobile displaces the streamlines in a uniform flow field in a way that depends on the shape of the automobile. Figure 14.1 shows the streamlines around the cross-section of an automobile in inviscid flow. Here the flow field has been simulated by conducting boundaries (the road and the car cross-section) on resistance paper (the air around the car) in order to visualize the streamlines, which are simply constant voltage lines plotted on the resistance paper.

The force-field and the object have a reciprocal relationship. If the shape of the object is known, it can be used to determine the field—the usual situation. But conversely, if the field is known, it can be used to determine the shape of the object. Essentially, the force-field "encodes" the object. If the object changes, so does the field. If the field changes, it must have been the result of a change in the object.

Here then is a way to inspect an object. Simply measure its force-field and correlate changes in the field to changes in the object. Figure 14.2 shows how the technique can be used for flow fields: the field around a car body determines variations in the underside shape of the car. Pressure transducers embedded in the roadway measure the pressure distribution at the road when a car passes

Figure 14.1 Streamlines Around the Cross-section of an Automobile in Inviscid Flow

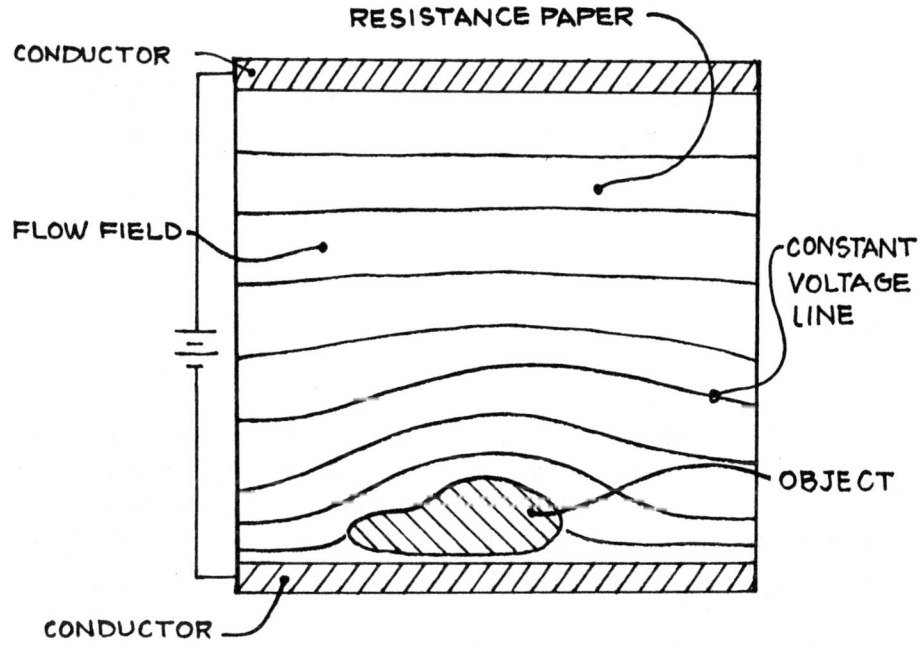

Figure 14.2 Variations in the Car's Underside Are Detected by Measuring the Pressure Distribution When the Car Passes Overhead

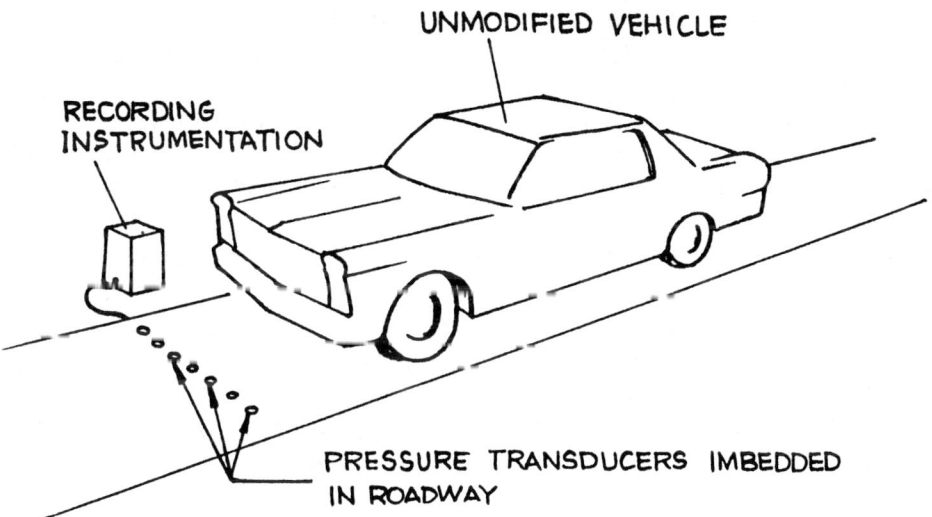

overhead. Thus, variations in the object's shape (the car's underside) are detected by variations in the force-field around the object.

As another example, consider an ordinary magnet. The magnetic force-field around the magnet can be seen by sprinkling iron filings on a piece of paper placed on the magnet (figure 14.3). If another identical magnet were placed under the paper, the pattern of iron filings would be identical, suggesting that the force-fields were identical. If the magnet changed, the pattern of iron filings would also change. Sensors that could detect the pattern of the filings could tell that the magnet was defective even though the paper covered it; the magnet's flaw is revealed by the distortion of the force-field around it. By detecting where and how much the field has distorted, the size and location of the flaw can be determined.

Force-fields such as the flow field in the automobile example and the magnetic field in the iron filing example are static fields. They do not change with time. When investigators at M.I.T. developed force-field sensing in the 1970s, they found that static fields could not be calibrated easily. Time-varying fields not only could be calibrated easily but lent themselves to analysis by analog and digital circuitry [6, 10].

Figure 14.3 Force-Field Changes Show Flaws in a Magnet

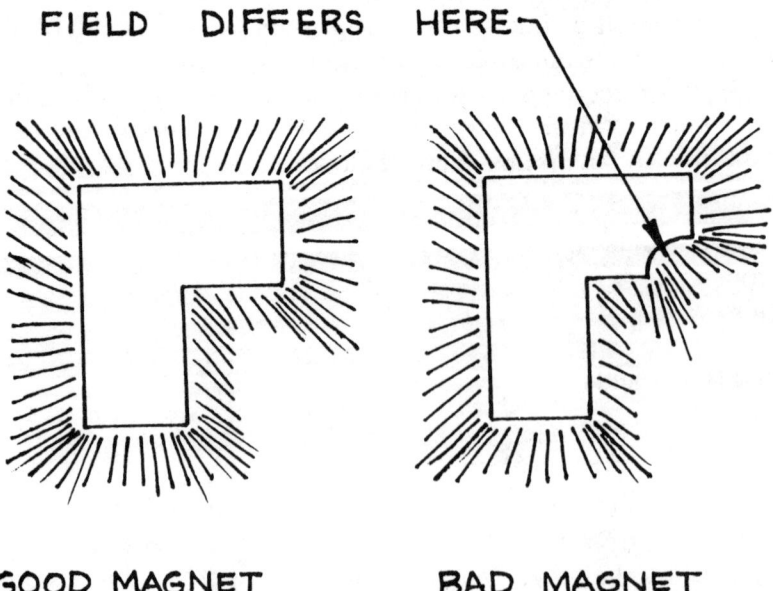

Force-Field Sensing

Two major classes of force-fields were investigated: pressure fields and electromagnetic fields. Each of the classes includes both static and time-varying fields, as shown in table 14.1

The first step in force-field measurement is to set up an inspection region. In this region, a field generator produces the force-field. For an acoustic field, an acoustic horn sets up the acoustic field in the inspection region. For electromagnetic fields, field generators consist of microwave antennas for microwave fields, coils for inductive fields, and capacitive plates for capacitive fields [15].

To inspect an object using force-fields, one simply measures the distortion of the generated field caused by the object. Because the object's information is encoded in the field, the field must be measured at many points. The M.I.T researchers found that the more points at which the field is measured, the better the field represents the object. The field's distortion is measured with an array of appropriate sensors: acoustic sensors for acoustic fields, microwave antennas in microwave fields, sensor coils for inductive fields, and sensor plates for capacitive fields. The more sensors used, the better the field describes the object that distorts the field.

Distortion of the force-field occurs when the object being inspected enters the inspection region. The entire object or only a portion of it can be within the inspection region. For example, in an automated assembly application, the entire part enters the inspection region on its way between assembly operations. In a sorting application of, say, 150-mm (6-inch) bolts, the bolts pass through a small inspection region a portion at a time—first the tip, then the shank, and finally the head. Each portion distorts the force-field in a different way.

An important aspect of force-field sensors is the amount of stand-off required: how far the sensors must be from the object sensed. The nature of the force-fields divides them into two flavors, as shown below:

- Sinusoidal force-fields
    - Acoustic
    - Microwave

- Exponential force-fields
    - Inductive
    - Capacitive

Sinusoidal force-fields (acoustic and microwave) have a field that diminishes sinusoidally with distance from the sensor, as shown in figure 14.4. Sinusoidal fields are characterized by the wave equation, and the important dimension on which to base stand-off is the wavelength of the field. For sinusoidal fields, the

FORCE-FIELD SENSING

Table 14.1 Classes of Force-Fields

Field Class	Force-Field	Type
Pressure	Flow	Static
	Acoustic	Time-varying
Electromagnetic	Magnetic	Static
	Inductive	Time-varying
	Capacitive	Time-varying
	Microwave	Time-varying

stand-off is typically a few wavelengths. So, for an acoustic field operating at 40 kHz in air, the stand-off between object and sensor is usually less than 25 mm (1 inch), because the wavelength is about 10 mm (.4 inch) [2]. Greater stand-off is possible but with reduced resolution. The same arguments apply to microwaves, typically in the 2-to-30-gigahertz band, where wavelengths are between 150 mm and 10 mm respectively.

Exponential fields (inductive and capacitive) have a force-field that falls off exponentially as the stand-off increases. These fields are characterized by the sensor dimension. Exponential force-fields have a stand-off approximately one-half the sensor dimension. An inductive sensing coil 20 mm in diameter will have a useful range (that is, stand-off) of 10 mm; a capacitive sensing plate 2 mm square will only sense the capacitive force-field within a millimeter of the plate.

Note that an object can be interrogated by several force-fields simultaneously. Each force-field is distorted by different aspects of the object [3]. An object's shape distorts an acoustic field. Its conductive characteristics distort an inductive field, and so forth (more on this later). Importantly, the force-fields do not

Figure 14.4 Force-Field Variation with Distance from Source

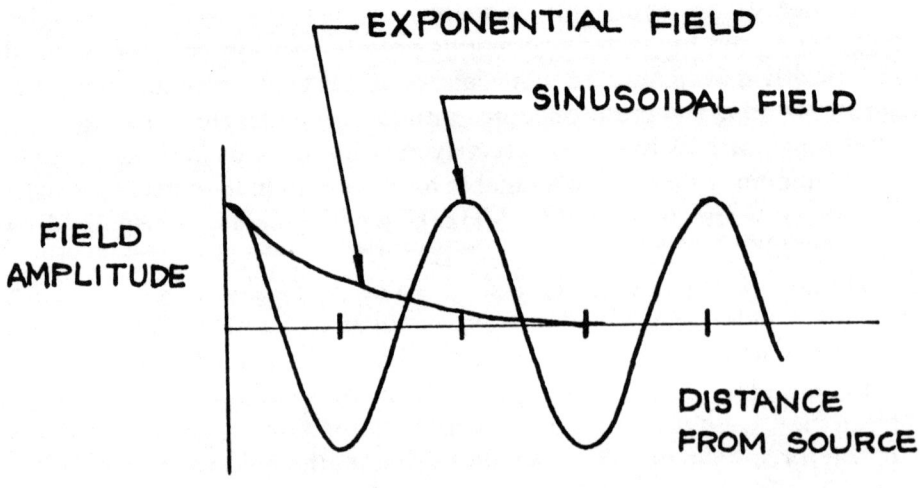

interact with one another, so acoustic distortions can be measured simultaneously with inductive ones, inductive with capacitive, and capacitive with microwave. For an object in an inspection region having several force-fields, distortions of each field provide different kinds of information about the object simultaneously.

Because only distortions in the various force-fields are measured, the effect of jigs and fixtures near the object can be eliminated. Consider the inspection region without an object in it. Each array of sensors will measure some residual field because of the transport mechanism that moves the object into the region, because of other sensors in the same array, and because of sensors and their fixtures from other arrays. It is not this residual force-field that is important but rather how it is distorted when an object is in the region. Moreover, the residual field is fixed, because the jigs, fixtures, and sensors are fixed. Self-calibration results from measuring the residual force-field from time to time with no objects present [12]. Measurement drift in the sensors due to environmental effects can be eliminated by assuring that the sensors measure only the distortion in the residual field, not the field itself.

Measuring Force-Field Distortion

Time-varying force-fields are most easily understood by thinking of them operating at a fixed frequency: the force-field varies sinusoidally with time. In actual operation, force-fields operate at multiple frequencies and are not restricted to sinusoidal variation. Analog and digital filters (similar to those used in Fast Fourier Transform [FFT] technology) separate the spectrum into various frequency components. Multiple-frequency or nonsinusoidal operation is an extrapolation of how force-fields work at a single frequency.

The frequency used by each force-field is not necessarily the same. Acoustic fields are typically driven at frequencies above 20 kHz (so we cannot hear them) to as high as 500 kHz (where it becomes difficult to match the sensor's impedance with the air). Microwave fields are driven at frequencies in the 2 GHz to 30 GHz band to minimize the cost of available hardware; inductive fields are driven at frequencies between 60 Hz and 10 MHz. Capacitive fields are usually driven at less than 400 kHz.

As a simplification, then, consider a single force-field—say, acoustic—at a single frequency. A field-generating horn sets up an acoustic field in the inspection region. An array of nearby acoustic sensors detect the acoustic field, which is distorted by an object—a bolt (figure 14.5). Because the field is time-varying at a fixed frequency, each acoustic sensor can determine only two values: the amplitude of the force-field and its phase shift. That is, the field varies sinusoidally

at a fixed frequency because the field generator (the acoustic horn) is driven at this frequency. The force-field grows and collapses at precisely the same frequency. Each sensor converts the force-field at its location into a voltage signal that fluctuates sinusoidally at the driven frequency. Although each acoustic sensor will have a different value of amplitude and phase shift, all the sensor signals vary at the same frequency—the force-field's driven frequency.

In general, the problem of determining the field distortion caused by an object is considerably simplified. One need only find two values for each sensor of the array, amplitude and phase shift. Typical arrays of sensors have a few hundred sensor locations. Although analysis of several hundred values may seem difficult, it is a simple task for modern "workstation"-grade computers. Machine-vision systems, by comparison, typically analyze half a million values during an inspection task [8].

The task of inspecting an object with force-fields is then divided into two subtasks. First, the information about the object—shape, composition, and so forth—is encoded into a force-field. Second, the force-field itself is encoded into a list of numbers (amplitudes and phase shift of each sensor) that describe the field. The more numbers, the better the object is described. However, the physics of force-fields are such that an object can be encoded into a list of relatively few numbers.

Returning to the simple example shown in figure 14.5, the shape of the bolt in the inspection region has been coded into a list of numbers, an amplitude value

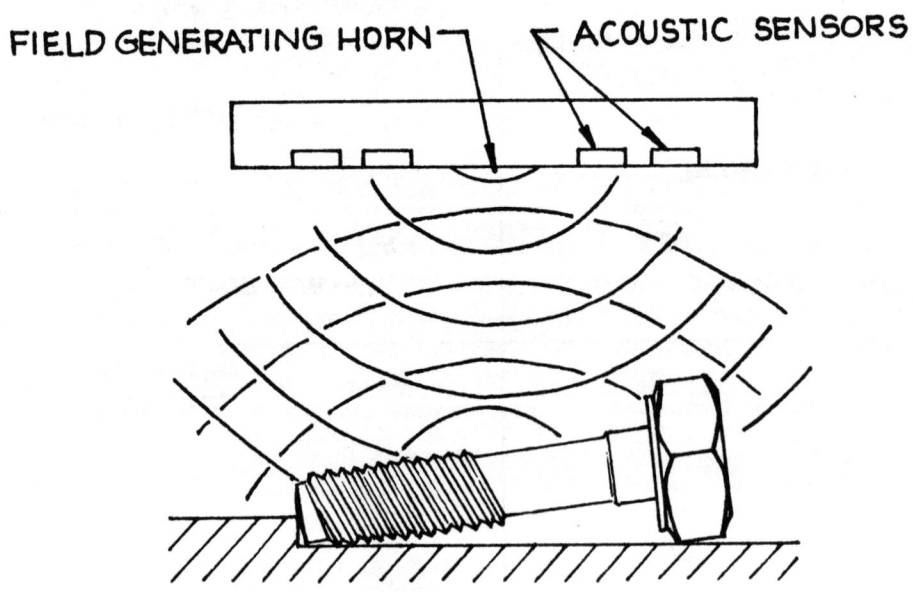

Figure 14.5 A Single Force-Field, Single Frequency Application

and a phase shift value for each acoustic sensor in the array. If exactly the same object were placed in exactly the same position in the region, one would expect the list of numbers to be identical as well. The acoustic field would be distorted in the same way. A different object placed in the same position would give a different list of numbers. But how different is different enough? Where and by how much should the list of numbers change before the object moves from the "good" or "acceptable" category to the "bad" or "unacceptable" category? Such a determination is called *pattern recognition*.

To understand how pattern recognition operates for force-field distortion analysis, the acoustic example above will be further simplified to only two acoustic sensors. In addition, only the phase shift of each sensor will be considered. Now let different bolts be placed against the stop in the inspection region to ensure that each bolt is placed in exactly the same position. Every bolt will produce two phase shift values, one from each of the two acoustic sensors in the array. Figure 14.6 shows these two values plotted against each other. A point on the graph represents a bolt placed against the stop in the inspection region. A graph such as figure 14.6 is a two-dimensional representation of *N-space* (also called *Euclidean space* or *pattern recognition space*). N refers to the dimensionality of the space, simplified here to two dimensions but in general having many more dimensions—one for each sensor in the array.

Because each bolt is slightly different (all parts have slight variations due to

Figure 14.6 Two Sensor Pattern Recognition

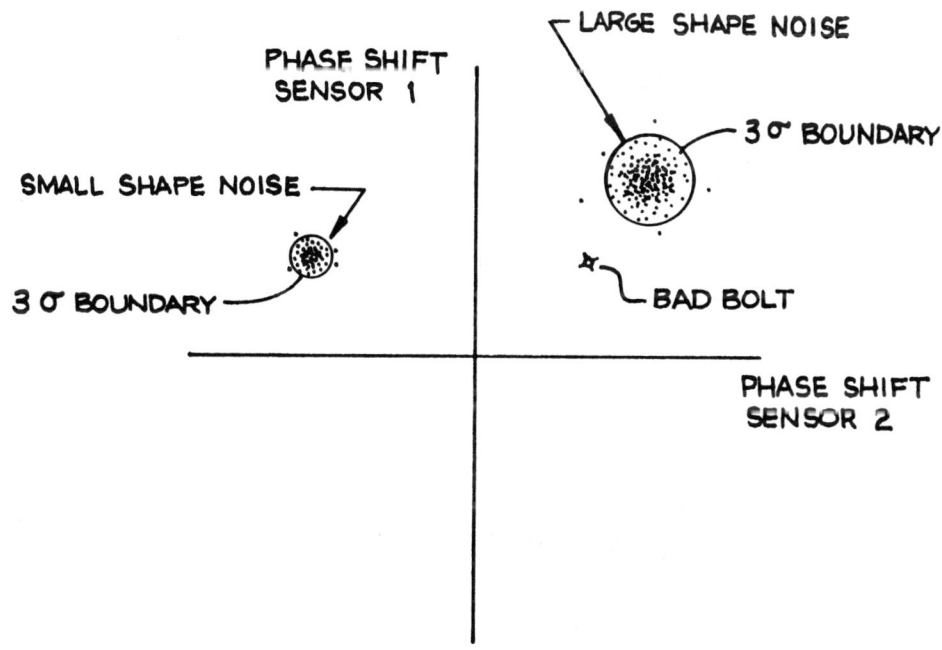

manufacturing tolerances), many bolts placed in the region gives a cluster of points on the graph. The "compactness" of the cluster represents the noise of the signal. Assuming that other variations of the two-phase shift signals (such as measurement noise and drift due to temperature and humidity changes) have been eliminated, the scatter in the cluster is related to the manufacturing variations of the bolts, or *shape noise*. Bolts made very exactly have small shape noise and are represented by a compact cluster on the graph. Bolts with large variations in their dimensions have high shape noise and are represented by a "loose" cluster—that is, points on the graph are spread out more from each other.

The compactness of the cluster can be measured using a concept from statistics, the standard deviation. Each point on the graph has a nearest neighbor—the point closest to it. If the distance from one point to every other point is calculated, the smallest of the values represents the distance between that point and its nearest neighbor. Performing the same calculation for each of the points in the cluster gives the nearest neighbor distance for every point. From these "nearest neighbor distances" a standard deviation can be calculated if we assume the bolt variations have a Gaussian distribution (usually the case for manufacturing variations).

In any inspection task, the idea is to accept the vast majority of the good objects but reject those that deviate from the norm. A good (that is, acceptable) bolt is simply one that is acceptably close to another good bolt. The measuring stick of how close is "close" is the standard deviation (also called a *sigma*). Generally an acceptable bolt is one that is within 3 sigma of bolts already known to be good. In geographical terms, the centroid of the point on the N-space graph is enclosed by a circle whose radius is 3 sigmas. Points that fall within the circle are acceptably close and those that fall outside are not.

Now suppose a bolt is placed against the stop in the inspection region. Is it a good bolt or a bad bolt? The phase shifts from each of the two acoustic sensors are measured; the two values represent a new point on the graph. If that point lies within a circle, the bolt is a good one. If it is outside the circles, it is a bad bolt—it differs unacceptably from the good bolts. Computationally, the procedure is as follows. The distance in N-space between the "unknown" bolt and the good bolt's centroid is calculated. The distance is divided by the 3-sigma limits determined by good parts to produce a percentage score. If the score is greater than 100 percent, the distance in N-space between the unknown bolt and the average good bolt is more than the allowable 3-sigma limits: the bolt is defective. If the score is less than 100 percent, the unknown bolt is close enough in shape to a known good bolt to be deemed acceptable.

In practice, the threshold (the 3-sigma limit, in this case) can be chosen to be more or less than 3. Figure 14.7 shows a plot of force-field "distance" values versus the frequency of bolts having that value. The plot is similar to the familiar bell-shaped curve (the Gaussian function), except that the values in figure 14.7

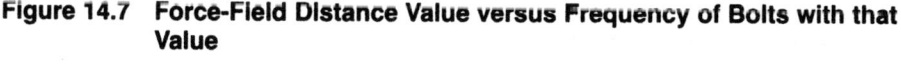

Figure 14.7 Force-Field Distance Value versus Frequency of Bolts with that Value

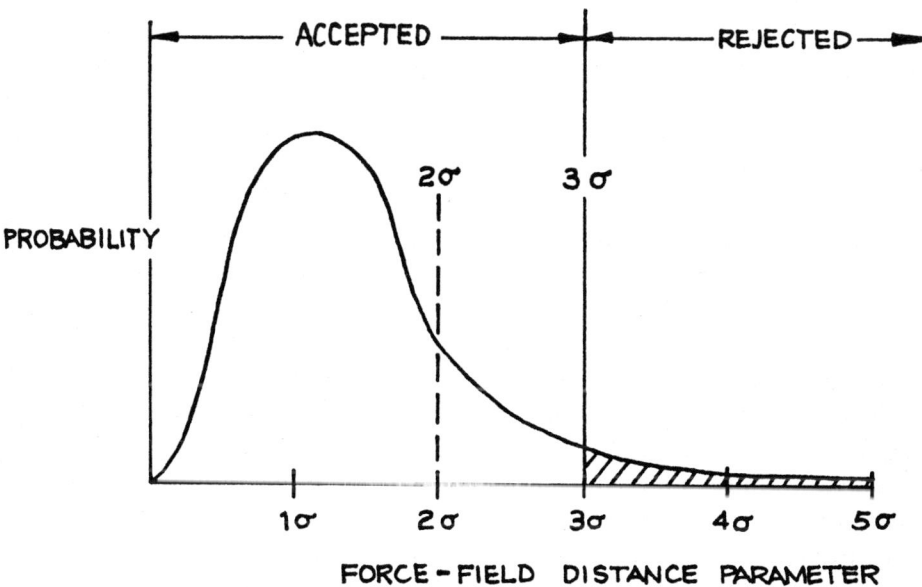

are all positive—no negative distances are allowed in N-space. The 3-sigma threshold is represented by a vertical line having a value of 3. Unknown bolts whose distance is less than 3 are acceptable, and those greater than 3 are not. For a Gaussian distribution of bolt dimensions, about 99 percent of the bolts shown will be accepted and 1 percent will be rejected. Those rejected are called "false rejects," because many of them are likely good bolts whose tolerances were close to the limits. For off-line applications of force-field sensing, a 3-sigma criterion is often used: the 1 percent of falsely rejected good parts is acceptable. In on-line applications, a higher criterion—4 sigma or even 5 sigma—is often used to reduce the number of false rejects. However, the inspection is not as accurate as at smaller sigma limits.

Sinusoidal Force-Fields

Sinusoidal fields—acoustic and microwave fields—are most commonly used for shape determination of objects. In all force-fields, the generated field interacts with the object in two ways: it will penetrate the object's boundary (and be absorbed or transmitted) or it will reflect from a boundary.

In the case of acoustic fields, the penetration is minute. Penetration depends on the density ratio between the object and the medium (air) in which the field is generated. Even low-density objects made of plastic have a thousand times the density of air. Hence, the vast majority of the field is reflected from the objects; little penetrates. Because little of the field penetrates an object using acoustic force-fields, the distortion is primarily the result of its shape rather than the result of flaws within the object's material.

In the case of microwave fields, a phenomenon called *skin effect* prevents the field from penetrating a conducting object. Nonconductors such as plastics, ceramics, and glass are penetrated by microwaves; their dielectric constant differs from that of air causing a distortion of the microwave field. Hence, defects in composite assemblies of metals and nonmetals such as electronic connectors and components can be inspected. In addition, moisture and density of food products, wood products, and pharmaceuticals can be determined with microwave force-fields.

Both acoustic and microwave fields are similarly sinusoidal in nature. Such fields are characterized by their wavelength. Important parameters such as stand-off (as we saw earlier) and resolution depend on wavelength. Sinusoidal fields are "wave-like"; they behave in three dimensions like water waves do in two dimensions.

Sinusoidal fields operate in two regimes: the reflection regime and the diffraction regime. Objects distort a sinusoidal field differently in each regime. The dividing line between regimes is based on the field's wavelength and the size of the object's surface under consideration. Because acoustic fields do not penetrate into an object (nor microwave fields into metal objects), they can interact only with its surfaces. The reflection regime comes into play when this surface is large compared to a wavelength. Thus, sinusoidal fields are most sensitive to dimensional changes in large surfaces. The diffraction regime, on the other hand, comes into play when the surface is small compared to a wavelength. Here, sinusoidal fields become sensitive to the *volume* variation (missing or added) rather than to variation in the object's surface.

By analogy, consider an ocean wave approaching shore. Its wavelength is perhaps 30m (100 feet). If it hits a breakwater many times longer than its wavelength, it reflects. If it hits the piling of a pier it passes by without being impeded; little reflection occurs, only diffraction. Diffraction is the "wrapping around" of waves that occurs at corners and small surfaces. Little distortion of the field occurs in diffraction, making force-field sensing less sensitive.

If the size of the object's surface is plotted against the sensitivity of measuring force-fields, the result is as shown in figure 14.8. The vertical axis is the sensitivity defined as the change in a force-field variable (amplitude or phase shift) per unit change in the displacement of the surface in question. The horizontal axis is the normalized area: the surface area divided by the wavelength squared. The reflection regime is the region on the figure in which the normalized area is

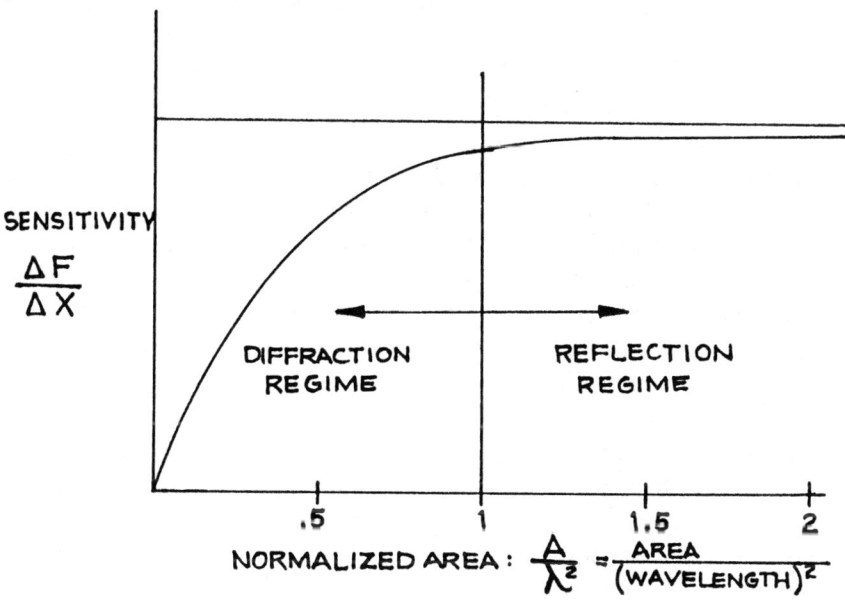

Figure 14.8 Regimes of Sinusoidal Force-Fields

greater than 1. In this region, the sensitivity is not only a maximum but also constant; the force-field sensitivity does not change as the area increases. Sensitivity depends not only on the object's surface area but also on the orientation of its surface normal, its proximity to other surfaces, and its curvature, among other factors. For values of the normalized area below 1, the diffraction regime comes into effect. Here, the sensitivity to a displacement of the surface falls off linearly as the normalized area approaches 0. That is, sinusoidal force-fields become less and less sensitive to a defect as the size of the defect (compared to a wavelength) is reduced.

As an example, consider a hex nut that is 8 mm (.3 inch) high, 13 mm (.5 inch) across flats, with a 6-mm (.25-inch) thread using acoustic force-field sensors operating at 40 kHz in air (figure 14.9). The wavelength is 10 mm (.4 inch). If the nut passes through the inspection region by sliding down a chute with the nut's hole facing up, the surface with the largest area exposed to the force-field is the nut's top face. The area of the top face is about 140 square mm, and its normalized area is 1.4 (excluding the hole). The normalized area is greater than 1, so sensing is in the reflection regime.

For force-field sensing, consider only the phase-shift component (amplitude changes behave similarly). If the nut is taller by .1 mm, the top face will be displaced away from the chute. Current commercial force-field equipment has a typical phase-shift sensitivity between 200 and 2000 mrad/mm depending on the orientation of the surface normal, the curvature, and other factors. At a nominal

Figure 14.9 Example of Acoustic Force-Field Sensing: Crimped Nut

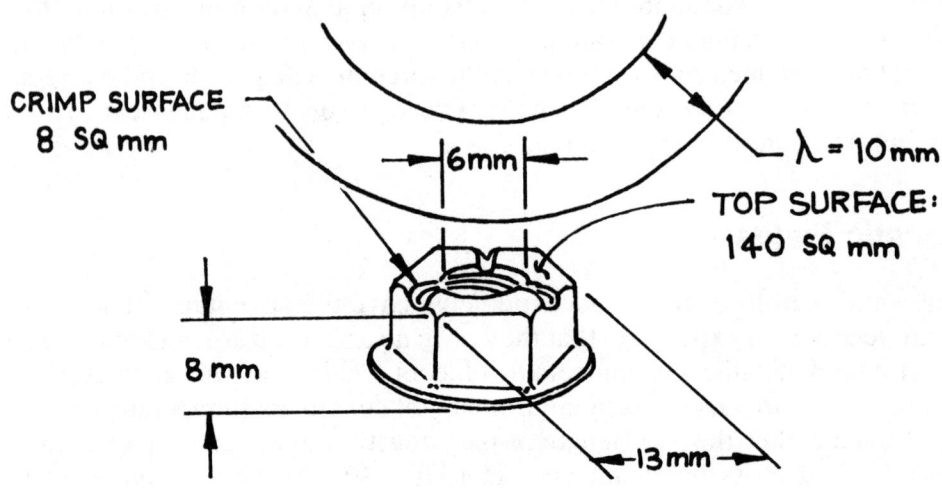

500 mrad/mm, the .1 mm taller nut will produce a 50 mrad variation in phase-shift signals. Because current equipment has a noise level of 5–10 mrad for phase-shift measurements, the taller nut can be detected easily: its signal is ten times the noise threshold.

When such nuts are used in automobile engines to hold the big end of the connecting rod to the crankshaft, the nuts are crimped—the top few threads are crushed to prevent the nut from spinning off. Each crimp is .4 mm (.016 inch) deep, 4 mm (.016 inch) long and 2 mm (.08 inch) wide. The area of a crimp is 8 mm squared, giving a normalized area of .08; sensing is in the diffraction regime, because the normalized area is less than 1. The sensitivity for such a small area will be much less than for the reflection case. Using the nominal reflection sensitivity of 500 mrad/mm, the diffraction sensitivity will be about 40 mrad/mm (that is, $500 \times .08 = 40$). The absence of the crimp means that the crimp surface will be displaced away from the chute .4 mm; the expected phase shift is 16 mrad (.4 mm $\times$ 40 mrad/mm). The measurement noise level is 5–10 mrad, so the crimp signal is barely discernible above the noise: acoustic sensing can detect the crimp, but barely.

For this example, now consider how the various surfaces of the same object interact. Suppose the nuts have a manufacturing tolerance of .1 mm (.004 inch) in their height, a quite common occurrence in nuts made with a nutformer. As we calculated above, the .1-mm (.004-inch) variation gives a 50-mrad variation in the phase-shift signal, but the phase-shift signal from the crimp is only 16 mrad. The nut's normal height variation swamps out the crimp signal. Without the height variation, the crimp can be detected; with it, the crimp signal is lost in the shape noise. Because the crimp and the nut's height are both part of the

same surface (the nut's top face), the two signals cannot be separated. In general, masking of small shape changes by acceptable shape changes of larger, nearby surfaces is common. Often the resolution limitation of sinusoidal force-fields is due to acceptable variations in the objects masking unacceptable variations, rather than measurement noise in the force-field amplitude and phase-shift measurements. Improvements in pattern-recognition techniques can help reduce, but not eliminate, the problem.

Acoustic Fields

Of the sinusoidal force-fields, acoustic fields have the advantages that the sensors are relatively inexpensive, that they pose no safety hazard, and that the field can sense both metallic and nonmetallic objects. Their major disadvantage is that they are subject to variations in environmental conditions (temperature and humidity), which alter the wavelength of the acoustic waves. The wavelength of a sinusoidal field is its dominant characteristic. Without proper compensation, wavelength variation due to even slight temperature or humidity changes can distort force-field measurements. The wavelength is the yardstick with which objects are measured—imagine trying to measure with a yardstick that stretched differently every time you tried to make a measurement.

Temperature has the greatest effect on acoustic force-field measurements. For each degree centigrade temperature change (1.6°F), the wavelength of sound changes by about .2 percent. In commercial equipment, the path length between the field generator and a field sensor is typically 20 wavelengths. A degree centigrade temperature change of the air through which the field is transmitted produces a 4-percent change (.2 percent per wavelength times 20 wavelengths) in the total path between generator and sensor. A 4-percent change in path length causes a 250-mrad variation in the field's phase-shift measurements (a similar argument holds for amplitude changes). By comparison, the measurement noise for the same variable is only 5–10 mrad. Clearly, even a single degree of temperature variation can dominate acoustic force-field sensing.

Why does temperature have such a big effect? It is because even though each wavelength changes length only slightly, the effect is multiplied by the number of wavelengths in the total path between generator and sensor. By analogy, consider the stretchy ruler again. If you measured a 20-cm object, the scale would read 20 cm. Now if each centimeter of the ruler expanded by 1 percent, the length change of each centimeter would grow by just .1 mm. The 20-cm object, however, would measure 2 mm short because the error in each centimeter "stacks up." Similarly, small changes in each wavelength can cause large measurement errors when many wavelengths stack up.

Fortunately, it is possible to compensate for most of the error due to temperature changes. Because industrial plants operate over a temperature range of

Figure 14.10 Waveguides Used in Acoustic Force-Field Sensing

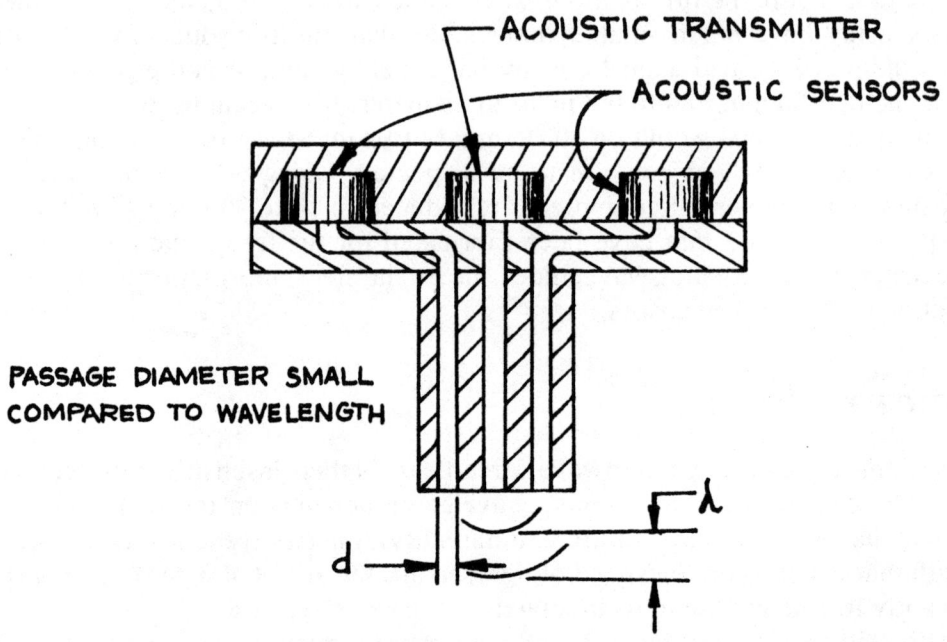

30°C (50°F), the first step is to control the temperature of the medium (air) using heaters designed to control ambient temperature to 1°C (1.6°F). Acoustic field sensing does not care at which temperature it operates, as long as that temperature is fixed. For simplicity, the operating temperature is usually fixed 5°C (9°F) hotter than any expected plant temperature. Some acoustic force-field systems first cool the air to below ambient temperature and then reheat it to a fixed temperature near ambient.

Once the air temperature is fixed to 1°C (1.6°F), further improvement requires software compensation to eliminate residual temperature variations as well as second-order effects due to humidity. Temperature and absolute humidity affect acoustic measurements in the same way—both affect the acoustic wavelength. By using the residual field values, the system can adjust the operating frequency (increasing the frequency shortens the wavelength), can add a correction factor, or can fine-tune the temperature to improve compensation. Acoustic force-field equipment with both air temperature control and software compensation can hold amplitudes to 0.01 percent and phase shifts to 1 mrad under laboratory conditions. Under factory floor conditions (30°C or 50°F temperature variation; 80 percent relative humidity variation), amplitudes can be held to .1 percent and phase shifts to 10 mrad.

Acoustic transducers—both field generator and sensors—are usually located at some distance from the inspection region. Narrow passages (narrow compared

to the wavelength) transmit acoustic energy from the transducer to the inspection region (figure 14.10). The passages, called *waveguides,* let the generator/sensor array have much smaller dimensions than the transducers themselves. For example, a typical acoustic array has a field generator and eight field sensors, each 10–20 mm (0.4 to 0.8 inch) in diameter. If waveguides were not used, the array dimensions would be 50–75 mm (2 to 3 inches)—too large for applications in which small objects are to be inspected. Using waveguides, array dimensions on commercial equipment are reduced to 10 to 20 mm (.4 to .8 inch). Arrays as small as 3 mm have been fabricated for the force-field inspection of objects .5 mm on a side; waveguides direct the field information from the inspection region to the sensors.

Microwave Fields

The major advantage of microwave force-fields is their insensitivity to temperature. Unlike acoustic fields, whose wavelength depends on the speed of sound (which changes with temperature and humidity), microwave fields have a wavelength that depends on the speed of light. In air, the speed of light changes insignificantly for the path lengths involved.

Although they do not have wavelength effects, microwave force-field equipment has typically been more expensive than acoustic. However, with recent advances in microwave integrated circuits based on gallium arsenide, the cost factor is becoming less significant. In acoustics operating at 20 KHz to 300 KHz, the voltage signal from the sensors can be easily sampled, converted to digital values, and filtered digitally. Not so with microwave sensors: the voltages vary too quickly to be digitized directly. With microwaves, other techniques must be used to digitize the amplitude and phase-shift values. Once digitized, the list of numbers is precisely the same as for acoustic force-field measurements.

The wavelength of microwaves at 30 GHz corresponds to the same wavelength as that of acoustic force-fields at 40 KHz: 10 mm. Microwave sensors are available commercially in the range between 2 GHz (150-mm wavelength) and 30 GHz (10-mm wavelength).

The power levels required in microwave force-field sensing are very low level—typically one tenth to one hundredth that of police radar equipment and microwave-based door openers—preventing the microwaves from harming operators.

The resolution of microwave sensors is typically .01 percent in amplitude and 1 mrad in phase shift. The signals do not drift with temperature or humidity as acoustic signals do; no heaters are required, nor is software compensation needed. As in acoustic force-field sensing, the dominant noise source is not measurement noise but "shape noise." The signal variation from one object to the next due to normal manufacturing tolerances usually produces greater differ-

ences in the amplitude and phase-shift measurements than does the equipment's inherent ability to measure amplitude and phase shift. Just because microwave sensors have more measurement resolution does not mean that microwave sensing can measure defects better than acoustic sensing. If shape noise dominates measurement noise—it usually does—then both systems would perform equally. However, microwave force-fields are sensitive to the polarization of the field, allowing improved resolution for certain antenna designs.

Exponential Force-Fields

As discussed exponential fields are either inductive or capacitive. In most applications, the exponential fields penetrate metal objects much more than in sinusoidal fields. For example, inductive fields (which operate at much lower frequencies than microwave fields) have less of a "skin effect" and can penetrate several millimeters into a metal object. Capacitive fields, most commonly used in inspecting nonconducting objects, completely penetrate the object. In general, sinusoidal fields apply to measuring the external shape of an object—the outside; exponential fields apply to measurements within the material of the object—the inside.

There are many exceptions, of course. Inductive fields at high frequencies (above 100 KHz) penetrate little into metal objects. Capacitive fields used with metal objects are affected only by the object's surface, not its internal flaws. Moreover, although exponential fields are usually used for detecting the "insides" of objects, external shape also affects the measurements. For instance, in the hex nut described earlier, the missing crimp could barely be detected with an acoustic field. Using inductive sensing, the missing crimp is easily detected despite shape noise such as nut height variation.

Inductive effects are also used in proximity sensors, in metal detectors (used in airport security and food-packing equipment), and in traffic-control sensors embedded in city streets. In each case, the size of the sensing coil varies depending on the sensing task. The sensor's range is about equal to its diameter, whether it is a 5-mm (.2-inch) proximity sensor or a 2-m (6-foot) traffic sensor. Capacitive effects are common in proximity sensors and in hand-held sensors that locate studs behind plaster wall board. Again the sensor's range is on the order of the size of its sensing plates. In force-field sensing with exponential fields, the same is true: range and stand-off are about the same as sensor size. Although wavelength characterizes a sinusoidal field, it is the sensor size that characterizes an exponential field.

Inductive Sensing

The history of inductive sensing began in the 1930s with work by Sperry in the U.S. to detect cracks in steel rails and by Foerster in Germany to detect cracks and hardness of steel tubing. Inductive sensing is also called eddy-current testing, because the field generator produces an electromagnetic field that induces in a metallic object currents called *eddy currents*. The induced current, in turn, produces its own magnetic field, which distorts the generated field; coils sensitive to magnetic fields detect the distortion. Inductive force-field sensing is distinct from eddy-current testing in that arrays of individual sensors are analyzed by pattern-recognition techniques.

Inductive sensors come in two distinct types: through coils and surface (or "pancake") coils. With through coils, the object passes through the coil—as you do when you pass through the inductive metal detectors at an airport. With surface coils, you pass over or near a coil—as you do when your car passes over the inductive traffic control sensors embedded in the street. In either case, the presence of metallic objects distorts a generated inductive field.

Two basic techniques are used to sense the field distortion using either through coils or surface coils. One technique is, as described above, for one coil to generate an inductive field and other coils to measure the force-field distortion produced by a metal object. This is called the *mutual inductance technique,* because the mutual inductance between two coils (the generator and a sensor) is measured. The second technique uses the same coil to generate the field and do the sensing. It is called the *self-inductance technique,* because the self-inductance of the coil (as distorted by the metallic object) is measured.

Commercial force-field equipment tends to use the self-inductance method, except in cases where "waveguides" are used. Inductive waveguides are not true waveguides as are used in sinusoidal fields; rather, they are a means of channeling the inductive field to the inspection region. Certain materials, such as ferrous metals, have high magnetic permeability; magnetic fields "flow" through these materials much more easily than they do through air and nonferrous materials that have low permeability. Hence, the inductive field tends to confine itself to the ferrous material. Guides made of ferrous material (ferrite is commonly used) can channel inductive fields much as waveguides or coax channel acoustic and microwave fields from the force-field generator or sensors to the inspection region. Such guides are appropriate when the inspection region is so small that coils could not be built easily. For instance, read-write heads for computer hard disks use ferrite guides to channel the inductive field to a tiny spot on the surface of the disk.

Inductive force-fields are affected by both the conductivity and the permeability of metal objects. The amount by which each affects the measurements depends upon the frequency of operation. For simplicity, objects can be divided into two groups: ferrous and nonferrous. Although various metals can differ in

conductivity by a factor of 10 (copper has ten times the conductivity of iron), permeability differs by a factor of 100. Ferrous materials (magnetic metals such as iron, nickel, and many of their alloys) have a permeability 100 times that of nonferrous conducting materials, such as copper, aluminum, stainless steel, titanium, and even graphite composites.

The high permeability of ferrous materials prevents the inductive force-field from penetrating into the object. However, penetration can be improved for ferrous materials by operating the force-field at a lower driven frequency. The division of inductive force-field sensing into ferrous and nonferrous materials, then, is really a division into frequency of operation. Low frequencies (60 Hz to 50 kHz) typically are used for ferrous materials; higher frequencies (50 kHz to 10 MHz) are used for nonferrous materials. The distinction is important, because the field generating/sensing coils cannot operate in both frequency ranges at once.

Temperature variation is the only environmental factor that seriously affects inductive sensing. Fortunately, it is easy to compensate for most of the errors caused by temperature. The biggest effect is due to the self-heating of the coils: the presence of a metallic object near a sensing coil changes its impedance, thus changing the current through it. But changes in the coil current cause the coil to either heat up or cool down, giving measurement drift. Piece part inspection is compensated for by adjusting the inductive measurements between parts—following the drift.

A more insidious temperature error is that of temperature variation of the objects themselves. Inductive measurements determine the object's conductivity and permeability; depending on the material, either or both of these change with temperature. Higher-frequency measurements (above 100 kHz) are particularly sensitive to conductive changes in a metal object. If parts being inspected have a variation in temperature, that variation contributes to the noise of good parts. If parts being inspected vary in temperature over a day's run, some of the later parts may be rejected falsely because their temperature has changed. Parts should stabilize to a fixed temperature for the most accurate results.

Another source of error for ferrous objects is residual magnetism. Often piece parts are magnetized by magnetic conveyors such as are common in industrial plants. A magnetized part sliding near an inductive coil acts like a generator, inducing unwanted signals into the coil. Depending on the accuracy of measurement required, the magnetized parts can either produce a large fraction of falsely rejected parts or can prevent the parts from being inspected at all. If necessary, the parts can be demagnetized by passing them through a degaussing coil prior to inspection.

The shape defects that inductive force-sensing can detect differ depending on whether through coils or surface coils are used (figure 14.11). Through coils detect changes in volume of the object (missing volume or added volume) at the cross-section sliced by the coil—such as acoustic sensing in the diffraction

Figure 14.11 A Through Coil and a Surface Coil for Inductive Sensing

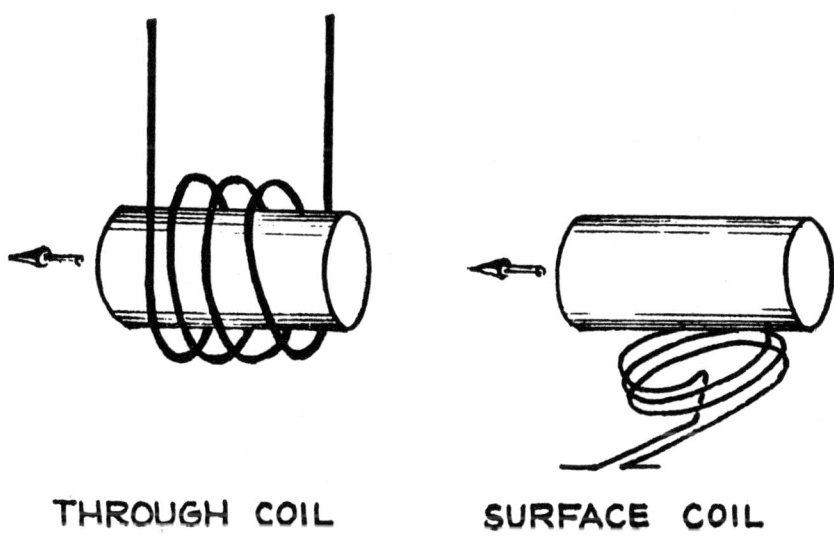

regime detects changes in volume. Surface coils detect missing volume, but they are also "distance-sensitive" as well. Because the response of an exponential field drops off quickly with distance from the sensor, surface coils are more sensitive to metal that is closer to the coil than to metal that is farther away. Consider the bolt example discussed earlier. If the surface coil was embedded into the surface on which the bolt was placed, a threaded bolt would have some metal—the tips of the threads above the coil—closer to the coil than if the bolt were not threaded there. Thus, unthreaded or partially threaded bolts can be distinguished from threaded ones.

Cracks in conducting objects can also be found with inductive force-field sensing. In a good object, the current induced by the field-generating coil flows through the object's outer surface. The depth through which it flows depends on the material (ferrous or nonferrous) and the generated field's frequency (the lower the frequency the deeper the current flows). If a crack blocks the induced current, the force-field will distort differently. Because the induced current in the object's surface flows in the same direction as the current in the field generating coil, the coil direction should be consistent with the expected crack direction. For example, a longitudinal crack in steel tubing is most easily detected by moving the tubing through a coil. The induced current flows around the tubing's circumferences; any longitudinal crack blocks the induced current, and the degree of distortion can be used to detect the crack. A radial crack in a ring-shaped object (such as a valve seat or a nut) is heat detected with a surface coil on which the object is placed or over which it slides. The induced current traveling around the ring is blocked by a radial crack.

Plating presence and plating thickness are detected in much the same way—using through coils and surface coils. Induced current sheets in the surface or "skin" are altered depending on the surface conductivity difference between the base metal and the plating. The frequency of the field should be chosen so that most of the induced current flows through the plating to give the most accurate measurements. Because force-field sensing uses arrays of sensing coils, the plating (or plating thickness) can be checked at various points on the object.

Material differences in metal objects can be detected with force-field sensing in the same way as plating differences. Currents that are induced into the surface (or "skin") of an object conduct differently for different materials. For example, copper, zinc, lead, and tin all have differing conductivity; objects of the same shape with different proportions of these constituents (the brasses and bronzes) can be distinguished.

Heat-treating of steel also has a strong effect on conductivity and permeability. Not only can heat-treated objects be sensed and separated from unheated objects, but the amount and location of heat-treating can be determined. On a typical steel bolt hardened to 40 Rockwell C, overhardening or underhardening of 5 points is practical. Core hardness variation of the same order is practical using lower-frequency force-fields (typically less than 2 KHz). Force-field measurements detect the inductive field distortion over the entire object as it passes through the inspection region. Hence, objects whose hardness varies at different locations of the object can be inspected at each location. Shafts with hardened middles and "soft" ends are an example of such parts.

Capacitive Sensing

Using capacitors for force-field sensors is similar to using inductive force-field sensors. Just as inductive sensing measures both the permeability and the conductivity of objects, capacitive sensing measures both the dielectric constant and the conductivity of objects. At lower frequencies, the signals primarily sense the object's dielectric constant; at higher frequencies, the signals mostly sense the object's conductivity. In general, both properties have some effect on the signals.

Consider the simplest case, that of a metal object whose conductivity is very high. When two plate sensors are near the object, the capacitive field near the object is distorted by the object's presence. For example, if the two plates are parallel and opposite each other, their mutual capacitance is very low—they are not closely coupled. A conducting object between the plates lets the two plates couple better, increasing their mutual capacitance, just as the intermediate plates of a tuning capacitor change its capacitance. With a nonconducting object (such as a plastic part) between the plates, the capacitive field is distorted by the part's dielectric constant. When no part is between the plates, the signal is based on the dielectric constant of air. When the part is present, the field's distor-

tion is approximately proportional to that portion of the object between the plates.

For either conducting or nonconducting objects, capacitive sensing is sensitive to volume variations: added volume or missing volume. As in all force-field sensing, the resolution of the change in volume (that is, the smallest detectable volume increment) depends on the volume variation of the parts themselves. In capacitive sensing, parts that have large volume variations because of normal manufacturing tolerances will have poorer resolution than parts with little variation because of manufacturing tolerances.

By analogy with inductive sensing, capacitive sensing uses the equivalent of through coils and surface coils. When the capacitive plates are opposed and the object passes between them, the entire object is sensed, much as a through coil senses the entire object (see figure 14.12). Similar to a surface coil, the plates may be on the same plane (typically one plate surrounds the other) and the object passes over or near the plates. The capacitive field falls off quickly with distance from the plane; it does not usually extend through the entire object. The same-plane configuration is "distance-sensitive," much as surface coils are distance-sensitive.

Capacitive sensing can be used for shape measurement of metallic objects. For metallic objects, charges in the metal can move freely to the outermost surface of the object in closest proximity to the capacitive plates. If this charge distribution differs from one object to another, the mutual capacitance of the sensors change. Because the charges are confined to the outer skin, capacitive sensing cannot detect the "insides" of metallic objects—only the shape distribution of the outermost surface. Metallic objects act to better couple one of the sensing plates to the other—the plates effectively are closer together when the object is present.

Figure 14.12 Capacitive Sensing Plates

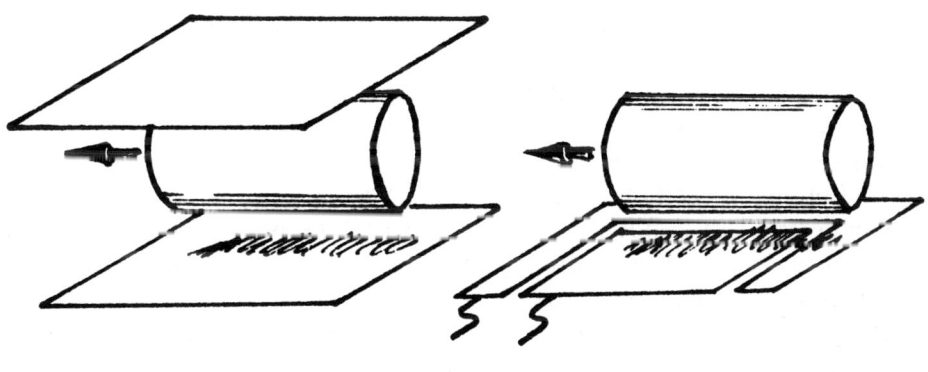

OPPOSED PLATES   SAME PLANE PLATES

Humidity is the biggest environmental concern with capacitive sensing. Because dry air has a different dielectric constant than most air, measurements drift as humidity changes. However, with proper compensation the effects of drift can be nearly eliminated. For piece part inspection, the compensation is relatively simple: the inspection chamber is measured when no objects are present—much as inductive sensing compensates for temperature variations. For continuous measurements, the humidity must be determined by independent measurement and compensated for in software.

Capacitive sensing is used most effectively for plastic parts. These parts have two common problems: short shots (the mold did not fill completely because of a cold mold or blocked injection ports) and flash (material flowed from between the mold halves because of overfill, worn molds, or material caught between mold halves when they close).

Short shots are detected by the missing volume of dielectric (plastic), using either opposed planes or same-plane capacitive plates. The size of the short shots that can be detected depends on the positional and shape variations of the part. Often the position of a short shot is known (the last portion of the mold which is filled). Improved resolution can usually be obtained if the expected position of the short shot moves past a "same-plane" capacitive sensor. Because the volume of the plastic inspected is reduced (only that portion within the strongest field where the plates nearly touch counts) the ratio of "defect volume to inspect volume" is improved, giving higher resolution for short shots.

Flash is usually the most difficult defect to detect on plastic parts. Its volume is usually very small, so only the grossest flash can be detected with capacitive sensing. However, if the parting line of the part slides against the part conveyor or gravity chute, the flash (which usually occurs at the parting line) can often be detected. The flash displaces the part away from embedded capacitive plates, changing their impedance and causing the part to be rejected.

Applications

Force-field sensing has been used to detect defects at several points in the manufacturing process. First are production processes—ensuring that components are correct as they are being produced. Second are inspection processes. Here, subcomponents, usually in bulk, are inspected either on-line (as part of a continuous production process) or off-line (stand-alone inspection machines operating in parallel with the production process). Lastly, assemblies are checked during the assembly process for either defective subcomponents or misassembly.

Production Processes

Stamping, forming, heading, and metal cutting are four production processes most appropriate to force-field sensing. Microwave and inductive sensing are used for production processes because of their insensitivity to environmental variations. On the other hand, acoustic and capacitive sensing are sensitive to temperature and humidity changes.

In stamping and forming operations, sensors inspect the parts as they are formed or after they are formed (as in progressive die stamping). Force-field sensing primarily determines shape variations during forming: double hits, misformed parts, and burrs on sheared parts. In headers, the sensors are positioned to look for defects in three areas: the parts after shearing from wire (short-feed check), the forming punches and dies (broken punch and die break-out check), and the transfer fingers (correct transfer and correct part shape). Microwave sensors are most appropriate, because their standoff from the parts and/or machine components is greater than in inductive sensing. In metal cutting, sensing is usually not done during metal cutting itself in order to avoid erroneous signals from chips. When cutting stops, a sensing head swings in to determine the part's shape consistency. The cutting tool can also be checked for edge build-up, correct tool, and tool diameter (performed at an inspection station associated with the tool changer).

Inspection Processes

When subcomponents have already been manufactured, force-field sensing is appropriate for both on-line inspection and off-line inspection. For on-line inspection, the parts typically are held in fixturing, as in dial, carousel, pallet, or lift-and-carry methods of transfer between operations. The parts are aready oriented.

In some on-line inspection, parts are conveyed by belt. Here, parts must be positioned accurately by adding a gently-angled side rail. Parts slide on the belt and position themselves against the rail for accurate inspection. The belt itself must vary by no more than a mil ($\pm$ .001 inch, $\pm$ .025mm) in the thickness along its length to assure the part is positioned properly in the vertical axis. The belt must ride over a fixed guide (typically twice the part length) during part inspection to assure belt warp is minimized. Usually the parts are separated from one another so that a part approaching the inspection region does not interfere with parts being inspected. The amount of separation depends on the sensors used: sinusoidal sensors need the biggest spacing and exponential the least.

When parts are required to go through secondary processes (such as plating, deburring, or heat-treating) or when they must be stored efficiently, parts are in bulk form and are unoriented. Inspection of bulk parts (often called *sorting*) is

usually done off-line. Bulk parts must be singulated (fed into the inspection region one at a time) to be sensed accurately. Most parts have only a few stable orientations, so force-field sensing must store the pattern of each stable state. Hence, if a bolt moves through the inspection chamber thread-first, it is compared to good bolts in the thread-first orientation; if it moves through head-first, it is compared to other head-first bolts [13, 14].

For sorting applications, the parts being inspected must be positioned accurately: the unknown parts must be located in the same position as the previously learned good parts. Typically, parts fed into the inspection region are located by gravity or other forces against two planes. For example, when parts are fed down a chute, gravity force components hold the part against the chute walls; when fed by belt, gravity force components hold the parts against the belt and fixed side walls.

Once located in two dimensions, the parts are located in the third dimension by sensors. Typically, through-beam light sensors are used, but other sensors are also appropriate: machine vision, inductive, or capacitive proximity sensors. The part is located in the direction of travel such that measurements are made "on the fly." Indeed, having the part move through a relatively small inspection region is equivalent to scanning the part and results in improved accuracy [1, 4].

Because the force-field information contains both position information and shape/electromagnetic information, eliminating the position variation improves the measurement resolution. In some situations where the position or rotation variations cannot be easily minimized (such as rotationally unsymmetric objects fed from bulk), software techniques can improve resolution. In general, the less positional variation, the easier the job of software compensation.

Besides sorting of bulk parts, force-field sensing is used for automated assembly, ensuring consistency during the assembly process itself. Consider an insertion device that picks up parts from a feeder and inserts them into an assembly at some station of an assembly operation (dial, carousel, lift-and-carry, or whatever). The "inspection region" becomes the region surrounding the insertion tip if appropriate field sensors are installed in the tip or nearby. Inductive and microwave sensors are particularly easy, because they can be simply epoxied into the insertion tip. The sensors set up force-fields in the vicinity of the insertion tip to check for consistency of the assembly process. If the insertion device misses the pick of the part, the force-fields detect it. If it drops the part during transfer, the force-fields detect it. If the insertion device mispositions the part on the assembly, or if the assembly was otherwise incorrect after the insertion, the force-fields detect it. Depending on the application, the force-fields are checked for consistency 10 to 100 times each second of operation [5].

The accuracy of the consistency check depends on the relative distance between the sensors and the objects that distort their fields. Accuracy improves as the distance diminishes. For the insertion device example above, the force-field measurements are most accurate—typically to a few thousandths of an inch

(.1 mm)—when the insertion tip is transferring the part or inserting it into the assembly. The measurements are least accurate when the objects of concern (the part and the assembly) are farthest from the sensors—when accurate measurements are least needed. Consequently, force-field sensing matches the requirements of automated assembly. It is accurate when accuracy is needed.

A third application of force-field sensing is in production equipment. Parts are monitored as they are being produced on metalcutters, forming equipment, presses, and headers. Force-field sensors measure the part's shape directly, rather than indirectly as in load-monitoring.

As an example of force-field sensing used in production equipment, consider a cold header, a machine used to form bolts. Several regions on a cold header are checked simultaneously for consistency. First, when the wire is sheared, inductive sensors check for cracks in the wire and "short-feed" conditions. Second, the punches and dies are checked for consistency with microwave sensors before they head the wire—has a punch broken, have sections of the die "broken out"? Third, the transfer of the part being headed from one set of dies to the next is checked: Did the transfer fingers grip the part properly? Was it transferred to the next operation correctly?

This third application of force-field sensing—sensing of parts in the production process—is of the highest accuracy because the objects are already oriented, both in translation and in rotation. Production equipment already has high-ac-

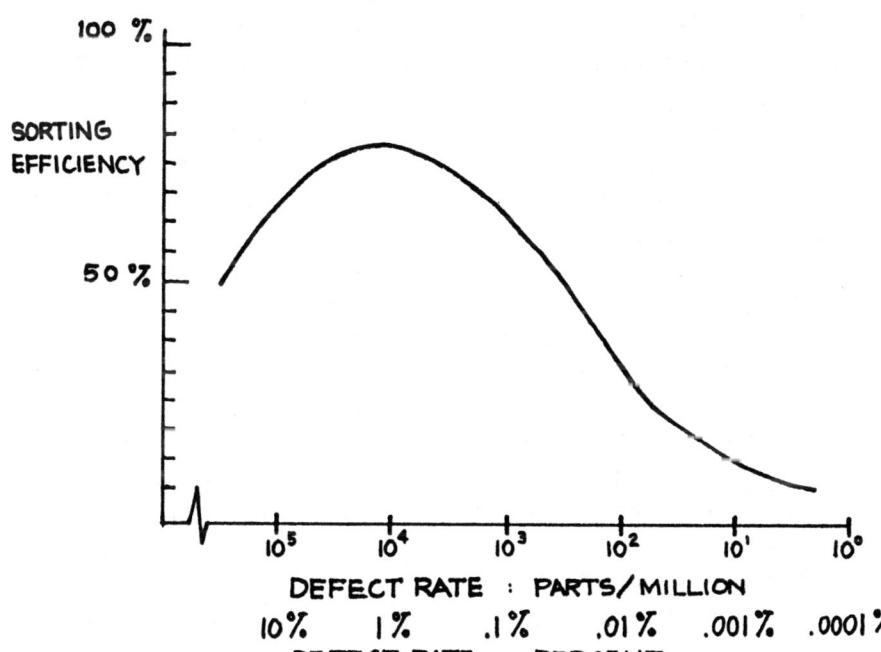

Figure 14.13 Manual Sorting Efficiency

curacy motion, typically to .001 inch (0.25 mm): the variation of good objects is small. Sensors are typically inductive or microwave to minimize the effect of cutting oil and environmental conditions. Encoders on the production shafts or proximity switches keyed to the machine's motion ensure that the force-field measurements are coordinated with the production process.

Conclusion

Force-field sensing is needed in high-volume manufacturing to ensure consistency of product. Most parts are used as components in assemblies. The assembly equipment is sensitive to jamming by defective parts or by mixed parts. As assembly equipment becomes more complex, the effect of jamming on production levels becomes critical.

The slightest percentage of defects can reduce the production efficiency enormously. Manual sorting of parts is not an acceptable solution, because people can eliminate, at best, only about 80 percent of the defects (figure 14.13). Statistical process control (SPC) does not solve the problem either. Defects that cause jamming are due to random errors in the manufacturing equipment or to mixed parts that usually enter a batch of parts as "leftovers" from a previous batch. Figure 14.14 shows a graph of part dimension as parts leave a process; high and

Figure 14.14 Random Errors and Mixed Parts in Production

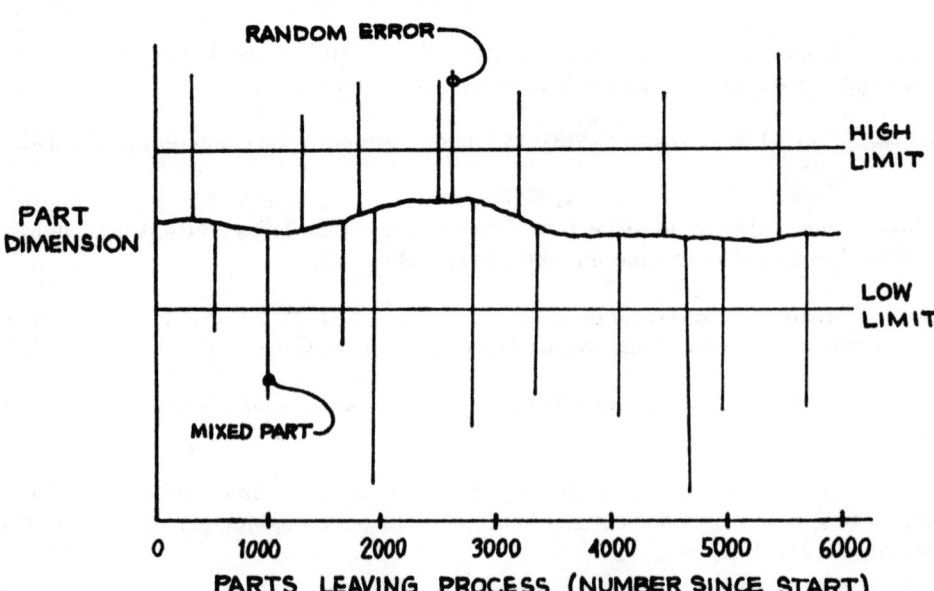

low limits indicate out-of-tolerance parts. SPC samples the part dimension occasionally to assure that its trend is correct. Equipment is adjusted if the trend is incorrect or the dimension is out of tolerance [11].

The SPC process is necessary to ensure that dimensions stay within bounds. Unfortunately, it seldom detects random errors and mixed parts. As shown on the figure, these errors cannot be picked up by sampling the parts. The errors occur at random times—the part before and the part after can be correct but still a defect is produced. Although SPC can predict the variation of dimensions (for example, 6-sigma limits), unfortunately, it relies on sampling methods and assumes a Gaussian distribution to predict dimensional variation. Only 100 percent inspection of each part by sensors of some sort can hope to reduce defect rates much below 1,000 PPM.

References

1. Buckley, Shawn. "100-percent Inspection of Fasteners with Sound Waves." FASTEC '87 Conference, Atlanta, GA, October 27–29, 1987.

2. ———. "Acoustic Inspection of Parts, Using Microprocessors." *Autofact West* vol. 1. CAD/CAM 8, SME, Anaheim, CA, November 17–20, 1980.

3. ———. "Automation Sensing Mimics Organisms." *Sensors* vol. 2, no. 6 (June 1985):27–30.

4. ———. "Continuous Wave Ultrasonic Inspection." 18th Annual Technical Symposium, Ultrasonic Industries Assoc., New York, NY, May, 1987.

5. ———. "Force-Field Sensing." SME MS 88-694. Autofact '88 Conference, Chicago, IL, October 1988.

6. ———. "Phase Monitored Inspection." Proceedings of the Third North American Metalworking Research Conference, Pittsburgh, PA, May, 1975.

7. ———. "Road Test Aerodynamic Instrumentation." SAE 741030. Society of Automotive Engineering, Automobile Engineering Meeting, Toronto, Canada, October 21–25, 1974.

8. ———. "Sorting Out Electronic Parts Sorters." *Tooling and Production* (September 1985):78–79.

9. Buckley, Shawn, and Edmund Lattone. "Airflow Beneath an Automobile." SAE 741028. Society of Automotive Engineering, Automobile Engineering Meeting, Toronto, Canada, October 21–25, 1974.

10. Buckley, Shawn, and Kim Stelson. "Phase Monitoring for Automated Inspection, Positioning, and Assembly." *Transactions of the Society of Manufacturing Engineering* vol. 6 (1978):56–63.

11. Cheng, Alex. "Coping with Assembly Downtime." *Assembly Engineering* (March 1987):16–18.

12. Glabicky, Martha. "Ultrasound Qualifies Parts." *American Machinist* (November 1985): 106–8.

13. McCarty, Lyle. "Ultrasonic Device Inspects Small Parts." *Design News* (April 6, 1987):130–31.

14. Minghelli, Giovanni. "How Sound Inspects Small Parts." *Industrial World* (October 1987):40–41.

15. Tavormina, Joseph J., and Shawn Buckley. "Automatic Positioning and Assembly Under Microcomputer Control via Acoustic Phase Monitoring." *Transactions of the Society of Manufacturing Engineering* vol. 6 (1978):448–54.

Chapter 15 Use of Ultrasonic Sensors in Level and Flow Measurements

Jack A. Perry

Introduction

Echo ranging with sound pulses, or *sonar,* was used by bats, dolphins, and certain birds long before it was imagined by man. Shortly after World War I, from 1920 through 1946, echo ranging was used for depth gauging and the location of submarines, fish, and other marine life in the oceans. After World War II, *echo-ranging* found extensive use in nondestructive testing of materials and in medical diagnosis. The plotting of ultrasonic echoes has applications in many other fields, including the testing of homogeneous metals and the charting of ocean beds. Ultrasound—or *sonograms,* as the technique is now called—is applied to several aspects of medical diagnosis.

The principle involved is to generate and listen for sound pulses and echoes. An alternating electric current is applied to a suitably housed piezoelectric crystal. The crystal vibrates at whatever frequency is applied. The vibration produces pressure waves in the medium surrounding the crystal, and these waves radiate outward at the speed sound travels through the medium. If the alternating current has a frequency above 20 kHz, the "sound" produced is well beyond the range of human hearing. The term *ultrasonic* refers to any sound wave above 20,000 Hz. Ultrasonic frequencies as high as 20 MHz are not uncommon in medical diagnostic instruments.

Ultrasonic sensors as they apply to the chemical process industries have a brief history compared to the differential pressure or float-on-a-cable methods. Ultrasonic sensors emerged following World War I in Europe. Early developments were hampered by the lack of electronic components, such as the LSI chip and the microprocessor. In the early 1970s, ultrasonic sensors were first applied to a variety of process control tasks. Applications such as point level, continuous level, concentration, and full pipe flowmeters are now widely ac-

Figure 15.1 Simplistic Sound Spectrum

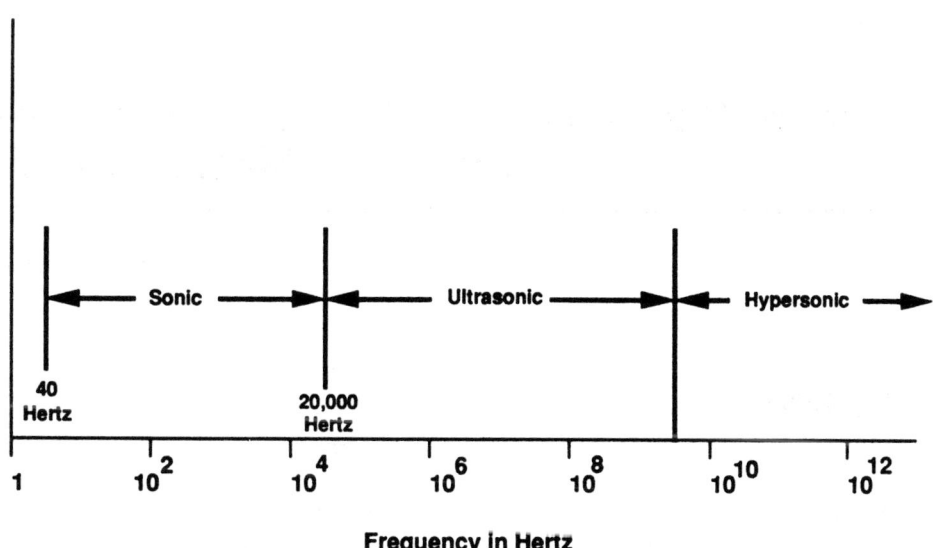

cepted. These sensors are applied to a variety of applications, for which they are, in many cases, better suited than other forms of instruments.

Ultrasonic process control instruments have four principal segments:

- Point level switches

- Continuous echo-ranging level metering

- Composition and concentration detection

- Transit-time or time-of-flight and Doppler full-pipe flow meters.

Open channel flow metering is a function of continuous level, because it is merely an interpretation of the head-to-flow relationship for any primary flow element.

Figure 15.1 is a simplistic illustration of the sound spectrum. Both sonic and ultrasonic frequencies are used in military and industrial applications of ultrasound to determine composition, distance, flow, level, and thickness. For our discussion of ultrasonic sensors, we will deal with a frequency range from 7.5 KHz to 5.0 MHz.

Figure 15.2 Application of Piezoelectric Effect

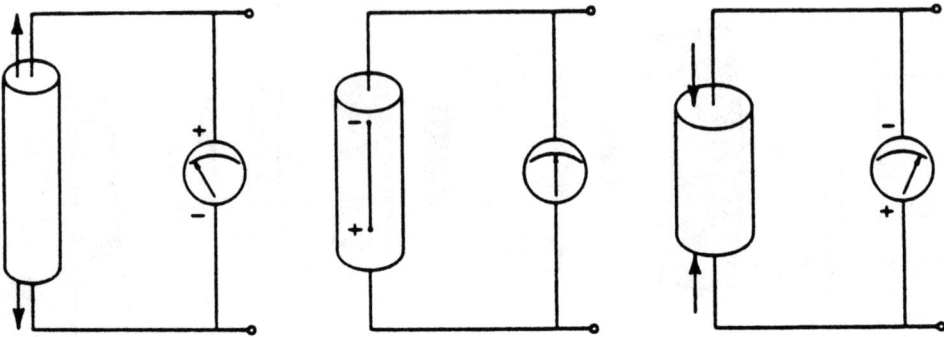

Ultrasonics

Piezoelectric Crystals and Their Function

Piezoelectricity is a means of converting mechanical energy into electric energy and vice versa. The prefix "piezo" is from the Greek verb meaning "to press." Figure 15.2 illustrates the application of the piezoelectric effect to ultrasonic echo ranging.

The application of compression or stretching forces (greatly exaggerated in the drawing) produces the voltages shown by the meters in the circuit. As the ceramic responds to the mechanical deformation shown, similarly, an alternating current will cause the ceramic to alternate in size. The latter case is the most interesting. In particular, the ceramic will have its own resonant frequency at which it vibrates most easily, the value of which is determined by its composition, size, and shape. If the ceramic is stimulated by an alternating current at this frequency, it will oscillate with efficiency, converting electrical energy into mechanical (acoustic) energy or sound pulses.

Generating Sound Pulses—Propagation

Propagation of sound waves through air, water, or metal is a mechanical process of compression and expansion initiated by a vibrating material. Vibration is induced by stimulating a piezoelectric crystal with an alternating current as illustrated in figure 15.3. This simple echo-ranging device for determining the distance from a piezoelectric crystal to a solid planar surface is fundamental to all ultrasonic echo-ranging sensors.

Figure 15.3 Ultrasonic Echo Ranging

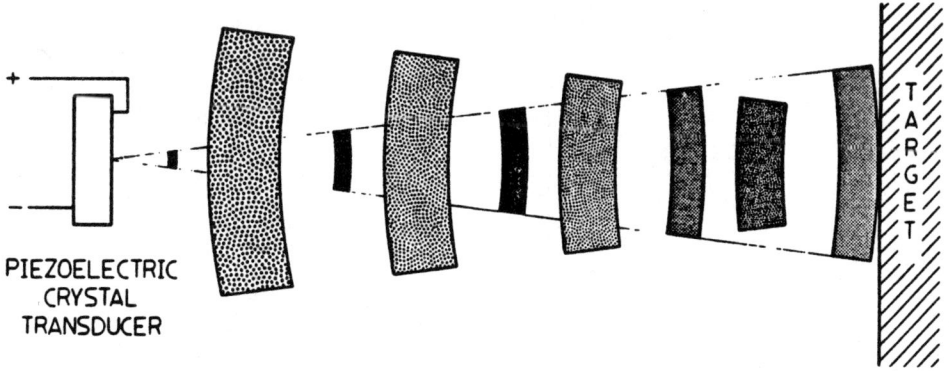

Figure 15.4 Ultrasonic Pulse Burst as Viewed on an Oscilloscope

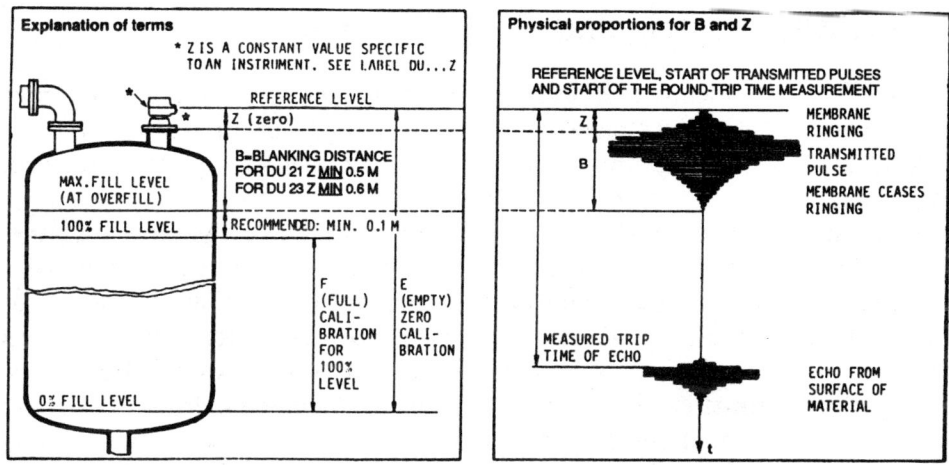

Figure 15.5 Distance Measurement by Ultrasonic Echo Ranging

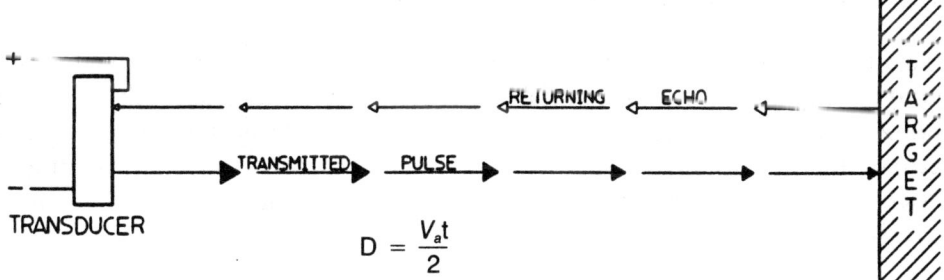

Figure 15.6 Liquid Level Measurement in a Water Tank

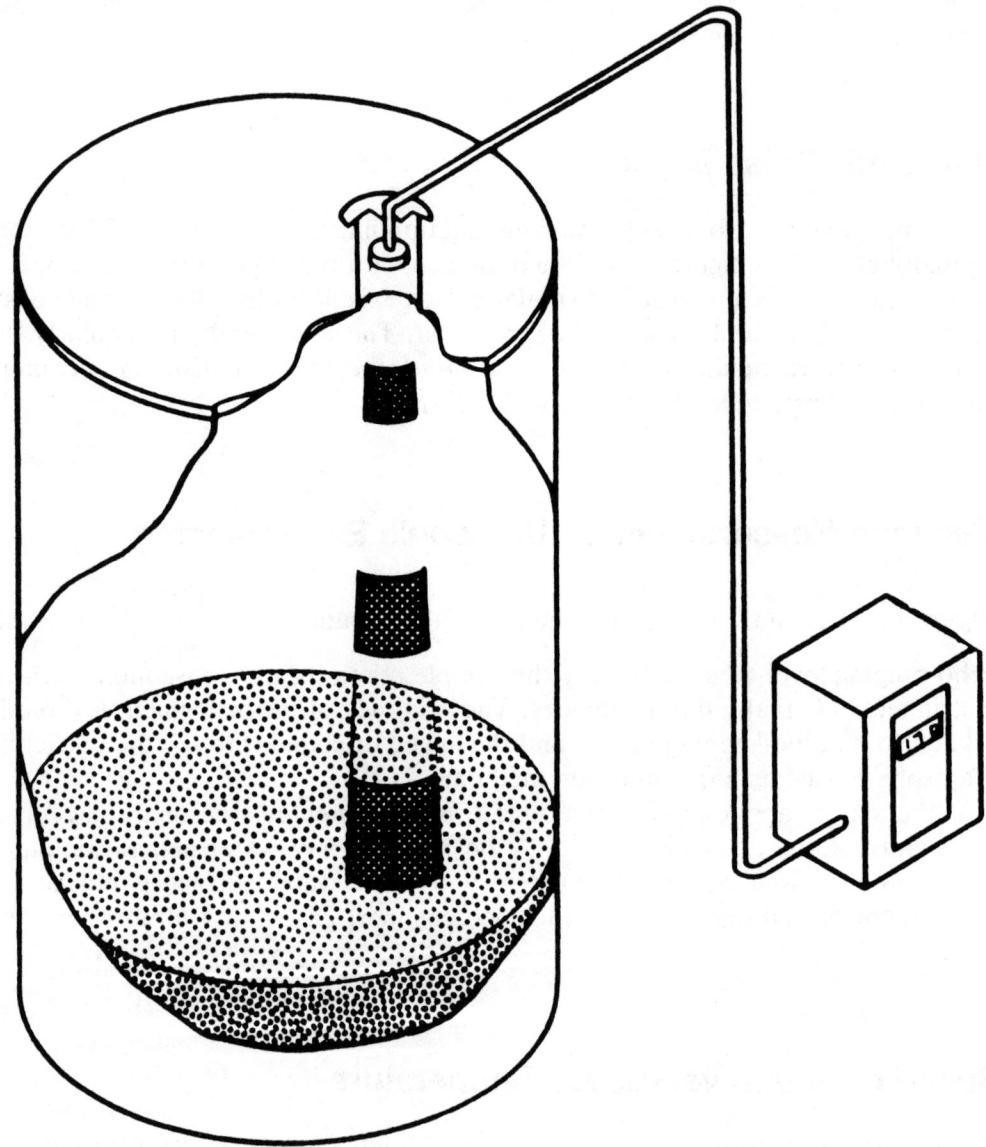

A fixed frequency voltage is applied to the sensor crystal, causing it to vibrate at a set frequency to produce pulsed sound waves that are directed at the surface of the target. The sound pulses are reflected by the target and returned to the crystal. The returning echo pulses vibrate the crystal, producing an AC signal that is fed back to the electronics for signal processing.

Figure 15.3 illustrates a simple pulse-echo-ranging transducer and its operation. The sound pulses start at the center surface of the transducer (crystal), travel out through the medium, and are reflected back to strike the crystal when they complete their return travel time.

Ultrasonic Pulse Burst

The conceptual ultrasonic echo ranging function illustrated in figure 15.3 is more factually defined by figure 15.4. When viewed with the aid of an oscilloscope, a *pulse burst* appears as a group of similar pulses except for the start-up and coast-down-to-rest front and back ends of the burst. These two ends, particularly the coast-down-to-rest end, dictate the *dead band,* the *blanking distance,* or, more precisely, the *ring time* of the crystal.

Distance Measurement by Ultrasonic Echo Ranging

Figure 15.5's purpose is to define the use of the equation $D = \frac{V_a t}{2}$. All ultrasonic echo-ranging level devices employ this simple relationship. Consequently, these instruments are really timing devices. The accuracy of the instrument is directly related to its time-keeping ability and the speed of sound through the particular atmosphere used as a transmission medium.

If the sensor application of figure 15.6 is implemented, reasonably accurate level and volume determinations may be made at any water height contained by the tank as long as the atmosphere above the water surface is normal air (79 percent N_2, 20 percent O_2, and 1 percent inert gases) at 1 atmosphere and 20°C.

Speed of Sound versus Air Temperature

No discussion of through-air ultrasonic level fundamentals is complete without addressing the fact that the speed of sound varies as the absolute temperature of the air through which it travels according to the equation:

$$V_s = V_o \sqrt{1 + \frac{C}{273}}$$

ULTRASONICS

Figure 15.7 The Speed of Sound versus Temperature

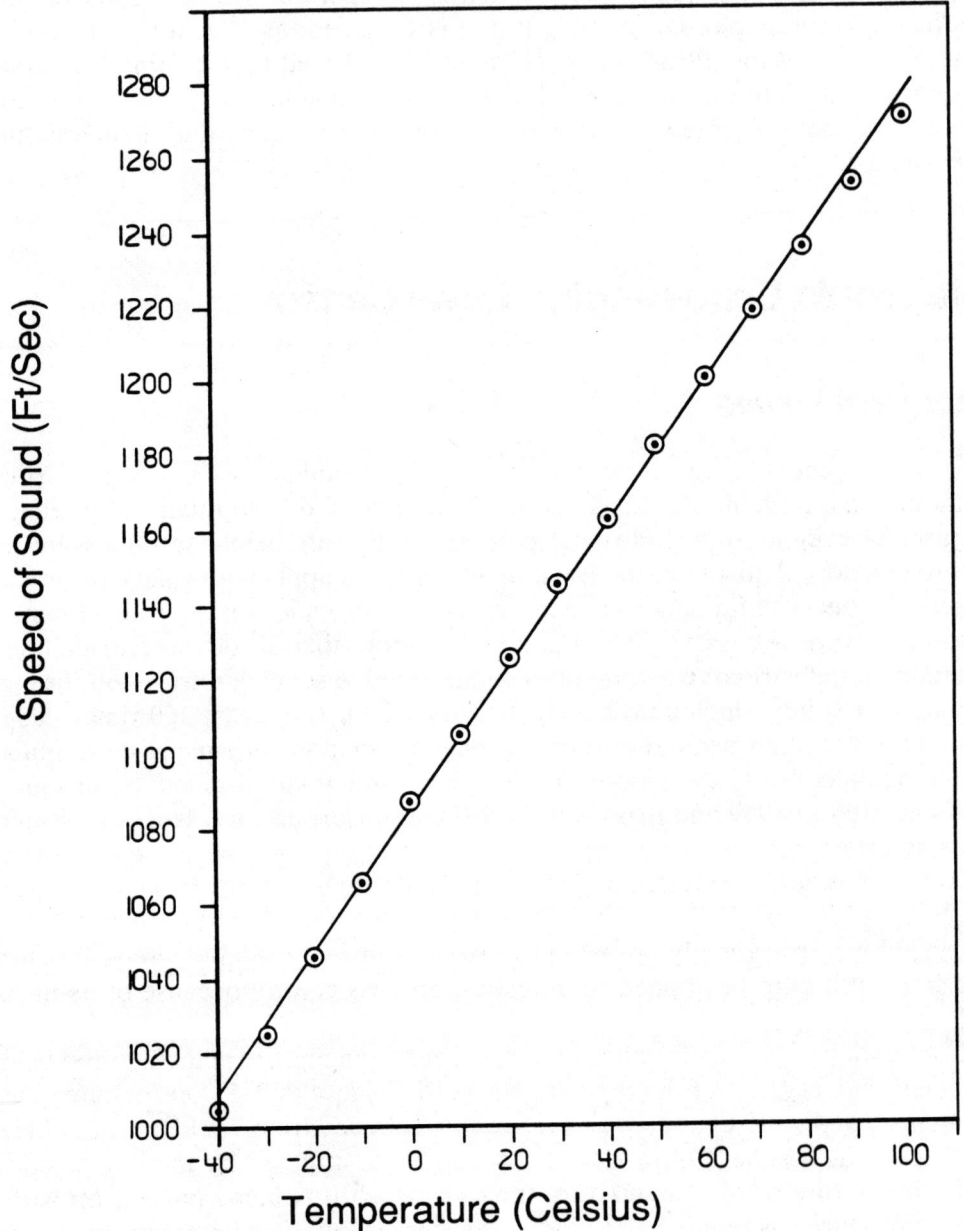

V_s is the velocity of the speed of sound through the media in question. This equals velocity of sound times the square root of one plus the temperature (in degrees centigrade) divided by 273. When the temperature versus sound velocity of this equation is plotted, a straight line is obtained, as shown by figure 15.7. The precision of the ultrasonic level meter is improved by factoring the proper sound velocity into the equation for distance shown in figure 15.5. Various techniques are used to achieve *temperature compensation,* and all of them are quite precise.

Ultrasonic Echo-ranging Level Sensors

Technical Issues

Ultrasonic echo ranging to obtain tank level determinations is not performed without some difficulties. It has taken a long time to develop uniformly reliable ultrasonic level sensors. Industrial process control ultrasonic sensors were the last to develop. Antisubmarine warfare and medical applications have been very successful because funding has been available to provide whatever development resources were necessary. It is important to note that all of these disciplines, including nondestructive testing ultrasound, involve sending ultrasound through liquids and solids—including human tissue—which is at least 100 times easier than it is to send ultrasound through normal air, let alone organic gases in industrial process control applications. The original through-air ultrasound transducer was patented in 1969 and is owned by Raytheon Corporation. It was a tremendous achievement.

Any discussion of through-air ultrasonic echo ranging must include notice of the Polaroid sensor, U.S. Patent 4,439,846 [7]. This transducer is one of the most advanced electrostatically operated ultrasonic sensors available today. It is limited in its ability to be applied to industrial process control because of its materials of construction.

Conventional sensors for ultrasonic level echo ranging are manufactured using piezoceramic crystals of the type known as PZT-4 and PZT-5. Sensors are made using both discs and cylinders and range in frequency from 7.5 kHz to 200 kHz.

Through-atmosphere ultrasonic echo ranging is affected by the composition and temperature of the gas mixture through which it is being pulsed. Moisture vapor, measured as relative humidity, has a significant effect upon the absorption of acoustic energy or sound loss. This occurs through the conversion of sound energy to heat and is more significant at higher sound frequencies. Figure 15.8 compares the effect of relative humidity on sound absorption for three typical through-air echo-ranging sensors. This phenomena explains one reason that

Figure 15.8 Absorption versus Frequency at Relative Humidity (RH)

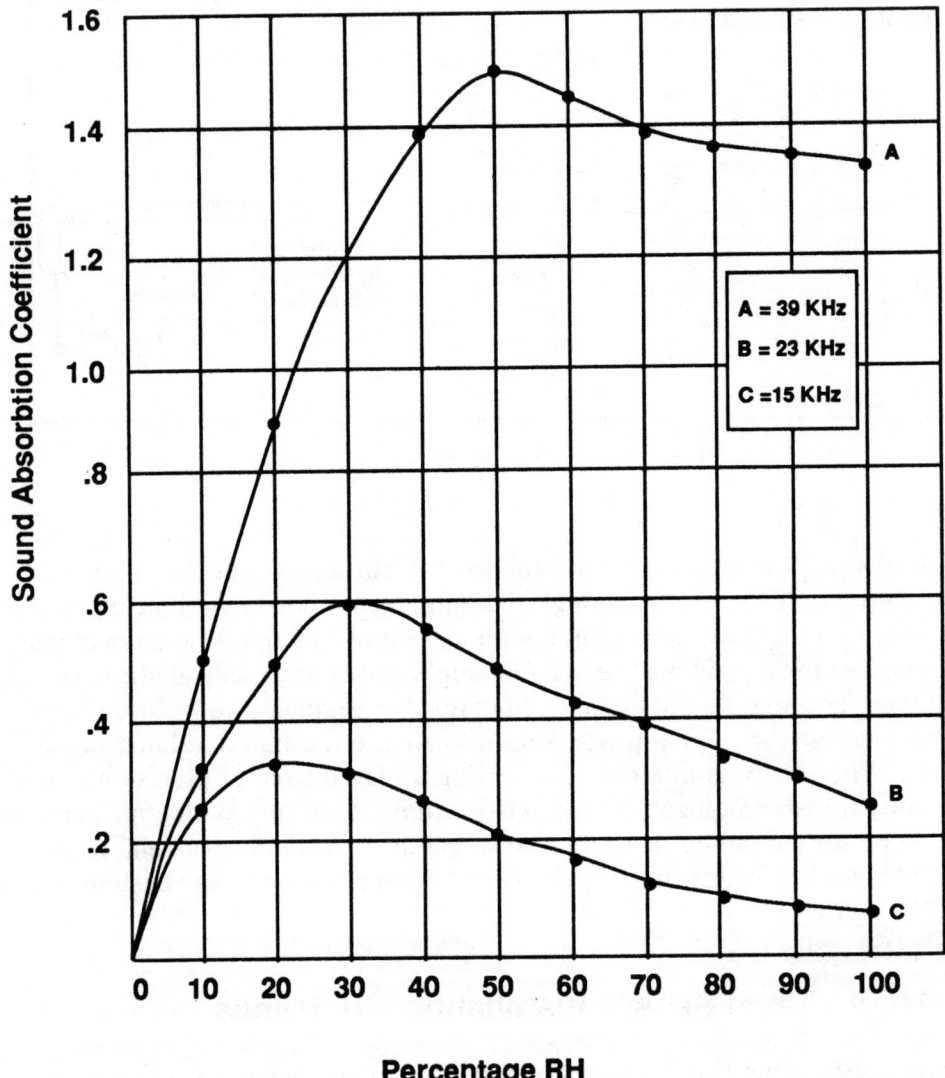

high-frequency echo-ranging sensors of this type have short distance spans, and conversely, why sensors operating in the 7-to-25-kHz range have longer spans.

Transmission medium pressure alone has little or no effect upon the speed of sound through a medium. Consequently, it is ignored for most through-atmospheric-air echo-ranging applications.

Figure 15.9 Sonar Level Gauging

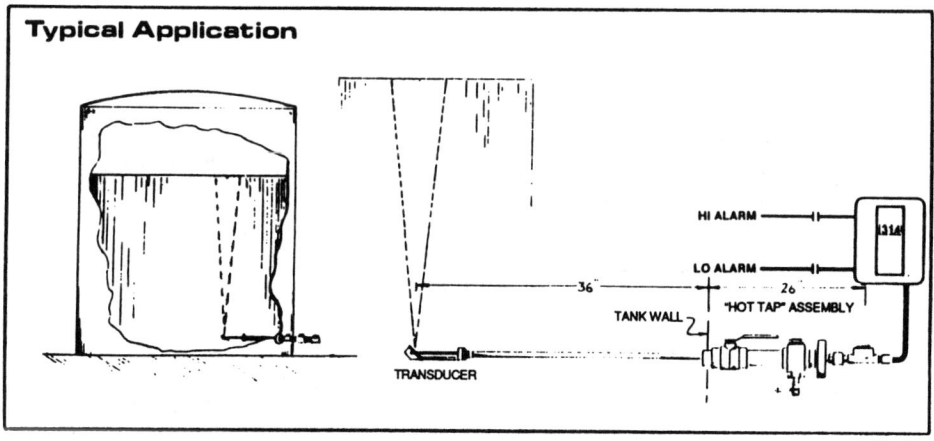

One of the most important applications for ultrasonic level or volume determination today is the use of through-the-liquid echo ranging as a means of gauging storage tanks. This technique, commonly known as *sonar*, was developed to a high degree for antisubmarine warfare applications and medical ultrasound applications. Through-liquid sonar techniques are beginning to be used with sophisticated software signal processing to measure the liquid volume in all size vessels. When there is interest in achieving a high degree of precision, such as in custody transfer applications for petroleum products and synthetic chemicals, this is a better technique. It is capable of yielding overall instrument accuracies of ±0.005 inch at spans of up to 50 feet. A typical *sonar gauge* system is illustrated in figure 15.9.

Ultrasonic Level Sensor Installation Guidelines

Industrial ultrasonic level sensor systems have been engineered to perform in a number of suitable applications. Because conditions vary widely for different installations, some general guidelines for the application of these sensors are provided in the following sections. A typical processing tank is illustrated in figure 15.10.

Placement of Sensor

The beam pattern of the sensor is a 7-to-14-degree cone (depending upon the ceramic type and the sensor construction used). The beam is projected from the

Figure 15.10 Typical Chemical Process Tank with Ultrasound Gauging

center of the sensor radiating face, which should be located so that material being conveyed into the top of a vessel does not fall into the beam path in any way. This location of the sensor will allow the instrument to detect the rise of the material in the vessel during the filling process without interference.

Irregularity of Tank Walls

When tanks are deep (more than 40 feet/12 meters) and the cross-section is small (less than 8 feet/2.4 meters), the signal transmitted by the sensor will strike the sidewalls. If these walls are not smooth, they will reflect some of the transmitted sound energy, causing spurious echoes that may be detected by some receivers. This can occur in tanks in which material attaches itself to the inner tank walls, as often happens with adhesives and sticky products. This may also occur when tanks are fabricated of steel and supporting members are mounted within the vessel. Microprocessor signal processing has virtually eliminated these difficulties, provided sufficient application information is available.

Influence of Stored Material

The ultrasonic reflections from liquids, powders, and granular solids differ. The material stored in the vessel to be measured must be considered before the application is made.

Liquids The interface between air and a liquid surface is well defined and is therefore a hard target for ultrasonic echo ranging. In some situations when the liquid is agitated, the sensor may receive one echo from the trough and another from the crest of the wave. Depending on the software signal process of the

instrument, the integral average of these two extremes can be processed and indicated. The more sophisticated electronic instruments provide such advantages as echo averaging, range gating, and adjustable dampening of the response time to determine and maintain stable instrument readings. Foam on the liquid surface will absorb the sound pulses in most instances, thus preventing any sufficiently processable signal from returning to the sensor for detection.

Solids Solid materials, such as grain, corn, plastic chips, coal, ore, etc., will not repose horizontally in a smooth surface. Instead, the surface usually forms into some angle of repose. These surfaces are also porous to ultrasonic sound burst, and they attenuate the pulses. In such cases, the reflected signal is complex, and the instrument reads an average level of the material. Experience and the microprocessor have made these granular determinations feasible.

Powders The surface of powdery materials in tanks or bins is always irregular. The level of these materials can be gauged by ultrasonics, except when the powder is excessively aerated, specifically where pneumatic transportation may have been used to convey it. A vessel containing this type of material should be allowed to settle before a reliable ultrasonic level reading is attempted and recorded.

Ultrasonic Echo-ranging Level Sensor Details

The following sections describe and explain some of the acoustic physics associated with ultrasonic echo-ranging level sensor operation. Understanding these is important to ensure successful application of all such instruments.

When a sound wave strikes the interface between two media of different physical properties (for example, air and water), some of the wave is reflected and some is transmitted through the new medium.

How much of the sound is reflected and how much is transmitted by the new medium depends on acoustic impedance:

$$\text{Impedance} = \text{Acoustic Density of Medium} \times \text{Velocity of Sound}$$

The greater the difference in impedance between the two media, the greater the reflection. Ultrasonics work extremely well when measuring the level of materials with significantly greater density than air, because density is a major factor in determining impedance.

As with the reflection of light waves, sound waves are reflected according to the following formula: Angle of incidence = angle of reflection. When the level of solids that do not present a uniformly flat surface is measured, some of the sound will be deflected away from the sensor. Strong transmit power can assure adequate return echoes in many cases.

Intensity

The intensity of sound (acoustic intensity) decreases as the distance from the source of sound increases, because a given amount of mechanical energy is spread out over an increasingly larger area.

Intensity increases with increased amplitude of vibration. This increase in intensity requires more energy. When transmit power is added to an ultrasonic sensor to achieve greater intensity, a longer effective echo range is obtained.

Intensity increases with the area of the vibrating object. For example, longer-range transducers employ cylindrical surfaced reflector-type sensors for added power without large, cumbersome size.

The intensity of sound for a given power source will be greatly increased if it is highly focused in a single direction.

Absorption

Absorption is the loss of sound energy through its conversion into heat, resulting in attenuation of the sound pulse. Absorption increases with an increase in frequency, so that, with a given power level, higher frequencies cannot travel as far and return with an adequate echo. The presence of steam and high humidity also increase the absorption of sound energy. The problems of absorption may be reduced with the use of increased transmit power and lower frequency.

Frequency

Transmitting frequency affects the performance characteristics of ultrasonic pulsed echo measurements as outlined in table 15.1

Diffraction

Diffraction occurs when a sound pulse bends around an object so that there is little or no reflection of echo generated. Diffraction increases with longer wavelengths. As the frequency of the sound wave increases (and the wavelength decreases correspondingly), the sound beam converges (for a transducer of a given

Table 15.1 Performance Characteristics

High Frequency	Low Frequency
Shorter wavelength	Longer wavelength
Greater resolution	Lower resolution (depending on signal processing)
Lower effective range	Greater effective range (without attenuation)

Reprinted by permission from *Sensors*. Copyright 1987, Helmers Publishing, Inc.

size) and is less easily diffracted. It is reflected by smaller and smaller objects. Ultrasonic sound, with its relatively high frequency, is therefore strongly reflected by most objects. Dust and liquid vapor can cause some diffraction—especially with higher frequencies. Added transmit power may help this to maintain sufficient echoes in some instances.

Transducer Frequency, Power, and Performance

Echo ranging through air (or other atmosphere) is severely hampered by the extreme difficulty with which sound is injected into any gaseous media by any ultrasonic sensor. This phenomenon has been termed *impedance mismatch*. To obtain one acoustic watt of power in air with an echo-ranging burst is extremely difficult. In water, this is done with ease. Other problems that plague through-atmosphere echo ranging are pulse spreading energy loss, energy absorption by the target, attenuation of the pulse, and reverberation. Table 15.2 defines some of the parameters that exist for transducers of various frequencies.

Echo Ranging Applications Issues

Echo Ranging in Organic Liquid Atmosphere

The closed tank contains a volatile organic chemical such as toluene. For simplicity, the "ideal gas law" applies to the atmosphere or vapor above the liquid level. At least on an instantaneous basis, it represents the mixture of air and

Table 15.2 Through-air Ultrasonic Echo Ranging

Transducer Frequency	Power Required	Distance Range	Resolving Power	Transducer Dead Band
150–200 KHz	200–400 VAC	0.5–8 FEET	0.02 INCH	3–6 INCHES
80–100 KHz	300–500 VAC	0.6–12 FEET	0.05 INCH	5–8 INCHES
35–40 KHz	400–700 VAC	1.0–35 FEET	0.25 INCH	15–24 INCHES
15–20 KHz	500–1,000 VAC	3.0–60 FEET	0.75 INCH	20–30 INCHES
7½–10 KHz	1,700–2,000 VAC	4.0–150 FEET	1.5 INCH	36–40 INCHES

Reprinted by permission from *Sensors*. Copyright 1987, Helmers Publishing, Inc.

Figure 15.11 Echo Ranging in Organic Liquid Vapor

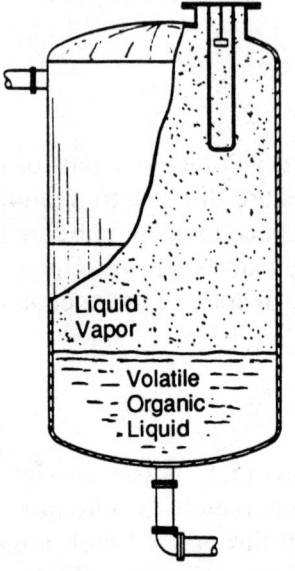

Ideal Gas Law

PV=nRT
Instananeously P, V. & T Are K

n = Number of Moles of Gas
R = Gas Law Constant @ Standard
Temperature and Pressure

Must Measure Sound Velocity

toluene vapor sufficiently for the purpose of echo-ranging level detection. Figure 15.11 illustrates such an enclosed tank whose atmosphere is some mixture of air and toluene vapor. This illustration shows a preliminary target, as described in figure 15.12. This enables continuous sound velocity determination to be substituted into the distance measurement equation: $D = \dfrac{V_a t}{2}$ where V_a is the actual

Figure 15.12 Measured Sound Velocity Calibration

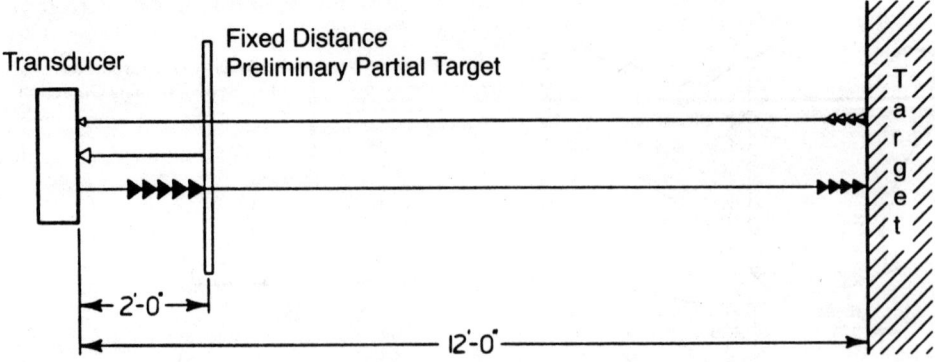

speed of sound on an instantaneous basis. What affects the speed of sound is *n*—the number of moles to toluene and air present. Because of the variability of the value of *n*, it is necessary to determine V_g, the speed of sound in the gas, on a continuous basis.

Measured Sound Velocity Calibration

Figure 15.12 illustrates one method of measuring sound velocity as a part of the "echo ranging" apparatus. However, such instruments are difficult to manufacture, calibrate, and install mechanically. They require space to accommodate the *blanking distance* or *dead band* of the echo-ranging sensor as shown. Once operational, this sensor system does the job satisfactorily in spite of its mechanical obstructions.

Continuous Sound Velocity Calibration

The composite echo-ranging sensor illustrated by figure 15.13 is one configuration that accomplishes sound velocity determinations, coupled with echo ranging on a continuous basis. It is compact and installs easily through a 4-inch nozzle opening. It is relatively simple to build in its designed embodiment, which will accommodate both Sodar[tm] and sonar level determinations with excellent overall accuracy, resolution, and repeatability.

Composite Ultrasonic Level Gauging Issues

Two transducer installation configurations are shown in figure 15.13. One is sonar and the other is Sodar. Other Sodar transducer-mounting techniques are possible and may be quite practical. Note the placement of the sonar transducer at

Figure 15.13 Autocal Echo Ranger

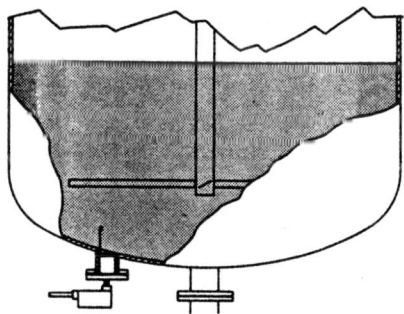
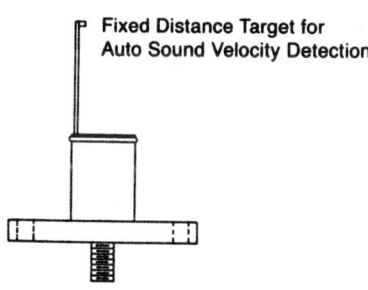

Fixed Distance Target for Auto Sound Velocity Detection

Figure 15.14 Speed of Sound versus Temperature for Nitrogen Gas Regardless of Pressure

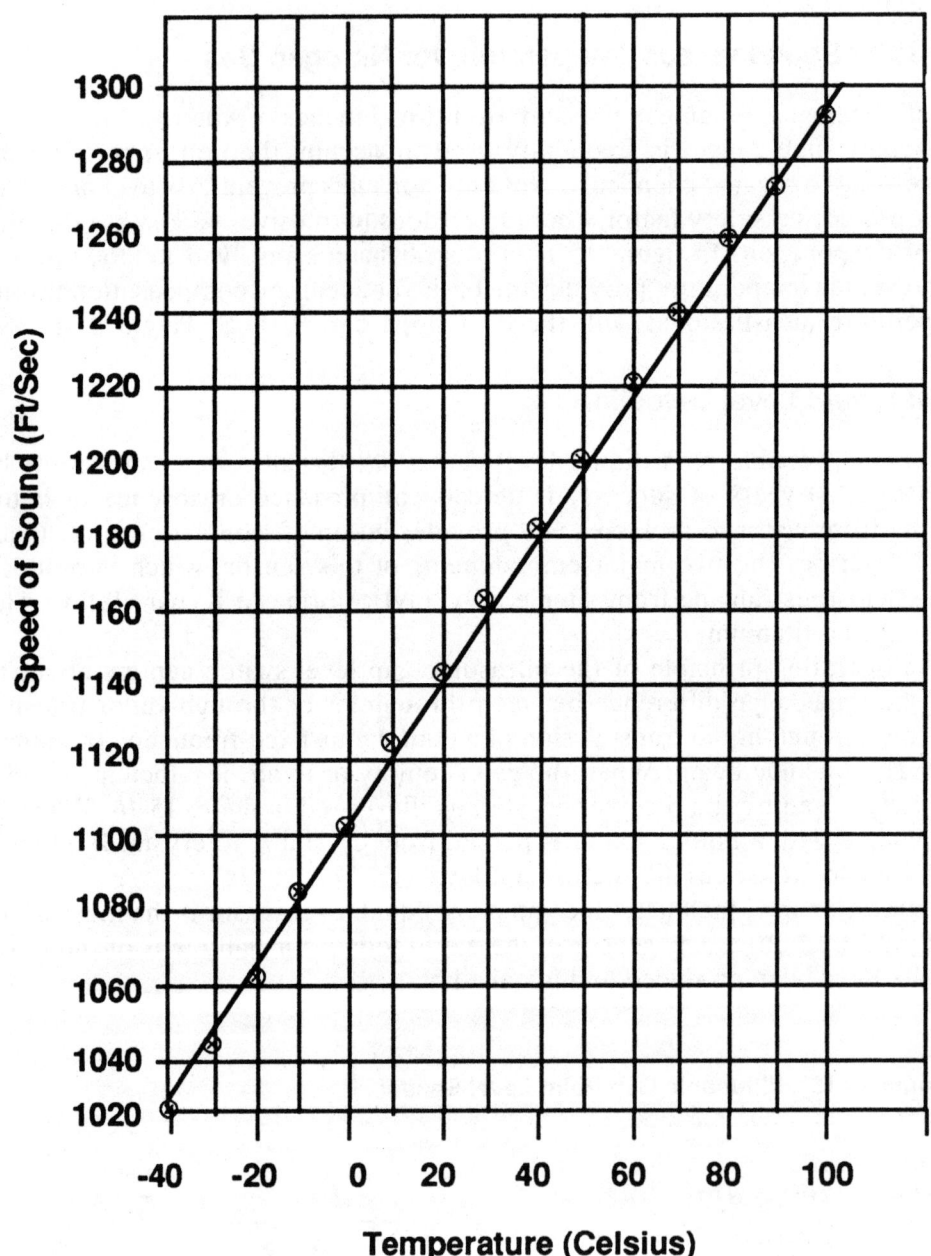

the bottom of the tank. These alternate techniques provide sufficient versatility to accommodate most storage tank applications in all of the chemical process industries.

Speed of Sound versus Temperature for Nitrogen Gas

Dry nitrogen gas, ranging in pressure from 1 to 2 inches of water to 3 to 4 pounds per square inch gauge, is frequently used to occupy the atmosphere in tanks above volatile organic chemicals. Not only does this prevent loss to evaporation, but it provides a safety factor where hazardous (explosive) vapors are the product of evaporation. In figure 15.14, the straight line resolved for the speed of sound versus temperature provides the basis for accuracy compensation through temperature measurement with the dual slope circuit (U.S. Patent 4,317,184).

Point Liquid Level Detection

For simple, reliable point liquid level detection, the ultrasonic gap sensor has more than 20 years of success. It detects the presence or absence of liquids ranging from water to molasses and provides an on/off contact closure. Figure 15.15 describes the two major embodiments of this sensor, which is produced with enclosures ranging from simple polyvinyl chloride to Kynar, Teflon, Hastellay C, and titanium.

The operating principle of the ultrasonic gap level switch centers about the acoustic impedance difference between through-air or through-vapor transmission and through-liquid transmission of a continuous fixed-frequency (nominally 1-MHz) ultrasonic beam. When the gap is empty or in air, insufficient sound (if any) is received by the receiver crystal, as illustrated in figure 15.16. When the gap is filled with a liquid, sound is passed from crystal A to crystal B and activates the electronic circuit to close a relay.

Unquestionably, the ultrasonic gap point liquid level sensor is the most widely used industrial ultrasonic sensor in the world today. Virtually tens of thousands of units have been produced and installed.

Figure 15.15 Ultrasonic Gap Point Level Sensor

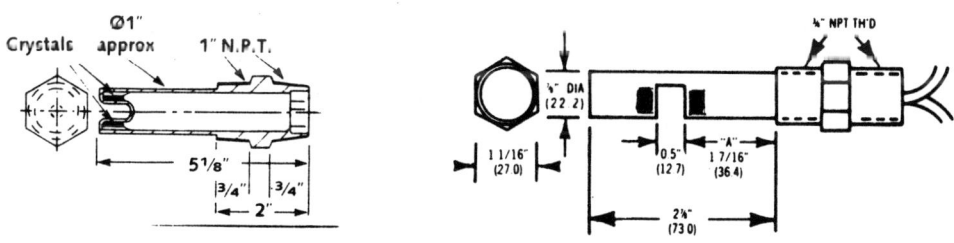

Figure 15.16 Ultrasonic Gap Crystal Function

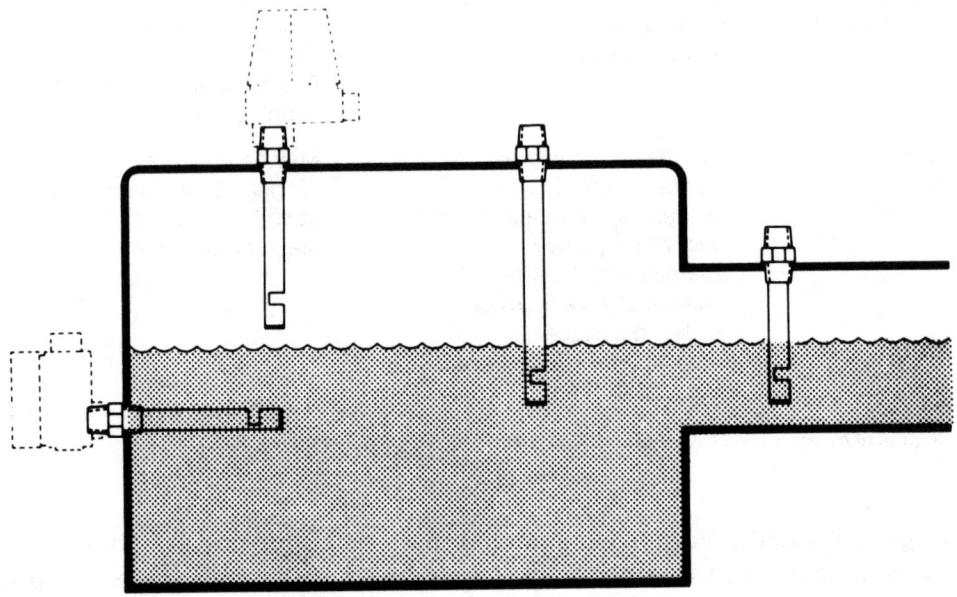

Ultrasonic Level Measurement—Dos and Don'ts

Experience has proven that 95 percent of the performance problems with ultrasonic level instruments are the result of misapplication of basically good products. From 1970 to 1976, successful ultrasonic level and open-channel flowmetering applications were those of a simple nature. Flumes and weirs were gauged without sound velocity temperature correction. Some suppliers began to achieve tank and silo level spans of 25–45 feet on both liquids and some granular solid materials. In 1978, microprocessor signal processing was applied to continuous ultrasonic level and open-channel flow. As the 1980s came in, so did *software signal* processing.

Because of the use of microprocessors for software signal processing and transducer improvements, ultrasonic level sensors provide level and volume gauging of materials in vessels ranging from a 55-gallon drum to a 1,000,000-gallon bulk storage tank. Granular solids levels in silos are measured at depths of 150–200 feet. Despite dust- and vapor-laden atmospheres within containers, reasonable gauging accuracies are achieved that facilitate process control and inventory management.

The introduction of sonar through-liquid echo ranging to the chemical process industries is a significant advance in accurate level gauging for the ultrasonic sensors. Such environmental requirements as leak detection in underground

Table 15.3 Comparison of Ranging Media

Method	Advantages	Disadvantages
Through-air, or Sodar	Noninvasive Minimum installed cost	High power required Short range Foamy surfaces fail to reflect sound pulses
Through-fluid, or sonar	Requires very low power for long distances (200–500 ft) Provides higher resolution due to higher frequency Determines tank level in the presence of a vacuum blanket over liquid surface Works when liquid surface is covered with foam	May be invasive Air bubbles in fluid cancel/absorb sound pulse and preclude operation

Reprinted by permission from *Sensors*. Copyright 1987, Helmers Publishing, Inc.

storage tanks and precision volume and mass determinations in above-ground large-volume tankage will see the use of automatic calibration sensors involving microprocessor-based software signal processing.

Table 15.3 compares through-air and through-liquid ultrasonic level gauging. The advantages of using sonar for liquid level gauging far outweigh those of Sodar in the chemical process industries. New transducer materials and techniques facilitate operating temperatures in excess of 400°F.

Table 15.4 provides a list of some of the product applications that have been made with various ultrasonic level sensors. In the evolution of this technology, products have been perfected that can be used as web guides, that can measure

Table 15.4 Some Ultrasonic Echo-ranging Instrument Applications

Liquids and solids level management

Vehicular sensing systems—eyes to the rear

Presence sensing—automatic door opener control

Electronic tape measure

Proximity-sensing for security systems

Camera focus control

Robotics position and alignment sensing

Conveyor belt material level

Railroad car fill profile

Web tension control by loop volume detection

the distance of a razor-sharp knife edge above a work product or from a transducer surface, and that can measure the thickness of a piece of metal or plastic to within .0001 of an inch at a distance up to 4 feet away. These capabilities are a direct result of work done in the fields of antisubmarine warfare, photography, and the medical area, as well as the application of the resultant techniques to industrial opportunities.

Flow Measurement with Ultrasonics

Ultrasonic Open Channel Flowmeters

The use of ultrasonic echo ranging to determine open channel flow is a major application of continuous level gauging. Flow is determined by gauging the head of the fluid flowing through a *primary flow element,* such as a flume, nozzle, or weir. Level measurements are correlated to the flow tables for the primary element, resulting in flow rate output from the electronics. The following definitions explain terms used in discussing ultrasonic open channel flow.

Open Channel	Any fluid flow conduit in which one surface of the fluid is free and unbounded. The free fluid surface is assumed to be in contact with normal air at atmospheric pressure.
Noninvasive	A term describing a technique in which the sensor used to gauge flow by open channel echo ranging will not be in direct contact with the liquid surface.
Flowmeter	Any electronic device that determines the volume of fluid flow through an open channel in a given period of time by interpreting gauging point head data. In this use, a flowmeter measures volumetric transfer and also transmits data to record flow information at a remote location for use in process monitoring and control.

Primary Flow Elements

A *primary flow element* is any conduit for channeling fluid flow wherein a simple head measurement may provide an indication of the free-flow fluid volume by solution of a specific flow equation. All primary elements create some restriction

Table 15.5 Summary of Open-Channel Flow Elements

Weirs—sharp crested

Rectangular

V-notch (90, 60, 30 and 22½ degrees)

Trapezoidal (including cipoletti)

Other—compound weirs

Flumes

Parshall

Palmer-Bowlus

Other

Trapezoidal

HS, H, HL

Open Flow Nozzles

Konnleon nozzle

Parabolic nozzle

California pipe discharge method

Reprinted by permission from *Sensors*. Copyright 1987, Helmers Publishing, Inc.

to flow, resulting in an increase in upstream head. This increase in head is directly related to the rate of flow. The mathematical relationship of head to flow volume is different for each type and size of primary flow element. Overall flowmeter and primary flow element accuracies of ±8 to ±10 percent of full scale are reasonable expectations.

The most common primary elements are listed in table 15.5. In general, sharp-crested weirs are suitable for liquids not carrying solid materials. Flumes are applicable for flows containing solid materials. The Parshall flume undoubtedly provides the best combination of range of measurement and tolerance of water-borne solids.

Details of Ultrasonic Open-Channel Flowmeters

Figure 15.17 illustrates an ultrasonic echo-ranging open-channel flowmeter operating in a Parshall flume. This microprocessor-based instrument converts head measurements obtained at H_a (the free-flow discharge gauging point for a normal Parshall flume) to a flow rate signal and performs such necessary instrument functions as determining flow rate output via a 4–20mA current loop; totalizing

Figure 15.17 Ultrasonic Open-Channel Flowmeter

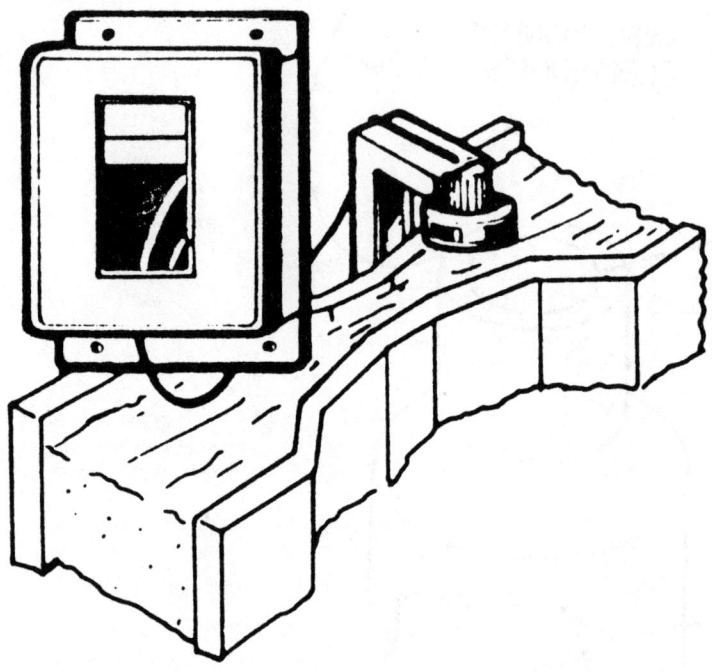

flow throughput; proportionally actuating a water sampler or chlorine dose monitor; and actuating high- and/or low-flow alarms. The display reads out flow in all common engineering units. Many other data manipulations are possible from modern microprocessor-based instruments.

In an effort to obtain greater accuracy and eliminate the head loss associated with the use of primary flow elements, Q = AV meters—Area times Velocity Equals the Quantity of fluid flowing instruments (Q = AV)—have been perfected. Figure 15.18 illustrates one such meter that is easy to install in any conduit and that gives far better accuracy (±2 percent of flow) than the combination of primary flow element and head gauge. Head is measured to determine the area of cross-section through which the liquid is flowing by ultrasonic echo ranging. One or more separate ultrasonic Doppler sensors determine flow velocity. A microprocessor-based receiver performs the calculation of Q = AV and outputs flow data. One area-times-velocity flowmeter is available with field switch selectable operation capability for circles, ellipsoids, and squares. This meter may be installed in a matter of hours. The accuracy and economy of these sensors have made them the current preferred choice for open channel flow installations.

Figure 15.18 An Ultrasonic Area Times Velocity Equals Flow

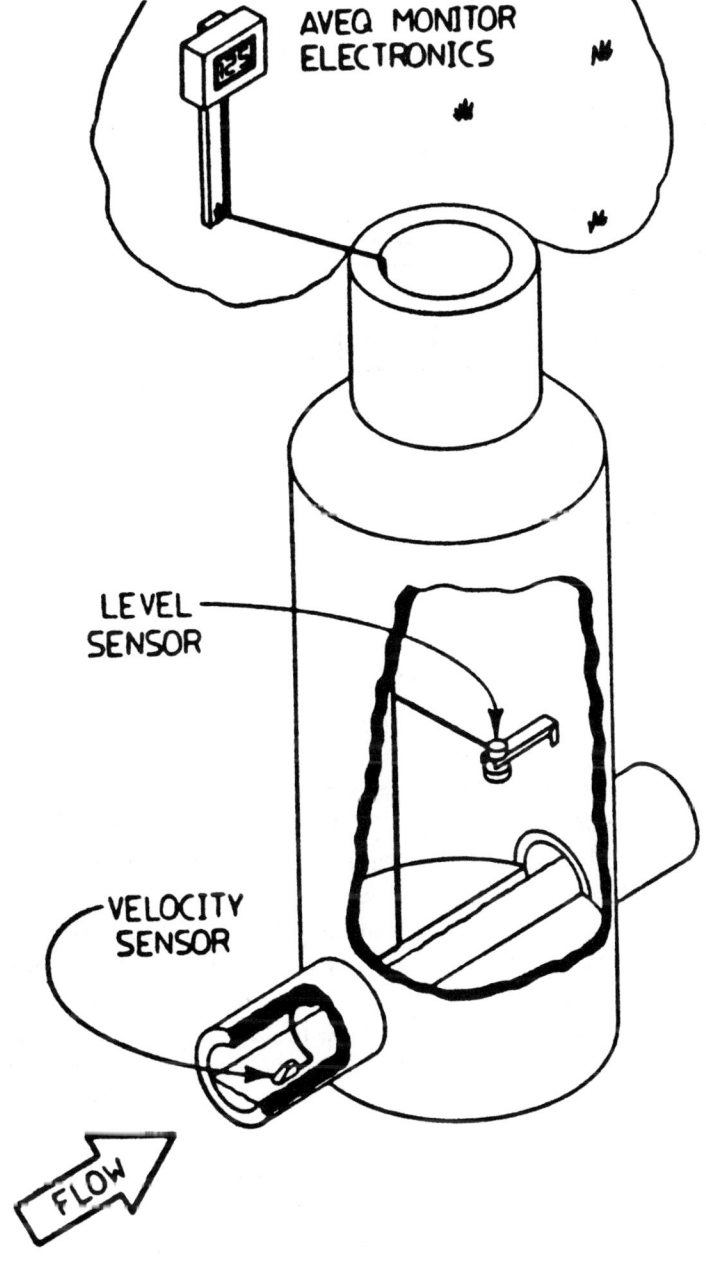

Figure 15.19 Ultrasonic Composition Sensor

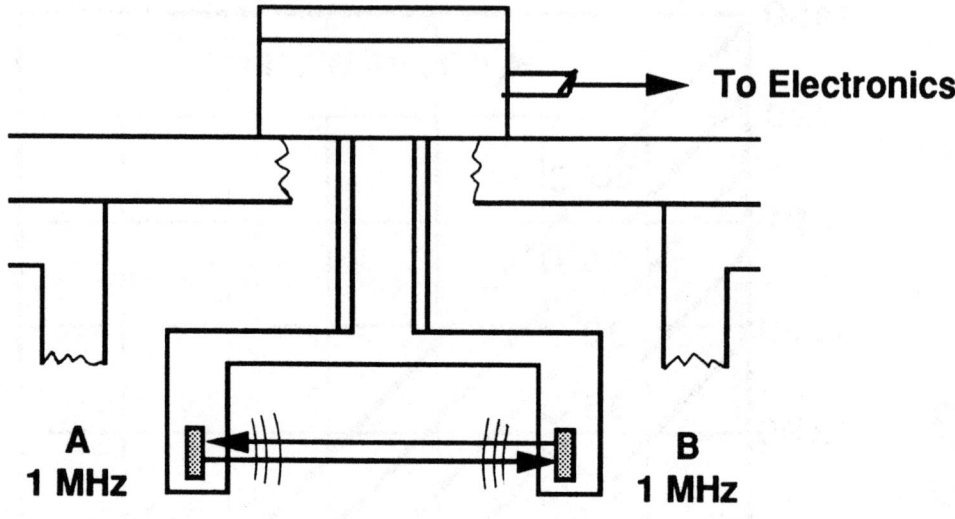

Composition Measurement

A wide variety of liquids, acids, bases, alcohols, and other aqueous solutions, emulsions, and suspensions may be characterized by determining the velocity at which sound travels through them over a fixed distance at constant temperature. Figure 15.19 illustrates a sensor system that performs this analysis. An accurate temperature sensor accompanies the "fixed-path" ultrasonic sound velocity transducer. This system is capable of performing over a temperature range of −40°C to +350°C under pressures up to 2500 PSIG. It is particularly constructed to perform in highly corrosive process media such as crude oil transfer pipelines.

An early application of this technology was to determine when a change in composition, such as from gasoline to fuel oil, occurred in a cross-country pipeline. Subsequent applications include the concentration of sulfuric acid and sodium hydroxide, as shown in figure 15.20. The *composition monitor* is another sensor that has been advanced because of the microprocessor and LSI memory chips that provide both signal processing and "look-up" table capacity.

Full-Pipe Ultrasonic Flowmeters

Beginning in the 1920s, activity was directed to perfect full-pipe ultrasonic liquid and slurry flow sensors. The early products were represented as anything from a solution for every flow metering challenge to a last-resort device, to be applied

Figure 15.20 Sulfuric Acid Concentration

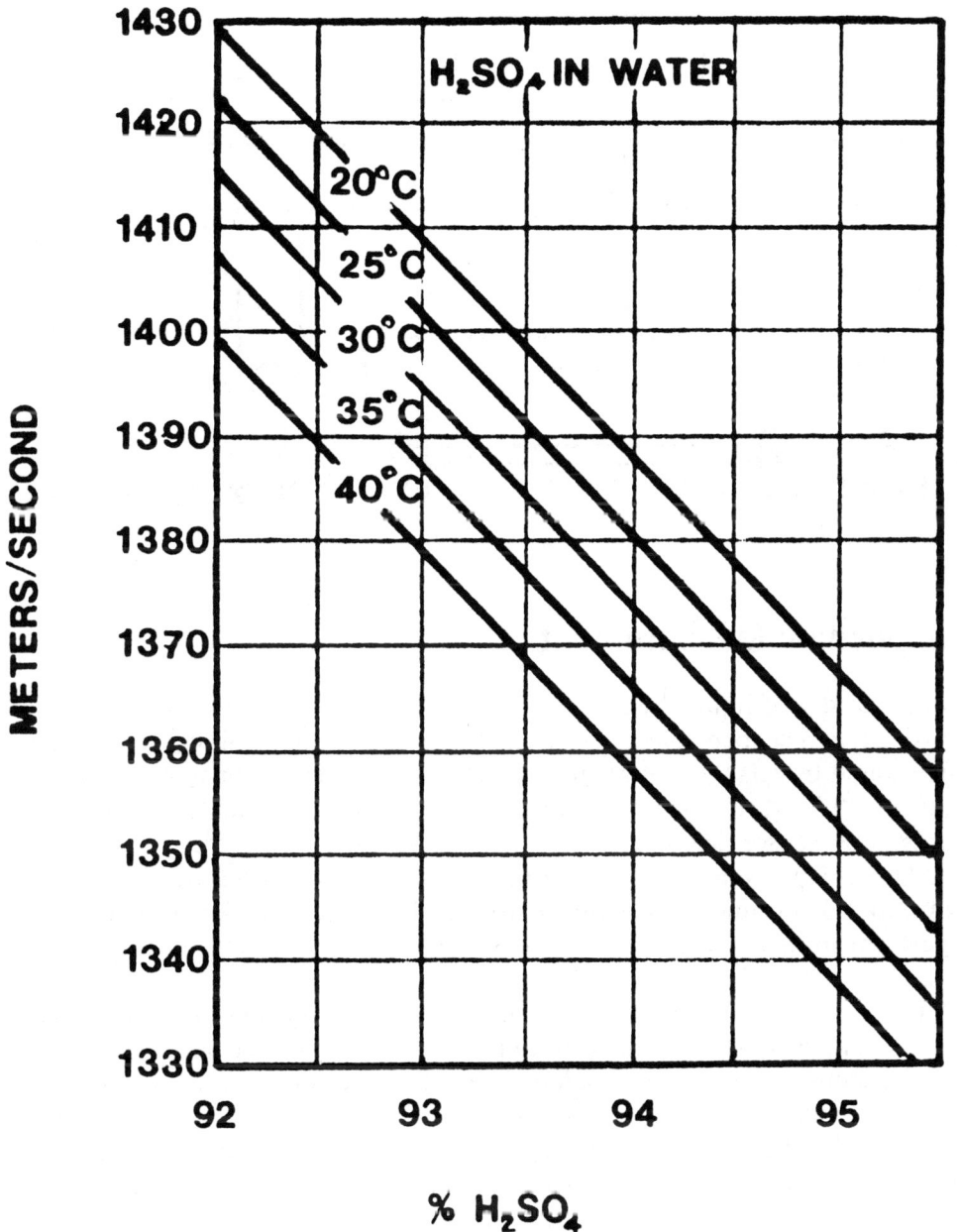

only when nothing else could do the job. An overall lack of applications understanding, and unrealistic claims by sales representatives and manufacturers, resulted in some products being regarded with great skepticism. The early lack of applications data and technique has been displaced by the introduction of high-quality smart sensors by competent applications engineers. Any decision to use an ultrasonic flowmeter should be made knowing both the advantages and the shortcomings of the particular sensor and its technology, as well as the application for which the sensor is to be used. Consider the following design and operations criteria:

- Each flowmeter consists of at least two distinct components:
  - One or more sensors
  - An electronic transmitter/receiver

- All ultrasonic flowmeters use piezoelectric crystals in either a pulse- or a continuous-tone mode to detect flow. Each sensor includes one or more piezoelectric elements. Considerably more technical skill is needed to produce reliable, accurate sensors than to produce a correspondingly good electronics package.

- Each type of ultrasonic sensor has specific areas of application. No single unit is available that fulfills all flow metering requirements.

Doppler Shift Flowmeters

When a fixed-frequency sound beam is directed at a moving object, it will be reflected, and a modified frequency will be observed. This frequency shift is known as the Doppler shift, and it is directly proportional to the velocity of the moving flow object. The *in-line-parallel* sensor has two crystals, one for transmitting and one for receiving (see figure 15.21).

The Doppler shift caused by the moving liquid is detected and processed in the electronics. The fluid must have two phases, or *acoustic density infaces,* to obtain Doppler shift. The interface may result from entrained air, suspended solids, or hydraulic density interfaces caused by the physical chemistry of the liquid. The major disadvantage of the Doppler flow sensor is its lack of response to single-phase fluid flows unless a secondary phase is introduced artificially into the flow stream. Aeration is the most common means by which this is achieved.

Quality Doppler flow sensors operate satisfactorily on fluids with very low suspended solids content, particles a few microns in diameter, and concentrations as low as 100 ppm. This sensor is suitable for measuring flow in most multiphased fluids and slurries, including sludges.

Figure 15.21 In-Line-Parallel Crystal Doppler Sensor

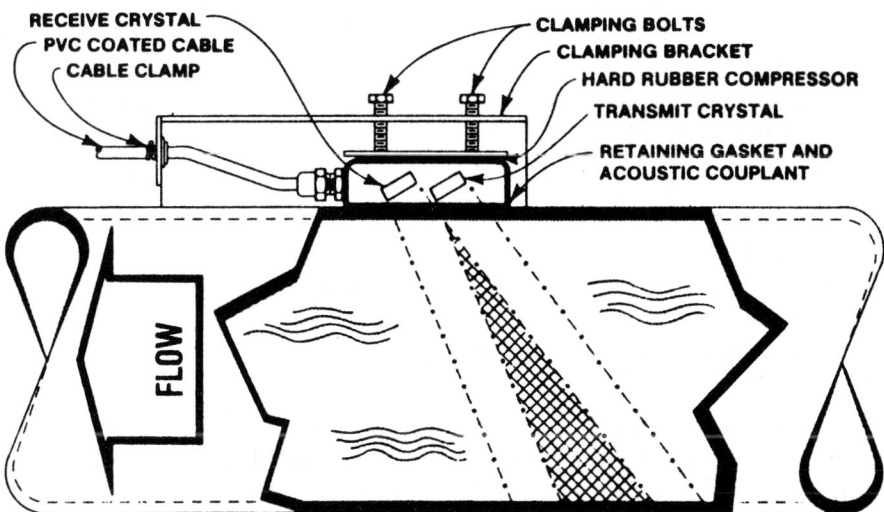

In the Doppler shift method, only some of the sound energy is reflected. One might conclude from this that only limited penetration of the fluid is achieved in high-solids slurry gauging. However, tests on pipe up to 72 inches in diameter, using two in-line-parallel sensors—one for transmit and the other for receive—has negated this hypothesis. The instrument performed equally well and was referenced against a differential pressure Venturi meter upstream in the line. If instrument tuning and calibration is implemented immediately upon installation, performance with accuracy comparable to that of a Venturi meter is readily obtained. In many installations, Doppler velocity sensors are operating quite successfully on pipes from 0.5 to 100 inches in diameter.

The angle at which the transmitted sound wave enters the fluid is fundamental to successful signal processing. Alignment of the Doppler transducer parallel to the axis of flow is mandatory. The transducer assembly must be clamped flat against an absolutely clean outer surface. A good ultrasonic couplant must be used to ensure maximum sound injection through the pipe wall into the flow stream.

It is important that a well-constructed and properly designed in-line-parallel transducer can give full-pipe flow-scanning accuracy and flow-profile integration. Of particular importance is this transducer's ability to accommodate low flow velocities. Meters using this transducer design are in operation on flow velocity spans ranging from 0.5–1.5 to 0.5–40 feet per second.

Figure 15.22 illustrates a *wetted* or *insertion* Doppler transducer. Its disadvantage is its invasive nature; some of its advantages are that it circumvents the

Figure 15.22 Wetted Doppler Flow Sensor

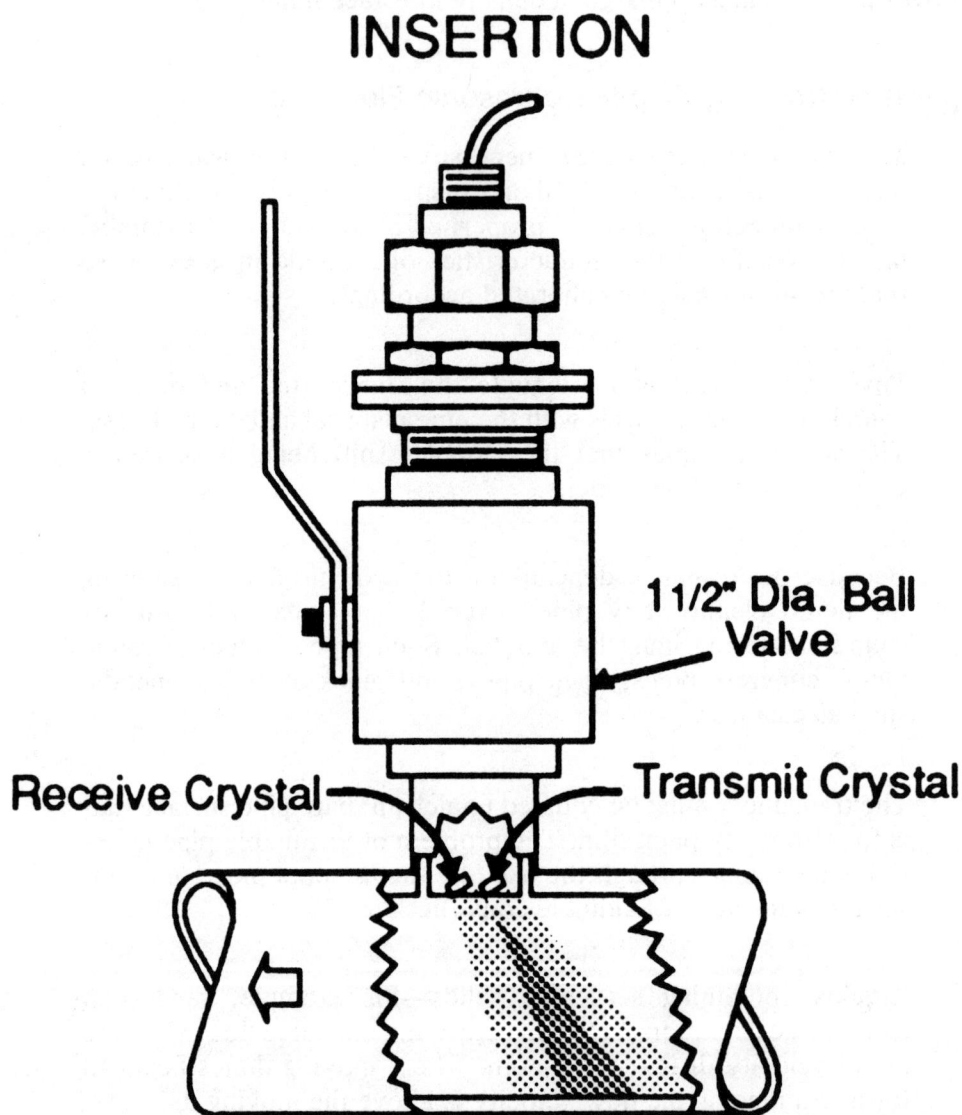

problem of pipe material through which a sound beam simply will not transmit (cement, glass lining, cast iron, and other porous composite materials) and it improves performance on marginal density interface fluids.

Application Notes on Doppler Ultrasonic Flowmeters

- Most Doppler sensors are of necessity calibrated on water-based flow systems. Both dissolved and suspended solids can affect the "sound reflection-velocity" properties of the water. It is important to specify all the characteristics of the fluid in question so that the sensor may be calibrated accordingly.

- Pipe walls refract and attenuate the transmitted and received sound. The degree varies with the pipe material and its thickness. The sensor assumes that the Doppler shift being measured is caused only by flow velocity.

- Because performance depends on the acoustic beam's entering the liquid cleanly, any pipe material that causes reflection or sound scattering must be avoided. Such pipes include ceramic pipes, concrete pipes, lined pipes, and pipes of porous metals, such as cast iron.

- The transducer must be coupled to a clean, bare pipe surface that is free from any paint film. The problem of unsuitable pipe material is overcome through the use of either a spool piece or an insertion transducer of suitable construction.

- Liquids containing settleable solids—for example, sand—can cause large deviations between actual and indicated flow when the liquid velocity drops to the point where moving dunes begin to form. As long as the flow velocity is above the moving dune formation point, there is no difficulty.

- Typically, Doppler flow sensors have been noninvasive. Consequently, existing piping can be fitted with flowmeters at a minimum cost. Instrument maintenance may be completed without plant shutdowns. Sensors made from exotic materials are not required for toxic or corrosive fluids, because no contact is made with the troublesome fluid.

Transit-Time Flowmeters

The first ultrasonic *upstream-downstream* or *time-of-flight* flowmeter was patented in Germany by Rutten in 1928. In 1954, H. P. Kalmus measured flow velocity in a pipe using externally mounted (clamp-on) transducers to generate and detect the contrapropagating sound waves. However, not until the 1970s were *transmit-time* flowmeters perfected for industrial flow monitoring. A typical clamp-on-sensor transit-time system is illustrated in figure 15.23.

The operating principle of a transit-time flowmeter is as follows: The velocity of a sound pulse traveling from sensor A to sensor B will be equal that of one from B to A in a still fluid in figure 15.23. When the liquid is pumped through the pipe, the speed of sound from A to B will increase, and that from B to A will decrease. This change is detected and processed electronically. The resulting analog signal is linear with respect to velocity.

Figure 15.23 Flowmeter Using Transit-Time Clamp-on Sensors

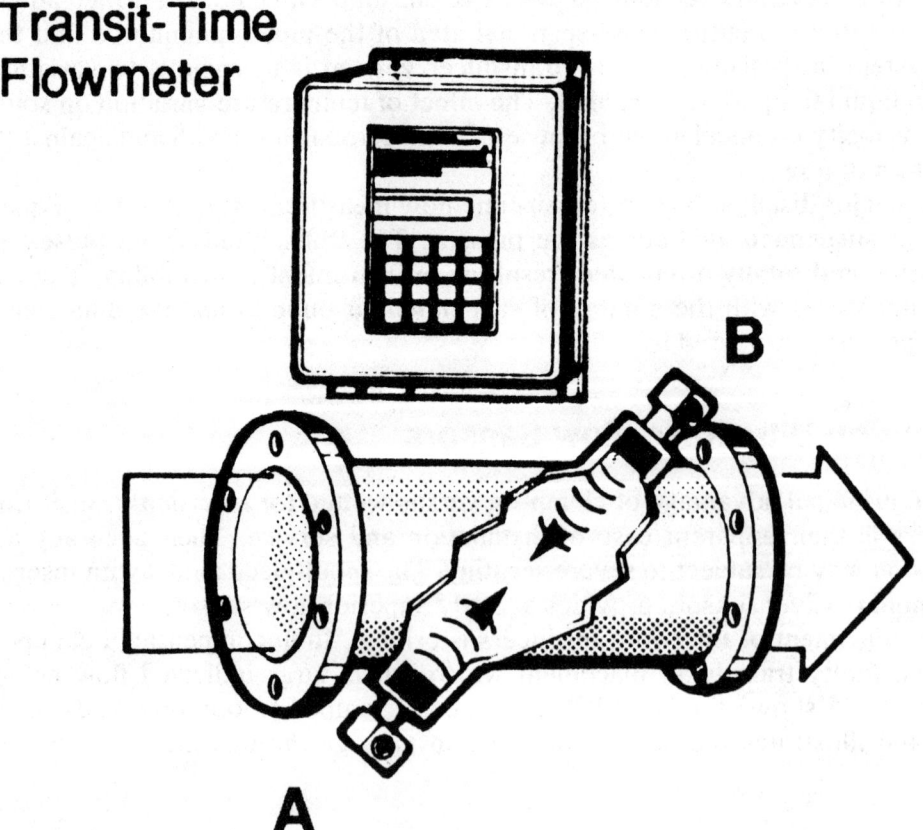

Figure 15.24 Transit-Time Flow Sensors

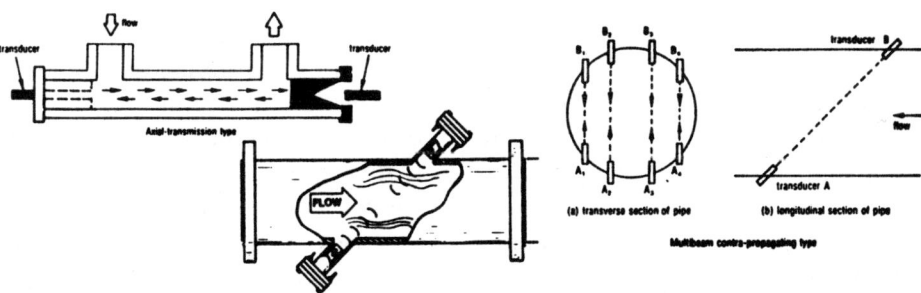

Other important forms of transit-time flow sensors, as shown in figure 15.24, are axial-transmission, longitudinal, and multibeam sensors. Both operating experience and mathematical evaluation have substantiated that the wetted-sensor version of the transit-time ultrasonic flowmeter is the most accurate and reliable.

The primary advantage of transit-time flow measurement is its pure liquid measuring capability. Deionized water is one important fluid. Further advantages are that the entire cross-sectional area of the pipe is monitored and that the system in its fixed insertion transducer version is insensitive to variations due to liquid temperature changes. The effect of temperature variation on sound pulse velocity is canceled out because of contrapropagation with and against the direction of flow.

The major disadvantage of transit-time flow measurement occurs when quantities of suspended air bubbles are present. The transmitted sound pulses are disrupted and totally attenuated, resulting in instrument inoperability. The cut-off point varies with the number of suspended air bubbles and the diameter of the pipe being measured.

Clamp-on Ultrasonic Flow Sensors

The principal advantage of clamp-on versus wetted (or insertion) transit-time sensors is their apparent ease of installation and service. Their accuracy and precision may be subject to severe scrutiny. The spool-piece model with inserted (but noninvasive) sensors provides a vastly superior flow sensor.

The alignment of the two transducers is critical. In uncompensated clamp-on meters, faulty transducer placement will result in large indicated flow errors. Figure 15.25 shows the A and B transducers clamped to opposite sides of the pipe and illustrates the pulsed sound beam passage through the pipe wall and fluid.

Figure 15.25 Sound Propagation with Clamp-on Sensors

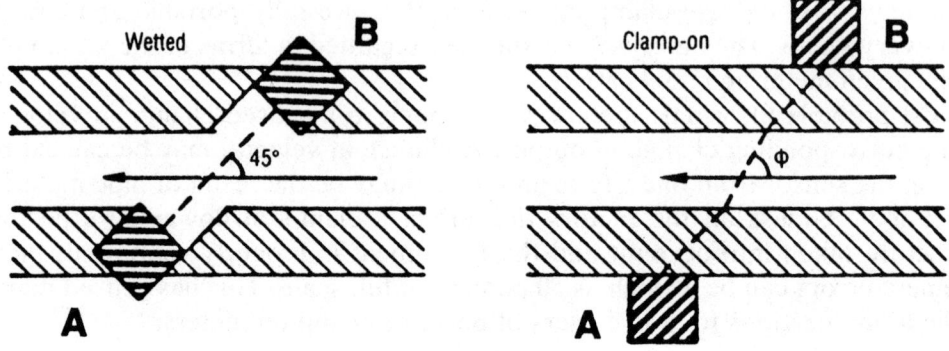

Sound Propagation Issues

An angle of insertion exists as a result of *shear mode wave propagation* by the sound beam as it enters the pipe material. The angle of entry must equal the angle of exit at the receiving transducer for acceptable performance. This dictates the need for precise transducer alignment upon installation, or for some automatic correction via electronic signal processing.

Both transit-time and Doppler flowmeters arrived with the same difficulties as liquid level and open channel flowmeters. There were a number of difficulties, most of them associated with the pipe material and the fluid flowing. Clamp-on flow sensors of both types were easy to use. Instrument and process engineers throughout the chemical process industries applied the early ultrasonic flow sensors because they were less costly and required little installation effort and expense. Early clamp-on applications were limited to those contained in table 15.6.

Table 15.6 Early Ultrasonic Full-pipe Flowmeter Applications

Doppler	Transit-Time
Waste water flows	Clear water or chemicals
Wood pulp slurry	120°F Max. temp.
Mining slurry	Large-diameter pipes
120°F Max. temp.	Gas-free liquids a must
±2.0% Full-scale accuracy	+ ½% Full-scale accuracy

Portable Ultrasonic Clamp-on Flow Sensors

It has been stated that because most Doppler and some transit-time flow sensors are noninvasive and use clamp-on sensors, they are fully portable and can be used everywhere. They are, if the results are regarded in terms of the variability of any given meter and application.

Most protable ultrasonic meters will respond to a sensed change in velocity with a corresponding change in output. A change in velocity may be caused by moving the sensor from one site to another or may be the result of pipe material differences. Unless all the factors that affect a clamp-on flowmeter's performance are taken into account and the instrument is properly calibrated, measurement errors can be as high as 50 percent of full scale. This has caused major application questions for some users of portable clamp-on meters.

Summary

In summary, it is essential that any user of ultrasonic full-pipe flow sensors keep the following guidelines in mind:

- The majority of acoustic flowmeters available are basically good instruments. Some products are more versatile than others.

- Do not use price as a criteria for purchase. You will only get what you pay for.

- The sensor or transducer is a major portion of the total instrument even though it may appear to be a small physical part.

- Technical support by the manufacturer's factory engineers may be of significant value to a successful installation.

- Do not deviate from the manufacturer's expressed instructions for installation, start-up, and operation.

- If it is the last thing you do, have the supplier send a factory service engineer to your plant for "start-up" or "installation certification" before you decide: "That ultrasonic flowmeter is no good!" The fault in a majority of cases lies in misapplication, improper installation, a faulty part, faulty calibration, or a misunderstanding.

Note: Today an ultrasonic flow sensor is applicable for almost any fluid, sludge, or slurry encountered in the chemical process industries. Two manufacturers have perfected gas (full-pipe) flow sensors using transit-time techniques.

Coupled with a composition sensor continuously monitoring the specific gravity of a fluid, a transit-time sensor may be an ultrasonic mass flow sensor of reasonable accuracy and precision. One reason such a sensor may not have been pursued on a more rigorous industrial scale was the perfection and introduction of the Coriolus mass flow sensor in the early 1980s.

References

Publications

1. Aronson, Milton A., ed. *Flow Handbook and Buyer's Guide.* Pittsburgh, PA: Measurements and Data Corp., 1985.

2. Bailey, S. J. "Level Sensing Technology Rises to Logistic Demand." *Control Engineering* (July 1986):87–94.

3. ———. "Mass Metering and Precision Volumetrics Abound in Flow Control." *Control Engineering* (March 1987):47–53.

4. Biber, C., S. Ellin, K. Shenk, and J. Stempeck. "The Polaroid Ultrasonic Ranging System." *Proceedings of the 67th Convention of AES,* October 31, 1980.

5. DeCarlo, J. P. *Fundamentals of Flow Measurement.* Research Triangle Park, NC: Instrument Society of America, 1984.

6. Donovan, John. "Looking at Sensors—A User's Perspective." *Plant Engineering* (September 25, 1986):60–65.

7. Hueter and Bolt. *Sonics: Techniques for the Use of Sound and Ultrasound in Engineering and Science.* New York: John Wiley, 1955.

8. Lazenby, Brian. "Level Monitoring and Control." *Chemical Engineering* (January 14, 1980):88–96.

9. Lowell, F. C., Jr., and F. Hirschfeld. "Acoustic Flowmeters for Pipelines." *Mechanical Engineering* vol. 101, no. 10 (October 1979):29–35.

10. Meinhold, T. F. "Liquid Flow Meters." *Plant Engineering* (November 21, 1984):46–60.

11. "Ultrasonic Flow Meters." *Measurements & Control* (October 1986):104–9.

12. *Ultrasonics for Medical Diagnostics*. Textbook for a professional course. Pittsburgh, PA: Medical Electronics, 1984.

13. Yost, Rod. "Doppler Effect Tied to Flow Rate." *Water/Engineering & Management* (March 1987):30–31.

Patents

1. Adams, et al., Ultrasonic Transducer with Reference Locator. U.S. Patent 4,130,018, issued December 19, 1978.

2. Dorr. Ultrasonic Apparatus for Determining the Amount of Liquid in a Container of Known Volume. U.S. Patent 4,715,226, issued December 28, 1987.

3. Fitzgerald, J. W., et al. Method for Determining the Constitution of Milk. U.S. Patent 3,040,562, issued June 26, 1962.

4. Lescheck, et al. Replaceable Element Ultrasonic Flowmeter Transducer. U.S. Patent Reissue Re 29,785, issued September 26, 1978.

5. Leszczynski, N. G. Dual Slope Compensation Apparatus. U.S. Patent 4,317,184, issued February 23, 1982.

6. Newman, R. A. Echo Location System for Measuring Liquid Level and Flow. U.S. Patent 4,145,914, issued July 25, 1977.

7. Polaroid Company. U.S. Patents 4,440,482 and 4,439,846, issued April 3, 1984, and March 27, 1984.

8. Raytheon Company. U.S. Patent 3,674,945, issued July 4, 1972.

9. Zacharias, Jr. Electroacoustic Transducer Assembly for Concentration by Sound Velocity. U.S. Patent 3,890,423, issued June 6, 1975.

Chapter 16 Sensor Fusion

David A. Dornfeld

Introduction

The Developing Needs of Sensors in Manufacturing Automation

Consumers are now demanding products that are reasonably priced, reliable, and tailored to their needs. As a result, manufacturers have had to develop manufacturing systems that are flexible and that can accommodate a variety of products promising high performance. According to Ayres [3], high performance demands precision and complexity of differing degrees and, because complexity is often accompanied by a higher likelihood of defects and errors, increased attention to monitoring and screening devices during production is also required.

The expense of automating manufacturing operations is high enough that operation around the clock is often required. These processes are necessarily untended or minimally tended because of the expense of labor or the lack of trained personnel to monitor the process. Thus, there is also a great demand for monitoring systems to ensure the safe and efficient performance of these systems during untended operation. Add to this the great diversity of materials, operating conditions, and tooling likely to be experienced over the range of workpieces produced, and it is highly likely that malfunctions will occur. In the absence of good models of these processes to predict performance, sensors have been utilized in these systems to reduce the likelihood of unexpected malfunctions. Studies have pointed out the pivotal role that sensing technology will play in the development of future factory systems (Ito [34]). As pointed out earlier, both processing and system conditions must be monitored to ensure optimum performance. Ito predicts that compact multiple-purpose sensors and sensors for "ambiguity factors" will be developed. Sensor fusion is a technique enabling both types of developments to occur.

Because sensor fusion is most often embodied in what could be referred to as an *intelligent sensor,* I will first discuss, generally, the concept of an intelligent sensor and then go into some detail on the sensor fusion strategies employed.

Intelligent Sensors Defined

Intelligent sensing systems have been associated most commonly with robot systems operating in unstructured environments. This has been motivated by the need to integrate multiple sensors for flexibility in control of the robot [63]. In these applications, information from only one sensor is generally insufficient to allow complete specification of the environment for task planning and execution. Multiple sensors are often employed for object location and recognition, for example, and they can employ cameras, infrared, ultrasonic, and tactile sensing devices. The integration of the data from all of these sensors operating simultaneously is the major challenge for sensor fusion methodologies in robot applications. A number of excellent references are listed at the end of this chapter for readers who want further information on this subject. Some of the fusion methodologies, as applied in manufacturing process monitoring, are described in more detail later in this chapter.

Figure 16.1 The Autonomy of Intelligent Machine Tool

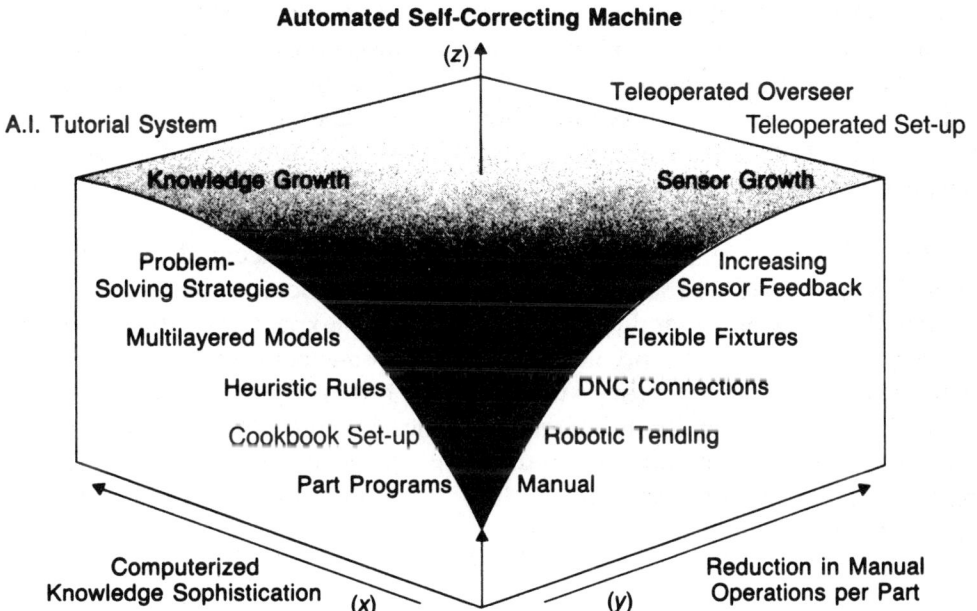

INTRODUCTION

Figure 16.2 Intelligent Control Architecture

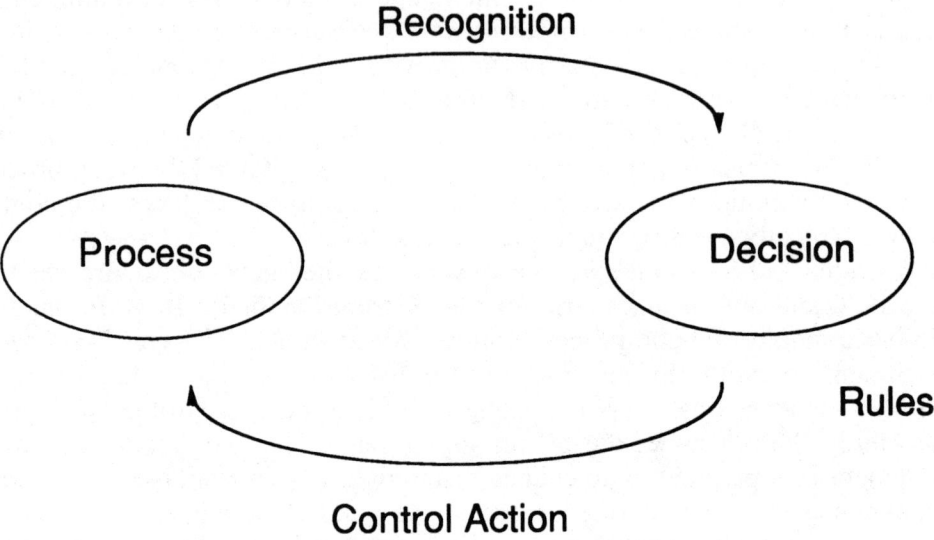

Figure 16.3 Distribution of Intelligent Control in a Machining Operation

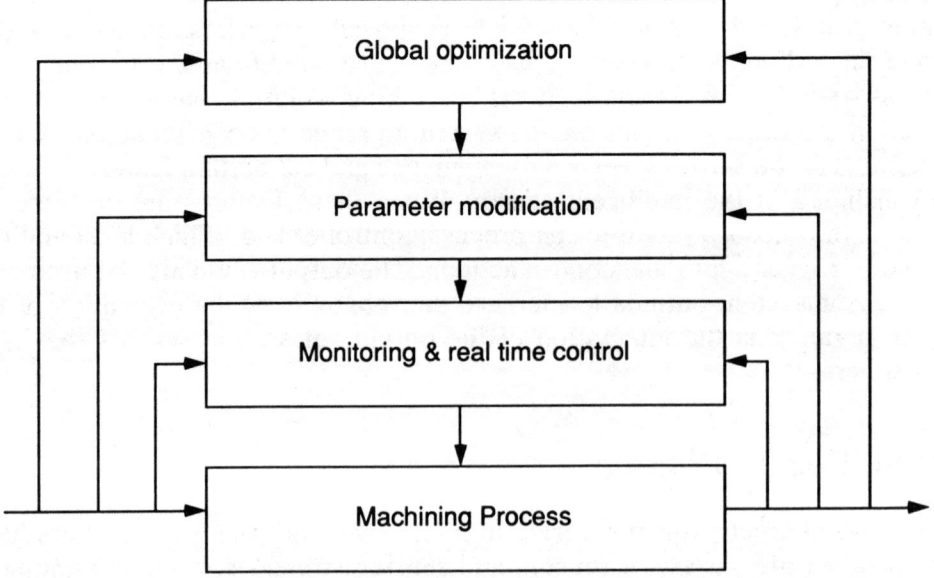

The focus in this chapter will be on the realization of intelligent manufacturing systems or, at the least, intelligent machines. Wright and Bourne [76] explore the anatomy and characteristics of intelligent machines. The development of these machines, which they term *automated self-correcting machines,* is in response to growing requirements for the growth in knowledge and sensor feedback in manufacturing operations (figure 16.1). A key part of any intelligent machine is control, which often serves to link the process function of the machine with the decision-making function. The second vital link between process and decision-making is the sensor feedback. In complex machines, the control functions typically are distributed over several layers.

Masushima and Sata [48] give one view of the intelligent control architecture (figure 16.2) and outline a scenario for this distribution (figure 16.3). In this scenario basic monitoring and process control (for example, feed speed control of a machining operation, in this case, in response to measured cutting force) are at the lowest level (fast response using a predetermined algorithm with fixed parameters), then intermediate processing of sensor-derived data for modification of algorithm parameters to change machining state in response to change in the machining environment (medium response), and at the highest level a global optimization that can suggest changes in more basic process set-up features, such as tool geometry or work material, in response to trends extracted from sensor and performance data accumulated over time (slow response). The highest level can also suggest changes in the algorithm used at the lower levels.

Yamasaki [79] also identifies intelligent sensors as part of the lowest layer in a multilayer control system for complex processes. In that work, which discusses feature extraction for speech pattern recognition, an intermediate layer that provides some control and optimization at the lower level as well is described.

Intelligent sensor systems have been proposed for process monitoring that include, in addition to the basic sensor and signal conditioning electronics usually associated with sensors, decision-making abilities based on feature-extraction techniques that enable the system to render a decision on the state of the process at the sensor level. Self-diagnostics and calibration features are also often included in the intelligent sensor. When these features are present, the output of the sensor system to the process controller is at a high level and can be used to trigger additional control actions. The output could also be used with other sensor system outputs to increase the reliability of the estimation of the process state. It is the integration of the outputs of several sensors that is of interest here.

Sensor Fusion Defined

With a specific focus for monitoring in mind, over the years, researchers have developed a wide variety of sensors and sensing strategies, each attempting to predict or detect a specific phenomenon during the operation of the process and

in the presence of noise and other environmental contaminants. Although these specific techniques have been able to accomplish the task for a narrow set of conditions, they have almost uniformly failed to be reliable enough to work over the range of operating conditions and environments commonly available in manufacturing facilities. Thus, researchers have begun to look at ways to collect the maximum amount of information about the state of a process from a number of different sensors (each of which is able to provide an output related to the phenomenon of interest, although at varying reliability).

The strategy of integrating the information from a variety of sensors with the expectation that this will "increase the accuracy and . . . resolve ambiguities in the knowledge about the environment" [6] is called *sensor fusion*. Sensor fusion is able to provide for the decision-making process data that has a low uncertainty because of the inherent randomness or noise in the sensor signals, that includes significant features covering a broader range of operating conditions, and that, through redundancy, accommodates changes in the operating characteristics of the individual sensors (because of calibration, drift, etc.). In fact, perhaps the most advantageous aspect of sensor fusion is in the richness of information available to the signal processing/feature extraction and decision-making methodology employed as part of the sensor system.

Sensor fusion is best defined in terms of the *intelligent sensor* [14, 15] introduced above, because that sensor system is structured to utilize many of the same elements needed for sensor fusion. These elements include the basic sensor hardware (transducer element and electronics, such as the piezo element and charge amplifier in a loadcell or bimetallic and reference junctions and Wheatstone bridge in a thermocouple) as well as basic signal conditioning, decision-making, and self-calibration and diagnostic capabilities. Middelhock and Hoogerwerf [50] define an integrated sensor along similar lines as a device with one or more transducer elements, signal conditioning and signal processing electronics, microcontroller, and communication circuitry integrated into the same package. The hardware implementation of these intelligent and integrated sensors are discussed in more detail later in this chapter.

Overview of Chapter

Although sensor fusion was developed principally in response to robots working in unstructured environments, it is quite applicable in other monitoring situations as well. It is impossible to cover in this chapter all of the potential automation applications in which sensor fusion is appropriate. The discussion in this chapter focuses on manufacturing automation and, specifically, metal-removal processes. This chapter includes background on the techniques of sensor fusion defined for the manufacturing environment, including a comparison of competing techniques. Specific examples of applications to manufacturing process sensing, principally metalcutting-related, are given, along with a discussion of the considerations that should be made with regard to using the specific fusion tech-

nique. A brief discussion of sensor fusion in other manufacturing automation areas is included. As a result, readers should be able to ascertain the basic principles of sensor fusion and sources of more detailed background for application to their areas of interest.

The remainder of this chapter includes a review of sensor technology for sensor fusion, signal processing and feature extraction techniques, fusion methodologies, hardware considerations, and some specific examples of applications of sensor fusion in the manufacturing environment.

Sensor Technology

Sensor Impact on Signal Processing and Fusion

Sensors are defined as devices that convert a physical phenomena into an electrical signal. If the overall goal of using multiple sensors is to ensure that the knowledge resulting from sensor integration is greater than the sum of the parts, we must have the capability to describe the information from the sensor. The use of a model of the sensor has been proposed to provide a description of the sensor's ability to observe the environment and derive a description of it [26]. The sensor model specifies the function, operation, and response performance of the sensor. Although model development is not part of this chapter, sensor performance is considered later. The effect of integration of sensor information on the uncertainty of that information must also be considered. Thus, it is important to be able to assess the uncertainty of the basic sensor output for any specific application.

Review of Sensors

There are a number of means for catagorizing sensors and the sensor. In manufacturing automation, the monitoring task is often a system of interconnected processes for which we are trying to provide real-time feedback on process state or regarding which we want to alert the control system to malfunctions (discrete) or gradual changes in performance (variable). Hence, four basic sensor concepts can be defined: preprocess, in-process, interprocess, and postprocess sensing [68], depending on where in the manufacturing system the sensor functions. We can also divide sensors into two large classes—contact and noncontact—depending on whether the sensing element is physically in contact with or touching the machine, tool, or object that is being monitored. Common contact sensors include low- and high-frequency accelerometers, strain gages, piezocrystal load cells, thermocouples, etc. One challenge in utilizing contact sensing is avoiding

SENSOR TECHNOLOGY

Table 16.1 Comparison of Direct and Indirect Sensing Methodologies

	Direct	Indirect
Measuring Principle	[Diagram: Measuring Device contacting Workpiece, or contacting Master Workpiece]	[Diagram: Workpiece with Measuring Device positioned separately]
Main Features	(1) Applicable to diameters within the limited range of the measuring devices	(1) Applicable to the wide range of diameters
	(2) Difficult to deal with internal diameters and complex shapes	(2) Applicable to internal diameters and complex shapes with limitation
	(3) Effects such as tool wear, machine errors and distortion, and workpiece distortion are all taken into consideration	(3) These errors strictly affect the measurement.
	(4) Measurements can deal with poor quality machine tools (retrofitable)	(4) Available techniques are very useful when applied to good quality machine tools.

From Shiraishi [68]. Reproduced by courtesy of Butterworth-Heinemann.

aliasing of the phenomenon under investigation by the physical presence of the sensor. Noncontact sensors include vision, infrared radiation, acoustic (audio and ultrasonic), etc. Other chapters of this book cover these sensors in detail.

Sensor systems can also be categorized in terms of the method of measuring the object or feature of interest—either direct or indirect. This generally refers to whether the feature is being measured directly from the workpiece, for example, or whether it is being inferred from other measurements of characteristics associated with the desired feature. Table 16.1 compares direct and indirect methods for measuring work diameter [68].

Table 16.2 Sensing in Machine Tools

Motivation for Sensing	Sensed Feature
Reduce scrap	
Dimension out of tolerance	Workpiece dimensions, profile, temperature
Surface roughness out of tolerance	Workpiece surface roughness tool condition, tool-edge location
Reduce total machine operating time per piece	
Machining time	Load, chatter threshold, tool-work approach gap
Tool-change time per piece	Tool wear rate, tool condition
Time to adjust tool at start change	Tool-edge location
	Workpiece size, temperature
Time lost due to tool break	Load, tool condition, chatter threshold
Time lost to clear chips	Chip breaking/congestion
Reduce average cost of cutting tool per piece	Tool wear rate
	Tool condition
Reduce average cost of broken tool holders per piece	Load, tool condition, chatter threshold
Reduce manufacturing lead time, lost sales, etc. when capacity constrained	System load and others depending on conditions
Avoid tool/work collision	Vision of scene, load, proximity
Avoid sudden machine failure	
Bearings	Temperature, vibration, sound
Gears	Temperature, vibration, sound
Lubrication	Flow, temperature
Coolant	Flow, temperature
Seals	Temperature
Avoid damage to work due to chuck/clamp malfunction	Jaw force, flow, hydraulic pressure
Extend equipment life	Overloads, excessive temperature or speed
Improve accuracy, reduce recalibration	Temperature of machine elements Lubricant, hydraulic fluid, coolant
Minimize startup time	Chip congestion

Sensor Specifications of Interest

Properties Sensed

The focus in this chapter is on sensors used to monitor and control machinery used in manufacturing, with special attention to metalcutting. In general, however, these classifications and criteria for specifying sensors can be applied over a wide range of processes by appropriately modifying the details of the application. To specify sensors for a process, we must understand basic features of both the process and the sensor in the application. For example, Birla [5] lists the reasons for sensing in machine tools (table 16.2).

Here the primary motivation for sensing is to improve the productivity of the machine system by avoiding the production of low-quality parts, avoiding wasting time through unscheduled downtime and reducing costs by minimizing tooling-related costs. A wide variety of sensors has been utilized to accomplish these tasks. Iwata [35] gives the results of a survey of machine tool builders evaluating needs of sensing systems for "accessories," tool functions, and workpiece functions associated with machining centers. The survey covers a variety of machine tools, including lathes, machining centers, and grinders, and applications ranging from pure machine diagnostics to in-process control.

Design Approach

The previous discussion centered on the objective of the sensor systems and common sensing methodologies. But how do we design the sensor system to reflect the needs of the machinery and the process being monitored as well as the capabilities of the sensors? This will be answered by looking broadly at how to pick the right sensor for the job and then what the role of sensor fusion is in meeting our design objectives.

The required performance of the system in which the sensor or sensors operate must be considered when a sensor is selected. The following points should be considered, according to Death [11]:

- Define the requirements—what is the system to accomplish?

- Determine the individual sensor functions—what needs to be achieved and where in the process can it be best accomplished?

- Determine the approaches to achieve those functions—which sensor will most efficiently achieve the required functions?

- Determine what interaction exists between functions and whether the chosen approach meets system requirements

Table 16.3 Sensing System Component Features

	Measurement Hardware Component			
GF	BM	HS	OE	C
Dimension	Force	Accuracy	Contact	Set-up
Metal removal rate	Static	Repeatability	Noncontact	Capital
Surface roughness	Dynamic	Reliability	Ruggedization	Operation
Cutting force	Magnitude	Bandwidth	Device size	Maintenance
Proximity	Direction	Range	Usability	Availability
Tool force	Strain	Resolution	Manual machine	Replaceability
Cutting torque	Torsion	Responsiveness	Semiautomatic	
Cutting power	Bending	Lifetime	Automatic	
Acoustic emission	Pneumatic		N.C.	
Workpiece size	Piezoelectric		Maintainability	
Workpiece surface finish	Piezoresistive		Reliability	
Cutting temperature	Telemetry		Placement	
	Optics		Remote	
	Vibration		Machine zone	
	Sound		Process monitoring	
	Power		Online	
	Temperature		Preprocess	
	Torque		Postprocess	
	Air flow		Lifetime	
	Capacitance		Environment	
	Voltage		temperature	
	Current			
	Resistance			

Digital Hardware Component

GF	BM	HS	OE	C
Multiplexing		Data rates	Ruggedization	Memory
Demultiplexing		Clock freq.		Processor
A/D conversion		Sampling freq.		Maintenance
		Programmable		Operating
		Memory size		
		Processor speed		
		Graphics		
		Memory structure		

Signal Processing Component

GF	BM	HS	OE	C
Remedial		Data rates		Algorithm development
Adaptive		Algorithm speed		Maintenance
Signal comparisons		Processor type		Operating
Noise elimination				
Noise rejection				
Self-teaching				
Robustness				
Nonlinearities				
Discontinuities				
Image processing				
Error checking				

From Stein and Dornfeld [71].

Table 16.4 Comparison of Features and Performance of Measuring Methods

Measuring Method		General Features	Best Example (res: resolution; acc: accuracy)	
			Direct	Indirect
Mechanical	Friction roller	• Easy to operate • Ease of signal processing • Reliable	res: 4–6 µm at 100 mm acc: 10 µm diameter • Industrial potential	
	Caliper type	• Wear of contact head • Relatively low gain and low resolution	res: 1 µm acc: ±3 µm • Successful application	
Optical	Optical micrometer, Light reflection, etc.	• High sensitivity • Remote sensing • Difficulty of system alignment • Difficulty of practical operation	res: 1 µm acc: 8–10 µm • Need countermeasures for disturbances	res: 0.5 µm acc: 5–10 µm • Need further investigation for reliability
Pneumatic	Back pressure detection, Flow rate detection	• High gain and practical • Low response and less robust • Narrow measurable range	res: 1 µm acc: 2 µm • Promising	res: 2 µm acc: 10 µm • Promising

Measuring Method	Best Example				Main Features	State of Development
	Resolution	Accuracy	Range (R_a)	Speed		
Ellipsometry	0.01 μm	0.1 μm	0.01–1.2 μm	Relatively fast	• Effective for smooth surface • Need careful system alignment	Need further investigation for measurement of engineering surfaces
Angular distribution	2 μm	±5 μm	Not specified	Slow	• Not practical • Need high speed data processing	Not promising
Light sectioning	1 μm	5 μm	2–20 μm	Slow	• Effective for relatively rough surface • Need high speed data processing	At the research stage but promising
[cf] direct method	0.5 μm	3 μm	2–80 μm	Fast	• Need careful system alignment • The accuracy depends on the light spot size	At the research stage

From Shiraishi [68]. Reproduced by courtesy of Butterworth-Heinemann.

- Test the system at least by simulation if a full-scale test is infeasible

Death also points out the necessity of determining the required performance characteristics expected in terms of what is to be sensed and under what conditions. This includes the operating environment (temperature, humidity, shock, vibration), power source and its stability, service life expected, and whether or not any industrial standards must be met (UL, NEMA, etc.)

Performance Specifications

Component Classification Performance specifications refer to the basic characteristics of the sensor system needed to perform the desired task. In view of the earlier discussion of the intelligent sensor, a convenient way to review specifications is to look at the hardware as well as the software aspects of the system. Stein and Dornfeld [71] have proposed a methodology for the design of sensor systems based on a classification scheme that identifies hardware functions as including the following:

- A primary sensing element

- A variable conversion element that converts sensed variables to more suitable units while preserving the information content

- A variable manipulation element that changes the numerical value of a variable according to some rule but that preserves the physical nature of the variable

- Data transmission elements

- Data-acquisition, storage, and processing elements.

Because the first four hardware functions above are not necessarily four separate physical elements, for the purpose of defining sensor components, the four functions and their associated hardware components are termed the *measurement hardware* component. The second component, termed the *digital hardware* component, consists of all necessary digital logic and computing hardware. The third component is termed the *signal processing* component and consists of software algorithms necessary for monitoring the given process. Five types of features have been defined to differentiate devices within each component category, as follows:

- General function (GF) features—manufacturing states or conditions that may be measured by making inferences from a more

basic measurement. (Example: Tool forces in machining can be inferred or derived from measuring strain at a specified location on the tool holder.)

- Basic measurement (BM) features—measurements that are generic in nature and the basic principles that constitute the measurement. (Example: force, voltage capacitance, and optics.)

- Hardware specification (HS) features—technical specifications of devices determined experimentally or taken from manufacturer's data. (Example: resolution, range, and bandwidth.)

- Operating environment (OE) features—factors that influence the use of a device relative to the machine tool. (Example: device size and operating temperature range.)

- Cost (C) features—factors that directly or indirectly influence the cost of obtaining, operating, and maintaining the device. (Example: availability, capital cost, and maintenance cost.)

Some device features may be classified under more than one category. A list of features for each component category appears in table 16.3, taken from Stein and Dornfeld [71].

Resolution and Accuracy The ultimate measure of the success of a sensing system is its accuracy and resolution. This varies with the basic measurement features of the sensor and its mode of application. Table 16.4 shows a comparison between several methods of measuring geometrical profiles, such as roundness and cylindricity of workpieces during precision machining [68]. This is a more complex task than simply measuring the dimension of the workpiece as the geometry profile affects the workpiece shape accuracy. Table 16.5 gives a similar comparison for surface roughness measurement techniques, ranging from those with near-term commercial potential to those still in the research stage [68].

Signal Processing and Feature Extraction

Introduction

Human monitoring of manufacturing processes can attribute its success to the ability of the human to distinguish, by nature of the physical senses and experience, between the "significant" information and the meaningless. Table 16.6 il-

Table 16.6 Use of Human Sensors to Monitor Machining Activities with Possible Sensor Solutions

Human Sense	Human Monitoring Activity	Possible Machine Sensors
Vision	Establish datum points between incoming workmaterial stock, fixtures, and cutting tools	Touch-trigger probe
	Watch for sudden breakage of cutting tools	Machine vision and touch-trigger probes
	Carry out between-pass visual checks of trends in flank and crater wear	Machine vision
	Detect tool temperature by studying chip color	Thermocouples
	Watch for changes in part surface finish	Machine vision
Hearing	Listen for excessive vibrations between tool and part	Accelerometers and dynamometers
	Listen for sounds of tools near or at failure	Accelerometers, dynamometers, and acoustic emission devices.
Touch	Feel excessive vibrations through floor or by touching fixtures	Accelerometers
	Approximately sense excessive cutting forces by touching fixtures or tool-holders	Dynamometers and strain gauges
	Touch surface finish and approximately gauge quality	Stylus measurements of surface finish
Smell	Excessive tool temperatures sometimes change the smell of cutting fluids	Chemical sensors
Taste		

From Wright and Bourne [76]. Reprinted with permission of the publisher.

Figure 16.4 Structure of Typical Pattern-recognition System

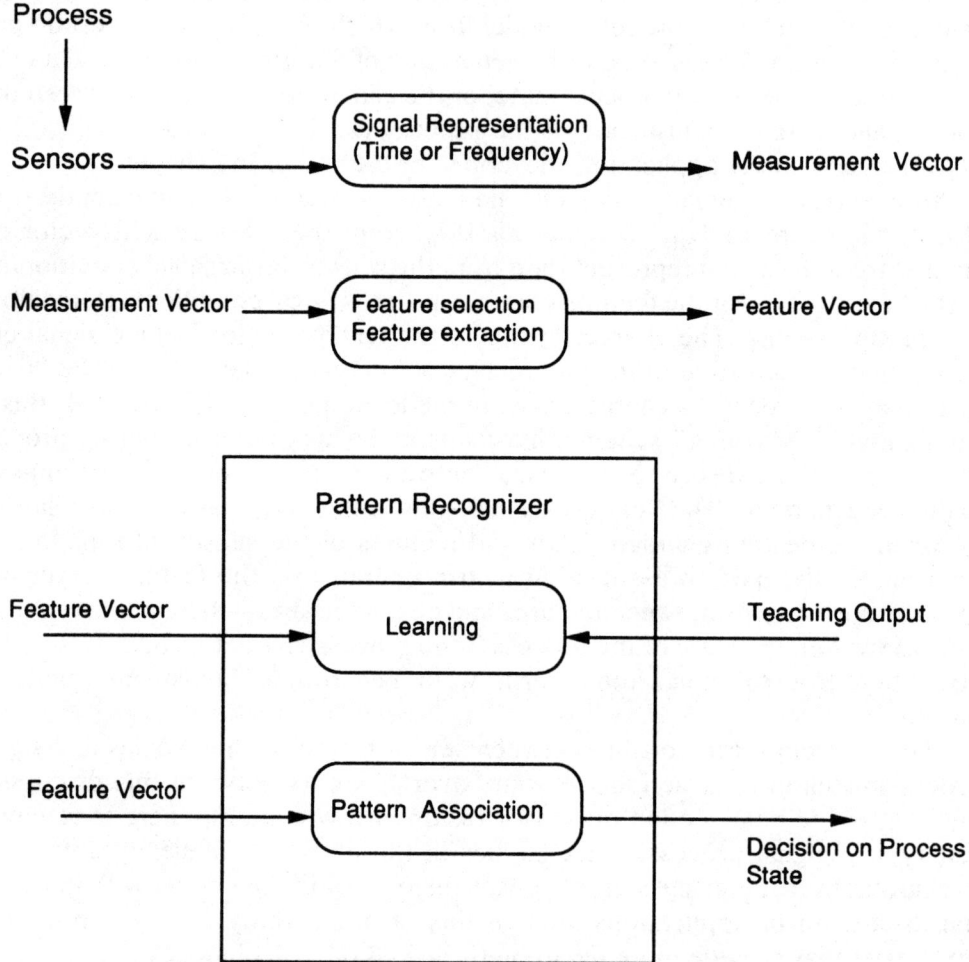

lustrates the human sense and monitoring activity along with possible sensor solutions [76]. In general, humans are capable as process monitors because of the high degree of development of sensory abilities, essentially noise-free data (unique memory triggers), parallel processing of information, and the knowledge acquired through training and experience [57]. Limitations are seen when one of the basic human sensor specifications is violated—something happening too fast to see, or happening out of range of hearing or visual sensitivity because of frequency content. These limitations have always served as some of the justification for the use of sensors. Sensors, of course, are also limited in their ability to yield an output sensitive to an important input. Thus, we need to consider the

use of signal processing, the variable manipulation element discussed above, and along with that feature extraction. In most cases, the utilization of any signal processing methodology has as its goal one or more of the following: the determination of a suitable "process" model from which the influence of certain process variables can be discerned; the generation of features from sensor data that can be used to determine process state; or the generation of data features so that the change in the performance of the process can be "tracked." This will be shown clearly in the applications described at the end of the chapter.

An overview of signal processing and feature extraction is conveniently summarized in figure 16.4, from Rangwala [57]. Here the measurement vector extracted from the signal representation from the sensor (basic signal conditioning) is the "feedstock" for the feature-selection process (local conditioning), resulting in a feature vector. The characteristics of the feature vector include signal elements that are sensitive to the parameters of interest in the process. The "decision-making" process is characterized in the lower portion of figure 16.4. Based on a suitable "learning" scheme that maps a teaching pattern (that is, process characteristics we desire to recognize) onto the feature vector, a pattern association is generated. The "pattern association" contains a matrix of associations between the desired characteristics and features of the sensor information. In application, the pattern association matrix operates on the feature vector and extracts correlations between features and characteristics—these are taken to be "decisions" on the state of the process if the process characteristics are suitably structured (for example, tool worn, weld penetration incomplete, material flawed).

There is a close relationship between sensor fusion methodologies and signal processing/feature extraction, so some overlap exists between this discussion and that in the next section on sensor fusion. We will attempt here to review a few typical signal processing techniques in the time and frequency domain as background for the discussion of sensor fusion. Additional detail will appear in the discussion of applications later in this chapter. Many excellent reference texts exist that provide more detail on these and other techniques.

Time Domain Analysis

Basic Statistics

The basic statistical analysis techniques learned in undergraduate studies are simple signal processing methods. Simple linear regression expresses the dependence of one set of observations on another set under certain assumptions (usually that the independent observations are independent or uncorrelated). The parameters of the regression, slope, and intercept give us some information on the interaction of the dependent and independent variables. Observing the change in these parameters under differing process conditions can allow us to

Figure 16.5 Illustration of Skew and Kurtosis Nomenclature

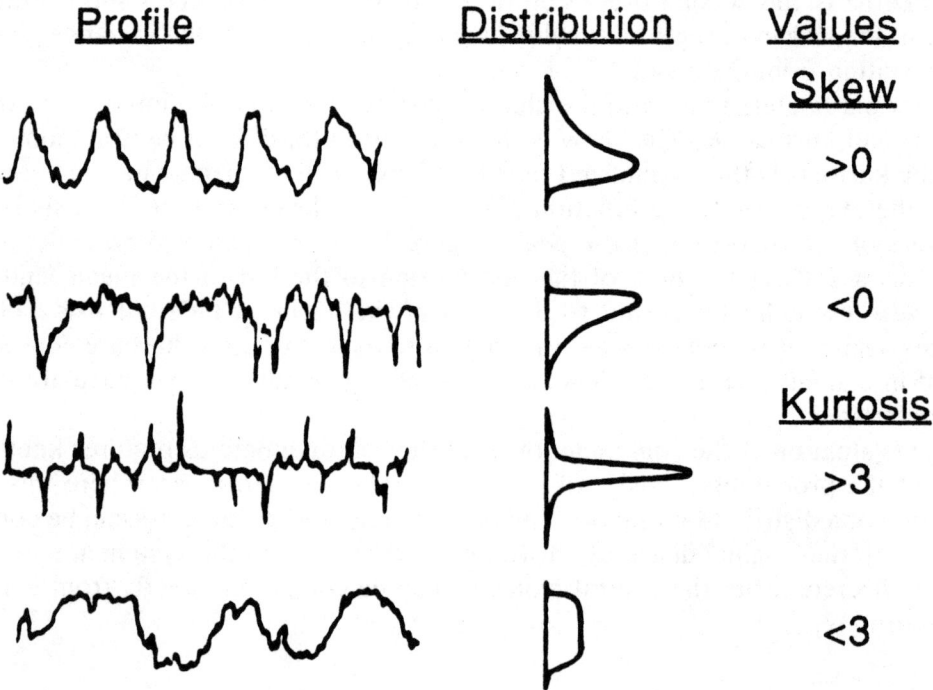

identify the state of the process or track its behavior. Observing the residuals from the regression can indicate to us when the process has changed dramatically, as evidenced by a significant trend in the residuals (skew, for example). If we have data that forms a series over time, such as a surface profile or a force trace during machining, we can calculate the mean and the standard deviation, and these parameters represent characteristics of the data useful for representation [51]. Using the parameters of the best-fitted model of sets of data (that is, mean and standard deviation based upon an assumed distribution with standard normalized mean and standard deviation), the spectral moments—that is, m_0, the variance; m_2, the variance of the slope; and m_4, the variance of the curvature—can be calculated and further related to physical characteristics of the process. Based on these parameters, skew and kurtosis of the distribution can be calculated (figure 16.5). This has been done successfully in a variety of manufacturing applications (for example, see Wu [77] and Kannatey-Asibu and Dornfeld [39]). Skew and kurtosis have been used effectively in surface profile characterization [73]. A more detailed discussion of the generation of these statistical parameters and their relationship to the form of the data (mean number of zero crossings or mean number of peaks, for example) follows.

The mean $\bar{x}$, or $E(z)$, of a function of a random variable is the first-order moment, the r.m.s. value is the square root of the second-order moment and the variance σ^2 is the second-order central moment. The mean gives the average value of the variable, the r.m.s. value gives the intensity, and the variance gives the deviation from the mean.

Other parameters related to the characteristics of the distribution of x are the skew S and kurtosis K. The skew is the normalized third-order central moment and the kurtosis is the normalized fourth-order central moment. The skew measures the symmetry of the function about its mean level, and the kurtosis is a measure of the sharpness of the peaks (figure 16.5). A negative skew generally indicates a shift of the bulk of the distribution to the left of the mean, and a positive skew indicates a shift to the right of the mean. A high kurtosis value implies a sharp distribution peak (in other words, most of the values are concentrated in a small area), and a low kurtosis value generally implies virtually flat characteristics.

The evaluation of the analytical forms of the central moments requires knowledge of the probability density of a given distribution. However, where this is not known, a distribution function can be assumed, if its parameters can be compared with the original distribution. If, however, data from the system are available in discrete form, the central moments can be computed directly from Korn and Korn [42]:

$$M_r = \overline{(x-\bar{x})^r} = \frac{1}{n} \sum_{k=1}^{n} (x_k - \bar{x})^r \qquad (16.1)$$

where n is the number of data points and the skew and kurtosis are, respectively:

$$S = M_3/M_2^{3/2} \qquad (16.2)$$

$$K = M_4/M_2^2 \qquad (16.3)$$

A further use of the spectral moments is for profile characterization because of the ease of physically interpreting the moments calculated [19]. For a surface having a Gaussian distribution of profile heights, it can be shown that at a level, H, above the mean of the profile (figure 16.6), the mean number of zero crossings (MNZC) is proportional to the ratio M_2/M_0 [10].

The spectral moments can be related to the physical profile characteristics $\bar{A}_H$ and $\bar{I}_H$, shown in figure 16.6, as follows:

$$\frac{\bar{A}_H}{\bar{Z}_H} = \left(\sqrt{\frac{M_2}{M_0}} \bullet f(H) \right) \qquad (16.4)$$

SIGNAL PROCESSING AND FEATURE EXTRACTION

Figure 16.6 Surface Profile Notation

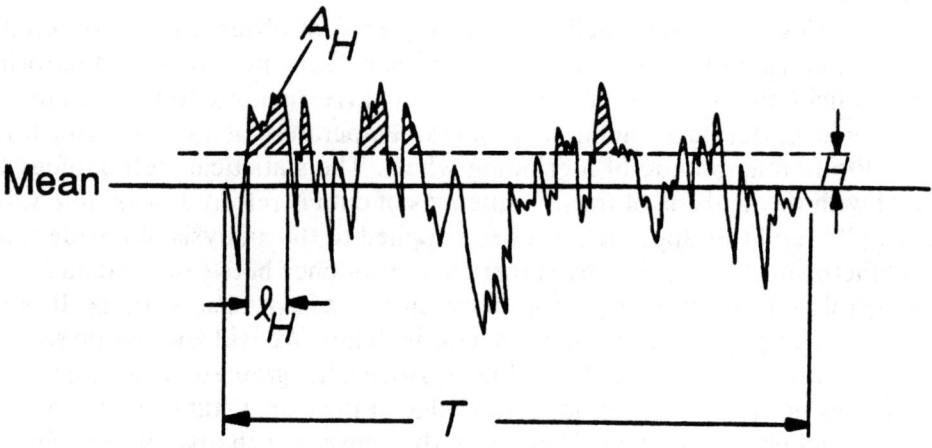

where

$\bar{A}_H$ = the mean area of a peak above level H

$\bar{l}_H$ = the mean length of a peak base at level H

$f(H)$ = a function of H, the profile height above the mean

or simply:

$$\frac{\bar{A}_H}{\bar{l}_H} = \frac{M_2}{M_0} \qquad (16.5)$$

This gives an indication of the profile peak sharpness, because for similar values of $\bar{l}_H$ for two profiles, an increase in $\bar{A}_H$ means a sharper peak. The assumption is made and verified by the profiles that a basic triangle peak shape exists. Thus, for equal base lengths, a triangle with a larger area must have a sharper peak than a triangle with a smaller area.

Time Series Analysis

It is sometimes possible to derive the mathematical model for a dynamic system based on physical laws, which then allows us to calculate the value of some time-varying quantity at any particular time. This type of model would be entirely deterministic. However, very few dynamic systems are totally deterministic, because changes due to unknown or unquantified effects may take place during the process. Thus, it is convenient to construct stochastic models that can describe

the dynamics from a probabilistic point of view. In this way, the underlying system physics or system characteristics can be studied or ascertained from experimental data.

A time series is generally defined as a sequence of observed data ordered in time (or other variables, such as space). In manufacturing process monitoring, we often encounter such ordered sets of data corresponding to the output of a force transducer during a machining process, temperature of a sheet during forming, or vibration amplitude of a grinding wheel. The statistical methodology associated with the analysis of these sequences of data is referred to as *time series analysis* [78], and this approach has been applied to the analysis of a wide range of manufacturing processes. Any statistical dependence between the data is seen in the correlation or autocorrelation between successive observations. It is impossible to discuss time series analysis here in detail. We will address one simple form, the autoregressive model using a stochastic gradient algorithm. This method does not require any prior knowledge of the signal statistical properties, and the modeling algorithm is adaptive in the sense that the parameters are updated at every time step, rather than being estimated only after a whole data set has been collected, as is done in batch algorithms. In the application of the time series modeling approach to in-process characterization of systems or processes that have fast time-varying dynamics or features, the modeling technique has to be adaptive so that the information contained in the measured data can be used promptly to reflect instantaneous system dynamics or features. Not only is the adaptability needed for real-time analysis but it also reduces the memory size required, because the oldest data point is discarded at each time step. An example of an application of this is given later in this chapter.

In an Nth-order autoregressive (AR) model for a time series $y(k)$, where k is the discrete time index, the current value can be predicted from the N previous values as

$$\hat{y}(k) = n(k) + \sum_{j=1}^{N} a_i(k)y(k-i) \qquad (16.6)$$

where $n(k)$ designates a white noise. In the present case, $y(k)$ is the measured signal at the transducer site and each a_i is a model parameter.

If the measured data value of $y(k)$ is different from the value predicted by using equation 16.6, some error will occur. The error signal, $e(k)$, is defined to be the difference between the model-predicted value $\hat{y}(k)$ and the actual sampled value $y(k)$:

$$e(k) = y(k) - \hat{y}(k) \qquad (16.7)$$

The behavior of output signal $y(k)$ is closely related to the model parameters a_is as well. During a cutting operation, when the acoustic emission signal

as a result of tool wear progression, the model parameters become time-varying and are utilized to track the tool wear. The model parameters are calculated from the sensor signal, $y(k)$, using the stochastic gradient algorithm.

With the stochastic gradient algorithm, the model parameters are adjusted every time a new data point is sampled. Each adjustment is an effort to minimize the square of the error signal at that instant, $e^2(k)$. The algorithm is given in a recursive form as follows [28]:

$$a(k+1) = a(k) + \beta e(k)y(k-1) \tag{16.8}$$

where β is a constant adaptation gain that determines the amount of change in a at each adjustment. The selection of adaptation gain is critical, because it governs both the stability of adaptation and the speed of convergence. A larger β will result in a faster convergence, and a smaller β will provide better adaptation stability. It can be shown that if β is larger than $2/\lambda_{max}$, where λ_{max} is the largest eigenvalue of the correlation matrix $\Phi(k)$ defined by this equation:

$$\Phi(k) = \text{Expectation } [y(k)y^T(k)] \tag{16.9}$$

then the error signal $e(k)$ will actually increase with time and the algorithm becomes unstable. In the application to real processes, the sensor signal is not generally statistically stationary, because its source mechanism varies with time and changes in the process. Therefore, the eigenvalues of $\Phi(k)$ do not remain constant with time. To keep the algorithm stable, β should be selected to be small enough that it is never greater than 2 over the "instantaneous" maximum eigenvalue of $\Phi(k)$. However, the trade-off for a more robust gradient algorithm is the reduction of convergence speed.

If some of the model parameters do not vary significantly with process state, or if the model order is so high that the real-time implementation of signal analysis is difficult, it becomes necessary to ignore some less important model parameters. In this section, the importance of a model parameter is evaluated based on its ability to discriminate different process states. A discrimination index associated with each parameter is formulated here to describe quantitatively the relative importance of that model parameter.

For any process state specified by A, an "ith parameter mean" can be defined for the ith model parameter as its mean value with respect to time:

$$a_{i,}{}^\circ A = \frac{1}{M} \sum_{k=1}^{M} a_{i,A}(k) \tag{16.10}$$

where M is the number of total adaptation time steps. One natural way to evaluate the capability of a parameter a_i in separating two different states A and B is

through the observation of its between-class variation $Q_i[A,B]$, defined as follows:

$$Q_i[A,B] = |a_{i,A}^\circ - a_{i,B}^\circ| \qquad (16.11)$$

When the variation of $a_i(k)$ between process states A and B is on the same order as its parameter mean, $Q_i[A,B]$ will decrease with increasing i. That is,

$$Q_i[A,B] \geq Q_j[A,B] \quad i,j = 1-N \text{ and } i \leq j \qquad (16.12)$$

Therefore, $Q_i[A,B]$ alone cannot represent the relative importance of a_i in distinguishing process states. To formulate a better index for the relative importance of model parameters, a within-class variation in the ith parameter for state A is defined as follows:

$$S_{i,A} = [\frac{1}{M} \sum_{k=1}^{M} (u_{i,A}^\circ(k) - u_{i,A}^\circ)^2]^{1/2} \qquad (16.13)$$

Similarly, $S_{i,A}$ decreases with respect to i as the variation of $a_i(k)$ between conditions A and B is on the same order as its parameter mean:

$$S_{i,A} \geq S_{j,A} \quad i,j = 1-N \text{ and } i \leq j \qquad (16.14)$$

A discrimination index $J_i[A,B]$ between the two conditions A and B based on the ith parameter can then be obtained by the normalization of $Q_i[A,B]$ with $S_{i,A}$ and $S_{i,B}$. That is,

$$J_i[A,B] = \frac{Q_i[A,B]}{[S_{i,A}S_{i,B}]^{1/2}} \qquad (16.15)$$

The discrimination index defined in this way does not necessarily decrease with i. A greater discrimination index implies that the difference in this specific parameter for two conditions is more pronounced, and that the parameter varies less within either of the conditions. Therefore, the discrimination index, $J_i[A,B]$, is a suitable indication of how successfully the two conditions, A and B, can be separated through the observation of the ith model parameter. The most important parameter is the one that maximizes the discrimination index. Parameter reduction can then be achieved by ignoring the parameters with small discrimination indices.

Frequency Domain Analysis

The representation of a signal from a transducer or sensor by sums of sinusoids or complex exponentials, commonly called a Fourier representation, is useful in signal analysis because it serves to emphasize evidence of certain properties of the signal that may be less obvious in the original signal. A definition of the time-dependent Fourier transform can be given as follows:

$$V(t,f) = \sum_{k=-\infty}^{\infty} w(t-k)v(k)e^{-jfk} \qquad (16.16)$$

where $w(t-k)$ is a moving windowing sequence that determines the portion of input signal that receives emphasis at a particular time t. Windowing sequences that are most commonly used are the rectangular window:

$$w(t) = \begin{cases} 1 & 0 \leq t \leq T \\ 0 & \text{elsewhere} \end{cases} \qquad (16.17)$$

and the Hamming window:

$$w(t) = \begin{cases} 0.54 - 0.46 \cos(2\pi t/T) & 0 \leq t \leq T \\ 0 & \text{elsewhere} \end{cases} \qquad (16.18)$$

The rectangular window corresponds to applying equal weight to all the samples in the interval from $(t-T)$ to $(t-1)$. The frequency response of a rectangular window with impulsive response given by equation 16.17 can be shown to be as follows:

$$W(e^{j\omega}) = \frac{\sin(\omega T/2)}{\sin(\omega/2)} e^{-j\omega(T-1)/2} \qquad (16.19)$$

The lowest frequency zero of equation 16.17 occurs at the following frequency:

$$\omega = 1/T$$

This is usually the cut-off frequency of the lowpass filter corresponding to a rectangular window. The bandwidth of the Hamming window is approximately twice the bandwidth of a rectangular window of the same length. The Hamming window gives much greater attenuation outside the passband than does the comparable rectangular window. Furthermore, the effect of increasing the window width is to decrease the bandwidth. With a narrow window, $V(t,f)$ will fluctuate

rapidly depending on the details of the signal waveform. If the window is too wide, $V(t,f)$ will change slowly and thus will not adequately reflect the changing properties of the signal $v(k)$.

Equation 16.16, the spectral density function, or the power spectrum, of a sequence of signal can be calculated as follows:

$$S(t,f) = \sum_{k=-\infty}^{\infty} R(t,k)e^{-ifk} \qquad (16.20)$$

where $R(t,k)$ is the short-time autocorrelation function defined as follows:

$$R(t,k) = \sum_{n=-\infty}^{\infty} v(n)w(t-n)v(n+K)w(t-n-k) \qquad (16.21)$$

The spectral density function calculated this way contains as many frequency components as half of the window width in the time domain. That is, using a window width of 2,048 points in the time domain, $S(t,f)$ will yield 1,024 spectral components in the frequency domain. Each of these components may vary with time. In order to characterize the frequency spectrum quantitatively as a function of time without having to trace the variation of each spectral component, select the mean, the standard deviation, and the averaged density of the spectra as parameters and compute them at different operation states. A "mean frequency" is defined as follows:

$$\bar{f}(t) = \frac{\sum_{i=1}^{N} f_i S(t,f_i)}{\sum_{i=1}^{N} S(t,f_i)} \qquad (16.22)$$

It represents the frequency that divides the spectral density function into two portions of equal area. Furthermore, the standard deviation of the frequency spectrum with respect to this mean frequency can be given as follows:

$$\sigma(t) = \left[\frac{\sum_{i=1}^{N} (f_i - \bar{f}(t))^2 S(t,f_i)}{\sum_{i=1}^{N} S(t,f_i)} \right] \qquad (16.23)$$

which is an indication of the frequency spread in a signal. A third parameter,

"averaged spectral density," $\tilde{S}(t)$, can be defined as the average of spectral density function over the frequency range of interest. That is:

$$\tilde{S}(t) = \frac{1}{N+1} \sum_{i=1}^{N} S(t, f_i) \qquad (16.24)$$

Fusion Methodologies

Introduction

This section reviews, briefly, several techniques for integrating information from several sources. These techniques are reviewed in light of the requirements for monitoring manufacturing processes. The objective of sensor fusion is to increase the reliability of the information so that a decision on the state of the process is reached. This tends to make fusion techniques closely coupled with feature extraction methodologies and pattern-recognition techniques. The problem here is to establish the relationship between the measured parameter and the process parameter. There are two principal ways to encode this relationship [57]:

- Theoretical model—the relationship between a phenomenon and the measured parameters of the process (say tool wear and the process) is determined.

- Empirical model—experimental data is used to tune parameters of a proposed model.

As mentioned earlier, reliable theoretical models relating sensor output and process characteristics are often difficult to develop because the complexity and variability of the process and the problems associated with incorporating large numbers of variables in the model. As a result, empirical methods that can use sensor data to tune unknown parameters of a proposed relation are attractive. These types of approaches can be implemented either by proposing a relationship between a particular process characteristic and sensor outputs and then using experimental data to tune unknown parameters of a model, or by associating patterns of sensor data with an appropriate decision on the process state without consideration of any model relating sensor data to the state. The second

approach is generally referred to as pattern recognition and involves three critical stages [1]:

1. Sampling of input signal to acquire the measurement vector

2. Feature selection and extraction

3. Classification in the feature space to permit a decision on the process state

These were illustrated previously in figure 16.4. The pattern-recognition approach provides a framework for machine learning and knowledge synthesis in a manufacturing environment by observation of sensor data with minimal human intervention. More importantly, such an approach allows information to be integrated from multiple sources (such as different sensors), which is the principal interest here.

Sata et al. [64] were among the first researchers to propose the application of pattern-recognition techniques to machine process monitoring. They attempted to recognize chip breakage, formation of built-up edge, and the presence of chatter in a turning operation using the features of the spectrum of the cutting force in the 0–150-Hz range. Dornfeld and Pan [18] used the event rate of the RMS energy of an acoustic emission signal, along with feedrate and cutting velocity, in order to provide a decision on the chip formation produced during a turning operation. Emel and Kannatey-Asibu [20] used spectral features of the acoustic emission signal in order to classify fresh and worn cutting tools.

The manufacturing process may be monitored by a variety of sensors, and typically, the sensor output is a digitized time domain waveform. The signal can then be processed in either the time domain (for example, by extracting the time series parameters of the signal) or the frequency domain (power spectrum representation). The effect of this is to convert the original time domain record into a measurement vector. In most cases, this mapping does not preserve information in the original signal. Usually, the dimension of the measurement vector is high and it becomes necessary to reduce this dimension because of computational considerations. There are two prevalent approaches at this stage: select only those components of the measurement vector which maximize the signal/noise ratio or map the measurement vector into a lower dimensional space through a suitable transformation. The latter approach is called *feature extraction*. The outcome of the feature selection/extraction stage is a lower dimensional feature vector. These features are used in pattern-recognition techniques and as inputs to sensor fusion. Discussed below are several "fusion" techniques.

Linear Discriminant Functions

The focus in this section is on linear discriminant pattern classifiers trained using the perception learning algorithm. These are often referred to as *perceptrons*. A detailed discussion of the perceptron learning algorithm and its application to machine learning can be found in Nilsson [55].

A state can be characterized by a set of measured numbers, $x_1, x_2, \ldots, x_d$, which form the pattern X for the state. A pattern classifier assigns the patterns into one of R different categories. A pattern can be viewed as a point in d-dimensional pattern space, with its components as the coordinates. The vector extending from the origin to the point can also be used to represent the pattern, called a *pattern vector*. Each pattern classifier can also be viewed as a set of surfaces, called *decision surfaces*, that partitions the pattern space into R different regions. The decision surfaces are defined implicitly by a set of functions containing R members, $g_1(X), g_2(X), \ldots, g_R(X)$, called *discriminant functions*, which are scalar and single-valued functions of the pattern X. The discriminant functions are chosen such that for all X in category i, $g_i(X) > g_j(X)$ for all $i \neq j$, and $i, j = 1, 2, \ldots, R$.

The block diagram in figure 16.7 illustrates how the classification works. A pattern, X, is presented to R discriminators, each of which computes the values

Figure 16.7 Basic Model for a Pattern Classifier

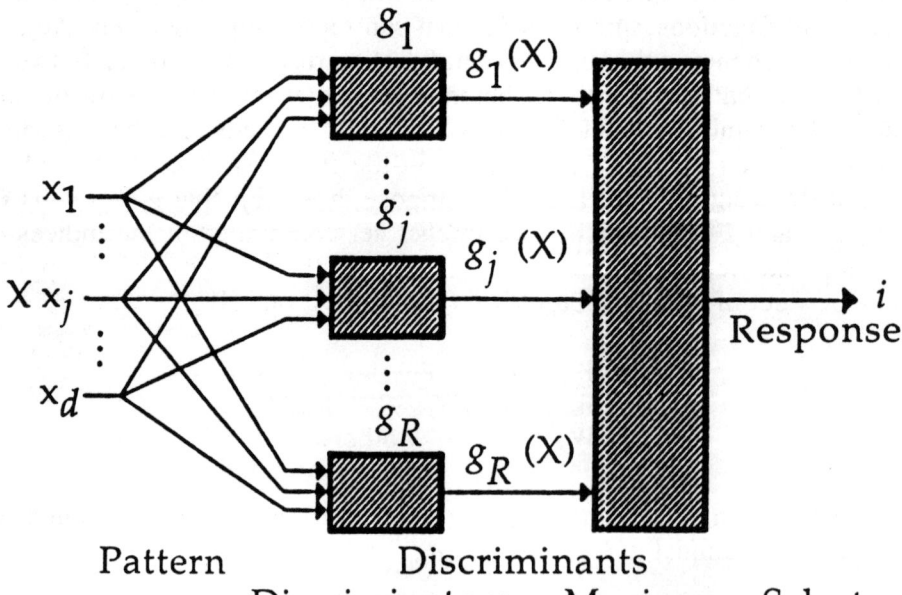

of a discriminant function. The outputs of the discriminators, called *discriminants*, are compared by a maximum selector, which indicates the largest discriminant, i. Then the pattern X is classified into category i.

Discriminant functions can be selected in a variety of ways. In a special case, the discriminant functions are linear and the decision surfaces are hyperplanes. This is the simplest form, the easiest for calculation and is especially good for real-time application, and, thus, may not be the most effective way for pattern classification. A linear discriminant function has the following form:

$$g_i(X) = W_i(X) = \sum_{k=1}^{k=d+1} w_k x_k \qquad i = 1, 2, \ldots, R \qquad (16.25)$$

where W_i = weight vector, $(w_1, w_2, \ldots, w_{i+1})$

X = pattern vector, $(x_1, x_2, \ldots, x_d, 1)$

The threshold margin, which is the minimum difference required between the largest discriminant and all others for making a classification, is embedded in w_{d+1}.

The weight vectors of all the discriminant functions are obtained by an adjustment process known as *training*. Typical patterns similar to those that the discriminant functions must ultimately classify are chosen to form a training set. All the classifications of the training pattern are known. In this discussion, the error-correction training procedure, a nonparametric training method, is described. The training procedure starts with arbitrary initial values for all W_is. Every pattern in the training set is presented one at a time in any sequence to the discriminant functions, and each pattern can recur infinitely often. Adjustments are made whenever the discriminant function responds incorrectly to any pattern. Suppose that a pattern, X_k, belonging to category i, is the ith pattern presented in the training sequence. If $g_i(X_k) = W_i W_k$ exceeds all other discriminants—that is, $g_i(X_k) > g_j(X_k)$, for all $j \neq i$—the response is correct, and no correction of the weight vector is made. Suppose, however, that $g_k(X_k) \leq g_j(X_k)$ for some $j \neq i$ and $j \in J$, which is an integer set containing all the indices of weight vectors that need to be corrected for X_k. Then the following rule is applied to obtain a new set of weight vectors from the present one (W_p):

$$W_p = \begin{cases} W_i + a_k X_k & p = i \\ W_j - \alpha_{jk} a_k W_k & P = j \in J \\ W_p & \text{otherwise} \end{cases}$$

The correction increments, a_k and α_{jk}, are allowed to vary with the number of corrections, k. There must exist constants $a_{\min}$ and $a_{\max}$, such that

$$0 < a_{\min} \leq a_k \leq a_{\max} \qquad k = 1, 2, \ldots$$

FUSION METHODOLOGIES

and α_{jk} must satisfy

$$\alpha_{jk} \geq 0; \text{ and } \sum_{j \in J} \alpha_{jk} = 1$$

The effect of the adjustment is to increase the value of the ith discriminant by $a_k|X_k|^2$, and to reduce the value of the jth discriminant by $\alpha_{jk}a_k|X_k|^2$. If the training set is "linearly separable"—that is, if there exists a set of linear discriminant functions that can classify all patterns correctly—the training method guarantees that the weight vectors are yielded after a finite number of corrections.

If only two categories exist—that is, $R = 2$—the classification is made by deciding which one, $g_1(X)$ or $g_2(X)$, is larger. It turns out that this decision can be implemented by evaluating the sign of a single discriminant function: $g(X) = g_1(X) - g_2(X)$. The single linear discriminant function has the same form as defined in equation 25. If $g(x) > 0$, X is placed in category 1; if $g(x) < 0$, X is placed in category 2. The two regions in the pattern space are separated by a decision surface $g(X) = 0$. The pattern classifier can be implemented according to the block diagram in figure 16.8. Such a structure, consisting of weights, a summing device, and a threshold element, is called a threshold logic unit, TLU.

Desirable properties of perceptrons are that they offer a means for machine learning based upon observations of training data and that they are suited for parallel operation because the weighted values of the different components of the feature vector can be computed in parallel. Thus, information from different features is combined to render a decision.

Once a pattern classifier has been trained, it should be able to associate in-

Figure 16.8 The Threshold Logic Unit (TLU)

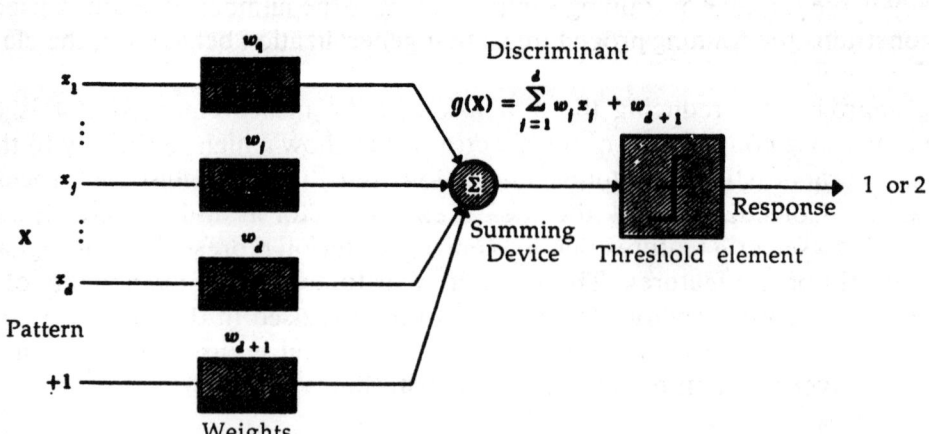

coming sensory patterns with a decision on process status. The degree to which correct associations can be made depends upon the following factors [57]:

- The quality of information available in the sensory features

- The type of processing that the raw sensory features are subjected to during the training and pattern-recognition phases

The first factor reflects the amount of discriminatory information contained in the raw sensor signal features presented to the pattern classifier. Ideally, good information implies that the features are very sensitive to the process characteristics of interest and insensitive to the effects of noise and process variables. In many situations, even though the raw signal features contain the necessary information for discriminating between two distinct states, it may be encoded in a complex manner or colored as a result of the effects of noise and process variables. In such cases, it becomes necessary to process the raw sensor information in order to extract features suitable for classification purposes and to reject noise. Some of the techniques discussed in the previous section do exactly that.

Earlier in this chapter, the sensor variable conversion element was introduced, the result of which (for example, a power spectrum of a sensor signal, like force which, as the component of a vector, represents the signal power at various discrete frequencies) is a measurement vector for that sensor. Although valuable information may be contained in the entire measurement vector, from practical considerations only a few of these components can be used for training and pattern association. This is because in training a pattern classifier such as a perceptron, the minimum number of training samples to be used is as follows:

$$N = 2(d+1) \qquad (16.26)$$

where N is the number of training samples and d is the number of features used. This constrains the training procedure so that generalization behavior of the classifier is acceptable.

The approach for reducing the dimension of the measurement vector is to retain only those components of the spectra which show a high sensitivity to the process characteristics of interest and a low sensitivity to noise or process parameters. Considering that the measurement vector is d-dimensional, the objective is to select d features that maximize a criterion representing the signal-to-noise ratio of the features. The selected d features are the components of a d-dimensional feature vector. The criterion function used in this case uses the concept of interclass Euclidean distance measures and is discussed in greater detail in Dejiver and Kittler [12]. A typical criterion is as follows:

$$J = \text{trace}(S_w\text{sup}-1 S_b) \qquad (16.27)$$

where S_w is the within-class scatter matrix and S_b is the between-class scatter matrix of the d-dimensional feature vector. S_w measures the scatter of data points within a class representing a process state, and S_b measures the distance between clusters representing data points in the d-dimensional feature space of different states. Intuitively, the value of J represents the signal/noise ratio of the feature vectors. Adding new features increases the J value, because additional features cause the distance between mean values of the clusters representing states to increase. A high value for J indicates that the clusters corresponding to two different process states are far apart and that the scatter within the cluster is small.

Neural Networks

Feature extraction and learning activities occurring at the same time is preferable, because this allows the extraction of optimal information from the features along with noise rejection. Such an approach is possible using neural network pattern recognizers. A neural network is a collection of simple, interconnected processors that operate in parallel and that store knowledge in the strength of the connections between the individual processors. Such parallel networks of computing elements crudely resemble processing activity in the brain and have been applied successfully to intelligent tasks such as learning and pattern recognition.

Artificial neural networks are an attempt to mimic the computational architecture of the human brain in electronic hardware, the objective being to incorporate intelligent functions such as learning and pattern recognition in computers. The human brain consists of a large number of interconnected neurons, each possessing very simple computational abilities. However, the interactions between the neurons allows for parallel processing of information, which greatly enhances the speed of computation and causes a large amount of knowledge to be brought to bear in processing this information [27]. A typical neuron consists of three components: the cell body, the input lines into the neurons (*dendrites*) and the output lines emerging from the cell body (*axons*). The axons of a neuron are connected to the dendrites of other neurons at points called *synapses*. This forms a highly interconnected system of neurons that communicate with one another via synapses. The synapses determine the strength of the connection between two neurons. A typical neuron receives inputs from various other neurons via the dendrites. The time-averaged sum of these inputs causes biochemical reactions inside the cell body, which results in pulses of electrochemical activity being transmitted over the axon lines of the neuron. The pulse rate depends on the magnitude of the input excitation to the neuron and is usually assumed to be a sigmoid function of the input (see figure 16.9). This is because the output saturates at extreme values of the input (the output pulse rate lies between 0 and 500 Hz for a typical neuron).

Figure 16.9 Sigmoid Firing Behavior

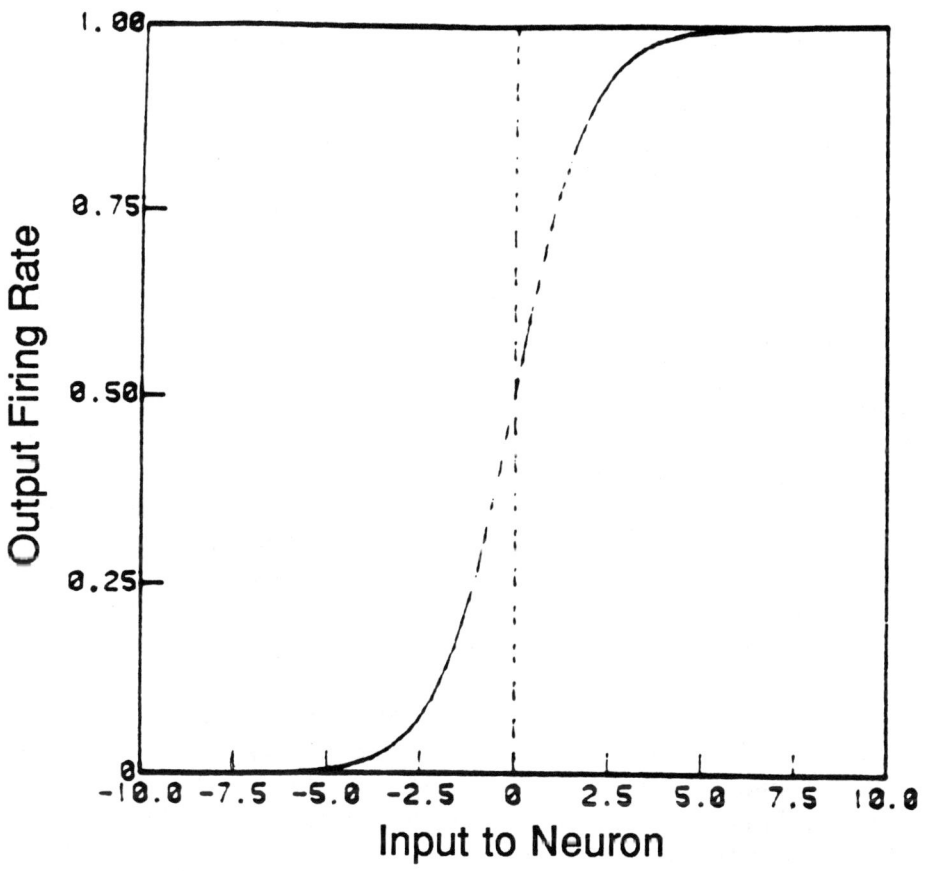

The synapse between two neurons may be excitory (in which case a high activity in one neuron causes a high activity in the other neuron) or inhibitory (in which case a high activity in one neuron causes activity in the other neuron to be suppressed). The synapses develop through learning processes in the brain; however, the exact mechanisms are not known at present. The information processing tasks at which the human brain excels, such as pattern recognition and the ability to retrieve memorized data based on partial or incorrect cues (content addressable memory), are made possible by the collective processing activity of a large number of interconnected neurons, operating in parallel and with the knowledge stored in the strength of the synapses between these neurons [29].

Artificial neural networks can be implemented by using amplifiers with a sigmoid input-output relationship as the "neuron" element and resistive connections between the amplifiers representing the synapses between the neurons. The

Figure 16.10 Behavior of Nodes in a Neural Network

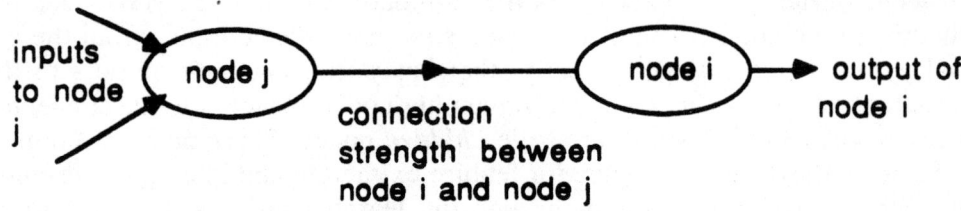

conductance values of the resistive elements represent the strength of the connection between the individual processors, and the sign of the conductance determines whether it is excitory (positive conductance) or inhibitory (negative conductance). The voltage output of the amplifier represents the activity level of a given processor, whereas the input to the processor is simply a current-summing operation on the outputs of the other processors. A schematic of two such interconnected processors is shown in figure 16.10. The connection strength between the jth and the ith neuron is represented as w_{ij} and is simply the conductance value of the connection between these processors. The input to the ith processor is given by the following:

$$\text{INPUT}_i = \sum_{j=1}^{N} w_{ij} \text{OUT}_j \qquad (16.28)$$

where N is the total number of processors connected to the ith processor and OUT_j is the output of the jth processor. The output of a processor is usually assumed to be a sigmoid function of the input, or in some cases, a threshold function may also be used (refer to figure 16.9).

The conductance values, or the *weights,* are the learning parameters of the system; they encode the knowledge in the system. These learning parameters are acquired through learning. Physically, this implies that the resistors should be able to change their resistance values in response to the learning process—that is, adaptive or programmable resistors are required. Current research efforts are aimed at these implementation issues, the main thrust being aimed at developing programmable resistors (Spencer [70], Owen et al. [56], and, on implementing vast arrays of interconnected processors in VLSI technology, Hubbard et al. [32]). A prototype of a VLSI network employing thin-film resistors has been demonstrated [22] for implementing a content addressable memory (CAM).

Computation in neural networks occurs by propagation of signals through the connections between the processors. Each processor is capable of simple func-

tions such as current summing and elementary arithmetic operations. In a general network, all the processors may be connected to one another, with the knowledge of the system encoded in the "strength" of connections between the individual processors. Some of the processors may receive inputs from the external world (*input nodes*), whereas others may transmit their outputs to the external world (*output nodes*). The remaining nodes, which are not connected directly to the external world, are called *hidden* nodes. These nodes are important because they are responsible for feature extraction and internal representation of the knowledge acquired through the learning process. One important feature of neural networks is that the knowledge in the system directly determines how the processors interact; in contrast, when processors are stored in a separate knowledge base, they must wait to be accessed sequentially by a CPU. Also, the knowledge is distributed over a large number of connections, which results in a fail-soft operation: a failure of some of the processors will cause graceful degradation in performance rather than a complete loss of the knowledge base.

Pattern-recognition tasks typically involve associating sets of patterns. In a neural network, the knowledge required to associate the correct sets of patterns is encoded in the values of the weights or connection strengths between the processors. Neural architectures proposed by Hopfield [29, 30] have been demonstrated to implement content addressable memories successfully; in such architectures, a system of interconnected processors can retrieve a complete memory given only a partial knowledge of the memory. Hopfield networks consist of a system of N processors, each processor connected to all other processors. The operation of such a network can be described as a dynamic system to which the network state converges. The state of the network is represented by the activation levels of the individual processors at a given instant of time and is an N-dimensional vector. The important point here is that the location of the attraction basins (or *equilibrium points*) can be controlled by suitable selection of the connection strengths between the processor states (which represent an incomplete or incorrect memory), and the network will converge to one of the attraction basins of the system. If the initial state is close enough to the desired state, the correct memory (represented by the converged state) will be retrieved. Hopfield networks have also been used to solve combinatorial optimization problems [31, 72].

One class of neural networks that has been shown to be successful at pattern-recognition tasks is the class consisting of multilayered, feedforward networks of the type shown in figure 16.11. As noted above, there are three kinds of processing units in such networks: input layer nodes that accept patterns from the external world, output layer nodes that generate outputs to the external world, and hidden nodes that do not interact directly with the external world. The role of the hidden nodes is to form internal representations of the patterns presented at the input layer. These networks perform pattern-association tasks in which a pattern presented at the input layer of the network is associated with a pattern

Figure 16.11 The Structure of a Feedforward Neural Network

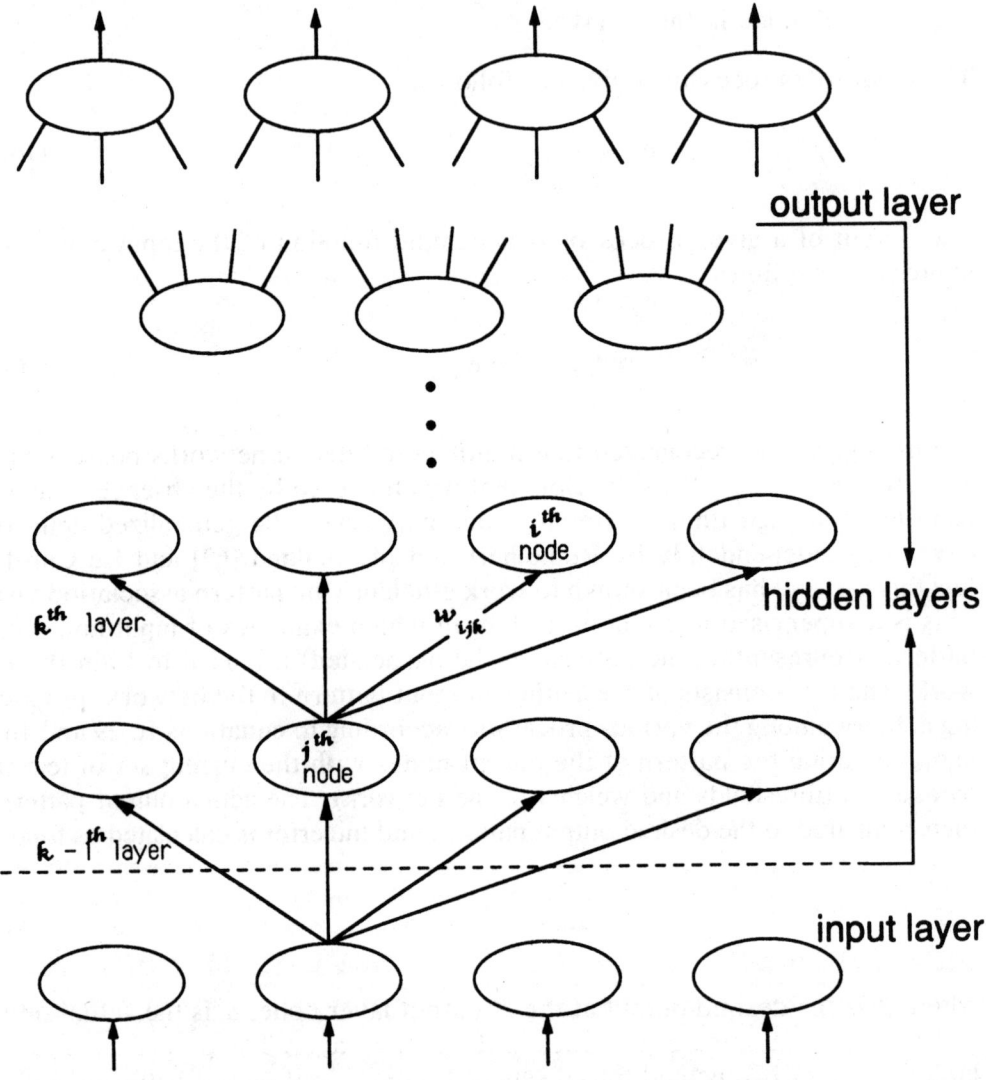

at the output layer. In these networks, information propagates from the bottom to the top layer, with connections existing only between processors in adjacent layers.

Let:

$w_{i,j,k}$ = weight between j^{th} processor in $(k-1)^{th}$ layer and i^{th} processor in the kth layer

$\text{net}_{i,k}$ = input to i^{th} node in the kth layer

$\text{out}_{i,k}$ = output of ith node in the kth layer

$t_{i,k}$ = threshold value associated with the ith node in the kth layer

The input to a processor is given as follows:

$$\text{net}_{i,k} = [\sum_j w_{i,j,k} \text{out}_{j,k-1}] + t_{i,k} \quad (16.29)$$

The output of a given processor is a sigmoid function of the input and can be expressed as follows:

$$\text{out}_{i,k} = F(\text{net}_{i,k}) = \frac{1}{e^{-\text{net}_{i,k}}} \quad (16.30)$$

Although it was recognized that multilayered neural networks possess many attractive properties, their development was hindered by the absence of an efficient learning algorithm for training such networks. The generalized delta rule developed independently by Rumelhart and McClelland [62] and Le Cun [44] fills this gap and has been shown to work efficiently on pattern association tasks. This is a supervised learning procedure in which examples of input and output patterns (representing the patterns to be associated) are used to train the network. The rule consists of presenting an input pattern to the network, propagating activity among the various processors according to equations 16.29 and 16.30 and computing the pattern at the output nodes with the current set of learning parameters (thresholds and weights of the network). The actual output pattern is then compared to the desired output pattern, and the error is calculated as follows:

$$E = \frac{1}{2} \sum_{i=1}^{q} (d_i - a_i)^2 \quad (16.31)$$

where d_i is the desired output at the ith output layer node, a_i is the actual output and q is the total number of nodes in the output layer. The procedure of calculating the error is repeated for all sets of training input-output patterns, and the individual errors are added to compute the total error. This constitutes the forward pass through the network.

Next, the error is propagated from the top to the bottom layer through the network to modify the weights and thresholds in such a way that the error term is minimized. This involves minimization of a nonlinear error function with respect to the threshold and weight values, using gradient descent. Computation of the error term with respect to each weight and threshold is accomplished using local information at each node, so that gradient calculations at each layer can be accomplished in parallel. For example, Rumelhart and McClelland [62] uses the gradient information to adjust the weights and thresholds as follows:

$$\Delta w_{i,j,k} = -\eta \frac{\partial E}{\partial w_{i,j,k}} \qquad (16.32)$$

$$\Delta t_{i,k} = -\beta \frac{\partial E}{\partial t_{i,k}} \qquad (16.33)$$

where η and β are the step sizes in the minimization process.

A linear network is one in which the output of a processor is a linear function of its input, with the input to a processor defined as in equation 16.29. For a linear system, the error surface is bowl shaped and has only one minimum point, so that convergence is guaranteed. In the present case, however, the error function is a nonlinear function of the learning parameters, so that any gradient descent scheme for error minimization is prone to terminating in a local minimum. There is no guarantee that a gradient descent procedure will find a set of thresholds and weights so that the error term is zero. However, as pointed out by Rumelhart and McClelland [62], this does not seem to present difficulties in practical implementations, because the number of hidden layers and number of nodes in each hidden layer can be chosen so that a set of weights and thresholds that drives the error to zero can usually be found for a given implementation. The final values of the learning parameters are randomized and usually lie between -1 and 1.

Once such a network has been trained using a set of training patterns, it can be used to associate patterns presented at the input layer with appropriate patterns at the output layer. The advantages of using these networks for pattern-recognition tasks are that learning can be accomplished purely by observation of sensor data; that learning and pattern recognition are accomplished using parallel computation; and that such networks can form internal representations of the raw sensory information independently. Internal representations are necessary because the raw information may be noisy and redundant and not suited for making pattern classification decisions. Another advantage of using such networks is that knowledge is stored in the connection strengths between the processors and directly determines how the network operates, rather than being stored in a database, waiting to be accessed by the CPU.

There are similarities between the perceptron-type network discussed in the previous section and the multilayered networks discussed here. In fact, multilayer networks have also been referred to as *multilayered perceptrons* [55]. The perceptron performs pattern classification by computing a weighted sum of sensor inputs and comparing it to a threshold value. In the case of a perceptron, there are only two layers of units, with the outer layer unit implementing a threshold-type function such as that shown in figure 16.9. The perceptron implements a hyperplane in feature space, with the hyperplane surface representing the decision surface. No processing of raw information is carried out. With multilayered neural nets, however, the raw input patterns undergo further process-

ing to filter out noise in these patterns. The training procedure forces the hidden nodes to perform feature extraction on the raw features so that as information propagates through the network, the noise is filtered out. The feature-extraction capability of the hidden nodes is developed during the training procedure so that the extracted features are better suited for the classification task. The last two layers of the neural network essentially implement a perceptron—however, the features used in this case are the internal features, which are relatively noise free. This leads to better generalization abilities of the classifier. A further difference between the perceptron and the multilayered neural network is that the perceptron can perform only a linear separation of the sensor features, whereas the feature-extraction abilities of the hidden nodes in a multilayered neural network allow the network to perform arbitrary mappings between input and output patterns.

Hardware Considerations

The techniques discussed earlier involving features selected from sensor outputs must, inevitably, be implemented in hardware for real-time utilization. At this point, it is necessary to confront the realities of architectures, interfaces, buffers, and the assorted digital signal processing hardware associated with sensor systems. Numerous constraints are imposed on these systems in terms of economics, reliability, resolution, data rates, etc. Most of the original development of sensor fusion systems was associated with robotics research, because vision was a major challenge to the implementation of robots in structured and unstructured environments and is a logical candidate for sensor fusion with multiple cameras. This section addresses some typical implementations of hardware-based sensor systems from the standpoint of architecture.

Most systems employing multiple sensors for monitoring or control are based upon architectures with either parallel or serial communications. That is, either the sensors are polled independently to form the basis of some decision or action, or data can be obtained from the sensors, features of importance extracted, and those features fused to form a consensus on which action is based. Most of the initial work in the development of these architectures was driven by the requirements of command generation for robots and involved the integration of information from sensors such as vision systems, wrist force/torque sensors, or acoustic ranging devices for object acquisition or motion. The multiple sensors provide redundancy between similar systems and allow variable control strategies in which one sensor might provide a more global view of the status and other sensors provided more details [63].

Henderson et al. [26] characterized individual sensors suitable for use in automated manufacturing operations (that is, those falling in the price range of $100–$1,000) as having the following features:

- Standardized interface

- Addressability, bidirectionality, and bus compatibility

- Self-testing and autoranging capabilities

- Digitally compensated, 12-bit output accuracy

- Operating temperature range: $-40°C$ to $+175°C$

- Single 5V supply

They also stated that these sensors will include internal storage of interface protocols, nonlinearity compensation, and slope/offset compensation. A review of sensor architectures for the third through the fifth generation of sensing systems for automated manufacturing is shown in figure 16.12. Figure 16.13 illustrates the VLSI fifth-generation integrated sensor showing provision for multiple sensors. Both figures are from Henderson et al. [26].

There have been several physical implementations of sensor systems meeting the characteristics of a smart sensor described above. A typical one that has an architecture suitable for use in automated manufacturing was proposed by Schoess and Castore [66] for the purpose of monitoring advanced aerospace systems. The details of that system are reviewed here. Schoess and Castore describe the development of a *distributed sensor architecture,* or DSA. The DSA attempts to provide a framework for transforming the logical representation of a multisensor system according to the logical sensor specification (LSS) proposed by Henderson and Shilcrat [25] into a hardware system capable of interpreting and fusing data from multiple sensors as well as controlling the activity of the sensors. The logical sensor is interpreted here as a network composed of subnetworks. Each subnetwork is viewed as a logical sensor as well. Communication is controlled via the data flow between subnetworks. Alternate input paths exist to the individual logical sensors, corresponding to equivalent (with respect to type of sensor) alternate subnets, and the subnets can provide back-up to other sensors in case of failure.

The DSA is organized into three levels of hierarchy: integrated sensors (IS), sensor supervisors (ISS), and supervisory communication and control. The integrated sensor at the lowest level incorporates several analog transducers, electronics for signal processing, and a microcontroller. These are all integrated on

Figure 16.12 Sensing Systems for Automated Control

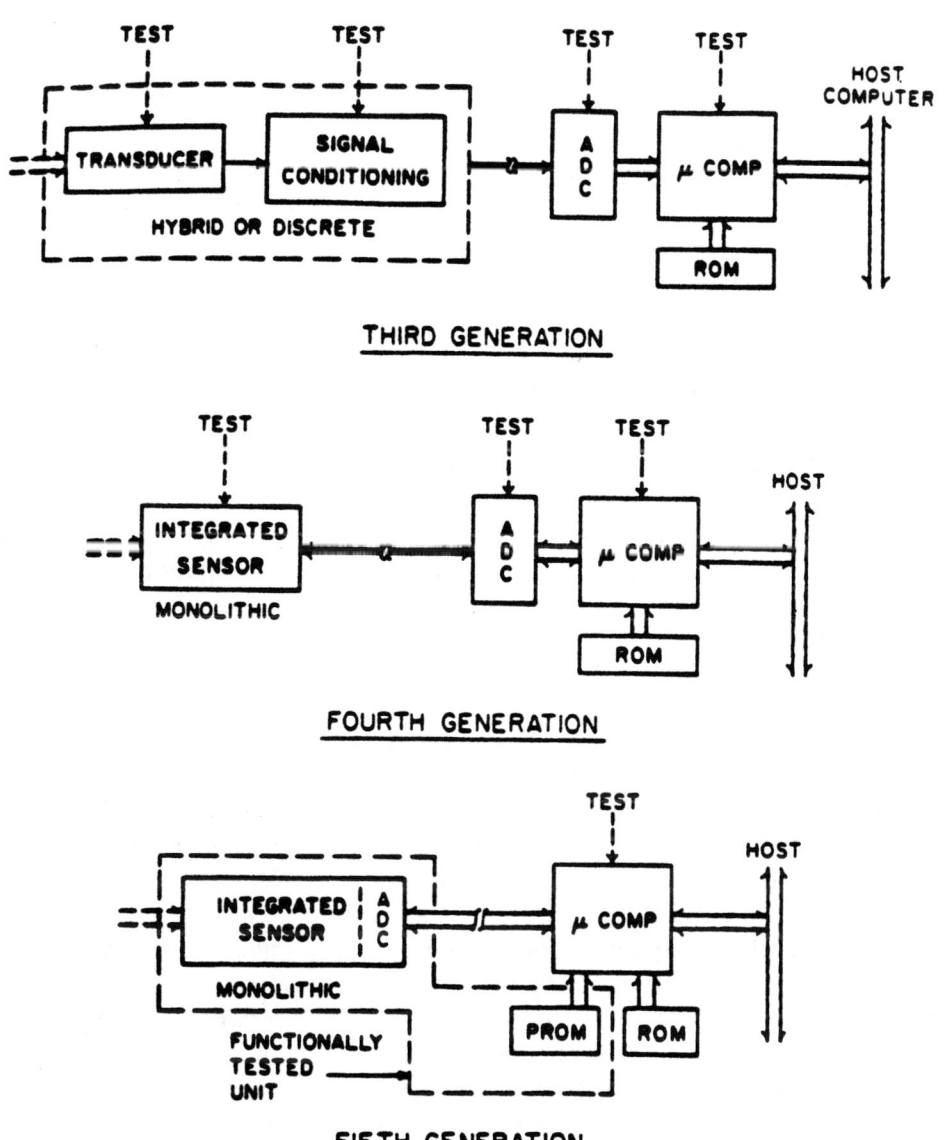

one or two integrated circuit chips. The sensor supervisor communicates with the integrated sensors over a serial communications bus. The function of the ISS is to provide sensor data interpretation and analysis, data-trend extraction, generation of control commands, and intersensor association. The DSA is shown schematically in figure 16.14.

Figure 16.13 VLSI Fifth-generation Integrated Sensor

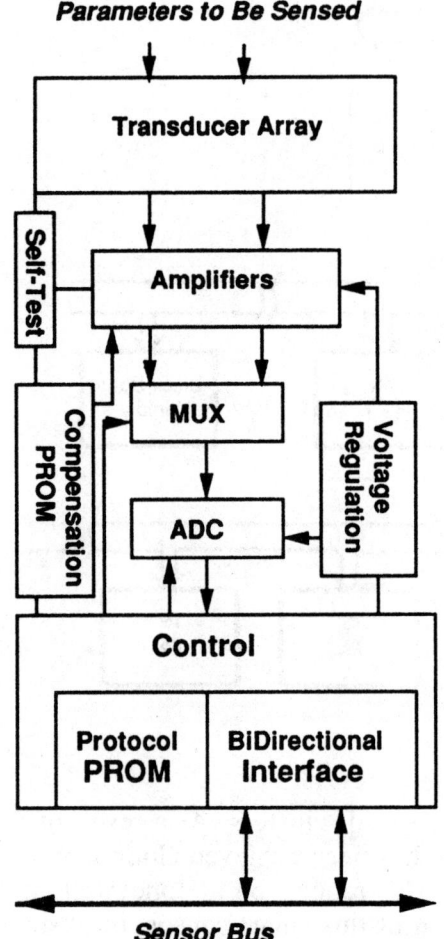

Sensor signal processing is distributed between several ISSs. A set of integrated sensors is allocated to each ISS depending upon functional requirements. The DSA architecture utilizes two "blackboard systems," one for sensor supervision and one for system operation. This allows sensor data fusion to occur within a single sensor cluster controlled by an ISS as well as among sensor supervisors and among subsystems. The ISS communication is via a shared memory accessed through a parallel high-speed bus. The sensor bus is a two-wire bidirectional serial bus utilizing a poll-response protocol. A local area network (LAN) facilitates communication between the DSA and other subsystems through the network interface unit (NIU). Using the bus structure, the ISS can

Figure 16.14 Distributed Sensor System Topology

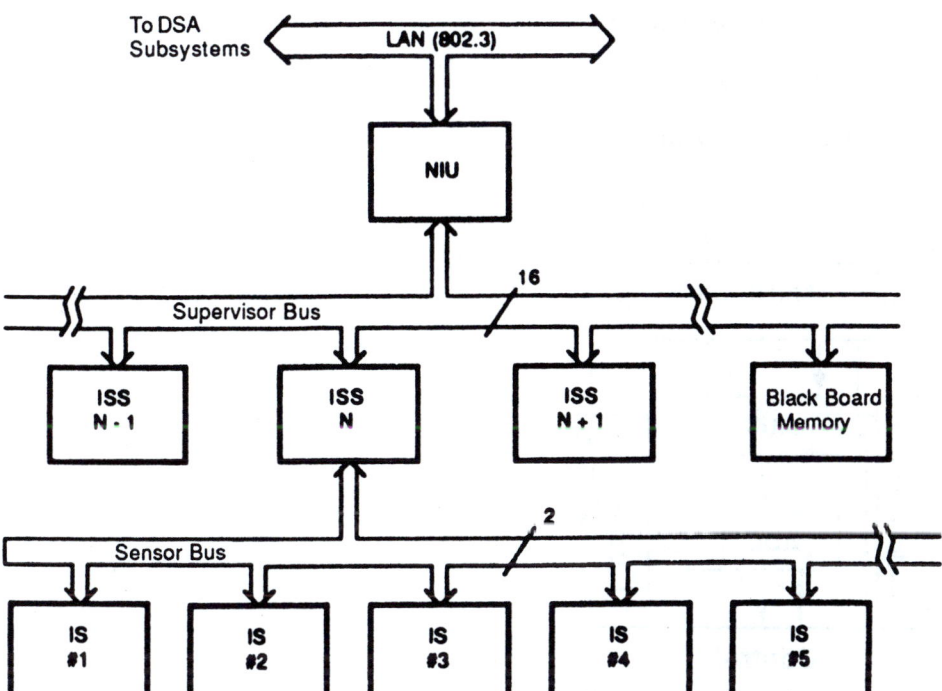

communicate to fuse data among interactive sensor clusters. As a result of this architecture, a high degree of fault tolerance has been achieved along with real-time monitoring of sensor outputs. Schoess [65] reports on a Honeywell study showing that, for a hardware implementation of this smart sensor, the "stand-alone probability" of fault isolation for this type of sensor, including built-in test features, is 97 percent, compared to 85 percent for conventional sensor systems (without smart sensors or the self-test feature).

The integrated sensor architecture is illustrated in figure 16.15. Middelhock and Hoogerwerf [50] define an integrated sensor as a device with one or more transducer elements, signal conditioning and signal processing electronics, microcontroller, and communication circuitry integrated into the same package. The integrated sensor shown in figure 16.15 is such a device, with the following features:

- Solid-state transducer array

- On-board signal amplification electronics

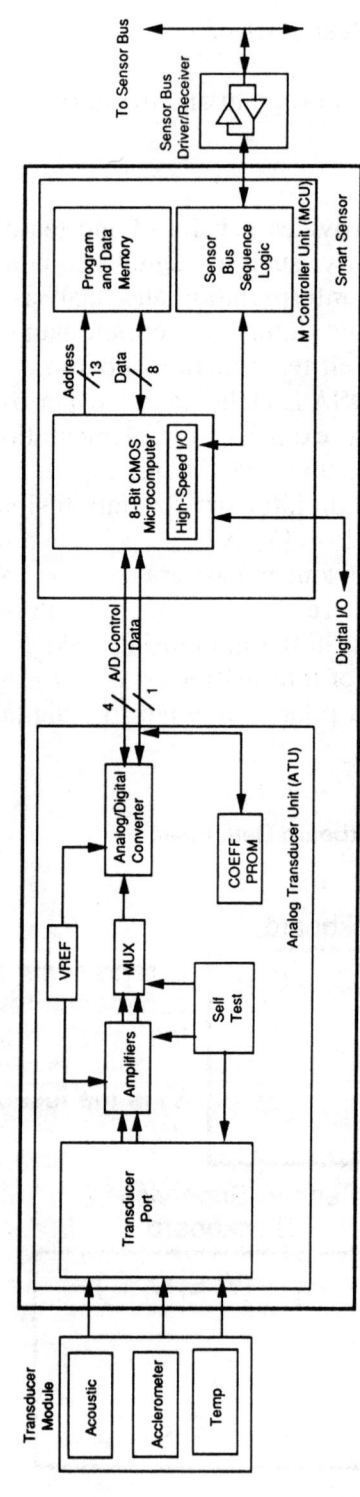

Figure 16.15   Honeywell Integrated Sensor

- A/D convertor and built-in sensor test electronics

- 8-bit microcomputer with associated program and memory

- Sensor bus electronics

The integrated sensors microcomputer provides several of the features previously identified by Henderson as necessary, such as digital compensation for sensor nonlinearity and slope/offset, data interpretation and analysis, data formatting and storage, time stamp referencing, interpretation and handling of supervisor commands, and periodic sensor self-test function actuation.

An example of sensor fusion using the DSA is included in a paper by Schoess and Castore [66]. Because it is an excellent example of implementation in software and hardware of sensor fusion, it is summarized here. Figure 16.16 gives an overview of the distributed blackboard architecture for data fusion. E is an unordered set of integrated sensors, S_i, or $E = (S_1, S_2, \ldots S_n)$. Each integrated sensor S_i is associated with a set of transducer elements, T_{ij}, or $S_i = (T_{i1}, T_{i2}, \ldots, T_{in})$. These transducer elements are the devices that output a signal proportional to the phenomenon of interest in the monitoring task. Each transducer element is described by four pieces of information (v, e, c, t_s), where v is a single data value representing a raw data point converted to a digital word, e

Figure 16.16 Example of Distributed Blackboard Data Fusion

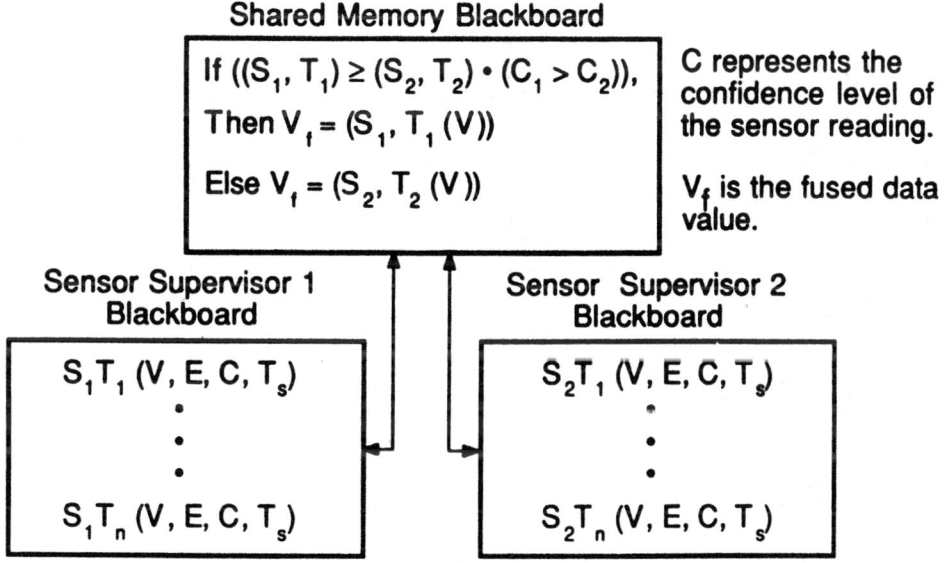

is an estimation of error based on estimated accuracy and the transducer transfer function, c is a confidence value based on the ability to assess process functions from v and the reasonableness of e, and t_s is a time stamp that is often useful when data to be fused is time-dependent.

Figure 16.16 shows a system with two integrated sensors, S_1 and S_2, with their respective transducer elements and the descriptive information v, e, c, and t_s. The value of the fused data, V_f, is calculated by comparing the data values for transducers 1 and 2 in a Boolean operation. V_f represents the data value for transducer 1 if (S_1, T_1) is greater than or equal to (S_2, T_2). If a conflict exists—for example, when two sensors give different readings but are essentially the same and are measuring the same physical phenomenon—it can be resolved by comparing the confidence, c, values.

Applications

Introduction

Three examples of applications of intelligent sensor signal processing and sensor fusion are presented here to illustrate the practical implementation of the methodologies discussed in earlier sections. The examples are drawn from research work related to process monitoring for manufacturing—specifically, metalcutting. However, the principles behind the applications are appropriate for a wide range of processes and problems. The methodologies presented include the linear discriminant function applied to metalcutting chip-form determination, adaptive autoregressive models for feature extraction for tool-wear monitoring, and neural network sensor fusion for tool-condition monitoring.

All of these examples rely on acoustic emission generated by the machining process as one of the sensor outputs observed during process monitoring. Acoustic emission (AE)—that is, stress waves spontaneously released in materials undergoing deformation, fracture, friction, rubbing, and/or impact—is usually of two distinct types, continuous and burst. Continuous type signals arrive at the transducer in large numbers (so that distinct events cannot be distinguished). Burst-type signals appear as series of bursts (related to distinct events such as growth of a crack or a fracture) that are distinctly separable. In the machining process, continuous AE signals are generated in the shear zone, at the chip-tool interface, and at the tool-work interface. Burst AE signals are generated as a result of chip breakage during or after chip formation or because of tool cracking or fracture.

Determination of Chip Forming States Using a Linear Discriminant Function Technique with Acoustic Emission

Introduction

One of the primary limitations of the further automation and optimization of manufacturing processes (metalcutting, in this case) is the availability of reliable, efficient, and cost-effective sensors. In automated factories, untended machine tools are required to operate for long periods of time with little or no operator supervision. Under these circumstances, it is crucial that chip control, which ensures that discontinuous chips are produced, be maintained. Continuous chips can cause catastrophic failure of tooling, can entangle and damage the workpiece, can hinder the efficient operation of mechanized chip disposal systems, and can interfere with automated tool-handling equipment. The problem of chip-form detection has been characterized by Nakayama and Ogawa [54] as one of the most serious problems in machine tool automation.

As a result of this challenging problem, many sensing devices have been proposed for the detection of chip form. One of the more promising of the proposed techniques uses the analysis of acoustic emission (AE) signals generated by the chips as an indication of chip form. The generation of acoustic emission from the fracture of discontinuous chips was suggested by Dornfeld [13] and has been confirmed experimentally in a number of studies [36, 17] (figure 16.17). These studies have shown that there is an excellent correlation between the event rate of the AE signal and the frequency of chip formation for discontinuous chip machining of steel and aluminum work materials (figure 16.18).

The "burst" AE activity due to discontinuous chip formation is superimposed over the continuous AE due to the plastic deformation and rubbing in the ma-

Figure 16.17 Acoustic Emission from Discontinuous Chip Formation

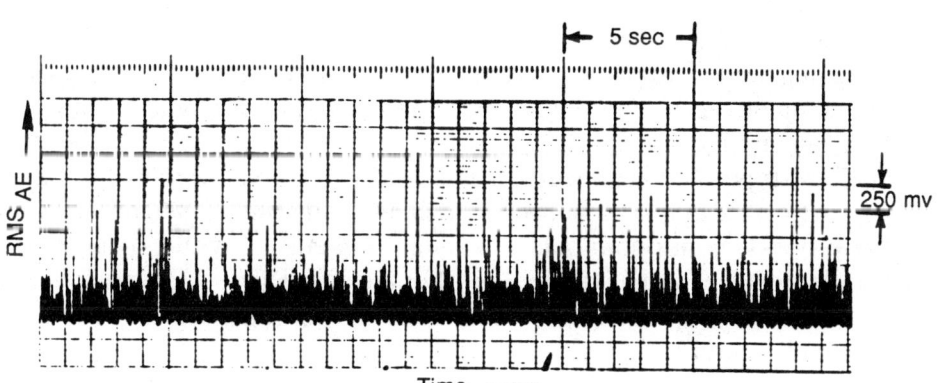

Figure 16.18 Average Event Rate of AE RMS and Estimated Chip Breaking Frequency versus Feed Rate

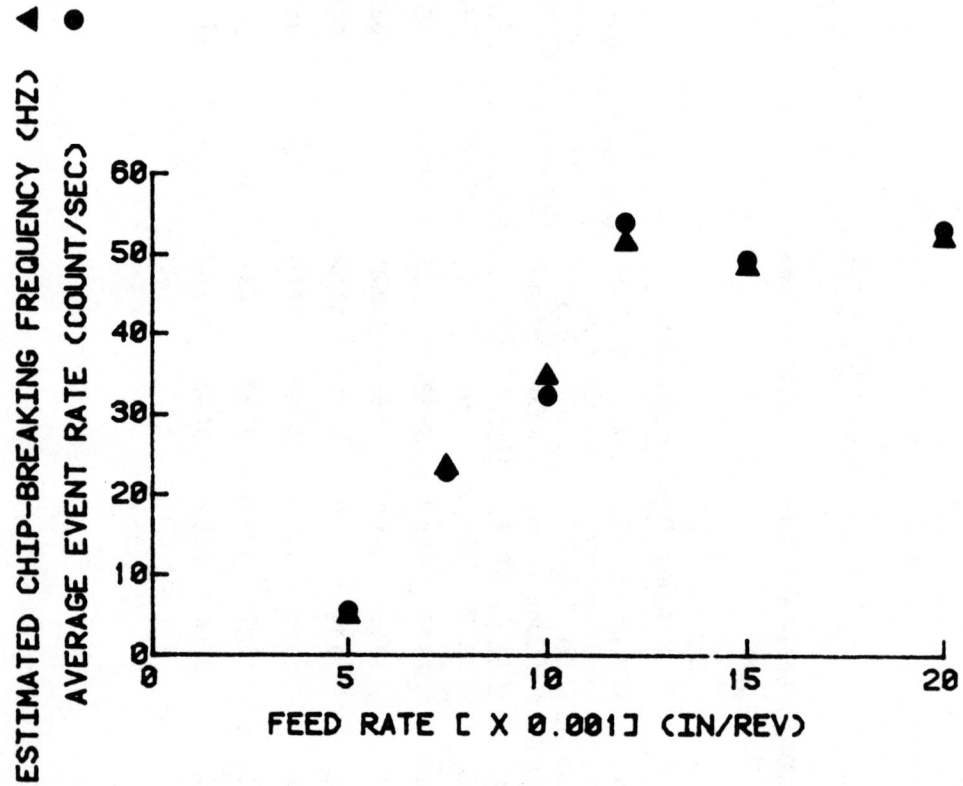

chining process. A methodology for analysis of this AE has been developed by Yee *et al.* [80] based on the event rate of the root mean square (RMS) voltage of the AE above a predetermined threshold to distinguish between continuous and discontinuous chip forms. It is difficult in some cases to identify the exact chip-forming condition near the transition from a continuous to a discontinuous chip based on any single factor. Further, under differing machining conditions, the definition of a desirable discontinuous chip form may vary. Thus, additional signal analysis capabilities are required.

The linear discriminant function introduced earlier in this chapter is adopted here to help distinguish the cutting states and identify the continuous/discontinuous chip forming boundary. Discriminant functions, including the event rate of the RMS of AE, are obtained through a training process using a set of pattern vectors, the classifications of which are known. The discriminant functions are then applied to the pattern vectors of test cuts. A more efficient discriminator,

Table 16.7 Chip Forms Classified by LDF for 6061-T6 Al, Cut by TPG-322 Carbide Insert Tool

Cutting Parameters			Discriminant Functions		2-Member Discriminant Function				TLU	
					With Depth of Cut as a Component		W/O Depth of Cut as a Component		With Depth of cut as a Component	W/O Depth of cut as a Component
Cutting Speed 1000 fpm	Feed Rate .001 ipr	Depth of Cut .01 in	Event Rate of RMS of AE; Hz	Chip Type (observed from cut test)	$g_1(X)$ (for Cont. chip)	$g_2(X)$ (for disc. chip)	$g_1(X)$ (for Cont. chip)	$g_2(X)$ (for disc. chip)	$g(X)$	$g(X)$
1.5	10	5	44.9	DISC.	−36.32	161.12	−7.01	121.81	122.23	74.42
1.5	6	5	11.7	CONT.	78.65	−28.25	38.37	2.03	−64.05	−18.80
1.5	12	5	44.4	DISC.	−13.36	141.16	8.59	109.21	94.97	58.59
1.5	14	5	45.9	DISC.	0.19	134.61	19.72	105.08	81.80	50.06
1.5	19	5	51.3	DISC.	16.01	137.59	36.60	107.00	72.35	41.77
1.5	16	5	46.9	DISC.	16.10	124.70	31.96	98.84	65.11	39.71
1.25	10	5	54.7	DISC.	−84.30	228.20	−31.46	165.36	192.97	112.65

1.5	14	6	47.4	DISC.	4.31	135.49	16.36	111.44	80.08	55.54
1.5	2	5	6.3	CONT.	62.84	−31.24	21.49	0.11	−54.60	−10.50
1.5	6	4	13.7	CONT.	58.07	−5.67	33.89	10.51	−37.68	−11.49
1.3	20	5	53.2	DISC.	26.18	134.82	44.83	106.17	63.39	36.65
1.5	6	6	12.7	CONT.	85.12	−30.72	36.13	6.27	−69.29	−15.15
1.25	8	5	37.6	DISC.	−24.46	130.16	−7.65	103.35	96.31	64.21
1.5	7	5	36.1	DISC.	−25.83	127.04	−9.03	100.24	95.87	63.30
1.8	8	4	5.9	CONT.	117.63	−76.23	68.84	−35.44	−118.43	−56.91
1.5	7	4	16.6	CONT.	54.73	5.47	34.63	17.57	−29.13	−7.91

From Dornfeld and Pan [18]. Reprinted courtesy of the Society of Manufacturing Engineers, Copyright 1985.

The criteria to distinguish chip form are as follows:

1. For two-member discriminant function
$g_1(X) > g_2(X) = \,$ > continuous-chip cutting; $\quad g_2(X) = \,$ > $g_1(X) = \,$ > discontinuous-chip cutting
2. For TLU
$g(X) < 0 = \,$ > continuous-chip cutting; $\quad g(X) > 0 = \,$ > discontinuous-chip cutting

the threshold logic unit (TLU), is also applied successfully to classification of chip form. The significance of the event rate of the RMS of AE as a component of the pattern vector for characterizing cutting states is evaluated.

Classification of Cutting States

Tests were done to distinguish the cutting states into their continuous or discontinuous chip formation [18]. The following parameters were selected to characterize a cutting pattern:

- Cutting speed ($\times$ 1000 fpm)

- Feed rate ($\times$ 0.001 ipr)

- Depth of cut ($\times$ 0.01 inch)

- Event rate of the RMS of AE, using 1.1 times average RMS level as threshold (Hz)

The training patterns were picked so that they represented machining at a variety of cutting speeds, feed rates, and depths of cut. Especially, cutting conditions near the boundary of continuous or discontinuous chip formation for this tool geometery and work material were included. Seven training pattern vectors were used to determine the weight vectors. The correction increment was selected to be equal to the inverse of the number of corrections—that is, with a minimum of .002. The following weight vectors (cutting speed weight, feed rate weight, depth of cut, weight, etc.) were obtained after 48 iterations:

- Continuous chip (7.50, 10.30, 11.17, -4.70, 4.76)

- Discontinuous chip (-5.50, -8.30, -9.17, 6.70, -2.76)

Cutting experiments were carried out under various conditions to check the validity of the recognition system for the cutting-state classification. Table 16.7 shows the results of the discriminant functions in 16 different cutting tests. The test cutting conditions are listed as well. The classifications are matched with the observed states for all the cases.

An analysis was carried out to identify the significance of each component of the pattern vector in the classification. New pattern vectors were formed by eliminating one component at a time—for example, using cutting speed, feed rate, and depth of cut (without AE event rate), or using cutting speed, depth of cut, and event rate of the RMS of AE (without feed rate) as parameters each time. The seven new training patterns were used to search for the discriminant

Table 16.8 Results of LDF Classification for Cutting Tests Excluding One Component at a Time

Case	Number of Iterations to Get Wt. Vector	Discriminant Function For	Weight of Cutting Speed	Weight of Feed Rate	Weight of Depth of Cut	Weight of Event Rate of the RMS of AE	Weight of Constant	Successful Rate of Test
No Cutting Speed in Pattern	524	Cont. chip Disc. Chip	— —	8.62 −6.62	12.61 −10.61	−3.85 5.85	5.93 −3.97	100%
No Feed Rate in Pattern	2200	Cont. Chip Disc. Chip	8.26 −6.26	— —	2.10 −0.10	0.23 1.77	5.29 −3.29	100%
No Depth of Cut in Pattern	49	Cont. Chip Disc. Chip	10.00 −8.00	7.24 −5.24	— —	−2.24 4.24	6.11 −4.11	100%
No Event Rate of the RMS of AE in Pattern	53	Cont. Chip Disc. Chip	4.65 −2.65	0.57 1.43	−4.43 2.04	— —	3.02 −1.02	87.5%

From Dornfeld and Pan [18]. Reprinted courtesy of Society of Manufacturing Engineers. Copyright 1985.

functions. Again, these classifiers were applied to the 16 cutting tests. Table 16.8 shows the number of iterations needed to obtain solutions, the weight vectors, and the successful rate of the classifications done on different types of pattern vectors. It shows that the classification is not reliable without the inclusion of the event rate of the RMS of AE as a pattern component, indicating the effectiveness of the AE technique in distinguishing chip form. Based on the number of iterations needed to obtain weight vectors, more effort is needed to get a set of discriminant functions without feed rate as a component. This verifies that feed rate is the second most important factor in chip-form classification. It was also the most effective parameter for changing the chip form during test cuts. However, the absolute value of the weight for each component does not really indicate the relative importance of each parameter. This is true for a variety of reasons, including differences in the selection of correction increments and in the relative scale factors (instrumentation gains, for example) among the components. The analysis above is a more suitable way to judge the relative importance of each component to the classification.

Because the basic classification needed is between continuous and discontinuous chip form in this study, the performance of the TLU was evaluated to simplify the process. With the five-component pattern vectors, it was assumed that the discontinuous chip state generated a positive discriminant and that the continuous chip state generated a negative one. Using the same training set as above with all parameters included, the weight vector was obtained after 69 iterations as follows:

$$(-6.98, -11.87, -12.28, 7.04, -3.34)$$

The discriminant function was applied again to the cutting tests and the classifications determined were correct every time, as shown in table 16.7. In two-category classification, the calculation is straightforward using a TLU because of the single discriminant function involved. This also implies that the classification scheme can be implemented in hardware for real-time application.

In most machining processes, the exact depth of cut is not always known without human observation or other sensor input, whereas cutting speed and feed rate are more easily obtained. Although the depth of cut has some influence on the chip formation, the effect is much less prominent in the pattern than feed rate or event rate of the RMS of AE, as discussed earlier. An analysis was done to see whether depth of cut could be eliminated from the cutting pattern without jeopardizing the performance of the discriminator. First, the two-member discriminant functions and TLU were obtained through the training patterns without depth of cut as a component. Next, classifiers were applied to the new patterns for the 16 cutting tests above, as shown in table 16.7. The test data indicates that the classification is still highly reliable without the depth of cut as a pattern component. When the difference between two discriminants in the

TLU is larger, the classification is more definite and less ambiguous. An examination of table 16.7 reveals that the different and absolute values of discriminants decrease for the classification without depth of cut included. It is apparent that depth of cut has some positive contribution to the classification and the new discriminant functions are less effective than the original ones. However, using only those easily obtained parameters (that is, no depth of cut) to distinguish chip form can work well in on-line monitoring according to the analysis.

Tool Wear Detection Using Time Series Analysis of Acoustic Emission

Introduction

Tool wear in a machining operation is highly undesirable because it severely degrades the quality of machined surfaces and causes undesirable changes in work geometry. From a process automation point of view, therefore, it is necessary that an intelligent sensing system be devised to detect the progress of tool wear during cutting operations so that worn tools can be identified and replaced in time. A fair amount of research has been devoted to the detection of tool wear. Techniques reported include the use of optical, electric, mechanical, audible acoustic, pneumatic, inductive, or capacitive transducers. These methods have various degrees of success in practical applications depending on their sensitivity, noise contamination, ease of use, and cost.

As was mentioned previously, during a cutting operation, acoustic emission is generated primarily by the deformation in the primary shear zone and the sliding friction in the secondary shear zone. As the cutting tool wears, additional frictional action between the tool flank and the workpiece also creates acoustic emission. The portion of AE that is attributed to friction on the wear land becomes more important when the flank/workpiece contact area increases as a result of tool wear. Acoustic emission generated from shearing and friction exhibit different signal characteristics, because the mechanisms by which AE is produced on these occasions are fundamentally different. As a result, the signal characteristics of acoustic emission are expected to change when the tool wear-land progresses.

The major advantage of using acoustic emission to detect the condition of tool wear is that the frequency range of the acoustic emission signal is much higher than that of the machine vibrations and environmental noises. Therefore, a relatively uncontaminated signal can be obtained easily by the use of a high-pass filter. In addition, acoustic emission can be measured by simply mounting a piezoelectric transducer on the tool holder. The transducer does not interfere with the cutting operation, and thus allows for continuous monitoring of the tool condition. However, because of their high-frequency nature and their sensitivity

to microstructural behavior of material, acoustic emission signals often have to be treated with additional signal processing schemes so that the most useful information can be extracted. The detection of tool wear using acoustic emission has been attempted by several researchers. The signal analysis methodologies reported include the RMS (Root-Mean-Square) measurement, the event count analysis, and the frequency analysis.

Using the first method, the RMS voltage level of AE is shown to increase in proportion to the amount of the flank wear [17, 37, 33]. In the second method, correlation is found between the amount of the flank wear and the number of accumulated counts of the AE signal whose amplitude exceeds some preselected threshold value [36]. RMS voltage level and event count based on a properly selected threshold are both representatives of the signal power content, which increases with wear-land in general. However, the crater wear, as a result of its influence on the tool effective rake angle, tends to reduce the sensitivity of AE energy content to progressive flank wear. Moreover, cutting parameters will change the AE energy content independently, because the AE power released is proportional to the strain rate in the cutting process. As a result of using a single parameter to characterize the signal, power-level analysis often fails to distinguish between the change of AE source mechanisms (such as the flank wear and the growth of crater wear on the tool rake) and the change of cutting parameters (such as feed rate, cutting speed, and depth of cut). Therefore, calibrations of AE signal power at all combinations of cutting parameters are necessary to implement the monitoring technique. In the third method, spectral characteristics are found to be a function of the tool wear condition [20]. However, difficulties usually encountered in the frequency analysis are the "signal coloring" effects caused by the propagation media, sensor frequency response, and instrumentation system function. Furthermore, the discrete Fourier transform introduces a large number of orthogonal parameters to characterize the AE signal; therefore, a parameter selection process has to be implemented before the spectral analysis can be carried out practically.

In this example, a time-series analysis technique is used to characterize the acoustic emission RMS signal with an autoregressive model. The model parameters are updated constantly according to the RMS signal dynamics, which are strongly dependent on the AE source mechanism. As a result, these time-varying parameters are expected to contain information about the condition of cutting tool wear. A description of the background and implementation of time-series modeling was given earlier in this chapter. The detection scheme illustrated monitors the time-series model parameters of the acoustic emission RMS signal generated during metal cutting. When the parameter pattern exceeds the preset allowable range, a severely worn tool condition is concluded and a tool change should take place. The merits of this technique are that the number of parameters to be monitored is much lower than in spectral analysis and that the method provides a large degree of freedom to describe the acoustic emission signal other than by just studying its DC power level.

APPLICATIONS 477

The RMS signal is a function of the AE low-frequency components and the total power contained in the individual bursts of AE generated during machining. To make the technique sensitive only to changes in the AE source rather than to the change of cutting parameters (RMS is proportional to cutting speed), the DC component of RMS voltage is filtered out. Thus, the autoregressive model tracks only the dynamic properties, not the mean energy level, of the AE signal. Because of this, an off-line parameter calibration procedure is needed only once under any cutting condition to map out the allowable range for the parameters, because the parameters will be affected by tool wear but not by the change of cutting velocity, depth of cut, or feed rate.

Experimental Evaluation

A series of experiments was conducted to test the performance of the proposed technique [45]. Figure 16.19 shows the experimental set-up and the signal-processing schematic. A Kennametal K68 tungsten carbide insert tool was mounted on a tool holder with 5-degree rake. The workpieces used were low carbon steel bars with diameters of 2 inches (5.08 cm). Experiments were performed under five different cutting conditions, as listed in table 16.9. Conditions 2 and 3 were the same as condition 1 except for different amounts of tool flank wear. Conditions 1, 4, and 5 were all conducted using fresh cutting tools but with different cutting parameters. No chatter, built-up edge, or rake face crater was observed during cutting.

A commercial piezoelectric AE transducer was mounted on the tool shank. The detected acoustic emission signals were amplified, high-passed at 50 KHz, sent through a RMS meter with a time constant of 10 ms, modulated to remove the DC component, and digitized at a rate of 5 kHz. The following experimental procedure was used:

1. Use a fresh tool to cut a workpiece for a short time. Measure the digitized acoustic emission during cutting and evaluate the autoregressive model parameters simultaneously.

2. Replace the workpiece used in step 1 with another piece of steel bar. Machine for approximately 30 minutes.

3. Stop the operation. Use a microscope to measure the length of wear-land on tool.

4. Use the worn tool to cut the workpiece used in step 1. Measure the acoustic emission and calculate the model parameters. The guideline here is to monitor the acoustic emission signal only when the identical workpiece is being cut. In this way, the surface

Figure 16.19 Experimental Set-up and Signal Processing Flow Diagram

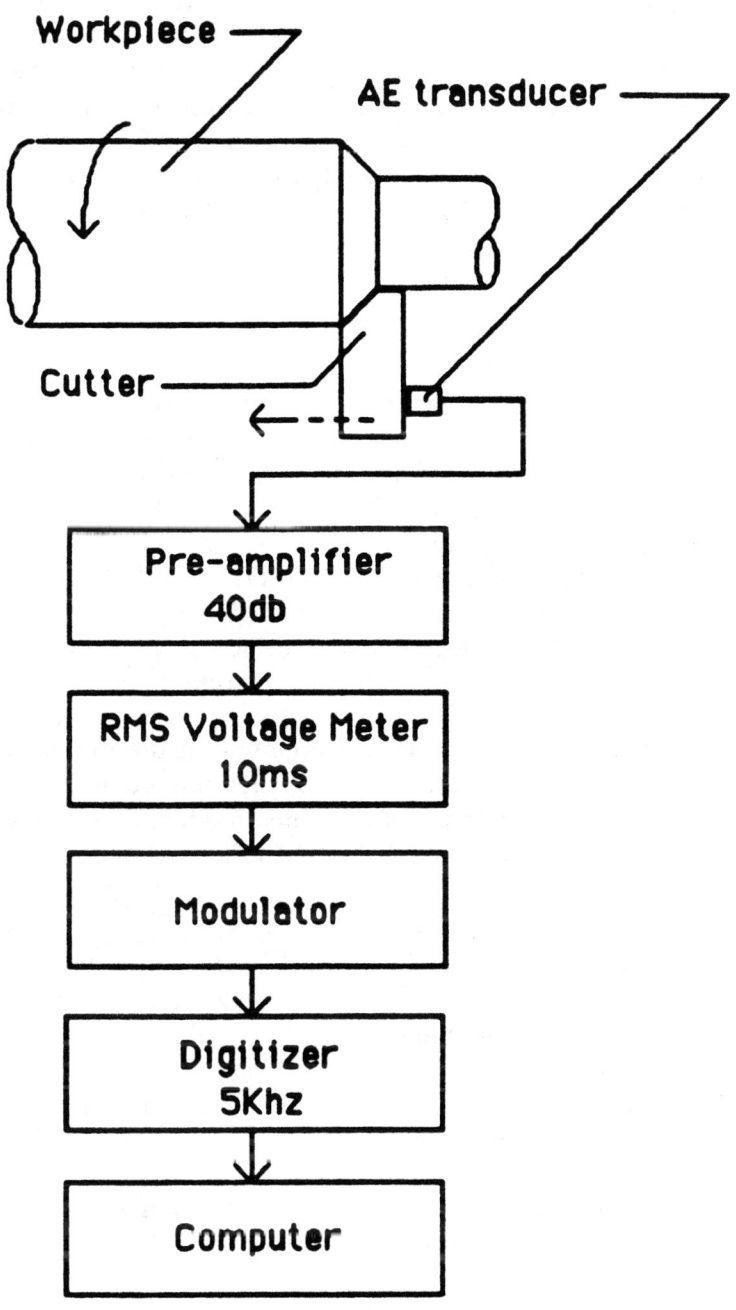

APPLICATIONS

Table 16.9 Experimental Conditions

#	Tool Condition	Cutting Parameters
1	Fresh	1000rpm, 0.008ipr (0.203mmpr) 0.02in (0.508mm) depth of cut
2	0.0078in (0.19mm) flank wear	Same as above
3	0.0197in (0.50mm) flank wear	Same as above
4	Fresh	1000rpm, 0.008ipr (0.203mmpr) 0.03in (0.762mm) depth of cut
5	Fresh	800rpm, 0.005ipr (0.127mmpr) 0.03in (0.762mm) depth of cut

From Liang and Dornfeld [45]. Reproduced courtesy of the American Society of Mechanical Engineers. Copyright 1989.

speed and material properties are guaranteed to remain unchanged.

5. Go back to step 2 and repeat the procedure until a wear land of 0.0197 inch (0.5 mm) is achieved.

Analysis

A typical time series of acoustic emission RMS signal recorded over 0.4 second is shown in figure 16.20. The DC level of the signal, normally about 300 mv, has been removed. Also plotted on this diagram is a dotted line that shows the predicted values of the AE RMS from a 6th-order autoregressive model with an adaptation gain of 1.0e-5. Some signal dynamics at the beginning of cutting were lost for just a short period while the adaptation began. However, the predicted values agree with the original signal extremely well, as the figure shows. Figures 16.21 and 16.22 show the time variation of the error signal and the first model parameter respectively. The decreasing trend in error signal with time is clearly shown. After 400 ms of adaptation, the error signal is confined within ± 5 percent of the measured signal. The first model parameter takes about 300 ms to achieve its optimal value. The time then required to track the time-varying optimal value will be much shorter than 300 ms, because the initial condition will always be the current value instead of zero.

If an autoregressive signal is modeled by an autoregressive model with sufficiently high order, the error signal should be white, because all the parameters are optimized in the sense of minimizing the mean-square error. The error signal

Figure 16.20 RMS of Acoustic Emission Signal (Solid, Experimental, and Points, Model-predicted Values)

The line and the dots are not clearly distinguishable because the model closely fits the measured data.

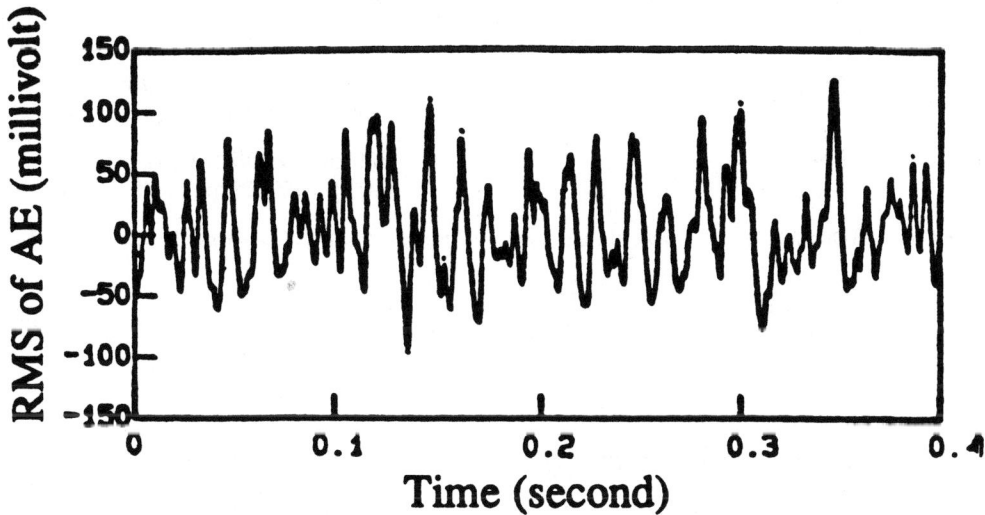

$e(k)$ shows no major autocorrelation. The existence of some minor correlated components indicates that (1) the acoustic emission RMS signal generated during metalcutting operation is not a purely autoregressive process, (2) the model order, 6 in this case, is not sufficiently high that the truncated higher order terms are incorporated into the error signal, and (3) based on the formulation of the stochastic gradient algorithm, the model parameters are not the exact solutions to the problem of minimizing the mean-square error but rather only approach the solution all the time. However, these limitations are not significant here.

Figure 16.21 Error Signal

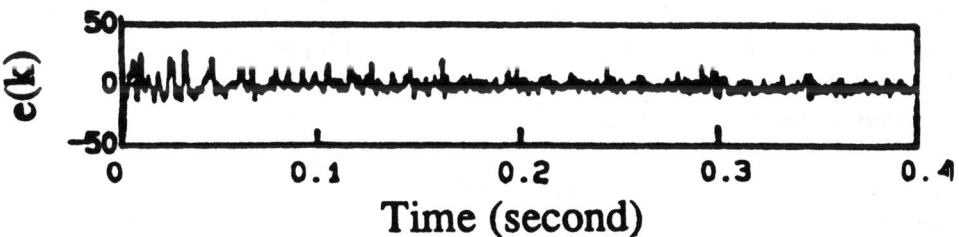

APPLICATIONS

Figure 16.22 First Model Parameter

A 6th-order autoregressive model was used.

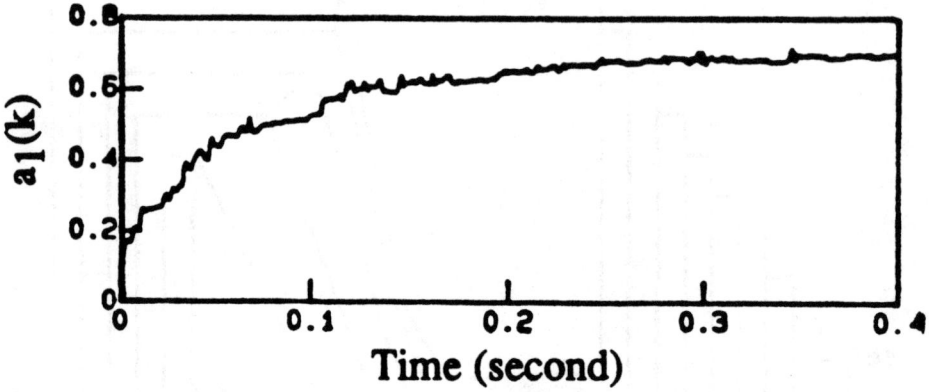

The modeling algorithm works on a preselected model order and adaptation gain, which are kept constant throughout the whole process. The guideline to the selection of the model order and gain are based on the minimization of the sum of square errors, defined as follows:

$$\text{S.S.E.} = \sum_{k=1}^{M} e^2(k) \qquad (16.34)$$

where M is a large number, 2,048 in this study. The correlation between model order, adaptation gain, and S.S.E. is shown in figure 16.23, in which the curved plane formed by lines of constant adaptation gain suggests that a larger adaptation gain in the region of low model order or a higher model order in the region of small adaptation gain will result in a smaller sum of square errors. However, a large adaptation gain associated with a high model order will cause unstable adaptation. An optimal order of 6 and an adaptation gain of 0.6e-5 were selected because they minimized the S.S.E.

The parameter vectors $[a_1, a_2, a_3, a_4, a_5 a_6]$ determined under test conditions 1, 2, and 3, which are listed in table 16.10, are shown in figure 16.24. Each time-varying parameter is averaged over a 0.1-second period. Figure 16.25 shows the parameters under test conditions 1, 4, and 5. Data in these diagrams exhibit the distinction between parameters for various tool wear conditions and the agreement of parameters under various cutting speeds, feed rates, and depths of cut.

The discrimination indices between classes 1 and 2, 1 and 3, 1 and 4, and 1 and 5 are calculated for each model parameter and listed in table 16.10. The results of these tests show that the separation attributed to changes in cutting

Figure 16.23 Dependence of Sum of Square Error on Model Parameter and Adaptation Gain

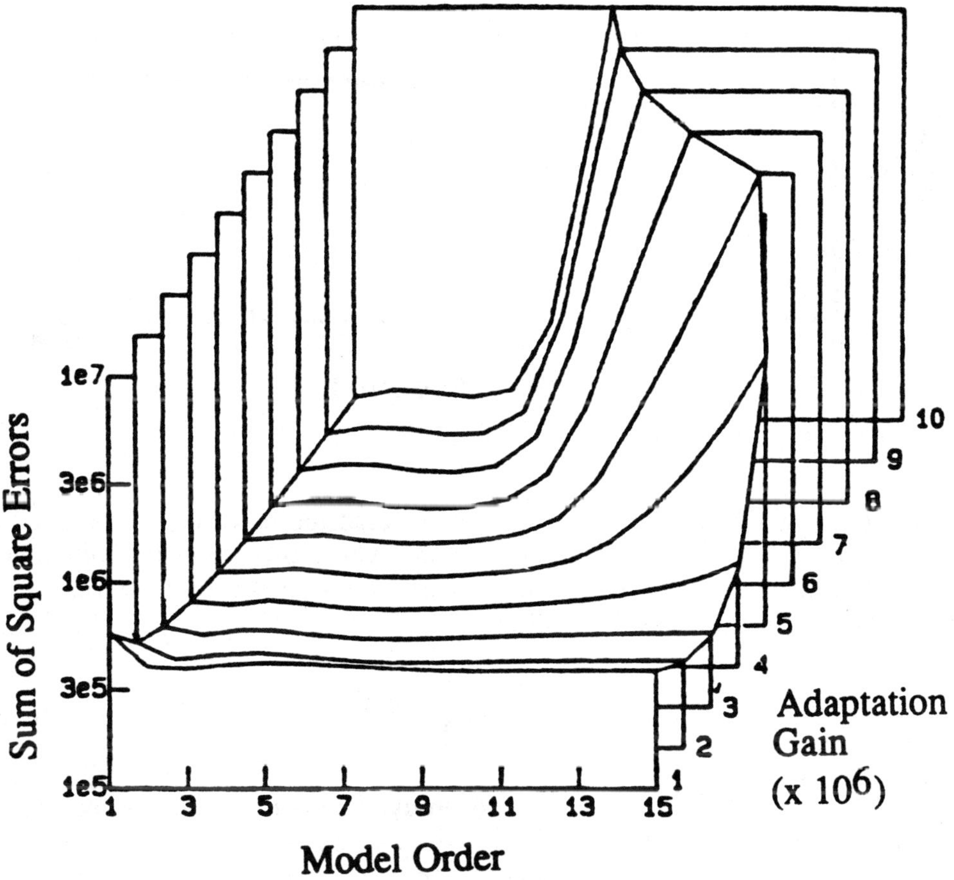

parameters is low, whereas the separation resulting from various states of tool wear is comparatively high. All data collected under conditions 1, 2, and 3 are then combined into a single class, 1+2+3, and the discrimination index is calculated. The discrimination indices between this class and conditions 4 and 5 are listed in table 16.10. The resulting discrimination indices are lower than they are in the cases when fresh tool conditions are not combined. This is expected from the fact that the combined class has a higher within-class variation. Based on the discrimination analysis, parameters 1 and 4 are shown to be the two most important features in terms of detecting and tracking the amount of tool wear while maintaining insensitivity to machining tool condition.

Figure 16.24 Model Parameters Under Conditions 1, 2, and 3

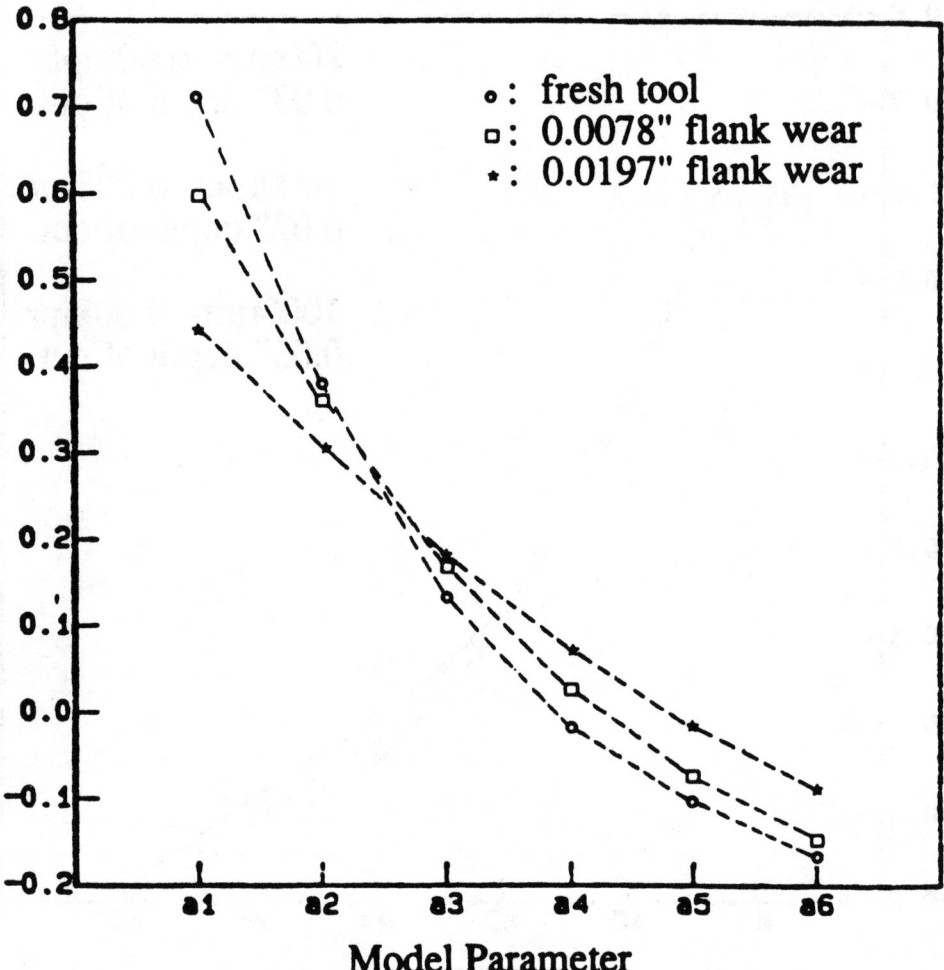

A two-dimensional parameter plane is constructed by plotting the fourth parameter against the first one, as shown in figure 16.26. Owing to the nonstationarity of the acoustic emission signal, the model parameters are time-varying and form clusters in the plane. However, these clusters, each representing a different tool wear condition, are clearly separable. As a result, the condition of tool wear can be detected effectively by monitoring the time trajectories of the model parameters. The parameter plane in figure 16.26 suggests that a tool change should be called for when $[a_1 a_4]$ goes beyond $[0.46, 0.07]$, because a 0.0197-inch wearland tool is considered damaged for these studies.

Figure 16.25 Model Parameters Under Conditions 1, 4, and 5

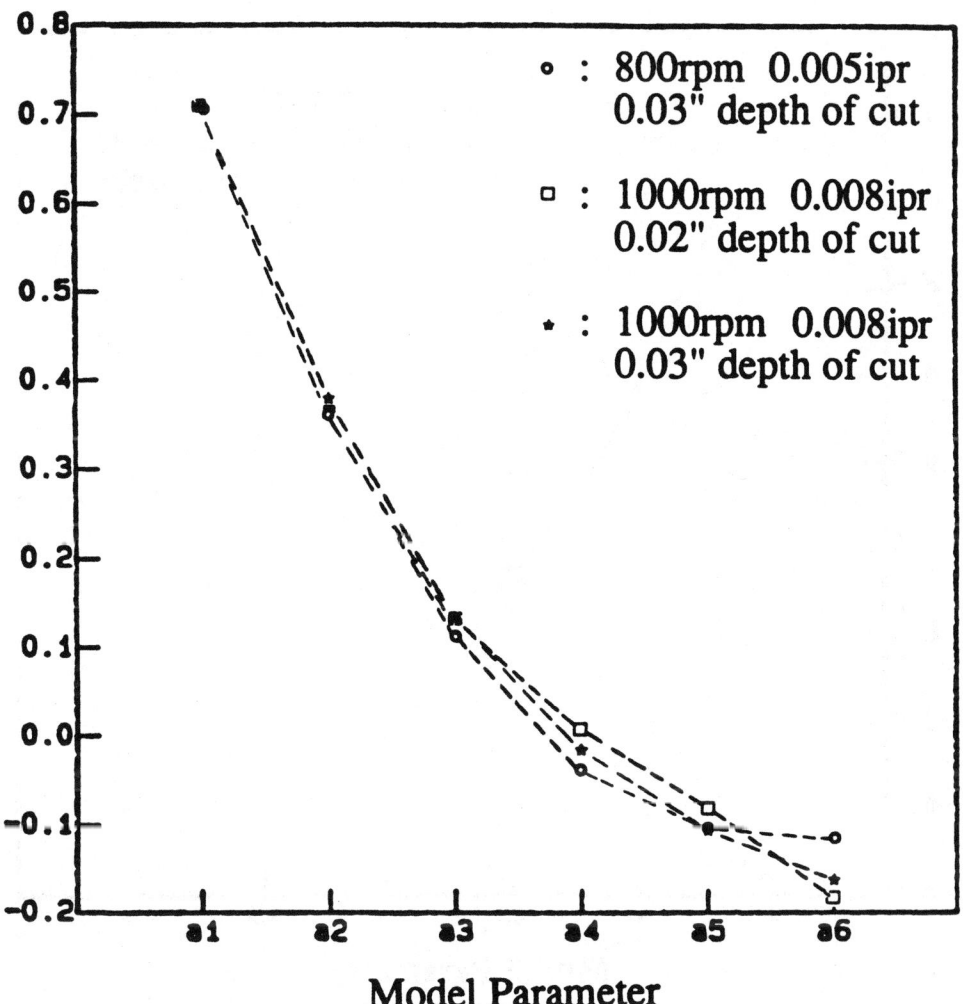

Sensor Integration Using Neural Networks for Intelligent Tool Condition Monitoring

Introduction

In this example, a technique for intelligent tool condition monitoring that employs information from multiple sensors is presented. This information is integrated via a neural network, a parallel computing architecture that can learn to

APPLICATIONS

Table 16.10 Discrimination Index J Between Different Experimental Conditions

	a_1	a_2	a_3	a_4	a_5	a_6
$J[1,2]$	8.84	2.84	5.34	1.90	4.39	2.58
$J[1,3]$	24.65	8.57	6.02	13.14	12.95	8.63
$J[1,4]$	0.97	3.58	0.19	3.65	4.13	4.08
$J[1,5]$	0.25	1.85	2.63	0.04	0.83	5.76
$J[1+2+3,4]$	8.23	1.06	4.93	3.26	2.36	0.86
$J[1+2+3,5]$	23.16	5.54	5.19	7.19	7.88	3.72

From Liang and Dornfeld [45]. Reproduced courtesy of the American Society of Mechanical Engineers. Copyright 1989.

Figure 16.26 Parameter Plane of the First and Fourth Parameters

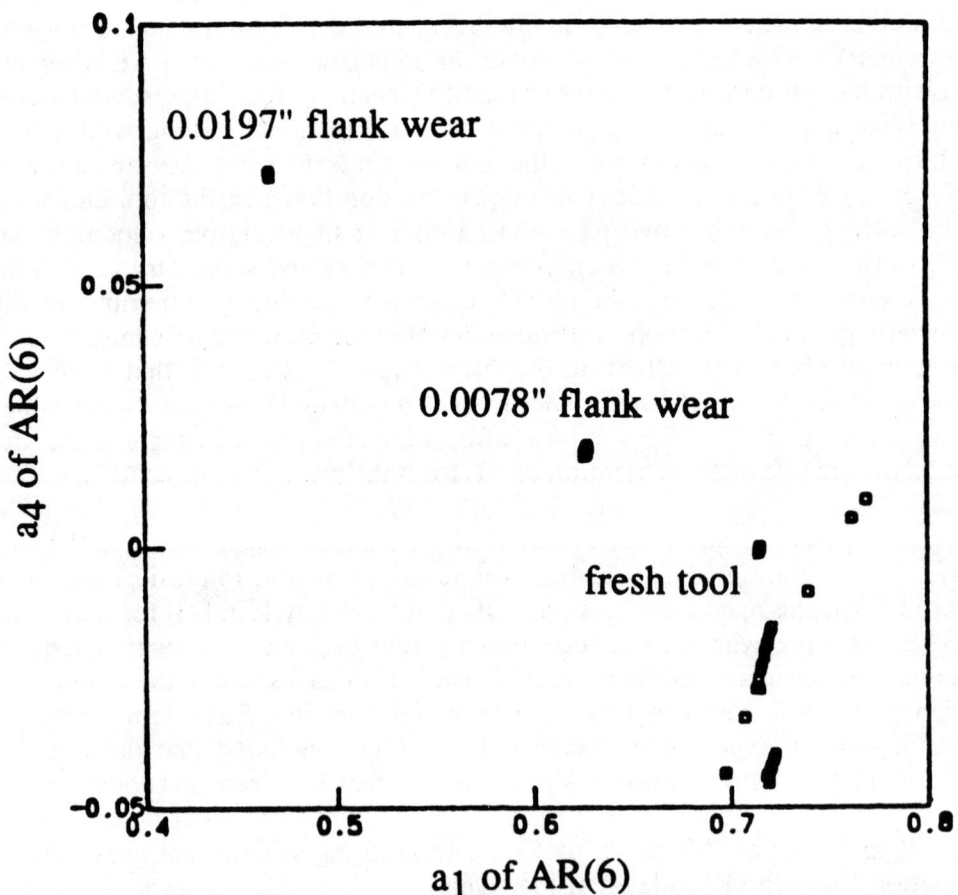

recognize patterns of sensor information and associate them with decisions on the tool-wear state. Initial efforts by Rangwala [57] and Rangwala and Dornfeld [60] demonstrated the feasibility of using neural networks for sensor integration in tool-wear monitoring tasks. The networks were used as learning and pattern-recognition devices and were able to successfully associate sensor signal patterns with the appropriate decision on tool wear. Chryssolouris and Domroese [7] performed simulations in order to study the learning capabilities of these networks. Based on the simulation results, they proposed the use of neural networks as the decision-making component in an intelligent tool condition monitoring system. As shown in this example, neural networks are able to filter out noise in the sensor data, which enhances their ability to perform successful pattern association tasks. These aspects are evaluated experimentally for tool wear monitoring in a turning operation, under a range of machining conditions.

Use of Multiple Sensors

In the application discussed here, it was decided to use AE and cutting force information in order to develop an intelligent tool condition monitoring system. The primary and secondary shear zones are important sources of AE when cutting with a fresh tool. Kannatey-Asibu and Dornfeld [38] have presented a comprehensive analysis for AE generation during orthogonal cutting with a fresh tool. In the presence of flank wear, the tool-work interface becomes an additional zone of AE generation because of intense friction between the tool and workpiece surfaces, which move past one another at high relative velocities. The effects of tool wear on AE generation in the primary and secondary zones must also be considered. Kobayashi and Thomsen [41] conducted experiments with artificially ground worn tools and concluded that the presence of a flank land did not have an observable effect on the shear angle. This implies that flank wear does not affect the AE characteristics in the primary and secondary shear zones. However, the presence of crater wear affects the effective rake angle of the tool, and this could affect the generation of AE from the primary and secondary shear zones.

The root mean square (RMS) level of the AE signal (V_{RMS}) measures the total power level of the signal and has been found to be sensitive to the degree of flank wear in a turning operation. Experiments conducted by Lan [43] for machining of SAE 4340 steel with carbide tools indicate that V_{RMS} increases with machining time because of increased flank wear. However, in cases where the crater wear is significant, V_{RMS} tends to decrease or remains constant. Because the presence of flank wear is expected to increase V_{RMS}, Lan concluded that the effect of crater wear is to cause a drop in V_{RMS}. The fact that V_{RMS} remains constant with increased tool wear because opposing effects of flank and crater wear makes it difficult to design an AE-based tool-wear monitoring system that uses only information about the RMS level of the signal.

Table 16.11 Effect of Velocity and Wear on AE

Condition	Total Power	Low Freq. Power	High Freq. Power	Mean Frequency	Standard Dev. of Frequency
Increased Velocity	+	+	+	−	+
Increased Wear	+	+	−	−	−

From Rangwala and Dornfeld [60].

Emel and Kannatey-Asibu [21] present experimental data that shows that the power spectrum is sensitive to tool wear and process conditions. Results for machining of AISI 1060 with carbide inserts [57] also indicated that the AE power spectrum was sensitive to the level of flank wear and process parameters such as the cutting velocity. Table 16.11, reproduced from Rangwala and Dornfeld [59] summarizes the qualitative effects of tool wear and cutting velocity on the AE power spectrum. The quantities f_m and σ are the mean and standard deviation of frequency of the power spectrum. The mean frequency, f_m, divides the total power of the spectrum into two equal parts, whereas σ indicates the spread in power content around the mean frequency. Table 16.11 shows that an increase in flank wear and cutting velocity causes an increase in the low-frequency (100–300 kHz) power of the AE signal. Other effects, such as feed rate and depth of cut changes as well as chip tangling and chip breakage processes, are also expected to affect the AE spectral characteristics. An important consideration for tool wear monitoring is that appropriate schemes should be used in order to identify spectral regions that show maximum sensitivity to tool wear under a range of process conditions.

The performance of an AE-based tool-wear monitoring system can be enhanced by complementing the AE information with information from other sensors mounted on the machine tool (for example, force or power sensors). The magnitude of the cutting force is sensitive to the occurrence of tool wear in a turning operation [2]. According to Wright [75], however, cutting force information by itself is inadequate for tool-wear detection, because its magnitude is also dependent on the cutting velocity. Another problem is that although flank wear tends to increase the cutting force, the accompanying crater wear tends to reduce it, so that the magnitude of the cutting force may not show any sensitivity to tool wear. Cook [8] and Martin et al. [47] have shown that the cutting force spectrum (which reflects the dynamic characteristics of the cutting force) is sensitive to tool flank wear. Vibrations in the direction of the cutting force are induced as a result of flank wear in high-frequency regions (> 5 kHz) and in lower-frequency regions (< 300 Hz). The former is the result of vibrations of the tool holder, and the latter is attributed to workpiece vibrations. The force spectrum is also dependent on process variables, such as cutting velocity, feed rate, and oscillations in the shear angle during chip formation.

The AE and cutting force information relate to different effects of tool wear. Acoustic emission is sensitive to the microscopic activities (and the resulting stress waves) related to plastic deformation and friction in the cutting zone. The cutting force spectrum is sensitive to the vibrations induced in the tool and workpiece because of the effects of flank wear. The advantage of using AE and cutting force sensors is that they provide information relating to microscopic (stress waves) and macroscopic (vibrations) effects of tool wear. This helps provide better signal features to the pattern classifier, allowing a greater reliability in making decisions about the state of tool wear.

Experimental Evaluation

To apply the neural-network-based machine-learning approach discussed earlier, a series of machining tests was conducted on a Tree lathe. A schematic of the experimental set-up is shown in figure 16.27. The work material was case-hardened AISI 1060 bars (hardened workpieces were used in order to induce faster tool wear). A Kennametal TPGF-322 insert of grade K68 was used. The bars were of nominal diameter 2 inches (50.8 mm) and 12 inches (305 mm) in length.

An acoustic emission transducer (type D9201) was mounted on the tool shank. The tool shank was mounted in a fixture instrumented with a Kistler force dynamometer (type 9251A). The fixture was mounted in the tool turret. The AE sensor output was passed through a preamplifier (with a fixed gain of 40 db), which high-pass-filters the incoming signal above 50 kHz. The preamplified signal was passed through an amplifier (5 db gain) and recorded on the video channel of a modified Sony recorder. The cutting force signal was passed through a charge amplifier and recorded on the audio channel of the Sony recorder.

The process variables were varied in the following range:

- Feed rate: 0.002 ipr–0.008 ipr (0.05 mm/rev–0.20 mm/rev)

- Depth: 0.01 inch–0.03 inch (0.25 mm–0.75 mm)

- Velocity: 278 sfpm–556 sfpm (85 m/min–170m/min)

No signals were collected while machining the hardened layer (approximately 1.5–2 mm thick) of the workpiece. Signals were collected only when the workpiece diameter was 45 mm (1.75 inch) or less. The tool flank land was measured using an optical comparator. The procedure used was to measure the flank land width after every two passes through the soft section of the bar and after every pass through the hardened layer. The tool wear was recorded at flank wear levels of 0.1 mm (0.004 inch), 0.125 mm (0.005 inch), 0.25 mm (0.01 inch), 0.5 mm (0.02 inch), and 0.75 mm (0.03 inch). Signals collected between these wear levels were

Figure 16.27 Experimental Set-up with Force and Acoustic Emission Sensors

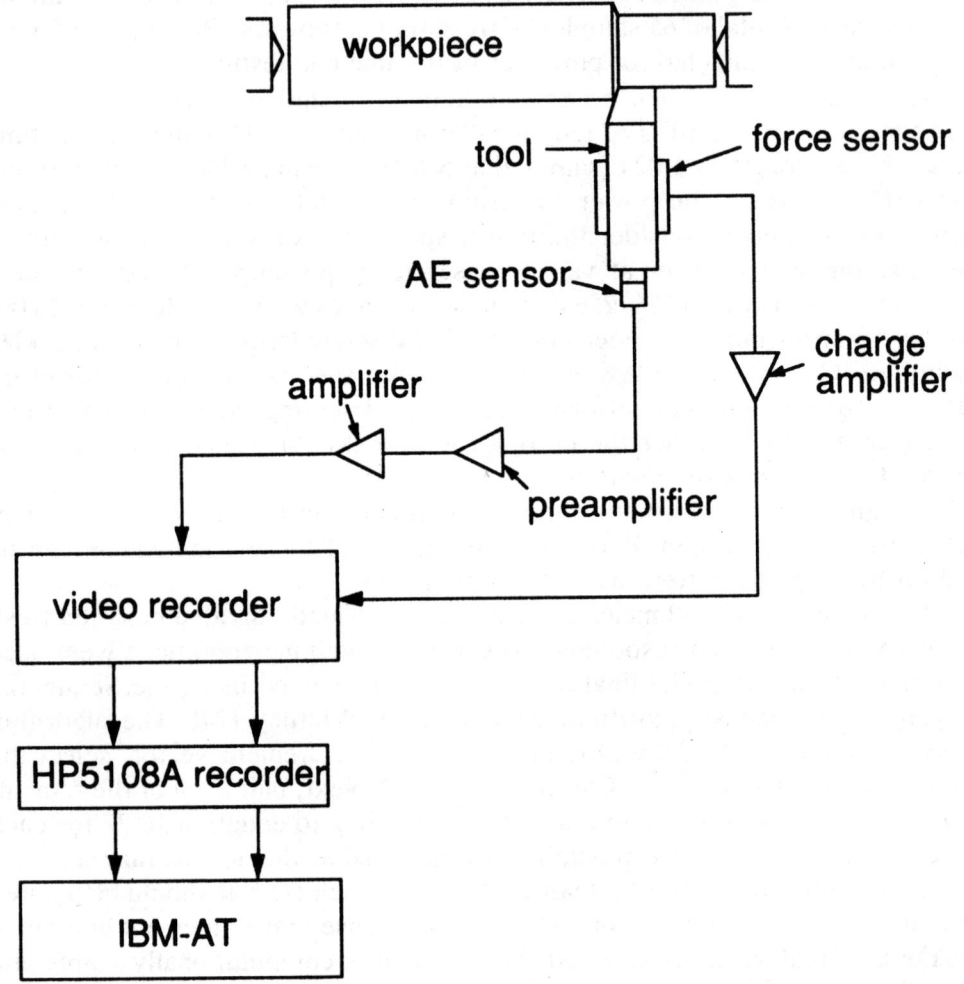

ascribed to the wear value at the lower end of the interval. For example, signals collected between 0 and 0.1 mm flank wear were assumed to be generated as a result of cutting with a fresh tool. Between wear levels of 0.25 mm and 0.5 mm, no signals were recorded, although cutting proceeded. Signals collected during cutting below 0.25 mm flank wear were assumed to belong to fresh tool cutting, whereas signals associated with a flank wear level of 0.5 mm were assumed to belong to the worn tool category.

During post-processing, the signals recorded on video tape were played back, filtered, and digitized on a HP waveform recorder. The digitized AE signals had

a record length of 1,024 points, sampled at 5 MHz, and the digitized force signals were of record length 512 points, sampled at 1 kHz. The sampled AE and force records were synchronized as closely as possible using the tape counter number as a reference. A total of 65 samples of fresh tool cutting and 58 samples of worn tool cutting were collected for purposes of training and testing.

A schematic of the signal processing activity is shown in figure 16.28. The force time domain record is of length 512 (sampled at 1 kHz) and the AE time domain record length is 1,024 (sampled at 5 MHz). Using a Fast Fourier Transform (FFT) program, the power spectrum representations of the time domain records are obtained. Consider the power spectrum as a vector whose components are the signal power at various discrete frequencies. The cutting force spectrum is of dimension 256 (256 discrete frequencies with a resolution of 2 Hz), and the AE spectrum is of dimension 512 (512 discrete frequencies with a 5 kHz resolution). Combining the AE and cutting force spectra yields a vector of dimension 768, each component of the vector representing the signal power at a discrete frequency in either the cutting force or the AE signal. This vector is referred to as the *measurement vector*.

Although valuable information may be contained in the entire measurement vector, from practical considerations, only a few of these components can be used for training and pattern-association purposes.

In the current work, 30 measurement vectors (equally divided between fresh and worn tool states) corresponding to various machining conditions were used to estimate S_w and S_b. The final d features were selected using the Sequential Forward Search (SFS) algorithm, developed by Whitney [74]. The algorithm works as follows: out of the D features in the measurement vector, select the one feature that maximizes J. Call this feature ζ_1. Next, pair each of the remaining $D - 1$ features with ζ_1 and compute J according to equation 16.27 for each of these pairs. The pair that maximizes J is selected as the new feature set. This procedure is repeated until all d features have been selected. It should be pointed out that the SFS algorithm is suboptimal in the sense that it does not guarantee that the best feature set is selected. However, it is computationally viable and yields feature sets whose signal/noise ratio is reasonably close to the optimal case [12].

It was decided that 30 samples (equally divided between fresh and worn tool cutting) would be used for purposes of training. According to the criterion in equation 16.26, the dimension of the feature vector was chosen to be 6.

Three feature sets were selected using the procedure discussed above. Set 1 features were selected using a combined measurement vector of the AE and force spectra. Application of the SFS algorithm yielded four AE and two force features in this case. Set 2 features were selected by considering the AE and force spectra as separate measurement vectors and selecting three features from each. In this case, the feature vector consists of three AE and three force features. Set 3 features were selected considering only the AE spectrum as the

APPLICATIONS

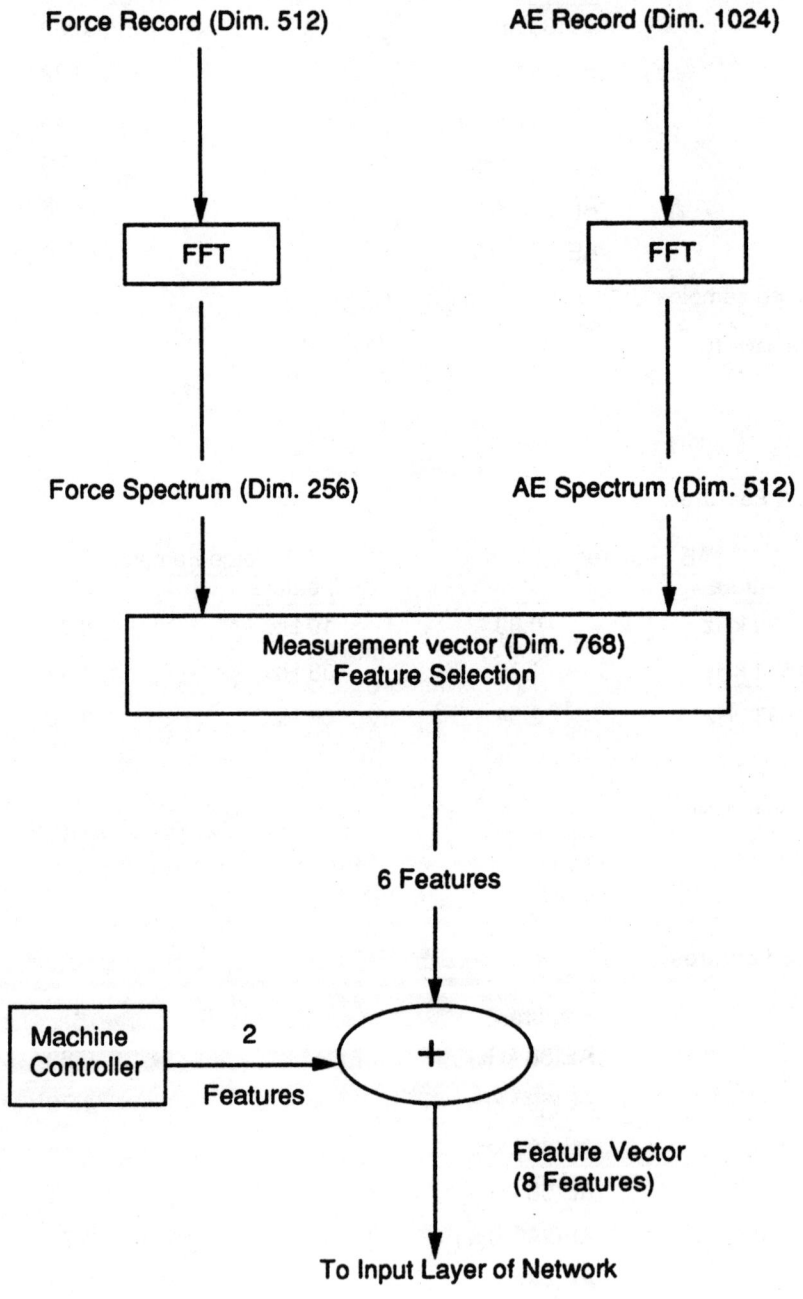

Figure 16.28 Signal Processing Flow Diagram

Table 16.12 Set 1 Features

No.	Feature	J*
1	AE(88 kHz)	0.89
2	Force(43 Hz)	3.22
3	AE(161 kHz)	5.33
4	Force(10 Hz)	8.76
5	AE(122 kHz)	12.76
6	AE(151 kHz)	20.10

*Based on 30 training samples

From Rangwala and Dornfeld [60].

Table 16.13 Set 2 Features

	AE Features		Force Features	
No.	Feature	J*	Feature	J*
1	88 kHz	0.89	10 Hz	0.56
2	504 kHz	1.79	33 Hz	1.17
3	493 kHz	2.54	39 Hz	2.00

*Based on 30 training samples

From Rangwala and Dornfeld [60].

Table 16.14 Set 3 Features

No.	Feature	J*
1	AE(88 kHz)	0.89
2	AE(504 kHz)	1.79
3	AE(493 kHz)	2.54
4	AE(68 kHz)	3.31
5	AE(293 kHz)	4.7
6	AE(449 kHz)	5.86

*Based on 30 training samples

From Rangwala and Dornfeld [60].

measurement vector. The selected features for each set and the corresponding J values as each additional feature is added are shown in tables 16.12–16.14. It is shown that adding new features increases J, because additional features cause the distance between the mean values of fresh and worn tool clusters to increase. Note that these values of J are based on estimates of S_w and S_b, computed using 30 samples of the measurement vector.

Because measurement vectors corresponding to different process conditions are used, the selected features should show a low sensitivity to changes in process variables. However, some sensitivity may still be present, so it makes sense to use the process conditions as additional features. Information such as the feed rate and cutting velocity is easily available from the machine controller and can be used as additional features. Depth-of-cut information is difficult to obtain on-line and is not used as a feature. Thus, a change in sensor feature values resulting from a change in the depth of cut has the effect of noise corrupting the sensor feature value.

Various design parameters affect the performance of the tool-wear monitoring system. These include factors such as the number of training samples, the number of sensors and sensor features used, and the structure of the neural network. The effect of these factors on the performance of the tool-wear monitoring system is evaluated next, and a design that yields the best performance is shown. Although the exact design will change for different situations, the methodology presented here will yield practical design strategies for implementing on-line process monitoring systems.

Discussion of Results

The perceptron training algorithm was used to train a linear classifier, using set 1 features. In order to reveal the effects of sensor fusion, perceptrons were also trained using set 2 and set 3 features. Unless otherwise specified, all training sets contained 30 samples, equally divided between fresh and worn tool cutting. The trained classifiers were then tested on the remaining 93 samples (of which 50 correspond to fresh tool cutting and the remaining correspond to worn tool cutting). The results are shown in table 16.15. Sets 1 and 2 yield comparable performance (88 percent and 87 percent classification success rates, respectively) whereas the performance of set 3 is lower (80-percent success rate). This indicates that feature sets composed of multiple sensor information provide better classification performance.

To reveal the effect of process variables on the sensor features, the relative influence of changes in depth of cut and tool wear on the first AE feature (88 kHz) was studied. We consider one group of samples (group F) corresponding to fresh tool cutting and seven groups of samples (groups W1–W7) corresponding to worn tool cutting. The exact machining conditions for each sample group are shown in table 16.16. The value of J for each fresh-worn sample group was cal-

Table 16.15 Perceptron Performance for Different Feature Sets

No.	Features	No. Misclass.	Success Rate (%)	J*
1	Set 1	11	88	1.02
2	Set 2	12	87	1.71
3	Set 3	18	80	0.72

*Based on 123 samples

From Rangwala and Dornfeld [60].

culated and is shown in table 16.17. It is shown that in all seven cases, the AE feature has zero sensitivity to tool wear (a J value of 0.001 or less is considered as zero sensitivity). Notice that group F samples correspond to a higher depth of cut than groups W1–W7 samples. Thus, simply looking at the AE feature would cause increases in depth of cut to be mistaken for a "tool worn" condition, and hence would lead to classification errors. The sensitivity of the force feature (10 Hz) to tool wear is also shown in table 16.17 and is revealed to be reasonably high, regardless of changes in depth of cut. Including the force feature would, in this case, reduce classification errors. Of course, additional AE features may also provide sensitivity to tool wear under these operational conditions (in fact, this is the motivation for using a large number of features). However, as larger numbers of features from one sensor are used, the information provided by them becomes highly correlated, so that a loss of sensitivity to tool wear in one feature

Table 16.16 Description of Cutting Conditions

Machining Condition	Tool Status	Feed ipr	Vel. fpm	Depth of Cut (in)	Flank Land (in)	Flank Land (mm)
F1	fresh	0.008	450	0.03	0.000	0.00
W1	worn	0.008	450	0.02	0.020	0.50
W2	worn	0.008	450	0.02	0.030	0.75
W3	worn	0.005	370	0.02	0.020	0.50
W4	worn	0.008	278	0.02	0.020	0.50
W5	worn	0.004	370	0.02	0.030	0.75
W6	worn	0.002	278	0.02	0.030	0.75
W7	worn	0.005	556	0.01	0.030	0.75

From Rangwala and Dornfeld [60].

APPLICATIONS

Table 16.17 Signal/Noise Ratio for AE and Force Features

Feature	F1 & W1	F1 & W2	F1 & W3	F1 & W4	F1 & W5	F1 & W6	F1 & W7
AE (88 kHz)	0.0	0.0	0.0	0.0	0.0	0.0	0.0
Force (10 Hz)	0.2	0.1	0.3	12.0	1.0	0.4	0.5

From Rangwala and Dornfeld [60].

is accompanied by a loss of sensitivity in other features of the same sensor signal.

Feature sets 1, 2, and 3 were used to train and test multilayered neural networks. Sensor feature values were normalized in order to prevent saturation of the sigmoid function. This was done by dividing the feature value by its maximum value in the training set. Neural networks with a single hidden layer and three nodes in the hidden layer were used. The number of nodes in the input layer is equal to the number of input features, which in the current case is eight (six sensor features and two process features). The output layer contains a single node, whose output level associates the current input pattern with a decision about tool wear. This yields a network with an 8-3-1 structure.

During the training phase, the target state of the output node was fixed at 0.01 for fresh tool patterns and at 0.99 for worn tool patterns. The minimization of the error was achieved by using conjugate gradient optimization, which adjusts the weights and thresholds in a direction that minimizes the error. The weights and thresholds were initialized to uniformly distributed random values lying between -1 and 1. During the testing stage, a pattern presented at the input layer was associated with a "fresh tool" decision if the output node activity was between 0 and 0.5; otherwise, the pattern was associated with a worn tool state.

A threshold value is associated with all nodes in the input, hidden, and output layers. The role of the threshold is to compare the weighted sum of inputs to the node and generate an output that depends on the difference between this sum and the node threshold. The threshold value thus acts as a filter for incoming signals. Theoretically, the learning procedure maps worn tool samples to an output node activity of 1, whereas fresh tool samples are associated with zero activity of the output node, so that the signal-to-noise ratio (measured by the value of the discriminant index, J) of the output node feature approaches infinity. In practice, this does not occur, because the output node error does not converge exactly to zero. Because it is sufficiently close to zero, however, each filtering step in the network is expected to suppress noise and increase the signal/noise ratio as the signal propagates through the network.

In order to reveal the noise-suppression behavior discussed above, the trained 8-3-1 network (set 1 features) was presented with all 123 samples, and the variation of the J value of the features at each layer was calculated. This is shown in figure 16.29. The value of J increases at every layer, implying higher separa-

Figure 16.29 Filtering Action of 8-3-1 Network

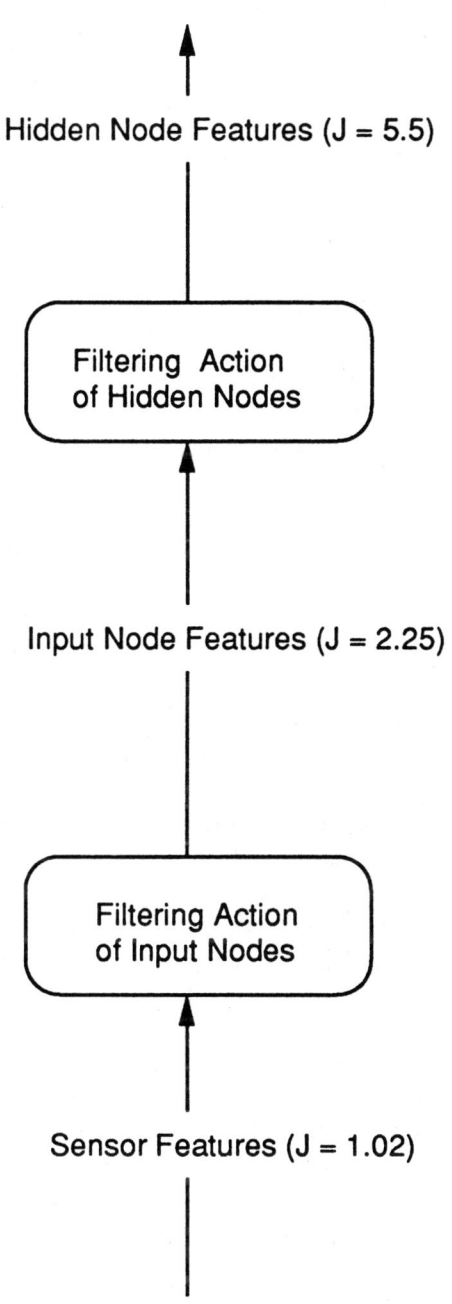

Figure 16.30 Two-dimensional Feature Space (Sensor Features)

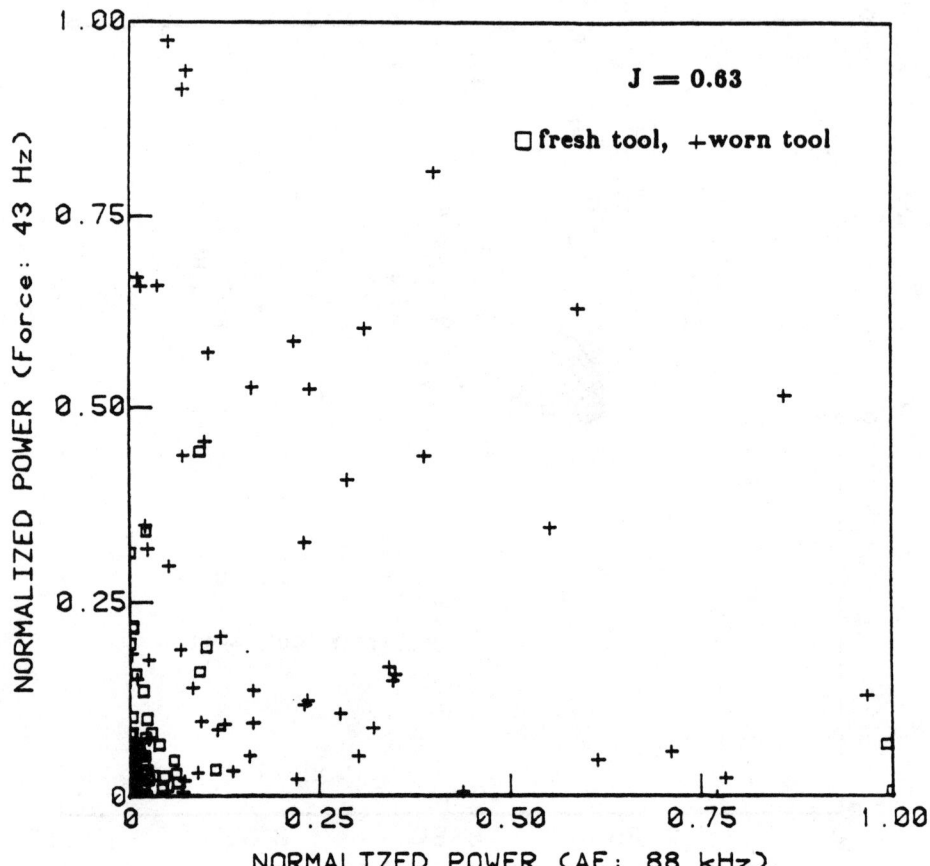

bility of the fresh and worn tool patterns at the decision layer. In order to show the increase in J graphically, a two-dimensional feature space was plotted for each layer of the network. The first two sensor features of the network (AE spectral power at 88 kHz and force spectral power at 43 Hz) are shown in figure 16.30. The value of J at this stage for this pair of features is 0.63. The input node feature pair corresponding to these features has a J value of 0.94. This pair of features is plotted in figure 16.31. Finally, figure 16.32 shows a plot of a pair of hidden node features with $J = 5.45$. At this stage, the fresh and worn tool clusters are clearly separated, allowing for greater reliability in decision making.

The classification success rate of the 8-3-1 network used above, based on 93 test samples, was found to be 94 percent. For comparison purposes, a perceptron network using the same normalized input features as the neural network

Figure 16.31 Two-dimensional Feature Space (Input Node Features)

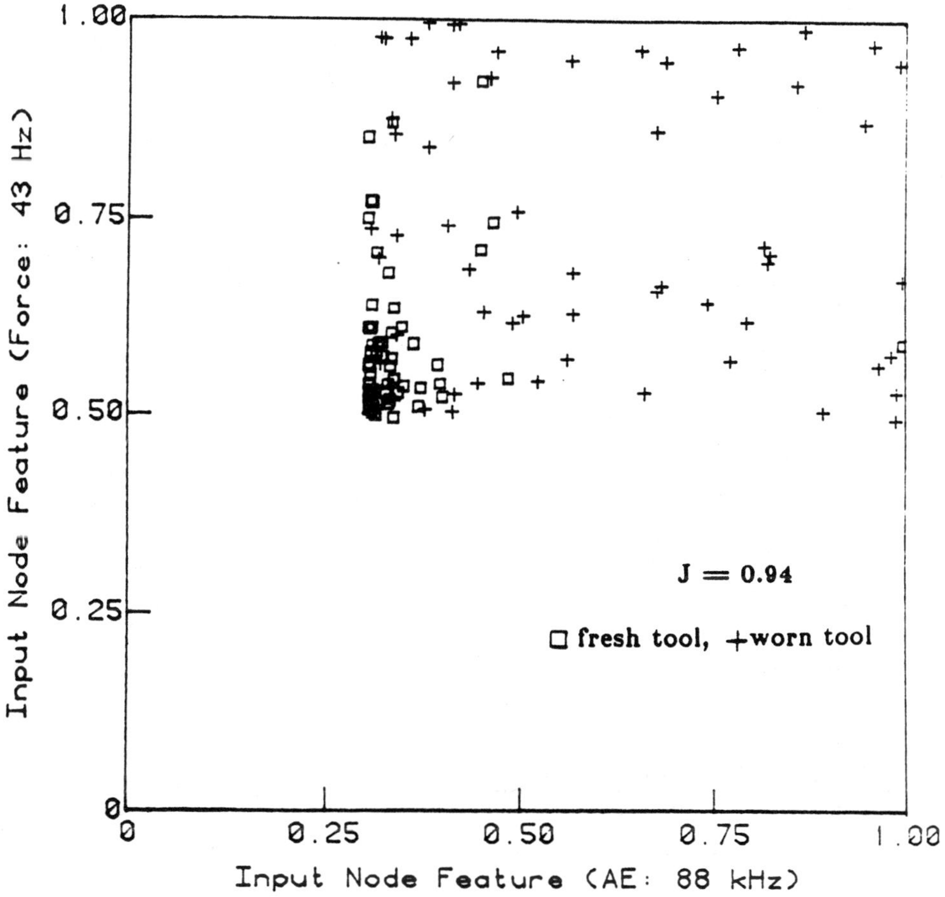

was also trained and tested. The classification success rate in this case was found to be 88 percent (similar to that obtained with non-normalized features). The superior performance of the neural network is attributed to their noise suppression abilities.

It is interesting to see how the classification performance is affected when the number of features presented to the input layer is varied. To reveal this, the least significant feature in the input feature vector was dropped sequentially. Process features were always included as part of the feature vector. The modified vectors were used to train and test the performance of a perceptron and a neural network.

The successful classification rate as a function of the number of sensor features used at the input layer of the network is shown in figure 16.33. It is shown

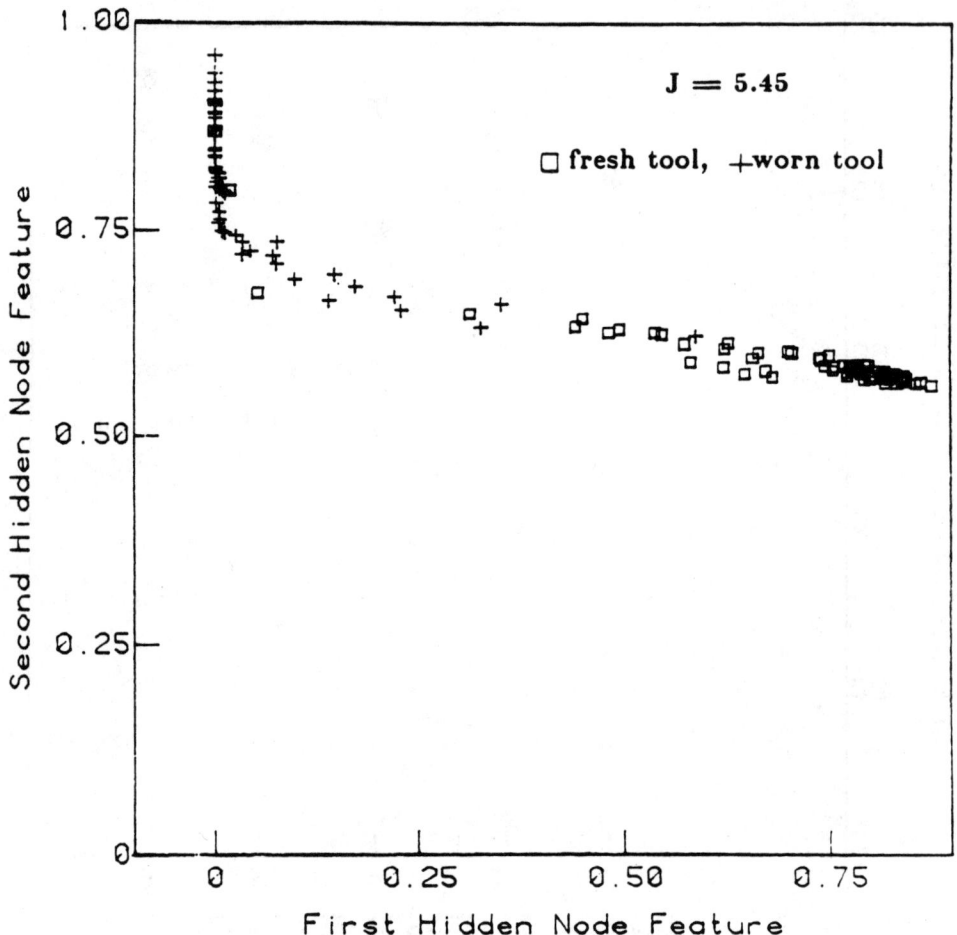

Figure 16.32 Two-dimensional Feature Space (Hidden Node Features)

that an increase in the number of features used at the input layer generally improves classification performance. For a given number of features, the performance of the neural network is shown to be superior to that of the perceptron. The effect of not using the process features is shown in figure 16.34, which reveals that the performance is adversely affected when the process features are not included. In this case, it is possible that changes in process conditions are confused with those resulting from changes in tool wear state, so that the classification error rate increases. In this case also, the neural network performs better than the perceptron network.

One aspect that is not fully explained is that although increase in the number

Figure 16.33 Classification Performance (with Process Features)

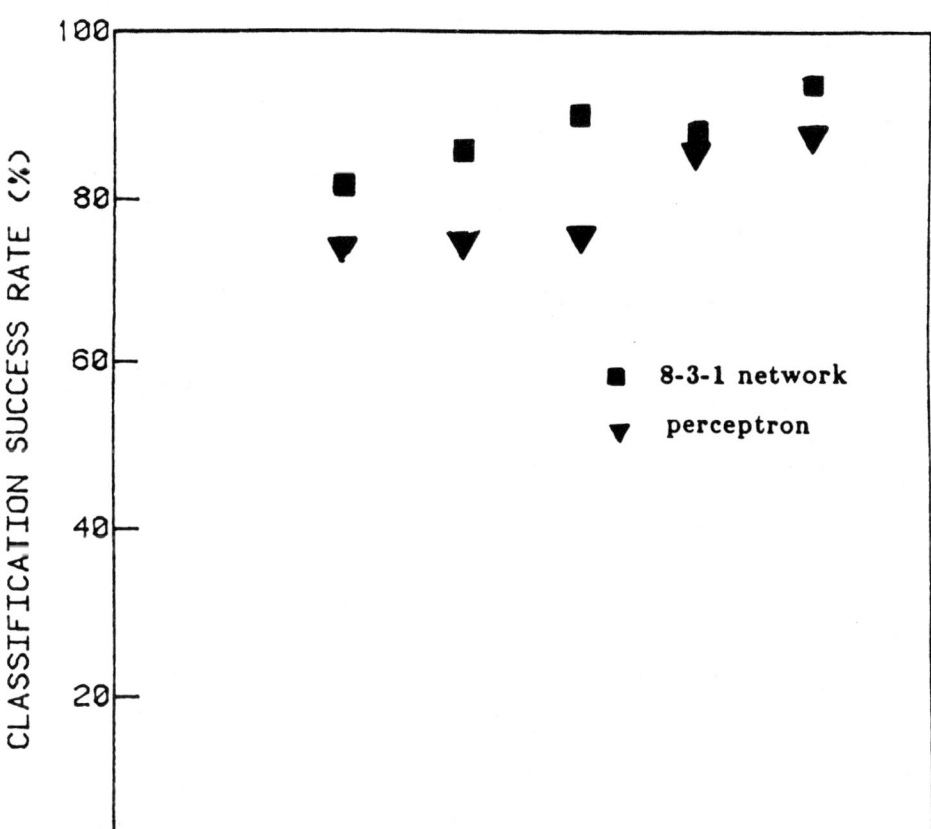

of sensor features generally improves performance, in some cases, the use of an additional feature causes a deterioration in the performance level. A possible reason may be that the training and test data statistics for that particular feature may be very different, so that the trained network may not be able to respond correctly to test data. Training anomalies may also contribute to this sort of behavior.

The performance of the 8-3-1 networks trained and tested using set 1, 2, and 3 features is compared in table 16.18. Set 2 features show the best performance (97 percent), and this correlates with the fact that the signal/noise ratio of the sensor features, as well as the internal features, is highest for set 2. On the other hand, set 3 features (which are very noisy) show poorer performance (84 per-

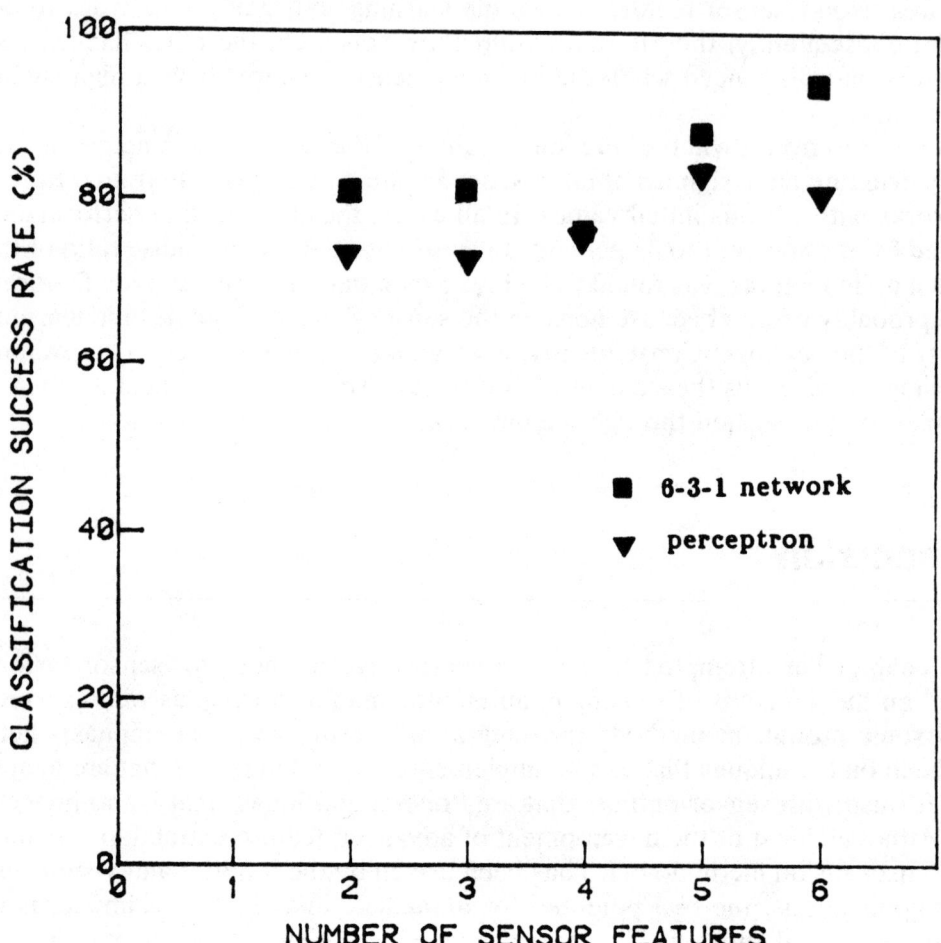

Figure 16.34 Classification Performance (without Process Features)

Table 16.18 Performance of Neural Network

Features	J Value (Sensor Features)	J Value (Input Node Features)	J Value (Hidden Node Features)	Success Rate (%)
Set 1	1.02	2.3	5.5	94
Set 2	1.70	3.6	11.5	97
Set 3	0.72	1.4	2.1	84

From Rangwala and Dornfeld [60].

cent). The data presented in table 16.18 suggests that the noise suppression ability of a neural network is a function of the amount of noise present in the sensor features. Noisy sensor features cause the learning ability of the network to degrade; consequently, the internal features are noisy. On the other hand, noise suppression is enhanced when the incoming sensor features have a high signal/noise ratio.

In order to reveal whether the initial values of the learning parameters or network structure have significant effects, set 3 features were used to train different networks with various initial values. In all cases, the classification performance ranged from 80 percent to 85 percent. In some cases, the signal/noise ratio of the hidden node features was found to be lower than that of the input node features. This probably occurs because noise in the sensor features degrades the learning ability of the network. Consequently, even though feature extraction on training set samples increases the signal/noise ratio, performance deteriorates when new samples are propagated through the network.

Conclusion

This chapter has attempted to place in perspective the need for sensor fusion, based on the demands of sensing in automated manufacturing, as well as to review some prominent methods for integrating sensor data. The emphasis here has been on techniques that can be implemented in real time and that are adaptable for use with sensor outputs that are "one-dimensional" that is, no images, etc. Although most of the development of advanced feature-extraction schemes and sensor fusion methodologies has been driven by the robotics and vision systems applications, the real potential for immediate and significant impact is in automated manufacturing. The examples given at the end of the chapter are designed to illustrate that potential.

References

1. Ahmed, N., and K. K. Rao. *Orthogonal Transforms for Digital Signal Processing.* New York: Springer-Verlag, 1975.

2. Andrews, G. C., and J. Tlusty. "A Critical Review of Sensors for Unmanned Machining." *Annals of the CIRP* vol. 32, no. 2 (1983):563–72.

3. Ayres, R. U. "Complexity, Reliability, and Design: Manufacturing Implications," *Manufacturing Review* vol. 1, no. 1 (March 1988):27.

4. Barash, M. "Computer Integrated Manufacturing Systems." In *Towards the Factory of the Future*, L. Kops, ed. New York: ASME, 1980, pp. 37–50.

5. Birla, S. "Sensors for Adaptive Control and Machine Diagnostics." In *Technology of Machine Tools—Machine Tool Task Force Report*. vol. 4: *Machine Tool Controls*. Rep #VCRL52960-1. R. V. Miskell, ed. Livermore, CA: LLNL, 1980.

6. Chiu, S. L., D. J. Morley, and J. F. Martin. "Sensor Data Fusion on a Parallel Processor." *Proc. 1987 IEEE International Conference on Robotics and Automation*, IEEE, Raleigh, NC, 1987, pp. 1629–33.

7. Chryssolouris, G., and M. Domroese. "Sensor Integration for Tool Wear Estimation in Machining." *Sensors and Controls for Manufacturing* PED vol. 33. New York: ASME, 1988, pp. 115–23.

8. Cook, N. "Self Excited Vibrations in Metal Cutting." *Transactions of the ASME, Journal of Engineering for Industry* (1959):183–86.

9. Cover, T. M. "Geometrical and Statistical Properties of Systems of Linear Inequalities with Applications in Pattern Recognition." *IEEE Transactions on Computers* vol. 14 (1965):326–34.

10. Cramer, H., and W. Leadbetter. "Some Fundamental Concepts and Results of Mathematical Probability Theory." In *Stationary and Related Stochastic Processes*, New York: Wiley, 1967, p. 19.

11. Death, M. "Sensors: Keys to Automation." *Manufacturing Engineering* vol. 96, no. 6 (1986):54.

12. Devijver, P. A., and J. Kittler. *Pattern Recognition—A Statistical Approach*. Englewood Cliffs, NJ: Prentice-Hall, 1982.

13. Dornfeld, D. A. "Acoustic Emission and Metalworking-Survey of Potential and Examples of Applications." *Proc. 8th North American Metalworking Research Conference*, SME, Univ. of Missouri, Rolla, MO, 1981, pp. 207–13.

14. ———. "Acoustic Emission Process Monitoring for Untended Manufacturing." *Proc. Japan-USA Symposium on Flexible Automation*, JAACE, Osaka, Japan, July, 1986.

15. ———. "Intelligent Sensors for Monitoring Untended Manufacturing Processes." *Proc. Second International Machine Tool Research Forum*, NMTBA, Chicago, IL, September, 1987.

16. ———. "Chip Form Detection Using Acoustic Emission." *Proc. 11th North American Manufacturing Research Conference*, SME, University of Wisconsin, Madison, WI, 1983, pp. 386–89.

17. Dornfeld, D. A., and M. S. Lan. "Experimental Studies of Tool Wear via Acoustic Emission Analysis." *Proc. 10th North American Manufacturing Research Conference*, SME, McMaster University, Hamilton, ONT, 1982, pp. 305–11.

18. Dornfeld, D. A., and C. S. Pan. "Determination of Chip Forming States Using a Linear

19. Dornfeld, D. A., and S. M. Wu. "An Investigation of Ground Wood Surfaces as Related to Pulp and Stone Characteristics." *Wear* vol. 42 (1977):163–75.

20. Emel, E., and E. Kannatey-Asibu, Jr. "Characterization of Tool Wear and Breakage by Pattern Recognition Analysis of Acoustic Emission Signals." *Proc. 14th North American Manufacturing Research Conference*, SME, University of Minnesota, Minneapolis, 1986, pp. 266–72.

21. ———. "Tool Failure Monitoring in Turning by Pattern Recognition Analysis and AE Signals." *Transactions of the ASME, Journal of Engineering for Industry* vol. 110, no. 2 (1988):137–45.

22. Graf, H., L. Jackel, R. Howard, B. Straghn, J. Denker, W. Hubbard, D. Tennant, and D. Schwartz. "VLSI Implementation of a Neural Network Memory with Several Hundreds of Neurons." *Proc. American Institute of Physics Conference on Neural Networks for Computing*, New York, 1986, pp. 182–87.

23. Hager, M. and M. Mintz. "Task-directed Multisensor Fusion." *Proc. 1989 IEEE International Conference on Robotics and Automation* vol. 2 (1989):1068–75.

24. Harmon, S. Y., G. L. Bianchini, and B. E. Pinz. "Sensor Data Fusion Through a Distributed Blackboard." *Proc. 1987 IEEE International Conference on Robotics and Automation*, IEEE, Raleigh, NC, 1987, pp. 1449–54.

25. Henderson, T., and E. Shilcrat. "Logical Sensor Systems." *Journal of Robotic Systems* vol. 1, no. 2 (1984):169–93.

26. Henderson, T. C., P. Allen, I. Cox, A. Mitchie, H. Durrant-Whyte, and W. Snyder, eds. *Workshop on Multisensor Integration in Manufacturing Automation*. Tech. Report UUCS–87–006. Salt Lake City, UT: University of Utah, Department of Computer Science, 1987.

27. Hinton, G., and S. Fahlman. "Connectionist Architectures for Artificial Intelligence." *UL IEEE Computer* (1987):100–9.

28. Honig, M. L., and D. G. Messerschmitt. *Adaptive Filters: Structures, Algorithms, and Application*. Hingham, MA: Academic Publishers, 1984, pp. 49–52.

29. Hopfield, J. J. "Neural Networks and Physical Systems with Emergent Collective Computational Abilities." *Proceedings of the National Academy of Sciences* vol. 79 (April 1982):2544–88.

30. ———. "Neurons with Graded Response Have Collective Computation Properties Like Those of Two-State Neurons." *Proc. National Academy of Sciences* vol. 81 (May 1984):3088–92.

31. Hopfield, J. J., and D. Tank. "Computing with Neural Circuits: A Model." *Science* vol. 233 (August 1986):625–33.

32. Hubbard, W., D. Schwartz, J. Denker, H. Graf, R. Howard, L. Jackel, B. Straghn, and D. Tennant. "Electronic Neural Networks." *Proc. American Institute of Physics Conference on Neural Networks for Computing,* New York, 1986, pp. 227–34.

33. Inasaki, I., and S. Yonetsu. "In-Process Detection of Cutting Tool Damage by Acoustic Emission Measurement." *Proc. 22nd Int'l Machine Tool Design and Research Conf.,* 1981, pp. 261–66.

34. Ito, Y. "Conceptualizing the Future Factory System." *Manufacturing Review* vol. 1, no. 4 (December):252–58.

35. Iwata, K. "Sensing Technologies for Improving the Machine Tool Function." *Proc. 3rd International Machine Tool Engineers Conference,* JMTBA, Tokyo, Japan, 1988, pp. 87–109.

36. Iwata, K., and T. Moriwaki. "An Application of Acoustic Emission Measurements to In-Process Sensing of Tool Wear." *Annals of CIRP* vol. 26, no. 1 (1977):21–26.

37. Kakino, Y. "In-Process Detection of Tool Breakage by Monitoring Acoustic Emission." *Proc. Int'l Conference on Cutting Tool Materials,* SCTE, Fort Mitchell, KY, 1980, pp. 29–43.

38. Kannatey-Asibu, E., and D. A. Dornfeld. "Quantitative Relationships for Acoustic Emission from Orthogonal Metal Cutting." *Transactions of the ASME, Journal of Engineering for Industry* vol. 103 (1981):330–40.

39. ———. "A Study of Tool Wear Using Statistical Analysis of Metal-Cutting Acoustic Emission." *Wear* vol. 76 (1982):247–61.

40. Klafter, R. D., T. A. Chmielewski, and M. Negin. *Robotic Engineering.* Englewood Cliffs, NJ: Prentice-Hall, 1989, pp. 314–15.

41. Kobayashi, S., and E. Thomsen. "The Role of Friction in Metal Cutting." *Transactions of the ASME, Journal of Engineering for Industry* vol. 82 (1960):324–32.

42. Korn, G. A., and T. M. Korn. "Mathematical Statistics." In *Mathematical Handbook for Scientists and Engineers.* 2nd ed. New York: McGraw-Hill, 1968, p. 671.

43. Lan, M. "Investigation of Tool Wear, Fracture, and Chip Formation in Metal Cutting Using Acoustic Emission." Ph.D. Dissertation, University of California at Berkeley, Department of Mechanical Engineering, 1983.

44. Le Cun, Y. "A Learning Procedure for Asymmetric Threshold Networks." *Proc. Cognitiva* (1985).

45. Liang, S., and D. A. Dornfeld. "Tool Wear Analysis Using Time Series Analysis of Acoustic Emission." *Transactions of the ASME, Journal of Engineering for Industry* vol. 111, no. 3 (1989):199–205.

46. Luo, R. C., M. H. Lin, and R. Scherp. "The Issues and Approaches of a Robot Multisensor Integration." *Proc. 1987 IEEE International Conference on Robotics and Automation,* IEEE, Raleigh, NC, 1987, pp. 1941–46.

47. Martin, P., B. Mutels, and J. Drapier. "Influence of Lathe Tool Wear on the Vibrations Sustained in Cutting." *Proc. of the 15th MTDR Conference,* Birmingham, UK, 1974, pp. 251–57.

48. Matsushima, K., and T. Sata. "Development of the Intelligent Machine Tool." *Journal of the Faculty of Engineering,* Univ. of Tokyo (B), vol. 35, no. 3 (1980):395–405.

49. Micheletti, G. F., W. Koenig, and H. R. Victor. "In Process Tool Wear Sensors for Cutting Operations." *Annals of CIRP* vol. 25, no. 2 (1976):483–96.

50. Middelhock, S., and A. C. Hoogerwerf. *IEEE Transducer '85 Digest* (1985):2–7.

51. Miller, I., and J. E. Freund. *Probability and Statistics for Engineers.* 3rd ed. Englewood Cliffs, NJ: Prentice-Hall, 1985.

52. Minsky, M., and S. Papert. *Perceptrons.* Cambridge, MA: MIT Press, 1969.

53. Nakamura, Y. and Y. T. Xu. "Geometrical Fusion Method for Multisensor Robotic Systems." *Proc. 1989 IEEE International Conference on Robotics and Automation,* vol. 1 (1989): 668–73.

54. Nakayama, K., and M. Ogawa. "Basic Rules on the Form of Chip in Metal Cutting." *Annals of CIRP* vol. 27, no. 1 (1978):17–21.

55. Nilsson, N. J. *The Mathematical Foundations of Learning Machines.* San Mateo, CA: Morgan Kaufman Publishers, 1990.

56. Owen, A., P. Le Comber, G. Sarraybarouse, and W. Spear. "New Amorphous-Silicon Electrically Programmable Nonvolatile Switching Device." *IEEE Proceedings* vol. 129, no. 2, part 1 (1982):51–54.

57. Rangwala S. "Machining Process Characterization and Intelligent Tool Condition Monitoring Using Acoustic Emission Signal Analysis." Ph.D. Thesis, Department of Mechanical Engineering, University of California, Berkeley, CA, 1988.

58. Rangwala, S., and D. A. Dornfeld. "Integration of Sensors via Neural Networks for Detection of Tool Wear States." *Proceedings of the Winter Annual Meeting of the ASME, PED* vol. 25, 1987, pp. 109–20.

59. ———. "Learning and Optimization of Machining Operations Using Computing Abilities of Neural Networks." *IEEE Transactions on Systems, Man and Cybernetics* vol. 19, no. 2 (1989):299–314.

60. ———. "Sensor Integration Using Neural Networks for Intelligent Tool Condition Monitoring." *Transactions of the ASME, Journal of Engineering for Industry* vol. 112, no. 3 (1990):219–28.

61. Rosenblatt, R. *Principles of Neurodynamics.* New York: Spartan Books, 1959.

62. Rumelhart, D., and J. McClelland. *Parallel Distributed Processing* vol. 1. Cambridge, MA: MIT Press, 1986.

REFERENCES

63. Ruokangas, C. C., M. S. Blank, J. F. Martin, and J. S. Schoenwald. "Integration of Multiple Sensors to Provide Flexible Control Strategies." *Proc. 1986 IEEE International Conference on Robotics and Automation,* IEEE, San Francisco, CA, 1986, pp. 1947–53.

64. Sata, T., K. Matsushima, T. Nagakura, and E. Kono. "Learning and Recognition of the Cutting States by Spectrum Analysis." *Annals of the CIRP* vol. 22, no. 1 (1973):41–42.

65. Schoess, J. "Smart Sensor Technology for Advanced Launch Vehicles." *Proc. 25th Joint Propulsion Conference,* AIAA, Monterey, CA, 1989.

66. Schoess, J., and G. Castore. "A Distributed Sensor Architecture for Advanced Aerospace Systems." *SPIE Proceedings on Sensor Fusion* vol. 931 (1988).

67. Shiraishi, M. "In-Process Measurement, Monitoring, and Control Techniques for FMS—Part 1: In Process Techniques for Tools." *Precision Engineering* vol. 10, no. 4 (1988):179–89.

68. ———. "In-Process Measurement, Monitoring, and Control Techniques for FMS—Part 2: In Process Techniques for Workpieces." *Precision Engineering* vol. 11, no. 1 (1989):27–37.

69. ———. "In-Process Measurement, Monitoring, and Control Techniques for FMS—Part 3: In Process Techniques for Cutting Processes and Machine Tools." *Precision Engineering* vol. 11, no. 1 (1989):39–47.

70. Spencer, E. "Programmable Bistable Switches and Resistors for Neural Networks." *Proc. American Institute of Physics Conference on Neural Networks for Computing,* New York, 1986, pp. 414–19.

71. Stein, J., and D. A. Dornfeld. "A Methodology for Classification of Sensors Used in Manufacturing Processes." Research Report, Engineering Systems Research Center, University of California at Berkeley and *Proc. Japan-U.S. Symposium on Flexible Automation,* ISCIE, Kyoto, Japan, 1989.

72. Tank, D., and J. J. Hopfield. "Simple Neural Optimization Networks: An A/D Converter, Signal Decision Circuit, and a Linear Programming Circuit." *IEEE Trans. on Circuits and Systems* vol. CAS-33/5 (May 1986):533–41.

73. Whitehouse, D. J. "Beta Functions for Surface Typology." *Annals of CIRP* vol. 27 (1978):491–97.

74. Whitney, A. "A Direct Method of Nonparametric Measurement Selection." *IEEE Transactions on Computers* vol. 20 (1971):1100–3.

75. Wright, P. K. "Physical Models of Tool Wear for Adaptive Control in Flexible Machining Cells." In *Computer Integrated Manufacturing* PED-vol. 8. M. R. Martinez and M. C. Leu, eds. New York: ASME, 1983, pp. 19–31.

76. Wright, P. K., and D. A. Bourne. *Manufacturing Intelligence.* Reading, MA: Addison-Wesley, 1988.

77. Wu, S. M. "Tool Life Testing by Response Surface Analysis." *Transactions of the ASME* series B, vol. 86, no. 2 (1964):105–16.

78. Wu, S. M., and S. M. Pandit. *Time Series and Systems Analysis with Applications.* New York: Wiley, 1983.

79. Yamasaki, H. "Intelligent Sensing Technology." *Journal of the Japan Society of Precision Engineering* vol. 55, no. 9 (1989):14–19 (in Japanese).

80. Yee, K. W., D. Blomquist, D. A. Dornfeld, and C. S. Pan. "An Acoustic Emission Chipform Monitor for Single Point Turning." *Proc. 26th Int'l Machine Tool Design and Research Conf.,* Univ. of Manchester, Manchester, UK, 1986.

Credits and Permissions

Chapter 1

Table 1.1—Copyright Kennametal, Inc., 1990, all rights reserved, William A. Kline, author

Figure 1.1—Copyright Kennametal, Inc., 1990, all rights reserved, William A. Kline, author

Figure 1.2—Copyright Kennametal, Inc., 1990, all rights reserved, William A. Kline, author

Figure 1.3—Copyright Kennametal, Inc., 1990, all rights reserved, William A. Kline, author

Figure 1.4—Copyright Kennametal, Inc., 1990, all rights reserved, William A. Kline, author

Figure 1.5—Copyright Kennametal, Inc., 1990, all rights reserved, William A. Kline, author

Figure 1.6—Copyright Kennametal, Inc., 1990, all rights reserved, William A. Kline, author

Figure 1.7—Copyright Kennametal, Inc., 1990, all rights reserved, William A. Kline, author

Figure 1.8—Copyright Kennametal, Inc., 1990, all rights reserved, William A. Kline, author

Figure 1.9—Copyright Kennametal, Inc., 1990, all rights reserved, William A. Kline, author

Figure 1.10a—Copyright Kennametal, Inc., 1990, all rights reserved, William A. Kline, author

Figure 1.10b—Copyright Kennametal, Inc., 1990, all rights reserved, William A. Kline, author

Figure 1.11a—Copyright Kennametal, Inc., 1990, all rights reserved, William A. Kline, author

Figure 1.11b—Copyright Kennametal, Inc., 1990, all rights reserved, William A. Kline, author

Figure 1.12—Copyright Kennametal, Inc., 1990, all rights reserved, William A. Kline, author

Chapter 2

Figure 2.1—Reprinted with permission of Newport Corporation and Deutsch ECD

Figure 2.2—Reprinted with permission of Newport Corporation and Deutsch ECD

Figure 2.3—Reprinted with permission of Newport Corporation and Deutsch ECD

Chapter 3

Table 3.1—Reprinted with permission. Copyright © Instrument Society of America 1985. From *Proceedings of the 31st International Instrumentation Symposium*.

Figure 3.1—Reprinted with permission. Copyright © Instrument Society of America 1985. From *Proceedings of the 31st International Instrumentation Symposium.*

Figure 3.2—Reprinted with permission. Copyright © Instrument Society of America 1985. From *Proceedings of the 31st International Instrumentation Symposium.*

Figure 3.3—Reprinted with permission. Copyright © Instrument Society of America 1985. From *Proceedings of the 31st International Instrumentation Symposium.*

Figure 3.4—Reprinted with permission. Copyright © Instrument Society of America 1985. From *Proceedings of the 31st International Instrumentation Symposium.*

Figure 3.5—Reprinted with permission. Copyright © Instrument Society of America 1985. From *Proceedings of the 31st International Instrumentation Symposium.*

Figure 3.6—Reprinted with permission. Copyright © Instrument Society of America 1985. From *Proceedings of the 31st International Instrumentation Symposium.*

Figure 3.7—Reprinted with permission. Copyright © Instrument Society of America 1985. From *Proceedings of the 31st International Instrumentation Symposium.*

Figure 3.8—Reprinted with permission. Copyright © Instrument Society of America 1985. From *Proceedings of the 31st International Instrumentation Symposium.*

Figure 3.9—Reprinted with permission. Copyright © Instrument Society of America 1985. From *Proceedings of the 31st International Instrumentation Symposium.*

Figure 3.10—Reprinted with permission. Copyright © Instrument Society of America 1985. From *Proceedings of the 31st International Instrumentation Symposium.*

Figure 3.11—Reprinted with permission. Copyright © Instrument Society of America 1985. From *Proceedings of the 31st International Instrumentation Symposium.*

Figure 3.12—Reprinted with permission. Copyright © Instrument Society of America 1985. From *Proceedings of the 31st International Instrumentation Symposium.*

Figure 3.13—Reprinted with permission. Copyright © Instrument Society of America 1985. From *Proceedings of the 31st International Instrumentation Symposium.*

Figure 3.14—Reprinted with permission. Copyright © Instrument Society of America 1985. From *Proceedings of the 31st International Instrumentation Symposium.*

Figure 3.15—Reprinted with permission. Copyright © Instrument Society of America 1985. From *Proceedings of the 31st International Instrumentation Symposium.*

Figure 3.16—Reprinted with permission. Copyright © Instrument Society of America 1985. From *Proceedings of the 31st International Instrumentation Symposium.*

Figure 3.17—Reprinted with permission. Copyright © Instrument Society of America 1985. From *Proceedings of the 31st International Instrumentation Symposium.*

Figure 3.18—Reprinted with permission. Copyright © Instrument Society of America 1985. From *Proceedings of the 31st International Instrumentation Symposium.*

Figure 3.19—Reprinted with permission. Copyright © Instrument Society of America 1985. From *Proceedings of the 31st International Instrumentation Symposium.*

Figure 3.20—Reprinted with permission. Copyright © Instrument Society of America 1985. From *Proceedings of the 31st International Instrumentation Symposium.*

Chapter 4

Figure 4.2—Reprinted with permission of Polaroid Corporation

Figure 4.3—Reprinted with permission of Digital Optronics Corporation (Boonton Township, NJ)

Figure 4.4—Reprinted from Wampler [28] by permission of MIT Press, Cambridge, MA. Copyright © 1984 by the Massachusetts Institute of Technology.

Figure 4.5—Reprinted with permission from SRI International and Arbotech Systems

Figure 4.6—Reprinted with permission of PFA, Inc.

Figure 4.7—Photo courtesy of Assurance Technologies, Inc. Sensor is no longer being marketed.

Figure 4.8—Photo courtesy of Assurance Technologies, Inc. Sensor is no longer being marketed.

Chapter 5

Figure 5.1—Reprinted with permission of Zygo Corporation

Figure 5.2a—Reprinted with permission of Candid Logic, Inc.

Figure 5.2b—Reprinted with permission of Candid Logic, Inc.

Figure 5.2c—Reprinted with permission of Candid Logic, Inc.

Figure 5.3—Photo courtesy of Selective Electronics, Inc.

Figure 5.4—Reprinted with permission of Rodenstock Precision Optics, Inc.

Figure 5.5—Reprinted with permission of Chapman Instruments

Figure 5.6—Reprinted with permission of GCA/Tropel

Figure 5.7—Reprinted with permission of Zygo Corporation

Chapter 6

Figure 6.37—Reprinted with permission of Hamar Laser Instruments, Inc.

Chapter 7

Figure 7.1—Courtesy of EDO Corporation
Figure 7.2—Courtesy of EDO Corporation
Figure 7.3—Courtesy of EDO Corporation
Figure 7.4—Courtesy of EDO Corporation
Figure 7.5—Courtesy of EDO Corporation
Figure 7.6—Courtesy of EDO Corporation
Figure 7.7—Courtesy of EDO Corporation
Figure 7.8—Courtesy of EDO Corporation
Figure 7.9—Courtesy of EDO Corporation
Figure 7.10—Courtesy of EDO Corporation
Figure 7.11—Courtesy of EDO Corporation
Figure 7.12—Courtesy of EDO Corporation
Figure 7.13—Courtesy of EDO Corporation
Figure 7.14—Courtesy of EDO Corporation
Figure 7.15—Courtesy of EDO Corporation
Figure 7.16—Courtesy of EDO Corporation
Figure 7.17—Courtesy of EDO Corporation
Figure 7.18—Courtesy of Mikron Instrument Company, Inc.
Figure 7.19—Courtesy of EDO Corporation
Figure 7.20—Courtesy of EDO Corporation
Figure 7.21—Courtesy of EDO Corporation
Figure 7.22—Courtesy of EDO Corporation
Figure 7.23—Courtesy of Mikron Instrument Company, Inc.

Chapter 9

Figure 9.1—Reprinted with permission of Macbeth
Figure 9.2—Reprinted with permission of Macbeth
Figure 9.3—Reprinted with permission of Macbeth
Figure 9.4—Reprinted with permission of Macbeth
Figure 9.5—Reprinted with permission of Macbeth

Chapter 11

Figure 11.4—Photo courtesy of D. M. Boyd, Battelle Pacific Northwest Laboratories

Chapter 13

Figure 13.1—Reprinted with permission of Physical Acoustics Corporation
Figure 13.2—Reprinted with permission of Physical Acoustics Corporation

CREDITS AND PERMISSIONS 513

Figure 13.3—Reprinted with permission of Physical Acoustics Corporation
Figure 13.4—Reprinted with permission of Physical Acoustics Corporation
Figure 13.5—Reprinted with permission of Physical Acoustics Corporation
Figure 13.6—Reprinted with permission of Physical Acoustics Corporation
Figure 13.7—Reprinted with permission of Physical Acoustics Corporation
Figure 13.8—Reprinted with permission of Physical Acoustics Corporation
Figure 13.9—Reprinted with permission of Physical Acoustics Corporation
Figure 13.10—Reprinted with permission of Physical Acoustics Corporation
Figure 13.11—Reprinted with permission of Physical Acoustics Corporation
Figure 13.12—Reprinted with permission of Physical Acoustics Corporation
Figure 13.13—Reprinted with permission of Physical Acoustics Corporation
Figure 13.14—Reprinted with permission of Physical Acoustics Corporation
Figure 13.15—Reprinted with permission of Physical Acoustics Corporation
Figure 13.16—Reprinted with permission of Physical Acoustics Corporation
Figure 13.17—Reprinted with permission of Physical Acoustics Corporation
Figure 13.18—Reprinted with permission of Physical Acoustics Corporation
Figure 13.19—Reprinted with permission of Physical Acoustics Corporation
Figure 13.20—Reprinted with permission of Physical Acoustics Corporation

Chapter 15

Table 15.1—Reprinted by permission from *Sensors*. Copyright 1987, Helmers Publishing, Inc.
Table 15.2—Reprinted by permission from *Sensors*. Copyright 1987, Helmers Publishing, Inc.
Table 15.3—Reprinted by permission from *Sensors*. Copyright 1987, Helmers Publishing, Inc.
Table 15.5—Reprinted by permission from *Sensors*. Copyright 1987, Helmers Publishing, Inc.
Figure 15.3—Reprinted by permission from *Sensors*. Copyright 1987, Helmers Publishing, Inc.
Figure 15.4—Courtesy of Endress & Hauser, FRG
Figure 15.18—Reprinted by permission from *Sensors*. Copyright 1987, Helmers Publishing, Inc.
Figure 15.21—Reprinted by permission from *Sensors*. Copyright 1987, Helmers Publishing, Inc.

Chapter 16

Table 16.1—From Shiraishi [68]. Reproduced by courtesy of Butterworth-Heinemann.
Table 16.3—From Stein and Dornfeld [71]

Table 16.4—From Shiraishi [68]. Reproduced by courtesy of Butterworth-Heinemann.

Table 16.5—From Shiraishi [68]. Reproduced by courtesy of Butterworth-Heinemann.

Table 16.6—From Wright and Bourne [76]. Reprinted with permission of the publisher.

Table 16.7—From Dornfeld and Pan [18]. Reprinted courtesy of the Society of Manufacturing Engineers. Copyright 1985.

Table 16.8—From Dornfeld and Pan [18]. Reprinted courtesy of the Society of Manufacturing Engineers. Copyright 1985.

Table 16.9—From Liang and Dornfeld [45]. Reproduced courtesy of the American Society of Mechanical Engineers. Copyright 1989.

Table 16.10—From Liang and Dornfeld [45]. Reproduced courtesy of the American Society of Mechanical Engineers. Copyright 1989.

Table 16.11—From Rangwala and Dornfeld [60].

Table 16.12—From Rangwala and Dornfeld [60].

Table 16.13—From Rangwala and Dornfeld [60].

Table 16.14—From Rangwala and Dornfeld [60].

Table 16.15—From Rangwala and Dornfeld [60].

Table 16.16—From Rangwala and Dornfeld [60].

Table 16.17—From Rangwala and Dornfeld [60].

Table 16.18—From Rangwala and Dornfeld [60].

Figure 16.1—From P. K. Wright and D. A. Bourne [76]. Reprinted with permission of the publisher.

Figure 16.2—From Matsushima, K., and T. Sata [48]. Reprinted with permission from Takuo Sugano and the Institute of Physical and Chemical Research.

Figure 16.3—From Matsushima, K., and T. Sata [48]. Reprinted with permission from Takuo Sugano and the Institute of Physical and Chemical Research.

Figure 16.4—From Rangwala [57]

Figure 16.7—From Nilsson [55]. Used by permission.

Figure 16.8—From Nilsson [55]. Used by permission.

Figure 16.12—From Henderson *et al.* [26]

Figure 16.13—From Henderson *et al.* [26]

Figure 16.14—From Schoess and Castore [66]

Figure 16.15—From Schoess and Castore [66]

Figure 16.16—From Schoess and Castore [66]

Figure 16.18—From Dornfeld and Lan [16]. Reprinted courtesy of the Society of Manufacturing Engineers. Copyright 1983.

Figure 16.19—From Liang and Dornfeld [45]. Reproduced courtesy of the American Society of Mechanical Engineers. Copyright 1989.

Figure 16.20—From Liang and Dornfeld [45]. Reproduced courtesy of the American Society of Mechanical Engineers. Copyright 1989.

Figure 16.21—From Liang and Dornfeld [45]. Reproduced courtesy of the American Society of Mechanical Engineers. Copyright 1989.

Figure 16.22—From Liang and Dornfeld [45]. Reproduced courtesy of the American Society of Mechanical Engineers. Copyright 1989.

Figure 16.23—From Liang and Dornfeld [45]. Reproduced courtesy of the American Society of Mechanical Engineers. Copyright 1989.

Figure 16.24—From Liang and Dornfeld [45]. Reproduced courtesy of the American Society of Mechanical Engineers. Copyright 1989.

Figure 16.25—From Liang and Dornfeld [45]. Reproduced courtesy of the American Society of Mechanical Engineers. Copyright 1989.

Figure 16.26—From Liang and Dornfeld [45]. Reproduced courtesy of the American Society of Mechanical Engineers. Copyright 1989.

Figure 16.27—From Rangwala and Dornfeld [60]. Reproduced courtesy of American Society of Mechanical Engineers. Copyright 1990.

Figure 16.28—From Rangwala and Dornfeld [60]. Reproduced courtesy of American Society of Mechanical Engineers. Copyright 1990.

Figure 16.29—From Rangwala and Dornfeld [60]. Reproduced courtesy of American Society of Mechanical Engineers. Copyright 1990.

Figure 16.30—From Rangwala and Dornfeld [60]. Reproduced courtesy of American Society of Mechanical Engineers. Copyright 1990.

Figure 16.31—From Rangwala and Dornfeld [60]. Reproduced courtesy of American Society of Mechanical Engineers. Copyright 1990.

Figure 16.32—From Rangwala and Dornfeld [60]. Reproduced courtesy of American Society of Mechanical Engineers. Copyright 1990.

Figure 16.33—From Rangwala and Dornfeld [60]. Reproduced courtesy of American Society of Mechanical Engineers. Copyright 1990.

Figure 16.34—From Rangwala and Dornfeld [60]. Reproduced courtesy of American Society of Mechanical Engineers. Copyright 1990.

Index

Absorptance 168
Absorption 27, 395
Acceleration 5
Accuracy 435
Acoustic 76
Acoustic birefringence 303
Acoustic emission 5, 15, 321, 448, 467, 475
Acoustic fields 366
Acoustic impedance 394
Acoustic intensity 395
Acoustic sensors 356
Alignment 111
Alignment laser systems 142
Alloy monitor 261
Amplitude 245, 251
Angular distribution 433
Angular errors 133
Annealing 39
Attenuation 27, 396
Attraction basins 456
Autofocusing 68
Axons 453

Band pass filter 180, 251
Bandwith limitations 27
Beacon navigation 68
Bearing monitoring 341
Binarizing 103
Blackboard system 463
Black body 207
Blanking distance 388
Boiler furnace flame temperature 35
Bolometers 172
Bond 321, 337
Bonding voids 216
Bore measurement 149
Brazing 33, 39

Brightness 99, 231, 234
Brinell hardness number 308

Cable splice 257
Capacitance 76
Capacitive 356
Capacitive fields 358, 369
Capacitive sensing 373
Case-hardened parts 315
Cell body 453
Centering errors 130
Character verification 106
Chatter 448
Chip breakage 448
Chip form determination 467
Chroma 224, 234
Chromaticity 234
CIE 233, 239
CIELAB space 234
Cladding 22
Classification 448
Coherent fiber bundles 23
Coil 300
Coil impedance 245
Collimated light 90
Collision detection 13
Color 100, 223, 225
Colorimetry 223, 239
Color inspection 228
Color order 223
Color standards 228
Color vision 230
Composition 384
Composition measurement 407
Concentration 384
Conductance 455
Conduction 206
Contact resistance 76

Continuous acoustic emission 335
Convection 206
Coriolus 417
Corrosion 295
Coupling alignment 156
Crack 217, 243, 295, 321, 336, 372
Crack development 266
Curie temperature 196
Cutting force 486

Data normalization 9
Dead band 388
Dead reckoning 82
Decision theoretic 105
Defect 243
Delaminations 216
Dendrites 453
Densitometry 238
Detectivity 176
Deterministic 105
Dial machine alignment 155
Diameter 88
Diamond pyramid 308
Differential pressure Venturi meter 410
Diffraction 363, 395
Diffuseness 432
Digital comparator 265
Digital imaging 33
Digital signal processing 9
Dimensions 87
Dispersion 27
Displacement 30
Distance 384
Distributed sensor architecture 461
Doppler 67, 384, 405, 409, 412, 415

Echo ranging 383
Eddy current 243, 307, 370
Eddy current senor 71
Edges 103
Electric 431
Electrical conductivity 288
Electrical/magnetic field 30
Electromagnetic acoustic transducers 286
Ellipsometry 433
Emission spectroscopy 49
Emissivity 163, 184, 193, 206
Encoders 66

Energy absorption 396
Energy loss 396
Equilibrium points 456
Euclidean space 360
Excitory 454
Exponential force fields 356, 369

Feature selection and extraction 448
Feedforward 456
Fiber optic infrared sensors 190
Fiber optic interferometer 68
Fiber optics 21, 34, 55
Filter 251
Filter colorimeters 232
Flame condition monitoring 37
Flame envelope control 37
Flame quality analyzer 35
Flame temperature measurement 33
Flash 375
Flatness 140
Flaw 295
Flow 384, 403
Flowmeter 403, 407, 412, 413
Fluid/flow 30
Fluorescence 237
FM radar 71
Force 5, 6, 72, 73
Force field 377
Force-field sensing 353
Forming 376
Frame store 101
Frequency domain analysis 445
Furnace control 33
Fusion methodologies 447

Global Positioning System (GPS) 68
Goodness of fit 105
Gouffe's analysis 168
Graded index 25
Gray body 207

Hardness 303, 307, 373
Hardness measurement under load 313
Headers 376, 378
Hearing 436
Heat-treated objects 373
Heat treating 282
Height 92

Hidden nodes 456
High pass 251
Histogram 103
Hopfield 456
Hue 224, 234

Image processing 101
Impedance mismatch 396
Indentation 307
Index of diffraction 178
Index of refraction 124, 144
Induced vibration 72
Inductance 76
Induction heating 275
Inductive 356, 369
Inductive fields 358
Inductive reactance 245
Inductive sensing 370
Inertial navigation systems 67
Infrared cameras 192
Infrared detectors 172
Infrared filter 180
Infrared microscopes 192
Infrared pyrometers 168
Infrared radiation 161, 204
Infrared sensors 161
Infrared sources 166
Inhibitory 454
Input nodes 456
Integrated sensor 464
Intelligent machine 422
Intelligent sensor 420, 422, 423
Interference 29
Interferometer 142
Interferometer laser 138
Intermodulation effect 257
International Commission on
    Illumination 229. *See also* CIE.
Isothermal 199

Justifying 107

Knoop geometries 308

Laps 295, 296
Laser alignment 113
Laser gyroscope 67

Laser plane error 135
Laser scanner 90
Laser speckle interferometry 33
Laser triangulation sensors 90
Leak 216, 321, 340
Level 120, 384
Lightness 224, 234
Light pipe 22
Light sectioning 433
Linear array 87
Linear discriminant pattern
    classifiers 449
Linear network 459
Line scan camera 49
Liquid light pipe 23
Load signature analysis 275
Logical sensor specification 461
Lorentz force 286
Low pass 251
Luminous intensity 234

Machine alignment 148
Machine monitoring 1
Machine tool 148
Machine tool alignment 120
Machine vision 377
Magnetic induction 76
Magnetostrictive 288
Manufacturing Automation Protocol
    (MAP) 11
Material dispersion 27
Materials characterization 302
Meander coil 290
Measurement vector 490
Mechanical 430
Mechanical vibrations 322
Metal analyzer 266
Metal cutting 376, 467
Metal removal 423
Metameric match 229
Metamerism 229
Microbending losses 28
Microindentation 308
Microstructures 243
Microwave 356
Microwave fields 368
Modal dispersion 27
Mode scrambling 28
Moisture 215
Monochromator 233

INDEX

Multiple sensors 9
Munsell 223
Munsell color space 225
Munsell value 234
Mutual inductance technique 370

Navigation sensor 67
Neural networks 453
Noise equivalent power (NEP) 176
Noncoherent fiber bundles 23
Normalized frequency parameter 26
Numerical aperture 26

Offset 159
Optical 430
Optical micrometer 144
Optical occlusion 76
Optical path 194
Optical reflectance 71
Output nodes 456

Parallel measurement 120
Particle Impact Noise Detection (PIND) 337
Passive filter 252
Passive infrared 189
Pattern classifier 451
Pattern recognition 9, 105, 456
Penetration 363
Penetration depth 244
Penta sweep errors 127
Perceptron 459
Perpendicularity 140
Phase 29, 245, 251
Phase digitizer 264
Phase measuring 69
Phase shift 360
Phase shift holography 33
Photoconductive 173
Photoelectric eye 33
Photon detectors 172
Photovoltaic 173
Piezoelectric 6, 76, 285, 288, 290, 325, 385
Piezoresistance 76
Pipes 297
Planck's equation 165
Planck's Law 185

Plane error budget 135
Plating 373
Plating thickness 243
Pneumatic 430
Pneumatic leak rate 76
Point level 384
Polarization 29
Polarization preserving 25
Polarization scrambling 28
Pose 82
Positional 106
Positions 87
Power 5
Pressure 30, 356
Pressure transducer 353
Preweld seam alignment 46
Primaries 231
Probabilistic 105
Process mill roll alignment 154
Profiles 87
Proximity sensor 71
Psychophysics 223
Pulse burst 388
Pulse echo 301
Pulse spreading 396
Punch press monitoring 345
Pyroelectric 172, 196
Pyrometer 35, 166, 201

Quantizing 99
Quantum detectors 174

Radar 70
Radiation 206
Radioactivity 5
Radiometer 178, 190
Range map 66
Range sensor 68
Reflection 363
Reflective optics 176
Reflectivity 168, 206
Refractive index 23
Refractive optics 177
Registration 106
Residual magnetism 371
Resistive 455
Resistivity 245
Resolution 435
Resonance scan control 264

Responsivity 176
Reverberation 396
Ring laser 68
Ring time 388
Robotics 63
Robot sensor 65
Rockwell hardness values 308, 311, 373
Rolling sensor 327

Sampling input signal 448
Saturation 225
Scattered light measurements 93
Scattering 28
Seams 295, 296
Segmentation 103
Self-inductance technique 370
Sensing coil 250
Sensing coil driver 264
Sensing frequency 264
Sensor 4, 424
Sensor fusion 419, 423, 447
Sequential forward search 490
Shade of gray 99
Shape 362, 374, 378
Short shots 375
Sigmoid function 453, 495
Signature technique 9
Single mode fiber 24
Sinusoidal fields 363
Sinusoidal force field 356, 362
Skin effect 363, 369
Slip 72
Smart sensor 461
Smell 436
Solid light pipe 23
Sonar 65, 68, 383, 392, 398
Speckle 432
Spectral analyzer 233
Spectral luminous efficiency function 229
Spectrophotometer 239
Spectrophotometry 233, 236
Spectroscopic 33
Specular reflectance 432
Stamping 376
Standard observer 231
Stefan-Boltzmann 165
Step index 24
Straightness 140, 147

Strain 30, 53, 73
Strain gauge 6, 76
Stress 30, 303, 322
Structural strain 33
Subpixel 99
Surface 296, 439
Surface acoustic waves (Raleigh waves) 296
Surface roughness 92
Surface uniformity 221
Synapses 453
Syntactic 105

Tactile force measuring 63
Tactile sensor 71, 76
Temperature 5, 30
Temperature measurement 243
Temperature monitoring 39
Temperature sensing 291
Texture 292
Thermal conductivity 81
Thermal detectors 172
Thermal signature 213
Thermal transfer 72
Thermistors 173
Thermochromism 237
Thermocompression bonding 336
Thermocouple 166, 190
Thermogram 205
Thermopile 172, 174
Thickness 92, 294, 373, 384
Thin film filter 180
Threshold 103
Threshold algorithm 9
Through-liquid echo ranging 392
Time domain analysis 438
Time series analysis 9, 441
Titanium welding 49
Tool breakage 2
Tool breakage detection 15
Tool monitoring 2, 18, 321, 467
Tool touch 343
Tool wear 2, 344
Tool wear detection 17, 475
Tool wear monitoring 467
Torque 72, 73, 81
Total internal reflections 23, 80
Touch 436
Touch sensor 72
Training pattern 459

Transducers 5
Transfer line 155
Transformation 66
Transformation of primaries 231
Transit-time flowmeter 413
Transmission 168
Transmissivity 206, 208
Tristimulus 233
Tristimulus values 231
Tubes 297
Tubing 294
Turbine alignment 150
Tow-color 201
Two-color pyrometry 42
Two-color temperature sensing 189

Ultrasonic 285, 295, 297, 383, 431
Ultrasonic contact impedance 310
Ultrasonic gap 400

Vacuum 297
Velocity 87
Vertical shaft alignment 151
Vibration 5
Vickers 311
Visibility function 229
Vision 436
Visual colorimetry 231
Voids 217
Volume profiles 92

Waveguides 368
Wavelength dispersion 27
Web 106
Weights 455
Wein's displacement law 166
Weld 297, 300, 321, 330, 346, 349
Welding 33, 49